THE FALL OF Boris Johnson

Sebastian Payne is the award-winning Whitehall Editor, columnist for the *Financial Times* and author of the acclaimed *Broken Heartlands* – *The Times* Political Book of the Year for 2021. Sebastian presents the *Payne's Politics* podcast, which was shortlisted for News Podcast of the Year at the 2020 National Press Awards. *The Fall of Boris Johnson* is his second book.

Also by Sebastian Payne
Broken Heartlands

THE FALL OF Boris Johnson THE FULL STORY

SEBASTIAN PAYNE

MACMILLAN

First published 2022 by Macmillan
an imprint of Pan Macmillan
The Smithson, 6 Briset Street, London EC1M 5NR
EU representative: Macmillan Publishers Ireland Ltd, 1st Floor,
The Liffey Trust Centre, 117–126 Sheriff Street Upper,
Dublin 1, D01 YC43
Associated companies throughout the world
www.panmacmillan.com

ISBN 978-1-0350-1664-8

1 3 5 7 9 8 6 4 2

A CIP catalogue record for this book is available from the British Library.

Typeset by Typo•glyphix, Burton-on-Trent, DE14 3HE
Printed and bound by CPI Group (UK) Ltd, Croydon, CR0 4YY

MIX
Paper | Supporting
responsible forestry
FSC® C116313

Visit **www.panmacmillan.com** to read more about all our books
and to buy them. You will also find features, author interviews and
news of any author events, and you can sign up for e-newsletters
so that you're always first to hear about our new releases.

For Bronwen,
who was and remains a slight Boris fan

Contents

'When a regime has been in power too long, when it has fatally exhausted the patience of the people, and when oblivion finally beckons – I am afraid that across the world you can rely on the leaders of that regime to act solely in the interests of self-preservation, and not in the interests of the electorate.'

— BORIS JOHNSON

Introduction –
Drinks at the Garrick Club

Boris Johnson shuffled into the mahogany and red dining room of the Garrick Club one cold November evening with a relaxed grin on his face. Scooping up a drink as the dinner was about to begin, he beamed at his former journalist colleagues. Rumours had been circulating that he would attend, but many were stunned not only that the prime minister had just walked in, but that he had done so on time (unlike the filing of his newspaper articles). Johnson had returned to a gathering to celebrate his spiritual home: among the comment writers of *The Daily Telegraph*. Fresh from the success of the COP26 climate conference in Glasgow, he could finally let his guard down.

Since 1831, the Garrick has wined and dined the great of London's cultural scene. From A. A. Milne to Stephen Fry, the institution inspires improbable passions among its members – with its garish salmon club ties and sumptuous Covent Garden surroundings (Johnson was not a member when he arrived for supper in late 2021). His choice of transport had been criticised; the optics were poor, jetting back from a conference about climate change. But he could not care less, he was among friends. After two years of the Covid pandemic he was the global statesman and at the centre of everyone's attention, something that he had craved since childhood.

In the private room, a broad table was set for around thirty

Fleet Street veterans who had worked with a colleague later to become the most powerful man in the country. The occasion was a reunion of columnists and leader writers whose careers stretched back to the 1960s. The dominant era represented was Charles Moore's, editor from 1995 to 2003; the occasion convened by Stephen Glover and Neil Darbyshire, both senior figures at the *Daily Mail* who had stints at the *Telegraph* in the 1980s and 90s when Johnson was becoming the paper's star political columnist.

The assembled diners – including editor of *The Oldie* magazine Harry Mount, former *Today* programme editor Sarah Sands and editor of ConservativeHome website Paul Goodman – were surprised and delighted to see Johnson was present. Guzzling roast pheasant[1] with Grand Marnier soufflé, washed down with hefty bottles of claret, the collected journalists celebrated what seemed to be the very best of times. Glover noted in his speech that the attendees were 'responsible for millions of words over the decade' and 'it would be impossible to calculate the damage we've done'.

At the prime minister's end of the table Dean Godson, the *Telegraph*'s former chief leader writer, impersonated his old proprietor Conrad Black attempting French; Johnson laughed so hard his friends feared he might crack a rib. One attendee said, 'The extraordinary thing is that I've known Boris in passing for thirty-odd years, but I've never seen him happier and laugh harder than that evening.' Another remarked, 'It was a triumphant homecoming, he had proven himself beyond doubt at having beaten us all.'

When Johnson spoke at the supper, after much wine had been consumed, he delivered a typically comic and self-deprecating speech where one attendee said he (improbably) claimed to have only penned two leaders for the *Telegraph*, the second of which was about the row between author Salman Rushdie and Ayatollah

Khomeini, then the supreme leader of Iran. After his editorial came down on the side of the Ayatollah, the paper's then proprietor Conrad Black informed Johnson he didn't need to write any more, so the yarn went. The hacks lapped it up.

The prime minister's 'very infectious' tone adding to the gaiety of the evening. He rapidly moved on to his favourite topic: his achievements. He paid tribute to the success points of his own government – delivering Brexit and the world-leading Covid vaccine rollout. Then came a heckle: one *Telegraph* writer shouted out that he had not been especially conservative. With his well-worn hangdog expression, an artful ruffle of his thatched hair, Johnson admitted they had a point. There was no malice, it was not an evening for serious policy debate, but to celebrate one of their own.

Johnson later stumbled out of the Garrick Club after the supper had concluded, wearing the same grey suit with blue tie he had donned hours earlier in Glasgow. Moore was photographed at his side, in a double-breasted suit with red tie. The wide grins on both their faces spoke not only to an enjoyable evening, but the decades of warm professional and personal relations. Repaying his early career patronage, Moore had been ennobled[2] by Johnson in 2020.

Moore's demeanour may have been jolly, but his concern for a close friend weighed heavily on his mind. Three days before the Garrick supper, he wrote a *Telegraph* column[3] on the case of Owen Paterson, the Conservative MP and former environment secretary who was facing a suspension from the House of Commons having been found guilty of 'paid advocacy', misconduct that would end his political career. During the investigation, Paterson's wife Rose had committed suicide and Moore made the case that Paterson was being hounded. Moore insisted he did not discuss the matter with the prime minister that night.

But weeks before the Garrick supper, Johnson's closest allies had voiced similar misgivings and had begun plotting a ruse to try and stave off the end of Paterson's career. In the Cabinet and the whips' office, those responsible for Tory party management were crafting a scheme that would disastrously backfire and create a fissure between Conservative MPs that would expose the flaws in Johnson's premiership and see the man feted by his former colleagues as a great leader heaved out of power within the year, rather than his stated desire of serving for at least a decade.

The botched plan to save Paterson was not cooked up at the Garrick alongside the pheasant, but one *Telegraph* alumni reflected on that supper later, 'He palpably felt so powerful and so popular that he thought "I can save Owen Paterson, I'm untouchable at the moment." He was certainly giving off that air. He looked like someone very much enjoying being prime minister at their peak of their powers.'

***

That Garrick supper took place thirty turbulent months after Johnson entered 10 Downing Street in July 2019, amid the Brexit wars and one of the Conservative party's deepest ever crises. The UK's febrile divisions had been tearing apart its politics and social fabric. Three years after 17.4 million Britons had voted to leave the EU, Westminster had failed to fulfil the result. The Tories were hurting: David Cameron had been turfed out as leader after his campaign to remain in the EU failed. Theresa May, his successor, failed and failed again to see through the UK's exit from the bloc. The nadir of her time as prime minister came in May 2019, when the Conservatives came fifth in the ludicrous set of European Parliament elections that took place while the UK's exit from the bloc was in progress. The party faced extinction.

Johnson had long been the bookmakers' favourite to be the next prime minister. From the day he announced[4] 'of course I'm going to go for it', there was an inevitability he would succeed May as the only contender who could reinvent and save the Tories. During the MPs' shortlisting process, where the Conservative parliamentary party selected the final two contenders to be voted on by the 150,000-odd members, he topped[5] each round with clear majorities. His rival, the subdued foreign secretary Jeremy Hunt, stood from the centre left of the party and made little impact. Nearly two decades after he first became an MP, three years since his first bid for prime minister failed, and the countless times he had been written off, Johnson garnered two-thirds of the party's vote. He finally rolled into Downing Street on 24 July 2019.

From the off, the drama and chaos scarcely let up. Outside Number 10 for the first time, Johnson pledged that the UK would exit the EU 'do or die' on 31 October that year. Members of Johnson's first Cabinet had a markedly more right-leaning bent than what had come before, with many of Johnson's long-time supporters handed prime secretary of state portfolios. A few days into power, the prime minister spoke[6] at the Science and Industry Museum in Manchester to pledge a new high-speed rail route from Leeds to Manchester, later known as Northern Powerhouse Rail (he has a lifelong devotion to infrastructure, as part of his quest to leave his physical mark on the country).

A few weeks before Johnson became prime minister, a meeting had taken place with a cabal of his friends and acolytes to figure out how prime minister Johnson would break the Brexit deadlock: without a majority in parliament to deliver a 'no deal' Brexit, or a plan to negotiate a new withdrawal agreement with the EU, he faced being the shortest-lived prime minister in history. Also present at the meeting was his young partner Carrie Symonds, a Conservative party activist who he began dating the previous year and would go on to become his most crucial sounding board. After an inconclusive discussion, one of Johnson's closest allies told him, 'You're going to need to send for Dom.' He duly visited the north London home of Dominic Cummings, the mercurial strategist behind the Vote Leave campaign.

After some persuasion Cummings agreed to come with him to Number 10, but the terms were onerous. He would report directly to Johnson; he would be de facto chief of staff without the title; he would exercise total authority over all politically appointed special advisors. With no alternative, Johnson acquiesced. The relationship was uneasy from the start. Each man felt innately superior and different to the other: Cummings the nerdish strategist and thinker, Johnson the charismatic politician and national figure. Cummings saw Johnson as his useful tool to smash the British state and rebuild it in his image, the prime minister saw Cummings as someone with the force of personality to break the Brexit deadlock.

Throughout his first summer in office, the Brexit deadlock remained and rumours abounded that Johnson would prorogue parliament to ensure it could not further delay the UK's departure. On 28 August, he duly asked the Queen to end the parliamentary session. This was later overturned by the Supreme Court as 'unlawful'[7] but the outrage prompted by suspending parliamentary scrutiny soon deprived Johnson of his working majority when twenty-one Tory MPs were expelled[8] for defying his orders to vote against leaving the EU without a deal – including the former chancellor Ken Clarke and Nicholas Soames, grandson of Johnson's hero Winston Churchill. These expulsions were a defining moment in his rise, a signal of Johnson's intent to break conventions, reshape the Tory party in his image, and do whatever it takes for Brexit.

In October Johnson struck a new agreement[9] with Brussels, albeit one that essentially raised a trade border between Northern

Ireland and the rest of the UK. Instead of approving the new deal, the House of Commons forced Johnson into yet another Brexit delay.

Johnson's calls for a general election to resolve the deadlock and to 'get Brexit done' ramped up. The country at last went to the polls on 12 December. With Tory MPs refusing to back his deal, only one option remained: a new parliamentary party in his own image. The result was the greatest electoral feat of his career. His status as the most compelling political campaigner of his generation was proven by winning the Tories their largest majority[10] since 1987. Jeremy Corbyn, the opposition's left-wing leader, stood no chance. When Johnson arrived in Sedgefield, the County Durham seat represented by Tony Blair for twenty-four years, he was greeted by crowds chanting his name. Working-class England buried reservations about the party and its leader to put him back in Downing Street. Once again, he had defied the consensus. By collapsing the so-called 'red wall' of former heartlands, Johnson was handed a generational chance to reshape the country. The UK finally left the EU on 31 January 2020.

The early days of Johnson's second term were marked by triumphalism. His Downing Street aides, led by Cummings, declared a war on the established media, the civil service and many of the country's respected institutions. In his quest to repay the trust of those first-time voters, Johnson pressed ahead with the High Speed 2 (HS2) railway in February,[11] followed by a Cabinet reshuffle that booted out those outside his inner circle. The most critical change, however, was the forced resignation of Sajid Javid. Johnson and Cummings ordered the chancellor to sack his team of advisors and replace them with Number 10's picks. Javid refused[12] and he was replaced by Rishi Sunak, the young chief secretary to the Treasury. This marked another inflection point of his premiership: had Javid remained chancellor, the most critical power nexus of his government could have been remarkably different.

The country's palpable relief of a stable government after the chaos of the Brexit years was soon shattered when Covid-19 was found in every nation of the UK by the start of March 2020. Johnson was initially slow to act, as the government bickered about the best way to tackle the pandemic. The first lockdown came[13] on 23 March, when Johnson ordered citizens to stay at home. All shops, schools and nonessential businesses closed; normal life ceased. Days later, Johnson himself was diagnosed with Covid. The prime minister was admitted to St Thomas' Hospital on 5 April and moved to intensive care two days later.[14] He recovered but the long fatigue and his brush with death left a deep mark on his premiership.

As the first wave of Covid abated, the first true scandal of his premiership arrived when it was revealed that Cummings had driven to the market town of Barnard Castle in the north-east of England when nonessential travel was forbidden. In a bizarre press conference in the Number 10 garden, Cummings claimed[15] he had travelled thirty miles from his family home to test his eyesight.

Johnson's one-year anniversary of entering Downing Street was marked by a gradual easing of Covid restrictions, albeit with rising fears that another coronavirus wave would hit the country. In September, the so-called 'rule of six' was introduced,[16] restricting how many people could gather indoors, followed by a convoluted system of tiered restrictions later that month. In late October, Johnson announced a month-long 'circuit breaker' lockdown[17] that largely mirrored the draconian restrictions of March. While society was shut down, Cummings left Downing Street after an acrimonious falling out[18] that neither would soon forget. The nation reopened with some restrictions still in place, on the same day Pfizer's Covid-19 vaccine was approved[19] by medical authorities, the first green-lighted jab in the world.

As Christmas dawned, Britons were advised not to travel and the third and final Covid lockdown came into force[20] on 4 January as the Delta variant of Covid spread rapidly. While the prime minister's legacy on Covid is mixed, the vaccine rollout of 2021 was an unadulterated success. His habit of claiming something British was world-beating was proven to be accurate for once. Lockdown ended on 29 March and life gradually returned to a semblance of normality as Covid abated. Riding off the success of the jabs, Johnson delivered a remarkable set of local election results for the Tories in April, including winning the northern seat of Hartlepool for the first time – proving that his electoral potency went beyond the events of 2019. In May, Johnson married Carrie in a small ceremony at Westminster Cathedral; they celebrated afterwards in the Downing Street garden.

Ominous signs, however, began to emerge that the glory of 2019 was fading, that Johnson's coalition stretching the breadth of England was beginning to collapse under the contradictions of governing. In June 2021, the Tories lost the leafy Buckinghamshire constituency of Chesham and Amersham to the Liberal Democrats – the first time the seat had not been represented by a Conservative – prompting party fears that his populist governing style was turning off the traditional Tory base. In July, all remaining Covid restrictions were abolished on 'Freedom Day' – a decision Johnson privately vacillated over for weeks. August brought the withdrawal of UK troops from Afghanistan and the fall of Kabul to the Taliban, a shambolic and shameful moment for all Western countries. Dominic Raab, his foreign secretary, was widely mocked for claiming 'the sea was closed'[21] when asked if he was paddleboarding as British troops were being evacuated.

Ignoring the growing warnings about his premiership, Johnson began the autumn political season with a bang by reshuffling his Cabinet again, promoting Liz Truss to foreign secretary, demoting Raab to justice secretary, creating a new ministry for the levelling-up agenda to tackle regional inequalities and tasking long-time minister Michael Gove to head it. The Cabinet shake-up had been planned for months, according to those involved, and was initially due to take place at the end of July. Several struggling ministers left government while devoted loyalists such as Nadine Dorries were handed new briefs, hers as culture secretary. A week later, Johnson announced a defence pact with America and Australia to counter the dominance of China, known as Aukus. As the economy geared up after the pandemic, however, a crisis in the UK's fuel supplies – triggered by the rise in energy prices – led to supply chain disruptions, soaring wages and thousands of job vacancies.

Johnson's post-pandemic zenith came at that year's Conservative party conference in Manchester, where his allies observed that he was 'pretty chipper'. The prime minister adopted the slogan of 'Build Back Better' from the pandemic and leaned into[22] rising wages, claiming that he wanted a highly productive, highly paid economy that would no longer rest on 'mainlining' cheap labour from abroad. It was typically ideologically and culturally diverse: invoking his political lodestars Churchill and Margaret Thatcher, channelling tennis star Emma Raducanu and praising the Dunkirk spirit for the Afghanistan evacuation. And there were plenty of jokes: Gove was nicknamed 'Jon Bon Govey'[23] after the Cabinet minister was videoed dancing at an Aberdeen nightclub. The prime minister seemed almost bored, hubristically so, by the lack of controversy. When he ran into veteran rebel David Davis in the conference hall, Johnson asked him,[24] 'Why aren't you causing me more trouble?' As they left Manchester, his advisors privately acknowledged 'this is as good as it gets'.

Across the media, journalists lauded Johnson as a phenomenon. Tim Shipman of *The Sunday Times* expressed the feelings of many when he observed,[25] 'Boris Johnson now squats like a giant toad across British politics. He has expanded the Overton window in both directions. Praising bankers and drug companies, while tight on immigration and woke history. Cheered for lauding the NHS and pro LGBT. Where does Labour find a gap?'

And a year later, he was gone. From that high point, the fall of Boris Johnson is the most remarkable political defenestration in modern British political history because so few believed it would ever actually happen. The so-called 'Teflon politician' had defied conventions and odds so many times few thought it could ever end. The parallel to Johnson is Thatcher, who similarly proved herself an election winner that transformed the political scene but eventually lost the confidence of her MPs. Like Johnson, her end was long in the making. It was a similar alchemy of policy and personality that ended her reign as the longest-serving prime minister of the twentieth century.

Was it always going to end this way? Could a better team, a stronger Cabinet, improved structures have resulted in better decisions, fewer mistakes, and a longer stint in power? Or did Johnson's personality and governing style, with its benefits but many flaws, mean his government was always going to come to an almighty smash ending? The answer lies in the story of what took place between the dinner on 2 November 2021 to his announcement on 6 July 2022 that he would resign as Conservative party leader. Although few were aware at the time, the Garrick Club supper marked one of the last true bright spots of Johnson's time in power. As Johnson laughed that night at the jokes and scrapes of his life as a journalist, some further successes lay ahead, especially abroad, but his gradual exit had almost impercept-ibly begun.

***

Owen Paterson was not a close friend or ally of Boris Johnson's. The sixty-six-year-old's temperament was one of an unyield-ing hardliner: he entered parliament in 1997 as MP for North Shropshire – an archetypal rural constituency with a vast Conservative majority. Paterson rose to become shadow secretary of state for Northern Ireland and he clashed with Cameron's modernising agenda, voting against same-sex marriage legislation.

His second and last role in government as environment secret-ary was even more jarring, underscoring his reputation as an anachronism that the party seemingly had left behind. Paterson's scepticism of climate change again clashed with Cameron's agenda, as did his brittle persona. During a failed badger cull in 2013, Paterson was ridiculed for claiming[26] 'the badgers have moved the goalposts'. It was no shock when he was booted out of the Cabinet as Cameron prepared to reorientate for the next election. On the backbenches, Paterson's campaigning efforts were focused on promoting Brexit.

Most of his time, however, was focused on promoting his bank balance. Paterson took up a part-time role in 2015 as a consultant for Randox, a health care company based in Northern Ireland for which he was initially paid £49,000, a sum that was to later double. During the Covid pandemic, Randox was awarded a £133 million contract for testing kits (no other company was offered the work). Paterson represented Randox in a call with James Bethell, the health minister then responsible for private sector contracts. Randox was awarded a further £347 million contract for testing work. Such lobbying was not enough for Paterson: in December 2016, he took up another role with Lynn's Country Foods, also based in Northern Ireland. Emails showed Paterson lobbied the Food Standards Agency about their 'naked bacon' produce.

To the casual voter, and those closely watching his outside interests, Paterson appeared to be a lobbyist first and an MP second. An inquiry by Kathryn Stone, the independent standards commissioner, was opened into Paterson's outside roles in October 2019 but as the investigation progressed, tragedy struck when Paterson's wife, Rose, committed suicide in June 2020. There was no definitive link between the investigation and her death, but the *Mail On Sunday* published emails[27] between Rose and a friend that included links to articles about Paterson and Randox. The investigation rumbled on throughout 2021.

The report, published on 26 October, was damning. It found that Paterson had breached rules on paid advocacy with his approaches to government ministries and agencies on behalf of Randox and Lynn's Country Foods. It recommended a thirty-day suspension from the House of Commons – a move that would have likely led to a recall petition and the end of his parliamentary career. Three days after Stone's report, Charles Moore published his *Telegraph* article defending Paterson. And three days later, Johnson dined with Moore at the Garrick Club.

The conduct of one backbench Tory would normally be a matter purely for the chief whip: Mark Spencer, a jolly rotund Nottinghamshire farmer liked, if not feared, by MPs.

Yet when Johnson met his Downing Street aides the following morning after the Garrick supper, dealing with the Owen Paterson affair had risen to the top of the agenda. Before the Garrick Club dinner, those around him said he was sceptical of intervening. One close aide recalled, 'I can remember in a couple of conversations with him after the dinner he definitely changed.

It was like this seed about Owen Paterson and the need to defend him had been planted.'

Johnson's inner circle of aides and ministers was split between those who felt Paterson should be assisted, and those who could see the pitfalls of trying to save an MP who had blatantly broken parliamentary rules. Two Johnson loyalists, Jacob Rees-Mogg, the patrician leader of the House of Commons, and Mark Spencer plus Declan Lyons, Johnson's political secretary and his critical link with the parliamentary party who was drafted in to facilitate their plans, had already begun plotting how the Paterson situation could best be handled with scant consultation among the wider party machine.

The Spencer–Rees-Mogg–Lyons trio presented their plan to Johnson: they had considered rejecting the report outright but suggested instead that the government would put forward a motion in the House of Commons that would delay a vote on the report and punishment, followed by forming a new nine-strong committee that would explore parliamentary standards and whether there should be a recourse mechanism. It was to be proposed by Andrea Leadsom, the former business secretary. The new committee would (peculiarly) be chaired by former minister John Whittingdale, who had been sacked by Johnson in the last reshuffle. 'God knows why John got involved,' one MP said.

Two individuals close to the Spencer–Rees-Mogg–Lyons trio said the cabal also looked at reducing Paterson's suspension to below ten days, which would have meant no automatic recall petition – a ploy that would have been fraught with the same image problem. 'It would have still created a row because it would have been transparently gerrymandering,' an official said.

Those involved with the plot insist the trio fully grasped that Paterson had broken parliamentary rules but ran two counter-arguments to merely accepting Stone's findings. First was that there was no appeal mechanism for the punishment (had it existed, it is unlikely Paterson would have won given the weight of evidence about his behaviour). Second was an argument from the heart, which found the most traction with Johnson. Spencer, Rees-Mogg and Lyons keenly felt that Paterson had paid a high enough price with the death of his wife and did not deserve to lose his political career too.

This debate took place while Johnson was abroad, physically absent from Downing Street – a theme that was to emerge in other later scandals. 'He was always away when stuff went wrong,' one colleague recalled. 'When you're travelling as PM, it's bizarrely impossible to get people on the phone and things run out of control very quickly.' Some in Number 10 blamed Dan Rosenfield, his chief of staff, for not ensuring he received proper written advice whether home or away. 'It was a fundamental process flaw,' one said. Another government insider said, 'It was the classic case of the PM not realising the significance of how big a problem it was because no one was really telling him.' Decision-making had shrunk to a fatally small clique.

Upon his return to Downing Street, the Paterson plot found favour with Johnson not just because of its supposed compassion but also because of its focus on reforming parliamentary stand-ards. Johnson had been previously investigated[28] over his declarations for a holiday to Mustique paid for by a Tory donor and he had little time for such pettifogging rules; to reshape them was his prerogative.

Johnson, the plotting trio and pro-Paterson MPs were all hopelessly naive. Throughout these weeks of discussions, they missed the obvious problem with the whole endeavour: the average voter could see that Paterson had been through a horrific personal situation, but they could also grasp that he had blatantly breached parliamentary rules. His significant sums of earnings were unlikely to garner much sympathy with the public. With the discussions taking place among no more than half a dozen aides and ministers, Johnson was isolated from further advice that may have persuaded him that saving Paterson and changing the parliamentary standards rules to do so was a terrible idea.

Before the scheme went public on 3 November, his chief of staff Dan Rosenfield and communications chief Jack Doyle instructed Johnson to actually read and contemplate the report, after it became apparent he had not bothered to do so. He also raised an obvious problem in his discussions with Spencer–Rees-Mogg–Lyons: would the Labour party play ball? If they opted out of working with the new committee to examine standards, its legitimacy would collapse. One official recalls Rosenfield asking, 'Why would Labour play ball with this? And what happens when Labour say, "Fuck off, I'm not putting anyone on the committee."' Rosenfield was assured by Spencer that the opposition were fully on side.

Among the wider Downing Street staff, knowledge of the plot to save Paterson was limited until that morning of 3 November. To the civil servants, it was presented as a fait accompli. One said, 'It was like "everyone's going to row in behind it, everyone's on board. It will be rough, but we'll push through".' A WhatsApp was sent to lobby journalists at 11.12 a.m. announcing what would happen. 'This isn't about one case but providing Members of Parliament from all political parties with the right to a fair hearing,' it said. 'Therefore the Commons should seek cross-party agreement on a new appeals process whereby the conclusions of the standards committee and the commissioner can be looked at. This could include judicial and lay member representation on the appeals panel.' The announcement of the plot shocked many at Conservative party HQ and the whips' office.

Motions on parliamentary standards are typically voted

through without objections or amendments so what happened that evening was unprecedented. In the Commons debate Rees-Mogg told MPs that concerns about the Paterson situation had become 'too numerous to ignore'.[29] He reiterated the point that it was not about the individual case but the system. 'It is not for me to judge him, others have done that, but was the process a fair one?' Tory MPs and opposition MPs saw the Paterson plot for exactly what it was: a Tory ruse to save one of their own.

During the vote that evening, senior MPs could scarcely believe what they were being ordered to do. Christian Wakeford, one of the more outspoken newly elected Tories who won Bury South for the first time since 1997, walked up to Paterson in the voting lobbies to call him a 'fucking selfish cunt'. The result showed the mess Johnson had waded into: thirteen Tory MPs voted against and ninety-eight abstained. As it was announced, opposition MPs heckled 'shame' and shouted at the government benches, 'What have you done to this place?'

Number 10's insistence that the motion was not about Paterson's case was moot. Hannah White, from the Institute for Government think tank, said, 'The decision to redesign the system and allow Paterson to appeal his case against whatever new rules are put in place vindicates the public view that there is one rule for MPs and another for the rest of us.' Or, as one Johnson ally put it retrospectively, 'It was patently obvious that Labour were not going to miss the chance to say, "The Tories are reforming the regime to protect themselves."'

Immediately after the amendment passed, Dan Rosenfield's prediction came true. Angela Rayner, Labour's deputy leader, announced her party would 'not be taking any part in this sham process or any corrupt committee'. The Liberal Democrats and Scottish National party followed suit. Following the vote, Rosenfield was in the prime minister's outer office with Lyons and Simone Finn, deputy chief of staff. Someone asked what would happen, Rosenfield responded, 'We're going to scrap it straight away because we have lost this fight.'

Johnson was stuck in the worst of all situations: a lame duck parliamentary committee and Paterson still on the hook. Either he would have to press ahead alone to try and reform standards with a committee of only Conservative MPs, or he would need to rapidly accept he had messed up. Spencer and Rees-Mogg spoke to him, ashen-faced, and admitted they had no plan. Lyons, who was chiefly drafted in to enact their instructions and marshall different sides of the arguments, awaited instructions. Johnson consulted with his aides overnight. One person he spoke to recalls the sentiment was, 'Look, we are clearly in a corner here, we've cocked this up and we need to change it.'

The final straw came in an interview Paterson gave to Sky News[30] where he showed no contrition at all, despite reassurances to Spencer. 'I wouldn't hesitate to do it again tomorrow,' the disgraced MP said. One ministerial aide watched him in horror: 'Owen was not behaving brilliantly at this time and that made it a lot harder.' Another government official recalled Johnson was 'totally furious' both at Paterson's behaviour and the whole ruse.

The next morning, the U-turn came – just one in a long history of rapid strategic or policy reversals that became a hallmark of Johnson's government. Rees-Mogg told the Commons on 4 November, 'I fear last night's debate conflated the individual case with general concern, this link needs to be broken,' and the changes to the standards committee would not go ahead. Those involved saw no alternative: 'We backed ourselves into a corner, there was no way that the committee could ever work.' Paterson soon announced he was off and quit politics – forcing a parliamentary by-election in his traditionally safe North Shropshire constituency that the Tories went on to lose to the Liberal Democrats.

Johnson was castigated. Friday's *Daily Mail* headline read 'On day of farce, Tories U-turn on disgraced MP Paterson after public fury . . . he quits . . . and a nation aghast at Boris's misjudgement asks . . . IS ANYBODY IN CHARGE AT No 10?' On Saturday, the former prime minister John Major, a long-time Johnson critic, told the BBC that the way the government had handled the affair was 'shameful'.

But it was not over. The Paterson scandal blew into a much wider debate about second jobs and whether Westminster should make MPs a full-time profession with no outside interests. Particular attention was paid to Geoffrey Cox, the former attorney general, who registered £970,000 for 705 hours of legal work during 2020. A week after Paterson announced he was quitting politics, the House of Commons endorsed a new code of conduct that banned MPs from acting as paid lobbyists.

The Spencer–Rees-Mogg–Lyons trio slowly grasped how much damage they had wrought. 'They bungled the handling of it obviously. It led to a by-election and damaged the prime minister hugely,' one senior Tory said. So why did Johnson make such an obvious mistake? Some MPs put it down to loyalty to his old *Telegraph* chums. One Cabinet minister told *The Sunday Times*,[31] 'The first rule of politics is that if you listen to Charles Moore and do the complete opposite of what he says, you won't go far wrong.' The same article noted that there was a spilt between different generations about whether to let Paterson off the hook. 'Younger MPs, many in red wall seats, are furious with the old guard – ageing Eurosceptics, Old Etonians and Johnson's former *Telegraph* colleagues.' In turn, the old blamed their youthful colleagues for the second jobs row that risked scuppering their retirement nests. Everyone, meanwhile, was seething at Johnson.

The Spencer–Rees-Mogg–Lyons trio were well intentioned in their efforts to save Paterson, but they failed in their duty to deliver the cold, realistic political advice Johnson desperately needed. With the hundreds of decisions across his desk each day, the Paterson plot should never have reached the prime minister. Equally, though, instead of listening to his former *Telegraph* colleagues, Johnson should have heeded the warnings from some of his aides that it would blow up and was impossible to sell to MPs and the public. Kathryn Stone's report should have been accepted but Johnson made the fatal decision to listen to a too tight group of advisors, instead of more widely consulting the Cabinet.

One senior Tory said, 'He was getting bad advice from the chief [whip] and Jacob at the time. He agreed to do it as, "This is my instinctive reaction, so it'll be fine." And then two days later it's, "Why the fuck has this happened, why did no one tell me?"' Others blamed Lyons, 'I don't think Declan had the nous to spot how big of a problem it was going to be.' A longstanding ally of Johnson piled in, 'He was surrounded by a very mediocre group because they all want to touch the orbit of the Sun King. He didn't think of the consequences of how people will react to this. There was no mechanism for a considered approach. He runs the government like an Oxford tutorial, when people float in with interesting ideas.' But one person who spoke to the prime minister said he was unhappy with his own decision-making as well as the advice he was receiving.

Ultimately, however, it was Johnson's decision to press ahead with the Paterson ruse. 'Boris's greatest fault, which ties into lots of other things, is that he's not ruthless enough,' one minister said. 'He's too kindly and you need to deal with unpleasant business that arises as a PM.' His lifelong desire to be liked meant he often tried to please everyone.

MPs were furious about being marched up the hill to vote for a scheme that cost them political capital for something that was then jettisoned within less than twenty-four hours. More so than the madness of the plot to save Paterson was the indecision. Throughout his premiership, delegation after delegation of MPs had made it clear to Johnson that the U-turns – characterised by Dominic Cummings's frequent use of a trolley emoji, which Johnson initially came up with to describe his own journey towards Brexit in 2015 – were ruining the government. One Tory aide said, 'They had made it clear that all the fucking U-turns had to stop. MPs told Number 10 they're happy to take brickbats, but not if we have to U-turn a few days later. It's one of the most corrosive, painful things you can ask MPs to do.'

The botched Paterson plot marked a turning point for Johnson. The shine of the party conference, the globetrotting premier and the Garrick Club supper was entirely worn off by the affair. Allies of Johnson said at the time that the prime minister 'admits it's a complete own goal'. The damage, however, went far deeper: it created a fissure with the parliamentary party that widened and was never addressed.

One of those tasked with smoothing over relations between Downing Street and MPs explained why the Paterson plot had such an impact: 'It opened up a lot of vulnerabilities in the parliamentary party because all Tory MPs are paranoid about being accused of sleaze. They didn't understand why there had been a sort of special pleading, in Owen's case, because they felt that nobody else would have been treated like that.'

To the party's strategists, Paterson also created a public image issue. 'It looked like Boris is not doing things in parliament that are relevant to me, they're looking after their mates, it's all about politics again.'

Having an eighty-seat majority had acted as a big cushion for Johnson and the government that could absorb its failings and U-turns. But it would not be long before the broken bonds that had begun with the Paterson affair would become an even greater problem, one that threatened to undermine his whole government at the very moment it faced two of its greatest threats to date.

1. Partygate and an Omicron Christmas

Boris Johnson was glum. It was Saturday 27 November 2021 and he was back in the Downing Street press briefing room, speaking to the nation again about the one topic he most wanted to avoid: coronavirus. A few days earlier Chris Whitty, the chief medical officer for England, and his scientific counterpart Patrick Vallance, had visited Number 10 to warn the prime minister's team that a new ominous Covid variant had emerged, one that that might evade the vaccine. 'It was one of those doom-monger moments,' one senior aide said.

Although only two Omicron cases had been detected in the UK, Johnson warned[1] in his televised address that a third wave was coming: 'It does appear that Omicron spreads very rapidly and can be spread between people who are double vaccinated.' The prime minister announced the return of restrictions to buy scientists time to understand whether the existing Covid jabs offered substantial protection. Day two tests for those arriving in the UK returned, along with enforced self-isolation for those who tested positive with Omicron. Face coverings in shops and public transport were reintroduced and Johnson announced that the booster programme for a third round of jabs would be hugely accelerated.

As the pandemic neared its two-year anniversary, daily Covid meetings still took place in Downing Street, usually at around 9 a.m. The cast was small and included Dan Rosenfield, the prime minister's chief of staff, his communications director Jack Doyle, health secretary Sajid Javid and a 'handful' of other aides who drifted in and out depending on the severity of the situation. Those who attended recalled there was often 'indecisiveness' from Johnson between the need to protect from Covid and his constant yearning for freedom. When Omicron arrived, the debate about what to do was no exception.

After three lockdowns, at least two of which Johnson was deeply sceptical about, his gut was against the return of restrictions – echoed by many advisors in his inner circle. One person involved said, 'There were some arguing, "You've been sold a pup" by the scientists, others who said, "You've got to take draconian measures, this is a Doomsday we're fucked scenario." Then there were the mainstream people who said, "Hang on, we have no idea how severe this is." . . . So we took the middle-ground approach.' When considering measures, Johnson's team gave little or no thought to Tory MPs – a repeated critical error.

But in parliament, a growing band of Conservative MPs felt much more strongly and were appalled, thinking that Johnson was making a historic mistake that would ruin the economy, destroy Christmas for the second year in a row, and curb liberties without due cause. A potent caucus emerged known as the Covid Recovery Group – led by arch-Conservative libertarians and former ministers Mark Harper and Steve Baker. The former, who was chief whip, was a longstanding Johnson sceptic who had challenged him for the leadership in 2019. But it was the role of Baker, one of the party's most feared campaigners who had played major roles in the defenestration of two Tory leaders, which concerned Downing Street the most. Johnson had offered Baker a junior ministerial role in his first government, but the MP had rejected it as *too* junior. Their relationship had always been strained, and Covid made it more so. Baker argued that the previous lockdowns were an error, and the government should be focused instead on 'living with' Covid. They were certainly not willing to give Johnson the benefit of the doubt on Omicron.

On 30 November, parliament voted on the new restrictions. Johnson failed to win over Tory MPs to the new restrictions: thirty-four of them opposed the return of self-isolation for those with Omicron and twenty-one opposed face masks in public spaces. Johnson's eighty-odd seat majority was almost eroded. In the chamber,[2] Baker attacked the scientists and data behind face masks: 'the issue is that we are taking away the public's right to choose what they do, based on flimsy and uncertain evidence.' For Baker, an evangelical Christian and messianic Brexiter, the debate was about more than Omicron. For him, it was 'how we react and the kind of nation and civilisation that we are creating in the context of this new disease. What is the relationship between the state and the individual?'

The votes on the first round of Omicron measures underscored the damage the Owen Paterson affair had done to Johnson's relationship with his party. In growing numbers, his party was no longer listening to him. 'MPs were waiting to give us a kicking at that point, and that was the point,' one government insider said. 'We'd lost the benefit of the doubt and everything we brought to parliament was going to be a row.'

Johnson was all too aware that if Omicron went wrong, either with collapsing the health service or thousands of excess deaths, it could undo all of the progress gained with the success of the UK's vaccination programme. But hours after the Covid vote on 30 November, a far greater political problem arrived on Johnson's desk. His communications chief Jack Doyle, along with the prime minister's spokespeople Rosie Bate-Williams and Max Blain, warned Dan Rosenfield that Pippa Crerar, the tenacious political editor of the *Daily Mirror*, was to publish a story that accused the prime minister and his staff of breaking Covid lockdown rules[3] the previous November. Rosenfield, who had not been in Downing Street at the time, asked all three what had happened. The sentiment of their discussion was that some things had gone on and that 'with hindsight, it's not something we should have done' but no one argued that restrictions were not observed. The aides then went to see Johnson, who needed no second invitation to get into a scrap with the left-leaning paper and take a firm line. With the pressure of deadlines, they sought to bat away what was initially seen as a one-day story.

The *Mirror*'s front page that night reported that Johnson had spoken at a 'packed leaving do' when the country was in lockdown in late 2020. It stated that another event took place closer to Christmas that year where officials 'knocked back glasses of wine' and played Secret Santa, at a time when London was under restrictions banning indoor gatherings. Crerar's report went on to state there were many more 'social gatherings' beyond these initial two. One of her sources spoke about the hypocrisy of what allegedly happened: 'While there was one message for the public, the prime minister gave the impression that it could be very relaxed in No 10.' Within Team Johnson, there was the widespread view that the story was briefed by former Number 10 officials close to Dominic Cummings, who were set on bringing down his premiership.

Crerar's story landed at a point when Johnson had just suffered a major rebellion, and while the country was facing another wave of Covid. The accusation of breaking rules was bad enough – playing into the perception that it had been one rule for the establishment, one rule for the rest of the country – but it came at a moment when the country was facing the return of restrictions, which made the story far more potent. It would take some weeks and a drip-drip of reports before the moniker 'partygate' was attached to the scandal, yet the deeply problematic response by Johnson's office was already forged. At the bottom of the *Mirror*'s first story, Downing Street said, 'Covid rules have been followed at all times.'

That line was lifted from the pages of the *Mirror* and repeated the next day in the House of Commons where Crerar's story was a prime focus at prime minister's questions. The preparation team – including cabinet secretary Simon Case, chief of staff Dan Rosenfield, levelling up secretary Michael Gove and a bevy of political aides – were all aware of what he was going to say. Johnson was asked about the gatherings, and bound by the ministerial code, which states that knowingly misleading MPs means resignation, he duly said,[4] 'All guidance was followed completely.' Every aide to the prime minister realised in hindsight that a fatal mistake had been made. From that first discussion in Number 10 with Rosenfield, no one questioned whether Crerar's story was the thin end of the wedge; whether there were more illegal gatherings that breached the government's own laws. No one thought to put together a scoping exercise to find the facts. No one thought to leave any room for flexibility in the press line. 'Of course we should have got someone to do a review, but it was already too late,' one insider said.

***

The end of 2021 for Johnson was dominated by the intertwining tales of partygate and Omicron, both of which exposed flaws in his character and how his Downing Street was run. The schism with Conservative MPs that started with the botched plot to save Owen Paterson grew and the prime minister's approval ratings began to drop rapidly. Although MPs baulked at the Covid restrictions they were being asked to vote on, it was the drip-drip of allegations about historic rule breaking at the heart of his government that was to cause the biggest headache.

A week on from the Covid rebellion, *ITV News* broadcast footage[5] of Allegra Stratton, Johnson's COP spokesperson, answering a question at a mock press conference about a party that breached Covid rules. Plans for holding televised press conferences, in the style of White House briefings in the US, heralded from the Dominic Cummings era, when his (and the prime minister's) desire to circumvent political journalists gave birth to plans for daily briefings where Number 10 could pump its slogans straight to voters. Cummings and the then director of communications Lee Cain wanted Ellie Price, a BBC reporter, to take the press secretary role. Johnson instead plumped for Stratton, previously a *Guardian* and BBC journalist before working for chancellor Rishi Sunak. Reportedly, Johnson's wife Carrie had privately advocated[6] for Stratton.

Although Johnson was initially keen on the idea of communicating directly to the country – particularly after the success of the pandemic press conferences – his aides were not sold on it. 'Boris Johnson is a good communicator and knows he is,' one ally said. 'Was he really going to subcontract his words to somebody else? This is a guy who writes his own speeches and articles.' Along with many others in Number 10, they felt the idea of putting an aide on screen to represent him every day was 'really stupid'. After Cummings and Cain left their jobs, plans for the daily press conferences were unceremoniously scrapped in April 2021.

In the forty-seven seconds of leaked footage, recorded in December 2020, Stratton was asked by a staffer, 'I've just seen reports on Twitter that there was a Downing Street Christmas party on Friday night, do you recognise those reports?' With titters of nervous laughter around the room, Stratton joked that this 'fictional party' was in fact a business event featuring cheese and wine. The clip gave the strong impression that Stratton and the other aides knew that the event in question – 18 November, the one Pippa Crerar had previously revealed – broke rules, contrary to the official Downing Street line.

That night, Johnson and his aides were reeling from the Covid rebellion in the House of Commons. When senior figures in Johnson's inner circle saw the leaked video footage on Twitter, many had no idea what Stratton was talking about. One said, 'My initial response was: what the hell is this? Where the fuck did this come from?' Given the turnover of officials after Cummings and his allies had left Number 10, those running the government had no idea Stratton had been holding practice press conferences. Once again, the finger of blame among Team Johnson was pointed in the direction of the Vote Leave cabal for leaking the footage. Universally it was acknowledged to be a disaster. Tory MPs soon picked up their phones to express their anger at Johnson, realising that the jovial nature of the clip hit a nerve.

After the initial *Mirror* story, communications director Jack Doyle had assured Johnson and chief of staff Dan Rosenfield that it was his belief that all the rules were followed in the press office. As one senior member of his team said, 'The Allegra video was the first point I think we realised this was going wrong and we had a big political problem.'

Only now were the reports about the 18 November party taken seriously and a limited fact-finding exercise began to figure out what had happened. Dan Rosenfield tasked his civil servants with exploring if any rules had been broken, but the inquiry did not span beyond a small team. 'Dan was always motivated to reduce the size of cast lists in meetings and close the loop on conversations because he wanted to protect information,' one colleague said. At the time, Johnson was constantly asking his aides, 'How much more of this is there to come?' A full answer never came. Rosenfield's fact-finding exercise produced a few sides of A4 paper; many of the events that were to prove most embarrassing to Johnson were not even mentioned.

Alongside frustration at the internal process, Johnson's inner circle believed external forces were seeking to bring down the government. Cummings had begun voicing his opinion that Johnson was unfit for the role, remarking[7] he was a 'a joke prime minister' and accused Number 10 of lying[8] about the Christmas parties. Johnson's team suspected that people involved in his Vote Leave gang had access to the archived footage of Stratton via cloud storage and had a role in leaking it to ITV (her former employer) to cause maximum damage. One insider said their first reaction was to realise Stratton was 'going to go through the absolute ringer', swiftly followed by 'a sense of preservation about what else do they have?'

Within Number 10, there was much sympathy for Stratton. The following day, in a tearful video outside her home, she announced her resignation from government. 'The British people have made immense sacrifices in the ongoing battle against Covid-19.' Stratton went on: 'I now fear that my com-ments in the leaked video . . . have become a distraction in that fight.' She added it was never her intention to make light of Covid rules. 'I will regret those remarks for the rest of my days and offer my profound apologies to all of you at home for them.' Stratton had taken the hit, but she had not even attended the 18 November party.

The following day, 8 December, Johnson addressed the House of Commons about the Stratton video. He told MPs he was 'furious' about the clip, but did not change his official response from the *Mirror*'s first report: 'All rules had been followed.' He was asked directly by Labour MP Catherine West, about whether another party had been held in Number 10 on 13 November 2020. His response was, 'No, but I am sure that whatever happened, the guidance was followed and the rules were followed at all times.' Whether Johnson said 'no' to telling MPs or 'no' to whether there was a party is still unclear and became key for the Commons' privileges committee's investigation into whether he knowingly misled MPs.

Some in his team were becoming nervous at the handling of the crisis. 'I remember being surprised it was such a clear-cut sentence,' one Number 10 aide said of Johnson's words in the Commons. A Cabinet minister was told by Downing Street that in response to questions about the Stratton video they should say, 'The rules were followed at all times.' He declined to do so. 'I never did say it because I thought it wasn't something you could be that categoric about.' The minister added, 'The PM was badly advised to be too certain about things in which you can't be certain – bearing in mind nobody really knew what the rules meant precisely.'

What Johnson should have done at this stage was to tell MPs that his team would look into what had happened and he would report back. Instead, the prime minister and his allies became 'like rabbits in the headlights', according to one official. 'They just got caught and went further and further with the denials.' The issue was that too many in the prime minister's core team were directly implicated in partygate. Within the Cabinet, it dawned that a real scandal was brewing. One member said, 'It's the classic Watergate lesson, the cover-up is worse than the event.' The blame was rightly portioned on both Johnson personally and those around him. 'The fundamental flaw for Boris was that his team are not strong managers,' one friend says. 'The lack of political management and understanding is at the core of it. Good leaders put around them people who don't exacerbate their weakness, they offset them. The people who are most loyal to him feed his weakness.'

Yet he cannot escape culpability. When Johnson asked Jack Doyle about whether all the rules had been followed, he did not question his aide's response, or ask him to investigate further whether any more illicit parties had taken place. On the other hand, his chief media aide should have given him the right advice. One senior Tory who observed Johnson at work said he consistently failed to consider the consequences of denying rules were broken. 'What you would normally do is you have a meeting and somebody would say, "Hang on, you can't sustain that argument." Boris would say, "We will get through this, we will get through this." No one bothered to tell him, "No you won't."'

After the leaked Stratton video, calls grew[9] from opposition MPs for the Met police to investigate whether Covid rules had been broken, but, at this stage, they declined. The police said that the footage and other material 'does not provide evidence of a breach' of Covid rules and said it would not retrospectively open an investigation. But it left open the possibility of an inquiry if further evidence of wrongdoing was found.

Johnson, however, was forced to act. On 8 December, the day after the Stratton footage was published, he announced that Simon Case, the head of the civil service, would carry out an inquiry into partygate and disciplinary action would be taken against those found to have broken the rules. The decision to appoint Case was 'rapid', according to those who spoke to the prime minister about it. 'It was just muscle memory. What happens when you need something sorting out? A cab sec's investigation. It's tried and tested.' Another aide close to Johnson felt otherwise: 'It was a really stupid decision.'

The prime minister knew he needed someone credible. 'It couldn't be a politician, it needs to be a civil servant,' one aide said. He considered a retired mandarin but decided that an external inquiry would risk becoming ungainly. Case, who had been appointed as the youngest ever head of the civil service under Dominic Cummings's auspices, was 'furious' at the position he was put in by the prime minister. Case fumed at Johnson's team, 'You're asking me to judge my colleagues. I'm going to do it, it's going to be difficult, and it will find things out that you don't like.'

***

Johnson and his team were also contending with another media storm around Omicron. On the morning of 8 December, Sajid Javid was due to tour the broadcast studios ahead of a major pandemic announcement, but knowing the focus of the questioning after the Stratton footage leaked, he asked Number 10 for a 'categorical assurance' that rules had not been broken. The health secretary did not hear back from Dan Rosenfield or the prime minister directly, so he cancelled the morning media tour.

On this same day of 8 December, before his Commons statement on partygate, Johnson accepted that more restrictions were necessary. An informal ministerial Covid quad of Johnson, Javid, chancellor Rishi Sunak and Cabinet Office minister Steve Barclay had formed around the daily 9 a.m. meetings to monitor the worsening situation. Johnson then lumbered into the Downing Street press room on the evening of 8 December to inform the nation that a 'Plan B' of measures would be introduced, including mandatory indoor face coverings in public places. Guidance to work from home would return. And, for the first time, nightclubs and large events would require vaccine certification or proof of a negative lateral flow test. It was the last measure that would prove particularly controversial with Tory MPs, who decided vaccine passports were a red line they were unwilling to cross.

Compared to the lockdowns of 2020, the measures were limited. 'Boris was never minded to do more than the minimum that could be negotiated,' one close colleague said. But he brought in the measures knowing fully that Tory MPs would not be happy. As one minister summed up: 'The path he ended up taking was not only very courageous and the right call, he did it knowing that the parliamentary party wouldn't be happy. He went in knowing that, but he thought it was the right thing to do to keep the economy open while slowing the spread of the virus.' When his position as prime minister was under threat in the months ahead, Johnson's allies often claimed he 'got the big calls right' and this was one instance when it was true.

It was not only MPs who were divided on vaccine passports, but the Cabinet too. One minister said, 'I was never convinced that certification makes any difference. In practical terms, it would be very hard to actually implement and to be meaningful.' Those in the discussions said Johnson was 'absolutely gang-busters' about introducing them. 'He thought it was a massive incentive to get vaccinated.' The eventual compromise was to allow individuals to show their testing status in lieu of their jabs history. Sajid Javid, who had to present the measures to parliament, focused on the compromise nature of the proposals in his (unsuccessful) efforts to tame the Tory rebellion.

The next day, 9 December, Rosenfield and Number 10 communications director Jack Doyle pleaded with Javid to tour the broadcast studios to sell the new package of Covid restrictions, aware that a major rebellion was brewing. Javid was told by Downing Street, 'You have to do it, otherwise we're up shit creek and it looks very bad.' But the health secretary was still concerned about partygate questions and how he would respond. Eventually Javid was assured there were no parties and no rules were broken – a line he trotted out on TV. But as one friend of Javid put it, 'It turned out to be total bullshit.'

If November's Omicron restrictions vote had damaged the government, the vote on the second round was much more severe – leading to the biggest rebellion of Johnson's premiership. Steve Baker, the ringleader of the Covid rebels, ominously warned[10] the government was 'creating a miserable dystopia'. Many of his colleagues agreed and followed his lead. On the night of the vote, Johnson was distraught, aware it would not pass with Tory votes. A total of ninety-eight of his own MPs rebelled against the measures. He was saved by the opposition parties, who supported the measures, but Johnson had lost his tribe.

Inside Number 10, a large rebellion was expected but not as high as it turned out to be. One Johnson ally said, 'The chief [whip] told us very clearly that it was going to be maximum eighty.' Declan Lyons and Ben Gascoigne, two of Johnson's closest political aides, cautioned against pushing ahead with the vote, telling the prime minister, 'We are going to get completely hammered.' One senior minister realised Number 10 was drifting away from the parliamentary party. 'It became overall Tory political correctness to be anti-lockdown. The vibe was simply against it.' Johnson's problem was that within the Conservative party and outside the government ranks, there was no organised support network for lockdown measures.

One government figure particularly disgruntled about 'Plan B' was David Frost. Known to all in Westminster as 'Frosty', he had taken the Brexit journey with Johnson from the Foreign Office as his special advisor, to the heart of Downing Street as the prime minister's chief negotiator for the revised withdrawal agreement and later negotiating the UK–EU free trade agreement. He was briefly considered to be the prime minister's national security advisor and nominated for a Conservative peerage. After a backlash, Johnson opted to make him a Cabinet Office minister overseeing the domestic and overseas consequences of Brexit. An unashamed right-winger, he became the prime minister's Thatcherite conscience.

In the summer of 2021, Frost had expressed[11] concerns that the Northern Ireland Protocol, which governs trade between the province and the rest of the UK, was broken. 'The EU needs a new playbook for dealing with neighbours, one that involves pragmatic solutions between friends, not the imposition of one side's rules on the other and legal purism,' he wrote of the very deal he negotiated. In October, the EU put forward a package of changes to the protocol that were soon dismissed by Frost as failing to speak to the scale of change required. The situation was deadlocked.

Johnson's team was aware Frost was becoming disillusioned over a range of policy areas, including the Northern Ireland Protocol, the rise in National Insurance, Covid restrictions but also Brexit. One senior government figure said, 'His frustration was that we weren't going far enough on regulation and Brexit opportunities. Number 10's response was, "That's your job, you're the Cabinet minister in charge so go and fucking do it." You've got all the latitude, you've got all the authority. If anybody gets in your way, we will take the Boris Johnson baseball bat out of the cupboard and swing it very hard at them for you.'

Throughout the pandemic, Johnson had ensured the tubthumping Frost was at the key Covid decision meetings to buttress Johnson's arguments against restrictions. At the time of Omicron, Frost felt the arguments made by Chris Whitty and Patrick Vallance were not credible and insisted that there was not enough data from South Africa, the source of the variant, to support more measures. 'He could never believe Boris would ever do it. But then it was rushed in overnight, Plan B was presented to the Cabinet as a done deal,' one minister said. After the package was agreed, Frost told Johnson he simply could not defend it.

Frost duly agreed he would leave government in January to avoid further drama, an acknowledgement of the precarious standing partygate had put the prime minister in. Yet on 18 December, the Sunday following the second Covid vote rebellion, news of his resignation leaked[12] and he was forced to quit immediately (Johnson's inner circle believe he leaked it, but Frost firmly denies this). In a hasty resignation letter, written in a tone more sorry than angry, Frost cited 'concerns about the current direction of travel' – in other words, concerns about Johnson's policy agenda.

Frost praised the prime minister's delivery of Brexit but urged, 'I hope we will move as fast as possible to where we need to get to: a lightly regulated, low-tax, entrepreneurial economy, at the cutting edge of modern science and economic change.' Frost echoed the language of Steve Baker in stating 'we need to learn to live with Covid' and said he was hopeful the country would be 'back on track soon'. His tone later hardened as he urged in a tweet to those in Downing Street[13] and to Johnson to sack 'the neo-socialists, green fanatics and pro-woke crowd', widely interpreted to be friends of Johnson's wife Carrie.

Frost's departure spoke to the wider mood of the party of Johnson's government, according to one of his ministerial colleagues. 'Covid fitted into a broader narrative: bureaucrats in the blob are thwarting Brexit, bureaucrats and the blob thwarting living with Covid. Frosty's critique of the government brought all those things together in one thread.' Although he had been on resignation watch for some weeks, Johnson was 'very very hurt' by his decision to quit. 'He felt it was a personal betrayal because he felt he had made Frost's career.'

***

The sole blessing for Johnson at this time was the vaccine booster programme. After the second vote, Johnson spoke to the country on 12 December where he unveiled the 'Get boosted now' slogan and announced a target of offering third jabs to every adult by 31 December. With the threat of the NHS being overwhelmed once again, his tone was sombre. 'I am afraid we are now facing an emergency in our battle with the new variant, Omicron, and we must urgently reinforce our wall of vaccine protection to keep our friends and loved ones safe,' he said. 'The evidence [is] that Omicron is doubling here in the UK every two to three days.' The military teams behind the first vaccination drives returned: clinics opened seven days a week, over forty planning units were deployed across Britain to deliver jabs into arms.

Johnson's scientific advisors were already warning him that the 'Plan B' measures did not go far enough. On 15 December, chief medical officer Chris Whitty said that Omicron was becoming a 'serious' threat and told people to limit their social interactions ahead of the festive season. One of the most important Cabinet meetings of Johnson's premiership took place on 20 December, a meeting to decide whether the UK would have a second Christmas disrupted by the pandemic – or whether it could go ahead at a risk to the health service.

Rishi Sunak, who was in California at the time, spoke to the prime minister by phone[14] to 'urge restraint' before flying back to London. The chancellor met with Johnson and Number 10's chief of staff Dan Rosenfield on his return to dissuade them on further measures. An official who was present said, 'Rishi privately argued strongly against any further lockdown. He said there was not enough evidence.' Johnson was nervous. If he publicly hinted at more restrictions, Tory MPs might move against him. If he came out strongly against restrictions, he risked losing the fragile support of Whitty and Vallance, both of whom had proved instrumental in maintaining confidence in the government's Covid strategy. 'Public confidence mattered far more than parliamentary confidence, and we came very close to losing Chris [Whitty] in that December,' one insider said.

Five days before Christmas, a much-anticipated two-hour-long Cabinet meeting that would decide whether a second festive season would be ruined by Covid took place virtually on Microsoft Teams. SAGE, the government's official body of scientific advisors, warned ministers that hospital admissions could reach 3,000 a day. Stephen Reicher, one of its associate members, said,[15] 'A circuit breaker is the way to save the NHS and the way to save Christmas.' Johnson was being squeezed both ways. 'In Number 10, the PM was under enormous pressure. He had people saying at this point "You must lock down now,"' one aide said. 'The rest were pretty against, arguing the data could not support what was on the extreme end of being discussed.'

The debate commenced with the customary frequent confusion over who was muted, then Chris Whitty told ministers 'just how bad' the infection rates of Omicron were. But there was a scrap of positive news: the existing Covid vaccines offered a decent degree of protection against the new variant, but not as great as the previous Delta strain. One Cabinet minister recalled Whitty stating, 'If the jabs were 95 per cent against effective Delta, even if they're 90 per cent effective against Omicron, that five percentage point difference in terms of hospitalisations, given its high infection rate will make a huge difference.'

The pro-measures camp was led by health secretary Sajid Javid and levelling up secretary Michael Gove. Javid was the most cautious, highlighting the SAGE modelling and threat of 3,000 admissions a day. But the health secretary did not ultimately back new measures. Pointing to the balance of risks, few of those arguing for restrictions were pushing for another lockdown, unlike some members of the SAGE committee. 'The less risky route in terms of the pandemic would have been more restrictions, but there was no discussion whatsoever by anyone, even from the officials, about lockdown-type restrictions,' a minister present said. Javid told ministers he was happy with whatever decision was made but 'the Cabinet must accept that it is a risk and we're going in with our eyes open'.

The anti-measures camp was led by Jacob Rees-Mogg, leader of the House of Commons. Johnson phoned him the evening before the virtual Cabinet meeting, aware of his longstanding lockdown-sceptic views and urged him to speak out – clearly in need of a comforting voice. Johnson came to Rees-Mogg early in the meeting, before more senior colleagues, and he duly stated that behaviour had already changed as a result of Omicron messaging. One minister present said his argument was essentially, 'We should let people decide for themselves.'

Sunak did not intervene significantly in the meeting, stating Johnson was aware of his views. But one Cabinet minister said the chancellor was 'very upset' with Simon Clarke, his number two at the Treasury, for taking the opposing view and favouring restrictions. Other ministers who spoke out included the business secretary Kwasi Kwarteng and transport secretary Grant Shapps. Oliver Dowden, chair of the Conservative party and an ally of Sunak, had privately told colleagues he was 'pro-freedom' but sat on the fence in the meeting.

The anti-measures ministers focused on the same point: many

of the Covid models had been wrong before and there was not enough data to ruin the nation's Christmas. Instead, they argued that vaccines and an abundance of lateral flow tests would protect Britons. Bizarrely, the decisive voice proved to be David Frost, who was present at the meeting despite having resigned two days before. Like Rees-Mogg, Johnson had asked him before the meeting to make the case against restrictions.

To the surprise of no one in Downing Street, Johnson sided with those who wanted more data before more restrictions. At the end, Johnson summed up 'okay, we're all agreed that we're not going to lock down' but he made it clear it was a risk and his ultimate decision. The prime minister was aware of an argument made by Rees-Mogg that you aren't rewarded politically for locking down. It was such thinking that had convinced Johnson that the previous restrictions had been too onerous and should not be repeated.

After the Cabinet meeting, Johnson delivered another press conference that came as a sigh of relief to the nation overall, but was of great concern to the doctors and staff of the NHS. Christmas would go ahead with no further restrictions. 'Naturally we can't rule out any further measures after Christmas. We're going to keep a constant eye on the data and we'll do whatever it takes to protect public health,' Johnson said, urging, 'but in view of the continuing uncertainty about several things . . . we don't think today that there is enough evidence to justify any tougher measures before Christmas.'

Had partygate not dominated the coming weeks, Johnson would have been able to claim a victory lap with the booster programme, which was 'pure Boris' according to his aides. Johnson was facing the potential collapse of the NHS 'without hyperbole and exaggeration' and the only thing that could save it would be the booster programme and more jabs. The Cabinet Office's marketing department disseminated the 'Get boosted now' slogan relentlessly across the country. Unlike some of the convoluted Covid messaging of the past, this wave came with a straightforward one: get jabbed or Christmas will be ruined.

The practical triumph of the booster programme, however, was almost entirely down to one individual, Emily Lawson, a senior civil servant who had won much favour with Johnson[16] overseeing the rollout of the first and second jabs in 2020. During the first waves of the pandemic, the highest number of jabs delivered by the NHS in one day was 800,000. During December 2021, a million boosters a day was hit consistently. 'We had never as a country done anything like that before,' one senior minister said. Vaccinations were even delivered on Christmas Day and Boxing Day.

Johnson's decision to put Lawson in charge of the booster rollout was inspired, a rare occasion where his grasp of management structures was correct. As with the government's vaccine taskforce, when Johnson hired Kate Bingham to oversee the procurement of Covid vaccines, a small swift team with confident leadership delivered results. Her team was not burdened with Whitehall bureaucracy or the Number 10 squabbling that dominated the rest of his inner circle. 'The brilliance of Boris's leadership came in,' an ally said. 'There is the positive side of never taking "no" for an answer. Boris was personally the one who said, "Nope, I want to go hell for leather, I want us to get everybody boosted by Christmas."'

January 2022 was a bumpy time for the NHS, with hospitalisations rising high just as Chris Whitty had predicted. But it did not tip over. One senior health service official said, 'There was a point in January when we were concerned about it, but thankfully it did level off.' The focus on Covid exacerbated the backlog of non-urgent work facing the health service, which continued to trouble Johnson for the rest of his time as prime minister. 'We knew there was going to be a price to pay to speak in terms of an even bigger backlog.' But out of those tortuous debates, another major Johnson gamble paid off. 'With the benefit of hindsight, Boris got it right when he decided against more measures or lockdown,' one minister said. 'By hook or by crook, in the end, he made that call on Omicron.'

***

Two other developments took place away from public eyes in December that were to have greater ramifications for Johnson's final months in office. During the debate on Covid restrictions, Johnson's allies became concerned that Rishi Sunak was increasingly unhappy – particularly during back and forth over Covid restrictions and the impact they would have on the economy. Throughout 2020, Sunak was briefly the most popular politician in recent British history due to his billions of pounds of economic support during the pandemic. Now he was chiefly worried about stalling the country's recovery.

While some close to Sunak say that he was never serious about his intentions, one figure close to Johnson claimed Sunak 'genuinely thought about going' and that a draft resignation letter had been written over Number 10's handling of the partygate allegations, plus the threat of more Covid restrictions. 'It was well known within Whitehall at a very senior level that he was thinking of going,' one government insider said. 'The PM called him multiple times and they had several long discussions, which stood him down from going. But it was definitely in the ether.' Sunak had taken soundings from his friends in the media at this time, while his campaign handily purchased ready4rishi.com.

The other significant change was in the media. The *Daily Mail*, one of the most influential newspaper in Conservative circles, saw a sudden change of editor. Out went Geordie Greig, the smooth Old Etonian socialite who was close to Johnson's nemesis David Cameron and had run a series of stories about the controversial redecoration of Johnson's Downing Street flat, known as 'wallpapergate', and in came Ted Verity, a protégé of legendary *Mail* chief Paul Dacre and a far more sympathetic editor to his premiership.

A senior Johnson ally said Verity's arrival marked a 'key turning point' in the government's fortunes. 'Geordie was totally hostile with Boris. For some reason, they clearly had a bad personal relationship . . . there was an animus between the editor of the *Daily Mail* and the prime minister, which is never a good mix,' the person said. Under Verity's editorship, the paper became one of Johnson's staunchest defenders until the very end. One government insider remarked, 'If the editor of the *Daily Mail* had changed six months earlier, before all the campaign about wallpapergate, that would have been helpful to us.'

In the background of Omicron, the trickle of partygate stories continued in the run-up to Christmas as political journalists delved into every possible avenue of rule breaking. On 9 December, the BBC reported that Jack Doyle, director of communications, doled out awards at a Christmas party the previous year. On 12 December, Downing Street confirmed that Johnson was part of a semi-virtual Christmas quiz at a time when indoor gatherings were banned. As each story was revealed, the picture painted for the public was that Downing Street seemed to be party central while the rest of the country was locked at home.

On 15 December, a photo emerged of a party at Conservative party headquarters featuring Shaun Bailey, the party's London mayoral candidate, and billionaire property developer Nick Candy. The picture showed that catering had been laid on, including a deeply unappetising selection of snacks. The partygate saga took another turn for the worse on 16 December, when reports emerged that Johnson had attended a do in May 2020, during the first lockdown. Downing Street explained it away as a work meeting. Three days after, a photograph emerged of the event that showed nineteen people drinking wine and sharing cheese in the garden. Dominic Cummings was present, along with Johnson's wife Carrie and their newborn son Wilfred. It patently did not appear to be a meeting.

Then, on 17 December, the final partygate bombshell of the year landed. Simon Case, who had been appointed by Johnson to investigate all the claims, was forced out of the inquiry after it emerged a party had been held in his own office the previous year. Once again, Johnson was furious with his aides, even though he had failed to ask Case if he was aware of any such parties. It was another example of the incurable combination of his aides failing to do due diligence, while Johnson failed to ask the right questions and think through the consequences of what he was doing.

There still seemed to be no strategy for dealing with party-gate, which his inner circle increasingly saw as a concerted campaign prosecuted by his former aides with an axe to grind. Johnson continued to tell his friends, 'This is inconsequential, it's ridiculous rubbish.' That dismissive instinct had served him well in the past, ignoring scandals that all eventually went away. It wholly failed with partygate because he failed to understand its scope and potency for a country facing a second ruined Christmas. Johnson, in the words of a close Cabinet colleague, 'broke every rule of how to deal with a scandal in politics – to first of all establish the facts to satisfy yourself absolutely and fully'.

At its heart, it was also a failure of communications. One strat-egist advised Johnson to make a public statement when the Case inquiry began, with full accounts of the other events and an apology along these lines: 'People who worked eighteen hours a day, seven days a week, did some things that they shouldn't have done, they had some drinks after work while no one else in the country was going into offices. We made mistakes, put our hands up.' The Tory official added, 'It would have been a bumpy couple of weeks, but we could have toughened it out.' Instead, Johnson continued to dismiss the problem until it was way too late.

Any sense that Number 10 could be able to control the direction of the official partygate inquiry disappeared with their choice of replacement. In Johnson's political team, the decision to ask Case to conduct the review meant they felt they had some ability to 'manage' the outcome. 'I don't think we would have been able to shape the views, but we would have had an understanding of where it was heading,' one official said. In his place, however, came one of Whitehall's most senior officials and adjudicators who would certainly take no notice of what Downing Street or the prime minister wanted. Her name, which was soon to be on lips across the country, was Sue Gray.

2. Sue Gray

On her way into the office, a petite, middle-aged civil servant made a regular stop at the Pret near St James's Park station to pick up breakfast. In normal times, no one would have taken any notice of her and the order, but Westminster was experiencing one of its fevered emotional breakdowns. Tony Diver, a political correspondent at the *Telegraph*, recognised Sue Gray in the coffee queue and tweeted out:[1] 'Black Americano. No sugar, no messing around. Ruthless.' The tweet was liked over 13,000 times.

Writing in *The Times* Polly Vernon mused:[2] 'Sue Gray ordering a black Americano in Pret A Manger weeks before finishing and releasing a report that might bring down the prime minister of the United Kingdom is the civil servant equivalent of a mobster doing a line of cocaine before shooting up the headquarters of a rival gang.' During the long gestation of her partygate report, Westminster and the media lost its marbles.

After Simon Case was forced to step aside from the partygate inquiry in December 2021, Johnson had few realistic choices about who could replace him. One close colleague said, 'When Simon stepped down, we thought immediately, "Fuck, we've got to get somebody to do this and do it quickly."' One option considered by Downing Street was a panel of experts, another was bringing in an external lawyer. But the prime minister wanted to keep the inquiry within Whitehall. It could not be the permanent secretary of another ministry – someone junior to the Cabinet secretary – nor could it be a partisan political figure. Gray was recommended for the task by Simone Finn and Henry Newman, both deputy chiefs of staff at the time.

Little is known about Gray and even her age is still a matter of dispute. She was born in 1957 or 1958 in north London, the daughter of Irish immigrants. After her father died of a sudden heart attack in her late teens, she abandoned plans to go to university and headed straight into the civil service. Little again is known about her early mandarin career, except that she took a highly unusual career break in the 1980s to run a bar in Newry in Northern Ireland's 'bandit country' with her husband Bill, a country singer. Some in Whitehall have speculated she worked in an intelligence role at the time, given that the career break took place during The Troubles, though Gray has denied it.

Back in London from 1987, after roles in the transport, work and pensions and health ministries, she joined the Cabinet Office in the late 1990s. Her most influential role came in 2012 as director-general of the propriety and ethics team – known as PET. Gray adjudicated on everything from pay and conditions for political special advisors, to all behaviour covered by the civil service code. Whitehall was littered with political bodies from her past findings: Andrew Mitchell, the former chief whip, was forced out following alleged comments to police officers at the gates of Downing Street. Damian Green, deputy prime minister, was also forced to quit following a Gray inquiry that concluded he misled colleagues over pornography on his work computer.

Gray's power flowed from her close working relationship with the then head of the civil service, Jeremy Heywood. Her influence was private but immense. In his memoirs, Oliver Letwin, a former Cabinet Office minister, wrote, 'Our great United Kingdom is actually entirely run by a lady called Sue Gray . . . unless she agrees, things just don't happen.' The BBC described her as 'the most powerful person you've never heard of'. Heywood praised her as 'user friendly' as she would typically give advice that ministers liked to hear. She is said to have a warm sense of humour, enjoys karaoke and has a passion for cats.

Those who have worked with Gray over the last decade praised her work ethic. Above all else, she existed to protect the civil service from political interference. One aide close to Johnson said, 'I'm fucking terrified of her but not for any real reason.' A Tory minister who worked closely with Gray said they assumed her private views were 'to the left of centre' but added it did not matter. 'She is absolutely dedicated to serving the government of the day.'

Her numerous critics, mostly external to Whitehall, argued that she was too secretive, too devoted to shoring up power for the administrative state. Gray had a reputation for not leaving any paper trails: when the Labour party wanted to nominate someone for a peerage, for example, they would call up Gray for a 'yes or no' on whether the person would pass vetting. No one questioned her advice, there were no records or explanations of her guidance. 'It's fairly obvious that very senior people are scared of her,' one Cabinet Office insider said. 'Everyone knows she can be utterly steely.'

In 2018, Gray abruptly left Whitehall to become permanent secretary of Northern Ireland's finance department, a surprising move for a civil service high-flyer. She then applied to be head of the Northern Ireland civil service but was unsuccessful – she later remarked,[3] 'People may have thought that I perhaps was too much of a challenger, or a disrupter. I am both.' Others reckoned it was political, suggesting her appointment was blocked by the Democratic Unionist party, who felt she was too close to the nationalist Sinn Fein ministers.

In May 2021, she returned to Whitehall to be the second permanent secretary at the Cabinet Office with special responsibilities for the union of the United Kingdom – working closely with the levelling up secretary Michael Gove. The appointment, at the age of sixty-five, suggested that her era as one of Whitehall's most senior figures appeared to be coming to an end. That was until she received the call from the prime minister's office in December 2021.

Gray's arrival into partygate came with Simon Case's blessing – the head of the civil service told colleagues he was relieved to no longer be involved. Her colleagues said she was 'acutely aware' of the balancing act she now had to oversee: go too easy on Johnson and she would be accused of a whitewash, go too hard and a civil servant would be accused of removing a democratically elected prime minister. Gray was nervous and later told colleagues she felt she had been misled by Case. 'She absolutely had no concept of what she was getting herself into. If she had, she would have said no to the inquiry. She was sold a pup by the Cabinet secretary,' one official said. Another added, 'Simon was very much figuratively rubbing his hands.'

The partygate investigation came with wide-ranging terms of reference: Gray was instructed to establish 'a general understanding of the nature of the gatherings', and it could include disciplinary action. There were certain prescribed events she would look at, including all the parties in the run-up to Christmas 2020. But there was a deep contradiction about what she was being asked to do. Catherine Haddon of the Institute for Government think tank summed it up: 'No matter how thorough her investigation, she has effectively been asked to investigate her own political boss.' Or as one senior Tory figure said, 'Cabinet Office inquiries never find the PM guilty.'

Gray's inquiries started before Christmas, while Downing Street was preoccupied with the pandemic. The focus, however, was starting to shift onto partygate. After the Owen Paterson scandal and the Covid vote revolts, Conservative MPs were unwilling to give Johnson the benefit of the doubt any longer. One Downing Street insider said, 'My conversations with MPs about partygate all became negative. I can remember thinking that unless we grip this situation very quickly in January, change the line and clarify our position, it will become a major problem with the parliamentary party.' And so it proved to be.

During the festive break, Johnson's two youthful Conservative strategists – the bearded Australian Isaac Levido and former journalist Ross Kempsell – sought a reset of the strategy for dealing with partygate. They were aware that the media was now chasing the story and would not leave it alone. Levido and Kempsell wanted a 'big war room', with outside legal advice, that would sift through all the evidence from throughout the pandemic to finally figure out what happened, how to repair public perceptions and protect the prime minister's standing. But their hopes were dashed when outside forces struck again and the partygate leaks resumed early in the new year.

***

Dominic Cummings was the first true digital native person to work at the top of a British government. After he left Downing Street, he returned to Twitter and created a Substack account, writing dense but enticing posts about his time in government, particularly now about the partygate scandal. With thousands of subscribers paying £10 each, it was a lucrative enterprise for an apparatchik who might have struggled to find work elsewhere. It became increasingly clear that Johnson's former chief advisor was hellbent on removing him from office and saw partygate as his weapon to do so.

On 7 January, Cummings posted an entry[4] that suggested Gray should focus her inquiries on an event that happened on 20 May 2020 that he said was heralded as 'socially distanced drinks'. His post dismissed *The Guardian*'s photo of the 15 May 2020 garden gathering, stating it was taken after a series of outdoor meetings. The long entry – full of dense language and repetition, a hallmark of his writing – reiterated many of Cummings's critiques of Johnson's decision-making during the pandemic and his long-standing criticisms of how the government was operating. But much of it was devoted to this hitherto unknown event.

Cummings wrote, 'I and at least one other spad (in writing so Sue Gray can dig up the original email and the warning) said that this seemed to be against the rules and should not happen. We were ignored. I was ill and went home to bed early that afternoon but am told this event definitely happened.' The post also marked the first time that he described Johnson as 'the trolley', in a reference to his habit of veering from side to side on policy decisions, akin to a wonky object in a supermarket. Cummings was explicit too that he wanted to remove the prime minister: 'The only way to avert this existential threat to many seats, including much of the "Red Wall", is to replace the trolley with a team that can actually deliver meaningful workforce changes.'

On 17 January, Cummings wrote a lengthy appendix to his blog about the 20 May party where he accused Johnson of lying when he said there were no parties and no rules were broken. 'No10 is throwing out as much confusing chaff as possible, such as nonsense about a "drinking culture" intended to shift blame,' he wrote. 'The events of 20 May alone, never mind the string of other events, mean the PM lied to Parliament about parties.' Cummings argued that Johnson's principal private secretary Martin Reynolds invited people to the drinks party, that he had checked with Johnson, and that both agreed it should go ahead and both attended the party.

Four days later, the invitation that Cummings had discussed handily turned up in public in another leak[5] to *ITV News*. Reynolds, who ran his private office, provided undisputable evidence that a party took place on 20 May 2020:

> *Hi all,*
>
> *After what has been an incredibly busy period we thought it would be nice to make the most of the lovely weather and have some socially distanced drinks in the No10 garden this evening.*
>
> *Please join us from 6pm and bring your own booze!*
>
> *Martin*

ITV reported that around forty staff gathered in the garden with drinks and picnic food. When the revelations had been leaked about the previous events, Number 10 had insisted they were purely work events, impromptu 'gatherings'. This one was impossible to pass off with a formal invitation where individuals were invited to 'bring your own booze'. The timing of the BYOB party was particularly embarrassing as hours before the bash began, the then culture secretary Oliver Dowden had delivered a press conference where he told viewers, 'You can meet one person outside of your household in an outdoor, public place provided that you stay two metres apart.' Gatherings in greater numbers were not allowed until a month later. Yet seemingly Number 10 had taken no notice of their own rules. When the invitation was leaked, there was no comment from Downing Street.

Inside Number 10, however, the atmosphere instantly became like a circular firing squad. The event had not appeared in the slender report into the parties ordered by Dan Rosenfield a few weeks prior, and he had no idea it even existed. Diaries were checked, though, and the ITV report was accurate: Johnson and his wife Carrie had attended. The prime minister was, again, utterly furious with his team, but apparently not at himself for attending the event. He felt his aides had let him down. In a crisis meeting, Johnson shouted: 'How has all this been allowed to happen? How has it come to this? How haven't you sorted this out?'

Much abuse that evening was naturally thrown in the direction of Reynolds from his colleagues. 'People went apeshit with Martin over that email, absolutely apeshit,' one senior civil servant said. 'Not that he had sent it, but at the fact he hadn't bothered to tell people when we asked around about what parties had taken place.' Some officials put the blame on decision-making structures in Number 10 'essentially collapsing' after Johnson suffered Covid, while others put the blame on Dominic Cummings, who had 'disengaged' after the Barnard Castle scandal according to colleagues. Reynolds told colleagues that some of the partying in Number 10 had even been self-medicating: 'When people drank excessively, they weren't doing it for fun.'

Civil servants within Number 10 were anxious they were going to be dobbed in during the Gray inquiry, which was now widened to include the BYOB party. 'People were all running scared, they didn't know who to trust and they had nowhere to go. It was a horrific, toxic atmosphere,' one said. Faced with potentially misleading parliament and lying to the public, Johnson's political team were unforgiving. 'The civil service chronically let the boss down,' an ally said. 'Nobody stepped up, Martin [Reynolds] or others. Nobody stepped up and said "We know things are happening that probably shouldn't have happened. Let's get it all out, let's pull it all together." Officials were giving the PM an incremental impression that it was going to be okay.'

Some vague attempts were made to figure out who had leaked the email. Johnson's closest allies blamed Cummings again, pointing out that the timing of his blog and the leaking of the email were 'too close to be a coincidence'. One ally said, 'It really was a concerted campaign of an extraordinary nature against a sitting prime minister by his previous closest advisor.' Others felt it was the civil service seeking revenge for Johnson dismissing their concerns. One close ally said, 'A lot of the partygate stuff was leaked by junior civil servants, particularly in the press office. There's about thirty of them, all quite young and junior. One person leaking had quit on bad terms the previous summer. Another was selling pictures to the *Mirror*.' Whoever was responsible, trust began to break down between the prime minister and those who were supposed to be running the country.

The following day, 12 January, Johnson appeared in the House of Commons to apologise for the second time. To a deathly silent chamber, the prime minister spoke without his usual rhetoric flourishes or ebullience. He told MPs about the BYOB event that he 'believed implicitly ... was a work event' but admitted 'with hindsight I should have sent everyone back inside'. The prime minister acknowledged the anger and anguish people will have felt 'when they think in Downing Street itself the rules are not being properly followed by the people who make the rules'.

Yet Johnson sought to justify the gathering, stating that Number 10 is a 'big department' with the garden used 'as an extension of the office'. Despite these excuses, the prime minister said he would take responsibility and there was little more he could say until the Gray inquiry was complete. Remarkably, Johnson's words were his own. While journalists took the 'believed implicitly' line to be the result of careful legal advice, to avoid misleading MPs, it was Johnson's effort. 'It wasn't a heavily legal-ised statement, that was the whole problem!' an aide said. 'The PM was writing a lot of these lines himself.'

After a bruising time at the Despatch Box, Johnson visited the members' tearoom – he typically turned up when things were going badly. Some MPs he chatted to recall he repeated his line that he had given to parliament, that he had personally done nothing wrong. Others said he looked 'almost ill' and showed contrition. The mood among the Cabinet was no better. Rumours began to surface that a major shake-up in his Downing Street staff would follow the full Gray report, whenever it was con-cluded, described by one MP at the time as 'the Night of the Long Scapegoats'.

The scandal took one of its routine turns for the worse the following day when *The Daily Telegraph* reported[6] on 13 January that yet another illegal gathering took place, this time on the evening of Prince Philip's funeral in April 2021. The imagery of this third party was the starkest yet: the evening before the Queen sat alone in the chapel of Windsor Castle when nationwide Covid rules forbade people from gathering in large numbers to attend funerals, not one but two boozed-up parties took place in Downing Street. A government official had been dispatched to a nearby Co-op supermarket to fill up a suitcase with wine. Once again, the parties had not appeared in Dan Rosenfield's previous fact-finding dossier of parties.

One party was for James Slack, Johnson's former director of communications, while the other took place for a personal photo-grapher. The *Telegraph* reported that 'excessive' levels of alcohol were consumed and guests danced late into the night. The Covid guidance at the time stated that indoor gatherings beyond house-hold bubbles were forbidden and it was impossible to justify this as a work meeting. Johnson was not present in Number 10 as he had travelled to Chequers, his countryside residence. For Slack's party, drinks were consumed in the press office before transferring to the garden. Staffers at the other do partied in the basement, with a raucous atmosphere. When the two events merged, music began blaring out of a laptop on top of a photocopier while someone played on a swing belonging to Wilf, Johnson's baby son. The seat was snapped off.

When the revelations became public, senior officials were incredulous. All of those in Downing Street were aware that the revelations about the Prince Philip party, where guests were reportedly 'lathered', made the partygate crisis far worse. 'It was the idea of the Queen sitting alone while everyone was getting drunk,' one insider said. At such a sensitive moment for the nation, Number 10 staffers had been reminded by the building's custodians that it was a time of national mourning and they should not exit the black door of Number 10 with grins on their faces. 'I didn't think anybody would need reminding not to have a massive piss-up in the garden,' one senior official said.

At this point, the partygate furore expanded beyond specific events with further revelations about the general culture in Downing Street. Reports emerged that 'wine time Fridays' had been commonplace for a decade, with the suitcase being used to smuggle booze into Number 10 since David Cameron was prime minister. The suitcase began as a carry-on bag, before gradually expanding into something sturdier with wheels. Under Johnson's premiership, a wine fridge was installed that could hold dozens of bottles.

Gray's report had been set up to explore failures by various individuals, but Tory MPs began turning on the prime minister – blaming him personally for allowing such lax standards. One long-serving ministerial aide said, 'There is no doubt the culture is set from the top. It would be impossible to imagine some of the pandemic parties happening under Theresa May or even David Cameron. It's hard to dispute that the atmosphere relaxed under Boris.' While there was still no sign of the Gray report, anticipation for her findings was building each day. Social media was full of memes around 'waiting for Sue Gray',[7] likening her to Mr Bean standing in a field, US Democrat Nancy Pelosi ripping up paper behind Donald Trump, and Gromit the dog, building a train track as he was gliding along.

Throughout January, as the leaks continued, Gray was in regular contact with Johnson's inner circle. While some close to Gray said she 'loathed' the attention and that it was 'the very worst' job she did in government, others in Number 10 thought she was lapping it all up. 'Sue loved being the centre of the story,' one said. 'She became obsessed about her status, her reputation, her position.'

When Gray picked up the partygate inquiry from Case, a fair chunk of work had been done by the Cabinet Office's propriety and ethics team, which Gray used to lead. Her successor Darren Tierney led the investigation day to day and although she conducted some of the interviews personally, for more senior individuals, Tierney and his team did the grunt work. One official on the Gray inquiry described it as a 'very pressured intense environment'. The officials were only too aware they were not just investigating their colleagues, but the most powerful people in the country. 'Sue was concerned, but her aim was not to bring down the government. It might sound old-fashioned but she just wanted to get to the truth,' one official involved said.

While waiting for Sue Gray to complete her work, Johnson desperately formed two new support networks of his closest confidants (his official political team was barely functioning). 'Operation Big Dog' was the first, consisting of minister without portfolio Nigel Adams, chief whip Chris Heaton-Harris, transport secretary Grant Shapps, his political strategist Ross Kempsell and Charlotte Owen, a special advisor who oversaw administration of the team. *The Independent* reported the existence of the gang but missed one key fact: the 'big dog' was not in fact Johnson but Nigel Adams – a humorous nickname for one of the prime minister's most loyal soldiers who is far from big in stature.

Operation Big Dog was a parliamentary operation to counter waning support for Johnson among Tory MPs. Their efforts were directed through a complex spreadsheet, masterminded by Shapps. It ranked Conservative MPs on their loyalty, voting record, constituency needs and how they could be expected to vote in a potential confidence vote to remove the prime minister. From early January onwards, the Big Dog team concluded it was 'inevitable' that the prime minister would be challenged. Unlike partygate, they wanted to be prepared. Dan Rosenfield and the formal Number 10 team welcomed the support. 'He didn't feel undermined or anything, he was happy for the help,' one aide said.

The second support organisation formed at this point was the 'Brains Trust', consisting of Tory strategists Isaac Levido, Lynton Crosby and Ross Kempsell, plus Will Lewis, Johnson's former editor at the *Telegraph*. The latter was brought in as a close friend of Johnson and communications expert. 'He was a very sensible guy and at that stage, the PM had very low trust in any of the actual team,' one person involved said. From the Brains Trust came a slew of policy announcements intended to regain his footing after Sue Gray: the end of all Covid restrictions, a major policy paper on the levelling up agenda to tackle regional inequality, freezing the BBC licence fee for two years. One minister said its efforts were broadly successful: 'The critique most MPs had was, "This Conservative government isn't doing anything that's conservative right now." They sought to change that.'

Two events during January gave Johnson a respite from party-gate. On 18 January, the first plot to unseat Johnson burst into the open thanks to the work of the 'Big Dog' team. Dubbed the 'pork pie plot', it was named after the ringleader Alicia Kearns, MP for the Rutland and Melton constituency, home to famous pies. It was formed of fifteen to twenty MPs from the 2019 intake who were plotting to force a no-confidence vote in Johnson. The membership of the plot was much disputed, but Gary Sambrook, MP for Birmingham Northfield and Chris Loder of West Dorset were both involved. One Cabinet minister said[8] of the plotters, 'They were only elected because of him [Johnson]. Most of them are a load of fucking nobodies.' Within Number 10, the plot brought some relief and comedy.' That was a good moment in party management because things began to swing back to us a bit,' one insider recalled. 'We also just laughed at how achingly bad they were.'

The second event came on 19 January, when the *Financial Times* broke the news that Christian Wakeford, Tory MP for Bury South, would be crossing the floor to the Labour party at prime minister's questions. Wakeford, one of the pork pie plotters who had sworn directly at Owen Paterson several months prior, cited partygate and the cost of living crisis for his reasons for defecting. Johnson received the Wakeford news (he was privately named 'Christian Wokeford' among Tory MPs) just as he arrived at the Palace of Westminster. The prime minister cheered. 'He immediately knew it was a win because it would allow us to claim that the pork pie plotters had committed the cardinal sin of going to Labour,' one senior aide said. Instead of further dividing the party, as Wakeford had hoped, his defection had a unifying effect.

Gray's investigations rumbled on with no hint of when she might be finished and what the final report would look like. And still the partygate leaks continued. On 24 January, *ITV News* reported that Johnson had attended a birthday party in June 2020 at a time when indoor gatherings were banned. The cast list at this particular party was said to have included the chancellor Rishi Sunak, Johnson's wife Carrie and Lulu Lytle, who was redecorating Johnson's Downing Street flat with furnishings financially out of reach for most of the population. The mood inside the government soured dramatically. 'It's death by a thousand cuts,' one Cabinet minister remarked. Other senior Tories came to the same conclusion as the Big Dog Operation: it was 'inevitable' that Johnson would face a no-confidence vote.

The efforts to defend all these parties became farcical. Conor Burns, the Northern Ireland minister and a devoted Johnson loyalist who was occasionally involved with the Big Dog team, was questioned on Channel 4 that evening about the birthday party. Burns argued that the prime minister 'was in a sense, ambushed with a cake' when staffers produced the dessert to celebrate his birthday. The ridiculous phrase entered the partygate lexicon, leading celebrity chef Nigella Lawson to announce[9] 'Ambushed By Cake' would be the title of her next book. When Johnson saw the clip of Burns's interview, he was 'massively pissed off' according to colleagues. There was cake at the birthday do, but it was never taken out of a Tupperware box. Still there was little contrition. Nadine Dorries, the culture secretary and easily the most ardent Johnson loyalist, mused, 'When people in an office buy a cake in the middle of the afternoon for someone else they are working in the office with and stop for ten minutes to sing happy birthday and then go back to their desks, this is now called a party?' The Brains Trust team was 'tearing its hair out at these shit lines', according to one official involved.

Had Gray's full inquiry been published at this point, a no-confidence vote in Johnson could have finished off his career.

With partygate, the prime minister had waded into quicksand and he was gradually being subsumed by each new revelation. Back in December, he could have grabbed a rope to safety by ordering a fact-finding exercise and perhaps sitting down for a comprehensive interview to sincerely apologise and take responsibility for what had gone wrong. Yet no internal fact-finding exercise had ever taken place and the press office never properly softened their response that no Covid rules had been broken and that there had been no parties.

And then, partygate went from a political problem to a criminal one. After weeks of vacillation, the Met police picked the last week of January to formally open an investigation. Gray's team had been passing information to the Met since December and were baffled as to why the police had so far opted not to investigate. One person close to her inquiry said, 'They could have feasibly started an investigation before Christmas, based on the photos and witness statements they received.' The civil servants put the Met's stalling down to incompetence or perhaps concern that it would look politically motivated.

On 25 January, the head of the Met, Cressida Dick, told[10] the London Assembly that her force would look into 'a number' of the parties. Johnson's inner circle was given warning a few hours before the announcement but in a Cabinet meeting that morning, Johnson did not tell his colleagues that he was now under police investigation as it was 'too sensitive' to be shared in advance – again a sign of the low regard he held of those purported to be loyal to him. Johnson's inner circle accepted they would have to cooperate '100 per cent' with the inquiry but most realised they had lost all control of the partygate strategy.

The decision came as a complete shock to the Cabinet Office, throwing Gray's inquiry into chaos just as it was about to conclude. 'From our perspective, they massively dropped the ball and then tried to do a huge overcorrection by kicking off when they did,' one official close to Gray said of the police inquiry. To her colleagues she expressed huge anger and frustration that the report was going to be delayed just as it reached the final drafting. Had the Met not launched their probe, the full Gray report was due to be out by the end of January. A codename was given to the Met inquiry: Operation Hillman.

One ally of the prime minister said they had no visibility of how the police work was going to pan out. 'We didn't know when it was going to end, when it was going to report, there was zero communication between the Met and Number 10. There was no sense of how long the process would take, how many people would be questioned. At this stage, we were massively out of control and the police were fully in the lead.' Some in Johnson's inner circle saw an opportunity to reset the narrative around partygate: with the police investigation underway, they could no longer answer questions from the media or from their own MPs. Everything was paused and stopped, or 'thrown into a bucket called "the Metropolitan Police investigation",' as one insider said.

Sue Gray, however, had other ideas. She told Number 10 that day she still intended to publish an interim report that would skirt around the Met's inquiries. That came as a huge frustration to Johnson's team, who dispatched Simon Case to try and persuade her to wait until the police inquiry was finished. She roundly told Case that was not going to happen.

On 31 January, Gray's dozen tersely worded pages came out. She concluded that many of the gatherings were 'difficult to justify', stating there had been 'failures of leadership and judgment by different parts of Number 10 and the Cabinet Office'. The interim report lambasted the culture of 10 Downing Street and the 'excessive consumption of alcohol' which she said was 'not appropriate in a professional workplace at any time'. Some government staffers had wanted to raise concerns about behaviour but felt 'unable to do so' due to the drinking culture at the time. Although more detailed findings would have to wait, she concluded 'there is significant learning to be drawn from these events which must be addressed immediately across government. This does not need to wait for the police investigations to be concluded.'

When copies landed in his Number 10 private office, the prime minister's reaction was relatively positive according to those in the room and it 'wasn't as hostile as it might have been'. 'He was mostly pleased it was not too personal,' one person present said. Another aide said, 'The interim Sue Gray report was the first time he had a comprehensive understanding of a lot of things that happened.' When setting out a plan to respond, the inner circle knew the only option was another apology – but one that came with a plan to reset the government.

Johnson returned to the House of Commons for his third partygate mea culpa. The prime minister told MPs he was 'sorry for the things we simply didn't get right and also sorry for the way that this matter has been handled' and said he would act immediately to fix some of the structural problems highlighted by Gray.

Despite his relative optimism at the interim report, the ensuing debate revealed that backbench support was draining away from his leadership. Theresa May, his grudge-holding predecessor, said that Gray's report had shown 'Number 10 Downing Street was not observing the regulations they had imposed on members of the public' and posed a question to Johnson: 'Either my right honourable friend had not read the rules or didn't understand what they meant, or others around him, or they didn't think the rules applied to Number 10. Which was it?'

The criticism in parliament went on for hours and Johnson had to take it. Andrew Mitchell, the former chief whip who had supported Johnson's leadership bid, said he had lost confidence in him. Aaron Bell, a 2019 red wall Tory MP, told the prime minister he had not attended his grandmother's funeral due to Covid restrictions. 'Does the prime minister think I'm a fool?' he asked. The testiest exchange, however, came with Keir Starmer, the opposition leader, who called Johnson 'a man without shame', saying, 'Just as he's done throughout his life he's damaged everything and everyone around him.'

In his response, Johnson made one of the most remarkable comments of his time in public life. He suggested that Starmer had failed to prosecute the notorious paedophile Jimmy Savile during his time as director of public prosecutions and that as such he would not be taking any lectures from him. It was untrue and not rehearsed beforehand but seemed to be picked up from Jacob Rees-Mogg, the leader of the House of Commons, who was beside him on the front bench and had yelled it across the chamber. 'People say stuff on the front bench and in the atmosphere of the Commons, you need ideas the whole time,' one Johnson ally said. 'He had a bad habit of repeating what others had said. He has no filter sometimes.' Back at Downing Street, his aides were stunned. Priti Patel, the home secretary, made it known she was 'livid'.

Gray's interim findings, though, allowed Johnson to launch a major reset of Downing Street, planned out by the Brains Trust team. First was structural: her report said 'as a matter of priority' there should be a major effort to address the fact Number 10 had 'not evolved sufficiently' to deal with the 'size, scale and range of responsibilities' that it now had. In response, Johnson announced that a new 'Office of the Prime Minister' would be created, hiving off half of the Cabinet Office's domestic functions to better support his position. 'The PM was genuinely seized of the need to reform how Number 10 was working,' one colleague said. 'He felt he'd been massively locked out of the system by those around him.' One example were the press lines on partygate. 'All of those lines being issued weren't repeatedly signed off by the PM, it wasn't reaching the PM. That was a big structural problem.'

The second part of the reset came on 3 February with the departure of three of Johnson's most senior aides. The first resignation was not planned: Johnson's policy chief Munira Mirza who had worked with him since his City Hall days, was a huge shock for Johnson and his team. In her resignation letter, she cited her reason for leaving as the Jimmy Savile slur against Keir Starmer in the House of Commons. 'This was not the normal cut-and-thrust of politics; it was an inappropriate and partisan reference to a horrendous case of child sex abuse,' she wrote in an excoriating letter that concluded, 'It is not too late for you but, I'm sorry to say, it is too late for me.' Mirza's departure was bitterly felt among Team Johnson, as a minister reportedly[11] said: 'If he's lost her, he really is screwed, there really isn't anyone left.'

Many officials in Johnson's inner circle remained puzzled as to why she quit. 'It certainly wasn't about Jimmy Savile,' one official said. 'When Munira didn't like something, you knew about it immediately. She didn't raise the Savile remark once.' One Johnson ally said, 'There is not a chance on God's earth that a remark about Jimmy Savile would have made a blind bit of difference to Munira. She is as hardcore as it comes.' One minister who worked with her said that the Savile remark was 'the straw that broke the camel's back in Munira's mind', adding that she privately shared Dominic Cummings's views of Boris. 'She loved him, still loves him, but was infuriated by his trolley-like leadership.'

Her departure, though, precipitated the Number 10 shake-up that had been planned for weeks. Martin Reynolds, who acquired the nickname in Whitehall 'Party Marty', after his infamous email about the BYOB email, quit. Dan Rosenfield was out as chief of staff and Jack Doyle was out as director of communications. Doyle had found himself at the harsh end of dealing with the partygate scandal and had fundamentally failed with the unyielding comments to the media he had overseen, and that left no room for manoeuvre. According to one colleague, 'Jack was hollowed out by then, he wasn't functioning in his job.'

Rosenfield realised his position had become untenable. Well before the Gray report, he had attempted to persuade Johnson of the need for some significant personnel changes in Number 10. After months of fruitless discussions, where he warned the prime minister if the calibre of advisors didn't improve it would cost him his job, he concluded it was not going to happen. The day of Mirza's resignation, he travelled in the car with the prime minister to Stansted Airport where the pair came to a mutual agreement he should go. 'Dan was humble enough to accept it was over,' one Johnson ally said. Johnson held no animosity towards Rosenfield and Doyle. The following day, Johnson gathered all Downing Street staff to discuss the shake-up and supposedly herald a new era of calm competence after the Gray report. He quoted[12] Rafiki from *The Lion King* that change was 'good and necessary'. There was no mention of Operation Hillman. The mood was unsettled, however, and it was unclear who or what was coming next.

Despite the reset, relations between Johnson and Sunak began to fray further. Following Mirza's resignation, the chancellor was asked publicly about the Jimmy Savile remark. 'Being honest I wouldn't have said it,' he said in a press conference. Johnson loyalists fumed that it was another sign of betrayal, that Sunak was drifting away from the prime minister's camp. The prime minister's inner circle became convinced that Sunak had again begun planning an exit from government in an attempt to seize the crown for himself. 'December had been an emotional wobble for Sunak, but in January he was strategising and organising a bid,' one ally said. The unhappiness went further when Sajid Javid was also publicly asked about the Savile remark and said he had 'absolute respect' for Starmer's work.

On 4 February, the Brains Trust met to map out what a new Downing Street would look like after the departure of Mirza, Rosenfield and Doyle. The meeting began with bacon sandwiches at 7 a.m. and ended with some 'godawful' takeaway food late that evening. To replace Jack Doyle as director of communications several seasoned political journalists were approached, including George Pascoe-Watson, the former political editor of the *Sun*, Neil Darbyshire (organiser of the Garrick dinner back in October), Andrew Porter, a former political editor of the *Telegraph*, and Sarah Sands, the ex-editor of Radio 4's *Today* programme. Johnson asked Will Lewis to take up the role, but he politely declined and opted to remain an informal advisor.

On Monday 5 February, the new Downing Street team was announced. Steve Barclay, who was appointed as Cabinet Office minister in September's reshuffle, was made Number 10 chief of staff, to run alongside his ministerial duties (something that had never been done before). He was not Johnson's first choice for the job: the Brains Trust tapped up a range of people who all rejected the role. One person involved said, 'We went through all the political advisors and they were all rejected for political or personal reasons.' Another senior official said, 'it was hard to find an advisor who was, by that stage, senior enough or respected enough, to take the job or who wouldn't piss off everybody else.' Grant Shapps was asked to take on the role and declined. 'We needed an outsider. Boris liked the idea of having a minister and he thought that Steve was a competent administrator.'

The other appointment was a familiar name in Team Johnson: Guto Harri, a former BBC political correspondent who worked with Johnson during his time as mayor of London, would be his new director of communications. The always cheerful Harri rapidly made his mark when he told Golwg360,[13] a Welsh-language news site, that he had enjoyed a brief rendition of Gloria Gaynor's 'I Will Survive' and 'a lot of laughing' during his job interview with Johnson. For good measure, Harri went on to insist that his new boss was 'not a complete clown' and a 'very likeable character'. Hari was sharply reprimanded by the prime minister, which did not portend well for their relationship.

The next piece of Johnson's government reset came later that week on 8 February with a mini Cabinet reshuffle that was to have severe consequences. The first aim was to deal with the ministers implicated in the Owen Paterson farrago: Mark Spencer was shifted from chief whip to leader of the House of Commons, while Jacob Rees-Mogg was moved to the Cabinet Office in a new role as minister for government efficiency and Brexit opportunities. Two core members of the Big Dog team were brought into formal roles: Chris Heaton-Harris was made chief whip and his friend and ally Chris Pincher was appointed his deputy.

Two final appointments capped off what would be Johnson's final Number 10 team. Andrew Griffith, a former Johnson aide, was made head of the Number 10 policy unit. Again he could not find a political appointee to fulfil the role but turned to the smooth, well-dressed MP for Arundel and South Downs, who had loaned his Westminster house for Johnson's leadership bid in 2019. Coming from the right of centre of the party, the Big Dog team tried to turn the fact he was an MP into an advantage.

'Andrew and the PM go back a long way with their personal relationship, they do speak and trust each other,' one official said. But those involved in the discussions were aware he was not universally popular. 'He rubs a lot of people up the wrong way,' a colleague said.

The last new figure to arrive in Johnson's orbit was David Canzini, a slight, goateed Tory party official who worked at Lynton Crosby's political consultancy firm, who was tasked to improve relations with Tory MPs. But unlike many of the appointees, he was not close to Johnson – the prime minister told colleagues, 'This guy Canzini, I don't know him.' One longstanding aide to the prime minister said Canzini was a 'very weird addition' to the team and 'it was not clear what he was there to do.' He was often to be spotted skulking around the glass atrium of Portcullis House, which MPs walk through to their offices.

The new team were soon faced with another crisis, this time not at home. With Omicron receding and the pandemic finally over, Johnson's attention turned to the worsening situation in mainland Europe. The first full-scale invasion of a European country since the Second World War would provide Johnson with what some would say were some of his greatest achievements as prime minister. As far as the daily news was concerned, Sue Gray and the Met drifted into the background as President Vladimir Putin drew up plans to invade Ukraine. Johnson would soon find himself playing a leading role on the world stage, as he had always dreamed.

3. Putin's Move

Boris Johnson was nudged awake at 4 a.m. on 24 February 2022 to hear the news he had been dreading but feared was coming. Jamie Norman, the prime minister's military assistant, informed him that Russian troops had crossed several borders into Ukraine from the north, east and south. Missile attacks from Russia had been launched on Ukraine's major cities including the capital Kyiv. What President Vladimir Putin termed a 'special military operation' was given its genuine name in Downing Street: an invasion. The prime minister pulled himself out of bed and Downing Street kicked into what officials termed 'crisis gear'.

For months, the military and intelligence apparatus of the British state had warned publicly and privately that the colossal build-up of thousands of Russian troops along Ukraine's border was not another bluff. Johnson had shared these concerns more widely and some had accused the prime minister of stoking the crisis; of seeking to focus on international matters in order to detract attention away from his growing domestic woes. Both of those accusations were proven false as the horror of Russia's disastrous invasion decision unfurled. The depth of planning that had taken place in Moscow to seek to collapse Ukraine as an independent, democratic state was now obvious to all.

In the early hours of that February morning, Johnson spoke to Ukraine's president Volodymyr Zelenskyy to reaffirm the UK's support for its vital eastern European ally – a partnership that would be central to the final months of his premiership and his legacy. The pair had established a relationship through a series of in-person and virtual meetings, and it was to evolve into one of the deepest geopolitical bonds of recent times. Johnson's critics argued that any British leader would have been forced to develop such bonds by the reality of the UK's foreign policy need to curb Russian aggression. Yet those who have been in the room with Johnson and Zelenskyy attest that their affinity is deep and personal.

Unlike the other crises that hit the UK during Johnson's time in office, such as the pandemic and partygate, the Ukraine war was one that the prime minister and his Downing Street team were well-prepared for. In the weeks leading up to the invasion, detailed plans were made for the prime minister to address the country, hold a debate in parliament, and slap waves of sanctions on Russia to penalise Putin. Johnson had even road-tested a snappy soundbite among senior Number 10 colleagues that he hoped would define the West's response to the invasion: Putin Must Fail. The plans were duly activated that morning.

In the televised address that lunchtime from Number 10, Johnson announced:[1] 'President Putin of Russia has unleashed war in our European continent. He has attacked a friendly country without any provocation and without any credible excuse.' The prime minister sought to differentiate Ukraine from other conflicts the UK had entangled itself with. 'This is not in the infamous phrase, "Some faraway country of which we know little." We have Ukrainian friends in this country; neighbours, co-workers.' He said that the UK and its allies could not allow the values of democracy and freedom to be snuffed out. Johnson summed up the UK's approach: 'Our mission is clear: Diplomatically, politically, economically – and eventually, militarily – this hideous and barbaric venture of Vladimir Putin must end in failure.' Those final words spoke to a lofty aim, but one that Number 10 believed, or hoped, was achievable. He did not, however, warn that the Russian invasion and the West's economic response risked a disastrous impact for consumers at home through the impact on the supply of goods and energy – something Tom Tugendhat, chair of the foreign affairs select committee had suggested. All Johnson said in reply was, 'We will of course do everything to keep our country safe.'

During the first day of the invasion, Johnson spoke to Jonas Gahr Støre, the Norwegian prime minister, and German chancellor Olaf Scholz, urging both countries to join forces with the UK for a coordinated approach with strong sanctions. Downing Street's robust approach was shared by the Foreign Office – typically far more cautious on diplomatic matters. Across the road from Downing Street, a testy meeting between foreign secretary Liz Truss and Andrey Kelin, Russia's ambassador to the UK, broke down[2] after a few minutes. She chastised the ambassador for the invasion, stating 'he should be ashamed of himself' after he 'spouted the usual propaganda'. Truss kicked him out of her office after warning Russia would become 'an international pariah'.

As Johnson prepared to set out the UK's sanctions that evening, he continued to seek a tougher response. The *Financial Times* reported Johnson pushed 'very hard' during a virtual call of G7 leaders that Thursday for Russia to be ejected from the international SWIFT payments system, making it almost impossible to move money in and out of Russia. But German chancellor Scholz did not support such a dramatic move at this stage. Number 10 warned after the call, 'The prime minister underscored that Western inaction or underreaction would have unthinkable consequences.'

The 'Putin Must Fail' sentiment was restated when Johnson addressed the House of Commons with trenchant rhetoric. 'I'm driven to conclude that Putin was always determined to attack his neighbour, no matter what we did. Now we see him for what he is – a bloodstained aggressor, who believes in imperial conquest,' he told MPs. Johnson went on to set out the 'largest ever' set of sanctions, including a ban on Aeroflot, the Russian airline, a full asset freeze on its second largest bank VBT, and export controls on equipment that could be put to military use. Over a hundred individuals would be sanctioned later, with a full range of measures applying to Belarus too, which had been the launch-pad for the invasion.

Over the following weeks, Johnson would garner some of the greatest praise of his premiership thanks to the confident response to the situation in Ukraine. At the close of 2021 and the start of 2022, Downing Street was still struggling with the chaos of partygate and the Sue Gray inquiry, as well as the instability within the prime minister's inner circle. But with the warning lights flashing on the government's diplomatic dashboard with increasing alarm in the lead-up to the invasion, Johnson's nimble foreign policy team guided him into the rare position of being fully briefed and prepared and, as a result, in the vanguard of global opinion. Unlike the unwieldy structures elsewhere at the top of his government, Johnson's approach to Ukraine was effective thanks to a small team dominated by expert special advisors and civil servants.

Led by his chief foreign policy advisor Professor John Bew, historian, academic and one of the world's foremost experts on realpolitik, the prime minister relied on a handful of advisors to navigate the UK's response to the most serious land war in Europe in a generation. Johnson's core Ukraine team included Jamie Norman, his civil service military aide, national security advisor Stephen Lovegrove and Simon Gass, chair of the joint intelligence committee. From the off, the core team wanted to go hard on Russia. 'Our job was to go around and push the envelope as far as possible,' one senior official said. Number 10's political and press team had minimal involvement – they were only drafted in for major media interventions, although Johnson continued to write most of his own speeches.

At cabinet level, Johnson was supported by two close ministers who shared his hardline approach: defence secretary, Ben Wallace, and foreign secretary, Liz Truss. Wallace was a long-time supporter of Johnson's political ambitions and had served in the Scots Guards for seven years; Truss had been promoted to the Foreign Office the previous year, importing her enthusiastic yet disruptive approach from the Department for International Trade. Both ministers were trusted by Number 10 during the crisis. 'We had an activist foreign secretary, who was very good, and an activist defence secretary with huge credibility on the issue,' a government insider side. 'It worked well because there weren't that many people involved.'

Since his tenure as foreign secretary, Johnson had taken a keen interest in Ukraine and was deeply engaged with its complex history. Unlike the often tedious management of Conservative MPs, or the exasperation he felt about Covid rules, his persona was fully engaged with the war. One senior Foreign Office insider said, 'Every time we got these giant maps out, Boris knew where everything was – the villages, historical moments, it fitted into a particular part of his brain.' An ally of Johnson said the conflict reflected on his admiration and aspirations of being a latter-day Winston Churchill; 'I genuinely suspect his worldview clicked with the subject. He has this great appreciation for the history of conflict and battles. It was all completely genuine.' None of his team sensed he was leaping into the subject to distract from his troubles closer to home. 'The suggestions that he was doing a cynical ploy to distract are rubbish,' one Number 10 insider said.

As with his views on almost any topic, Johnson's foreign policy stances had shifted and morphed over the years. During his years editing *The Spectator*, he set out its editorial line[3] as 'always be roughly speaking in favour of getting rid of Saddam, sticking up for Israel'. He had supported the invasion of Iraq and Afghanistan, but sharply criticised Tony Blair's handling of the conflicts. Officials who sat through crisis meetings on Ukraine stated, 'He's not an instinctive hawk, he's not a Russophobe. His basic theory of international relations is cultural and civilisational respect. He is not a kind of shrill neo-con.'

Since Russia's invasion of Crimea in 2014, the UK was at the forefront of the Western military response. Following the annexation, David Cameron's then government offered[4] nonlethal equipment at the request of the Ukrainian government. The following year, the UK launched Operation Orbital, a programme to train nonlethal Ukrainian armed forces with a focus on logistics, medical and intelligence support. In March 2015, the Ministry of Defence ramped up its supply of equipment. Michael Fallon, then defence secretary, said, 'Ukraine is our friend, it is in need and we should respond to requests.' Any requests for help were fulfilled by the UK in coordination with its NATO allies, but an early divide opened up: America supplied lethal equipment early on, France and Germany openly opposed arming Ukraine. Britain fell somewhere in the middle.

In March 2016, the UK and Ukraine signed a fifteen-year agreement on closer defence cooperation, intelligence sharing on potential threats and further cooperation in the training of armed forces. The UK government gifted Ukraine £2 million of military equipment between 2015 and 2017. By the time Boris Johnson became prime minister in July 2019, the defence ties between the two nations were already strong and he sought to make them even firmer, urged on by his advisor John Bew. As well as humanitarian and moral concerns, taking a leading role in the Western defence in Eastern Europe was part of his 'Global Britain' foreign policy.

In October 2020, Zelenskyy visited Johnson at Downing Street to sign[5] a deeper strategic defence partnership that the Atlantic Council think tank described[6] as 'the most consequential foreign relations act of his presidency to date'. It was a full state visit: after meeting Prince William at Buckingham Palace, the Ukrainian president visited one of the UK's gigantic aircraft carriers in Portsmouth and nodded approvingly at the Operation Orbital training of Ukrainian troops. Both countries' defence ministers signed a dense agreement promising £1.25 billion to help rebuild the Ukrainian Navy following early signs that Russia may have been looking to attack from the south. Johnson welcomed Ukraine's move towards NATO membership with 'enhanced opportunities partner' status and pledged whatever further support he could offer.

Johnson and Zelenskyy had grown closer as the threat from Russia increased. In June 2021, the partnership between the two nations had been further deepened with supplies of lethal military aid, the UK following in the steps of the US. Britain agreed to supply two refurbished Royal Navy minehunter vessels, along with the sale of missiles. NATO's largest member matched Johnson's commitment: that summer, US president Joe Biden pledged $150 million of security assistance, which was followed by another package of lethal and nonlethal equipment that autumn.

Come September, Johnson addressed the UN General Assembly (UNGA) and warned 'the adolescence of humanity is coming to an end'. While his message was driven by the impact of climate change as head of the COP26 climate summit in Glasgow, Ukraine was on his mind too. The prime minister met

Zelenskyy for a meeting on the sidelines of the summit, where British diplomats began to stress that the threat from Russia was real and urged Ukraine to supercharge its preparations for an invasion. Zelenskyy's public reticence to acknowledge or discuss how he would cope with an invasion alarmed many in Downing Street, but it later turned out to be a mask for comprehensive private preparations.

One of Johnson's closest aides who witnessed their UNGA meeting said, 'He had a real rapport. We joked that a politician who's famous for playing the piano with their penis is naturally going to get on with Boris,' a reference to a comedy sketch[7] from the Ukrainian president's days as an actor and comedian.

Washington and London were increasingly fearful that war was coming. Biden and Johnson made it clear that additional support for Ukraine could be available well beyond what was already being offered, but the prime minister's affinity with Ukraine was not entirely shared by the Whitehall foreign policy establishment. When intelligence reports suggested in late 2021 that a Russian invasion was a serious prospect, Ben Wallace and Johnson pushed for a further significant increase in the UK's assistance. Although the Foreign Office was seen by some as 'hawkish' on Russia – a topic that crossed the Remain and Leave divide – officials remained concerned at prodding the Russian bear, particularly about the decision to supply 'lethal' weaponry to Ukraine. Events were to prove Johnson correct. 'He and Ben Wallace got it right quite early on against a lot of resistance,' one senior Downing Street insider said.

***

Russia had built up troops along the Ukrainian border previously in March and April 2021 that had not resulted in an invasion. But when the second build-up followed in the autumn, British intelligence believed that an invasion was no longer a bluff. Over 100,000 Russian personnel were deployed – including forces in neighbouring Belarus and navy assets in the Black Sea. London's concerns were shared in America: Joe Biden was visited by his military and diplomatic chiefs in October[8] to inform him that their assessment had changed from uncertainty to alarm that military action was imminent. The US president was told, as was Johnson, that Putin had almost everything in place for an invasion. According to *The Washington Post*, Biden was informed of a plan with 'staggering audacity' that threatened to destabilise NATO and rip up Europe's post-war security model.

Bedecked in white tie, on 15 November, the prime minister used the annual Lord Mayor's Banquet to warn[9] that Western nations would face the unenviable choice between safeguarding their principles and energy supplies. 'A choice is shortly coming between mainlining ever more Russian hydrocarbons in giant new pipelines and sticking up for Ukraine and championing the cause of peace and stability,' he told the City of London's great and good. Downing Street had said earlier that day that the situation on Ukraine's border was 'concerning' and reiterated 'unwavering support' for its territory. Johnson criticised Belarus for being an enabler of Russia's aggression and accused it of engineering an 'abhorrent' migrant crisis. Russia still denied any plans to attack.

All Western military nations sought to strike the delicate balance between the classified nature of their intelligence, while continuing to plan for an invasion. Intelligence sharing by NATO members suggested that Russia would initially focus on an invasion from the north, heading for Kyiv with plans to seize the city within several days. Putin hoped to remove Zelenskyy and install a more Kremlin-friendly regime. Further attacks would follow in the east and the south. One US national security official said,[10] 'It did not seem like the kind of thing that a rational country would undertake.' Biden and Johnson were both receiving analogous intelligence and were left in no doubt that Putin was hugely determined. This time, the UK and US felt that an invasion was going to happen.

Johnson and Biden urged Ukraine to take the threat seriously and to prepare for war. 'The British and Americans were alarmed they were not taking the intelligence seriously enough,' one government insider said. 'It turns out they weren't telling us much about their plans. They were actually better prepared than we presumed at that point.' Another senior official involved in the response said that Ukraine was eager not to give any sense that the invasion was 'imminent or inevitable'.

On 7 December, Putin and Biden held a virtual summit, where the Russian president suggested[11] that NATO's expansion in the east was the reason behind his plans to send troops to the border – essentially that he was guarding his own territory. The US president countered that Ukraine was not on course to join the Western defence alliance. Biden advised there would be severe economic costs if Putin duplicitously proceeded. Johnson spoke to Putin on 13 December. Putin told him Russia wanted clear agreement that NATO's border would not expand at all. Johnson later told the House of Commons how he had responded during the call,[12] 'If Russia were so rash and mad as to engage in an invasion of sovereign territory of Ukraine, then there would be an extremely tough package of economic sanctions, mounted by our allies, mounted by the UK and our friends around the world.'

A few days later on 12 December, a communique[13] was issued by the G7 foreign leaders of France, Germany, Italy, Japan, the EU, US and the UK calling on Russia to 'de-escalate, pursue diplomatic channels, and abide by its international commitments on transparency of military activities'. The statement echoed Biden's message that any military aggression would be countered with 'massive consequences and severe costs in response'. But throughout December Russia continued to build up its presence on Ukraine's border and the US significantly ramped up its supplies of arms, along with the deployment of more of its troops to Europe.

Early in 2022, Ben Wallace, the defence secretary, pushed hard against opposition at the Ministry of Defence to send 2,000 'next generation light anti-tank weapons', known as NLAWs, to Ukraine. Wallace succeeded in his aims and British personnel were sent with the weapons to instruct soldiers how to use the equipment. Wallace said[14] he would not shy away from sending more NLAWs if required: 'I will keep the question of sending more defensive weapons to Ukraine under close review. I do not rule anything out within helping Ukraine deliver self-defence.'

In Downing Street, the rising crisis in Ukraine became the primary focus, yet all the while Johnson was distracted with his growing domestic woes around the partygate inquiry as a potential no-confidence vote loomed. Given his warning at Mansion House, specifically referring to forthcoming problems with energy supplies, it is a surprise that perhaps more was not done early in 2022 to prepare for such difficulties. Downing Street was aware of what was likely to come, yet there seemed little preparation for a short-term solution to energy security and rising prices. An energy security white paper[15] was prepared, which was chiefly focused on nuclear power and other projects that would take years to come to fruition.

On 24 January, Johnson warned[16] that any invasion would be 'painful, violent and bloody'. Based on the joint US and UK intelligence, the prime minister outlined how the conflict could be very rapid: 'The intelligence is very clear that there are sixty Russian battle groups on the border of Ukraine. The plan for a lightning war that could take out Kyiv is one that everybody can see.' Despite the darkening storm, the prime minister still hoped sense and peace could prevail. And if it did not, the UK was preparing to punish Russia.

The following day, 25 January, when the Met police announced their criminal investigation into Covid rule breaking at the heart of his government, Johnson insisted in[17] the House of Commons he was not distracted from Ukraine. 'I and the whole government are focused 100 per cent on dealing with the people's priorities, including the UK's leading role in protecting freedom around the world.' He reminded MPs that the UK had trained 21,000 Ukrainian troops under Operation Orbital since 2015, along with supplying anti-armour missiles and training personnel. But a sign of Whitehall's concern was evident in its decision to 'temporarily' evacuate some diplomats from the embassy in Kyiv.

At this moment, ministers were clear that the UK would not provide 'active military support', nor would it countenance a no-fly zone – which would considerably raise the possibility of direct conflict with Russia. Within Johnson's foreign policy team, a significant debate took place about whether the UK should mirror the US in supplying military equipment that went beyond defensive needs. One senior government insider said, 'The internal debate was whether we announce another tranche of nonlethal aid, or do we move it beyond what we've done already?' Again, the domestic and international collided. Johnson was scheduled to speak to Putin on 30 January, but the call was cancelled as the prime minister was forced to make a statement to MPs on partygate. The Kremlin enjoyed the distraction and declined to immediately rearrange.

On 1 February, Johnson visited Zelenskyy in Ukraine to but-tress the UK's 'unwavering commitment to Ukraine's sovereignty, independence, and territorial integrity within its internationally recognised borders'. As he flew across Europe, 135,000 Russian troops had now amassed on the border with Ukraine – increasing by thousands every week. Officials who accompanied the prime minister recall the visit as bittersweet. 'I'll never forget that trip,' one senior aide said. 'It was very sad because Kyiv is the most beautiful city – it's very Western and not what I expected.' A senior diplomat said that pro-British sentiments were strong during that visit. 'Everyone in Kyiv was obsessed with Brits. If we went to a bar, we were definitely getting drinks because we were British. They thanked us for training their troops and being really supportive.'

As Johnson landed in Kyiv, Poland announced it would supply Ukraine with lethal weaponry – including surface-to-air missiles and artillery shells. While Putin met with Hungary's Viktor Orbán at a ludicrously long, socially distanced table, Johnson's headline announcement was £88 million to fight corruption within Ukraine. In a joint press conference with Zelenskyy, he dismissed the notion that a war was being talked up. 'Someone said we were exaggerating the threat, that the US and UK are trying to big this up. It's not the intelligence we are seeing. It's a clear and present danger.'

After their press conference, the leaders enjoyed an upbeat but focused dinner with their closest aides. One person present said, 'We went to a restaurant, I remember jousting with Zelenskyy, we talked about NATO membership. Our overall impression that night was the Ukrainians weren't fully prepared for what was coming. Our intelligence picture suggested it was really bad.' But the Ukrainian president might have had good cause for dampen-ing the prospects of war. 'What Zelenskyy kept saying was if they spoke out in a way that caused a flight of capital, Putin might be able to get what he wanted, which is regime collapse and a massive crisis without even having to step a foot in Ukraine,' one government insider said.

On 10 February, the Ministry of Defence announced supplies of more defensive equipment – including body armour and helmets. But in another sign that the Brits expected an imminent invasion, all military trainers were withdrawn. The British state threw all of its diplomatic might at the crisis to ensure every option was exhausted. Having missed the Kyiv visit after catching Covid, Liz Truss made a futile trip to Moscow on 10 February, touted as a last major UK peace effort. The trip was a disaster: the foreign secretary was on the receiving end of a belligerent attack from Russian foreign minister, Sergey Lavrov. 'The conversation turns out to be between the dumb and the deaf,' he said, standing right beside her. 'We seem to listen, but we do not hear.' The press conference ended when Lavrov simply walked off and left Truss alone. From her perspective, the only positive was a photo in Red Square, wearing a faux-fur hat that seemingly channelled a visit by Margaret Thatcher thirty-five years earlier.

The same day, Johnson visited NATO headquarters in Brussels and warned the crisis had reached 'the most dangerous moment' as Russia's military build-up reached its climax. The delegation was well received, as Johnson's warnings proved prescient. 'Boris was quite strong,' one civil servant said. 'We'd spoken to the Dutch delegation, we felt like the leaders of this diplomatic campaign – members of the Ukrainian parliamentarians were coming over to hug Boris and get photos.' The last-ditch diplomacy with Russia was rounded off on 11 February when defence secretary Ben Wallace visited Moscow. He warned his Russian counterpart Sergei Shoigu that an invasion would be a 'lose–lose' situation and the UK had 1,000 troops on standby. Cooperation had reached 'close to zero'.

The UK's role as an interlocuter came to the fore. Johnson was 'locked in' on a tough no-compromise stance by this point, according to his aides, and there was 'much scurrying around' to ensure all Western nations were on the same page. 'Boris's role to bang heads together at this stage was quite important, he did his best to ensure everyone moved in lockstep in case the worst happened,' a diplomat said. Several groupings were at play. The core 'quad' of NATO defence powers spoke regularly: France, Germany, America and the UK. It was occasionally expanded to a 'quint' to bring Italy into the discussions. France and Germany may have operated around Johnson at certain times, but his close relations with the Baltic countries proved important.

All of the diplomatic efforts ultimately failed, as they were perhaps always going to. A sham vote took place in the Russian Duma on 15 February to recognise the Donetsk People's Republic and Luhansk People's Republic as separatist regions from Ukraine. Putin continued to insist 'of course' he did not want a war, and Russia muddied the waters by withdrawing some troops from the border. Johnson signalled there may be a 'diplomatic opening' but warned their foes were sending 'mixed signals'.

That following weekend, Johnson attended the Munich Security Conference – the annual gathering for Western political and military leaders. Johnson had a conversation on the sidelines with US Republican senator Lindsey Graham, who assured the prime minister, 'During a crisis, when shit hits the fan, the Brits and Americans are in one place.' John Bew and the Number 10 team were eager for smooth relations with Washington. One official explained, 'It was our job to get the Americans in the best possible position. We had to stay close because we know their heft does far more than anything we can achieve.'

Johnson's keynote speech proclaimed that Britain would always defend freedom and security around the world, reiterating his core message from the start of the conflict: 'If dialogue fails and if Russia chooses to use violence against an innocent and peaceful population in Ukraine . . . then we at this conference should be in no doubt that it is in our collective interest that Russia should ultimately fail and be seen to fail.' Zelenskyy received a standing ovation during his call for peace in his twenty-minute address and lambasted Western leaders for failing to fulfil their security pledges.

Johnson held bilateral meetings with Zelenskyy and delegations from Estonia and Poland. With Brexit still dominating the UK's foreign policy approach to Europe, he had struggled to find a new role until this crisis. 'Until that point, we didn't have a massively activist Europe policy,' one insider said. What alarmed Johnson's team the most was complacency among some other leaders. 'We thought everyone was being very complacent in Munich, we're like, "What the fuck is going on here?"'

The trigger for the invasion came gradually, then suddenly. On 17 February, Johnson said that the shelling of a nursery in Ukraine's Donbas region could be part of a 'false-flag' operation to destabilise the Zelenskyy government and offer Russia a pretext for an invasion. 'We fear very much that that is the kind of thing we will see more of over the next few days,'[18] he warned. A Kremlin disinformation campaign ramped up to purportedly show Ukrainian forces killing Russian troops. On 21 February came the official 'recognition' of the Donetsk and Luhansk republics, followed by tanks moving into the Donbas on 23 February. Russia evacuated its embassy in Ukraine and at 4 a.m. the following morning, the war began.

The UK immediately significantly increased its aid to Ukraine. On 9 March, Ben Wallace told MPs over 3,600 NLAWs had been delivered to Ukraine – along with anti-tank Javelin missiles. He insisted[19] all of the weapons were defensive and the supplies were 'calibrated not to escalate to a strategic level'. Wallace, who had not had the smoothest of relations with Downing Street under the Dominic Cummings regime, was lauded by Johnson's inner circle for ensuring the weapons were delivered. 'Ben broke the mould and Boris explicitly pushed the state further with each step,' one senior official said. 'We didn't realise at the time but he was being advised, "If you want to do this, we should be cautious." That happened on a number of issues during the escalation.' Another senior government insider said they felt Johnson's response on weapons and sanctions showed his gut political instincts at their best: 'It was guts, a willingness to take risks, commit resources and be difficult. He showed genuine leadership.'

***

After the invasion, Johnson pushed on with diplomacy. On 29 February, he visited Estonia and pledged[20] the 'biggest possible' offer of doubling the number of British troops to help protect Eastern Europe. He later went on to Estonia and met British troops stationed in Tallinn. Along with Jens Stoltenberg, NATO general secretary, and Estonian prime minister Kaja Kallas, he praised their efforts as 'fundamental for the safety and security of all of our nations, but also of our values – freedom, democracy, independent sovereign nations'. The prime minister privately picked up an NLAW for the first time during that trip, but photographs were forbidden.

On 1 March, he arrived in Poland and faced Ukrainian anger and frustration directly for the first time since the invasion had begun. Daria Kaleniuk, an activist who had fled her country when the war broke out, told Johnson in a highly emotional appearance, 'You're coming to Poland, you're not coming to Kyiv because you are afraid, because NATO is not willing to defend, because NATO is afraid of World War III, but it has already started.' Kaleniuk urged the prime minister to introduce a no-fly zone to stop 'the bombs and missiles which are coming from the sky' that would kill women and children. A pained-looking Johnson responded, 'I'm acutely conscious that there is not enough that we can do, as the UK government, to help in the way that you want,' explaining why a no-fly zone would result in the Royal Air Force shooting down Russian planes. He was deeply moved by the encounter according to colleagues. 'He was so emotional,' one official said. 'On the flight back to the UK, we were being told to avoid further escalation and be calm. That really pissed him off too.'

On 7 March, Johnson published[21] a six-point plan in *The New York Times* to try and rally an international response – including a humanitarian coalition; supplying more defensive equipment; going further on sanctions (including expelling Russia from the SWIFT banking system); preventing any 'creeping' normalisation of what Russia has done; remaining open to diplomacy and de-escalation; and looking to strengthen NATO. The Biden administration informed Number 10 through backchannels that it did not appreciate the intervention, but it spoke to the pugilistic approach Johnson was taking. He also felt vindicated by the US response; 'It was a conscious decision, we're willing to disrupt and make ourselves unpopular,' one ally said.

All of Johnson's worlds came together on 8 March when Zelenskyy addressed the House of Commons. Quoting the prime minister's political hero Winston Churchill, he told MPs, 'Just in the same way you didn't want to lose your country when Nazis started to fight your country, you had to fight.' Channelling the famous pledge to fight 'on the beaches', the Ukrainian president pledged, 'We'll fight in the forests, on the shores, in the streets.'

More than almost any other topic during his premiership, Johnson was emotionally invested in the conflict. He would often call his foreign policy aides late in the evening, after the 10 p.m. news bulletin, and ask them: 'Why aren't we doing more on x when there's atrocities happening?'

During the frequent rounds of the G7 leaders' calls in the first weeks of the invasion, Johnson did not seek to be a harmoniser. One diplomat said, 'Boris was always willing to piss people off in a way that does slightly go against the conceived wisdom that he always wants to be liked. Quite a few people in the diplomatic establishment were uncomfortable with it and would report back that [Olaf] Schultz or [Emmanuel] Macron were unhappy. But the PM would just come back and say "We're not doing enough."'

As the UK's financial sanctions gradually tightened in further rounds targeting oligarchs and key figures linked to Putin, Johnson's foreign policy team felt they had won the argument – especially when Germany announced it would freeze the Nord Stream 2 gas pipeline. 'We dealt in primary colours, we were explicit,' a British diplomat said. 'We didn't move an inch, whereas Macron or Schultz thought in terms of settlements and realpolitik.' Johnson's constant slogan of 'Putin Must Fail' was eventually adopted by other leaders (Number 10 officials were amused when Canada's liberal prime minister Justin Trudeau emphatically endorsed the slogan in one meeting). 'There was no backsliding by our senior partners. We felt we'd had a huge policy success because everyone landed on our position,' one insider said.

Johnson's central role in the West's response to Ukraine was confirmed on 9 April, when he made a surprise visit to Kyiv as 'a show of solidarity' soon after Russian troops had pulled back. British security officials opposed the visit, arguing it was too dangerous. Johnson overruled them. During a remarkable walk around the city, surrounded seemingly by half the army, Number 10 undertook meticulous planning to ensure no one knew he'd gone. 'It was the most satisfying trip to pull off, it never leaked,' one of his inner circle said. Johnson was cut off from Downing Street for twenty-four hours – except for a burner phone for emergencies – so the last his team heard of him was from a train in Poland. He was videoed greeting ordinary Ukrainians, many of whom embraced and thanked him. Later, at a press conference, Johnson praised Zelenskyy for his 'resolute leadership and the invincible heroism and courage of the Ukrainian people'. He added, 'Ukraine has defied the odds and pushed back Russian forces from the gates of Kyiv.' During the trip the UK increased its loan guarantee to £770 million and pledged yet more military support. One senior official in Zelenskyy's office said, 'The UK is the leader in defence support for Ukraine, the leader in the anti-war coalition, the leader in sanctions against the Russian aggressor.'

The personal rapport between Johnson and Zelenskyy as witnessed in that visit baffled some in Downing Street. One official who saw the pair closely said, 'I find it difficult to say why they get on so well because often his [Zelenskyy's] English isn't perfect and a lot of the time they speak through a translator. It's quite difficult to really understand their relationship. But I don't think it was a romance of convenience.' Another senior official added, 'Zelenskyy admired Boris as a politician and Boris has a sense of Zelenskyy as a significant figure. Boris has a whiff of the zeitgeist and Zelenskyy captured it.' It was arguably Johnson's finest hour as prime minister.

He would remain closely engaged with the Ukraine war throughout the rest of his time in Downing Street, although Johnson was unable to see through to victory his slogan that 'Putin Must Fail'. Officials in his foreign policy team admit now that 'there's no easy way out' of the conflict and that in late 2022 things on the ground are moving towards stalemate. One senior government insider said, 'No one thinks that is acceptable. With the initial Russian invasion against Kyiv repelled, the Donbas has been slightly stabilised and much of the war is now about access to the Black Sea and the land strip. That's really where the question is. If you froze it, Ukraine would not have the ability to function as a state.'

Another person said that it was 'completely possible' that the war could result in some form of disputed territory stalemate with Ukraine. 'There's so much political build-up, you can't go from full-scale war into a sort of neat solution,' the official said. 'Can you have a peace that theoretically may stop short of Ukraine's headline war aims, which is where life was before February 23? Yes.'

***

The Ukraine war had two consequential impacts on Johnson's premiership. The first was to heighten his personal interest in defence matters beyond his previous instincts on foreign policy. During a visit to an NLAW factory in Belfast in May 2022, the prime minister impressed the manufacturers with his 'quite detailed knowledge about the whole weapons systems'. One of his inner team said, 'He got far more into defence.'

The conflict also further developed his foreign policy views. 'Many of Boris's views are instinctive and quite emotional and I think that's probably also the way the British people see it,' one ally said. 'The way the invasion happened is such an egregious insult, all the things we're taught that were bad about the Second World War we thought had gone away. It was a shocking moment.' Although he faced much scepticism from the Whitehall establishment over his support for Brexit, the Ukraine conflict improved his mastery of foreign relations – leading some in the UK's diplomatic establishment to conclude he could turn to an international role after exiting Downing Street. 'He's quite well orientated, he's got a solid sense of it. After three years as foreign secretary, he's got a smell for it and knows the leaders,' one diplomat said. His foreign policy advisors think 'quantum leaps' were made with relations with Japan, South Korea, Australia – as well as the Baltics, Nordics and Poland – during his time as prime minister.

His relationship with Joe Biden was publicly somewhat distant, not least due to the US president's Irish heritage tying into the dispute over the Northern Ireland Protocol. Yet Whitehall officials who listened in on the pair's calls said that the two leaders would often find 'they're completely of the same mind', especially when they spoke one to one outside a formal setting. The protocol did not feature as heavily in their relationship as some reports suggested. 'The whole time Biden never ever mentioned Northern Ireland to Boris once, not once,' a senior diplomat claimed. One of Johnson's closest allies said that the war delivered him one fundamental insight: 'This crisis exposed and reaffirmed the massiveness of the United States and it's vital importance for all our security.'

One foreign policy area that was not resolved was Europe. Relations over the UK–EU trade deal came close to collapsing over the opposing approaches of Brussels and Westminster to the Northern Ireland Protocol. Johnson's team were acutely aware that their hopes of reconstructing Anglo-French relations were unfulfilled. As Johnson entered his final months in office, his foreign policy aides had hoped things may shift. 'I thought we turned the corner,' a senior official involved said. 'We had agreed to reset. That's one of the tragedies, we threw the boomerang really hard and fast and it didn't have time to come home.' Despite the difficulties of Brexit, Johnson's inner circle believed his right calls on Ukraine had left him with a respectable foreign policy legacy. 'His reputation in the world is strengthening, although some may still regard him as a bit untrustworthy. The UK is now more of a player, we are seen to act strategically instead of going along with the pack.' With Liz Truss's pledge to raise defence spending to 3 per cent of GDP by 2030, her approach is likely to follow much of what Johnson pursued. 'That gives us real heft and leverage.'

At the start of the Ukraine war, Johnson warned that the conflict would have a huge impact at home – but few realised the extent to which it would trigger inflation and expose the decades of policy mismanagement of the UK's energy security. When the first rounds of sanctions were discussed, Johnson's team were disgruntled by warnings from Rishi Sunak. One minister recalled the chancellor told the Cabinet, 'Of course we can do sanctions but we should be careful because this will have economic consequences.'

In the subsequent Cabinet debates, Johnson found an ally in Liz Truss as the most hawkish on action. One Number 10 insider said, 'It would always come back to us "Liz wants to push harder" and Boris would always go for the hardest position.' Ministers present said Sunak would not actively argue against action, but saw it as his job to flag the political and economic side effects. 'He didn't push hard, he never undercut what we decided,' one said. Johnson's foreign policy team also dismissed the notion that the UK could opt out of sanctions. 'If we'd sat the whole thing out, first it was politically implausible. Second, we'd all still be suffering from the economic crisis anyway. There's no specific UK sanction that's been self-harming, it's the Western sanctions collectively.'

Sunak was later to state[22] that he never opposed any sanctions but noted they came with consequences: 'I remember saying at the beginning of this thing: "Defending freedom is important, but you've got to tell people that it is likely the energy bills go up to £4,000 or £5,000 in the worst-case scenario . . ." I was like: "You need to go into it knowing that is what might happen. You've got to prepare the country for it, make sure that everyone is on board with that."' He was right that not enough groundwork was done to explain to Britons the potential cost at home, of inflation, of rising energy bills, of correcting the failures in energy security.

The immediate political effect of the Ukraine crisis revived Johnson's standing. By the end of March, most of the decline in his popularity by partygate over Christmas and into the new year had been restored. Pollsters Redfield & Wilton reported[23] in early March that Johnson's popularity had increased by eleven points at home. His approval ratings were even higher abroad: in Ukraine it was 50 per cent. The Number 10 political team were not intimately involved with the war, but his fixers appreciated a different topic to talk about. 'Everything got better politically – there was a period where the media focused on Ukraine and the heat was off on partygate. At that time, we thought, "We are going to get through this,"' one Tory strategist mused. Another senior Tory party figure said, 'It did significantly move the news agenda on. He did demonstrate incredibly good instincts.'

A Cabinet minister close to Johnson argued Ukraine was his 'Falklands moment' akin to Margaret Thatcher's decision to send the navy halfway across the globe in 1982. 'Nobody other than Boris would have set off on this course. The PM was truly world leading in this. It all goes back to the agreement to send arms to Ukraine which started some months before despite enormous official opposition. He took on the blob and won, it was a shame he could not do it on other matters too.' Another minister who observed him closely in the Ukraine response said, 'It showed him at his genuine best. Boris's strengths and weaknesses are the same thing, it just depends on which way the wind is blowing. He's crashing through with "I'm going to lead on this, I don't care about the norms and sort of hesitations about moving too fast on things and not considering them."'

Throughout his premiership, Johnson sometimes failed to demonstrate the knowhow on bending the civil service to his way. Ukraine was the notable exception. 'When the PM pushed something, we'd discover there had been a big internal fight within Whitehall,' one senior Number 10 figure said. 'I remember a top civil servant saying all the time, "Oh, well it's on you then." On a couple of occasions with Ukraine in general, on sanctions, there was a bit of stress transference. We felt in the Number 10 team, we were absolutely at the sharpest point. But we'd also fight, fight and fight for the toughest measures.'

Those who worked with him on the Ukraine conflict could still see the flaws that would bedevil other parts of his government, but felt he was more temperamentally suited to the crisis. 'He was nice to work with,' a Western diplomat said. 'He's obviously flawed in organisational ways. But he can listen to reason, listen to challenge. I sometimes worried he wasn't challenged enough by some seniors around him, but he certainly was on Ukraine.' Whereas Johnson's legacy on Covid and Brexit will be disputed, Ukraine is harder to quibble with. 'We did change the course of international opinion on Ukraine,' one government insider said.

Unfortunately for Johnson, his new-found popularity over Ukraine was short-lived. Partygate had not disappeared, the Met police's inquiries had continued throughout February and March while he was often abroad. His political standing in the UK would rapidly crash back down to earth when an email dropped in his

personal inbox one April morning from the Met police, inform-
ing him of a penalty notice, bringing all of his troubles back into
the limelight.

4. Operation Hillman

Boris Johnson's fifty-sixth birthday party was probably the most miserable of his life. Around 2.40 p.m. on 19 June 2020, the prime minister wandered into Downing Street's grand Cabinet room to discover a select, surprise gaggle of colleagues and those close to him – including his wife Carrie, the Cabinet secretary Simon Case and chancellor Rishi Sunak. Laid out on the coffin-shaped table was a tray of pre-packaged Marks & Spencer sandwiches, with big jugs of orange and apple juice, and cans of beer.

The gathering had not appeared in Johnson's official diary and he was not aware of it before it took place. The morning of 19 June was like many others for the prime minister: work commenced at 7 a.m. with eight meetings in Number 10 – including the daily Covid update. Johnson went off to visit a primary school in Hemel Hempstead, which had reopened earlier that month for the first time since the pandemic. Johnson chatted to the pupils,[1] joined a socially distanced class and was photographed on the playground demonstrating the two-metre rule, his arms raised up on either side. Before returning home, he posed for a photo with a luscious strawberry birthday cake, with dark chocolate oozing down the sides. The image would haunt him again and again during every subsequent partygate story.

According to Sue Gray, the gathering that would see Johnson becoming the first ever British prime minister to have broken the law while in office lasted no more than twenty minutes. Those attending consumed food and drink and 'some drank alcohol'[2] she would conclude. The leaked photos of the gathering present a rather lame sight: aside from Johnson holding aloft a small beer, birthday merriment was thin on the ground. One Tory aide present in the room said it was 'ridiculous' to describe it as a party. 'People were too fucking busy, it was the height of the pandemic.'

A few months shy of the two-year anniversary of this birthday do, Johnson, Carrie and Sunak were issued fixed penalty notices (FPNs) by London's Metropolitan Police for their attendance. The fines, issued on 12 April 2022, could have been challenged but all three instantly accepted and paid the £50 required of them. That evening, Johnson offered a 'full apology'[3] in a pained televised clip from Chequers. 'I have to say in all frankness, at the time, it did not occur to me that this might have been a breach of the rules,' he said. Johnson did not hint at any thought of resignation. 'Now I feel an even greater sense of obligation to deliver on the priorities of the British people.'

His remorseful sentiments were echoed by Carrie who also offered 'unreserved' apologies for breaking Covid rules. Sunak said the same in his public apology':[4] 'I understand that for figures in public office the rules must be applied stringently in order to maintain public confidence. I respect the decision that has been made and I have paid the fine. I know people sacrificed a great deal during Covid, and they will find this situation upsetting.' Surprisingly, the Cabinet secretary Simon Case was not fined, despite being photographed opposite Johnson. There was no pattern as to who the police fined or not: other Number 10 employees in the room also avoided a fixed penalty notice.

The penalties issued to Johnson and Sunak were easily the most significant result of Operation Hillman. The Met commenced its criminal partygate investigation back in January 2022, just as Sue Gray was preparing to release her full report. The Met had often seemed disinterested in investigating historic Covid law violations but with a stipulation that significant evidence would change that. As the leaks and reports of rule breaking stacked up, pressure from the opposition parties undoubtedly played a significant role in their decision to investigate. The police warned that if regulations were violated without a 'reasonable' excuse, then penalty notices would be issued – with fines increasing significantly with each breach.

Within Downing Street there was dismay at the criminal investigation. 'We were all assured for a long time by senior people that this wasn't going to happen,' one civil servant said. When the Met's inquiry began, the then chief of staff Dan Rosenfield gathered the thirty-odd political special advisors in the Cabinet room to reassure them about the inquiry, likening the prospect of any fixed penalty notice to a speeding fine. Despite the reassurances, 'It became a very anxious time for everyone who walked into the building because you were waiting to see if you or the person next to you was going to be fined,' one insider said.

When Operation Hillman began, Johnson's allies were strikingly upbeat that he could avoid a fine. Those close to the prime minister told[5] the *Financial Times* there was a 'good chance' that his reasonable excuses for the events he attended would hold because he considered them to be work gatherings. 'Legally the situation is not as black and white as it might seem. Some of the gatherings may have become full-blown parties later on but not while the PM was in attendance,' one ally said. Unlike some of his previous statements, Johnson took legal advice to oversee his response.

Despite these optimistic briefings to the media, the reality inside Johnson's political team was different. 'Nobody had a fucking clue what was going to happen with the Met,' one figure close to the prime minister said. 'There was no specialised knowledge on what was happening with the investigation, there was no back channel to the Met. People were theorising about what would or wouldn't happen out of thin air.' Throughout March and April, Johnson was constantly asking his aides – often on a daily basis – 'What's going to happen? What's going to happen?' His team simply did not know. The Met communicated only through Sue Gray and the Cabinet Office. Operation Hillman was so secretive that most of it was carried out on paper in a sealed room at New Scotland Yard.

The process took the Met's legendary opaqueness to new highs. At the end of January, the force helpfully said it would not name those issued with the fixed penalty notices, which only succeeded in creating a media witch-hunt to track down the rulebreakers. A few weeks into the inquiry, it was announced that ninety people would be sent questionnaires. Number 10 confirmed on 11 February that Johnson had received one, with the requirement for it to be returned 'truthfully' within a week. These forms held the same status as being interviewed under caution, meaning Johnson became the first prime minister to acquire this dubious accolade (one of his predecessors, Tony Blair, said he would quit if questioned under caution during the 'cash for peerages' scandal).

The forms, with some dozen questions,[6] asked individuals to provide a 'lawful exception' or 'reasonable excuse' for attending the event under investigation. The questions, which included the timings of the person's attendance at the gathering, included the following:

- Did you participate in a gathering on a specific date?
- What was the purpose of your participation in that gathering?
- Did you interact with, or undertake any activity with other persons present at the gathering? If yes, please provide details.

The Met said individuals could remain silent and answer 'no comment' to the questions, provide written responses, or attach a statement in their own words. Downing Street declined to say how Johnson had answered. But junior civil servants were petrified, fearing that the responses they had given to Sue Gray would be used against them in a criminal investigation – in turn, she allowed those who had spoken to her inquiry to review her notes before filling in the questionnaires.

Johnson's inner circle felt that the most problematic event would be the event that took place in May 2020, the 'Bring Your Own Booze' party, although their argument that the prime minister did not see Martin Reynolds's email invite ultimately held. The birthday party in June 2020 was far from the top of their radar: his allies insisted there would be no fine because it involved work colleagues and was not pre-planned. As the Ukraine war dominated the news, Downing Street had some breathing space from the restive Conservative MPs. 'The rage was gone so it didn't feel that bad,' one insider recalled.

But the fines kept coming and the scale of law breaking at the heart of the British state became apparent. By 29 March, twenty fines had been issued – and again the Met did not clarify who had received the £50 notices. The *Telegraph* reported that the first batch of fines covered the infamous 'Prince Philip' leaving party for James Slack, previously Johnson's director of communications. Another notable figure fined was Helen MacNamara, Sue Gray's successor as the Cabinet Office's director of propriety and ethics who procured a karaoke machine at one party that ended with a physical altercation between guests. She apologised[7] for 'the error of judgement I have shown'.

By 12 April, a batch of thirty FPNs were issued – including the ones issued for Johnson, his wife and chancellor. When the Met tipped off Downing Street that the fine was coming, the response was summarised by one press office aide to another as 'Fuck fuck fuck.' There was 'complete bafflement' as to why the Met had gone for that particular event. 'It was mad,' one insider said. 'Any objective person looks at that event and would say "What the hell is this?"' Johnson's closest colleagues concluded the fine was due to the presence of non-government staff.

Many in Downing Street felt sorrow that Johnson was taking responsibility for the rule breaking of others. 'I did feel a bit sorry for the PM because he was carrying the can,' one close colleague said, 'but Covid was something which literally every single person in the country related to because it affected their lives in a very bad way.' The sympathy for the prime minister extended into the Cabinet. 'Boris was as much a victim as anyone,' one minister said. 'The fine was ridiculous. His legal defence, which I think is right, was that he was demonstrating leadership. Boris doesn't even particularly like parties, when he went to all these events, he was doing it genuinely because he thought "These guys have been working hard and I've got to say thank you."'

The bewilderment was shared at the Department for Levelling Up. Sue Gray, who had returned to her day job until the police work was complete, privately expected Johnson to be fined but not necessarily for the birthday party. 'Sue had not put the birthday party at the top of her list,' one colleague said. 'There wasn't a surprise [among the team] that he was issued a fixed penalty notice, but there was surprise it was that event – particularly those who had seen the photos and all of the witness statements.'

Gray's team was privately quizzical that Simon Case, who was photographed laughing at Johnson raising a can of beer, had not received an FPN. 'Nobody understands that,' a senior official recalled. 'The only credible assumption is that they filled out the forms differently.' Johnson and Case did not coordinate their responses and took separate legal advice. Another person close to the process said, 'It can only be that there was sufficient doubt or excusable factors about Simon's actions, which is remarkable because they were all in the same room, for the same thing, for the same amount of time.'

The following week, Johnson was questioned in the House of Commons about the fine. Keir Starmer accused him of using the Ukraine war as a 'shield' to stave off resignation. Johnson admitted[8] he had been mistaken about the Covid rules: 'It did not occur to me then, or subsequently, that a gathering in the cabinet room just before a vital meeting on Covid strategy could amount to a breach of the rules.' Starmer, irate, retorted that his response was a joke and accused him of being dishonest (he was forced to withdraw the remark by the Commons speaker). On the Tory benches, Mark Harper, the former chief whip and one of the successful organising forces behind the Omicron rules rebellion the previous December, called on Johnson to resign.

Later that day, Johnson addressed a meeting of the 1922 Committee of Conservative MPs to stabilise his position – telling them, 'We're going to get on with our one-nation Conservative agenda.' Plenty of Johnson critics within the party piled into him. One advisor said that the fine became 'another excuse for people who wanted him to go' but they did not believe that a confidence vote was imminent. Tory strategists were increasingly aware that voters were becoming fed up with the story. 'The thing that people were most pissed off about partygate was the distraction from the things they actually cared about,' one said.

Among Johnson's closest allies, a visceral anger towards the police festered. Some of his supporters put the decision to investigate the parties down to internal leadership issues within the Met. One Johnson ally, who called the partygate investigation 'an abuse of power' and a 'waste of taxpayers' funds', mused, 'The Metropolitan Police was going through a bad time.

It was used as a distraction to give the commissioner some political strength by saying, "You can't get rid of me as commissioner now I'm investigating you.'"

But what was done was done. Johnson had broken the law and accepted the punishment. It may have been a minor infraction, yet his standing was undoubtedly harmed. Throughout partygate, the prime minister and his core team failed to understand why there was so much anger about parties that in normal times would never have been considered parties at all. In essence, they did not experience the same pandemic as the rest of the country with many of the 400-odd staffers in Downing Street continuing to work in the office, due to security issues and practical reasons, and as such they never suffered as much of the isolation and loneliness as the rest of the nation.

Johnson's failure to emotionally grasp the exceptional situation led to an over-optimistic sense that the fine would not be lethal to his career. Once again, his core political team miscalculated the mood. 'There was a consensus in Number 10 that it would be impossible for the police to fine the PM because it would be a massively political thing. Most people in Number 10 thought it wasn't going to happen. Turned out that was total bullshit.'

***

As well as worsening relations with his MPs, the strained relations between Johnson and Sunak sunk even further. The day after the fines were issued, *The Times* reported[9] that the chancellor devoted seven hours to debating his own future, having also told parliament that no Covid rules were broken. The paper reported that Sunak thought both he and Johnson should go, but 'friends warned him that his resignation could be considered an act of regicide against Johnson and damage any chances that Sunak might have of succeeding him'. One Sunak ally said he 'feels very badly let down by being dragged into this' and it was only natural for him to consider his position.

Relations between Number 10 and Number 11 Downing Street also faced policy pressure during the spring statement on 23 March when the cost of living crisis came to the fore. Due chiefly to the Ukraine war and the pandemic, inflation was soaring – reaching a four-decade high of 8.7 per cent. The Office for Budget Responsibility, which produces the UK's economic forecasts, warned that the country would suffer its biggest fall in living standards in sixty-six years.

To burnish his tax-slashing credentials within Tory circles, Sunak announced a 5p cut in fuel duty – in a publicity stunt he was later photographed filling up a Kia Rio in a Sainsbury's car park, only for it to later emerge the car was borrowed. It backfired when another photo suggested he could not use a contactless card machine. He also preannounced a 1p cut in the basic rate of income tax for 2024, something that Johnson's team thought was 'mad' when informed of it hours before the spring statement was delivered. 'That stupid income tax cut in two years was entirely on the Treasury's shoulders,' one Johnson ally said. 'They wouldn't even share with us what was in it until the morning.'

Rising inflation meant rising tax receipts, handing Sunak an extra £30 billion of 'headroom' that could be saved for a rainy day. Yet instead of spending it immediately, as some in Team Johnson wanted, he banked it to weather the turbulence ahead. Number 10 was 'attracted' to cutting VAT on energy bills in the spring statement, but was blocked by the chancellor according to those involved in the conversations (curiously Sunak went on to make this very pledge during his leadership bid). The package was widely judged as underwhelming, particularly the fuel duty cut. The shine was rapidly wearing off Sunak, who had briefly been wildly popular during the pandemic.

A far bigger problem, however, was emerging: Johnson and Sunak had fundamentally opposed economic views and approaches to governing. These differences were masked during the pandemic but had now come to the fore. Number 10 felt that the Treasury had to be dragged 'kicking and screaming' into taking action to tackle the cost of living crisis. One senior Johnson aide said, 'You can really tell when the Treasury are forced to do stuff they don't believe in. We didn't get the data, it was a very poor process.' After the spring statement, both sides openly criticised each other. Sunak's supporters said[10] the prime minister was 'unreliable and unpredictable'; Johnson's allies retorted Sunak was a 'privileged billionaire' and his energy offering was 'absolutely rubbish'.

Sunak's political woes were to rapidly worsen a fortnight later. *The Independent* broke the news[11] on 6 April that Akshata Murthy, Sunak's billionaire tech heiress wife, had held non-dom tax status while he was chancellor, living in the UK while stating that her home residence was in India. This revelation, which suggested she paid £30,000 to avoid an estimated[12] £20 million in taxes (according to the Labour party) could scarcely have been more toxic. A leak inquiry was duly launched, as Sunak's tax affairs were held tightly in Whitehall. Aides close to the chancellor believed that a civil servant leaked it to the Labour party, who in turn passed it to the media in order to discredit the chancellor.

After the revelations, some Number 10 officials admitted 'slight schadenfreude' after being on the receiving end of negative briefings from Team Sunak. The chancellor spoke to Johnson when the story was first published to reassure him that 'his wife was not going to be a political problem'. Yet Johnson's team were alarmed at both how badly Sunak's team had handled the story and the fact they had not anticipated what was to come next. 'It was very naive,' a Johnson ally said, adding that the timing ultimately benefited Sunak's future leadership hopes. 'In hindsight, they must be very glad that came out when it did, not in the summer' when Sunak was running for leader.

The following day, 8 April, Number 10 had reason to become even more exasperated when it emerged that Sunak had held a US Green Card, a route to permanent residency in the United States, for a significant period of time while he had been chancellor. Sunak had deep connections to America: he studied at Stanford University from 2004 to 2006, where he met his wife. Sunak's response was pugnacious: he gave a testy interview to *The Sun*[13] claiming the stories were a smear on him and his wife. 'She loves her country. Like I love mine, I would never dream of giving up my British citizenship. And I imagine most people wouldn't,' he said.

The chancellor called several newspaper editors to try and smooth the situation but decided that transparency was the best solution. Sunak referred himself for an investigation by Christopher Geidt, the government's independent advisor on ministerial interests, who later cleared him[14] of any wrongdoing and praised him for being 'assiduous in meeting his obligations and in engaging with this investigation'.

Johnson publicly defended Sunak, stating he was doing 'an absolutely outstanding job' and echoed his long-held personal views that families should be kept well out of politics. But behind the scenes, trust was thin. One senior Downing Street figure admitted the Sunak–Johnson relationship was 'always a bit tricky', adding, 'The PM did really value his relationship with Rishi and put a lot of time into it, even though he knew they were very different characters.' One of Johnson's closest aides argued that the difficult relations between Number 10 and Number 11 'dominated everything'.

That ally added that Sunak's unscheduled arrival in the Treasury, replacing health secretary Sajid Javid in February 2020 after he refused to sack all of his aides at the behest of Dominic Cummings, was a critical juncture in Johnson's premiership: 'If I was going to pick one moment that set the fate of the entire government, I would pick out the arrival of Sunak because it meant the PM lost control of the Treasury. He didn't have a close ally in the Treasury from day one.' The person added that Sunak's appointment was advocated by Cummings, and Johnson did not know him well. 'They met him a few times on the campaign and knew him as a talented young minister. But he didn't have a close personal relationship with him like he did with Saj.'

When relations deteriorated further in the months ahead, Johnson's team became convinced that Sunak had forged 'an alternate powerbase in Whitehall' from next door. Those close to the prime minister denied they had anything to do with the tax leaks. 'It was not planned. They dealt with it as if it was a crisis,' a colleague said. Another added there was no capacity to work at destabilising the chancellor: 'There was barely an operation in Number 10 to try and protect the PM, let alone doing in the chancellor.'

As the spring of 2022 drifted towards summer, the combination of the Operation Hillman fines, the policy differences over the spring statement and Sunak's struggles with revelations about his personal finances, meant the relationship that defines all British governments between the prime minister and the chancellor became 'very, very strained'. One figure close to Johnson concluded, 'The fines destroyed it. Rishi blamed the PM for creating this environment.'

***

Beyond the Conservative party, the Hillman fine brought another problem to a head. After Johnson accepted the fine, his MPs were braced for the opposition parties to refer the prime minister to the Commons' privileges committee for an inquiry on whether he had misled parliament. The investigation would be serious: if the bipartisan group found Johnson had knowingly misled MPs, he could face a suspension. And if that suspension was over ten days, that could in turn lead to a recall petition and a by-election. So if the inquiry investigation was successful, Johnson would plausibly face the end of his career.

With a direct echo to the Paterson saga, Johnson's political team hatched a plan to buy time before an inquiry could begin. On Tuesday 19 April, the day the fines for Johnson and Sunak landed, the Commons' speaker Lindsay Hoyle granted a request from all the opposition parties – including Labour and the Liberal Democrats – to refer the question of misleading the house to an investigation into whether Johnson was in contempt of parliament. The vote would take place two days later.

Much like the Paterson scandal, when Johnson was in Rome and Glasgow, Johnson was due to be out of the country and away from a moment of political danger. A thrice-rescheduled trade junket to India had been planned for the same day as the vote – a trip the prime minister was eager not to miss after the pandemic. The third iteration of Johnson's political team, with a new chief whip, the thinning-haired and efficient Chris Heaton-Harris, would need to stay behind and help Johnson wriggle out of his latest hole.

The motion,[15] proposed by Keir Starmer on Wednesday 20 April, noted that Johnson had told MPs the following: 'All guidance was followed in No. 10', 'I have been repeatedly assured since these allegations emerged that there was no party and that no Covid rules were broken', 'I have been repeatedly assured that the rules were not broken' and 'guidance was followed and the rules were followed at all times'. It said the words 'appear to amount to misleading the Commons' and called for a privileges committee to investigate whether his conduct 'amounted to a contempt of the House'. Finally, it said that the inquiry would not begin until Operation Hillman was concluded.

It was over to Heaton-Harris to produce an amendment that would allow Johnson to manoeuvre his way out of another inquiry. The chief whip devoted the afternoon speaking to concerned backbenchers[16] who might be minded to back the opposition motion, including former chief whip Mark Harper and Tom Tugendhat, chair of the foreign affairs select committee. Both influential MPs had called on Johnson to go and were not minded to give the government the benefit of the doubt. More junior whips spoke to a wider selection of MPs and it became clear the government did not have a majority. One Tory whip said, 'Our eighty-seat majority was gone, we couldn't vote down the investigation.'

On the Wednesday evening, Heaton-Harris produced a solution: the privileges committee investigation would go ahead, but not until the full Sue Gray report was published. The amendment would buy Johnson a little more time, but he would still ultimately face an investigation that could end his parliamentary career. One government insider said that they were eager to avoid the mistake of the Paterson saga: 'A neutral motion designed to kick the can down the road suited most Conservative MPs at that point.' Another Johnson ally said, 'The chief's view was that we didn't have the numbers to completely knock it back. But he thought an amendment was more doable. That was not gerrymandering, it was just saying, "Wait till the police report."'

But mistrust was so deep between Downing Street and the parliamentary party by this point that it became rapidly clear that Heaton-Harris's amendment would not work. One senior MP said, 'Overnight our inboxes filled up accusing us of providing a cover-up and minds begin to turn.' By Thursday 21 April, the government's majority had shrivelled and Heaton-Harris had to announce another U-turn – the single thing Downing Street had been seeking to avoid after realising how much MPs loathed such situations. 'I remember thinking "that's insane" because we have done it again,' one Downing Street insider said. "We've marched the parliamentary party up the hill to do something, we'd been briefing them for two days that they were going to have to back this. And then we abandoned them.'

Speaking from Ahmedabad on day two of his trade trip to India that morning, Johnson said, 'I'm very keen for every possible form of scrutiny . . . I don't think that should happen until the investigation is completed.' Heaton-Harris struggled to get in touch with the prime minister that day but the pair eventually spoke at 4 p.m. The chief whip said he could not guarantee the government would win the motion – and even if they did, it would lead to another huge rebellion that would further damage his government's standing. The pair agreed that he would climb down in a televised clip from India. Johnson stated: 'The House of Commons can do whatever it wants.' Watching the clip from Downing Street, one of his aides remarked, 'Another disastrous decision because he was away.'

Inside Downing Street, the mood was 'utter chaos' as they waited to hear confirmation from Johnson and Heaton-Harris that the climbdown had happened. One official remarked to another, 'This makes no sense, why are we such morons?' The climbdown on the privileges committee investigation was not made public until minutes before the Commons debate on the privileges investigation was due to begin. Having spoken to

Johnson, Heaton-Harris shuffled onto the frontbench and passed a note to Mark Spencer, his predecessor who had botched the Owen Paterson scandal and was now leader of the Commons. The green benches were sparsely attended and the vote meekly passed.

The vote itself came on the Friday morning, but recriminations had already begun in Downing Street. One senior official said to another that morning, 'Why the fuck are we causing ourselves absolute pain again? We've spent the whole of yesterday saying we're doing this because we should wait for the Sue Gray. Everyone had coalesced around the fact that that was an okay place to be. Then the chief told us actually no, we can't do that.' The answer was that the Tory whipping operation had failed, and relations had further soured between Downing Street and Tory MPs, just as more no-confidence letters in Johnson began flowing to the 1922 Committee.

***

Throughout the partygate scandal, the prime minister's allies insisted the saga was primarily a concern of the Westminster bubble and that 'real' voters were anxious about other priorities. The opinion polls told a different story. The last time the Conservatives had led in the polls was reported[17] on 8 December 2021 by Redfield & Wilton, before a run of leads for the Labour party that remained unbroken until Johnson left office in September 2022. Even when Ukraine temporarily boosted Johnson's ratings in March, the Tories never regained their lead. By mid-April, as the campaign for the local elections began, the party fell as far as eleven points behind.

Conservative party HQ was aware they were facing a shellacking at the elections. Although they set expectations high, journalists were frequently briefed that, given the last local elections came three years since the last general election, losing 800 council seats would be a good outcome for the Tories. There was particular concern among strategists that the party would lose its remaining council footholds in London and bleed votes to the Liberal Democrats in prosperous southern England, where partygate was proving particularly unpopular.

As the results filtered through overnight on 5 May, many of their fears were confirmed: Wandsworth in south-west London, praised as Margaret Thatcher's favourite council, went red for the first time. Westminster council also flipped to Labour, as did Worthing and Southampton on the south coast. The Tories lost control of scores of councils across their traditional home counties heartlands including West Oxfordshire and Tunbridge Wells. The party lost 485 councillors and control of 11 councils, yet the results were not spectacular for Labour who only gained 108 councillors. The real winners were the Lib Dems, returning as a significant political force with 224 gains.

Johnson was fortunate that the order of the results meant the worst did not arrive until the next morning. 'We were helped because the overnights were okay,' one Johnson ally said. 'Then, as we went through Friday, they got steadily worse. We actually lost a lot of seats but the narrative was we were doing okay.' The prime minister spoke constantly to Ross Kempsell, one of his strategists, to calibrate a response. He also spoke to party chairman Oliver Dowden after the results for Sunderland council in the north east of England landed, where Labour fell back by one seat. Overall the Tories did not capitalise on their previous gains in pro-Brexit England but Johnson voiced the opinion to Dowden, 'It was not such a bad night.'

One senior Conservative party official said partygate was to blame for the losses. 'It was broadly where we expected it to be, which was shown by the expectations management ... But obviously, it was not a good night.' Johnson's position remained precarious, but his inner circle felt assured a challenge was not forthcoming. 'We knew it wasn't going to be the locals that killed him, the results were all in the ballpark of what [David] Cameron suffered,' one insider said. The losses did frighten Conservative MPs facing off a Lib Dem challenge in their seats. 'It continued to scare the shit out of Lib Dem-facing MPs,' one Tory strategist said. 'On the doorstep, they were hearing "I'm sending a message to Boris Johnson."'

Any possibility of an uprising at this point, however, was thwarted by an announcement on Friday afternoon from Durham Constabulary: Keir Starmer would be investigated for potentially breaking Covid rules. A new scandal was born: 'beergate'. Its origins lay in events that had taken place in April 2021, when the opposition leader was reported to have quaffed a beer and enjoyed a curry after a day of campaigning in Durham when indoor socialising was banned under Covid rules. Soon after, a grainy video of Starmer, beer in hand, was published. The Starmer clip was eventually sent to anti-lockdown activists who posted it on social media. It was largely ignored, with the media focused on Johnson's Covid troubles.

In January 2022, the *Daily Mail* ran on its front page a still from the video footage and called Starmer 'the Covid Party Hypocrite' but in February Durham police cleared Starmer over allegations of rule breaking. Deep within Conservative party HQ, the footage was put in a metaphorical filing cabinet until the party decided to unleash it to try and score political points. The Conservative Research Department revisited the story in April to help Johnson's ailing position. 'We were desperate at that stage for something that the PM could actually use at PMQs as a tactical distraction,' one person involved said. A dozen people were set to dig into the matter to find evidence to refresh the story. They hit upon a Facebook post on the Durham constituency Labour party showing a quiz had taken place that night.

After Johnson's fine in April for attending the birthday party, the Conservative MP for North West Durham, Richard Holden, wrote to Durham police arguing there was 'a strong public interest' in reopening the investigation and that the Covid rules should apply equally. Via Conservative HQ, Holden provided the police with the Facebook post promoting a quiz night; the Labour party said Starmer had not been involved but the Tories' efforts to turn beergate into a scandal analogous to partygate seemed to have come to pass when Labour had to issue a statement admitting that its deputy leader Angela Rayner had attended the event, having previously stated that she hadn't been present.

Durham Constabulary said it had 'significant new information' and an investigation would commence. Much like the Met's inquiries into partygate, Durham did not state how long it would go on for and whether its thresholds would equal what happened in Downing Street.

Starmer could not bat away the scandal as a smear because he had called on Johnson to resign as soon as he was investigated by the Met police. The pressure from Tories for him to quit began. One senior MP said, 'Keir Starmer had called for Boris to resign, so by his own standards, he'd should have resigned on the day the police announced they were investigating. I thought he was a complete hypocrite, the stuff that he was doing was almost identical to the stuff the PM was doing.'

With willing help from the *Daily Mail*, the story was splashed in the paper for over ten consecutive days. Even senior Tories acknowledged that the prominence of beergate became 'ridiculous'.

What the scandal did, however, was to provide the government with some respite from partygate. The opposition party's attacks on Johnson were blunted and the message to voters became 'they're all the same'. Further beergate allegations came in May, when a leaked schedule[18] showed that the takeaway was planned in advance. It was also reported[19] by several outlets that Starmer did not return to work after the curry and some junior Labour staffers were drunk. After days of stories and pressure, Starmer announced on 9 May he would resign as leader of the opposition if he received an FPN to show 'different principles to the prime minister'. Rayner also said she would resign as deputy leader.

While the police investigated, Conservative party HQ continued to pour resources into keeping the beergate story alive to distract from partygate. One person involved said a lengthy 'war book' on beergate existed that included much information that was never published. The scandal was aided by sources inside the Labour party – one known in Tory HQ as 'red throat' – who 'wanted to do Starmer in' and provided the media with details and reports on what happened in Durham. Conservative officials believed 'there was quite a high chance' Starmer would be fined and had legal opinions to back it up.

For some weeks, it appeared Starmer might have made a major miscalculation. He and Rayner received police questionnaires on 31 May. Conservative MPs piled pressure on Durham police not to be lenient given the Met's treatment towards Johnson. The prime minister enjoyed the focus on his rival, dubbing Starmer 'Sir Beer Korma' during the investigation. But on Friday 8 July, the police announced the investigation was finished and no fixed penalty notices would be issued. Durham police said:[20] 'A substantial amount of documentary and witness evidence was obtained which identified the 17 participants and their activities during that gathering . . . it has been concluded that there is no case to answer for a contravention of the regulations, due to the application of an exception, namely reasonably necessary work.'

The Tories pushing beergate discussed seeking a judicial review of the outcome. 'There was an inconsistency in approach between Durham and the Met. If Starmer was looked into by the Met I think he would have been fined,' one person involved mused. But events soon overtook any such plans. Starmer pivoted back to partygate and drew a clear moral line with Johnson. 'For me, this was always a matter of principle. Honesty and integrity matter. You will always get that from me,' he tweeted.[21] Rayner said, 'The contrast with the behaviour of this disgraced prime minister couldn't be clearer.'

***

Throughout this time, the number of fines for partygate kept rising. On 12 May, the number of FPNs reached one hundred. There was much speculation Johnson would be fined again, and with it would come more pressure from MPs. Operation Hillman concluded on 19 May with 126 fines issued[22] to 83 individuals. The Met's conclusions were opaque and confusing: it is unknown who the other eighty-odd persons fined were, or which of the dozen events they attended.

The investigation had been significant in terms of time and resources. A total of twelve police detectives worked on Operation Hillman, sifting through 345 documents passed in their direction from Gray's team – including internal emails, diary entries, security door logs and witness statements. A whopping 510 photographs and pieces of CCTV footage were submitted. None of the fines were contested, but the Met said, 'We took great care to ensure that for each referral we had the necessary evidence to prosecute the FPN at court, were it not paid.'

Crucially for the prime minister, he received no further penalty notices, leading his internal critics to herald that the 'greased piglet' – former prime minister David Cameron's nickname for Johnson – had wriggled free once again. Charles Walker, a veteran Tory MP, predicted in February it was 'inevitable' he would be forced out. By May, Walker said,[23] 'He's a bit like that cricket all-rounder who's been written off time and time again, and then grabs the bowling ball and takes five for 15, or smashes a hundred, or does both things in the same match.'

Johnson had some political breathing room, but it did not last long. With the police work complete, the country reverted to waiting for Sue Gray; there were no further obstacles for her full investigation into partygate to be published. Throughout Operation Hillman, Gray had returned to the Department for Levelling Up and the inquiry was 'put into storage' until the all clear was given from the police.

The Met did not inform Gray of who had been issued with penalties, posing a challenge for the redrafting of her report. On Monday 16 May, though, three days before the public announcement, the Met privately told Gray that Operation Hillman was soon to be wrapped up. She called colleagues to inform them 'the Met think they might be done on Thursday' and rapidly reassembled her team and began the redrafting of the initial 'full fat' report that was meant to be published in January. But it was not until Wednesday 18 May that her team was certain that the police were done. The reaction by officials on her inquiry was, 'Oh shit it's actually coming.' According to those involved, around 10 to 20 per cent of the report was reworked following Hillman fines, with 'a lot of toing and froing over bits of the wording'. A critical sticking point was whether photos should be included: some officials were pressuring Gray against, others felt it was necessary to

Boris Johnson and
Charles Moore, former editor
of *The Daily Telegraph*, leaving
the Garrick Club.

Owen Paterson looks
on in the Commons
as MPs debate an
amendment calling
for a review of his
parliamentary
punishment.

The press conference
where Boris Johnson
announced the first
Omicron cases had
been found in the UK.

Allegra Stratton announcing her resignation.

Sue Gray – the shadowy civil servant who led the partygate inquiry.

The three senior aides who departed Downing Street
after Sue Gray's interim report was published.

Dan Rosenfield, chief of staff.

Jack Doyle,
communications director.

Munira Mirza, director of the
Number 10 policy unit.

Boris at the Munich Security Conference, which took place as Russian troops massed on the Ukrainian border.

Johnson and Volodymyr Zelenskyy walking through the street of Kyiv.

Rishi and Boris at the latter's infamous birthday party during Covid restrictions.

Cressida Dick arriving at Scotland Yard the day the investigation into rule-breaking parties in Downing Street was announced.

Key members of Johnson's support network.

Grant Shapps,
transport secretary.

Chris Heaton-Harris, chief whip.

Nigel Adams, minister
of state without portfolio
and chief fixer.

Ross Kempsell, key strategist.

Will Lewis, key fixer.

Graham Brady of the 1922 Committee announces
the vote of no confidence result.

Chris Pincher, whose alleged
behaviour was the final scandal
that led to Johnson's fall.

Sajid Javid's resignation
letter as health secretary.

New ministers that were appointed to prop up Johnson's government.

Nadhim Zahawi had one of the shortest tenures as chancellor in history.

Michelle Donelan became
education secretary for
forty-eight hours.

Steve Barclay escaped Number 10
to become health secretary.

Boris announces his resignation.

Liz Truss and Rishi Sunak at a debate as they vie to be Conservative leader.

Boris Johnson gives his farewell address outside Number 10.

show that the inquiry was not a whitewash. A decision on this was not immediately reached.

The publication of her report, however, did not go smoothly. A month before its release, Gray had an 'informal catch-up' with Samantha Jones, a civil servant who was appointed chief operating officer of Number 10 in February's shake-up. At the end of their meeting, Jones suggested to Gray it would be a 'good idea' if she caught up with Johnson at some point. Gray responded that she was more than happy to do so and Jones (perhaps oddly) suggested she should 'stick it in the diary'. In a brief moment that would later become significant, Gray forgot to revert to Jones and was soon chased for a date. One colleague said, 'The fact Sam then chased Sue to say "Can you please sort this invite out?", you could either interpret as Sam being efficient or having a reason for Sue to arrange a meeting.'

Given that Johnson has the largest diary team in Whitehall (and probably the country), it was natural to assume his office would have arranged it. The crunch meeting eventually took place in Johnson's private office, with Gray and Jones in attendance with Steve Barclay, his chief of staff and Cabinet Office minister. Much of the meeting was a 'general discussion' about the Met's inquiries, what Gray knew about their progress, and how ready she would be to publish when Operation Hillman concluded. The question of whether photographs should be included was not raised.

But there was a 'throwaway comment', according to officials, about whether the report needed to be published at all. 'By that point everything had been leaked,' one Downing Street insider said. 'It was almost a question asked to the air.' Gray's team did not take it seriously but thought the Number 10 officials were being 'very careful not to be seen to be suggesting that directly, but they were looking for Sue's reaction.' Gray did not take the suggestion seriously, until a senior official approached her after the meeting and said, 'I understand you had a meeting with the PM where the idea that you wouldn't publish a report came out?'

Gray was furious and insisted it was not seriously discussed. Johnson's political team suggested Steve Barclay had raised the prospect of binning the report in the meeting. 'Steve had this big idea that he was going to be able to prevent the publication of the second part of the report. I don't think anybody seriously thought that that was possible,' one ally said. 'No one serious thought that we could get away with not publishing the report.' One person who worked with her said, 'Sue was massively angered with this suggestion, but it was quickly quashed. The idea that the report would be binned was stamped out immediately.' Another colleague said, 'she was cross because there were only four people in that room.'

On Saturday 21 May, two days after the Met concluded their inquiries, Sky News reported[24] that the Johnson–Gray meeting had taken place. That weekend, a furious internal row broke out between Gray's team and Number 10. Guto Harri, Johnson's director of communications, insisted Steve Barclay was not present when he in fact was. Harri also stated that Gray had instigated the meeting, which she had not. Harri finally also suggested photographs had been discussed, which they had not. Gray became deeply concerned that Downing Street was attempting to discredit her and the report. One colleague said, 'Sue was enormously upset. From her point of view this was a hit job, this was Number 10 coming out trying to discredit Sue and all of her work.'

Gray's team took the highly unusual step of issuing an on-the-record statement saying that she had not instigated the meeting, which conflicted with Downing Street's account. Harri called Gray's spokesperson, a civil servant, and gave him 'the hair-dryer treatment' and accused him and the inquiry team of causing damage to the government. The battle ended in stalemate: Gray's spokesperson was forced to step back from the inquiry and Number 10 capitulated in agreeing that Gray had not organised the meeting. Whether Barclay's remark was a deliberate plot to discredit Gray that was botched, or just a silly offhand comment, their efforts at neutering the report failed.

On Monday 23 May, as anticipation for the full report hit fever point, leaked photos were published. Johnson was merrily seen in one raising a cup of wine[25] at the November 2020 leaving party, surrounded by the blurred-out faces of civil servants. With the photos in the public domain, Gray had no choice but to include them. And finally on Wednesday 25 May, six months since the inquiry began, the full Sue Gray report was published. Across sixty pages, her findings covered sixteen events between May 2020 and April 2021 in meticulous detail.

Gray wrote that many of the parties were rowdy and continued into the early hours of the morning. She was excoriating on the culture in Downing Street, particularly the political and civil service leadership. She accused officials of knowing what they were up to, renaming 'parties' as 'events' in email chains to make sure they were not caught out. She described how some tried to warn that the parties were a bad idea – the 20 May 2020 BYOB gathering was labelled a 'comms risk' by one staffer. Out of the 300 photographs submitted to the inquiry, only eight were published. Much of the detail in the full Gray report had been public for months, thanks to all the leaks. The most striking new finding was 'unacceptable' behaviour towards Number 10's cleaning and security staff from senior aides. Gray said they have been routinely rude. Johnson soon apologised to the staff. One ally said, 'Boris was totally horrified to hear that. He got up especially early the next morning to apologise in person to the cleaners and custodians.'

The report was problematic for Johnson and his team, but for the mandarins too. 'It's just as bad if not worse from the civil service point of view,' a senior figure said. One Downing Street figure said, 'It was a pretty grim read in all of its gory detail.' Gray only named the most senior officials who had attended events, including the Cabinet secretary Simon Case and Martin Reynolds. Civil servants were criticised as much as the politicians about who was to blame. One Johnson ally said: 'I don't subscribe to the idea Boris Johnson led a frat house. The report made it clear Martin was responsible for what happened in the house [Number 10] because he fundamentally led the civil service side.' Others said the report highlighted Johnson's consistently flawed judgement in who to trust. 'Fundamentally, there was a sort of person Boris wanted beside him. Appointing Party Marty, someone who was lax about such things, is much of a reflection on him.'

For Gray, the end of the report prompted relief. Although many in Number 10 believed 'she enjoyed the limelight a little too much', her colleagues insisted it was not a happy time. 'I think she regrets ever having taken it on.' Gray returned to her role as the second permanent secretary at the Department for Levelling Up and for a quieter life. She has never spoken publicly about the ordeal or the findings of her report. Her colleagues say she never intends to. But for Johnson, the moment of reckoning with his MPs had finally arrived. Throughout 2022, the prime minister's tedious and tenuous line that everyone should 'wait for Sue Gray' no longer held. It was time to see whether his colleagues had forgiven him over partygate, or whether they no longer had confidence in his position.

5. The 41 per cent

The House of Commons had scarcely heard Boris Johnson so humble. Addressing the chamber soon after the publication of the full Sue Gray report, his contrition put Uriah Heep to shame. He was 'humbled', had 'learnt a lesson' about his behaviour, and took 'full responsibility for everything that took place on my watch'. The prime minister set out the 'context' of partygate that he had been so eager to explain for months: Number 10 was full of hard-working staffers, who had made mistakes, but put in long hours in the office during the pandemic. 'I appreciate this is no mitigation,' he said to a torrent of heckling from MPs.

From the government Despatch Box on Wednesday 25 May 2022, Johnson corrected the record on partygate:[1] 'When I came to this house and said in all sincerity that the rules and guidance had been followed at all times, it was what I believed to be true. But clearly this was not the case for some of those gatherings after I had left, and at other gatherings when I was not even in the building.' His statement was followed by more jeers from MPs who believed he was once again avoiding responsibility and trying to create a narrative that took himself out of the picture.

The prime minister went on to emphasise the structural changes that had taken place in Number 10 since Gray's interim report earlier that year. Downing Street had a new chief of staff in Steve Barclay, a fresh director of communications in Guto Harri, a new principal private secretary to replace Martin Reynolds as well as a bevy of newly hired efficient officials.

Johnson concluded he would work 'day and night' to deliver his mission of tackling the cost of living crisis, the war in Ukraine and create 'high wage, high skilled, high employment' that would improve the UK's economic standing. He would not be resigning.

After the statement, there was no immediate rebellion from Conservative MPs, and Johnson had seemingly wriggled out of yet another hole, the accepted wisdom went. The only notable Tory critic was Tobias Ellwood, chair of the Commons defence committee and a longstanding Johnson opponent. He asked his fellow MPs: 'Are you willing day in and day out to defend this behaviour publicly? Can we continue to govern without distraction given the erosion of the trust with the British people? And can we win the general election on this current trajectory?' For his exhortations, Ellwood was heckled by Johnson's supporters.

In some parts of Downing Street, there was relief. They concluded that the trickle of leaked partygate stories and the elongation of Sue Gray's work meant that the moments of pressure had all been relieved. One Number 10 insider said, 'We thought he had basically survived Sue Gray albeit massively damaged – a 7 to 10 percentage hit to his polls that was probably permanent.' The fact he had not received another penalty notice added to the sense that Johnson had survived the storm. MPs had repeatedly said they wanted partygate and Sue Gray to just 'go away' and now perhaps they both had.

Those who thought Johnson had got away with it also did so because of the vast range of other scandals he had survived over the months. According to one senior Tory figure, '70 to 80 per cent of the parliamentary party came to the conclusion that if he'd made it through January – as bad as that was with morale so low – what's left to bring him down?'

Others in Johnson's inner circle believed severe trouble lay ahead. One close ally said that sceptics told Johnson that the terminal 'underlying problem' was him having lost his grip on the parliamentary party. 'It was day after day after day of bad headlines. MPs had very little for them to tell their constituents that they were doing positively,' one aide said. 'It was like sand running through our hands the whole time.'

Immediately after the prime minister's statement, his allies and aides devoted hours in parliament to seeing streams of Tory MPs and seeking to calm their nerves. The whips had told them in advance to prepare for resentment. The aim of that immediate post-Gray operation was to stabilise the situation and see Johnson through the following six weeks until summer recess, when the political temperature could cool. One Johnson ally said, 'There was a bit of complacency in Number 10. It was still a view among many that if we got into conference [in the autumn], we were probably safe.'

Yet Johnson's core political team, led by aides Declan Lyons and Ben Gascoigne, with assistance from the Brains Trust outriders, were convinced a vote of no confidence in Johnson by Tory MPs was approaching and urged him to be ready. 'There was so much parliamentary stuff going on, we were whirling for a vote coming,' one Tory official said. 'I'd always thought the greased piglet thing never aligned with the full situation among MPs. Sue Gray simply brought everything to a head again.' After Johnson's Commons statement, Downing Street kicked into survival mode in case enough MPs moved against their man.

To oust a leader of the Conservative party, 15 per cent of the parliamentary party must submit no-confidence letters to the chair of the 1922 Committee – the informal trade union of Tory MPs. In June 2022, that was 54 MPs required to write to Graham Brady, the portly genial grandee who had chaired the committee for over a decade. Brady entered parliament in 1997 and made the seamless journey from bright young spark to veteran backbencher without skimming ministerial high office. Out of sorts with David Cameron's modernisation efforts, he devoted himself to being the house master of the parliamentary party. His first no-confidence vote was in Theresa May four years prior and MPs widely thought he handled the tricky process with aplomb and tact.

The letter-writing process is even more opaque than the Met's partygate investigations. There is no public record of who has submitted letters; they are locked in the safe of Brady's expansive office on the top floor of Portcullis House on the parliamentary estate. Whenever the Westminster village becomes bored with the topic of the day, speculation typically rises that letters are being submitted and another Tory confidence vote is approaching. Such reports are nearly always off the mark, as Brady has a long-held principle of never commenting to MPs or journalists about how many letters are in his possession.

One reason the media often overestimates how many no-confidence letters are submitted is due to the transient whims of MPs. Many Tories made a hoo-hah about submitting them – the left-leaning Roger Gale and Brexiter headbanger Andrew Bridgen being two of the most notable culprits. Others visit Brady at a moment of angst to submit a letter, encouraging a few more colleagues. Then events rapidly change and the letters are withdrawn out of a fear that the timing is unhelpful for the government or party. There was one Tory MP who publicly announced they had submitted a letter, publicly stated it was withdrawn and then publicly resubmitted it, without ever actually writing one.

One senior Tory who served on the 1922 six-strong executive committee said the process is a 'fascinating' insight into how colleagues think, describing it as, 'A swirling current where the tide ebbs and flows.' Another party grandee said, 'People don't always feel the need to publicise the fact they have withdrawn their letter. That's why you get a lot of the media miscalculation on numbers – from counting them when they go in but not knowing when they've been withdrawn.'

Back in January 2022, when partygate hit its first peak, Conservative MPs were convinced that a confidence vote was imminent. One longstanding backbencher, who has experienced several such votes, said, 'The velocity was such that it might have happened. It did not necessarily go right up to the edge in terms of numbers in January.' Another member of the 1922 executive described that moment as, 'The mood of the herd. You got a series of people writing letters in very short order. And then just at the point where you thought it's going to happen, it petered out.' As usual, Brady made no public comment.

Johnson was fortunate that there was no coordinated effort in January to oust him. With 358 fellow Tory MPs, convincing 54 of them to remove their leader was not straightforward. Such an endeavour requires several wings of the party to have unified goals and strategies. When Theresa May faced her confidence vote in 2018, it was a coalition of hardline Brexiters and disgruntled centrists that tipped the letters over the threshold. Johnson did not face such a coordinated coalition against him. In the early months of 2022, a drinks party for Tory MPs took place in parliament where the prime minister's future was the topic du jour. One MP present recalled, 'I stumbled into a conversation with a leading light of the One Nation group [left-leaning Tory MPs] and the other of the 1992 group [right-leaning Tory MPs]. They both said nothing was being coordinated at all.'

As partygate wore on, a trickle of MPs publicly called on Johnson to go. In February, it was the former education minister Nick Gibb[2] who said voters were 'furious about the double standards' Johnson had demonstrated during the pandemic. Come April, backbench MP Nigel Mills joined him[3] after Johnson had been fined, stating voters 'had a right to accept higher standards'. The most notable by far was then Steve Baker, the formidable former chair of the European Research Group who had played a key role in bringing down the last two Tory leaders. On 21 April, Baker told[4] the Commons, 'the gig is up' and Johnson should be 'long gone by now'. Following the full Sue Gray report, nineteen Tories had publicly said he should go – including former health minister Stephen Hammond.[5] By 30 May, it was up to twenty-seven.[6]

Downing Street had hoped that the week of the Queen's Platinum Jubilee would offer respite from the threats, with MPs and the nation focused on celebrating the monarch's seventy years on the throne. Two significant figures, however, announced they had lost confidence in the run-up to the Jubilee bank holiday weekend: Jeremy Wright, the former attorney general who said[7] Johnson had done 'lasting damage' to the party, and Andrea Leadsom, the former business secretary who had worked closely with him during the Vote Leave campaign. She did not explicitly state Johnson should go, but wrote that leadership failings 'are the responsibility of the prime minister' and said Tory MPs 'must now decide on what is the right course of action that will restore confidence in our government'.

It seemed inevitable that the confidence vote predicted by Johnson's core allies was getting closer. As the Jubilee weekend dawned, forty-one Tory MPs had questioned[8] Johnson's position before glumly decamping to their constituencies for the celebrations. One Cabinet minister said, 'There was a growing view amongst MPs that this stain won't be wiped clean.' Support for Johnson began to waver in the Cabinet too, but few felt there was an alternative. Another minister said, 'I knew all his flaws but thought he's still capable of winning the next election, he's still got the energy, the animal spirits. and I'm not convinced that there's any obvious alternative.' Rishi Sunak, who was widely seen as the most viable replacement for Johnson, was struggling due to his partygate fine, the lacklustre spring statement and the row over his Green Card and his wife's tax affairs. 'He had been tarnished in the public mind and lost his mojo, so I just thought we're better off with Boris,' the minister said.

Even if Johnson survived this moment, a difficult pair of by-elections lay ahead at the end of the month – plus there was the spectre of the privileges committee's investigation into whether he had misled the house and which raised the prospect of further upheavals and distractions.

Instead of offering Johnson some political respite, the Jubilee celebrations ended up providing the moment that may have resulted in the threshold of fifty-four no-confidence letters being hit. On Friday 3 June, Johnson and his wife Carrie stepped out of their armoured Range Rover at St Paul's Cathedral for a thanksgiving service. A crowd of ardent loyalists lined the City of London to catch a glimpse of the Royal Family. Many other political dignitaries, including opposition leader Keir Starmer and foreign secretary Liz Truss, had arrived with little reaction from the crowd. But during the walk from their car to the entrance of St Paul's, an audible chorus of boos was picked up on TV. Johnson, seemingly unaware, smiled and nodded as he walked into the church but the moment was captured by the BBC and then shared widely on social media. It received almost eleven million[9] views.

When Johnson returned to Downing Street after the service, he was unaware of what had happened. 'When he was going in, he was quite far away from it,' one Number 10 insider said. 'Boris didn't know what it sounded like on the microphones.' His aides soon showed him the clip. Several senior MPs also saw the moment after it was widely shared on WhatsApp, which further unsettled their nerves. One senior Tory said, 'These were not *Guardian*-reading Islington dwellers, they're arch-monarchists. If we had lost those people, our core base, everything was gone.' Another MP said, 'It was that moment I realised just how unpopular Boris had become.'

One Tory strategist said, 'The clip clearly had an effect on some MPs putting their letters in – the spectre of him getting booed walking into St Paul's.' Johnson's inner circle were scathing of the BBC, which they claimed 'pushed it very hard'. Culture secretary Nadine Dorries, Johnson's most steadfast defender said,[10] 'There were far, far more cheers, but that doesn't make a good headline does it?' In response, *ITV News*'s royal editor Chris Ship tweeted, 'The facts are, and I was there, the boos were very loud indeed. No escaping that.'

Number 10 was dismissive about those who cared about the booing. 'I think it sums up a lot of the MPs, it's such a shallow analysis,' one senior aide said. Another Johnson ally said, 'A lot of these MPs pay far too much attention to this kind of stuff rather than the actual fundamentals of politics. That's why they're bad at their jobs. If you shit the bed every time something doesn't go exactly to plan, it's no wonder everything came crashing down.' The number of no-confidence letters rose over the bank holiday weekend. After the thirty-second clip went viral, the countdown to the confidence vote commenced.

***

Sunday 5 June was the pinnacle of the Jubilee celebrations, a regal pageant featuring military parades, cultural 'highlights' from the Queen's seventy years on the throne and a street carnival.

Alongside the most senior members of the Royal Family, the Queen came to the balcony of Buckingham Palace to greet the crowds belting out the national anthem, in what would be one of her final public appearances. Boris Johnson was seated in the VIP section with his wife Carrie, beside the opposition leader Keir Starmer, and behind the Duchess of Cambridge and her children. As Prince Louis bounced around, slightly bored, the prime minister was photographed smiling. There was no indication he now knew he could be out of a job the very next day.

Between the St Paul's booing and the Jubilee pageant, Conservative MPs were agitated but fearful about upsetting the celebrations. 'A large number of colleagues were very edgy about being seen to balls up the Jubilee,' one senior backbencher said. Several contacted Graham Brady to say they would be sending no-confidence letters but asked him to be cautious around the announcement. Through a backchannel of a senior Tory MP, Downing Street made it known to Brady that Johnson was 'really keen that the Queen's party was not interfered with'. Brady passed a message back that he was well aware of how to do his job.

Just before Johnson left for Buckingham Palace on Sunday lunchtime, he received the call his political advisors had long predicted – Declan Lyons, political secretary, told Johnson before the bank holiday that a no-confidence vote was 'likely' the following week. Graham Brady informed the prime minister that fifty-four letters of no confidence had now been submitted and a vote would need to take place 'as soon as reasonably practical'. One person with knowledge of the call said Johnson responded by 'spending a little while explaining why this was an extreme folly on the part of colleagues.'

Johnson did not tell a single person in Number 10 what had happened. Instead, he hopped straight into his motorcade to the party. One close advisor said he did not have the time to inform aides, but he may have had reasons to keep it private. 'When you're dealing with that kind of information your first concern is that it will leak and if it does, you've lost any ability to control the information.' Another official said, 'He was digesting it throughout the pageant.' By historical precedent, the mere fact that a confidence vote was happening suggested his time as prime minister was drawing to an end. No previous Tory leader had survived a confidence vote and gone on to win another election.

After the finale performance of Abba's 'Dancing Queen' by the cast of *Mamma Mia*, Johnson returned to Downing Street and sent a message out to the Big Dog team that the vote was coming. The team assembled in his luxuriously decorated flat that evening to plot over cups of tea – no food or alcohol – on how best to save his position. The aides present included chief whip Chris Heaton-Harris, political fixer Nigel Adams, Tory strategists Lynton Crosby and Ross Kempsell, plus director of communications Guto Harri. One person involved said, 'The plan was to give the PM the best possible chance in the confidence vote. The Big Dog group had been planning since January, it was obvious it was coming.'

But some junior aides were frustrated more had not been done in the days before the bank holiday weekend. 'On the Friday before the vote, there was a drip-drip of letters, notably from Andrea Leadsom. I really don't think anyone spotted it until Graham called the PM on Sunday. We could have bought ourselves an extra four days,' one Number 10 insider said. Johnson did not minimise the threat. One of the first questions he asked the assembled Big Dog team was how big the rebellion was going to be. Nigel Adams told him that their infamous spreadsheet, collated by transport secretary Grant Shapps, suggested it would be in the region of 150. The aides hoped to 'chip away' at those minded to vote against the prime minister, while chiefly ensuring their base did not collapse.

Brady had told Johnson he wanted to agree a timetable for the vote as soon as possible. The 1922 Committee does not have any formal guidance on when a confidence vote should take place. In 2018, Theresa May had been abroad when the threshold was reached and Brady requested a meeting with her the next day. Someone in the Number 10 team had leaked the information that Brady wanted to see Johnson, hence why he decided to make the call immediately to Johnson. One senior figure on the 1922 executive said, 'if Graham had asked to see him, it would have been tantamount to saying it's on.' After discussions with the Big Dog group, the prime minister texted Brady that evening to say, 'Let's crack on with it tomorrow.' The pair agreed an announcement should be made early on Monday 4 July and the ballot would take place between 6 and 8 p.m., with the result an hour later. No more than ten people knew.

Before an official announcement was made on that Monday, Johnson received another blow when Jesse Norman, a former Treasury minister widely respected among MPs, published a blistering letter explaining why he had lost confidence.[11] The prime minister's fellow plummy voiced Old Etonian (and long-standing ally who lost his job in a reshuffle) accused him of allowing 'a culture of casual law-breaking' in Downing Street and called his response to partygate 'grotesque'. Norman lambasted the government's policies too: the privatisation of Channel 4 was 'unnecessary and provocative' and plans to reform the controversial Northern Ireland element of his Brexit deal 'economically very damaging, politically foolhardy and almost certainly illegal'.

At 8.20 a.m. on Monday, Brady issued a press release stating: 'The threshold of 15 per cent of the parliamentary party seeking a vote of confidence in the leader of the Conservative Party has been exceeded.' He made a brief TV appearance on College Green, a patch of grass opposite the Palace of Westminster that morphs into a village of pop-up broadcast studios and shouty political protesters during moments of crisis, to explain the time-table. That morning, Sajid Javid was representing the government on the morning broadcast round. Downing Street had alerted the health secretary that Brady's announcement would likely take place while he was on air. Javid was in the tricky spot of acknow-ledging it could be imminent, without egging on the threat.

Before taking to the cameras and microphones on Monday morning, Javid consulted with his wife and aides about whether he personally still had confidence in Johnson. In these discussions, Javid was torn: on the one hand he was frustrated with the integrity of Johnson's operation and still angry at how he had been misled earlier in the year over partygate. But ultimately, with no successor or alternative ready, Javid decided to give the prime minister the benefit of the doubt and went out to defend the government. He was not prepared to run for leadership again himself.

In Downing Street, the efforts to shore up Johnson's position began early – led by the Big Dog group in conjunction with the formal advisory team. Their first task was to prepare letters for every Conservative MP pleading with them not to vote against their leader. One of Johnson's aides performed a mail merge and he spent hours topping and tailing 358 letters by hand with a fountain pen. The printer in Downing Street was slow and kept jamming. An assortment of aides folded and sealed each letter, including Johnson's wife Carrie and deputy chief of staff Simone Finn. Some aides thought it was a 'nuts' idea, a waste of time that could be better spent speaking to MPs.

When all the letters were signed, they were driven over to the lower whips' office in the House of Commons to be delivered.

Chris Pincher, deputy chief whip, was running a 'naughty and nice' operation that day in parliament with a mixture of threats and love-bombing MPs. One whip said, 'Pinch ran a tight ship: getting all those letters out, constant phone calls, in-person meetings. Boris came in and spoke to the right people, it was incredibly efficient.' A briefing note, written by Ross Kempsell, was dispatched to MPs emphasising his electoral record and warning that three months of party infighting would only benefit Labour.

Some of Johnson's most supportive ministers, including Conor Burns and Tom Pursglove, were dispatched by Pincher to speak in turn to their closest friends – a complex network of influence based on Shapps's multi-layered spreadsheet. One whip said of Shapps's work that, 'It was hugely comprehensive to ensure we had the right level of knowledge about what people wanted, what relationships they had in parliament, in terms of who could talk to whom. It was bloody good for getting that information quickly and keeping it up to date. It was the only way to keep the show on the road.'

While Johnson geared up for the battle of his political life, the work of being prime minister went on – including a call with Ukraine president Volodymyr Zelenskyy on the Monday morning where the leaders discussed the latest supplies of British military equipment and worries about grain exports. Some commentators suggested the timing seemed suspect, given Johnson's political woes, but civil servants insisted there was no chance it was impromptu. 'The Zelenskyy call was in the diary for a while, you can't change these things around. There's about fifty Foreign Office officials on the call and it takes a week to set up,' one official said.

The next unhelpful intervention for Johnson was one his team had long expected. Jeremy Hunt, who challenged him for the Tory leadership back in 2019 and came a distant second place, had made it clear he wanted another crack at the leadership. At 10.50 a.m., the former health secretary tweeted: 'Conservative MPs know in our hearts we are not giving the British people the leadership they deserve.' Hunt said the vote of no confidence was an opportunity for 'change or lose' and he would be opting for the former. Yet Number 10 was not concerned: one aide described Hunt as 'entirely insignificant' and his support in the parliamentary party was limited. His proto-leadership campaign had been running for months in the private dining rooms and bars of Westminster: Philip Dunne, the former junior health minister, was acting as his de facto manager, along with former Cabinet ministers Andrew Mitchell and David Davis, who were sounding out support.

Johnson scoffed at the suggestion Hunt was behind a major coup, if only based on knowing the profiles of those behind it. One close ally explained: 'Philip was never going to be the leader of a great political coup. Jeremy was busted flush and had no support. Andrew has no mates and David Davis has become a figure of some absurdity.' In a sign of how split the Tory party was becoming, the 'blue-on-blue' fighting went public. Nadine Dorries, the increasingly slavish culture secretary, publicly condemned Hunt[12] for being 'wrong about almost everything' including how to deal with the pandemic. 'Your duplicity right now is destabilising the party and the country to serve your personal ambition,' she added for good measure.

***

As Monday wore on, as the WhatsApp messages became more frantic, it became clear to Johnson's team there was no coordinated effort to oust him and the fifty-four threshold for confidence letters had 'tipped over by accident', as one government insider said.

'None of the rebels were actually organised. If they were actually coordinating, they should have known that they were going to tip over the Jubilee without the votes to win the actual ballot. They should have withdrawn twenty letters until they had the numbers.' The whips knew that better coordination could have 'easily' lost them the vote. One senior rebel who wanted Johnson out said their best weapon was the transactional nature of his support: 'People supported him precisely because he was popular and a winner. I might think he's a rogue and a charlatan but he also keeps us in power. When your support is that transactional, it can just fall away. That's what was happening.'

With less than twelve hours to win the vote the whips had to prioritise who to call, which naturally led to some MPs complaining they had been forgotten, further stoking their unhappiness. 'On a vote of no confidence day, you don't waste time phoning people who you know are either going be unhelpful or are probably going to vote for you,' one whip said. 'If you're a waverer who might be persuadable, you do get a call but of different seniority. It might be from a minister, it might be from the PM – he was on the phone all day. You have to persuade those who you absolutely need to come over to survive. There were hundreds of people to target.'

Four disparate groups of Tory MPs wanted Johnson out. First were the 'pork pie' plotters from the 2019 intake of MPs who instigated the failed coup of January 2022. Second was the Covid Research Group of libertarian-minded anti-lockdown MPs. Then there were the rebellious left-leaning One Nation MPs such as former immigration minister Caroline Nokes. And finally, and most importantly, were all the former ministers. After a decade in power, over a hundred ex-members of governments who had been fired or demoted were festering on the backbenches. There was also a smattering of Brexit rebels who believed Johnson had gone soft on the Northern Ireland dispute. Altogether, one Johnson ally called them 'quite a powerful cohort of disgruntled colleagues'. The situation was worsened because Johnson had wholly failed to manage these groups since becoming prime minister.

That afternoon, Johnson addressed a 1922 Committee meeting of the Conservative parliamentary party, an idea that came to fruition late in the day. The prime minister arrived to the traditional banging of tables by his keenest advocates, mostly for the benefit of the hundred-odd journalists crammed outside trying to hear what was going on. In that packed, sweaty, overly filled room, Johnson was bullish: he warned MPs that removing him would unleash 'some hellish Groundhog Day debate' about returning to the single market (prompted by a lone suggestion from the irreconcilable MP Tobias Ellwood that the UK should tear up Johnson's Brexit deal). Johnson reminded them he had won the Tory party its biggest election victory in forty years. His message in short was: I have won before and I can win again. Despite the sour mood, he told colleagues 'the best is yet to come' and made a vague pledge about cutting taxes. During the meeting, longstanding Covid rebel Mark Harper openly criticised Johnson's conduct that had led to the vote. He replied, 'I humbly submit to you that this is not the moment for a leisurely and entirely unforced domestic political drama.'

Despite the vying efforts that day of the rebels and Johnson's whipping and Big Dog teams, very little shifted. Team Johnson failed to see off the substantial rebellion; the damage was deep and had grown for months. 'We kept it to exactly where we were on the Sunday night,' one ally said. But those seeking to oust him failed to coordinate tactics and ran conflicting strategies, failing to make much headway towards the 50 per cent mark needed to oust Johnson and put in train a leadership contest. Before the vote, Grant Shapps took one last look at his spreadsheet and placed his prediction for the rebellion in a sealed envelope: 149.

The confidence vote commenced at 6 p.m. in the Palace of Westminster's opulent committee room 14 – where Theresa May, Iain Duncan Smith and Margaret Thatcher had all faced confidence ballots that precipitated the demise of their careers. Coming less than four years since May's vote, Brady followed the same procedures. MPs drifted in and out of the room, dismissing the heckles of journalists who lined the wood-panelled corridor to try (and fail) to ascertain whether Johnson was going to survive. Few of them exited with cheerful looks or any sense of confidence about where their party was heading.

Graham Brady and the 1922 Committee executive entered committee room 14 at 9 p.m. to announce the result. The room packed with journalists and MPs, he declared that out of 359 MPs, 211 had confidence in Johnson and 148 did not. The 41 per cent of rebels had delivered a hugely damaging result. It was a worse outcome than Theresa May (she was out within six months), worse than John Major in 1995 (he lost the election two years later), and worse than Margaret Thatcher in 1989 (out within the year). Johnson was braced for it: the result was just one vote off Grant Shapps's prediction. The only positive news was that the 1922's formal rules meant he could not be challenged again for another twelve months.

As the results came through, a group of Tory MPs were watching the results over drinks in Michael Gove's official residence in Carlton Gardens, just off Pall Mall. Kemi Badenoch, local government minister, was present along with chief secretary to the Treasury Simon Clarke, skills minister Alex Burghart and junior ministerial aides Laura Trott and Claire Coutinho. All present had voted for Johnson, but felt the result was a terrible outcome for the party. One said, 'We were all sad because we thought it's not going to end the pain. It's not "Oh my god Boris is going" or "Boris is safe", it was the worst possible zone: more agony.'

Johnson was unwisely muscular in his response to this slight victory. 'I think it's an extremely good, positive, conclusive, decisive result which enables us to move on, to unite and to focus on delivery and that is exactly what we are going to do,' he said in a televised statement. The prime minister later went further, arguing the result represented 'a new mandate from my party' that showed a wider level of support than the shortlisting process in the 2019 leadership race. This was not welcomed by his advisors. 'We did quite badly and then we tried to pretend it was a success,' one said. Another added, 'It wasn't the tone that some of us advised him to take.' William Hague, the former Tory leader, offered the ominous counter view: the result showed 'a greater level of rejection than any Tory leader has ever endured and survived'.

Johnson's mood throughout the vote of no confidence was defiant, but history suggested it was a question of when, not if, Johnson would be out. 'We were in a very bad situation after that result with the parliamentary party,' one Cabinet minister said. 'A lot of us thought it was a matter of time, but we also thought the PM is the kind of guy who can do impossible things. There was still the sense that maybe this is going to be the first Tory leader who gets through that and who is going to redefine that.'

The whips and the Big Dog Operation were disappointed. 'We'd love to have had it under one hundred,' one official involved said. Despite his public bravado, Johnson's political aides urged him to seize the moment and conduct a major Cabinet reshuffle, much bigger than the one that had taken place in February, as an olive branch to MPs. Had Johnson made it through to July, a new Cabinet would have been brought together before parliament's summer recess. Declan Lyons and Nigel Adams had drawn up a preliminary plan that would have seen Chris Pincher moved out of the whips' office – 'he had done his job to bring some order, he didn't want to stay' one aide said – while local government minister Kemi Badenoch would have been promoted to the top table.

Even though Johnson loathed reshuffles – he was terrible at delivering bad news to those being demoted – he accepted the need for a reset. Members of the 2019 intake of Tory MPs would have been made ministers for the first time, according to Lyons's plan, while the whips' office would be refreshed. The plan would have 'built some bridges' by bringing back sacked ministers from the more liberal wing of the party, such as former justice secretary Robert Buckland. 'It was time to show some humility and bring people into government who had not been necessarily support-ive,' one whip said. There was another reason for a reshuffle too: based on the scale of the rebellion, the whips office concluded that not everyone in government had voted to save the prime minister.

In the days after his near miss, Johnson's team became paranoid that chancellor Rishi Sunak was masterminding an operation to oust him – despite the fact there was clearly no coordinated putsch in the confidence vote. One close colleague of Johnson said, 'The agitation against Boris back in January, when it was pork pie plotters, was from amateurs. By the time we got to the confidence vote, it was far more sophisticated. The Sunak lot knew what they were doing, they were running an alternative whipping operation by that stage.' Instead of Jeremy Hunt, the only senior Tory to state Johnson should go, the prime minister's loyalists were focused on the chancellor. 'The main problem was Sunak and his people,' one said.

Another minister close to Johnson said Number 10 believed Sunak had drawn up 'a detailed strategy' on how to replace him – suggesting Sunak himself may have had a role in leaking the details about his wife's tax affairs and his Green Card to pave the way for a future leadership challenge. 'I think he decided to get the issue about his wife out of the way because that was very confidential information and very tightly held,' one minister claimed. Those close to Sunak strongly deny he was plotting against Johnson and said it was 'totally ludicrous' to suggest he would have leaked a damaging story about himself.

Instead of focusing on his neighbour, Johnson might have been better off improving relations with MPs who had become despondent following the vote. 'It wasn't like the white-hot rage we had over partygate,' one government insider said. 'MPs were realising that we were onto our third team running Number 10 and it still wasn't working. If the aides kept on changing and the problems kept on happening, there's one fundamental problem. They came to a reluctant conclusion that he's got to go.'

After the vote, Graham Brady's tally of no-confidence letters was reset to zero but it did not remain so for long. Immediately after the 41 per cent result, the most hardline Johnson rebels resubmitted their no-confidence letters – even though another vote could not take place until June 2023 under the 1922 Committee's rules. But Brady began to receive delegations calling on him to change the leadership contest guidelines to allow another vote as soon as possible. For now, Brady declined and told them it would be unfair to move the goalposts halfway through a match.

During that week's Cabinet meeting on Wednesday, ministers told Johnson in private he had reached the last chance saloon. Sajid Javid had a one-to-one discussion with the prime minister after the Cabinet meeting. The health secretary told him 'this is a really shit result' and reminded him that four out of ten colleagues wanted him gone. Javid summed it up: 'It's huge. PM, this is your last chance. If things don't change now, it's over. You've got to put all this chaos behind you and show people things can change.' Ben Gascoigne, one of his longest-serving political aides, told Johnson, 'Now we can change or die.'

A strategy for an organised reset was the last thing on Johnson's mind. Downing Street was in total crisis. The best he could do was survive each day and hope that the Cabinet would remain firm and there would be no resignations from his government. Instead, another pair of catastrophes were soon to strike.

***

Christopher Geidt was one of the most curious appointments of Johnson's administration. Previously a private secretary to the Queen, he became the independent advisor on ministerial interests in April 2021 – the official Whitehall arbiter of the ministerial code that governs the conduct of those in government. Geidt was the ultimate steady pick: a lifetime devoted to public service through the military and the Royal Family before taking a seat in the House of Lords. 'A man very much of the establishment in the nicest possible way,' one senior civil servant said.

He took up the role in inauspicious circumstances. Alex Allan, his predecessor, resigned from the role after Johnson disagreed with his conclusion that the home secretary Priti Patel had bullied officials. Throughout his career, Johnson had shown little regard for the rules and established norms, and as the most powerful person in the country, there was little chance he was going to do so now. After several senior Whitehall figures were approached and firmly rejected the job, the Cabinet secretary Simon Case beseeched Geidt to take it. The pair had worked closely in the Royal household and Case argued he would be able to protect him from Johnson's capricious nature and that Geidt was the best placed person to restore trust in the ministerial code. His time with the Royal Family had prepared him for working in sensitive circumstances full of rampant egos. Their discussions took 'weeks and weeks', according to those involved, until Case eventually pushed him over the line.

Immediately after he took up the role, Geidt told colleagues he had made a mistake. He was forced to carry out a series of investigations into Johnson's personal financial affairs, notably into whether the ministerial code had been broken over the refurbishment of his Downing Street flat. Stoked by a series of leaks to the *Daily Mail*, the wallpapergate scandal suggested Johnson had not been straightforward in declaring a loan from David Brownlow, a Tory donor, to pay for over £100,000 of decorating work. Geidt initially cleared Johnson of breaking the ministerial code, but considered resigning eight months later when it emerged Johnson had not been wholly forthcoming as to how the Brownlow donation had been solicited.

Geidt then became embroiled in the partygate scandal and was increasingly exercised that Johnson had broken the ministerial code – namely the sections on honesty and truth – over his statements to parliament that there had been no parties and all rules had been followed. Following the Met police fine, Geidt stated there were 'legitimate' concerns about whether the code had been breached. In a meeting with Johnson, he demanded an explanation of how Johnson had been truthful; the prime minister replied[13] that his breach of Covid rules had been 'unwitting'. Across Whitehall, the advisor was on 'constant' resignation watch as he had belatedly realised Johnson had little care for his role and had no desire to face the consequences for his actions.

However, it was not the parties that ultimately pushed Geidt to quit but a peculiar row about steel tariffs. He was asked by

Johnson to consult on whether deliberately breaking World Trade Organisation commitments over a dispute with China on steel trade would count as a breach of the ministerial code. In his resignation letter, Geidt said the request put him in 'an impossible and odious position' given the prime minister was suggesting 'a deliberate and purposeful breach of the ministerial code'. He warned it would make a 'mockery' of his role.

Johnson's allies thought it was 'eccentric' that Geidt decided to go over this issue. The following day, Geidt clarified that his departure may have also been linked to the dispute over the Northern Ireland Protocol. The steel tariff request was 'simply one example of what might yet constitute deliberate breaches by the United Kingdom of its obligations under international law, given the government's widely publicised openness to this,' he said. Civil service colleagues said Geidt was 'genuinely torn' between two principles: 'Genuine concern for public service duty and to be a person in there upholding the office, and the total shitshow that was going on in Downing Street.'

After his departure, Geidt told colleagues he tried his utmost but ultimately concluded Johnson would never follow the codified structures of the ministerial code. The prime minister had lost two ministerial ethics advisors – adding to a sense among Tory MPs and the public that Johnson was leading a government that had little care for standards. Johnson could or would not find a replacement for Geidt. When he left Downing Street in September 2022, there was still no arbiter of ministerial standards in place.

The next problem struck a far stronger note with MPs. On 23 June, a pair of by-elections took place that tested both ends of the Conservative party's voting coalition. One was in Tiverton and Honiton, a traditionally safe blue seat in Devon that returned a 24,239 majority in the 2019 election; the other in Wakefield, a pro-Brexit former Labour heartland in West Yorkshire that went Tory for the first time under Johnson. Both were prompted by Tory scandals: in Tiverton, MP Neil Parish was forced to resign after admitting to watching pornography in the House of Commons (he insisted he was searching for a tractor range called the 'Dominator'). In Wakefield, Imran Ahmad Khan was forced to quit after being convicted of child sexual abuse and being jailed for eighteen months.

Given that both votes were prompted by disgraced Tories, holding them in normal circumstances would have been a challenge. With Johnson's sinking popularity – his net approval ratings had sunk[14] to -45 in June – it was impossible. Johnson's keenest supporters hoped that his popularity in pro-Brexit northern England would stifle Labour's majority, and that the sheer size of the Tory majority in Tiverton and Honiton would insulate the party from a massive swing to the Liberal Democrats, the seat's traditional challengers.

Prior to the votes, the *Financial Times* reported[15] that senior Tory strategists were braced to lose both. And so it came to pass: Tiverton and Honiton flipped to the Liberal Democrats on 23 June with a 30 percentage point swing[16] away from the Tories, while Wakefield returned to the Labour party with a 13 percentage point swing.[17] Although Labour's 3,358 majority was lower than the party might have hoped, there was particular alarm at the swing towards the Lib Dems in the south. 'I didn't realise things were going to be so bad in Tiverton and Honiton,' one Cabinet minister said. 'The South had turned against us and Boris in particular.'

Johnson's inner circle justified the results as just an example of how mid-term governments tend to lose by-elections. But the pair of results were another example of Johnson losing his electoral potency, which in turn frightened Tory MPs. 'The cost to the party was political capital,' one senior Tory party official said. 'Losing both types of seats we represent was especially painful. Bear in mind with Boris the biggest attraction is his ability to win elections. Once that's gone, there's nothing.' One of Johnson's closest officials said, 'He expected the results to be as bad as they were. He did not expect the Dowden bombshell.'

At 5.35 a.m. on 24 June, Oliver Dowden became the first Cabinet-level casualty of Johnson's final decline. The Conservative party chairman had been ill at ease for some time; it was well known within the government that he was unhappy at being moved sideways from culture secretary in the previous reshuffle. 'He didn't like the move to chairman,' one Cabinet minister said. 'He wasn't suited to that role, he quite liked to go to the opera, the premieres and all the fun stuff of being culture sec.' A briefing to the *Mail On Sunday* that reported that he was likely to be demoted in the next reshuffle had stoked his annoyance. In his letter, Dowden said[18] he must take responsibility for the losses. 'We cannot carry on with business as usual. Somebody must take responsibility and I have concluded that, in these circumstances, it would not be right for me to remain in office,' he wrote, insisting it was a personal decision.

One person close to Johnson said it came as 'a huge surprise'. On Wednesday 22 June, the day before the by-election, Dowden had assisted Johnson with his preparations for prime minister's questions. He was also lined up to do the morning broadcast round straight after the by-election results. As was often the case, Johnson was out of Westminster when the crisis hit. He received the call from Dowden while in Kigali, Rwanda for a meeting of Commonwealth leaders. Downing Street told journalists he had received the news after an early morning swim. Back at Number 10, suspicions turned on Dowden's close political friend who Team Johnson feared (again) may have stoked the resignation and could be next to quit: Rishi Sunak.

The Big Dog team believed Dowden's resignation was part of an effort to destabilise the prime minister. Grant Shapps had recorded him on the spreadsheet as an MP who could not be counted on in a confidence vote and that a move somewhere else in government, or potentially a sacking, was in the ether if the potential reshuffle had taken place later that year. One Johnson ally said, 'Those of us who were close enough to the situation knew he was disloyal. His resignation was the public awareness of the Sunak plot, which had been running for months beforehand. Sunak and Dowden were very personally close.' Sunak's allies deny this, suggesting it was paranoia on behalf of Team Johnson.

Another Cabinet minister close to the prime minister described Dowden's departure as, 'an act of great personal treachery because the chairman of the Conservative party, in that role when you're in such trouble, should be one of your closest allies.' But one minister close to Dowden said it was nothing to do with Sunak. 'Oliver's frustration was that he was offering advice in a variety of areas as party chairman. It was either not taken, countermanded or only partially implemented. He felt the people in the Number 10 operation who are not directly responsible for running the party were overriding him.'

Immediately after Dowden put the phone down, Johnson spoke to the chief whip Chris Heaton-Harris to begin finding out whether a full Cabinet coup was taking place and whether Sunak was involved (the prime minister was later furious with his communications chief Guto Harri when reports of the ring round emerged, as it looked like Number 10 were panicking). Johnson spoke to home secretary Priti Patel, who convinced him she was steadfastly loyal. He then spoke to Sunak, who professed to having no knowledge of Dowden's resignation. One official close to Johnson said the prime minister was not convinced, while another said, 'I don't think Rishi was dishonest.'

Johnson also tried to speak to Sajid Javid, but the health secretary was delivering a speech on suicide prevention with his phone on silent. It was vibrating in his pocket throughout the morning, but the calls were ignored. When he later emerged from the event, Javid saw an escalating series of missed calls from senior figures in Downing Street who feared he was about to quit. Javid rapidly rung back Heaton-Harris and assured him he was going nowhere.

Until the by-election losses, the rebellion against Johnson had remained among MPs – many of those unrequited malcontents who were never going to be won over by his leadership. But the resignation of Dowden brought the problem directly into the Cabinet. With Johnson on edge that further ministers may soon quit, the Big Dog Operation was closely watching Rishi Sunak and all the while pressure was rising for the 1922 Committee to allow another confidence vote. The government could not afford any more mistakes – the head of steam had been building for over six months and it could easily blow. It needed a period of stability and calm, and yet a week later, one of Johnson's most volatile ministers visited a Pall Mall gentlemen's club for drinks with colleagues. What happened next set in train the final fall of Boris Johnson.

6. Drinks at the Carlton Club

On Thursday evenings, after parliament has wrapped up for the day, a certain partying sort of Conservative MP heads to the Carlton Club. Situated halfway up St James's Street, one of London's most salubrious addresses, membership is open to those who pledge a vow to Conservative values, and it is considered a safe space for Tories. Around 1,500 members pay fees[1] of £1,700 a year for the privilege of membership, which allows access to its luxurious dining rooms and bars named after former prime ministers. Having long given up any formal role in the party, many of its fundraising activities are directed towards elections.

The Carlton has long had a dubious reputation. The Duke of Wellington once remarked,[2] 'Never write a letter to your mistress and never join the Carlton Club.' It lacks the social cache of, say, the nearby Boodle's gentlemen's club, or the strong ties to the governing class as the Travellers Club. For newly elected MPs, however, it is an embodiment of the party's illustrious past – as well as somewhere to relax without interlopers earwigging on any plotting. In January 2022, serial Johnson critic William Wragg (a member of the 1922 executive) was reported[3] to be 'holding court' one night with a hundred fellow MPs at the club supposedly to discuss the ongoing partygate revelations and whether Johnson should be challenged. Nadine Dorries, culture secretary and arch-Johnson loyalist, also happened to be in the club.

Underneath the grand staircase of 69 St James's Street, there is an 'inviting corner' of dark leather armchairs beneath the Tory blue carpeted staircase. One observer* described the area as 'The spot where male members could stand to stare up the skirts of female guests walking up and down the stairs.' And it was here where Chris Pincher, Boris Johnson's deputy chief whip, ended up late on Thursday 29 June as part of a typical cabal of Tory MPs and acquaintances who had gone to the Carlton for drinks after parliament had finished sitting. The club was busy that night as a party was being held in aid of the Conservative Friends of Cyprus.[4]

Born in September 1969,[5] Pincher was first elected to parliament in 2010 for the seat of Tamworth in Staffordshire, which he won from the Labour party. A compact, bearded and impeccably dressed MP, his innate love of parliament and the political game meant he was destined for the whips' office. He became a junior whip in July 2016, rising up to become assistant chief whip. But Pincher's career came to an abrupt halt when Alex Story, a former Olympic rower-turned-Tory candidate, alleged he had massaged his neck and discussed 'his future in the Conservative party' before changing into a bathrobe. Story described[6] him as a 'pound shop Harvey Weinstein'. Pincher was also alleged to have made advances towards Labour MP Tom Blenkinsop who told him[7] to 'fuck off'. Following the allegations of these unwanted advances, Pincher promptly resigned from the whips' office and referred himself for an official investigation.

After several months, Pincher was cleared by the Conservative party of breaking the party's code of conduct. Of the allegations, Pincher said, 'If Mr Story has ever felt offended by anything I said then I can only apologise to him.' He rejoined Theresa May's

---

* Seth Alexander Thévoz, author of *Behind Closed Doors: The Secret Life of London's Private Members' Clubs*.

government in January 2018 and was promoted to deputy chief whip[8] where his reputation as an effective party manager burgeoned during the long collapse of her government. Pincher remained in this role until Johnson became prime minister in July 2019. As a keen supporter of the prime minister's leadership bid, he was then promoted into several government departments in crucial roles: first as Europe minister, then as housing minister.

When Johnson encountered his first serious leadership turbulence in early 2022, there were widespread rumours that Pincher would gain his coveted Cabinet job of running party management, but Number 10 suspected Pincher himself was responsible for putting such stories around. Chris Heaton-Harris, chief whip, plus Nigel Adams, Johnson's closest fixer, appreciated his talents and Pincher was called upon, but returned to his old role as deputy chief whip. As an adjunct member of the Big Dog Operation and loyalist to Johnson, he was perfectly placed to help prop up support for the government. During those 'relentless' evenings in January and February, when Johnson's allies were preparing for a confidence vote at the peak of the first partygate crisis, Pincher was omnipresent along with transport secretary Grant Shapps and his intricate spreadsheet.

His appointment as deputy chief whip was not universally welcomed. One Cabinet minister said Pincher was 'obviously unsuited' to the role but 'desperate to get it', adding, 'I went to a lot of the meetings where Pincher had to shore up Boris's support. He had poor manners and was really quite rude to some of the supporters. He told somebody in the 2019 intake that he had a face for radio. That may be a funny thing to say to your closest friend, but it's not funny when you're senior and he's junior.' Craig Whittaker, another senior Tory whip, refused to serve with Pincher and quit when he heard of the appointment, although told his local paper that he left due to 'personal reasons'. But one other person involved in his appointment explained why he was chosen, saying, 'He was ruthlessly brilliant as deputy chief whip, especially his attention to detail. There was not much else in his life: politics and parliament were Pincher's life.'

Rumours about his personal conduct, however, swirled at the time of his appointment, including the chatter of further sexual harassment incidents beyond the Alex Story allegations. Steve Barclay, Number 10's chief of staff, fought for four hours against the appointment that Adams and Chris Heaton-Harris wanted to make. Meg Powell-Chandler, one of Johnson's aides, flagged his behaviour with Barclay during this debate, telling him, 'I've heard something bad about Chris Pincher, something else.' The allegation she had heard was that Pincher had acted inappropriately towards two Conservative MPs at a party conference in 2017. The new chief whip asked the Cabinet Office's propriety and ethics team whether there were any red flags about Pincher and he also spoke directly to the MP involved. The appointment was delayed for several hours, much to the confusion of the media who were widely expecting it. Yet the mandarins gave Pincher the go-ahead and did not raise any concerns.

Johnson was initially reluctant to give Pincher the job, but told colleagues, 'I don't know anybody else.' One person involved said, 'Boris gave in like he always does.' Another aide said, 'The reality was everyone agreed that he was the best man for the job.' But as with other past problems with the running of his operation, Johnson and his team seemed to be aware of rumours, or had a partial grasp of the issues, but were not aware of the full facts and did not seek to find them out. One official said, 'There were discussions about "Oh, there's an allegation about somebody who did something at a party" but no one would provide the details. Boris would never demand the information either.' It was a mixture of incuriosity and complacency that would ultimately cost him his premiership.

One Cabinet minister close to Johnson argued that the issue was the prime minister was 'too kind' towards his colleagues, adding their spin that, 'He will never give up somebody on the basis of rumours.' But they also went on to say that, 'There is a level of rumour on everybody – some of it unfair, some of them are absolute nonsense. But there comes a level of rumour where you have to say, "I just cannot take this risk as an act of self-preservation." That was what I felt on Pincher.' A close ally of Johnson admitted, 'He never should have been appointed.'

A mere six months later, the fears about appointing Pincher were realised. That June evening at the Carlton Club, he arrived at 8 p.m. to join over a hundred Conservative MPs to hear a lacklustre speech from the former environment secretary, Theresa Villiers. Over canapés of smoked duck, goat's cheese mousse and pulled pork on sourdough, the real focus of the evening was the gossip about Johnson's future and whether the prime minister could make it to the summer. Waiters were on hand to top up glasses of wine. Pincher was spotted with a flute of prosecco. One fellow whip said Pincher most likely went along for 'good intel', adding, 'When he was deputy chief whip, he would instruct colleagues to go to a drinks party, make sure we've got someone there and report back. It's perfectly good whipping.'

After the party finished around 9 p.m., Pincher took to the 'cad's corner' underneath the Carlton's staircase and settled in for further drinks with fellow MPs and hangers-on. Pincher became increasingly inebriated, according to those present, and during the course of the following couple of hours he allegedly groped two men – including grabbing a victim's left buttock and groin after buying a round of drinks. When he was spotted in the club's Macmillan Bar even later, one MP claimed he was lurching towards people and propositioning them. The *Daily Mail* reported that he was 'Clearly trying to seduce several young men', including parliamentary aides. Some urged him to drink water to sober up but he took no notice. He was eventually told to leave the club by Mark Fletcher, the Tory MP for Bolsover, a young red wall MP who had every incentive to avoid conflict with the party hierarchy. One Tory present, who was on the receiving end of Pincher's behaviour, reported him to Sarah Dines, a fellow whip, who made the situation worse by inappropriately asking the alleged victim if he was gay. She later said that she was attempting to establish exactly what happened.

Dines passed her account of that evening to the chief whip Chris Heaton-Harris. There was despair in the whips' office and among the Big Dog team at Pincher's actions. 'Our response was, "Fucking hell Chris Pincher, what have you done?"' With Johnson's position still fragile after the 41 per cent of Tory MPs had rebelled against him a few weeks before, his supporters were nervous about any further scandals. The next morning, Thursday 30 June, Heaton-Harris spoke to several MPs and staffers who had been at the Carlton. He summoned Pincher to explain himself, who confirmed his behaviour had crossed a line.

Yet no formal complaint was made and no formal action was taken against Pincher, until *The Sun* approached Downing Steet with the allegations that afternoon. Team Johnson realised Pincher would have to quit as deputy chief whip, which he did at 8 p.m. that evening as the story went public. In a short resignation letter,[9] Pincher told Johnson, 'Last night I drank far too much ... I've embarrassed myself and other people which is the last thing I want to do and for that I apologise to you and those concerned.' The fifty-two-year-old said quitting was 'the right thing to do' and said he would continue to support the government from the backbenches. *The Sun* reported that Pincher would remain a Tory MP as those in government believed he had 'done the right thing' by falling on his sword. It was a huge misstep: as with the other botched responses to scandals, the first stage – as with grief – was always denial.

With his resignation from government, some in Downing Street hoped a line had been drawn under the situation. Several aides, however, told Johnson and Guto Harri, his director of communications who was handling the response to Pincher, 'You're going to have to suspend him.' But Harri was concerned for the MP's state of mind and resisted. In a crisis Number 10 meeting on Friday morning, Harri compared Pincher to David Kelly, the chemical weapons expert who killed himself following leaks about the Blair government's handling of the Iraq war. One official present said, 'Guto told the press office that they needed to be nice because it would be their fault if he did anything wrong. I was not happy at all about our position on someone who was an alleged predator. You can't put the onus on people like that, saying if they disagree, you might be risking Pincher's mental health.'

Another factor too was that Conservative party HQ was reluctant for yet another by-election. After the dual losses of Wakefield and Tiverton and Honiton the week before, one senior official told Number 10, 'We can't have any more.' Pincher's 19,634 majority in Tamworth would almost certainly have collapsed and the seat would have flipped to Labour, as it had in the dog days of John Major's government in 1996, when a previous iteration of the same seat fell on a huge swing. Tensions were running high throughout the day. One Johnson aide said the mood was 'frustrated and angry' because Pincher was still a Tory MP facing the most serious of allegations. 'We spent five days on the wrong side of sexual misconduct. It comes down to "Whose side are you on?" And for some reason . . . the government was seen as being on the side of the sex pest rather than the victim.'

That Friday morning, the Welsh secretary Simon Hart was given the chore of the morning media broadcast round and made it clear he thought Pincher should lose the whip. 'I know what I'd like to see happen – you can probably tell what that is by the way I'm trying to avoid answering your question . . . I think we might be having a very different conversation as the day goes on.' It was an uncharacteristic act of insubordination from an otherwise scrupulously loyal Cabinet minister that exposed just how far Johnson's stock had fallen so quickly. Only with increasing numbers of Tory MPs publicly saying he should be suspended, was it dawning on Number 10 how serious the Pincher situation was. 'Nobody thought his behaviour would be as significant as it was,' one Johnson ally said. 'The press office completely fucked it up. The David Kelly comparison was insane.' The internal anger at the mishandling of Pincher outstripped any of the previous errors. One senior aide said, 'when the incident happened at the Carlton Club, I screamed "For fuck's sake!" at people. First, it was happening again, we were defending the indefensible. And second, our response was utterly insane.'

Ahead of Downing Street's first encounter with journalists, the line of the questioning became obvious. Given all of the rumours about Pincher's behaviour: what did Johnson know and when about his misconduct? And were there other allegations he had not acted on? It had been reported that Pincher had even been assigned a minder to prevent him from drinking too much. Later that morning, Westminster's political journalists gathered in the media suite for a painful briefing where Pincher was the only topic. The prime minister's spokesperson told the media Johnson was not aware of any allegations at all about Pincher. That was not true, as Steve Barclay had flagged Meg Powell-Chandler's concerns in February when the Cabinet Office's PET team were ordered to dig into their files to see if there were any red flags.

The spokesperson realised his error and rapidly corrected the line to any 'specific' allegation against Pincher. But the civil servant would not repeat what specific allegation Johnson was supposed to be aware of. When this line became public, one senior Tory MP texted a colleague, 'What the fuck is wrong with these people? Have they learned nothing?'

When asked about any allegations surrounding Pincher's appointment in February, the spokesperson said, 'In the absence of any formal complaint it was not appropriate to stop the appointment on the basis of unsubstantiated claims.' Within Number 10, there was some doubt whether the spokesperson had all the facts about Pincher and what Johnson and his team had known. 'He was told by Guto that the PM didn't know about any specific allegations. But I'm pretty sure he didn't check that with the PM,' one government insider said. Johnson later on expressed his deep annoyance at Hari for the public statements. As the lobby briefing concluded, the official was asked over and over whether Johnson made an error in appointing Pincher. The Number 10 spokesperson stuck to a well-trodden but increasingly implausible answer: 'The prime minister always looks to appoint those who he thinks are the best fit for different positions in government, he has done that throughout his time as prime minister.'

As the Friday wore on, Johnson's aides Declan Lyons and Ben Gascoigne told the prime minister 'this is not going to hold' and warned he would have to backtrack on keeping Pincher in the Tory party. Pressure was building on all sides from MPs, the Cabinet, the civil service and the party. Caroline Nokes and Karen Brady, former ministers under Theresa May's government, wrote to Heaton-Harris to warn of 'serious reputational damage' to the party if Pincher remained an MP. The pair called for a zero-tolerance approach on sexual harassment and a 'thorough investigation' of any allegations. 'Anyone subject to such an investigation should not be allowed to sit as a Conservative MP and represent the party in any capacity,' they wrote.

With the anger swelling from MPs, Johnson realised he had made another bad call. 'The PM was open to taking the whip off him, there wasn't some sort of massive internal thing about defending him,' one ally said.

Some in Johnson's inner circle insisted they did not want to remove the whip until a complaint was made. One government insider said, 'When there are allegations of wrongdoing, it is difficult to remove the whip until there is a formal complaint.' With hindsight, almost everyone in Downing Street admitted they should have acted much sooner. One of Johnson's key advisors made it clear to the prime minister they should be more honest about the situation, that Number 10 was aware of some allegations but had not fully investigated the matter.

In a clear echo of partygate, no one in Downing Street had put together all the details of what had taken place with Pincher before the press response was formed. One ally of the prime minister said, 'Even at that stage, the work hadn't been done so Boris was making decisions with half information, without timeline explanation of what had actually taken place.' Steve Barclay, his chief of staff, and long-time confidant Lynton Crosby told Johnson directly the whip would have to be taken away, but until late in the day, the prime minister resisted.

Later that afternoon, though, the inevitable U-turn came. A formal complaint against Pincher was made by one individual present at the Carlton Club through parliament's Independent Complaints and Grievance Scheme and the Conservative whip was withdrawn. Pincher would sit as an independent MP while the allegations were investigated. But another twenty-four hours of damage had been wrought on the Johnson government. After defending the prime minister over the Owen Paterson saga, partygate, the Met police fine, the privileges committee investigation, Cabinet ministers had finally had enough. One senior member of the Cabinet said, 'I'd completely had it by this point. I didn't get into politics to defend a sex pest, which is what we were being asked to do.'

And just as with the privileges committee fiasco in May, Tory MPs were furious that they had to defend Johnson only for the rapid U-turn to come. 'This was where the anger really tipped over into ministers in the Cabinet, because Number 10 did exactly the same thing,' one senior party advisor said. 'All this time, people were asking what they knew about parties. Everyone in Westminster knew about Pincher and so the ministers saw straightaway that Number 10 was lying again. The system was not working.'

The wider implications of what had taken place were difficult to avoid for Johnson. Pincher was the fifth Tory MP to face such allegations over the past twelve months. Neil Parish, who had resigned in Tiverton and Honiton, had watched pornography in the House of Commons chamber. David Warburton, MP for Somerton and Frome, faced sexual misconduct allegations from three women. Imran Ahmad Khan, Wakefield's MP, was sent to prison for child sex abuse. Another anonymous MP was arrested on suspicion of rape. The prime minister's spokesperson denied the Conservative party had a problem. 'It's regrettable that we've seen a small number of people not meet the expectations that people would expect of MPs, which is why the prime minister is keen for everybody in parliament and across all the political parties to work together to improve that culture.' But the Pincher affair was far from over.

***

It was well over a year and a half since Dominic Cummings had left Johnson's side but he was observing the end of Johnson from afar with glee, offering up frequent contributions on social media, hauling up tales from his Number 10 past to cause further embarrassment. On Saturday 2 July, the prime minister's ex-chief aide took to Twitter[10] to highlight the mess Johnson had got himself into over Pincher: 'If [Johnson] didn't know about Pincher as he's claiming, why did he repeatedly refer to him laughingly in No10 as "Pincher by name Pincher by nature" long before appointing him . . .?' Cummings claimed Downing Street was 'lying again' over its knowledge of Pincher's behaviour. One Johnson ally admitted, 'It sounded very much like something he could have said.'

The following day, Sunday 3 July, the *Mail On Sunday* reported[11] that Johnson had told colleagues of Pincher back in 2020, 'He's handsy, that's a problem.' The paper also said that Johnson had been told of claims Pincher had made unwanted advances towards a fellow Tory MP, plus the revelation Pincher made unwanted advances towards a twenty-four-year-old in 2012. Number 10's line that Johnson was not aware of allegations before appointing him deputy chief whip was falling apart. The *Mail On Sunday* also featured disturbing details that Pincher threatened to report a Tory staffer to her superiors when she attempted to stop his 'lecherous' advances at a party conference event. Pincher denied all the allegations.

Almost every newspaper that day featured claims about Pincher's past conduct. *The Independent* spoke[12] to one Conservative MP who was groped by Pincher on two occasions – first in December 2021 and again in June 2022. 'He put his hand on my crotch and moved it around. I shook my head and said "No, I don't want that" but he [Pincher] just smiled . . . he carried on until I was able to move away,' the MP said. Pincher again firmly denied the allegations, but the damage to his party was growing. After months of sex-pest stories, the Tories were rapidly gaining the potent stench of sleaze, just as it had in the late 1990s before heading to a landslide defeat.

The most damning details came in *The Sunday Times*, which had been attempting to publish an exposé on Pincher for several months, only to encounter legal obstacles. As soon as the Number 10 press office received their inquiries, some aides urged Johnson to act immediately, before the stories were published. 'I kept saying, "Why are we not removing the whip?"' one government insider recalled. 'The end result was the end of Pincher, so why don't we do it now?' Some in Number 10 were hoping the paper would publish so they could finally remove him. 'Each week it went on without them publishing, the more difficult it was for us – about what we had known for how long. Had it all come out earlier, the Carlton Club wouldn't have happened and there wouldn't have been more victims,' one official said.

On 3 July, *The Sunday Times* published[13] what had been originally flagged to Steve Barclay in February when Pincher was appointed deputy chief whip. It reported that Pincher slid his hand down an MP's inner leg, who 'considered it an unwanted physical pass, and quickly reached down and removed Pincher's hand'. The victim met with his whip and urged them to monitor Pincher's mental health, but did not think the incident warranted a formal complaint. Through his lawyers Pincher denied acting inappropriately. The accusers were critical of Number 10's handling of sexual harassment allegations and admitted they had not taken it any further because 'this is something that happens in Westminster'.

The poor sod put up by the government to comment on all these troubling reports was Thérèse Coffey, the serious and steady work and pensions secretary and Number 10's reliable go-to media minister whenever a dead bat response was required.

Her aim was to say as little as possible, and not further implicate the prime minister. Speaking to Sky News's *Sophy Ridge On Sunday* programme, she channelled the hapless Manuel from *Fawlty Towers* with a range of interviews that could be summed up by his catchphrase: 'I know nothing.'

When asked about the (accurate) reports that the Cabinet Office's PET team had been asked to look into Pincher, Coffey replied, 'There's an element of a bit of vetting that goes on – but ultimately the decision is that of the prime minister. I'm not part of those individual conversations.' By the time she took to the BBC to speak to Sophie Raworth on their *Sunday Morning* programme, her line had softened. Coffey said to the 'best of my understanding' Johnson had 'not been aware of specific allegations'. Coffey was then asked how she knew the prime minister was not aware of the claims against Pincher. 'I have not spoken to the prime minister,' she curtly admitted, pointing out Johnson had been abroad at the G7 and NATO summits. Once again, another scandal and another party management meltdown was taking place with the prime minister abroad. So who had told Coffey? 'Somebody from the Number 10 press office,' she stated. 'As usual, one gets briefed on a wide variety of topics when you come onto a show like this today.'

Despite almost twenty-four hours of equivocation on keeping Pincher in the Tory party, Coffey implausibly argued Number 10 had been decisive. 'What's important . . . [is] the specific allegations were made and a very proactive decision was made to remove the whip as well, as Chris had already resigned from government.' On the *Mail On Sunday* allegation in which Pincher was described by the prime minister as being 'handsy', she stated she had not spoken to anyone in Number 10 about this. Coffey did her best with the information she had been given by Downing Street, but Johnson's political team were still not clear on what exactly happened with

Pincher and another series of media responses was given without the full facts, making the scandal even worse. The prospect of an umpteenth U-turn was approaching, yet Johnson's team repeated the same error in failing to see it coming.

That evening, the Cabinet Office's PET found a formal note about an examination into Pincher's behaviour during his time as Europe minister. Number 10's insistence it had not known about any allegations was ruined. Simon Case, head of the civil service, communicated to the prime minister's office they would have to change the line.

In a brief interlude from the Pincher scandal, Johnson had dinner that Sunday with Rishi Sunak to thrash out plans for a joint economic speech about their vision for the country. In his typical manner of dismissing media storms, the prime minister did not spend the weekend figuring out a response but was focused instead on his next endeavour. Relations between Johnson and Sunak had reached their lowest ebb and Number 10 was nervous about the meeting. Only the two men were present, no aides or partners attended.

The supper did not go well. One government insider said the pair clashed because 'there was a fundamental disagreement over the direction of the government'. Johnson made the case for tax cuts more quickly which Sunak refused. Johnson argued VAT should be slashed immediately to boost growth which Sunak rejected. It was a similar debate to the one that would later take place between Sunak and Liz Truss in the summer's leadership race.

The Pincher row was, however, briefly discussed. According to one government insider, Johnson asked Sunak what he made of the row. One Johnson ally said, 'The chancellor said nothing helpful, he just didn't offer any view at all.' The prime minister was frustrated that his chancellor appeared unwilling to engage with his plight and Johnson was fearful that Sunak was disconnecting from the government.

That night, another meeting took place that would be critical in Johnson's future. Sajid Javid had watched the unfurling reports about Pincher's behaviour with dismay. The health secretary continued to harbour deep anxieties about Johnson and Javid thought he might have reached the point when he no longer had confidence in him. Javid invited two of his special advisors to his home that evening and spoke to a handful of Tory grandees to assess their views. For the first time, Javid seriously contemplated resigning. All of his confidants told him 'the time is coming', but that he should stay put for now. For the final time, he gave Johnson the benefit of the doubt and decided to see if the prime minister could make it through the summer in the hope a reshuffle would improve things. As with many others in Johnson's orbit, Javid seemed to keep on making the mistake of assuming Johnson could change the way he operated.

When Monday 4 July dawned, the Number 10 press office arrived at work early to figure out how they could reset their public position following the PET discovery that Pincher's behaviour had been formally known about. That morning, children's minister Will Quince was sent out onto the airwaves to defend the government. Despite the urgent debate in Number 10, however, he reiterated the same lines as Coffey the day before – declining to comment on 'speculation, gossip or rumour'. Quince told[14] the BBC he had asked Number 10 on both Sunday and Monday 'firmly and clearly' what had happened and what they knew; he was given a 'categorical assurance that the prime minister was not aware of any specific allegation or complaint made against the former deputy chief whip Chris Pincher.'

Just as Sajid Javid had been sent out by Number 10 earlier in the year to state there were no parties and no rules had been broken, Quince was inadvertently not telling the truth. One senior advisor said it 'wasn't so much a conspiracy as a cock-up' and there was a breakdown between the press office and a little-known team in Number 10: the briefing team. Before government ministers head off on a media round, this small team of aides provide lines to take – this usually happens around 5.30 a.m. before the first interviews start an hour later. One veteran Whitehall official said the ineptitude of this team was to blame for many of the Johnson government's failures: 'The briefing team was always terrible in this administration. They take their instructions from the press office, but they consistently messed up the lines that secretaries of state took on the [broadcast] rounds.'

In the case of Quince, the briefing team were acting on incomplete information. They had not been aware of developments over the weekend and relied on the same press lines that had been used in Friday's briefing and given to Thérèse Coffey on Sunday – unaware that a major shift had occurred. 'It wasn't so much they had deliberately withheld information from Will. They were constantly twenty-four hours behind what was happening, so they kept giving ministers the old lines,' one insider said.

At 11.30 a.m., the daily lobby briefing for political journalists commenced. The Downing Street media suite was full of reporters eager to push the prime minister's chief spokesperson on what they knew about Pincher's behaviour. Number 10 finally had to admit that:[15] 'The prime minister was aware of media reports that others had seen over the years and some allegations that were either resolved or did not progress to a formal complaint, but at the time of the deputy chief whip's appointment he was not aware of any specific allegations.' The complaint in question was the incident in the Foreign Office.

More details on what had happened in February came out, including about Pincher's appointment: 'He [Johnson] did take advice on some of the allegations that had been made, but there was no formal complaint at that time and it was deemed not appropriate to stop an appointment simply because of unsubstantiated allegations.' The sudden shift in position alarmed ministers and MPs, and lost Downing Street what little credibility it had left. If they hadn't already, from this briefing onwards, the media and the wider public stopped believing what they were being told.

And still more allegations about Pincher emerged: Mark Dabbs, a marathon runner in Pincher's Tamworth constituency, claimed on 4 July[16] the MP 'was brushing his hand across my bottom' when the pair posed for a photo in 2018. Dabbs said his behaviour was 'bordering on sexual assault' and told *ITV News*[17] that Pincher made a series of suggestive and inappropriate comments during their meeting. Pincher again denied any wrongdoing.

***

Tuesday 5 July would prove to be a momentous day in Johnson's time as prime minister. It began in the wooden and marble grandeur of Westminster Hall, where much of Britain's political class attended the National Parliamentary Prayer Breakfast. Over coffee, pastries and orange juice, hundreds listened to the Reverend Les Isaac, founder of the Street Pastors movement, who spoke on the pertinent theme of 'serving the common good'. Boris Johnson was present, along with the opposition leader Keir Starmer and dozens of senior ministers, including health secretary Sajid Javid, who had carefully heeded the Reverend Isaac's message on honesty and integrity. While the politicians were aspiring to improve their spiritual standing, a longstanding opponent of Johnson sought to ruin his political one.

Simon McDonald was the embodiment of the Whitehall establishment that the prime minister loathed. He joined the Foreign Office in 1982, straight out of Cambridge University, and served as British ambassador in Israel and Germany. After decades of diplomatic service, he was appointed as the department's permanent undersecretary and head of the diplomatic service in 2015. When Johnson arrived as foreign secretary the following year, the pair clashed over Brexit – one of the prime minister's allies described him as 'a rabid anti-Brexiteer.' When Johnson, now prime minister, announced that the Foreign and Commonwealth Office would merge with the Department for International Development, Johnson informed McDonald he would be retired early.[18]

Two years later, McDonald delivered his revenge. That Tuesday morning at 7.30 a.m., he tweeted his letter[19] to the parliamentary standards commissioner about Number 10's utterances on the Pincher affair, accusing them of 'still not telling the truth' about Pincher's behaviour. The mandarin said a complaint had been made in the summer of 2019 about Pincher – regarding actions similar to what happened at the Carlton Club – and it had been discussed with the Cabinet Office. 'An investigation upheld the complaint; Mr Pincher apologised and promised not to repeat the inappropriate behaviour.' Critically McDonald claimed that Johnson 'was briefed in person about the investigation and outcome of the investigation' and said this constituted a formal complaint. In six brief paragraphs, McDonald had accused the prime minister and his team of lying and in doing so he plunged the government into its deepest crisis to date. Coming on the record from one of Whitehall's most senior figures gave the claims substantial heft.

One Number 10 insider said, 'It was reported as more in sorrow than anger. He was a trusted source, while everything we said was complete bollocks.'

Dominic Raab, the deputy prime minister and justice secretary, was not at the prayer breakfast but had the unlucky job of representing the government on Tuesday's media round. He was ambushed with McDonald's letter live on *BBC Breakfast* – the country's most watched morning programme. Looking decidedly prickly, Raab said,[20] 'That is news to me, that the prime minister was briefed on the specific complaint that was made and then the outcome, precisely because it didn't lead to a formal disciplinary grievance process, let alone formal action.' Raab said he had spoken to Johnson directly, who had assured him he had not been directly told about Pincher's misconduct.

When Johnson returned to Downing Street from the breakfast, he scrambled his political and press team for a crisis meeting on how to respond. The aides gathered in the Cabinet room with a palpable sense that the situation was becoming lethal. One aide said, 'There was a long and deep personal animus between them [Johnson and McDonald] but at this stage, things felt very out of control.' Team Johnson only had a few hours to prepare a public response: as well as the 11.30 a.m. press briefing, an urgent question was granted by the House of Commons speaker on the Pincher affair. Michael Ellis, a junior Cabinet Office minister who had often seemed to be the one made to defend the indefensible in parliament, was chosen to respond.

Finally, five days into the crisis, the prime minister's inner circle sought to figure out what they knew and when about Pincher. 'We had five days of being confused about what exactly happened,' one government insider said. It emerged that Helen MacNamara, the former head of the Cabinet Office's PET team, had briefed Johnson on the investigation. One official explained:

'There's a wider problem that people are a little bit hazy with Boris because they think he doesn't do stuff formally so they can be less formal. If you're going to have that kind of discussion with the prime minister you need to provide written minutes to make sure it's done properly.' Whether Johnson forgot, or whether his press chief Guto Harri had failed to properly check with him before announcing the government's position previously, was unclear. But the public position would have to shift.

Ellis and the prime minister's spokesperson agreed they would not say he 'forgot' as it would open the prime minister up to ridicule. Although there was anger at the Cabinet Office, the finger was not pointed internally – one official present said, 'The PM did not know of any specifics about the Foreign Office incident, it was a total cock-up by the Cabinet Office.' Instead the pair agreed on the line that the Foreign Office matter was discussed in a brief chat a number of years ago. Johnson's inner circle were furious about how the McDonald letter was being reported.

As journalists gathered in the media suite for yet another packed briefing, tensions were high. Johnson's official spokesperson Max Blain wearily began setting out the prime minister's diary. But before he could take questions, Jason Groves of the *Daily Mail* asked him, 'Are you planning on telling us the truth today?' The spokesperson sheepishly responded: 'We always seek to provide the information we have at the time,' noting the facts 'take time to establish'. The spokesperson confirmed Johnson knew about the formal complaint about Pincher's inappropriate behaviour. 'The prime minister was informed but not asked to take any action as a result. As a result of that action, the minister carried on serving in that department for a number of months.' The emphasis was placed on the fact it was not a formal complaint – contrary to McDonald's letter – and it was a 'brief conversation' three years ago that was buried deep in the prime minister's memory. The briefing was the most painful of Johnson's time in government.

At the same moment, Ellis lumbered up to the Despatch Box to deliver a similar message to MPs. 'Last week, when fresh allegations arose, the prime minister did not immediately recall the conversation in late 2019 about this incident. As soon as he was reminded, the press office corrected their public line.' He went on, 'The position is that the prime minister acted with probity at all times.' He did not use the word 'forgot' but in exchanges with Labour MPs, it was clear what he meant. One Cabinet minister watching him in the Commons remarked, 'The Number 10 line was he basically forgot. When that came out, I thought "This is seriously bad and lame."' Downing Street had wanted to rebut some of McDonald's claims but, after shifting their line several times, they had lost the right to be heard. 'The ship had sailed,' one official said.

As the Number 10 team failed to mount a response, the Big Dog and Brains Trust teams were activated again to ring round MPs and defend the government's position. Johnson's inner circle were flailing around. 'By Tuesday lunchtime, the wheels were coming off,' one ally said. 'There was no strategy to deal with the crisis. Internecine warfare took hold inside Downing Street, with officials telling journalists that the operation was collapsing. 'Number 10 began briefing about people in Number 10 which made it an even worse atmosphere to work in,' one insider said. A bunker mentality began to take hold. 'We were all raging, but our position just wasn't cutting through,' one senior official recalled. 'At that point, none of us had any access to the PM so it was getting harder to formulate a response.'

Later that Tuesday, Downing Street inexplicably allowed cameras in to film footage of the weekly Cabinet meeting. Every minister around the table seemed uncomfortably glum or furious or a mixture of both. Thérèse Coffey, who had been sent out on Sunday to propagate false information on behalf of Number 10, looked especially stern. Even loyalist ministers such as Jacob Rees-Mogg and Nadine Dorries were expressionless. Levelling up secretary Michael Gove and health secretary Sajid Javid appeared haunted. Chief whip Chris Heaton-Harris stared down at his papers, while attorney general Suella Braverman resolutely focused on the wall in the middle distance. Even though Pincher was not raised at the Cabinet meeting, he was present in spirit. Simon Case, head of the civil service, had his head bowed throughout.

The ensuing discussion was scarcely more positive than their demeanour. After his inconclusive supper with Rishi Sunak the previous Sunday, Johnson wanted to define the government's overall economic strategy that could counter rising inflation, the cost of living crisis and lacklustre growth. Following his inadequate spring statement, Sunak was forced to announce a £15 billion package[21] at the end of May that almost doubled energy bill support, particularly for poorer households. All homes would be given a £400 discount on energy bills, in addition to a £150 council tax rebate for many others. The offering was highly redistributive, aiding less well-off households, but it was not well received by Tories concerned with fiscal probity.

At the start of the Cabinet meeting, Johnson told ministers he was planning to hold a regular series of 'economic press conferences' that would set out what the government was doing to help people. He drew a parallel with the frequent broadcasts during the coronavirus pandemic that were credited with effective messaging. But no one was clear what these press conferences would achieve. Michael Gove, levelling up secretary, said whereas the government had a clear message on Covid – punchy slogans such as 'stay at home, protect the NHS, save lives' – there was no agreement around the table about what the government's central economic messaging would be.

The Cabinet broke out into a debate on what the economic message should be and it was immediately apparent no one agreed. Kwasi Kwarteng, business secretary, heartily argued that the government 'must cut taxes now'. Michelle Donelan, the universities minister, readily agreed. Sajid Javid, health secretary, talked up supply-side reforms to boost growth. Sunak shot back that now was not the time to cut taxes with inflation soaring. Kwarteng tried to sum up with, 'There's no disagreement, we all believe we should cut taxes.' Gove interjected to say, 'Literally the chancellor doesn't, so we don't have a coherent message.' Johnson was having none of it and said 'no, no, no' – so incredulous that the ministers began laughing. Not a single person mentioned Pincher, the mistruths and the chaos unfurling around them.

***

After the Cabinet meeting, Johnson's inner circle bickered about whether or not he should front a televised message to apologise for Downing Street's mishandling of the Pincher saga. Johnson had almost lost confidence in Guto Harri and the press office's ability to get a message out there. One close aide said, 'He was pushing for a clip, it was really his only option at this point to try and get it done.' Other aides disagreed. 'I told him this was a bad idea,' one advisor said. 'He said, "Why?" And I said, "I'm not entirely clear what it is you are trying to get across."' Johnson dismissed these concerns and insisted he had to clear up the mess. Once again, the facts were not clear.

Preparations were duly made for the BBC's political editor Chris Mason to come to his House of Commons office that afternoon to film a short clip that would be broadcast on the 6 p.m. news bulletin. His team agreed he would say sorry for appointing Pincher deputy chief whip – another U-turn on the previous days – and explain that the Foreign Office complaint was made in passing three years before. Johnson would also apologise for not looking into the matter further.

At the same time, half a mile away across Westminster, Sajid Javid concluded after the Cabinet meeting that he had had enough. Following his unhappiness on the previous Sunday evening and the revelations from the McDonald letter, the health secretary and his team discussed whether they had reached the moment to go. One person with knowledge of the conversations said, 'We all agreed that the PM and his team lied, they had done it again. The general feeling was "How can this just continue now?"' Javid took further soundings: he texted Rishi Sunak that afternoon, but the pair never found time for a call. He also spoke to education secretary Nadhim Zahawi about the situation. Javid instructed Samuel Coates, his closest aide, to draft a resignation letter. After speaking to Michael Gove, Javid made his decision and signed the letter.

He was not the only minister contemplating their future. Next door to Johnson in Number 11 Downing Street, Rishi Sunak had reached the same conclusion. The chancellor was despairing not only at the government's Pincher response, but also at the economic incoherence of the government's policy. The Cabinet meeting had confirmed in his mind that he held irreconcilable views on the economy as to the best way forward from Johnson. As with Javid, he had taken soundings over the weekend from his advisors, supporters and family, who similarly concurred that his time in government was drawing to a close. One MP close to Sunak said, 'Rishi was properly fed up and decided that afternoon he could no longer defend the government.' But he was cautious too, fearing that quitting abruptly could endanger his leadership hopes.

Some senior Tories with contacts to both men think that Sunak and Javid coordinated their actions in some way, but aides close to the pair insist that they did not speak that Tuesday afternoon and there was no communication about their plans to resign. Johnson's inner circle also didn't believe it was a coordinated coup. 'I can't see how it would have helped Rishi to have coordinated with Saj. As you saw during the leadership contest, the narrative of being the man who sunk the knife in is not particularly helpful. If it was coordinated it was a very silly thing to do. What Sunak should have done is stayed and let Sajid do it.'

Johnson returned to the Palace of Westminster in his motorcade that afternoon to record the BBC clip. With the camera crews setting up in his suite, he practised his apology in Sunak's House of Commons office – at the very moment the chancellor was penning his resignation letter elsewhere. As the prime minister prepared to meet Chris Mason, one of his aides informed him that Javid had requested an urgent one-to-one meeting. Instantly they knew he was about to quit. One senior Number 10 figure said, 'For months when people asked what would happen with Cabinet, I'd always said Sajid was the weak link. He'd quit it before . . . he wanted to be prime minister, which is not an ignoble ambition, but he wanted to run for it.'

After the broadcast crew had left, Johnson and Javid met in the prime minister's office. Steve Barclay, Johnson's chief of staff, was floating around but the health secretary insisted he wanted to speak to Johnson alone. The pair chatted for almost half an hour, but having stated his intention Javid did not budge. One official involved said, 'He didn't want Saj to go, but he knew he'd made up his mind and understood where he was coming from.' Javid walked down the corridor to his own parliamentary office to make his resignation public.

As Johnson was conversing with his aides about handling Javid's resignation, around fifty of his closest MP supporters were gathered in the conference room of his parliamentary office for a thank you drink for their assistance during the vote of no confidence. The room was 'packed', according to those present, with the assembled Tories gossiping about the Pincher affair – unaware of what was about to happen. The prime minister and his political team watched the 6 p.m. news where his apology was the lead item. Looking red-faced, sweaty and flustered, Johnson said it was 'bad mistake' not acting on the complaint and admitted that he should not have made Pincher deputy chief whip: 'I apologise for it.' Speaking about his frustration at his Number 10 team and McDonald's letter, Johnson told the BBC he was 'fed up with people saying things on my behalf'.

Johnson put forward his explanation of what had happened: 'About two and a half years ago I got this complaint, it was something that was only raised with me very cursorily but I wish that we had, I in particular, had acted on it and that he had not continued in government because he then went on, I'm afraid, to behave, as far as we can see, according to the allegations that we have, very, very badly.' The prime minister concluded he was, 'Sorry for those who have been badly affected by it.' Yet two minutes into his apology, as it was being broadcast on the 6 p.m. news, Sajid Javid tweeted his resignation letter. Several floors above the party in the parliamentary press gallery, journalists glued to the TV screens screamed aloud at what had just happened. The BBC production team struggled to work out how to cover the moment while the prime minister was still speaking: their caption led on the prime minister's apology, then it shifted to 'BREAKING . . .

Sajid Javid resigns', while Johnson continued to fluster through the pre-recorded clip.

In his letter, Javid spoke of his longstanding private concerns about the integrity of the government he was part of – he was later to say that the sermon at the prayer breakfast had shaped his thinking. 'The British people also rightly expect integrity from their government. The tone you set as a leader, and the values you represent, reflect on your colleagues, your party and ultimately the country,' he wrote. 'Sadly, in the current circumstances, the public are concluding that we are now neither. The vote of confidence last month showed that a large number of our colleagues agree.' Javid said Johnson had not shown the 'humility, grip and new direction' required and he had concluded, 'It is clear to me that this situation will not change under your leadership – and you have therefore lost my confidence too.' Johnson and his team knew it was coming, but the drinks party were unaware. A wave of shock rippled through the room next door, as the assembled MPs balanced their glasses of wine alongside their phones to squint at his letter.

Nine minutes later, Javid's resignation was toppled from the news headlines. When his resignation was made public, a scramble took place in Number 11 to print off Rishi Sunak's resignation, and deliver it next door so he could publicly declare it. At 6.11 p.m., Sunak resigned as chancellor. It is unclear whether he alerted Johnson: Sunak's colleagues said he attempted to call the prime minister on WhatsApp and he did not pick up; Johnson's team insisted they had no idea he was resigning. What Team Johnson had feared for almost six months had come to pass.

In his letter, Sunak wrote, 'The public rightly expect government to be conducted properly, competently and seriously. I recognise this may be my last ministerial job, but I believe these standards are worth fighting for.' The chancellor said he had been loyal and supported Johnson publicly even when they had disagreed, especially on economic policy. 'I firmly believe the public are ready to hear that truth. Our people know that if something is too good to be true then it's not true. They need to know that while there is a path to a better future, it is not an easy one.' Sunak concluded, 'In preparation for our proposed joint speech on the economy next week, it has become clear to me that our approaches are fundamentally too different.'

As the news broke, Johnson exploded in front of his aides with a diatribe of four-letter words. Javid's resignation was instantly brushed away. Sunak's resignation posed a far bigger problem. After months of their disintegrating relationship, Johnson saw his departure as a 'personal betrayal' and it was universally believed by Johnson and his aides that Sunak had resigned to challenge him for the Conservative party leadership. 'Boris was very, very upset. He thought the [resignation] letter was a tissue of lies about their relationship.'

A close ally explained, 'The difference with Saj is that the PM and Rishi worked very closely. The PM did everything to involve Rishi in everything – not just economy stuff – but he was going to the Number 10 morning meetings, throughout. The PM wanted Rishi to know everything he was thinking and made so much effort to bring him in. That is why it hurt so much.'

After his outburst, Johnson faced two pressing tasks: one to shore up the rest of the Cabinet, second to fill the gaps in his government. But before any of that, he had to immediately face an increasingly agitated room of his supporters, ploughing through the complimentary wine. Johnson entered the room to raucous cheers and banging on the tables. The prime minister delivered a classic stump speech. 'I want to thank everybody, everyone has done a fantastic job. We fight on,' he shouted. He sought to cast Sunak and Javid's resignation in a positive light.

'Those of you who champion free markets and tax cuts might find in light of the very recent news that we might be able to deliver some of those now,' to greater cheers. Even his closest aides were stunned at the performance. 'His ability to turn the room around was amazing,' one MP present said. Another MP said, 'It was incredible given the fact he had just lost his health secretary and chancellor, he was just brilliant.' After the meeting, his supporters queued up to lay into Sunak, with several telling Johnson it was 'good riddance'.

After leaving the party, Johnson instructed his chief whip Chris Heaton-Harris to phone round the Cabinet to ensure no one else was quitting. One of their chief fears was Michael Gove, who Johnson's team saw as close to Sunak and Javid and who could be on the verge of quitting. The levelling up secretary was unreachable: he was at the Royal Opera House watching *Cavalleria Rusticana* (about a blood feud in Sicily) and *Pagliacci* (about the downfall of a clown). When the news of the resignations came through, Gove was chatting to Theresa May. The pair agreed no one could take on the role of chancellor with much credibility. Gove was forced to abruptly leave the opera house and publicly said he had no plans to do anything.

Johnson hopped back in his motorcade to Downing Street, where the Big Dog team was summoned to start shoring up his standing. An emergency reshuffle was required that night to find a new chancellor and health secretary. The mood was rapidly darkening. 'I thought it was bad with Saj's resignation,' one senior government insider said. 'But when Rishi went I thought it was terminal.' When Johnson arrived at Number 10, he told aides that as long as he could form a government, he would stay on and that he had absolutely no plans to quit, yet the prime minister's final twenty-four hours as undisputed leader of the country and the Tory party had begun. Both Johnson and his inner team adopted a bunker mentality to try and rebuild his government, to avoid further major resignations and to keep him in office for as long as possible. But privately, nearly all of them knew the end was almost nigh.

7. The Bunker

The education secretary, Nadhim Zahawi, was enjoying supper on Tuesday 5 July when he received an abrupt message from Boris Johnson's chief fixer, Nigel Adams: 'Get your arse over here'. With the precipitous departure of the chancellor and health secretary, Zahawi sniffed a promotion in the air. As his ministerial Jaguar wormed its way through the traffic to 10 Downing Street, Zahawi's eagerness got the better of him and he repeatedly texted Adams to ask, 'What am I getting Nige?' Either job would have been a promotion, but Zahawi sensed it might be the big one. Adams shot back it was not for him to say and that he would just have to wait.

Fifty-five-year-old Zahawi was one of the most prominent faces of Boris Johnson's government, first as the media-friendly vaccines minister during the coronavirus pandemic and latterly as education secretary. Born in Iraq, Zahawi's family moved to the UK when he was eleven years old, his story encapsulating what might be called 'the British dream'. From refugee to millionaire, he gained huge financial success as a founder of the pollster YouGov. Zahawi's parliamentary career began in 2010 and he gained junior ministerial office under Theresa May's government in 2018. As a long-term backer of Johnson since his mayor of London days, Zahawi's career took off when Johnson became prime minister. He was also frequently mooted as a potential successor.

Zahawi was one of three names that evening to be in contention to be Johnson's third chancellor of the exchequer. Leaving the drinks party for his loyalist MPs, Johnson returned to Number 10 where the Big Dog team had been scrambled to work through a Cabinet reshuffle. The usual cast of Johnson's crisis managers were present: fixer Adams, strategist Ross Kempsell, chief whip Chris Heaton-Harris, his old *Telegraph* editor and confidant Will Lewis. From the formal Downing Street team were his political advisors Declan Lyons and Ben Gascoigne, plus director of communications Guto Harri and chief of staff Steve Barclay.

One other senior aide was present at the reshuffle. David Canzini, Number 10's deputy chief of staff, had been decidedly absent from most of the inner circle crisis meetings that had taken place previously, but he found his way to the centre of the events that evening at the prime minister's request. Some in the Big Dog team were puzzled: 'Canzini got himself in the room and I do remember thinking, "What the fuck is he doing here?"' Within Number 10, opinion about Canzini, who had been brought on board in 2022, was mixed. A range of glowing media profiles had not boosted his standing internally, with suspicions he had briefed them himself.

Crammed into the prime minister's private office, the assembled aides pondered how to restack the government. Should they seek two immediate replacements for Rishi Sunak and Sajid Javid? Or should they push for a much bigger reshuffle – the sort Declan Lyons had sketched out for later in the summer? Soon, however, the room concluded that Johnson did not have the political capital and authority to undertake a major reconstruction. The task, therefore, was to prove the Johnson government was still functioning and not hand his rivals any further ammunition. 'People were saying, "There's no way he can function, he's got to go, we want him marched out of the door with his wife and kids." So we had to get a functioning and competent government,' one insider said.

The first spot to be filled was the most straightforward. In his motorcade back from parliament to Downing Street, Johnson decided Steve Barclay should replace Javid. His chief of staff (previously a junior health minister) was mooted for the role a year before when Matt Hancock was forced to resign for breaking Covid rules for embracing his aide Gina Coladangelo. The smooth and assured fifty-year-old Barclay had shown a keen interest in health policy while in Number 10: monitoring reams of official statistics behind the NHS and talking up the government's manifesto commitment to forty new hospitals. He had essentially put himself forward for the role. One senior official said, 'Steve was obsessed with data and waiting lists, he's very into the technical details of health policy. So he volunteered himself. He also obviously wanted to get the fuck out of Number 10.'

Johnson asked his chief of staff to leave the room while his fate was pondered. He soon returned; the deal was swiftly done, and the pair emerged into the Cabinet room as the prime minister declared, 'Meet our new health secretary!' Barclay looked delighted and relieved, according to those present. They shook hands and the health secretary departed for his new ministry. It may have seemed insignificant at that moment but Johnson had just lost his third Downing Street chief of staff in almost three years. There wouldn't be a fourth.

Next came chancellor. Number 10 were not blessed with a range of options for the role that would be judged as credible by the markets when they opened the next morning. The three names in contention were foreign secretary Liz Truss, police minister Kit Malthouse and Zahawi. Truss was a serious candidate, but Johnson opted to keep her at the Foreign Office given the fragile geopolitical situation. 'There was a discussion about Liz but on balance the PM decided the Ukrainian situation was sufficiently important that she should stay focused on the international stuff,' one official said. Another person close to Johnson said, 'Liz could have easily done the job. He would have liked to appoint her chancellor, but he felt if there was any road left he wanted to keep her as foreign secretary.'

Malthouse's name soon fell by the wayside and so Zahawi was the consensual choice. As Zahawi was waiting to see the prime minister, Johnson's office had rapidly asked the Cabinet Office's propriety and ethics team to do due diligence to ensure Zahawi was suitable for such a high-profile role. Their work was questioned as days later it was alleged[1] that Zahawi was under investigation by the National Crime Agency and HM Revenue and Customs, something he later denied. He was taken into the Cabinet Room by Johnson for a lengthy one-to-one chat. Johnson did not want the same schism to open up between prime minister and chancellor that had developed with Sunak.

Zahawi was sympathetic with Johnson on the need to cut taxes and implement supply-side economic reforms to boost growth. 'It felt for a brief moment we finally had a Number 10 and Number 11 team that could work well together,' one ally said. 'The mood that night was, "Actually this is a good thing, now we have a chancellor who will get stuff done."' In their discussion, Johnson and Zahawi agreed to a set-piece economic speech in the near future – a rehash of what the prime minister had sought to do with Sunak weeks before. Their bonhomie would not last long.

As Zahawi accepted the job, Johnson's team had already lined up his replacement as education secretary: Michelle Donelan, the eager universities minister. The thirty-eight-year-old arrived at Number 10 quarter of an hour after Zahawi and was desperate for a Cabinet role: while in a waiting room, she texted Nigel Adams almost directly asking for education secretary. 'She went into the Cabinet Room, where the PM was appointing ministers, begging for a Cabinet job. She was jumping up and down like a pogo stick with excitement,' one person present said. Johnson's team had no qualms about appointing her; as universities minister she had impressed Number 10 and was already primed for a promotion in the July reshuffle. 'She was impressive, she would be another woman at the top table, she was the right choice,' one minister said. Very soon, however, Donelan would earn the dubious record of being the shortest-serving Cabinet minister in British history.

While Number 10 was busy filling the three top slots, resignations from the government had continued – albeit of a more junior level than Sunak or Javid. At 7 p.m., Andrew Murrison resigned[2] as the government's trade envoy to Morocco, citing Simon McDonald's letter (his letter to the prime minister was photographed so poorly that it was likened to a notice of repossession in the window of a fried chicken restaurant, and he had to repost it twenty minutes later so the press could read and report it properly). Next came Bim Afolami, who resigned live on TalkTV[3] as vice chair of the Conservative party when the presenter guided him to the conclusion he had lost confidence in Johnson. Five junior ministerial aides from the 2019 intake of MPs followed: Jonathan Gullis, Saqib Bhatti, Nicola Richards, Virginia Crosbie and Theo Clarke. The trickle of departures, which soon turned into a torrent, suggested to Johnson that the effort to oust him was gathering unstoppable momentum.

The last departure of 5 July had been long expected in Downing Street. Alex Chalk, solicitor general, had been on resignation watch for months and had told almost any MP who would listen that he was unhappy and about to walk – not least over Johnson's partygate fine. In his letter,[4] the Cheltenham MP said he could no longer defend the culture and course of the government: 'The cumulative effect of the Owen Paterson debacle, Partygate and now the handling of the former Deputy Chief Whip's resignation, is that public confidence in the ability of Number 10 to uphold the standards of candour expected of a British Government has irretrievably broken down.'

Team Johnson mostly dismissed these resignations as ungrateful nonentities, many of whom had not supported the Johnson project to begin with. Under Guto Harri's direction, the press office pumped out a series of media briefings that heralded their two big new appointments: Zahawi was described as a 'class act', someone who would reset economic policy. 'For the next stage, we need a plan for growth and not just balancing the books. He represents the government's values and commitment.' Barclay was heralded[5] as a 'massive upgrade' on Sajid Javid: 'He has a first class forensic brain, great clarity of thought and will use data to drive improvement.' There was one final barb at Sunak from Downing Street: 'He had no real plan for growth [and was] just obsessed with balancing the books.' Johnson and his political team were exhausted and fearful of what would lie ahead. One insider said, 'We left that night with a sense that the situation was very difficult but at least we've plugged the holes. We could say that we had a functioning Cabinet.' Another senior official said, 'That night it was feeling okay.' But another said, 'I was still extremely worried.'

There was very little sleep, however, for Zahawi who had been put forward for the morning broadcast round of interviews on Wednesday 6 July. Having left Number 11 for home, the new chancellor was WhatsApping colleagues until 3 a.m., digesting his new brief and finalising how exactly he would summarise his long, rambling discussion with Johnson on the government's new economic agenda. He grabbed two hours' sleep before waking at 5.30 a.m. to travel into the studios. One government insider said,

'When you become chancellor, you get a load of briefings and he was doing his best to brief himself. Nadhim did that media round with barely any preparation or sleep.'

July 6 began with Zahawi adopting a more conciliatory tone for the Johnson government after the dual major resignations the night before. The new chancellor said the prime minister was 'right to apologise'[6] over the appointment of Chris Pincher as deputy chief whip: 'When the prime minister realised he'd made a mistake, he came out and explained that. He said with the benefit of hindsight that he made a mistake. I think that's good leadership to come out and say that, to say: "Look, you know, I don't get every decision right."'

Zahawi also made a clear break with the Sunak era on the economy. Steve Swinford, political editor of *The Times*, summarised Zahawi's broadcast round as[7] 'the most expensive in history', as he went about reversing key policies from the previous era with plans to splash cash far and wide. The new chancellor strongly hinted that a rise in corporation tax due in 2023 from 19 to 25 per cent would not take place, which would lose the government a cool £16 billion a year. Zahawi also suggested a future income tax cut, at £5 billion, and reiterated his pledge to deliver a 5 per cent pay rise for teachers. Were that to be replicated across the public sector, it would add £12–15 billion to government expenditure. Such profligate spending was exactly what Johnson had wanted in a chancellor, but there was a notable absence of a plan on how it was going to be paid for.

As the interviews took place, though, it became clear that the new chancellor would not only have to answer questions about spending plans. While he was live on Radio 4's *Today* programme, the schools minister Will Quince resigned – his anger over the mistruths he was told to propagate over the Pincher affair came to a head. One senior Tory who spoke to Quince said he felt under 'so much pressure to resign from his family and friends'. His politics were firmly on the left of the party, but he remained loyal to Johnson throughout. His resignation soured the mood in Number 10. 'He just felt Boris couldn't continue, it wasn't a move to bring Boris down,' one friend said. 'Will wanted Boris to stay, but his resignation created momentum against the PM.' Ambushed live on air with news of his departure, Zahawi mournfully said he was sorry to see Quince go. 'He was a great minister, all I would say to colleagues is people don't vote for divided teams, we have to come together,' he said.

Number 10 was relieved Zahawi had not committed any major gaffes. 'Given the pressure he was under, at least he didn't have a car crash,' one official said. 'But the situation was becoming farcical.' While Zahawi was still on the *Today* programme, Laura Trott, an aide to transport secretary Grant Shapps, also quit, so he was forced to use the same words that he had used about Quince, that he was sorry she had quit and everyone needed to pull together.

The dam had broken. At 9.43 a.m., schools minister Robin Walker quit. At 11.06 a.m., it was city minister John Glen. At 11.43 a.m., it was prisons minister Victoria Atkins, who expressed concerns that the values of 'integrity, decency, respect and professionalism' had fractured. Johnson's inner team again shrugged them off. 'None of these people were a surprise,' one ally said. The loss of faith in Johnson was also spreading to Tory MPs. Rob Halfon, chair of the education select committee and a popular blue-collar Tory, also withdrew his support that morning, stating 'the public have been misled' over both partygate and Pincher. He was joined swiftly by Lee Anderson, a former member of Arthur Scargill's National Union of Mineworkers and now Tory MP for Ashfield in Nottinghamshire, who posted on Facebook:[8] 'It is my belief that our PM has got all the big decisions right and guided us through the most difficult time in my life time and I have always backed him to the hilt. That said, integrity should always come first and sadly this has not been the case over the past few days.'

While outwardly stating that this was all manageable, a sense of foreboding took hold in Number 10. Conservative MPs had started to leave the Johnson support group on WhatsApp. One senior government insider said, 'I'm a relentless optimist and we kept going. We still had the MPs' support team, we still had good numbers, they were still there. They still want to show they were loyal.' But the situation for Johnson was soon to take another turn for the worse. As he was beavering away in his private study, ignoring the junior resignations and preparing for what was undoubtedly going to be a bruising session of prime minister's questions, he was about to receive a visit from an old university chum who had some especially grave news to deliver in a deadly soft fashion.

***

After his interrupted evening at the opera, Michael Gove had mulled over the resignations of Rishi Sunak and Sajid Javid, both close Cabinet compadres.

Gove and Johnson had an especially intertwined and turbulent past. Their political psychodrama began when Gove was Johnson's campaign manager for the Oxford Union presidency in the 1980s. Both developed careers as budding journalists on different publications in the 1990s and then became parliamentary colleagues in the 2000s. Their relationship broke down in 2016, when Gove declared Johnson was unfit to be prime minister and became responsible for sinking Johnson's first Tory leadership campaign. Even though Johnson brought him back into government as one of his most senior ministers, first at the Cabinet Office then as levelling up secretary, the prime minister's most ardent loyalists never forgave Gove.

That Wednesday morning, the levelling up secretary spoke to dozens of Tory MPs and ministers and many told him that Johnson's time as prime minister was drawing to a close. He had come to the same conclusion. Gove was concerned that Downing Street had developed a bunker mentality and that Johnson was not receiving good advice about his prospects, so he decided to do something about it. Gove contacted Simone Finn, Number 10's deputy chief of staff (and a close friend and former partner), to ask for five minutes alone with Johnson before or after the prime minister's questions' prep. Throughout the Johnson premiership, Gove had been part of the team that role-played questions, quips and quibbles for the weekly jousts with opposition leader Keir Starmer in the House of Commons (as one of parliament's strongest, most amusing debaters, he had done the same throughout David Cameron's leadership too). He arrived at 10 Downing Steet early and was told by Finn he could have a brief word before the prep session begin.

Johnson did not know he was seeing Gove. Nigel Adams, his perennial fixer, was in Johnson's office when a knock came on his door at 10.25 a.m. Finn said, 'Michael is here, he wants to see you.' Johnson responded, 'But he's going to see me in a minute because we're doing PMQs prep.' She insisted. Gove walked into the prime minister's private office and the Number 10 aides filtered out.

He looked straight at Johnson and delivered the fatal blow for the second time in six years: 'Boss, I'm really sorry to say this but I think you should announce you're standing down today.' According to those briefed on what happened, Gove went on 'it's up to you obviously how' and he explained how he saw events panning out based on his conversations that morning. 'There are going to be a slew of junior ministerial resignations, many more than you may have been told. I anticipate they will include some of the best people in the party, people who are huge fans of yours. But you will not be able to get an administration together, it will be insupportable. If you survive that, the 1922 [Committee] will change the rules and you will lose a vote of confidence. I don't want to see you go that way.'

Johnson sarcastically thanked Gove: 'You've delivered the bullet in a polite way,' and he responded with a tale about one of his uncles who had 'failed to take his meds one day'. The man was a planning officer in East Ham and ended up in a dispute with his superiors, so barricaded himself into the town hall with a shotgun. The uncle was eventually bundled out by the police. 'That is going to be me,' the prime minister said. 'I'm going to fight, they're going to have to prise me out of here.' Gove, slightly stunned, responded, 'Okay, I totally understand prime minister.' Johnson told him he disagreed with his analysis of the situation; that there was no strong alternative leader. 'I think it would be bad for Ukraine, bad for Brexit, bad for the economy.' Gove acknowledged those reasons and explained they were why he had remained in government 'under stress' in recent weeks.

According to colleagues, Gove decided to tell Johnson the game was up because he thought it was impossible for him to go on. 'Michael wasn't going to run for leadership, he wasn't in anyone's camp, so he could tell him as the most senior minister in terms of experience. He felt it was his duty to do so – not to say anything would have been colluding in an illusion.' Gove did not issue an ultimatum for Johnson or threaten to quit himself, he told the prime minister he would not discuss the meeting with anyone.

Johnson did not see Gove's intervention in such a pure or positive way. The prime minister afterwards told only a handful of his inner circle what Gove had said and was 'absolutely furious' – particularly at the timing. Many saw it as Gove's final, ultimate treachery. One close colleague said, 'It was a deliberate knife in the front before a key moment'. Another claimed that the Gove meeting 'fucked his mindset' ahead of the Commons: 'Wednesday morning is all about the psychology of the PMQs and Gove knew exactly what he was doing.' Johnson's aides were equally angry. 'Literally before he's about to do PMQs, he's stabbed him in the fucking back – again,' one said. Then, in one of the most totally bizarre moments of a tumultuous day, Gove joined the prime minister's questions preparation session at 10.30 a.m. as if nothing had happened.

Johnson's special advisor Leonora Campbell role-played Keir Starmer as normal. Gove, who had told Johnson a mere ten minutes before that he should quit, made several observations on how to deal with difficult questions about his future. One aide asked how he would respond if Rishi Sunak popped up to ask something. Guto Harri responded, 'Oh I'm sure he's living in California already' and started humming 'All I Wanna Do' by Sheryl Crow which includes the line 'Until the sun comes up over Santa Monica Boulevard'. Not everyone was willing to go along with the charade: Nigel Adams entered the PMQs prep session knowing what had happened in Johnson's meeting with Gove, saw Gove was present, and walked straight back out.

After the preparation session, Gove returned to his ministry across Westminster and told colleagues that Johnson had 'utterly lost it' and had gone 'mad'. Johnson went to the House of Commons for what would be his penultimate prime minister's questions. That lunchtime, Johnson was determined to carry on through sheer effort of will. He felt the storm would pass, as so many others had. One colleague recalled a conversation Johnson had with Geoffrey Cox, the attorney general, during the 2019

Brexit wars in parliament. The lawyer said to him at one stage, 'Prime minister, you just can't do that.' Johnson replied, 'Geoffrey all my life people have been telling me "you can't do that". And I've always proven them wrong.'

***

Prime minister's questions is one of the most divisive aspects of Westminster politics. To its detractors, it is the worst kind of ya-boo politics, where serious debate is substituted for cheap laughs, petty point scoring and childlike behaviour by MPs. For its supporters, it is a vital moment of accountability, where every week both party leaders are put under intense scrutiny for half an hour to assess their capabilities and standing. Are their policy positions coherent? Can they rival their opponent with their arguments and rhetoric? And, most crucially, does the leader have their MPs behind them? The volume of support – in cheers, the customary Tory shouts of 'yeah yeah yeah' and the 'ahhs!' at moments of surprise – can make or break a leader's momentum. It scarcely matters outside the political bubble, but has a lot of traction within it.

When Johnson slid onto the green benches that Wednesday lunchtime, the response was muted from Conservative MPs. His most loyal supporters – ministers Nadine Dorries and Jacob Rees-Mogg on the frontbench, MPs such as Conor Burns, James Duddridge further behind – attempted to muster some customary cheers. But from the moment he arrived, it was palpably clear that Johnson's political authority was rapidly draining. From the press gallery, the government benches looked glum, the opposition side of the Commons were openly laughing at Johnson, perhaps the most damaging response for a leader to be receiving.

Keir Starmer began by reading out, chapter and verse, the allegations against Chris Pincher. He wanted to 'remind people propping up this PM how serious it is'. The question he then posed to Johnson was: 'Why did the prime minister promote Chris Pincher knowing he had been guilty of predatory behaviour?' Johnson replied that Pincher was no longer whip and was under investigation over the complaints, before adding that he 'abhors' the abuse of power, in his or any other party. Having dodged the specific question, Starmer tried again asking why he was promoted. He also asked whether Johnson had used the phrase 'Pincher by name, Pincher by nature'. Once again, Johnson dodged the question and said he was not going to 'trivialise the matter' and he reiterated, 'I greatly regret that he continued in office.' His lame efforts to pivot to 'hearing about other jobs' and new employment figures fell flat.

Starmer remained lawyerly focused, noting that Johnson had not denied using the 'Pincher by name' phrase. His fire was turned back on Conservative MPs, who he claimed were acting as if the Pincher scandal 'did not matter'. Johnson responded he had acted immediately by removing the whip (this was not true, he had waited almost twenty-four hours before kicking Pincher out of the Tory party). The opposition leader moved onto the mass of resignations, describing it as 'the first instance of sinking ships fleeing the rat'. Johnson tried to rebut Starmer by stating he had no right to talk about integrity as he had campaigned for Jeremy Corbyn to be prime minister; that he voted forty times against Brexit; and that he had faced a police investigation over the beer-gate saga. 'Pathetic,' Starmer responded, to a torrent of jeers from the Labour benches. Such attacks had worked for Johnson six weeks ago, whipping up cheers from his backbenchers, but now they were met in almost silence.

The opposition leader summed up the Pincher affair as 'awful behaviour, unacceptable in any walk of life ... he ignored it'. Starmer said the Tories remaining in his government were 'the charge of the lightweight brigade' – a line that even Johnson found amusing. He painfully went through all of Downing Street's shifting stances on Pincher, dismissing the prime minister's team as 'a Z-list cast of nodding dogs'. Struggling to find an adequate response, all Johnson could muster was that he wanted to 'get on with our job' and focus on topics that he felt mattered to the public. Starmer wrapped up the session by referring back to his days as director of public prosecutions and listening to evidence of victims, like those alleged to have been abused by Pincher. Johnson's finale was stating that eight of Labour's shadow Cabinet ministers voted to get rid of Trident nuclear deterrent. Again, it fell flat.

The two most damaging moments came during questions from his own team. First, ex-minister Tim Loughton asked Johnson if he could think of 'any circumstances in which he should resign?' The prime minister stated that if he was unable to help the people of Ukraine or deliver on his mandate then he might go – a hint that being unable to form a government might prove to be a red line. Then Gary Sambrook, the Conservative MP for Birmingham Northfield and a member of the 1922 executive, in a truly shocking interjection, recalled an exchange in the member's tearoom when Johnson had said openly: 'There were seven people, MPs, in the Carlton Club last week and one of them should have tried to intervene to stop Chris from drinking so much.' In complete silence, Sambrook went on, 'As if that wasn't insulting enough to the people who did try and intervene that night. And then also to the victims that drink was the problem.' He called on Johnson to 'take responsibility' and quit.

And for good measure, one last senior Tory called on Johnson to quit. David Davis, the former Brexit secretary, reiterated a sentiment he had made back in January, during the peak of the first partygate crisis. Davis had reiterated one of the most iconic lines in British political history, from Leo Amery (quoting Oliver Cromwell) speaking to former prime minister Neville Chamberlain in the famous Norway debate: 'You have sat there too long for all the good you have done. In the name of God, go.' On this occasion, he was more muted: 'I ask him to do the honourable thing and put the interests of the nation before his own interests.'

Immediately after PMQs came a personal statement from Sajid Javid. Every resigning Cabinet minister is granted their moment to have a say in the House of Commons and while Rishi Sunak did not put his name forward, the outgoing health secretary took up the opportunity. Mutters among MPs that morning were that Javid was hoping to reiterate what Geoffrey Howe, the former foreign secretary, had done to Margaret Thatcher in November 1990, when his devastating critique hastened the end of her premiership. Javid did not reach those heights, but his speech was another deep blow: he recalled the prayer breakfast the morning before, where the Reverend Les Isaac spoke. 'I will never risk losing my integrity,' Javid said. 'I believe a team is only as good as a team captain and a captain is only as good as their team, so loyalty has to go both ways. Events of recent months have made it increasingly difficult to be in that team.' The former health secretary warned that 'the problem starts at the top' with the prime minister. He told MPs: 'At some point, we have to conclude that enough is enough. I believe that point is now.' Johnson was forced to sit and listen to his speech, stony-faced.

And still the ministerial resignations continued – so much so that Sky News began a rolling ticker in the corner of the screen throughout that day's news coverage. One minute into PMQs, Jo Churchill resigned[9] as a junior environment minister with a personal attack on Johnson: 'Recent events have shown integrity, competence and judgement are all essential to the role of prime minister, while a jocular self-serving approach is bound to have its limitations.' Soon after PMQs finished, housing minister Stuart Andrew was the next to go:[10] 'Our party, particularly our members and more importantly our great country, deserve better.' But the most consequential resignation came at 2.24 p.m. when five prominent ministers from the 2017 intake quit as a group: Kemi Badenoch, Lee Rowley, Neil O'Brien, Julia Lopez and Alex Burghart. These ministers were seen as central to the future of the party. When Gove told Johnson some of the best Tory MPs were due to quit, he may have had Badenoch and O'Brien in mind, both having served in his department. The MPs wrote, 'It has become increasingly clear that the government cannot function given the issues that have come to light and the way in which they have been handled. In good faith, we must ask that, for the good of the party and the country, you step aside.' Johnson was said to be 'particularly hurt' by Burghart giving his notice as he had formerly served his chief parliamentary aide. Just twenty minutes later, at 2.47 p.m., the former international trade secretary Liam Fox withdraw his support. At the exact same moment, employment minister Mims Davies also resigned.[11]

After PMQs, the Downing Street press team gathered for their usual huddle with political journalists outside the Commons chamber. They were bombarded with question after question about Johnson's future. His press secretary claimed he still maintained the support of a majority of MPs. Would Johnson fight a confidence vote? 'Yes.' Did the prime minister think he could win a confidence vote? 'Yes.' Would new ministers be appointed? 'Yes, over the coming days.' But events were overtaking Downing Street's narrative: as the press briefing took place, John Stevens of the *Daily Mail* broke the news[12] that Gove had visited Johnson that morning and told him to quit.

Back in Downing Street, the mood shifted to disbelief as it became apparent that it would be impossible to fill the widening ministerial gaps opening up in his government. 'It was absolutely insane,' one aide said. 'That feeling only got stronger and stronger as the day went by.' Another close Johnson ally said after PMQs, 'It was done by this point, it was irrelevant what happened next because the course of events was set.' After the solemn response from MPs to Johnson's lacklustre Commons performance, the mood in the Tory party whips' office was bleak. 'That lunchtime was when I started getting really anxious that this could be it,' one insider said.

Yet Johnson disregarded the chaos unfurling around him and focused on his next duty: a two-hour appearance in front of parliament's liaison committee. Roughly three times a year, the prime minister of the day appears in front of a special committee formed of select committee chairs to take evidence on any topics the senior MPs see fit. Even in happier times, for Johnson these sessions were testy affairs, where rivals would seek to take chunks out of him and he would sometimes struggle with policy detail. It was already proven to be far from his best speaking platform. Hunkered down in his House of Commons office, Johnson prepared for two hours for the approaching session with his team, seeking to ignore the resignations going on around them – a 'totally surreal' situation one person present recalled. Johnson was not on his best form either, one official present said: 'It was a dire prep session. The boss wasn't being given good enough or accurate enough information, and his answers weren't forensic enough.'

The session commenced at 3 p.m. Johnson was immediately asked whether it would be possible for his government to function with thirty resignations; he responded there was a 'wealth of talent' on the Tory benches. Stephen Crabb, the former work and pensions secretary, mooted that he might struggle to replace those who had gone. Given the unfolding background news, and the sense that the government was collapsing about him, the committee afforded a strange experience to those watching. Johnson was having to answer detailed questions about policy and world events, such as grain supply in the Bosporus and the phasing out of petrol cars by 2030, yet there was an increasing sense that unless he was able to urgently respond to the flood of resigning MPs these were issues he was unlikely to be in office to deal with. As his core political team watched the session in his House of Commons office, the mood was 'grim' as the news of more resignations came through.

Johnson was questioned as to whether he would require the Queen's permission to call an election, or whether he would inform her, an indication some MPs were becoming concerned at some of the rumours emanating from his supporters. He dodged the question and said no one wanted an election. He was asked how important the truth was. 'Very important,' Johnson responded. At the session, as well as Ukraine and partygate, Pincher was a constant topic: Johnson acknowledged what had been obvious to all of his colleagues for nearly a week, Number 10 should have immediately established a timeline about the Pincher matter and it was 'by mistake' that many of the government's public responses had been incorrect.

As the liaison committee session drew to a close, with two more ministers resigning during proceedings, Labour MP Darren Jones informed Johnson that the BBC, Sky News and *The Times* had reported that a delegation of Cabinet ministers were waiting for him back at Downing Street, likely to tell him that his position was untenable. 'So you say,' he retorted. Jones was right: over the two agonising hours of questioning, some of the most senior members of Johnson's government had gathered, demanding to see him as soon as possible. Johnson was soon back in his motorcade on his way to hear what they had to say.

***

When Johnson arrived at Downing Street the atmosphere at Number 10 was sombre, with some staff in tears realising that the end was in sight. His deputy chief of staff David Canzini confirmed that half a dozen Cabinet ministers were waiting upstairs to see him. The cabal consisted of chancellor Nadhim Zahawi and education secretary Michelle Donelan – both of whom had been appointed by Johnson less than twenty-four hours ago – with Wales secretary Simon Hart and policing minister Kit Malthouse. Some of Johnson's staunchest defenders also visited Number 10 during the Wednesday evening: transport secretary Grant Shapps, who saved Johnson several times with his spreadsheet of loyalty, international trade secretary Anne-Marie Trevelyan and home secretary Priti Patel.

Northern Ireland secretary Brandon Lewis also wanted to see him, but was flying back from Belfast, while business secretary Kwasi Kwarteng had made it known he thought Johnson should step aside. Of the most senior ministers in his Cabinet, only foreign secretary Liz Truss did not tell Number 10 that Johnson should go, but then handily she was in Indonesia for a G20 foreign ministers' summit. With such a breadth of ministers calling time on his premiership, it was difficult to see how he could continue.

But the prime minister was not giving up. During the afternoon, a team had been scrambled to a cosy but well-appointed room known as the study – Margaret Thatcher's favourite place to work, where Johnson had punched the air to celebrate his 2019 election victory. The gathering became known as 'The Bunker' and featured members of all of Johnson's support networks including the Big Dog team, the Brains Trust and his closest Number 10 advisors, assembled for one final heave to try and save his premiership.

From the Big Dog team, there was Nigel Adams, minister without portfolio and Johnson's chief fixer, Conservative party HQ's Ross Kempsell, chief whip Chris Heaton-Harris and his aide Charlotte Owen. From the Brains Trust, Tory strategist Lynton Crobsy was in communication from Australia, his protégé Isaac Levido was present, plus Will Lewis, Johnson's former editor and friend. And from the Number 10 team, director of communications Guto Harri was present along with political aides Declan Lyons and Ben Gascoigne. Plenty of others attempted to join, knocking on the door to try and influence what was happening but everyone was denied entry in an effort to control the chaos. Shelley Williams-Walker, Number 10's head of operations, drew up a cast list and gave it to one of the building's custodians to keep nonessential aides away.

While the prime minister was taking questions from the liaison committee, The Bunker team had assembled a list of everyone who had not quit and remained loyal to Johnson. Will Lewis looked at the list and stated, 'This is enough, it's a lot of names we've got here.' Number 10 also asked the Cabinet Office just how small a government could be and still function. One Whitehall official said, 'We looked at whether to go for a broad reshuffle or slim it down to the bare minimum.'

But some in The Bunker had privately concluded the exercise was in vain – and perhaps for the first time this was something that Johnson himself had begun to privately moot to a select number of people when he returned to Number 10 at 5.30 p.m. 'Once he came back from liaison, he was making the decision that it was over. Boris wasn't saying it out loud to many people, but he was talking about how futile the situation was becoming.'

Before Johnson could see the waiting ministers, two other meetings took precedence. The first was with Graham Brady, chair of the 1922 Committee. The committee's official rules meant Johnson was technically safe from another challenge until June 2023. With tremendous pressures for another ballot, however, its executive committee had met that afternoon. The eighteen-strong group expected Brady to propose changing the rules for another contest, yet he was concerned about the legitimacy of such a move, given that the executive's year-long term had almost finished. He had an alternative: the 1922 would bring forward its annual elections to the following Monday, which would renew their mandate from Tory MPs, before rule change was discussed. One senior Tory said, 'Graham thought it looked dreadful that we were pushing out the dregs of our year in elected office on something so important.' His proposal was agreed.

At 6 p.m., Brady strode determinedly in his trademark royal blue suit out of the parliamentary estate and past the Red Lion pub filled with early-evening drinkers, in the direction of Downing Street. In a failed effort to avoid photographers, he circled up the right-hand side of Whitehall, crossing the road, and returning back down towards the Cabinet Office's white palace at Number 70. He avoided walking up Downing Street, conscious of the image he would create entering the famous black door. After walking through the Cabinet Office to Number 10 – through the notorious link door that physically separates the political side of government from the civil service – Brady went into the Cabinet Room to see Johnson at around 6.15 p.m.

The pair sat opposite each other, with chief whip Chris Heaton-Harris at the far end of the long table taking notes. The mood was business-like, with little of Johnson's jovial patter. The prime minister was expecting Brady to tell him that the rules had been changed and another confidence vote was happening. Instead, Brady explained the decision to elect a new 1922 executive, with the outcome due in five days. But Brady gravely told Johnson this was far from a reprieve: 'In my honest assessment, given the mood in the parliamentary party, it is inconceivable that the new executive would be more averse to changing the rules.' Brady informed Johnson it was 'almost inevitable' a vote of confidence would take place on the Tuesday. 'It is fairly obvious you would lose it,' he added.

The prospect of pushing the leadership question into the following week gave Johnson an opening to keep going. The prime minister was in a 'firm frame of mind', Downing Street insiders said, up for a fightback against MPs. He delivered Brady a robust defence of his record; speaking of 'all the great things' he still had left to do with the 2019 election mandate. 'Boris was firmly of the view that if Conservative MPs wanted to stand in his way and prevent him from fulfilling his duties to the British people, they should be made to do it. They should have a confidence vote,' one ally said. Brady politely told him, 'It would be better for the country, the party and for you personally if you didn't push it to that point.'

Johnson's allies had discussed and prepared for such an outcome and their solution was to try and rebalance the 1922 Committee in his favour, hoping they could thwart a rule change and confidence vote. The political team decided early on not to challenge Brady but to take a shot at replacing two vice chairs: William Wragg and Nus Ghani, both arch Johnson critics. They instead supported the candidacy of Sheryll Murray and Miriam Cates, MPs deeply loyal to the prime minister. One senior member of the 1922 said, 'Their assumption was they were going to heave out the disloyal people.' But the collapse of Johnson's standing in the party made such efforts futile – in fact, it risked emboldening the anti-Johnson factions.

Brady bid the prime minister farewell just before 6.30 p.m. and left Downing Street in a pre-booked car – just as he had done following his fateful meeting with Theresa May in 2019 – to avoid media attention. Brady promised the prime minister he would not speak to journalists about their meeting and a formal announcement was made that the 1922 executive elections would take place the following week. Later that evening, though, the substance of Brady's meeting leaked, much to his annoyance. James Duddridge, Johnson's parliamentary private secretary, was later heard boasting on the House of Commons terrace to MPs, 'We're calling Graham Brady's bluff.' But the chief whip told[13] Johnson that Brady was correct: he no longer had the numbers to win a confidence vote.

Before returning to The Bunker, Johnson spoke to the Queen at his weekly audience with her. Whereas most items in the prime minister's diary are flexible, the constitutional link between Downing Street and the monarch is not. 'It's a diary fixture every Wednesday evening at 6.30 p.m., he just had to do that,' one senior official said. No one except Johnson and the monarch know what was discussed on that phone call, although it seems implausible that his dire political situation was not a topic. The timing of their chat, however, stoked fears among Tory MPs that Johnson was about to make one last throw of the dice and to try and call a general election.

One of Johnson's inner circle confirmed 'every possibility' was war-gamed in The Bunker, including a snap poll. One person involved said, 'The election was mentioned because the thing that freaks out the 2019 MPs the most is the idea of an election. They're terrified because they've never been back to their patches at the ballot box.' An ally of Johnson confirmed it was 'inevitable' that the idea was discussed in the final hours. Jacob Rees-Mogg, Brexit opportunities minister, made it clear to colleagues that he thought the idea was unwise. Johnson rejected the proposal, according to those present. 'It was never going to happen,' one ally said.

However, such were the fears within Whitehall that Johnson may do something reckless if his position was threatened that secret planning had taken place in the preceding months at the most discrete and deep levels of the British state, in case he asked the Queen to dissolve parliament. In the lead-up to Johnson's final days, there was much media chatter about the Lascelles Principles: a constitutional convention from 1950 that defined the circumstances in which a monarch could reject a prime minister's request for an election. From 2011 to 2022, the sovereign's prerogative power to dissolve parliament was handed to politicians through the Fixed-term Parliament Act – a wholly destructive invention that set an election for every five years and was responsible for much of the turmoil during the Brexit wars. In one of his more welcome legacies, Johnson's government revoked the legislation and the de facto power returned to the monarch.

The Lascelles Principles were defined by Alan 'Tommy' Lascelles, King George VI's private secretary, in a pseudonymous letter[14] (under the sobriquet 'Senex') to *The Times*. He set out the three criteria when an election request could be rightly rejected:

1. The existing parliament was still vital, viable, and capable of doing its job.
2. A general election would be detrimental to the national economy.

3. He [the King] could rely on finding another prime minister who could carry on his Government, for a reasonable
period, with a working majority in the House of Commons.

Even during the chaos of Johnson's final days, all three of those
conditions would have surely been met. Parliament was still
viable, thanks to the Conservative party's eighty-seat majority
and there was no danger it would lose a confidence vote – MPs
were terrified of being wiped out by Labour. Soaring inflation
and the cost of living crisis would mean that a six-week campaign
would harm the economy. And there were plenty of viable interim
Tory leadership contenders who could have commanded a majority in the House of Commons.

How would this have been communicated to Johnson? For the
Queen to reject an election request outright would have prompted
a full-blown constitutional crisis and have put the monarch in the
most perilous position of her reign. One senior Whitehall figure
said, 'It was a question that couldn't be put to the Queen because
the Queen would have to say "yes". The PM cannot ask the question to which she ought to say "no" by the convention.' Instead, a
'magic triangle' of senior establishment figures had ensured it
would never reach that point. Graham Brady, representing the
parliamentary Conservative party, Simon Case heading up the
civil service, and the Queen's chief courtier Edward Young had
private channels of communication to ensure safeguards were in
place. This scenario had been discussed previously between
Brady, Case and Young when Theresa May's premiership hit the
buffers in 2019. During that time, Brady worked with Buckingham Palace to ensure the leadership timetable would minimise
inconvenience for the Queen.

As Johnson's grip on power became more precarious, one
senior Whitehall insider said of the moment, 'If there was an

effort to call an election, Tory MPs would have expected Brady to communicate to the Palace that we would be holding a vote of confidence in the very near future and that it might make sense for Her Majesty to be unavailable for a day.' Another senior official confirmed it would be politely communicated to Downing Street that Her Majesty 'couldn't come to the phone' had Johnson requested a call with the intention of dissolving parliament. One senior government figure said the 'magic triangle' had such a scenario mapped out. 'The Queen would never be asked a question to which she will say "no" to, because the magic triangle will ensure that the prime minister doesn't ask.' One Johnson ally said he knew it was a fruitless idea too, that 'the Palace would have wanted to see if there were others who could command confidence instead of accepting his call'.

At this juncture, Brady would have been politely asked by the Palace if his party could decide on another leader who would have parliament's confidence. All the guidance was informal and never tested, as Johnson opted not to push the election button.

Aside from a snap election, another idea mooted in The Bunker was whether a rule change by the 1922 Committee could be legally challenged. That again was swiftly ruled out, given that past legal opinion confirmed the Conservative party does not have locus on the committee and how it operates – the '22 is a members' association without a constitution that is run on convention. The only formal element is its chair, who has a place on the Tory party board. 'It would be like standing outside a golf club, of which you are not a member, and dictating its new constitution,' one senior Tory said.

The last bold move discussed in The Bunker was another major apology outside Downing Street by Johnson for his handling of the Pincher affair. 'That was quickly rejected because we'd already done about fifty of them,' one official said.

While Johnson spoke to Brady and then the Queen, The Bunker was preparing options to form a new government. Yet the resignations were totting up: by 7 p.m., thirty-nine ministers had quit government. At one point, Scotland secretary Alister Jack entered the study to ask whether Ruth Edwards, his parliamentary private secretary, was on the list. One official responded, 'I don't think she's loyal anymore.' Jack insisted she was – 'No, no she's still viable.' A few ministers later, he returned to the room, asked for Ruth Edwards's name, and tore the paper in half. She had just resigned from the government.

But it seemed the only option left for Johnson was to try and rebuild his government. Before that, though, he would have to see the ministers who had been waiting several tedious hours for a private audience with him. He returned to his study to prepare to see these colleagues, or the 'self-appointed death squad' as one of his aides called them.

***

The small dining room can be found on the second floor of Downing Street, above the prime minister's office and the Cabinet Room, and a couple of corridors along from the study, which had become The Bunker. Stewing in and around this wood-panelled room for nearly three hours, with increasingly cold pots of tea, were Nadhim Zahawi, Anne-Marie Trevelyan, Grant Shapps, Simon Hart, Michelle Donelan and Kit Malthouse. After separately voicing their disquiet to Chris Heaton-Harris over the events engulfing Johnson, Heaton-Harris had invited them all to Downing Street. The security convention that phones should be left at the entrance of Number 10 had been abandoned, as the ministers oscillated between watching Johnson's liaison committee appearance, looking at social media, reading the news, and

WhatsApping MPs and their private offices with thoughts about when the government would collapse.

Number 10 aides were sent to mind the ministers, trying to ensure they did not work themselves up into more of a frenzy. Simone Finn, deputy chief of staff, took turns with Charlotte Owen, an aide to Johnson and the chief whip. One official who witnessed the scene said, 'There was the most awkward silence, it was like a tea party. We kept pouring more and more cold tea because we had to do something. Because the aides were there, they didn't want to talk amongst themselves.' The ministers and officials tried to make light conversation. There was frustration in The Bunker team that the ministers refused to leave.

David Canzini, deputy chief of staff, popped into the dining room on a number of occasions and according to those present he pulled ministers aside and muttered that he too privately felt the PM needed to resign. The Downing Street team had begun to split: the likes of Canzini wanted to focus on a handover time-table while the Big Dog team wanted to fight till the very end. Others who felt he must stay on included Andrew Griffith, head of the Number 10 policy unit, director of communications Guto Harri, and Ben Elliot, Tory party chairman (who popped into the dining room). As Wednesday afternoon drifted into the evening, the scene became more fraught; no one was sure exactly why they were being made to wait so long and what the prime minister was doing. News of his discussion with Brady had not made it up the staircase.

Those present assumed they would be seeing Johnson as a group. Along with Johnson's strategist Ross Kempsell, the chief whip Chris Heaton-Harris decided, however, that they should go in and see Johnson one by one – an echo of the Cabinet procession which went in and saw Margaret Thatcher individually as she questioned their loyalty. 'By going in one by one, he was able to make slightly different pitches to everybody,' one Cabinet minister said. 'Had we all gone in as Chris Heaton-Harris had originally planned, it would have been over by 6 p.m. on Wednesday evening. The PM would have gracefully left, but they rolled the dice another time.'

Before the ministerial meetings began, the consensus in the small dining room was that it was over for Johnson and the chats would be about persuading him to exit gracefully. One minister said, 'There was not a single person in the [dining] room, not one, who suggested that the PM should stay, with the possible exception of Ben Elliot.' The person added that even firm loyalists such as Anne-Marie Trevelyan and Priti Patel had concluded it was done. 'There was no dissent between any of us that the number was up.' Before the audiences took place, though, Johnson told his aides he was not rolling over. 'His view was "I'm not going, if they want me gone, they're going to need to dip their hands in blood and do it themselves,"' one aide said. The meetings may have slowed down Johnson's exit, but did not stave it off. Having lost the support of the Cabinet, his public bullishness did not tally with the reality of the situation.

One of the ministers insisted to Johnson that even if he survived this crisis, there were many others ahead. One told him, 'We're going to be going through this agony over Christmas and the New Year, a little more than a year out from the 2024 election.' The calculation of those gathered was that they needed to cooperate quickly 'in order to give as much opportunity as they could to repair the situation, bed down a new regime, and put all of this behind them so they had a possibility of a compelling argument'. Johnson's base within the party had been almost entirely transactional, based on his election appeal. With that gone, his closest colleagues turned on him.

The first minister to see Johnson was Nadhim Zahawi.

According to those who waited with the newly appointed chancellor, he was the most emphatic that Johnson should quit, and that despite his patronage he was the 'leading advocate for instant resignation' as one colleague said. Facing Johnson and with his fixer Nigel Adams present, Zahawi was full of brio and confidently told Johnson that it was over. Yet the prime minister persuaded him that there remained a path through. The pair returned to their favoured topic of economic reform and agreed to a joint major speech in the coming days. 'By the end of the meeting they were shaking hands, hugging, and saying they were going to launch a new financial strategy,' one insider said.

Zahawi was not seen again by the ministerial delegation and returned straight to the Treasury. The first the delegation heard of how it had gone was when it emerged that the chancellor was planning a joint press conference with the prime minister. 'We were a little bit surprised, given Nadhim Zahawi's vociferous position on all of this,' a minister said. Next in to see Johnson was Grant Shapps, transport secretary, who was 'reasonable' and did not say he should go, but argued the situation was problematic. When news filtered through to The Bunker that Shapps was part of the group, the aides were particularly dispirited. 'The moment that killed me was when Grant came in,' one official said. 'I thought, if Grant thinks it's done, it's done.'

Two of the meetings were particularly long and did not reach a firm conclusion. Education secretary Michelle Donelan was in with Johnson for 'absolutely ages' and caused much chagrin. 'She fucking U-turned massively and went in saying she wanted to give up the education job,' one official said. Johnson responded in disbelief saying, 'You were only just appointed to it twenty-four hours ago!' She rapidly climbed down and remained in post for that evening. Policing minister Kit Malthouse was in with Johnson for the longest period, almost an hour. 'He was waffling on and on about whether he did or didn't support him. He obviously didn't but it was going around the houses,' one aide said. Another person said Malthouse, who had been a deputy mayor during Johnson's stint in City Hall, went in to tell him that it was over but was convinced otherwise. Meanwhile, The Bunker became increasingly irritated by David Canzini, who, as one person there recalled, 'was talking with these secretaries of state, talking bollocks . . . saying "He's a goner" while we're downstairs convincing them to stay'.

Priti Patel, home secretary, became upset during her audience. She did not tell Johnson to go but said she concluded it was over. 'She didn't put the knife in,' one insider said. More Cabinet ministers arrived for informal chats with Johnson, including the deputy prime minister, Dominic Raab. Raab awkwardly told Number 10 staffers he had to attend a white-tie dinner at Mansion House that evening, but required assistance with the outfit. An attendant was found with the skills to fix his bow tie. After he was dressed he saw Johnson, who found his outfit highly amusing. One insider said Raab offered a rare moment of levity: 'Are you actually going to walk out of the front door to the world's media in white tie?' Johnson asked, and Raab responded, 'You're finding this far too funny.' He ended up exiting the building by a side entrance.

Throughout the meetings, culture secretary and Johnson loyalist to the end, Nadine Dorries, was ever-present in the corridors of Number 10 together with his policy chief Andrew Griffith, drumming up enthusiasm and discussing how to keep the PM in place. Not everyone appreciated their efforts. 'It was blind loyalty to the PM. They were nodding dogs, completely lacking any sort of common sense,' one senior official said. Later that evening, one of the last ministers to see Johnson was Wales secretary Simon Hart, who had waited close to five hours in the upstairs dining room. Their meeting was to prove one of the more consequential that evening.

When Hart eventually saw Johnson, the prime minister told him: 'I've got a plan, just give me till Tuesday. I can turn this around. We owe it to the fourteen million people who voted for us.' The minister responded, 'I love your optimism but I don't think we're there anymore. That was an argument that might have worked six weeks or six months ago. But I think we're past that point.' Hart told Johnson that if the 1922 Committee didn't move against him soon, they would find a way to 'nail you to the floor one way or another'. He then pointed to the privileges committee investigation in the autumn. 'Every time we do this, we lose more ground, we lose more credibility and we're getting ever closer to an election. I think the game is up,' Hart said.

By now, it was dawning on Johnson that his hopes were shrinking. 'I realise I've only got a tiny chance of survival but it's one I prefer to take,' the prime minister said. As Hart left Downing Street, he pulled Heaton-Harris aside and handed him his resignation letter. 'If circumstances have altered overnight and he comes to the view this is unsustainable, chuck my letter in the bin and we'll say no more about it. But if this thing is still raging in the morning, I will have to step aside.' Heaton-Harris thanked him for not quitting that night and Hart left for the pub for a much-needed pint with his special advisor.

The press office briefed that evening[15] that Johnson had told ministers, 'It was a choice between a summer focused on economic growth, or chaos of a leadership contest followed by massive pressure for a general election' that would mean[16] 'almost certain defeat.' Journalists were also briefed that Johnson believed a lost general election would break up Britain, thanks to a potential Labour–Scottish nationalist coalition. 'He's not going to resign and he has a lot of things he wants to say this weekend before we even get to any [confidence] vote,'[17] one ally said. But the ministers had uniformly delivered the same message: his political authority was shot and regaining it would be impossible. If he did not go, some (like Simon Hart) hinted they would have to quit. Just as with Thatcher, the ministerial delegation had made the decisive difference. He would fight on for a few more hours, but Johnson realised there was likely no way out. He returned to The Bunker to see if it still might be possible to form a new government.

***

Upstairs in the study, The Bunker officials had wheeled out the reshuffle whiteboard and had begun planning to fill the empty slots within the government. The number of resignations had risen above forty and, although no further Cabinet ministers had quit, they needed to find new secretaries of state for Wales and Northern Ireland (the prime minister had not seen Brandon Lewis but anticipated he would quit). The Bunker team spoke to James Cleverly, a Johnson stalwart at the Foreign Office, who agreed he would take education. Shailesh Vara, who had previously served as a junior Northern Ireland minister, was lined up to take over the secretary of state role if Lewis went. 'Boris popped in to say "yes" and sign off all these roles,' one official said. 'We had to have a functioning Cabinet that night, whatever happened.' After Steve Barclay had moved to health secretary, a new Cabinet Office minister was also required.

There was one other Cabinet-level change Johnson was adamant to pursue immediately. Johnson had festered throughout the day about Michael Gove's pre-PMQs intervention and decided he wanted revenge. With the events of 2016 back in his mind, Johnson decided to boot out his levelling up secretary.

'That was his decision alone,' one ally said. 'It was the pre-PMQs meeting: the PM felt he was very treacherous, an unnecessary personal blow on a day that was clearly terminal. Boris felt he really didn't need to do that.' A rumour had arrived at The Bunker that Gove was to resign that evening, fuelling Johnson's ire. The prime minister was urged, 'Don't let him do this, you need to fire him.' So he left the study with Guto Harri and Nigel Adams to call up Gove.

Gove had spent the rest of Wednesday in his department, avoiding a Commons vote at 7 p.m. 'He didn't think he would be a welcome presence in the voting lobbies,' one colleague said. He had returned to his official residence at One Carlton Gardens just off Pall Mall. He invited several friends, including Theodore Agnew, a Tory peer who had resigned from Johnson's government over its failure to address Covid fraud, for drinks and to chew over the day's trauma. Gove noticed a missed call from Johnson on his phone at around 9.20 p.m. and several with no caller ID, which he assumed to be the Downing Street switchboard.

He returned the calls and asked Johnson if he was resigning. 'No Mikey mate, I'm afraid you are. I'm going to have to ask you to step back from your role as levelling up secretary. I'm reconstructing the government.' In shock, Gove replied, 'So you're not resigning?' Johnson said, 'No, you are.' Gove told him, 'No, I think it should be you. I think you have lost the confidence of the party.' Johnson disagreed and told him, 'I'm sure you can understand after our conversation this morning.' He wrapped up the call by thanking him for his service. Gove, bewildered, told his colleagues Johnson had lost it: 'Poor Boris is going to be gone tomorrow, so there's no particular point me doing anything.'

Number 10 took glee in the sacking, telling[18] the media, 'You cannot have a snake who is not with you on any of the big arguments who then gleefully briefs the press that he has called for the leader to go.' Gove's aides strongly denied leaking his meeting with the prime minister that morning. Johnson's allies also briefed out they believed Gove had been plotting for weeks previously. The 'snake' comment, though, was unpopular among some senior figures in Number 10, who wondered if Guto Harri had acted alone. 'I thought the whole affair was uncivilised, especially the aggressive briefings. Whether you like him or not, Gove has contributed massively to Conservative politics over the last decade.'

Johnson returned to The Bunker and to reconstructing his government. Eventually, Brandon Lewis arrived at Downing Street. Johnson ducked out to perform the same turnaround job on the Northern Ireland secretary that had worked on Kit Malthouse, Nadhim Zahawi and Michelle Donelan. Not only did Lewis maintain his job, but he was able to blag a promotion. Despite the tight security in the study, Lewis breezed into the room and took a look at the reshuffle board. Sensing the weakness of the team that was being assembled, Lewis argued he should get a grander job and was offered Chancellor of the Duchy of Lancaster and Cabinet Office minister. He initially accepted and went home.

With the 10 p.m. news bulletin approaching, Team Johnson wanted to have new ministers to announce and to stabilise his standing. Die-hard supporter Nadine Dorries took to social media to state Johnson was going to carry on:[19] 'The PM's priority is to stabilise the government, set a clear direction for the country and continue to deliver on the promises he made and the British public voted for.' James Duddridge, Johnson's parliamentary aide, gave an interview to Sky News, fresh from the House of Commons terrace, where he insisted new ministers including 'major appointments' would be announced that night. The Number 10 press team, however, had gone home. 'There was no point hanging around for something that was never going to happen. We were ready to announce stuff but it transpired rapidly, there was nothing to announce,' one official said.

As the minutes ticked down, the phone calls became increasingly frantic. The Cabinet secretary Simon Case advised The Bunker that Buckingham Palace would soon be unable to approve the appointments that night. Johnson faced the prospect of further ministers resigning and the nation waking up on Thursday 7 July to a half-empty government. Johnson's team were struggling to persuade MPs to take up the jobs; it was reaching the point where he could not form a credible government. Greg Hands, energy minister, was apparently dragged into Downing Street from a dinner in Chelsea to be offered the post of party chairman. He refused. And still the resignations continued, reaching forty-three by 10 p.m.

The Bunker made a major misstep at this point, which resulted in an immediate Cabinet resignation. Simon Hart received a call from his chum David TC Davies, the junior Welsh office minister, who said he had been asked to go to Number 10 to succeed him as secretary of state. 'I didn't think you'd resigned,' Davies told Hart, who responded, 'I haven't.' Davies said he would not take the role and thought it was 'disgraceful' they were trying to ease him out. Hart thanked him and said, 'You go do whatever, you're not obliged to show me any loyalty.' Number 10 assumed Hart would quit in the morning but among all the chaos they had acted too soon.

Hart left the pub and called up Chris Heaton-Harris, fuming 'You've already offered my job to someone else, so we might as well call it quits now.' The chief whip profusely apologised and said it should not have happened. Hart sat on a park bench to tweet his resignation letter, when a Tory apparition appeared in the form of Charles Moore, Johnson's former *Telegraph* editor who had organised the Garrick Club dinner the previous October. Moore asked Hart, 'Oh Simon, what are you up to this evening?' He responded, 'If you wait fifteen seconds, I'm literally resigning.' Hart's letter on Twitter said:[20] 'Colleagues have done their utmost in private and public to help you turn the ship around, but it is with sadness that I feel we have passed the point where this is possible.'

With Brandon Lewis having talked himself into leading the Cabinet Office, the team needed to find a new Northern Ireland secretary, as well as a levelling up secretary to replace Gove. For the latter, officials scrambled to get hold of Simon Clarke, chief secretary to the Treasury and another fervent Johnson supporter. Around 10.30 p.m., he did not immediately answer his phone. When Number 10 reached him, Clarke 'ummed and ahhed' and said he would prefer to stay in the Treasury rather than take a promotion to a full Cabinet role. One aide in The Bunker said, 'I thought even him, Simon, the super-loyal guy, was showing a bit of reticence. He must have been thinking "shit, they might not even be able to get through to tomorrow."'

And at this moment, Johnson finally realised it was over. When Clarke refused to take levelling up secretary, other names were mooted in the study, including one close Johnson ally who had served him loyally as a minister several times. After hearing the name of the minister being seriously suggested, Johnson told the room, 'It's not fair on the nation to give them a D-list government.' Levelling up was his *Grand Projet*; if he could not find someone willing and able enough to see it through, the prime minister concluded he had finally, after months of struggling on, reached the end of the road.

Team Johnson concluded they had failed on a basic constitutional principle: they could not form a viable Cabinet to run the country. Advice had been taken on just how slimline it could be. 'We could have probably fudged it, it's not like it's some hard and fast thing. If you have an attorney general you're okay basically,' one senior official said. In 1834, the Duke of Wellington occupied the role of prime minister, sole secretary of state and leader of the House of Lords for a month, with only a lord chancellor for support. Being in the House of Lords, he did not occupy the office of chancellor of the exchequer, which was left vacant and filled pro tempore by the lord chief justice.

Johnson left The Bunker with a departing message: a plan for a Cabinet would have to be ready for the following morning, the government would still have to function. But it would not be with him at the head. 'I can't do this, it's all too ghastly, it's not me,' he announced. After weeks and months of fighting, Johnson had finally given up.

At 11 p.m., The Bunker dissolved. The aides went home. Chris Heaton-Harris and Nigel Adams, who shared a flat in Westminster, collapsed on their sofa while trying to speak to attorney general, Suella Braverman. They realised she had just announced on ITV's *Peston* programme that she would run for the Tory party leadership – but was not resigning from the government. Heaton-Harris was furious and gave her a piece of his mind down the phone. That night, Heaton-Harris and Adams, who had done more than any other minister to shore up Johnson's position, realised the end was nigh and no further politicking could save him. One Tory whip said, 'Chris reached the conclusion that evening that it was coming to an end, that we couldn't stop the fucking tide.' Instead the best they could hope for was to secure a functioning government the next morning and ensure Johnson left on his own terms.

Johnson returned to the Downing Street flat after his aides had gone home. He spoke with his wife Carrie, who was supportive and did not offer advice either way; she told him, 'Do whatever you think is right.' He phoned Lynton Crosby, his closest and longest-serving advisor, to ask for his advice from Australia. 'Mate, I've been thinking about it, what do you think? I think this is unsustainable,' Johnson said. 'I don't want to destroy the Conservative party.' Crosby responded, 'I think you're right. My advice, based on everything I know, is that it's irrecoverable.' Crosby told him he would be better focusing on his exit terms rather than facing the indignity of being heaved out by the 1922 Committee. One of The Bunker team said, 'That night, by the time he'd gone up to the flat, I think he'd made that decision. It wasn't that he wanted to go, it was a case of "the fuckers are not going to throw me out the door."'

The Bunker team had told Johnson they would support him until he personally decided it was over. 'We were always going to fight to the end for him because we owed it to him,' one close ally said. Even if a government could have been formed that Wednesday night, the aides knew it would not last long. 'We couldn't sustain any more attacks. People were still resigning, people weren't answering the phone. People were refusing jobs. We couldn't do it. Boris told us, "The country deserves better."'

Throughout the day, the prime minister had told aides that he owed the fourteen million who had voted for him in the 2019 election to deliver on their priorities. His pledge would only be partially complete: Johnson had taken the UK out of the EU, seen it through the coronavirus pandemic, taken a world-leading role in the Ukrainian war, but his administration had collapsed. Johnson slept on his decision to leave the job he had dreamt of since childhood.

8. Hasta la vista, baby

On Thursday 7 July, Boris Johnson got up and decided that the decision of the previous night still stood. As with all his previous major speeches, the prime minister began drafting his resignation address on his own before meeting with The Bunker team to talk through the details of his departure. Most of the team arrived back in the study around 7 a.m. His most inner circle did not want the news of his resignation to leak, so The Bunker team locked the door when everyone had arrived. Nigel Adams, his chief fixer, called Graham Brady at 7.30 a.m. to let him know that he should expect a call from the prime minister 'fairly soon' about his departure. Brady told Adams he thought it was 'the right decision' adding, 'It is a sad day when the prime minister goes.'

Over strong coffee and bacon sandwiches, the first draft of the speech was read out to the room before editing began in haste. Johnson's fixer Adams and strategist Ross Kempsell were present, along with the chief whip Chris Heaton-Harris, political advisor Ben Gascoigne, Tory party chairman Ben Elliot, his friendly outside advisor Will Lewis and Number 10's director of communications, Guto Harri. After the dreary sombreness and despair of the past evening, the mood in The Bunker had lightened. 'He was pretty jovial at that stage because the decision had been made. He was joking around much more,' one person present said. But in an odd way, Johnson's core team had yet to fully comprehend he was actually leaving. 'It was surreal,' one said, although another

Number 10 aide added, 'It had to end on Thursday morning. It was obviously incredibly sad, but also a relief.'

Several insiders who saw the first draft of Johnson's speech said it was originally 'far punchier' than the version he went on deliver outside Number 10. 'It shone through that he was very angry,' one ally said. Early drafts contained references to MPs and ministers 'going to beaches and sun loungers' as if to suggest that if he could have got through the summer their attitudes on his longer-term prospects would have changed. His aides suggested it struck the wrong tone.

While The Bunker was preparing for his departure, the ministerial resignations continued. Brandon Lewis, having first accepted then rejected the offer of Cabinet Office minister, quit the Cabinet at 6.47 a.m.,[1] telling Johnson that his government was 'past the point of no return'. Junior Treasury minister Helen Whately followed him out of the door two minutes later[2] stating, 'There are only so many times you can apologise and move on.' At 7.30 a.m., the security minister Damian Hinds also resigned,[3] stating there had been a 'serious erosion' of standards and 'we must have a change of leadership', followed swiftly by science minister George Freeman who said the UK had reached a 'constitutional crisis'. David Frost, the former Brexit minister, popped up to argue[4] that Johnson should go immediately with an interim leader installed until a leadership contest was finished. Even though the prime minister had not announced his decision to quit yet, his position had become wholly untenable.

Johnson made the call to Brady at 8.30 a.m. and told the chair of the 1922 Committee, 'I've reflected on our conversation yesterday and I've changed my mind.' Brady thanked him and they discussed the timetable of how the forthcoming leadership contest would play out. Both agreed that a new leader should in place by the Tory party conference in early October and the prime minister would have a graceful path out of Downing Street. Although he had technically resigned as Tory leader at that moment, there was no discussion with Brady about exiting Number 10 immediately or about an interim prime minister being installed. Johnson also made a courtesy call to Windsor Castle to inform the Queen he would be stepping down.

Publicly, there was no knowledge of his departure and the pressure continued to grow. Nadhim Zahawi, who had been health secretary on Monday 4 July, appointed chancellor by Johnson on the Tuesday, called for him to go and then on Wednesday changed his mind, U-turned one final time. In a letter on Treasury notepaper at 8.43 a.m.,[5] Zahawi said he was 'heartbroken' that Johnson had not heeded his advice and 'you must do the right thing and go now'. Johnson's inner circle were scornful of his decision. 'Nadhim made one of the greatest political miscalculations and misjudgements in history,' an ally said. 'But for that letter he could have been a serious contender in the leadership race.' Another Johnson aide said, 'Being prime minister is 95 per cent judgement. He showed a catastrophic failure of it.'

Another Cabinet U-turn came at 8.51 a.m., when Michelle Donelan announced[6] 'with great sadness' she was also quitting after less than forty-eight hours in the role. The Bunker team agreed that Johnson's departure would need to be announced immediately to avoid any further embarrassment. 'We needed to get it out there otherwise the parliamentary party was going to try and remove him that day – the chief whip and others thought that's where it was going,' one senior government insider said. 'We needed to make it clear to the world that he wasn't going to stay.' Chris Mason, the BBC's political editor was live on an extended Radio 4 *Today* programme when he received the call from Guto Harri. After taking a brief moment off air, at 9.10 a.m.

Mason announced 'the prime minister has agreed to stand down' and that he would be making a speech at lunchtime.

Immediately, pressure mounted on Johnson to leave straight away. The timetable had not been agreed, but the prospect of the prime minister remaining in office until October was met with a backlash after the traumatic events of the previous forty-eight hours. Kwasi Kwarteng, business secretary, tweeted, 'What a depressing state of affairs. So much needless damage caused.' He called for a new leader to be installed 'as soon as practicable'. Former education minister Nick Gibb called[7] for him to go immediately: 'After losing so many ministers, he has lost the trust and authority required to continue. We need an acting PM who is not a candidate for leader to stabilise the government while a new leader is elected.'

One senior member of the '22 committee said deputy prime minister Dominic Raab would have been the obvious choice. 'It would have constitutionally straightforward, made easier by the fact that Raab wasn't planning to stand for leadership,' the MP said. But Johnson's allies in The Bunker team moved quickly to ensure this did not happen. One insider said, 'We needed to show there had never been a precedent for a caretaker prime minister. We were running around the building trying to find Simon Case to put out some kind of statement saying it's not going to happen.' Ultimately there was no need for Case's letter; much of the parliamentary party was unhappy with Johnson staying on but such were the speed of events that the focus was already moving on to who would be the next prime minister.

The Bunker team discussed whether his speech should be delivered in the Downing Street garden or outside the Number 10 black door. Shelley Williams-Walker, head of operations, was keen for it to happen on the street with a lectern and Johnson agreed.

With the announcement having been made and the speech ready to go, the Bunker team worked to form a new functioning government. 'As soon as that briefing went out, people started accepting Cabinet jobs and picking up the phone,' one aide said. The whiteboard from the previous night was refreshed. 'We had to ensure there was a Cabinet and working government by the time he went out on the steps. Otherwise if the government collapsed, it would have given Labour the chance to say you need to call an election,' an insider said.

The new Cabinet was proclaimed before the statement. Greg Clark was the first shock name[8] to be made public. The dry but competent former business secretary, who was one of the twenty-one MPs Johnson had booted out of the party in 2019 for voting against leaving the EU without a deal, replaced Michael Gove as levelling up secretary. James Cleverly, the junior Foreign Office minister and close Johnson ally, was promoted to education secretary. Kit Malthouse was elevated to Cabinet Office minister. Robert Buckland returned to government as Welsh secretary, while Shailesh Vara was named as the new Northern Ireland secretary. There was relief when the gaps were filled.

Andrew Stephenson, who worked with the Big Dog support group, was made Conservative party chairman. Later, scores of junior ministers were announced, including many who had resigned such as Will Quince, returning as education minister. The appointments were a mixture of Johnson loyalists and figures from the centre of the party – with a dollop of implausible MPs who would never normally be ministers. One Johnson ally remarked, 'He may have finally ended up with the Cabinet he should have had all along.'

At midday, a message went out around the Downing Street offices that anyone available was welcome to gather outside to hear the speech. Officials beyond Johnson's core team were torn as to whether to appear. 'I thought "fuck that" because I was so fucked off about how undignified his demise was,' one official said. But another said, 'I was really proud of some of the things that we achieved with Covid and Ukraine. It was a moment of history so I decided I might as well go out.' A notice also went out to Johnson's support network of MPs and around a dozen MPs turned up including Conor Burns and Andrea Jenkyns (who was photographed sticking her middle finger up at a crowd of protesters outside the Downing Street gates). Carrie Johnson, together with their baby girl Romy, joined the crowd with Tory chairman Ben Elliot. 'It wasn't perfect, we were absolutely exhausted and had about an hour to invite everybody. But it was better than him standing alone,' one insider said.

At 12.30 p.m., Johnson bounded out of Number 10's black door and met the wall of cameras with a cheery 'good afternoon'. The prime minister said it had become clear that the will of the Conservative parliamentary party was that there should be a new leader and prime minister, with a temporary Cabinet in place. He heralded his electoral gains, the biggest Conservative party majority since 1987 and rattled through his achievements, from Brexit to Ukraine, to the Covid vaccine rollout. The tone throughout was upbeat, if testy. Given all of those achievements, Johnson set out why he was off:

'In the last few days, I tried to persuade my colleagues that it would be eccentric to change governments when we're delivering so much and when we have such a vast mandate and when we're actually only a handful of points behind in the polls, even in midterm after quite a few months of pretty relentless sledging and when the economic scene is so difficult domestically and internationally. I regret not to have been successful in those arguments and of course it's painful not to be able to see through so many ideas and projects myself. But as we've seen, at Westminster the herd instinct is powerful, when the herd moves, it moves.'

Johnson's anger at the ousting was palpable, despite the toning down of the original speech. He referenced the 'vast mandate' his party had and noted the Tories were merely 'a handful of points behind in the polls'. He accepted Westminster life would go on without him: 'My friends in politics, no one is remotely indispensable and our brilliant and Darwinian system will produce another leader, equally committed to taking this country forward through tough times.' He concluded, 'I know there will be many people who are relieved and perhaps quite a few who will also be disappointed. And I want you to know how sad I am to be giving up the best job in the world.' With a final Johnsonian flourish, he finished with 'but thems the breaks'.

His speech was not wholly well received. Many commentators noted there was no apology for his mishandling of partygate and the Chris Pincher affair, and that instead it was a valedictory for his achievements in office. Some judged it as proof he privately harboured hopes of returning to high office in the future. Soon after the address, the foreign secretary Liz Truss took to social media to say he had 'made the right decision' and echoed his core message. 'The government under Boris's leadership had many achievements – delivering Brexit, vaccines and backing Ukraine. We need calmness and unity now and to keep governing while a new leader is found.' That process began immediately; the herd had moved on.

***

Johnson's leadership had been in so much trouble for so long that the proto-leadership campaigns of his successors were in a chaotic state. From the end of 2021 and throughout 2022, furtive conversations had taken place between potential contenders and Conservative MPs. The questions asked in private were always the same: would you back me if I stood? Should I stand? Do you think I have a chance? Are you taking soundings too? Do you have any good donors I could tap up? Who is good in the media to speak to?

The structure of the race was the same as the 2019 contest that had elected Johnson and consisted of two distinct stages. All campaigns would have to meet a threshold of support among MPs to make it onto the ballot paper. A rapid series of shortlisting rounds would take place among the parliamentary Conservative party. When the field was narrowed to two contenders, the contest would move out to the wider Tory party with televised and regional hustings for members. Getting a basic campaign running, with slick communications, and targeting MPs was all that mattered in the first stage of the race.

The abrupt end of Johnson's premiership meant that none of the major contenders had fully fledged campaigns, slogans or policies in place – although informal networks of MP supporters had been built up over months, if not years. This explained why the first two candidates to publicly declare were lesser known. First was the attorney general Suella Braverman, who announced her intention to stand on ITV's *Peston* programme before Johnson had even resigned. As one of the most hardline Brexiters in the Tory party, Braverman made an early pitch for the right bloc. Second came Tom Tugendhat, chair of the foreign affairs select committee and a long-time Johnson critic. In an article[9] for the *Telegraph*, Tugendhat talked up his military experience and said it was a moment for renewal: 'I have served before, now I hope to answer the call as prime minister.'

Having witnessed the brutal sacking of Michael Gove the previous Wednesday evening, Rishi Sunak realised the end was nigh for Johnson, that a leadership contest was finally inevitable and that he would run. 'When Gove was fired, it looked mental from the outside, it was like *King Lear* in there,' one Sunak ally said. On Thursday 7 July, the day Johnson resigned, Team Sunak scrabbled around to find a discreet venue to crank up their nascent campaign. A suite was booked at the luxury Conrad Hotel opposite St James's Park Tube station. Mel Stride, chair of the Treasury select committee, began working through MPs, along with Rupert Yorke, one of Sunak's special advisors. Oliver Dowden, the former Tory party chair, assumed a chairman-like role, while Liam Booth-Smith, Sunak's chief of staff at the Treasury, took on the same role for the campaign.

In the temporary 'Ready for Rishi' headquarters, his team crammed into the hotel suite to script and film a launch video, which they planned to post as soon as possible. Contrary to the perception that a sophisticated video had been in the works for months it only came together at this point, with Sunak's wife Akshata spending much of the day digging through old family photos. The first take of his video was filmed against an upturned mattress in the suite. His team credited Cass Horowitz, Sunak's social media manager, for pulling it together. 'It's a tribute to Cass on his social media team, who were fabulous, in how quickly they turned the whole thing around,' one insider said.

That Thursday also marked the highlight of Westminster's social calendar: *The Spectator*'s summer party. Hundreds of politicos, journalists, advisors, senior civil servants and hangers-on poured into the magazine's clammy bijou garden at 22 Old Queen Street for hours of free-flowing champagne and biting intrigue. With Johnson's resignation earlier that day, the party became the first major event of the leadership contest. Sunak was persuaded to attend the party by Nerissa Chesterfield, his long-time media advisor, who chaperoned him. Dressed in a well-fitted suit and open-collar white shirt, Sunak worked his easy charm on the guests with a glass of juice in hand (he is one of politics' rare teetotallers).

Guests could hardly move without bumping into a confirmed or likely leadership contender. Chancellor Nadhim Zahawi was present, guided to the key faces by his parliamentary aide David Johnston. Tom Tugendhat attended alone, hobnobbing for a brief period, as did Kemi Badenoch, the recently departed local government minister. All corners of the Tory establishment were present, including recently sacked minister Michael Gove, Graham Brady and former Cabinet ministers David Davis and Matt Hancock. Gove's aide Josh Grimstone had a full-blown row with Guto Harri in the middle of the garden over Gove's sacking, calling out Number 10's behaviour[10] as a 'fucking disgrace'. The talk of the party was that the race could be Sunak's to lose, but many guests remarked that there was a notable absentee – a Cabinet minister who had long been a fixture of the party circuit.

Almost 8,000 miles away in Indonesia, Liz Truss was attending a G20 foreign leaders' summit. The foreign secretary had jetted off on Wednesday 6 July after much debate among her team about whether being physically absent from Westminster would damage her chances if Johnson fell, or whether she would be criticised for putting ambition over duty. 'It was a really difficult call. Even at that point, we thought the PM might be fucked. But similarly, he could have made it through to conference,' one ally said. 'As soon as she landed, I knew we'd fucked up. We told Liz to get home as soon as possible.' Being out of the country showed she was loyal to Johnson, which was to prove hugely beneficial later in the race. Truss was privately clear she had to go but when Johnson did quit on the Thursday lunchtime, she returned.

As Truss was travelling back on an official government plane, she was notionally forbidden from undertaking any party political work. The foreign secretary's (relatively) small aircraft had to refuel in Dubai, giving Truss a useful four-hour window to start calling her key allies and MPs, rapidly kickstarting her campaign from the deserted airport lounge. She spoke initially to Thérèse Coffey, her close friend and ally in building parliamentary support, who was assisted by Iain Duncan Smith, the former party leader. When she landed back at Stansted Airport on the Friday evening, the calls started again. Having missed the *Spectator* party, her campaign was already forty-eight hours behind her rivals.

On Friday 8 July, with the odd sore head, Sunak's campaign team gathered at their new office on Smith Square, opposite the Conservative party's historic former central office. From 7.30 a.m., two final takes of his launch video were shot and rapidly edited. Sunak's campaign decided he would be the first major candidate to declare. 'We thought just go early, be the first out, pick up some momentum,' one insider said. From the off, however, his advisors warned him it was going to be an 'uphill fight'. Few chancellors make the journey from Number 11 to Number 10 Downing Street, as they face the difficult task of defending an economic record; Sunak would be no different. He would have to contend with his having raised taxes to their highest level in seven decades – plus his prominent role in the defenestration of Boris Johnson (who remained popular among activists).

Sunak's launch video went live that afternoon,[11] playing heavily on his family backstory. 'Let me tell you a story. About a young woman, almost a lifetime ago, who boarded a plane armed with hope for a better life and the love of her family,' it began. The former chancellor made a coded attack on Johnson's economic record. 'Do we confront this moment with honesty, seriousness and determination?' he asked. 'Or do we tell ourselves comforting fairy tales that might make us feel better in the moment but will leave our children worse off tomorrow?' Johnson's allies retaliated, accusing Sunak of treachery. One told the *Financial Times*,[12] 'Rishi will get everything he deserves for leading the charge in bringing down the prime minister.' The prediction turned out to be more prescient than even Johnson's most vindictive allies could have hoped.

That weekend, several other contenders announced bids, but one expected candidate opted out. Ben Wallace, the defence secretary who had played a vital role in the Ukraine war, said on Saturday 9 July he would not stand 'after careful consideration'. He added, 'It has not been an easy choice to make, but my focus is on my current job and keeping this great country safe.' Had Wallace stood, he would have likely been the favourite to gain the feted status of Johnson's anointed successor. In a succession of surveys by ConservativeHome, a highly influential website edited by former MP Paul Goodman, he was the clear pick[13] of the party's grassroots.

As Wallace opted out, a surprise contender opted in with a bid that would capture the Tory party's imagination. Kemi Badenoch, who was present at the *Spectator* party, set out her plans[14] in the Saturday edition of *The Times*. She argued forcefully against 'relative decline' and called for hard truths and discipline. Her pitch leaned heavily on cultural issues, including free speech, combined with fiscal discipline. Badenoch summarised her decision to stand: 'I'm putting myself forward in this leadership election because I want to tell the truth. It's the truth that will set us free.'

Having recovered from her delayed entry to the race, Truss's campaign team gathered in the kitchen of her Greenwich home on the Saturday morning – including work and pensions secretary Thérèse Coffey and trade minister Ranil Jayawardena, alongside strategists Jason Stein and Ruth Porter, press secretary Adam Jones and close advisor Sophie Jarvis. Her house became a revolving door of supporters – local neighbours Kwasi Kwarteng and James Cleverly visited and pledged their support, neither insisting on jobs in return. Greville Howard, a Tory peer, and Jon Moynihan were appointed as the campaign's treasurer and chairman to use their longstanding networks to raise the necessary funds.

Team Truss spread out around her house to make call after call to MPs to regain lost time – at one point, Truss was perched on a tiny chair in her daughter's bedroom. One campaign insider described the first days of her bid as chaotic. 'We were so far behind, we had nothing because Liz would not let the campaign get up and running before Boris had gone. There was no policy, no people, no MPs.' During that Saturday, Truss dictated the framing for her campaign. She told the assembled aides in Greenwich, 'It's going to be me versus Rishi. Rishi is not cutting taxes. I don't need to go nuts, but I need to cut a bit to set the parameters. We're going to scrap the NI rise, scrap the corporation tax rise, and we're going to scrap the green levies.'

The race rapidly became crowded with candidates who had little chance of winning. Grant Shapps, the number-crunching transport secretary, launched his bid with a piece in *The Sunday Times*[15] on Sunday 10 July, a staunch defence of Johnson. The same day, former health secretary Jeremy Hunt launched his campaign with a pledge to cancel the corporation tax rise due to take place in April 2023. The oddest entry came from Rehman Chishti, previously Johnson's special envoy on religious freedom. In a low-key video[16] that seemed to have been taken by himself in his garden, he explained, 'For me it's about aspirational conservatism, fresh ideas, fresh team for a fresh start taking our great country forward.'

Monday 11 July marked the formal start of the contest when the rules were confirmed after negotiations between the 1922

Committee and the Conservative party's board. Graham Brady wanted a quick process, but representatives of the voluntary wing of the party hoped for as many regional hustings as possible. 'They thought having twenty-five-odd events was more important than having a new prime minister and Cabinet in place for the next prime minister's questions in September,' one senior Tory said. Brady argued for the process to be wrapped up by mid-August, the voluntary party wanted to push it out until October. A compromise was reached with a dozen hustings and the result being announced on 5 September. The threshold to make it onto the ballot paper was twenty MPs in the first round, up from eight in the 2019 contest, and rising to thirty in subsequent rounds.

Two campaigns launched that day. As a scorching heatwave hit London, the former health secretary Sajid Javid set out his bid in a tiny corner of the Cinnamon Club, an upmarket Indian restaurant at the heart of Westminster, with a message focused on values, 'Over the last couple of years, our reputation on values and policies has slid away.' The other was more notable: Liz Truss's launch video was published that Monday, shot in her Greenwich back garden with a much lower-key feel than Sunak's slickly produced offering. Her core message was about delivery, referencing her five Cabinet positions and her record in striking trade deals and navigating the Ukraine crisis. 'To win the next election we need to deliver, deliver and deliver for the British people,' she said. Truss simultaneously published an article in the *Telegraph* setting out her trio of tax-cutting policies 'from day one' in Downing Street.

MPs' nominations opened and closed on Tuesday 12 July, with eight candidates on the ballot: Kemi Badenoch, Suella Braverman, Jeremy Hunt, Penny Mordaunt, Rishi Sunak, Liz Truss, Tom Tugendhat and Nadhim Zahawi. Three early contenders were out: Grant Shapps, Sajid Javid and Rehman Chishti, the last of whom failed to gain the backing of a single MP. There was speculation that Zahawi would struggle to get onto the ballot, especially as his launch speech had a similar social mobility pitch to Sunak: 'From the little boy who spoke no English to a husband, father, self-made businessman, vaccines minister, education secretary, and now chancellor of the exchequer. With a plan to deliver, and a track record of success, I am running to be your next leader.'

Wednesday 13 July brought the first round of voting, along with Penny Mordaunt's campaign launch. Jammed back into the tiny room at the Cinnamon Club on one of the hottest days of the year, the trade minister pledged a return to core Conservative values with a heavy dollop of patriotism. She likened the Tory party's plight to Paul McCartney's triumphant performance at the recent Glastonbury Festival. 'We liked hearing those new tunes but we really wanted to hear the old favourites.' Combining social liberalism with a pro-Brexit stance found much favour with MPs and party members.

A pair of critical endorsements also came that day. As they exited Downing Street following one of Johnson's final Cabinet meetings, Brexit opportunities minister Jacob Rees-Mogg and culture secretary Nadine Dorries endorsed[17] Liz Truss – granting her the semi-official status as the continuity Johnson candidate. With the backing of the Tory party's most ardent pro-Boris ministers, any questions on Truss's loyalty to the outgoing leader were quashed. One senior figure in Truss's campaign said, 'That was the first moment when I thought "Fuck, we might actually do this."'

In the first shortlisting round, Sunak came top as widely expected with the endorsement of eighty-eight MPs. But a shock second place came with Penny Mordaunt, who garnered sixty-seven supporters, usurping Liz Truss who came third on fifty. Kemi Badenoch put in a strong showing with forty MPs, followed by Tom Tugendhat on thirty-seven. Suella Braverman came third from last with thirty-two, followed by Nadhim Zahawi on twenty-five and Jeremy Hunt last on eighteen. The former health secretary, who had been the first to call on Johnson to quit back in June, was out of the running, as was Nadhim Zahawi – quite the fall for a contender who was widely expected to be a frontrunner to succeed Johnson had it not been for his flip-flopping.

Mordaunt had established herself as the insurgent: the pollster YouGov said 27 per cent of members backed her to be the next prime minister. ConservativeHome reported she was the top choice of activists. In a series of head-to-head run-offs, the survey also predicted Mordaunt would beat every other candidate – including thrashing Sunak 67 per cent to 28 per cent. The Truss campaign were taken aback by Mordaunt; one ally put her success down to being a 'blank canvas' for other senior Tories. 'She was a fresh start and everyone was able to project onto her what they wanted the prime minister to be,' an insider said.

The contest picked up pace on Thursday 14 July when Liz Truss formally launched her campaign event. Her speech echoed the core messages of her launch video, serving up red meat to the party's low-tax pro-Brexit wing. The foreign secretary pledged to slash the tax burden, shrink the state and take a tough line with Brussels over the Northern Ireland Protocol dispute. Truss praised Boris Johnson and said she would take up his mantle with the war in Ukraine. However, it was an awkward event, as Truss's delivery was robotic and stilted, and when leaving the stage, she turned the wrong way and struggled to find the exit. That night, the second round of MPs' shortlisting took place. Sunak came top again, with 101 supporters, and Penny Mordaunt came second with eighty-three backers. Truss made gains with sixty-four MPs now behind her campaign. Tom Tugendhat and Suella Braverman trailed last with thirty-two and twenty-seven backers respectively. Failing to meet the required threshold of thirty supporters, Braverman was out, handing the right flank of Tory MPs an opportunity to unite around one candidate. When Braverman endorsed Truss, she delivered the party's substantial Brexit bloc — including the European Research Group of ardent Brexiters.

Mordaunt's momentum still perplexed and troubled Truss's camp, who feared the trade minister could pick up more supporters in the coming rounds that would make it impossible for Truss to catch up. Facing the real prospect of not making the final two shortlist, Team Truss dispatched David Frost to take chunks out of Mordaunt. Speaking to TalkTV,[18] the former Brexit minister expressed surprise she was a viable candidate: 'I'm sorry to say this, I felt she did not master the detail that was necessary when we were in negotiations.' Frost also took a swipe at her pro-Brexit credentials: 'She wouldn't always deliver tough messages to the EU when that was necessary.'

Friday 15 July marked the first week of the race with a televised debate on Channel 4. The surprise winner was Tom Tugendhat, the only candidate to decline to say Boris Johnson was an honest man. He called on the Tory party to fix the collapsing trust in politics:[19] 'I've been holding a mirror to many of our actions and asking those in our party, those in our leadership positions, to ask themselves, "Is that what the public really expects?"' A snap poll found 36 per cent of viewers thought he performed best, followed by Sunak on 24 per cent and Penny Mordaunt on 12 per cent. Liz Truss came last on 7 per cent.

Truss's campaign put her bad performance down to a (misguided) assumption that the debate would not take place. Conservative party HQ had mediated discussions with the broadcasters and the Truss team thought Sunak would not participate, so giving them a proviso to opt out. But when the former chancellor announced he would be attending, they had no choice; they did not have the momentum or supporters for victory to be assured. Truss was simply not ready for a prime-time debate. 'She was nervous. We had done no prep,' one ally said. Over at Sunak's campaign headquarters, his team were confidant in their core message: 'Our plan was keep it simple, keep it to the economy because we've got the best plan,' one insider said. With their MP's lead growing in every shortlisting round, they did not have Truss's concerns. Some MPs wondered if he was lending votes to help Mordaunt and damage Truss, but his campaign strongly denied it.

Two days later, on Sunday 17 July, a slew of attacks appeared against Mordaunt in the *Mail On Sunday* and *The Sunday Times*, the result of some dark arts. The rival campaigns had combed through her past statements, particularly her post-Brexit manifesto book *Greater* and comments on trans issues she had made. 'We thought she was fucked then,' one opposing campaign official said. 'The trans stuff was toxic, so we just had to deploy it at the right moment.' That night was the second televised debate, this time on ITV. The so-called 'blue-on-blue' attacks between the candidates increased significantly. Sunak was repeatedly lambasted for raising taxes, while he in turn attacked Truss for 'fantasy economics of unfunded promises'. He also suggested that Mordaunt was more radical than Labour under its former leader Jeremy Corbyn. Sunak did better and was crowned the winner of the debate by a snap poll, coming first with 24 per cent. Tugendhat also put in a good performance and came second, but failed to reclaim the magic of his first turn. Truss put in a significantly better performance on 15 per cent. After a full day of prep, she was calmer and more confident.

In the third round of voting on Monday 18, Tugendhat was eliminated. But Team Truss remained concerned that they had yet to see a clear path to challenging Sunak in the final two. Kemi Badenoch was still gaining momentum, picking up nine supporters from Suella Braverman, putting her total of fifty-eight within touching distance of the foreign secretary's seventy-one backers. But Mordaunt's tally dropped back by one, suggesting that the attacks had stalled her momentum. 'Penny was still fifteen MPs ahead of us but losing one vote. That was it, she was done for. You can't ever go backwards,' one Truss ally said.

On the fourth shortlisting round the following day, it was Badenoch who was out. With Truss and Mordaunt bunched together, it was not at all clear who would go up against Sunak in the final two. Truss had gained fifteen supporters and was closing the gap with Mordaunt – yet she remained in third place. The night before the final vote, Truss's allies thought it was going to be 'on the wire' if she made it through. Come Wednesday 20 July and the final shortlisting vote, Truss gained twenty-seven new supporters from Badenoch's backers and jumped ahead of Mordaunt. The Truss campaign credited Thérèse Coffey and Iain Duncan Smith's whipping operation for getting her over the line, combined with the efforts of her close advisor Sophie Jarvis. The final race was set: the next prime minister would either be Johnson's foe Rishi Sunak or his anointed acolyte Liz Truss.

Johnson was entirely absent from the race, making few public utterances and no comment on the contest. On 18 July, he spoke at the Farnborough Airshow[20] about a recent flight he had taken in an RAF Typhoon – a video later emerged showing Johnson living out his *Top Gun* fantasies somewhere over the North Sea. At his last prime minister's questions on Wednesday 21 July, he told the House of Commons it had been 'mission largely accomplished' and he offered some advice for his successor,[21] 'Number

241

one, stay close to the Americans, stick up for the Ukrainians, stick up for freedom and democracy everywhere. Cut taxes and deregulation wherever you can and make this the greatest place to live and invest, which it is ... focus on the road ahead, but always remember to check the rear-view mirror. And remember above all it's not Twitter that counts, it's the people who sent us here.' In his last words as prime minister from the Despatch Box, he thanked his staff and the speaker. In a way no other previous prime minister could get away with, he signed off by channelling Arnold Schwarzenegger: 'Hasta la vista, baby.'

***

If Rishi Sunak triumphed in his first televised clash with Liz Truss, the dynamic flipped when the pair went head-to-head for the BBC debate on 25 July. The former chancellor may have come first in the MP shortlisting stage but, as his campaign team anticipated, the party's 170,000-odd members would prove more difficult to convince. From the start of the second stage of the contest, all available data suggested he was on course to lose. Days before the debate, YouGov put Truss twenty-four points[22] ahead of Sunak. Sensing that the momentum was slipping away, the former chancellor chose to take a markedly more aggressive approach on primetime national television to stir up the race's dynamics.

In the run-up to the BBC debate in Stoke-on-Trent, one of the former Labour heartlands won by the Tories for the first time in the 2019 election, Truss was incredibly nervous once again. Senior officials on her leadership campaign acknowledged 'she doesn't like debating' so a whole day had been blocked off for pre-preparations – with her advisor Jason Stein role-playing Sunak and Rob Butler, the MP for Aylesbury and a former TV presenter, tasked with improving her presentation. She knew the stakes were high: a solid performance would affirm her standing as the leading candidate to be prime minister. Yet if she did badly, it would raise questions about whether she could withstand the pressures of Number 10. When she left her Greenwich home for the debate, confronted with a full camera pack at her front door, one aide said, 'It almost felt like she was going off for war.'

Before the debate, Team Truss decamped to the Port Vale football club for further preparations with Stein, Butler and her policy aide, Jamie Hope. The room was so cold that at times Truss had to wrap herself in a blanket. Her team reckoned they did a total of twenty-four hours of preparation for one hour of television, a sign of how seriously she took the occasion. Truss's team arrived at the venue late to ensure there was minimal time for her to stew on the daunting task. Before she left her green room for the stage, the sounds of Bruce Springsteen's 'Dancing in the Dark' were heard, followed by Mark Ronson's 'Uptown Funk'. As one campaign insider put it, 'Liz went on in the optimum state of mind and Rishi fucked it.'

The exchanges between the two were the testiest to date. As in the first parliamentary stage of the race, it was the economy that dominated. Sunak posed a question to Truss about why she sought to 'cause misery to ordinary people' by risking higher inflation by borrowing billions to fund her tax cuts. She hit back that he was 'scaremongering' with 'Project Fear', a reference to the Remain campaign during the 2016 Brexit referendum. Sunak used the opportunity to remind the audience he had voted to Leave and she had not: 'I remember the referendum campaign and there was only one of us on the side of Remain and Project Fear and that was you.' But despite this moment on the attack, Sunak spent most of the evening on the back foot. He was even forced to defend his dress sense, following an attack earlier in the day by

Nadine Dorries who had compared his supremely tailored suits to Truss's '£4.50 earrings'.

Any hope that the blue-on-blue attacks would cease had disappeared. Many commentators noted that Sunak frequently spoke over Truss. In the green room, her campaign team grew increasingly furious with his attitude, resulting in a campaign comment reported by Steve Swinford of *The Times*:[23] 'Rishi Sunak has tonight proven he is not fit for office. His aggressive mansplaining and shouty private school behaviour is desperate, unbecoming and is a gift to Labour.' The Truss campaign believed Sunak made a fatal error that evening in the way in which he aggressively debated, and which would define the rest of the race. 'They'll know what a massive mistake they made because for days, people would come up to Liz, it was always a woman over fifty-five, a core Tory voter who had seen golf club sexism. They watched Rishi and thought, "He's every fucking knobhead who has ever shouted at me in my life,"' one insider said.

Sunak now appeared to be floundering, whereas Truss was improving. The next ConservativeHome leadership survey put Truss thirty-two points[24] ahead of Sunak. Over the next six weeks of the campaign, he never came anywhere near to closing the gap.

One final TV clash took place on Tuesday 26 July, hosted by TalkTV. The event was marred when halfway through the debate itself, co-host Kate McCann dramatically fainted (to the extreme horror of Truss,[25] which was captured on camera) and the event was called off. It was not rearranged and neither Sunak nor Truss would debate each other directly again.

The rest of the Tory leadership contest was dominated by a dozen hustings organised by Conservative party HQ. Across the UK – from Perth to London, Belfast to Norwich – Sunak and Truss were interviewed by a range of journalists, including this author in Exeter. Each event took the same format: Truss and

Sunak were introduced by a prominent MP supporter, delivered a ten-minute stump speech and were interviewed individually with an audience Q&A. Although they continued to take lumps out of each other's policy positions, Teams Sunak and Truss agreed through backchannels that further blue-on-blue attacks were bad for the Tory party's wider standing and further personal conflict should be avoided.

August brought a handful of notable policy interventions, followed by trip-ups from both contenders. On 27 July, Sunak sharply reversed his position on no tax cuts and announced he would scrap VAT on energy bills to ease the cost of living crisis – the very policy he had blocked while serving as Boris Johnson's chancellor. Business secretary Kwasi Kwarteng, who went on to become Truss's chancellor, described[26] it as a 'screeching U-turn'. The policy gave Sunak a talking point, but it shredded his fiscal credibility pitch. He had conceded the argument on the need for tax cuts to Truss but left an opening for her larger and better developed offering.

From the last weekend of July, Truss's team rolled out what was termed 'Operational Rolling Thunder' to announce a series of prominent backers. Masterminded by Mark Fullbrook, a Tory strategist since Margaret Thatcher's days in power who worked on Nadhim Zahawi and Penny Mordaunt's bids before going on to be Truss's chief of staff, a new prominent name was lined up each day. On Saturday 30 July, Tom Tugendhat was splashed in *The Times* as backing Truss[27] – citing her tough stance on China and foreign policy. On Sunday 31, it was former Northern Ireland secretary Brandon Lewis. Chancellor Nadhim Zahawi soon followed, as did former health secretary Sajid Javid. Tugendhat, Lewis and Javid were more natural Sunak supporters, coming from the left of the party, and yet each affirmed Truss as the frontrunner.

Penny Mordaunt, however, was the endorsement Truss's team were happiest with. The trade minister texted Truss on Friday 28 July, while Rishi Sunak was taking a pasting by Channel 4's Andrew Neil and while Truss was hosting a pizza dinner in Deptford with her husband, two daughters and core campaign team. Team Truss suggested Mordaunt could be the surprise guest at the Exeter hustings on 1 August. She was sneaked into the venue without the organisers or Sunak's team realising what was coming. There was one endorsement, however, that Truss failed to bag. Priti Patel had taken soundings early in the contest had decided not to run. She had a proto-campaign ready to go but it never happened. After the BBC debate, Truss called and texted the home secretary but never heard back. 'That was a sad one,' a campaign insider said. In an early draft of Truss's first Cabinet, Patel was lined up to be justice secretary, but she would ultimately end up returning to the backbenches.

It was not all smooth going for Truss. Her campaign posted a press release on 1 August proposing regional pay boards for the public sector to 'tailor pay to the cost of living where civil servants actually work'. In effect, her proposals would slash pay for millions of teachers, nurses and armed forces. Outside the south-east of England, the average cut would be about £1,500 per person. By midday on 2 August, the plan was ditched and the Truss campaign admitted she had not intended to cut pay. Internally, the blame game was visceral. 'A policy was made up and sent out. Liz went fucking tonto,' one insider said. 'At least it was easy to U-turn on a policy that she didn't know existed.' Truss told her team to U-turn immediately because she did not believe in it: 'My whole brand is that I don't say things I'm not going to do.' Her campaign moved the agenda on when the *Daily Mail* endorsed Truss[28] after weeks of positive front pages. She was also endorsed by *The Daily Telegraph*,[29] brokered by Nadhim Zahawi who arranged a breakfast between

Truss and the Barclay family, who owned the paper. Sunak's only major media endorsement came from *The Times*.

Truss's next major campaign intervention landed on Saturday 6 August, when she told the *Financial Times*[30] she rejected 'handouts' to ease the cost of living crisis, preferring instead to focus on tax cuts and radical economic reform. 'Of course I will look at what more can be done. But the way I would do things is in a Conservative way of lowering the tax burden, not giving out handouts.' Her team said they felt 'very confident' about the announcement, but Truss's campaign was forced in later weeks to soften the stance after widespread alarm among MPs. Penny Mordaunt claimed[31] she was 'misinterpreted' and was making a general point about preferring cuts to further spending. At the Norwich hustings on 25 August, Truss was similarly criticised for saying 'the jury is out' on whether France's Emmanuel Macron was a friend or foe. 'If I become prime minister I'll judge him on deeds not words,' she told the audience. Yet these weak moments failed to dent Truss's standing. From the BBC debate onwards, she was seemingly destined for Downing Street and thrived at the members' events. One Truss ally said the hustings were akin to 'a giant garden party'. 'It's just her talking to Tory members, these are her people. The TV debates were just not her comfort zone at all.'

Despite pressure to wrap up his campaign early, Sunak continued to fight all the way through to 5 September. He picked up a prominent endorsement from Michael Gove,[32] but lost Welsh secretary Robert Buckland[33] and his predecessor Alun Cairns who flipped to Truss. Losing endorsements publicly was without precedent in recent Tory leadership races and only served to reinforce Westminster's consensus that the race was a done deal. At every hustings, he was quizzed about his role in Boris Johnson's downfall and struggled to combat the sense he had acted ignobly – speaking to the cliché of Michael Heseltine who said of his part in Margaret Thatcher's downfall, 'He who wields the knife never wears the crown.' He sought some final momentum with a long interview with *The Spectator* magazine speaking about the pandemic response, claiming it was 'wrong to scare people' and that the government's advice on Covid had come from too narrow a pool of advisors. In his final campaign interview, Sunak told the *FT*[34] he had 'won the argument' and warned that he 'struggled' to see how Truss's sums would add up. The global financial markets, if not the Tory membership, would agree with him.

Sunak's campaign were phlegmatic about their failure. 'History will be very kind very quickly to Rishi,' one ally said. 'As the economic crisis bites, the party will realise he was right.' Despite their failure, one senior Sunak official concluded, 'I don't think there's anything that we did wrong. We could have taken on the Boris treachery argument head on.' But after the betrayal narrative set in from the parliamentary stage of the campaign, and having almost no support from the Tory press, Sunak's campaign never showed any momentum. 'We didn't get much of a channel to make our argument,' one insider sighed.

***

And where was Boris Johnson? Despite his aides forcefully arguing he should stay as prime minister until September, he did surprisingly little during his final weeks in office. On 30 July, the prime minister and his wife Carrie hosted a wedding party in the Cotswolds, having been forced to move it from Chequers after his defenestration. On the vast property of Anthony Bamford, Tory donor and tycoon of construction equipment giant JCB, whose diggers provided the most memorable visual representation of

Johnson's 2019 landslide by smashing a 'Get Brexit Done' wall, guests enjoyed drinks on hay bales and South African street food.[35] Despite the trauma of his departure, several close political allies attended, including Jacob Rees-Mogg, defence secretary Ben Wallace and his long-time fixer Nigel Adams. A leaked video on social media showed Johnson joyfully cavorting around the dance floor to Neil Diamond's 'Sweet Caroline' with his wife and son Wilfred.

Throughout August the country was gripped by fears about the cost of living crisis and energy bills, but Johnson was bound by convention not to make any major new policies. He was criticised by his political opponents for taking two holidays, in Slovenia and Greece, while the leadership contest was rumbling on. In the last weeks of his premiership, he made one final visit to Ukraine to see President Volodymyr Zelenskyy and toured the country for a series of photo opportunities and speeches. The only substantial announcement came with his decision to sign off the construction of Sizewell C nuclear power station in Suffolk.

Johnson's allies remained concerned that he could soon be out of parliament as well as Downing Street. With the privileges committee investigation looking into whether he lied to parliament ramping up in early September, his allies argued it was a sham process. On 7 August, culture secretary Nadine Dorries mused, 'If this witch hunt continues, it will be the most egregious abuse of power witnessed in Westminster. It will cast serious doubt not only on the reputation of individual MPs sitting on the committee, but on the processes of parliament and democracy itself.' Such attacks were decried by senior Tories, who argued it was an apolitical parliamentary process that must take place. The Truss campaign dodged whether they would back a serious punishment for Johnson that could lead to a by-election, arguing it was 'not a row we want to have'.

Relations between Johnson and Truss were cordial. Johnson spoke to the foreign secretary in the last week of July where in effect the pair discussed a job swap and his potential return to the Foreign Office to concentrate on the Ukraine war. But ultimately, Johnson and Truss agreed it would be too complicated. They had breakfast on 29 July in his Downing Street flat – Truss was surprised to find there was no gold wallpaper, contrary to all the stories about the expensive redecoration of his residence. Johnson gave her plenty of 'good advice', according to her allies, which was followed up by a later visit to Chequers with political thoughts on the campaign, as well as setting in motion the handover of power. Such invitations were not extended to Sunak.

Team Truss were only too aware that she was succeeding in the contest thanks to her predecessor's patronage. Johnson made it clear he would not be leaving public life and would continue to speak up on topics that mattered to him. One Truss ally drew an analogy that Johnson would be the Margaret Thatcher to her John Major, where the early years of his premiership were blighted by her backseat driving. Their fears were heightened when polls throughout August suggested the Tory party had 'sellers' remorse' about what had happened to Johnson, while he continued to refuse to rule out a political comeback. Their hope was the political caravan would move swiftly on and policy delivery would establish her position. One senior Truss ally said her team was confident he would soon come to terms with losing office. 'Once he leaves parliament, his mind will wander and he'll give less of a fuck about coming back. Once he leaves the bubble of being PM, and starts earning money, he'll start to think, "This is not such a bad life."'

At 12.30 p.m. on Monday 5 September, the results of the contest were announced at the Queen Elizabeth II conference centre in Westminster. In the very same room Johnson was crowned Tory party leader three years earlier, Truss was confirmed as his successor after beating Sunak with 57 per cent to 43 per cent – a smaller margin than her team had hoped. In her victory speech, the fourth Tory prime minister in six years pledged to deliver a 'great victory' for the Tories at the 2024 election. She stated, 'we will deliver, we will deliver, we deliver', albeit on a markedly different platform to Johnson. Whereas he was focused on investment and levelling up, Truss pivoted to the liberty-inspired message that dominated her leadership bid: 'I know that our beliefs resonate with the British people: our beliefs in freedom, in the ability to control your own life, in low taxes, in personal responsibility.'

The next morning, 6 September, Johnson stood outside Number 10 for the final time as the storm clouds literally gathered above Downing Street. Before he jetted off to tender his resignation to the Queen at Balmoral, he offered some parting words to the Tory party. 'Well, this is it folks,' he surmised, with a last pop at MPs for ending his leadership earlier than he hoped. 'The baton will be handed over in what has unexpectedly turned out to be a relay race. They changed the rules halfway through.' After rattling through his policy achievements, he left the country with a final metaphor for his future hopes. 'I am now like one of those booster rockets that has fulfilled its function and I will now be gently re-entering the atmosphere and splashing down invisibly in some remote and obscure corner of the Pacific. And like Cincinnatus I am returning to my plough.' It was missed on absolutely no one that Johnson had keenly likened himself to a fifth-century statesman who left Rome for his farm, only to be called up to return to the capital for a second time, albeit as a dictator. A subtle hint for his future it was not. Few other departing prime ministers left Number 10 with their eye already on a comeback.

Epilogue –
Was it always going to end this way?

'All political careers end in failure,' so goes the trope of the infamous Conservative MP Enoch Powell. Be it failure at the ballot box by losing an election, or failure through scandal, few recent British prime ministers have quit Downing Street at a time of their choosing. Boris Johnson certainly had no intention of leaving Number 10 when he did: as recently as April 2021, he was plotting a decade in power with aspirations to beat Tony Blair and Margaret Thatcher's three election victories. Just over a year later, his dream was over.

Through the forty hours of interviews with Cabinet ministers, senior civil servants and Johnson's closest confidants I conducted throughout July and August 2022, I posed the same question to each one: was it always going to end this way? Was it inevitable that his premiership was going to come to a crash, ending in outrage and scandal? Or was there an alternative universe where different decisions were made, with a more capable set of advisors, where his vision of a decade in power could have been fulfilled? Were Johnson's flaws too deep to offset his abilities? Was he ill-suited to the immense role that being prime minister has become?

Johnson was well known as a celebrity politician before he became prime minister; he was chosen by the Conservative party precisely because he did not fit the norms and would break convention to deliver Brexit. It was no surprise that he did not govern in a conventional sense, but few anticipated just how chaotic it would be. Through three Downing Street operations, he failed to make the job fit with his personality. During the last nine months of his government, he found great success in tackling the Ukraine war but spent most of his time fire-fighting internal blow-ups. The fatal flaw had been allowing a fissure to develop with Tory MPs, which eventually and inevitably spread to the Cabinet. The fact that his personal poll ratings tanked – along with those of the Tory party – led to his party losing faith in the prime reason he was elected leader in 2019.

One senior Conservative MP said it was 'no surprise' among the parliamentary party that Johnson's premiership ended with scandal, not least as he had failed to cultivate a support base. 'He was always living on his wits, close to the edge, taking risks, blagging his way through, and relying on personality rather than preparation. It is a recipe for the wheels falling off.'

Johnson's critics focus on his relationship with the truth, which led to the privileges committee investigation into whether he was in contempt of parliament. Politicians were lying and bending reality with rhetoric long before he became a frontline figure, yet he took a more cavalier approach than his predecessors. But again, that was well known before he became prime minister. In power, those who detested him had their fears confirmed; those who worshipped him were happy to accept his highly pragmatic approach.

Then there is attention to detail. Before he was elected Tory party leader, it was widely agreed among MPs that his best hope would be for a chairman-like role, where he would be supported by a crack team of top advisors and ministers who would oversee the day-to-day details of governing. Mark I of Johnson's Downing Street team under Dominic Cummings failed because Johnson was unwilling to let him have the power and total control he desired (the court also split as the Vote Leave supporters railed against the prime minister and Carrie). Mark II under Dan Rosenfield collapsed because he did not have Johnson's ear, or the know-how to rebuild the Downing Street operation during the partygate scandal.

And Mark III under Steve Barclay buckled due to the weight of further scandals, the contradictions of having MPs running the government, plus the collapse in relations with Tory MPs. Each of the teams had some successes – the Covid vaccine programme under Cummings and the Ukraine response under Rosenfield and Barclay – but they all failed to contend with the myriad of challenges that face a typical government every day. The evidence suggests there was no variant that could have ably supported Johnson, yet his closest allies envisaged a Mark IV that was successful, but never able to be tested. Throughout the upheaval, staff morale crumbled in Number 10 and was never rebuilt.

After their success in propping up Johnson throughout the final difficult months of 2022, the Big Dog and Brains Trust teams mooted that had they been in charge, it could have turned out differently. Johnson's outriders delivered six extra months in office from the start of the partygate scandal, but it is not at all certain they could have staved off a chaotic end to his premiership.

Within those three operations, miscommunication and chaos reigned. The policy successes of the Johnson government were thanks to small teams that were well led and empowered to take fast decisions. Whether it was the vaccine taskforce under Kate Bingham, the vaccine booster programme led by Emily Lawson or the Ukraine response under John Bew, this model worked for specific issues, but Johnson failed to replicate this successful model elsewhere in Downing Street.

One politico who worked closely with Johnson mused that by the time he reached Number 10, he had run out of officials willing and competent enough to work at the top of government. 'He never quite got the team in the way that he did when he was mayor. Boris, with all the iterations of his career, burned people. So by the time he became prime minister, the pool of people he could draw from was just getting smaller and smaller.' Some of Johnson's supporters believe he was temperamentally ill-suited to be prime minister in the twenty-first century, with the always-on demands so high.

The most strikingly consistent theme to the crises that engulfed his government was Johnson's absence at key moments. For Owen Paterson, he was in Glasgow. For the privileges committee vote, he was in India. For the by-elections and Oliver Dowden's resignation he was in Rwanda. It may have been fate or a coincidence, but too often communications broke down between Downing Street and the prime minister's travelling pack, while he was undoubtedly distracted by his travel engagements. His physical distance from Westminster added to the alienation from the parliamentary party; Johnson's preference (and indeed talent) for playing statesman on the world stage meant he neglected parliamentary politics, to which he had never really been suited.

Based on his flaws, the natural conclusion to the question as to whether it was always going to end this way then is 'yes', it was always going to come to a premature and sticky end. One senior Downing Street advisor said, 'The situation that we found ourselves in was exactly what I expected this prime ministerial tenure to look like. He was actually ten times better than I expected.' Another senior government official who worked closely with Johnson said, 'I remember Dom Cummings saying to me, "He got in there because he was the guy that could get Brexit done," but no one ever really thought about it as the Boris Johnson premiership. It was probably always going to happen because of the character flaws everyone knew he had.'

Johnson's younger allies, who had devoted less of their lives to being in his orbit, gave a more emphatic 'no' as to whether it was always going to end this way, arguing that the prime minister could have survived if the Cabinet had held their nerve. One senior ally said, 'If we had got to the summer and [Chris] Pincher had not done what he did, we'd have had a reshuffle, we'd have brought some people back, we would have had a fresh start into conference. I do think that would have been a likely scenario.' But his inner circle were also aware that his enemies would keep gunning for him, particularly those associated with the Vote Leave campaign who had lost faith in his leadership.

Within those who have worked closely with Johnson in government, there is little consensus on whether it was his personality that was responsible for the collapse of his government. One of Johnson's close political aides argued strongly there was no 'fatal flaw' in Johnson's personality that made him ill-suited to be prime minister. 'Those of us who served him made mistakes, it's always fundamentally going to happen in a building like Number 10. We were in such a defensive crouch for so long, we could never get back on the front foot in this period and start scoring runs.' With this way of thinking, had the pandemic never happened, had the errors of Owen Paterson and partygate been avoided, his tenure would have been much lengthier.

But even those who worked closely with him and insisted he got the big calls right, acknowledged he was never a details leader, that he was unable to show much interest in the mechanics of running a government. 'It is true, the great cliché of getting the big calls right, but he just couldn't get the smaller stuff, you have to sweat the small stuff in these jobs,' one aide said.

One of the senior officials drafted into Johnson's support network concluded, 'All administrations end in some form of disappointment and varying levels of crisis' but argued Johnson's did not have to end in such a brutal manner. 'There was a catastrophic series of misjudgements, mainly around communications and parliamentary handling, that led to the outcome that we got to. There was never a sufficient grip on either of those crucial elements. Everybody shares a bit of the blame – there were outstanding individual performances by people who did a great job under a lot of pressure.'

Then there is the role of Rishi Sunak. Johnson's loyalists believed his arrival in the Treasury was critical in his downfall. One close ally painted a scenario in which he survived: 'If Saj [Javid] had stayed as chancellor and people who had genuine affection and loyalty to the PM had been in Number 10, he could have been alright. The cardinal sin was the loss of the Treasury; that created Sunak as a problem. It created economic policy as a problem that could never be managed.' From the partygate scandal onwards, the chancellor decoupled from the prime minister and began to pursue his own agenda, seen through the series of wobbles that culminated in his resignation and leadership bid. There was paranoia among Team Johnson about his manoeuvres, which was not entirely misplaced.

If the fall of Boris Johnson is to be pinned on the individual, his character judgement has to be called into question. Too often, Johnson put trust in those who did not have the skills to deliver on his best interests and instead spent much of their time protecting themselves instead of the prime minister. Whether it was the ruse to save Owen Paterson, or giving Chris Pincher the benefit of the doubt, it is hard to dispute that Johnson failed because he followed ill-conceived, often politically naive advice. A minister close to Johnson said, 'You have to question some of the people he put huge trust in. He finds it hard to discipline and fire people, especially when others see as clear as day that person's in the wrong job. He just doesn't like confrontation. He likes to be liked.' One of Johnson's most ardent supporters in the Conservative parliamentary party was more direct and remarked to a colleague the week after his resignation, 'There's only one person responsible for Boris falling and that is Boris himself.'

Reflecting on the three Ps that brought down the prime minister – Paterson, partygate and Pincher – all of these crises suggested Johnson and his advisors had a difficult relationship with conventions and norms. To his critics, Johnson has debased the office of prime minister (and political discourse generally) by pushing the boundaries of truth, lying more obviously than any other politician in Britain. 'Shock news, politician lies! Do you think voters really care?' one Tory strategist said. But those who worked with Johnson throughout his career said he has a particular view on probity. 'The charitable interpretation is that he has a pragmatic view of things like honesty and the truth – that we're all in the gutter and all of us are misleading in one way or another. And we all just need to get on with it,' the aide said. 'In some respects, he was right about the hypocrisy of parliamentarians and of government. But obviously, it just goes to say, you get a drip-drip of scandals and it just reached a tipping point.'

Throughout the interviews, one consistent theme emerged, and that was that Johnson resists the idea that he has to bother with the consequences for his actions that normal people have to contend with. 'It may be there is something deep in his personality that resists the idea that he has to face up to the same reality as the rest of us,' one colleague said. Some point to his school and university days, when Johnson was rewarded for being exceptional. When the consequences of his decisions on partygate, Owen Paterson and Pincher came to a head, he refused to engage with them. But one long-term Johnson supporter dismissed the idea he was a politician who broke the boundaries of conventional politics: 'Some people say he's a Teflon politician but I've got a Teflon frying pan. It's smooth to start with but after a few years, you use it a bit, you get a little scratch and sometimes it sticks and then you get another scratch because you used the metal utensil instead of a plastic one. Then every time you cook an omelette, it sticks. Then you bin it. No one is 100 per cent Teflon, just like no frying pan lasts forever.'

Even in his final hours as prime minister, Johnson was bartering with his Cabinet ministers for one last chance. 'That was always his view: buy more time,' a colleague said. 'There was a world in which Ukraine plus the economy turns in 2024 and suddenly it looks very different.' Johnson won the 2019 election in part by pledging to end political games and focus on priorities seemingly more important to ordinary people. But from October 2021 onwards, his administration was also entirely focused on firefighting, as one Cabinet minister said: 'This is why Owen Paterson and the handling of partygate were so significant, because it was people playing politics. It looked like your bog-standard politicians messing about with politician issues.'

Johnson will be remembered as a consequential prime minister. To his supporters, he was the champion of Brexit; the leader who saw the country through the pandemic and led the world during the Ukraine war. To his enemies, he was a populist cad who debased moral standards. But neither would dispute Johnson mattered, more so than any leader since Tony Blair. His policy achievements were small but substantial. He may have only lasted three years in Downing Street, but his actions will have consequences for decades to come. His allies believe that the 'sellers' remorse' that has settled in among Tory MPs will become more pronounced in the years ahead: 'I do think in a decade's time, even sooner, they'll see they replaced an enormous figure in British politics for what people will come to regard as slightly trivial reasons.'

One of the most intriguing notions put forward by a colleague of Johnson's is that his view of politics is shaped by his adoration of the classics. Whereas most budding British politicians take to dry biographies of Disraeli and Gladstone, his cultural touch-points go much further back. 'He's a more Greek or Roman leader, than he is Judeo-Christian leader – he likes big things, big symbols,' the friend said. Such an attitude explained why he constantly ignored details and the small issues, focusing instead on the grand historical sweep, which simply does not work in a modern democracy. Enoch Powell, who made that famous elegy for political careers, was similarly a classical scholar.

Johnson once told a colleague he left the media for politics 'because they don't put up statues for journalists'. During his time as mayor of London, Johnson half-jokingly suggested a statue of himself on the M4 as it enters the city 'so they know when they're coming to London'. No statues of Johnson currently exist, so he will have to take heart that dozens of streets across Ukraine are now named after him. Long after he exits politics, the rights and wrongs of the last six months of Johnson's time in office – along with his abrupt departure – will still be debated. As the most mercurial prime minister in a generation, it was always likely his time in office was going to end this way. But as Johnson himself proved, it did not have to be.

Johnson was far from at ease about the end of his premiership and harboured hopes he would return; that the Tory party would see the error of its ways and come calling when it needed a proven election winner. But far greater events would conspire to make any yearning for the past fanciful. At lunchtime on Thursday 8 September, forty-eight hours after Johnson had tendered his resignation, Buckingham Palace issued a rare statement on the monarch's health: 'Following further evaluation this morning, The Queen's doctors are concerned for Her Majesty's health and have recommended she remain under medical supervision. The Queen remains comfortable and at Balmoral.' At 6.30 p.m., the Palace announced that she had died and King Charles III had ascended to the throne.

Her death prompted a wave of grief, mourning and national unity that most Britons had never experienced. Liz Truss was thrust onto the international stage, leading the nation's tributes to the Queen and welcoming in a new era. Emoting was not her natural arena; the prime minister's initial remarks outside Number 10 were likened by one commentator to 'reading the Queen's Wikipedia page'. But her tribute in the House of Commons fared much better, when Truss reminded MPs, 'It was just three days ago at Balmoral that she invited me to form a government and become her fifteenth prime minister.'

Johnson would have longed to be the omega to Winston Churchill's alpha, the bookend to the second Elizabethan age. Instead that honour went to his successor. One of his close allies said, 'it felt all so unfair, that moment was made for Boris'. Had the Queen's health taken a different turn, or had Johnson struggled on through the summer, he would have paid tribute to her as 'Elizabeth the Great', praising her service, humility, work ethic and sense of history. The tribute would have gone: 'so unvarying in her polestar radiance that we have perhaps been lulled into thinking she might be in some way eternal – but I think our shock is keener today because we are coming to understand in her death the full magnitude of what she did for us all.' We know this because these very words were delivered by Johnson, albeit in the House of Commons as a backbench Tory MP, not as prime minister outside Downing Street.

At Elizabeth II's funeral, which demonstrated all the pomp and grandeur of the British state at its best, six of the Queen's prime ministers were present – four Tory, two Labour. Johnson arrived at Westminster Abbey with his wife Carrie, but there was a slight mix-up in the ordering as he came to the doors before his two predecessors, David Cameron and Theresa May. Instead of taking his pew, he was ushered to step aside and join the end of the queue for an exclusive club that no one wants to be a member of, and from which there is no escape. Johnson was now visibly an ex-prime minister, in the same category as John Major, Tony Blair and Gordon Brown. The Tory party may still turn back to its former leader – far stranger things have certainly happened in Westminster – but his departure, coinciding with the dawn of the third Carolean age, suggested he may belong to Britain's past.

Notes

Introduction – Drinks at the Garrick Club

1 www.thetimes.co.uk/article/tory-grandee-owen-pattersons-allies-plot-to-slash-his-suspension-th2t3zt8d
2 lordslibrary.parliament.uk/new-lords-appointments-in-july-2020/
3 www.telegraph.co.uk/news/2021/10/29/hounding-owen-paterson-sets-dangerous-precedent-parliament/
4 www.bbc.co.uk/news/uk-politics-48299424
5 www.theguardian.com/politics/ng-interactive/2019/jun/13/conservative-leadership-election-full-results
6 www.bbc.co.uk/news/uk-england-49132477
7 commonslibrary.parliament.uk/decision-of-the-supreme-court-on-the-prorogation-of-parliament/
8 www.bbc.co.uk/news/uk-politics-49563357
9 www.ft.com/content/cdb2dadc-ec40-11e9-a240-3b065ef5fc55
10 www.bbc.co.uk/news/election-2019-50765773
11 www.theguardian.com/uk-news/2020/feb/11/hs2-to-go-ahead-boris-johnson-tells-mps
12 www.ft.com/content/a15c78ec-4e3f-11ea-95a0-43d18ec715f5
13 www.gov.uk/government/speeches/pm-address-to-the-nation-on-coronavirus-23-march-2020
14 www.bbc.co.uk/news/uk-52192604
15 www.bbc.co.uk/news/av/uk-52801667
16 www.gov.uk/government/news/coronavirus-covid-19-what-has-changed-9-september
17 www.bbc.co.uk/news/uk-54763956
18 www.ft.com/content/6f0fc7a4-becc-474a-9924-57d9c8419551
19 www.gov.uk/government/publications/regulatory-approval-of-pfizer-biontech-vaccine-for-covid-19

20 www.gov.uk/government/speeches/prime-ministers-address-to-the-nation-4-january-2021

21 www.standard.co.uk/news/uk/dominic-raab-foreign-secretary-kabul-taliban-sky-news-b952228.html

22 www.ft.com/content/271fe3a6-58c7-4633-a05f-c4ac3c1b54f0

23 www.thesun.co.uk/news/16343362/boris-michael-gove-belting-total-eclipse-heart/

24 www.thetimes.co.uk/article/boris-johnson-is-enjoying-his-party-but-may-soon-be-facing-a-hangover-0wsclsm9l

25 twitter.com/shippersunbound/status/1445711840378511360

26 www.bbc.co.uk/news/uk-england-24459424

27 www.dailymail.co.uk/news/article-10173141/Rose-Paterson-told-article-linking-corruption-allegations-hours-taking-life.html

28 committees.parliament.uk/committee/290/committee-on-standards/news/156428/report-on-the-conduct-of-rt-hon-boris-johnson-mp-published/

29 news.sky.com/story/owen-paterson-former-minister-saved-from-suspension-as-tory-mps-back-standards-process-overhaul-12458870

30 news.sky.com/story/owen-paterson-labour-leader-sir-keir-starmer-accuses-boris-johnsons-government-of-corruption-after-vote-to-protect-mp-from-being-suspended-12459400

31 www.thetimes.co.uk/article/will-boris-johnson-get-away-with-sleaze-scandal-7qdqvwpwf

1. Partygate and an Omicron Christmas

1 www.gov.uk/government/speeches/pm-opening-statement-at-covid-19-press-conference-27-november-2021

2 www.glasgowtimes.co.uk/news/national/19753733.boris-johnson-facing-scrutiny-omicrons-spread-festive-concerns-flagged/

3 www.mirror.co.uk/news/politics/boris-johnson-broke-covid-lockdown-25585238

4 hansard.parliament.uk/commons/2021-12-01/debates/A0E282CF-039D-4F26-8F16-946B8C6E2ABC/Engagements

5 www.itv.com/news/2021-12-07/no-10-staff-joke-in-leaked-recording-about-christmas-party-they-later-denied

6   www.thetimes.co.uk/article/how-calm-ellie-was-dumped-in-favour-of-risky-allegra-on-carries-orders-00jtjskjg
7   www.theguardian.com/politics/video/2021/oct/12/a-joke-prime-minister-cummings-slams-johnson-over-handling-of-covid-video
8   www.theguardian.com/politics/2021/dec/06/dominic-cummings-very-unwise-for-no-10-to-lie-about-christmas-parties
9   www.theguardian.com/uk-news/2021/dec/08/met-police-say-they-will-not-investigate-downing-street-christmas-party
10 news.sky.com/story/covid-19-pm-facing-major-revolt-over-coronavirus-curbs-amid-authoritarianism-warning-12493843
11 www.ft.com/content/eb35a108-6186-42a4-b401-5e1df0e2c64a
12 www.reuters.com/world/uk/uk-brexit-supremo-frost-resigns-blow-johnson-mail-sunday-2021-12-18/
13 www.thetimes.co.uk/article/boris-johnson-must-sack-downing-streets-woke-crowd-says-lord-frost-dhs2jwz2r
14 www.dailymail.co.uk/news/article-10455739/How-Cabinet-stopped-Boris-insane-plan-cancel-Christmas.html
15 www.thetimes.co.uk/article/problems-mount-as-boris-johnson-ponders-next-move-on-covid-7bvm6997l
16 www.standard.co.uk/news/uk/boris-johnson-kate-bingham-prime-minister-lawson-oxford-b922775.html

2. Sue Gray

1   twitter.com/Tony_Diver/status/1519209812512358401
2   www.thetimes.co.uk/article/what-your-coffee-says-about-you-are-you-a-sue-gray-americano-or-a-taylor-swift-latte-m8kt69cqv
3   www.bbc.com/news/uk-northern-ireland-57173404
4   dominiccummings.substack.com/p/parties-photos-trolleys-variants
5   www.itv.com/news/2022-01-10/email-proves-downing-street-staff-held-drinks-party-at-height-of-lockdown
6   www.telegraph.co.uk/politics/2022/01/13/two-parties-held-downing-street-queen-country-mourned-death/?
7   www.indy100.com/politics/sue-gray-downing-street-memes

8   www.thetimes.co.uk/article/dominic-cummings-boris-johnson-lied-to-parliament-about-lockdown-party-cwzhk2kcc

9   twitter.com/Nigella_Lawson/status/1486092328867663877

10 www.ft.com/content/8f849ae3-d8d0-4460-bf1e-43a35acb2ec1

11 www.thetimes.co.uk/article/paralysed-in-no-10-are-the-pm-and-his-wife-ready-to-let-it-go-2kdcnrhss

12 www.thetimes.co.uk/article/downing-street-party-crisis-johnsons-lion-king-pep-talk-fails-to-rally-aides-or-mps-in-survival-battle-fpqszmmgj

13 www.bbc.co.uk/news/uk-politics-60289339

3. Putin's Move

1   www.itv.com/news/2022-02-24/boris-johnsons-address-to-nation-in-full-after-russia-invades-ukraine

2   www.theguardian.com/politics/live/2022/feb/24/uk-politics-live-boris-johnson-sanctions-russia-invasion-ukraine-latest-updates?page=with:block-6217a3758f0814262e7ca129#block-6217a3758f0814262e7ca129

3   web.archive.org/web/20110123065155/http://www.independent.co.uk/news/media/the-blond-bombshell-540261.html

4   researchbriefings.files.parliament.uk/documents/SN07135/SN07135.pdf

5   www.gov.uk/government/news/pm-meeting-with-president-zelenskyy-8-october-2020

6   www.atlanticcouncil.org/blogs/ukrainealert/britain-and-ukraine-unveil-new-strategic-partnership/

7   twitter.com/AmySpiro/status/1498085663786344452

8   www.washingtonpost.com/national-security/interactive/2022/ukraine-road-to-war/

9   www.theguardian.com/politics/2021/nov/15/west-must-choose-between-russian-gas-and-supporting-ukraine-pm-warns

10 www.washingtonpost.com/national-security/interactive/2022/ukraine-road-to-war/

11 www.washingtonpost.com/politics/biden-putin-to-discuss-ukraine-in-video-call-amid-growing-tensions/2021/12/06/e089e36a-5707-11ec-a219-9b4ae96da3b7_story.html?

12 www.independent.co.uk/news/uk/boris-johnson-ukraine-bernard-jenkin-prime-minister-mps-b1976852.html

13 www.gov.uk/government/news/g7-foreign-ministers-statement-on-russia-and-ukraine

14 www.dailymail.co.uk/news/article-10420277/Britain-send-weapons-Ukraine-Defence-Secretary-Ben-Wallace-pledges-support.html

15 www.gov.uk/government/publications/british-energy-security-strategy/british-energy-security-strategy

16 www.theguardian.com/world/2022/jan/24/johnson-warns-of-painful-and-violent-ukraine-lightning-war

17 www.gov.uk/government/speeches/pm-statement-on-ukraine-25-january-2022

18 www.itv.com/news/2022-02-17/pm-russian-attack-on-ukraine-nursery-was-false-flag-operation

19 ukdefencejournal.org.uk/britain-sending-anti-aircraft-and-javelin-missiles-to-ukraine/

20 www.ft.com/content/35b3fdf0-6ed6-444f-849e-4076d0139d4b

21 www.nytimes.com/2022/03/06/opinion/boris-johnson-russia-putin-ukraine-war.html

22 www.spectator.co.uk/article/sunak-treasury-predicted-energy-price-hitting-5-000

23 reaction.life/boris-johnsons-popularity-in-ukraine-is-rubbing-off-at-home/

4. Operation Hillman

1 www.watfordobserver.co.uk/news/18528913.boris-johnson-visits-bovingdon-primary-academy/

2 assets.publishing.service.gov.uk/government/uploads/system/uploads/attachment_data/file/1078404/2022-05-25_FINAL_FINDINGS_OF_SECOND_PERMANENT_SECRETARY_INTO_ALLEGED_GATHERINGS.pdf

3 www.gov.uk/government/speeches/pm-statement-12-april-2022

4 www.bbc.co.uk/news/uk-politics-61083402

5 www.ft.com/content/b685482a-82f3-4602-bd02-41bb561161d7

6 www.itv.com/news/2022-02-22/revealed-itv-news-obtains-leaked-police-partygate-questionnaire

7   www.bbc.co.uk/news/uk-politics-60983517

8   twitter.com/BBCPolitics/status/1516449510679064590

9   www.thetimes.co.uk/article/rishi-sunak-apologises-after-agonising-over-future-rpf33tvdr

10 www.thetimes.co.uk/article/7c67289e-ac7e-11ec-b5dd-c16e85f55725?shareToken=b77c2d8db690a30878715486c9e137c3

11 www.independent.co.uk/news/uk/politics/rishi-sunak-akshata-murthy-non-dom-wife-tax-b2052251.html?r=68930

12 www.theguardian.com/politics/2022/apr/07/rishi-sunaks-wife-says-its-not-relevant-to-say-where-she-pays-tax-overseas

13 news.sky.com/story/rishi-sunak-says-his-wife-is-being-smeared-and-has-done-nothing-wrong-in-row-over-her-non-dom-tax-status-12584832

14 www.politicshome.com/news/article/rishi-sunak-cleared-over-us-green-card-by-independent-adviser

15 commonsbusiness.parliament.uk/document/56344/html#_idTextAnchor005

16 www.theguardian.com/politics/2022/apr/21/how-senior-tories-frantic-efforts-failed-to-block-boris-johnson-inquiry

17 redfieldandwiltonstrategies.com/latest-gb-voting-intention-8-december-2021/

18 www.telegraph.co.uk/politics/2022/05/07/keir-starmer-beergate-event-planned-leaked-memo-appears-show/

19 www.politico.eu/newsletter/london-playbook/scoops-drunk-staff-at-keir-curry-loto-xmas-party-invite-khan-dont-quit/

20 www.theguardian.com/politics/2022/jul/08/keir-starmer-cleared-durham-police-breaking-lockdown-rules-beer

21 www.bbc.co.uk/news/uk-politics-62095955

22 www.thetimes.co.uk/article/met-police-end-partygate-inquiry-with-126-fines-handed-out-f0rnpjh6c

23 www.thetimes.co.uk/article/sue-gray-report-on-downing-street-lockdown-parties-frustrated-by-police-secrecy-sxrllvrgd

24 news.sky.com/story/sue-gray-and-boris-johnson-had-private-meeting-to-discuss-handling-of-partygate-report-sky-news-understands-12617829

25 www.itv.com/news/2022-05-23/exclusive-pm-pictured-drinking-at-downing-street-party-during-lockdown

5. The 41 per cent

1 www.gov.uk/government/speeches/pm-statement-to-the-house-of-commons-25-may-2022
2 www.theguardian.com/politics/2022/feb/04/nick-gibb-becomes-latest-conservative-mp-to-call-for-boris-johnson-to-resign
3 www.bbc.co.uk/news/av/uk-politics-61100346
4 www.reuters.com/world/uk/influential-uk-lawmaker-tells-pm-johnson-gigs-up-2022-04-21/
5 www.londonworld.com/news/politics/wimbledon-mp-stephen-hammond-prime-minister-boris-johnson-quit-3710810
6 news.sky.com/story/partygate-three-more-tory-mps-urge-boris-johnson-to-quit-how-many-now-want-him-to-resign-12624248
7 www.bbc.co.uk/news/uk-politics-61636151
8 www.thetimes.co.uk/article/more-tories-challenge-boris-johnson-in-revolt-over-parties-d33gh6qj6
9 twitter.com/vicderbyshire/status/1532660093489119233
10 twitter.com/NadineDorries/status/1532778456072732672
11 twitter.com/jesse_norman/status/1533699235417403393
12 twitter.com/nadinedorries/status/1533763409627566080?lang=en
13 www.thetimes.co.uk/article/lord-geidt-threatens-to-resign-as-boris-johnsons-ethics-chief-over-parties-99gcp9fbq
14 yougov.co.uk/topics/politics/trackers/boris-johnson-approval-rating
15 www.ft.com/content/9d8b3793-7953-4f12-896e-9cb60069545a
16 www.middevon.gov.uk/your-council/voting-elections/2022-elections/tiverton-and-honiton-parliamentary-election-2022/the-results/
17 www.wakefield.gov.uk/elections/wakefield-constituency-parliamentary-by-election
18 www.theguardian.com/politics/2022/jun/24/oliver-dowden-resigns-as-conservative-party-chair-in-wake-of-byelection-losses

6. Drinks at the Carlton Club

1   www.theguardian.com/politics/2022/jul/01/cads-corner-and-mark-francois-holding-court-inside-the-carlton-club
2   www.alistairlexden.org.uk/news/conservative-party-and-carlton-club-partnership-nearly-200-years
3   twitter.com/eyespymp/status/1483552752106156036
4   www.dailymail.co.uk/news/article-10974593/How-night-Carlton-Club-ended-Chris-Pincher-frogmarched-door.html
5   policymogul.com/stakeholders/10401/christopher-pincher
6   www.mirror.co.uk/news/uk-news/like-pound-shop-harvey-weinstein-11469572
7   www.thesun.co.uk/news/4844822/bathrobe-wearing-tory-whip-chris-pincher-made-pass-at-ex-olympic-rower-and-touched-up-labour-mp-tom-blenkinsop/
8   web.archive.org/web/20180129140433/http://www.tamworthinformed.co.uk/chris-pincher-promoted-re-joins-government/
9   www.thesun.co.uk/news/politics/19054116/tory-whip-resigns-following-groping-allegations/
10 twitter.com/dominic2306/status/1543208854325977088?lang=en-GB
11 www.dailymail.co.uk/news/article-10976589/Boris-knew-Tory-MP-faced-lurid-allegations-TWO-YEARS-appointing-senior-post.html
12 www.independent.co.uk/news/uk/politics/chris-pincher-mp-grope-allegations-b2114382.html
13 www.thetimes.co.uk/article/tories-rallied-round-pincher-by-name-pincher-by-nature-in-spite-of-warnings-99r5gj5lm
14 www.bbc.co.uk/news/av/uk-politics-62049610
15 news.sky.com/story/politics-live-shocking-allegations-againt-chris-pincher-damage-reputation-of-parliament-boris-johnson-not-aware-of-serious-specific-allegations-12593360?postid=4116461#liveblog-body
16 www.mirror.co.uk/news/politics/marathon-runner-claims-tory-chris-27393078

17 www.itv.com/news/2022-07-04/bordering-on-sexual-assault-pincher-accuser-on-horrific-experience-with-mp
18 news.sky.com/story/foreign-office-boss-sir-simon-mcdonald-to-step-down-early-after-department-merger-plan-12010313
19 twitter.com/SimonMcDonaldUK/status/1544206976820854784
20 www.telegraph.co.uk/politics/2022/07/05/dominic-raab-boris-johnson-not-told-complaint-against-chris/
21 www.ft.com/content/8a56a22e-bcbe-4d7f-82ca-ebf2c8350a6e

7. The Bunker

1   www.ft.com/content/a57b6f7d-003f-4651-a6b8-3e880293efc1
2   www.andrewmurrison.co.uk/news/andrew-resigns-pms-trade-envoy
3   www.youtube.com/watch?v=gJ5Lq3eBkkc
4   www.gloucestershirelive.co.uk/news/cheltenham-news/cheltenham-mp-alex-chalk-resigns-7297122
5   www.ft.com/content/0ea7c729-b095-4796-8f34-e8cd49ba5747
6   www.theguardian.com/politics/2022/jul/06/boris-johnson-resignations-nadhim-zahawi-will-quince-laura-trott
7   twitter.com/Steven_Swinford/status/1544624832360357888?s=20&t=PIPmfNSExISEczZAAThYcw
8   www.facebook.com/LeeAndersoninAshfieldEastwood/posts/pfbid0bXnAhUrpoYy6urRn3svhdSYYVP4s1TzQUSf8ucJqFtxEHzHeB8ShCsXqjntAfSJ1l
9   twitter.com/Jochurchill_MP/status/1544637770169307137
10 www.leeds-live.co.uk/news/yorkshire-news/pudsey-mp-stuart-andrew-quits-24414405
11 twitter.com/mimsdavies/status/1544674148080910338
12 www.mailplus.co.uk/edition/news/politics/199324/exclusive-michael-gove-tells-pm-its-time-to-go
13 www.bloomberg.com/news/features/2022-07-08/boris-johnson-s-downfall-the-inside-story-of-how-his-government-collapsed
14 Turpin, Colin and Adam Tomkins, *British Government and the Constitution: Text and Materials*, p. 364. (Cambridge University Press: 2007)

15 twitter.com/AnushkaAsthana/status/1544752417757138949
16 twitter.com/JasonGroves1/status/1544757157089902594
17 twitter.com/MrHarryCole/status/1544759456088850432
18 twitter.com/ChrisMasonBBC/status/1544778322973949953
19 twitter.com/NadineDorries/status/1544780226307264512
20 twitter.com/Simonhartmp/status/1544796759645454342

8. Hasta la vista, baby

1   twitter.com/BrandonLewis/status/1544921034368901122
2   twitter.com/Helen_Whately/status/1544921576449183745
3   twitter.com/DamianHinds/status/1544928142854340608?
4   twitter.com/DavidGHFrost/status/1544930119461965824
5   twitter.com/nadhimzahawi/status/1544950219657330688
6   twitter.com/michelledonelan/status/1544952139549708288
7   twitter.com/NickGibbUK/status/544968333333876737
8   twitter.com/Steven_Swinford/status/1544987569733214209
9   www.telegraph.co.uk/politics/2022/07/07/tom-tugendhat-have-served-now-hope-answer-call-prime-minister/
10 order-order.com/2022/07/08/it-kicked-off-between-goves-spad-boriss-spin-doctor-at-the-spectators-party/
11 twitter.com/RishiSunak/status/1545426650032111616
12 www.ft.com/content/ea706ae0-284c-43f3-adb8-55c3ad8bc250
13 conservativehome.com/2022/07/03/our-survey-next-tory-leader-wallace-leads-mordaunt-by-two-votes-in-over-seven-hundred/
14 www.thetimes.co.uk/article/kemi-badenoch-i-want-to-set-us-free-by-telling-people-the-truth-85sk8prm9
15 www.thetimes.co.uk/article/tory-leadership-race-next-prime-minister-contenders-candidates-gglrzntp3
16 twitter.com/Rehman_Chishti/status/1546240922043695107
17 www.theguardian.com/politics/2022/jul/12/jacob-rees-mogg-and-nadine-dorries-back-liz-truss-for-tory-leadership
18 www.independent.co.uk/news/uk/politics/penny-mordaunt-brexit-lord-frost-b2122877.html
19 www.dailymail.co.uk/news/article-11018717/And-social-medias-debate-winner-Tom-Tugendhat-Tory-MP-makes-audience-laugh-quoting-Dumbledore.html

20 www.itv.com/news/meridian/2022-07-18/boris-johnson-attends-farnborough-air-show-in-hampshire

21 news.sky.com/story/terminated-boris-johnson-signs-off-with-hasta-la-vista-baby-in-final-pmqs-12655569

22 yougov.co.uk/topics/politics/articles-reports/2022/07/21/liz-truss-holds-24-point-lead-over-rishi-sunak-amo

23 twitter.com/Steven_Swinford/status/1551671228808708103

24 conservativehome.com/2022/08/04/conhomes-tory-leadership-election-survey-truss-58-per-cent-sunak-26-per-cent-12-per-cent-undecided/

25 www.mirror.co.uk/news/politics/liz-truss-looks-shocked-loud-27584139

26 www.theguardian.com/politics/2022/jul/27/rishi-sunak-vat-energy-bills-screeching-u-turn-kwasi-kwarteng-liz-truss

27 www.thetimes.co.uk/article/rishi-sunak-suffers-new-blow-as-tom-tugendhat-backs-liz-truss-for-leadership-wndbd8xqg

28 www.mailplus.co.uk/edition/news/politics/208330/mail-backs-truss-for-pm

29 www.telegraph.co.uk/opinion/2022/08/01/liz-truss-right-choice-tories/

30 www.ft.com/content/0d4e8e8c-a9f5-409b-86b8-884304ce0568

31 news.sky.com/story/liz-truss-misinterpreted-over-no-handouts-remark-her-supporters-say-12667655

32 www.thetimes.co.uk/article/michael-gove-liz-truss-rishi-sunak-pz67ggl9z

33 inews.co.uk/news/robert-buckland-becomes-first-Cabinet-minister-to-switch-support-from-rishi-sunak-to-liz-truss-1794189

34 www.ft.com/content/dd35044a-c568-41bc-bcdf-adf659c485d6

35 www.telegraph.co.uk/politics/2022/08/06/inside-boris-carrie-johnsons-secret-wedding-party/

Acknowledgements

When Pan Macmillan half-jestingly suggested that my second book could be on the fall of Boris Johnson, my response was that he would not be going anywhere anytime soon. But, when events rapidly conspired against my prediction, I returned to my writing desk sooner than expected.

The Fall of Boris Johnson is chiefly thanks to two superb mentors: Matthew Cole, my steadfast and patient editor at Pan Mac, and David Evans, as trustworthy and wise of an agent as anyone could ask for. With such a quick turnaround, Mike Jones made sense of the early drafts. Many thanks also to James Annal for the fine cover, Josie Turner and Hannah Corbett for their publicity prowess, and Becky Lushey for her marketing efforts.

Two comrades have contributed more than anyone else. Nathan Boroda has been a supreme researcher: his eye for detail and accuracy, combined with an overwhelming keenness for the project, was beyond reproach. Patrick Maguire was generous with his advice, proffering pints with encouragement and sage words.

I was fortunate to have several manuscript readers who helped polish the politics and the prose. Thank you to Matthew Elliott, Paul Goodman, Robert Shrimsley and Alex Wickham, plus my fantastic boss George Parker for their learned thoughts. My colleagues at the *Financial Times* were all fantastically understanding; with thanks to Roula Khalaf and Tobias Buck for allowing me to write it.

Acknowledgements

The back of this book was broken in the gorgeous Devon village of Brixham, with enormous gratitude to Emily Warburton-Brown and Sam, Michael and Fiona Roseveare for their hospitality over the warm summer. Christian May and Eliza Filby's hospitality was also much appreciated at a crucial moment.

I am fortunate in having the very best of friends. Thank you to Liz Ames and Chris Murray, Adam Atashzai, Katy Balls, Toby Coaker, James Kanagasooriam, Lucy Fisher, Charlotte Ivers, Ed Leech, Ed Macdonald, Luke McGee, Matt McGrath, Duncan Robinson, Laura Trott, Tom Tugendhat, Rhiannon Williams, Hugo Wiseman and Nicky Woolf for their unyielding support. A special thanks also to Sophia Gaston for all her patience, understanding and kindness.

My family have been as loving and supportive as anyone could ask. Bronwen Payne, to whom this book is dedicated, has given unwavering faith and kindness to the project, along with the keenest reading eyes. Dan Jackson provided some very good times on Tyneside.

Above all, this book owes a huge debt to Greg Callus, who has been a personal rock and judicious guide throughout the researching and writing. Without his steadfast support, friendship and counsel, it simply would not have been completed.

And finally, thank you to all those politicos who kindly gave me their time. Many of Boris Johnson's team had to contend with losing their jobs alongside my pesky requests. As a first draft of recent history, not everything can be exact. But I have sought to accurately portray events as the interviewees narrated them, so I hope all feel it fairly reflects a most unruly period in British politics.

Sebastian Payne, October 2022
London

Picture Credits

Page 1 top © Tim Anderson/Daily Mirror via Mirrorpix
Page 1 middle © House of Commons/PA Archive/PA Images
Page 1 bottom © Hollie Adams/Stringer via Getty Images
Page 2 top © Jonathan Buckmaster/Daily Express via Mirrorpix
Page 2 bottom and page 7 bottom right © Ian Davidson/Alamy Stock Photo
Page 3 top and page 4 middle © ZUMA Press, Inc./Alamy Stock Photo
Page 3 bottom left and right and page 6 top and bottom left © PA Images/Alamy Stock Photo
Page 4 top © Pool/Pool via Getty Images News
Page 4 bottom left © Photo Handout/UK Government via Getty Images
Page 4 bottom right © Dan Kitwood/Getty Images
Page 5 top left and page 8 middle © REUTERS/Alamy Stock Photo
Page 5 top right and page 8 bottom © MARTIN DALTON/Alamy Stock Photo
Page 5 middle left © Tayfun Salci/ZUMA Press Wire
Page 5 middle right courtesy of Ross Kempsell
Page 5 bottom © ANDY RAIN/EPA-EFE/Shutterstock
Page 6 bottom right © Sajid Javid/Twitter
Page 7 top © Allstar Picture Library Ltd/Alamy Stock Photo
Page 7 bottom left © photo-fox/Alamy Stock Photo
Page 8 top © Guy Bell/Alamy Stock Photo

Contents

The contributors

Oga Steve Abah is Professor of Theatre for Development at Ahmadu Bello University, Zaria, Nigeria. One of Abah's main interests is the exploration of different methodologies, especially Theatre for Development (TfD) and Participatory Learning and Action (PLA) in doing citizenship research. He is the Nigeria Country Coordinator for the Citizenship Development Research Centre.

Vaijanyanta Anand is a Social Worker and a Scholar at the Department of Sociology, University of Mumbai. She is a Senior Faculty Member at the College of Social Work, Nirmala Niketan, University of Mumbai. She is also Honorary Director of Nirman, an NGO working with unorganised labour. Her interests are issues of corporate accountability, environment and labour.

Hasrat Arjjumend is a freelance researcher on development issues. He is based in India.

Andrea Cornwall is a Fellow at the Institute of Development Studies at the University of Sussex, UK. A Social Anthropologist by training, her current research focuses on the history and politics of participation in development. Her publications include *Realizing Rights: Transforming Approaches to Sexual and Reproductive Wellbeing* (edited, with Alice Welbourn, Zed Books, 2002) and *Gender in Africa* (James Currey, 2004).

Silvia Cordeiro is a feminist, a doctor, and general coordinator of the Women's Centre of Cabo de Santo Agostinho, Municipality of Sao Paulo, Brazil. She was President of the Municipal Health Council of the Cabo de Santo Agostinho for two terms, representing users of health services.

Carlos Cortéz, Doctor in Anthropology, is a Postgraduate Professor of Rural Development at the Autonomous Metropolitan University (Universidad Autónoma Metropolitana) in Mexico. He coordinates an interdisciplinary research programme on human development. He has undertaken research and published on social strategies for development, on governmental policies and on action-research oriented methodologies.

Nelson Giordano Delgado is a Professor of the Graduate Programme on Development, Agriculture and Society (CPDA) of the Federal Rural University of Rio de Janeiro in Brazil. He has published articles and essays on agriculture and macroeconomic policies, public policies for rural development, international trade regimes, the World Social Forum, and democracy and public spaces for participation. He has been a consultant for several public agencies in Brazil, and has worked with numerous international agencies, NGOs and grassroots movements.

Harsh Jaitli holds an MPhil in American Studies from Jawaharlal Nehru University, New Delhi, and has 16 years of extensive experience in capacity building, socio-economic research, impact assessment, policy analysis and advocacy, conflict resolution, project management and evaluation. He is currently working at PRIA as Programme Director of PRIA Consultants. His research has focused on occupational and environmental health and safety and sustainable industrial development. He has been actively developing methodologies for participation and corporate accountability.

Naila Kabeer is Professorial Fellow at IDS and a member of the Poverty and Social Policy Team. Her research interests include gender, livelihoods and labour market issues. Recent books include *The Power to Choose: Bangladeshi Women and Labour Market Decisions in London and Dhaka* (Verso, 2000) and *Gender Mainstreaming in Poverty Eradication and the Millennium Development Goals* (Commonwealth Secretariat/IDRC, 2003).

R. D. Sampath Kumar is an Associate Professor at the Department of Social Work, Andhra University, India. His field of expertise is social research methodology and his areas of work are child abuse, child labour, human resource management, labour welfare and unorganised labour.

Rohit Lekhi is Head of Research at Research Republic, a public policy research consultancy, and Honorary Research Fellow at the Ahmed Iqbal Ullah Race Relations Resource Centre, University of Manchester.

Stephanie Luce is an Assistant Professor at the Labor Center, University of Massachusetts-Amherst. She is the author of *Fighting for a Living Wage* (Cornell University Press, 2004), and co-author with Robert Pollin of *The Living Wage: Building a Fair Economy* (New Press, 2000). She researches and teaches labour economics, economic development, and low-wage labour markets. She received her PhD in Sociology from the University of Wisconsin-Madison.

Simeen Mahmud studied Statistics at the Dhaka University and Medical Demography at the London School of Hygiene and Tropical Medicine. She joined the Bangladesh Institute of Development Studies after completing her Masters and is currently Senior Research Fellow in the Population Studies Division. Her past research has been on demographic estimation methods; the relationship between women's work, status and fertility; micro credit and its impact on women; and group behaviour. Her current work on social policy focuses on health and education; citizenship and rights; demographic transition under poverty; and globalisation and its implications for women workers in the export sector.

Lyla Mehta is a sociologist and has worked as Research Fellow at IDS since 1998. She has conducted research on the dynamics of water scarcity, forced displacement and resistance to large infrastructure projects, and conceptual issues around the 'public' and 'private' nature of water. She has extensive field experience in India and more recently has begun research in South Africa. She uses the case of water to explore questions around knowledge/power linkages, social differentiation in natural resource management, rights to resources, and how competing forms of governance shape people's rights and access to resources. She is the author of *The Politics and Poetics of Water: Naturalising Scarcity in Western India* (Orient Longman, 2005).

Peter Newell is Senior Research Fellow at the Centre for the Study of Globalisation and Regionalisation, University of Warwick. Prior to this he has held posts as Fellow at IDS, Visiting Researcher at FLACSO, Argentina, Lecturer in International Studies at the University of Warwick and Researcher and Lobbyist for Climate Network Europe in Brussels. He is the author of *Climate for Change: Non-State Actors and the Global Politics of the Greenhouse* (CUP, 2000), co-author of *The Effectiveness of EU Environmental Policy* (MacMillan, 2000) and co-editor of *Development and the Challenge of Globalisation* (ITDG, 2002) and *The Business of Global Environmental Governance* (MIT Press, 2005). His main research interests are the political economy of environmental governance and the politics of corporate accountability and regulation.

Celestine Nyamu-Musembi is a Kenyan Lawyer with a background in legal anthropology who is currently a Fellow at IDS. She researches and writes on land relations and gender equity in resource control, the functioning of formal and informal justice institutions at the local level, implementation of international human rights standards, rights-based approaches to development, and integrating participatory approaches to rights advocacy. Her geographical focus is Eastern Africa.

Jenks Zakari Okwori is a lecturer in Drama at Ahmadu Bello University, Zaria. As one of the lead researchers at the Citizenship Development Research Centre in Nigeria, he has focused on exploring questions of identity in Nigeria, as well as developing new communication strategies.

Luisa Paré is an anthropologist, and works as a full-time Researcher at the Instituto de Investigaciones Sociales, Universidad Nacional Autónoma de México. She currently works on environment, natural resources management and local development issues.

A. B. S. V. Ranga Rao is on the faculty at the department of Social Work, Andhra University, Visakhapatnam, Andhra Pradesh, India.

Carlos Robles is an economist specialising in rural development. He has worked in urban and rural participatory planning, transfers of technology for sustainable production, and the creation of spaces for grassroots territorial management organisations, emphasising the relationship between quality of life, environmental quality and informed social participation.

Joanna Wheeler is the Research Manager of the Development Research Centre on Citizenship, Participation and Accountability (Citizenship DRC), a collaborative initiative working on how rights and citizenship matter. She has worked for ten years with NGOs and research initiatives in Brazil, Argentina and the US on issues of citizenship, gender and exclusion. Prior to joining IDS, she conducted postgraduate research on gender and citizenship in Rio de Janeiro as a Fulbright scholar. Her recent publications include *Developing Rights?* (*IDS Bulletin*, 36, 1), co-edited with Jethro Pettit in 2005, and 'New Forms of Citizenship: Democracy, Family, and Community in Rio de Janeiro, Brazil' in *Gender, Development and Citizenship* (Oxfam, 2004).

Abbreviations

AFL–CIO	American Federation of Labour – Congress of Industrial Organisations
ANDM	Alfred Nzo District Municipality
APEN	Asian Pacific Environmental Network
ASK	Ain O Salish Kendra
BGMEA	Bangladesh Garment Manufacturing and Exporters Association
BIGUF	Bangladesh Independent Garment Workers Union Federation
CNA	Comision Nacional de Agua (National Water Commission)
COHRE	Centre on Housing Rights and Evictions
COMPITCH	Indigenous Medical Organisations of Chiapas State
CONANP	National Commission for Protected National Areas (Mexico)
CSR	corporate social responsibility
DC	District Commissioner
DDT	Dichloro-diphenyl-trichloroethane
DfID	Department for International Development
DRC	Development Research Centre
DWAF	Department for Water Affairs and Forestry
EJ	environmental justice
EPA	Environmental Protection Agency
EPZ	export processing zone
FBW	Free Basic Water
GATS	General Agreement on Trade in Services
GDP	gross domestic products
GEAR	Growth, Employment and Redistribution
GNA	good neighbourhood agreement
HSRC	Human Sciences Research Council
ICESCR	International Covenant on Economic, Social and Cultural Rights
IEN	Indigenous Environmental Network
IFC	International Finance Corporation
ILO	International Labour Organisation
IMF	International Monetary Fund

INGO   international non-governmental organisation
INTRAC   International NGO Training and Research Centre
JV   joint venture
MFA   Multi-fibre Arrangement
NGO   non-governmental organisation
NHP   National Hydraulic Programme
NNPC   Nigerian National Petroleum Corporation
NRM   natural resource management
NTPC   National Thermal Power Corporation
ODC   Ogulaha Development Council
PCB   polychlorinated biphenyl
PDP   People's Democratic Party
PFL   Partido da Frente Liberal
PLA   participatory learning and action
PMDB   Partido do Movimento Democrático Brasileiro
PNA   protected natural area
PPP   Plan Puebla Panama
PROCEDE   Programa de Cesión de Derechos Ejidales (Programme for
                Cession of Ejido Rights)
PRODERS   Regional Development Programmes
PROFEPA   Procuraduría Federal de Protección al Ambiente
RDP   Reconstruction and Development Programme
RMG   ready-made garments
SEMARNAT   Secretaría de Recursos Naturales y Medio Ambiente
                (Ministry of Environment and Natural Resources)
SINAP   System for Protected Natural Areas (Mexico)
SNEEJ   Southern Network for Economic and Environmental Justice
SPDC   Shell Petroleum Development Company
SSC   Solidarity Sponsoring Committee
STPP   Simhadri Thermal Power Project
SUS   Sistema Único de Saúde
TFDC   Theatre for Development Centre
TNC   transnational corporations
TRIPs   Trade-Related Intellectual Property Rights
UCC   United Church of Christ
UNDP   United Nations Development Programme
UNICEF   United Nations Children's Fund
US   United States
USAID   United States Agency for International Development
USAS   United Students Against Sweatshops
WSSA   Water and Sanitation Services Africa
WTO   World Trade Organisation

Acknowledgements

We would like to acknowledge the support and contributions of a number of people to this volume. We are hugely grateful to John Gaventa as director of the Centre and as an enthusiastic and supportive colleague. He has tirelessly encouraged us throughout the production of this book and during the research programme which preceded and underpins it. Rohit Lekhi and Stephanie Luce deserve thanks for getting involved in the work of the programme in its latter stages, contributing invaluable 'Northern' insights and experience which helped to broaden, challenge and enrich our understanding of the accountability politics we were exploring in the global South. Mike Kirkwood and Lucila Garcia Lahitou provided invaluable copy-editing, administrative and editorial support in the final stages of producing the book. Reviewers of individual chapters, as well as the overall manuscript, helped to improve the coherence of the volume significantly, for which we are hugely thankful. We hope we have all been able to do justice to their comments. We are grateful to Robert Molteno as commissioning editor and to Anne Rodford for seeing the book through the final stages of publication.

We owe an enormous debt to the team of researchers that made up the 'Rights and Accountabilities' programme of the Development Research Centre on Citizenship, Participation and Accountability, whose work made this volume possible. We would like to thank them for their commitment to, and engagement in, an ever-evolving research programme over a number of years and in a number of countries, requiring attendance at numerous meetings and patience with the endless stream of editorial demands!

We would like to dedicate this book to Lucila Garcia Lahitou and Rob Worthington for their patience and love, without which our right to produce ambitious volumes such as this would not be realised and whose role in holding us to account for our duties as responsible partners, as well as active researchers, was critical to the maintenance of sanity.

Peter Newell and Joanna Wheeler
Brighton, February 2006

Foreword

JOHN GAVENTA

'Accountability' is one of the latest buzz words in development. It may be used variously to refer to the relationship of states to their citizens, NGOs to their members, elected representatives to their voters, corporations to their stockholders, and government departments to one another. In the development context, the argument is that through greater accountability aid will be channelled to those for whom it is intended, governments will move from clientelistic to more inclusive and transparent practices, corporations will become more responsible to social, environmental and ethical concerns, and large NGOs will become answerable to the publics they claim to represent. Achieving accountability is essential if the Millennium Development Goals are to be met or if the core planks of the Make Poverty History and Global Campaign Against Poverty for more aid, less debt and fairer trade are really to make a difference to the lives of poor people.

In many of its more conventional uses, accountability is often reduced to a somewhat technical process of 'accountancy', to be achieved through clear procedures, transparency of information, and compliance with legal processes and regulations. Strategies for accountability may also involve a focus on systems of auditing and monitoring through 'counting', be it of indicators and performance targets, funds and expenditures, or legal offences and violations.

This book, the third in the series on Claiming Citizenship, challenges the conventional, technocratic view. While good management, disclosure of information and legal process are important, they are not enough. Like other aspects of citizenship, accountability is not only created from above through institutional procedures or mandate, but also must be constantly claimed through strategies of mobilization, pressure and vigilance from below. Ultimately, the book argues, accountability is about power. In a context of globalisation and neoliberalism where configurations of power are rapidly changing, so too the sites and strategies for realising accountability are in flux. Where once we might have expected the state to regulate markets and to ensure accountability for its citizens, increasingly citizens themselves play an important role in monitoring state activities, regulating the behaviour of corporations, and claiming responsiveness from local, national and international institutions.

While accountability is seen as an important strategy for overcoming poverty and social injustice, it cannot be separated, the book also argues, from contests over the realisation of rights and the distribution of resources. Rights must be understood in practice as well as in the law. Through case studies of grassroots struggles to claim diverse sets of rights – be they to water in South Africa or Mexico, to shelter in Kenya, to a safe environment in Nigeria, to health in Brazil, to a 'living wage' for low-income workers in the United States, or to 'dignity and daily bread' for garment workers in Bangladesh – the book shows the enormous gap that can exist between internationally proclaimed rights discourses and everyday life, and between global standards and local circumstances. At the same time, in each of these areas, the case studies reveal a range of exciting and imaginative ways in which poorer groups mobilise to claim their rights and to construct mechanisms of accountability with the state, the private sector and international institutions, and within civil society itself.

For poor and marginalised groups, struggles for accountability gain traction when they involve access to the basic resources and services that are necessary for survival and for sustainable livelihoods. We see in this volume multiple examples of the ways in which resources and livelihoods are being destroyed by unchecked practices of corporate actors, be they chemical companies in minority communities in the United States or the tribal regions of India, oil companies in the heart of the Niger Delta, bioprospecting companies in Chiapas, or land speculators in Kenya. Yet we also see the myriad formal and informal ways in which citizens mobilise to hold corporations and global investors accountable, including the use of peoples' hearings as well as the courts in India, popular theatre and direct action in Nigeria, participation in government fora and mass protest in Mexico, and appeals to international legal frameworks and mobilisation of the media in Kenya. Each of these cases suggests that while corporate responsibility and accountability are critical in an era of growing privatisation, they are unlikely to be attained through voluntary compliance of the corporate sector or through regulation by increasingly weakened governments alone. Rather, citizen mobilisation and action form a necessary and important part of any corporate accountability strategy.

Like the previous volumes in this series, this volume has been supported by the Development Research Centre (DRC) on Citizenship,

Participation and Accountability, an international research network based at the Institute of Development Studies in the UK, with partner institutions in Brazil, Bangladesh, India, Mexico, Nigeria and South Africa. Founded in 2000, the Citizenship DRC is funded by the research division of the UK Department for International Development (DFID), with additional funding from the Rockefeller Foundation, which has enabled the inclusion of Northern case studies in its work. (See www.drc-citizenship.org for more information about the Citizenship DRC and for other publications.)

Also, as in the previous volumes, the chapters in this volume aim to bring understanding and insight to international debates on rights, participation and accountability through concrete, empirically grounded case studies from both South and North. The cases in this book were not produced in a one-off commissioned fashion, based on pre-set hypotheses or concepts, as is often the case with international research projects. Rather, the questions that the book addresses evolved over time, as researchers and activists associated with the Rights and Accountability Working Group of the Citizenship DRC came together to discuss their contexts, concerns and experiences, often in one another's countries, where they could also observe firsthand some of the realities about which they were writing. The research process was an iterative one, in which concepts and questions were developed, applied to local settings, and then re-discussed and refined. From an initial focus on accountability, the programme of work expanded to explore the multiple ways in which poorer groups could use rights-based claims to hold more powerful groups to account across a range of settings and resources.

The research process also has been enriched by bringing together a mix of academics and activists from eight countries and from a range of disciplines and backgrounds. Many of the cases featured in the book – especially those from Mexico, Nigeria and India – have involved action research approaches, in which the authors and the organisations they represent have engaged over time with the cases being studied, and therefore also have a stake in the accountability struggles they recount. For almost all of the cases, the chapters in this book represent only one of the products of the research. Other more popular means – such as videos, theatre, posters, newsletters, newspaper interviews, policy briefings and workshops – have also been used to communicate the results of the research to those with whom it was conducted.

The volume is also the result of a highly collaborative process amongst the contributors, which evolved its own forms of feedback and critique, learning and solidarity in places as diverse as Abuja, Oaxaca, Delhi, Cape

Town, Barra do Sahy (Brazil) and Brighton. Over time, the relationships that grew among the participants were not only important in themselves, but allowed a coming together of perspectives and disciplines, across contexts and institutions, that rarely can be achieved through individual research projects alone.

As the editor of the Claiming Citizenship series, I want to thank the editors of this volume and each of the chapter contributors for the effort which they invested in this project. It represents a degree of commitment far beyond the resources that were received. Thanks also to all those who assisted in the process, including research assistants Lucila Lahitou and Alex Hughes and, of course, our colleagues and editors at Zed Books, whose support for this series is greatly appreciated.

John Gaventa
Director, Development Research Centre on Citizenship,
Participation and Accountability
Institute of Development Studies
December 2005

No Power without Accountability

Lost my job, my car and my house
when 10,000 miles away
Some guy clicked on a mouse
He didn't know me, we never spoke
He didn't ask my opinion
Or canvass my vote.
Gotto find a way to hold them to account
Before they find a way to snuff our voices out.

The ballot box is no guarantee
That we achieve democracy
Our leaders claim their victory
When only half the people have spoken
We have no job security in this global economy
Our borders closed to refugees
But our markets forced wide open

Can you hear us?
Are you listening?
No power without accountability

Billy Bragg

CHAPTER 1

Rights, resources and the politics of accountability: an introduction

PETER NEWELL AND JOANNA WHEELER

Many conflicts in development can be understood as struggles by the poor to hold the powerful to account. Contests over the rights and responsibilities of actors in development are increasing in intensity amid clashes between the promotion of a rights-based approach to development and market-based notions of access and entitlement to resources. How these conflicts are played out has enormous implications for efforts to tackle poverty and achieve the Millennium Development Goals. Understanding how the poor claim their rights and demand accountability for the realisation of those rights becomes critical.

This book contributes to such an understanding by exploring how poorer groups mobilise around rights to resources in a diversity of settings, employing a broad range of strategies to achieve accountability. It places accountability at the intersection between rights and resources, asking: what is the relationship between greater accountability and people's ability to realise their rights to resources? Struggles over key livelihood resources such as health, housing and labour, as well as natural resources such as water and oil, provide the backdrop to an enquiry into the ways in which poorer groups hold powerful state, corporate and civil society actors to account. The process of claiming rights provides one (but certainly not the only) way in which they do this.

Accountability has come to assume a central place in contemporary development discourse over the last ten years in the context of increasing donor attention to the idea of good governance. Its association with this agenda has meant that the politics of accountability has been reduced to questions of state reform. Whilst of course state reform is crucial, this book shows that accountability cannot be achieved through institutional reform alone, and it is often the case that state institutions act as rights violators as well as rights enforcers. The conventional focus on the state has created an over-reliance on the law as a mechanism to generate positive social change, without looking at the ways in which social mobilisation also changes the law.

Accountability is not an apolitical project. The leading global actors promoting accountability initiatives, despite claims to the contrary, have a political stake in advancing some forms of accountability and some groups' rights over others. For example, a narrow focus on questions of financial reporting and accountancy fails to address the political processes by which the powerful insulate themselves from accountability to the poor and efforts to promote the private provision of state services without addressing accountability to the poor often serve to create accountability deficits. The global reach of actors such as the World Bank and other leading donors, however, means that accountability models have often been transplanted from one setting to another with little regard for local context.

An explicitly political framing of accountability in development, on the other hand, requires a different approach. Where earlier work on accountability emphasised change through legal reform and tech-nocratic notions of governance, here we advance an understanding of accountability that is more directly relevant to the lives of the poor, where power assumes a central place. Despite the current fashion for the term accountability in development debates, the term and the relationships it seeks to describe have a much longer history. Contexts of globalisation and neoliberal reform have, nevertheless, fundamentally changed the division of rights and responsibilities between states, market actors and civil society in ways that directly affect the liveli-hoods of the poor. As the roles and power of key actors in development change so, therefore, do the processes by which people seek to hold them to account. This book documents the strategies they employ to do this: formal and informal, legal and non-legal, collaborative and confrontational.

Capturing this new landscape of accountability politics requires us to look at a range of state and non-state actors, going beyond traditional preoccupations with state reform. Here we look at struggles for corporate accountability in the absence of state protection of marginalised groups, and we explore mobilisations around rights that are conferred by the state but unevenly realised in practice. We explore the role of community-based organisations and the accountability strategies they adopt to challenge the state and civil society organisations claiming to act on their behalf. Rarely is the state absent in such conflicts, even if its presence is often felt as a failure to act. This being so, it is unsurprising that marginalised groups often claim accountability from below, rather than relying on the state to provide it from above. The challenge is to map the web of accountabilities that flow between these actors in specific contexts in order to understand the directions from which opportunities for change are most likely to come.

Reflecting these new political dynamics also means emphasising accountability processes. These are the strategies, tactics and repertoires of mobilisation by which movements and communities seek to realise rights to livelihood or to express their citizenship. While often hoping to trigger changes within the state or other actors, such strategies can also be an end in themselves, aimed for example at raising awareness about rights or articulating citizenship through accountability claims. Abah and Okwori (Chapter 10) explore the role of theatre as a tool enabling people to express the barriers they face to realising accountability in their day-to-day lives, while Newell *et al.* (Chapter 8) show how NGOs in rural India are creating new platforms and arenas for the articulation of accountability claims through informal public hearings and the construction of 'Peoples' Development Plans'. These are a few of the many different methods for demanding accountability that this book will explore.

Understanding the nature of accountability struggles means appreciating the historical, material and cultural contexts in which they take place. By looking at cases in the global North and South and across a range of livelihood resources, we build up an eclectic view of the diverse ways in which disenfranchised groups pursue accountability claims and the context-specific circumstances that enable or frustrate their ability to do this. The cases here also cover a range of institutional contexts which are politically, socially and culturally diverse. We have situations in which a strong state is present (India, the United States, Brazil); in which litigious legal cultures exist (South Africa, the United States); and where inequalities are being challenged through social movement mobilisation (Mexico, Brazil, India). In other contexts, corporations have become the dominant actors, with direct implications for accountability (Nigeria, Bangladesh).

A grounded empirical assessment of which accountability strategies work, when, and for whom provides an important antidote to the inappropriate export of accountability models from one setting to another without sufficient regard for key political, social and cultural differences. Each chapter seeks to reflect on those elements that were important to the outcome of the accountability struggle they describe. The chapters are framed around the following key questions:

- Does the strategy used achieve greater accountability in relation to access to resources?
- When does it work? Under what conditions? (Historically, institutionally, economically, culturally?)
- For whom does it work? Who benefits?
- What are the implications for contemporary debates about accountability in development?

The book includes examples of mobilisations around a range of resources from more narrowly defined notions of natural resources to broader notions of livelihood resources such as housing and health, for example. We are able to compare struggles around resources such as oil and water with campaigns for better working conditions, access to health services, and housing provision in order to draw conclusions about how different types of resources influence the nature of accountability.

Rather than viewing the lack of accountability as a problem that only afflicts developing countries, we explore 'global' experiences of accountability struggles from North and South. Despite differences of context, there are many interesting parallels, for example, between the experience of mobilising for worker rights in the United States and in Bangladesh, as well between struggles for corporate accountability in the United States and India. Lessons can be learned about accountability strategies in ways that transgress geographical and sectoral distinctions. In so far as they seek to address patterns of inequality and marginalisation that are globally present, but manifest themselves in distinct ways in local settings, accountability strategies aimed at challenging power resonate with poor peoples' experiences the world over.

The next section maps out the relationships between rights, resources and accountability that emerge from the cases in this book.

Rights, resources and the politics of accountability

There is a complex and overlapping relationship between rights, resources and the politics of accountability. Figure 1.1 shows how each is intimately related to the other in a dynamic way. In many ways, the nature of a resource, and who has access to it, defines possibilities for justice, redistribution and change. In this book, resource struggles and efforts to realise key developmental rights, such as the right to housing and water, provide the anchor for an exploration of the relationship between rights and accountability. The centrality of resources to the livelihoods of the poor means questions of access and entitlement are imbued with relations of power and conflict. Hence, while the deprivation of a resource may be predominantly economic in character, gaining the right to access resources and the right to claim accountability is a political project, with citizenship at its core.

The chapters in this book show how resources are not a politically neutral variable in the relationship between rights and accountability. Beyond a deterministic, single-dimensional understanding of the relationship between resources and politics, we focus on the impact of the dynamics of institutional practices and cultural values upon the realisation of resource rights. Questions of access, management and distribution vary, depending on whether we are talking about water, oil or health. Each implies a different infrastructure, brings different actors into conflict, implies different sensitivities and is symbolically and culturally understood in a distinct way. Themes we pick up throughout the book on the materiality of resources, the importance of law and institutions and competing cultures of accountability help us to explore these themes.

Mobilisations to claim rights can produce new forms of accountability, just as the ability to claim rights and have them realised assumes relations of accountability between the state and citizens. For example, the trajectories of mobilisation around rights in India, Brazil and South Africa have informed and shaped the meaning of rights within those

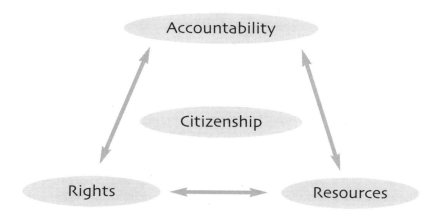

FIGURE 1.1   THE RELATIONSHIP BETWEEN RIGHTS, RESOURCES AND ACCOUNTABILITY

countries, from the way rights are used in practice to the encoding of specific rights in national constitutions (Pettit and Wheeler 2005). The relationship between rights and resources hinges on issues of access in terms of who controls and benefits from particular resources. The relationship between resources and accountability is informed by power, as more powerful groups monopolise control over resources and undermine accountability. This book focuses, then, on rights as a tool of accountability, where disenfranchised and marginalised groups use rights claims around key resources in order to demand greater accountability from state, private sector and civil society actors.

Cutting across processes of demanding accountability and claiming rights over resources, and at the centre of the triangle that we use (Figure 1.1) to describe the relationships between rights, resources and accountability, is the notion of citizenship. Citizenship relates to the claims that people believe they should be able to make of institutions, as well as their entitlements to access to material resources. We return to this theme in the conclusion to this chapter. Given the broad nature of this overview of the triangular relationship between rights, resources and accountability, the next section explores each of the dimensions of this relationship in more detail.

Rights and accountability
It is perhaps the case that more people are now claiming more rights than ever before (Jones 1994). The proliferation of types of rights claims is occurring in parallel with the increasingly salient discourse of rights in development (Cornwall and Nyamu-Musembi 2005). Though rights-based approaches have gained in popularity among some in the development community, their value, application and reach remain contested (Piron 2005). On the one hand, rights claims can provide a greater degree of access to justice. The long history of mobilisations around rights shows that they have the potential to provide a measure of access to justice that regulation does not, to support claims that other legal procedures do not recognise, and to ignite a level of activism that claims grounded in other discourses often fail to achieve. Framing a claim in the language of human rights gives it a certain status, legitimacy and moral weight; it constitutes a title which, at least in theory, others must recognise and respect (Dworkin 1978). On the other hand, 'rights talk' has increasingly been adopted in development debates in ways that render it vacuous and abstract. 'Rights talk is both pervasive and exciting ... rights talk is also frequently confused and inconclusive' (Merills 1996: 25). This has serious implications for those whose rights have been

denied or who are seeking to have their rights protected and respected (Pettit and Wheeler 2005).

Like accountability, rights and rights-based approaches, therefore, have a complex role within development. They have the potential to oppose technocratic top-down interpretations of accountability discussed earlier, but, as some of the chapters in this book show, powerful groups have also used rights discourse to advance their own agendas. Nonetheless, a conception of rights is at the heart of many mobilisations for accountability, a fact that becomes particularly clear in relation to struggles for resources. Our interest in rights here is guided by the ways in which poorer groups employ them to secure accountability from key actors, claiming basic development rights and rights to resources in order to enhance their livelihoods. We suggest that the right to claim accountability is fundamental to making other social and economic rights real, an idea we explore further in the final section of the chapter on citizenship. Hence, in considering rights in relationship to accountability, it is important to ask:

- How do marginalised or excluded groups use rights as part of a strategy for improving accountability?
- Under what conditions do rights enhance accountability to the poor?
- What is the relationship between the right to demand accountability and the protection of a broader set of economic and social rights?

Many rights, in and of themselves, are not *de facto* accountability tools; they have to be fashioned as such through processes of claiming, mobilisation and struggle. This becomes clear in Mexico, where obstacles to accountability are derived from the highly politicised disputes about different meanings and interpretations of rights (Paré and Robles, Chapter 4; Cortéz and Paré, Chapter 5). Similarly, in Brazil and South Africa, it was through sustained social protest that formal legal recognition for rights was achieved (Mehta, Chapter 3; Cornwall *et al.*, Chapter 7).

Since accountability is not just about promoting answerability but also about delivering enforceability, the process of how these rights can be realised is important. It is in this context that we encounter the limits of an (over-)reliance on rights. Many of the accountability strategies and tools that we explore in this book take as their starting point the lack of recognition or implementation of rights of particular groups, such as the right to water in South Africa, to adequate housing in Kenya and to a living wage in the United States. There is a difference, therefore, between *rights in theory* and *rights in practice*. Our concern is more with the latter and the ways in which poorer groups secure rights through a multitude of formal and informal creative strategies of accountability. The diverse forms of mobilisation that we explore in this book are reflective of this dynamic. In so far as the law is the medium through which rights-based claims are traditionally expressed, our work helps to explain the limitations of legally based constructions of rights and the ways in poorer groups often employ 'living' notions of rights that reflect more adequately the material deprivation or social exclusion they experience (Clark, O'Reilly and Wheeler 2005). The lack of protection provided by the law to poorer communities of colour in the US – despite civil rights claims – has given rise to notions of environmental justice that better embody people's experience of environmental harm (Lekhi and Newell, Chapter 9).

Nevertheless, claiming a right is not a short-cut to avoiding, pre-empting or reducing conflict over resources. Rights claims compete; they have to be balanced or reconciled, as the cases from Chiapas and Veracruz clearly show (chapters 4 and 5). There is also a political risk that attaches to efforts to politicise claims by invoking rights claims; the attention of rights violators, whether they be states or private actors, is drawn to vulnerable groups who may suffer the recriminations of high-lighting the negligence of powerful actors, as the cases from India demonstrate (Chapter 8). The value of a resource subject to conflict may mean that political freedoms are often denied and strategies of intimidation and violence invoked as the chapters from Mexico, India, and Nigeria show (chapters 4–5, 8 and 10). Particularly when confrontations with powerful actors are implied by an accountability struggle, the merits of action over silence or acquiescence need to be carefully evaluated. Accountability claims, therefore, are not easily made. Neither are they free of the costs and trade-offs that characterise other forms of mobilisation and claim making.

Rights are just one, albeit very important, means by which the poor seek accountability from those that exercise power over them. Social actors have to be clear about what is to be gained by framing a question in terms of rights and whether the same result could not be achieved equally well by other means. The choice of which strategy to pursue is a critical one for community-based organisations such as the tenants' association in Mombasa, Kenya with very limited resources and ambitious goals (Nyamu-Musembi, Chapter 6). The appeal of global reach should not mislead us into believing that the process of realising those rights demonstrates uniformity across the world. The limits of attempts to secure workers' rights through supplier-imposed labour standards in Bangladesh are a case in point (Mahmud and Kabeer, Chapter 11).

This is not just a book about how the poor claim, contest and secure rights, however. It is also a book about the rights of the powerful, used to defend their privileges, control of resources and access to power. At issue here is not just the rights of the state to claim land in the public interest for industrial development, as we see in the India case, or the right to admit investors to locate in economically impoverished but resource-rich areas of a country (Chapter 10). It is also the rights that have been conferred upon corporations, or in some cases assumed by them, to relocate their operations without offering compensation to communities that host them, to invest where they choose and to socialise costs while privatising profit. The struggles we explore in this book about campaigns to secure a living wage (Chapter 12) or to contest the social, economic and environmental effects of capital mobility and the economic blackmail that is used to suffocate communities' rights claims (chapters 8 and 9), provide evidence of attempts to challenge the privileging of rights to profit over rights to welfare and social justice.

Rights and resources

Contests over rights of access to resources and to the benefits that derive from their exploitation define many contemporary and historical struggles in development. They affect the interests of the powerful and the poor simultaneously, often bringing them into conflict with one another. The political and economic histories of resources and commodities as diverse as oil, sugar and coffee offer, in microcosm, a history of colonialism, capitalism and the origins of the modern order (Mintz 1986; Wild 2005; Evans, Goodman and Lansbury 2002). We see in the Nigeria case, for example, how contemporary accountability problems have been exacerbated by the country's experience of colonialism. Contests over how resources are to be used, for what, and by whom assume fundamental relations of social power. The chapters in this book suggest that it is this social power, related as it is to political and material power, that defines the context determining who is in a position to hold who to account and the means by which they are able to do so.

What emerges, then, is a *political economy of rights* in which questions of access to and distribution and production of resources are paramount. A focus on resources changes the way we think about the relationship between rights and accountability. The challenge is not to over-emphasise the material dimensions of this relationship and to acknowledge instead that economic rights are in many ways indivisible from social, political and cultural rights. Realising the former is in many ways contingent on having access to the latter rights. Though it is often a felt deprivation of resources that drives accountability demand making, the right to claim accountability presupposes all other claim making.

Indeed, it is often the absence of responsiveness from states, corporations or even community-based organisations that fuels situations of conflict around resources. For example, in Nigeria, the juxtaposition between the extreme poverty in the Niger Delta and the large amounts of wealth generated by oil extracted from the region is the starting point for many of the struggles over accountability. When people are denied shelter as in the case from Kenya, unable to get access to water or fail to receive compensation for land taken from them as in the cases from Mexico and India, they seek redress by locating responsibility for upholding that right or providing that service.

Increasingly this process takes place across different arenas and levels of decision making. In the case of the Tuxtlas Reserve in Mexico, there are multiple and overlapping institutions involved and establishing lines of accountability becomes very difficult. Even those conflicts which appear to be local in scale and orientation are often implicated in, and affected by, broader regional and global dynamics. For example, in Bangladesh, global standards set by powerful international buyers and trade unions can undermine the ability of groups of garment workers to define and claim labour rights they judge important. Efforts to conserve biospheres in Mexico illustrate how regional and global agendas make themselves felt at the local level, changing the balance of accountability relations.

Our concern here is less with key civil and political rights, though these often form the bedrock of future activism: the givens and prior enabling conditions of a broader social struggle. For example, the right to equal treatment and non-discrimination in the United States is the premise for mobilisations around environmental racism (see Chapter 9). We look instead at material struggles for subsistence and survival focused on resources such as water and oil, and rights such as those to health, housing and a living wage. Clearly this constitutes a broad spectrum of rights and ensuing chapters will show that there are important differences between these rights in terms of how claimants articulate and mobilise around them, and how *justiciable* and *realisable* they are.

The limitations of a notion of legal indivisibility of rights should not be confused with the interrelatedness of particular rights in practice and the struggles around them. In Kenya, for example, attempts by the tenants' association to uphold the right to shelter are difficult to separate from political rights to organisation and information, as well as citizenship defined by having access to a legitimate residence. Resource rights, therefore, are often indivisible from other forms of rights claims. In a close parallel to the India case, Zarsky (2002: 45) notes that 'Worker exposure to hazardous chemicals, for example, is at once a labour rights and an environmental concern. The expropriation of indigenous peoples from ancestral lands to make way for a mining operation has implications for both human rights and environmental protection.' These inter-relations help us to understand the coalitions that activists form, recognising and consolidating these links.

Resources and accountability

This book takes a broad approach to resources, where cultural under-standings of resources, the political economy of who has rights to resources, and the varied institutional configurations that mediate societal relations make for very different forms of accountability politics. Though much of our work explores accountability struggles around key resources such as oil and water, we are anxious not to draw conclusions about the possibilities of pro-poor action that are unduly determined by the nature of a resource, as in debates on the resource curse reviewed in Chapter 10. Our emphasis, instead, is on the ways in which institutions and the relations of social power that underpin them mediate the relationships between rights, resources and accountability.

Accountability challenges do, nevertheless, differ according to the resource in question. There are important differences between the politics of access, process and redress, depending on whether the struggle is for resource rights, rights to environmental protection or rights to welfare in the form of health and housing. Factors such as the centrality of a resource to a country's economy or, in turn, the location of that country in the global marketplace can have a strong bearing on which accountability mechanisms can be utilised and by whom. The seasonality of the garment industry in terms of fashion cycles and corresponding orders gives some advantages to workers demanding their rights, as they can use pressures from buyers on delivery deadlines to extract gains from factory owners (Chapter 11). The high value attached to oil, and its location in often remote and disputed territories, places it at the centre of many conflicting rights claims around land, livelihood and compensation (Chapter 10). Oil production both reflects and reproduces divided communities and petro-states complicit in rights violations, inevitably constructing a particular type of accountability politics in its wake where violence and intimidation are the tools of enforceability. Sometimes, it is not merely the material value attached to a resource, but competing perceptions of its worth and cultural significance that generate accountability conflicts. Radically different understandings of the environment and nature as a resource, when combined with institutional complexity in Mexico, create a context where accountability is very difficult to achieve through institutional design.

Just as people clearly attempt to demand accountability from different starting points, so too institutions and the élites that manage them feel different degrees of responsiveness to those they claim to represent. While in Mexico and Brazil, for example, there are legal provisions for citizen participation in major sectors of public policy such as health, in contrast, the state structures of Bangladesh and Nigeria are not orientated towards a significant level of accountability towards their citizens. While accountability towards poor and marginalised groups is imperfect in every case, the scope for particular states to respond to accountability demands varies enormously. It is when rights claims come into conflict over specific resources that we are able to see which accountability ties pull strongest, and power reveals itself.

Beyond issues of materiality or the nature of a particular resource and the institutional structures that mediate access to resources, there is also a cultural politics of resources: processes of constructing and attributing meaning to resources, which generate expectations about rights, duties and, therefore, accountabilities (Baviskar 2003; Mehta 2003). These can be derived from societal givens, religious and spiritual beliefs in ways which fundamentally alter the practice of accountability politics. They derive from the 'complex material and symbolic dimensions of how "natural resources" come to be imagined' (Baviskar 2003: 5051). For example, indigenous perceptions of water and the sacred meanings associated with water in Veracruz have informed the nature of accountability politics there. Hence there are symbolic as well as material dimensions to conflict, partly derived from the fact that 'Each resource has distinctive use values that emerge in relation to particular modes of production' (Baviskar 2003: 5052). In this sense, culture itself becomes a site of struggle where inequalities and exclusions around resources get challenged and reproduced.

Earlier work on the role of environmental movements in broader struggles over democracy and development (Garcia-Guadilla and Blauert 1994) and studies of the democratising potential of social movements in redefining notions of development (Peet and Watts 1996; Escobar and Alvarez 1992) have drawn attention to the politics of these struggles. As the chapters in this book on Mexico, South Africa and Brazil show, such campaigns are often focused on specific resources, mobilised around certain rights or targeted at specific institutions. There is increasing attention, however, to the global political dynamics of such mobilisations[1], reflecting the increasing implication of globalised actors in local resource struggles – as shown by the chapters on the living wage in the United States, the garment industry in Bangladesh, and disputes over knowledge rights in Mexico. This book reinforces the idea that people's experiences of and struggles over social and environmental rights are globally lived but locally felt (Eckstein and Crowley 2003: xiii).

The next section develops the links between these themes further through reference to cross-cutting themes that are developed in the book, summarising what we learn about accountability from the case studies and setting us up to explore the implications of this for contemporary debates about accountability and development in the final section of the chapter.

Key themes

Accountability aims and outcomes

Existing work on accountability suggests there are two key dimensions to effective accountability mechanisms: answerability (the right to make claims and demand a response) and enforceability (mechanisms for delivering accountability, for sanctioning non-responsiveness) (see Chapter 2). Accountability, in many of the cases in this book, is not an end in itself. It is a means to achieving a wider set of goals such as broader forms of social and political change, including greater justice, equity and the redistribution of resources. This is an important point, given the often-technocratic and target-driven approaches to accountability, and the often-apolitical approaches to rights in development (see Pettit and Wheeler 2005).

We see in this book how accountability is not only an outcome, but also a process, where both answerability and enforceability are achieved through ongoing engagement between citizens and institutions. This is a crucial point in cases where the formal or legal mechanisms are in place for accountability, but the enforcement of these rights and standards is weak. Mehta explores how, in South Africa, the constitutional provision of 20 litres of free basic water for all is unevenly translated in practice – and has led to a series of court cases to establish lines of accountability between different levels of government in fulfilling this right. As Luce shows in her contribution, the victories of the US labour movement in the first half of the twentieth century have been eroded: campaigns for a living wage have had to struggle for new labour rights legislation to be adopted, and then use leverage over the municipal governments to enforce living wage standards. The chapters in this book explore the complexities of both accountability processes and accountability outcomes, and the ways in which processes inform outcomes.

Struggles for accountability driven by different aims and processes inevitably lead to the construction of distinct forms of accountability politics. If the aim of the struggle is to expose state corruption, gaining media attention – as the tenants' associations seek to do in Mombasa – is an appropriate strategy. If, on the other hand, legal recognition of the right to housing is also an aim, then drawing on international legal agreements to secure that right is the preferred choice. This point is further illustrated in Luce's chapter, which looks at the difference between standards and rights in terms of the living wage campaign in the United States. The standard of the minimum wage in the United States has been drastically eroded. As a result, living wage campaigns have organised around the right to a living wage, which is contextually determined. Standards provided important gains in labour rights, but have not been sufficient to guarantee substantive rights to a living wage.

Several of the chapters in this book show how the presence of multiple actors involved in any accountability struggle serves to blur lines of accountability. Cortéz and Paré explore how, in the biosphere reserves in Southern Mexico, a tangled web of actors including indigenous groups, international conservation NGOs, pharmaceutical companies, and state and federal government agencies all have competing interests in relation to the environment, inhibiting the development of clear accountability mechanisms between them. Local accountability conflicts are increasingly embedded in global politics in a context in which relations between public/state and private/market actors are undergoing change. The commodification and commercialisation of resources (water, indigenous knowledge, oil, labour) is accelerating these changes – and catalysing conflict over rights to resources. This produces gaps and deficits, creating accountability challenges across multiple levels from community organisation up to global institutions as global market penetration creates more opportunities for actors to encounter one another in new ways.

Another crucial theme is the way in which many of the actors and stakeholders involved in accountability politics often perform contradictory roles. The cases of India, Kenya, Mexico, Nigeria and the United States illustrate how the state can act as both the guarantor and the violator of rights. Caught at the competing intersection of rights-based and market-based approaches to the provision of water, the South African government engages in 'sins of omission and commission', as Mehta puts it, enabling some rights while denying others. Newell *et al.* show how the government in India, far from being a buttress against corporate irresponsibility, is implicated in acts of negligence resulting in serious environmental degradation that disproportionately affects tribal and lower-caste groups. Similarly, in cases where the state apparatus is weak or being eroded (such as Bangladesh and Nigeria), the increasing influence and power of corporate actors diminishes the ability of the state to act as the enforcer of accountability.

Contradictory and competing obligations are not just issues faced by states and corporations. Within particular communities, the very people who are demanding accountability can themselves undermine it, as in Nigeria where internal divisions between traditional authorities and youth groups have led to increasing cycles of violence. The chapters in this book explore the many dimensions of accountability – from different meanings and goals, to the variety of actors involved. Overall, this points to the importance of context in understanding how accountability can lead to real gains in social, economic and political equity.

How does context matter?

It is clear that context matters in understanding struggles for accountability and rights, but certain elements of context have greater salience in explaining the conditions and prospects for improving accountability. First, the institutional complexity described above is an important contextual factor. We see throughout the book how a wide range of institutional actors with responsibilities for accountability can generate confusion and disable action. These actors often represent a diverse and shifting set of interests cutting across private and public spheres, so the strategies for achieving accountability and the types of accountability relationships that can be established are also shifting. In her chapter on the Mombasa tenants' association struggle, Nyamu-Musembi suggests that one of the most difficult challenges for grassroots organisations is to gauge the appropriate strategy given their goals and the rapidly changing map of actors and political interests. As Paré and Robles emphasise in the Veracruz case, changes in government administrations can easily undermine years of careful work to build stable relations of accountability between different institutions and actors.

Legal settings and traditions also have important implications for increasing accountability to the poor. This book challenges assumptions that law generates social change by looking at ways in which the reverse is equally true. Approaches to accountability that rely solely on legal reform are unlikely to appreciate the limits of the law, in terms of access and reach, for the majority of the world's poor. For example, constitutionally guaranteed rights (as with the right to water in South Africa and the right to health in Brazil) can create new possibilities for demanding accountability. Yet the difference in how these rights fit into legal traditions is critical. In Brazil, social mobilisation around constitutional provisions has provided an entry point for political struggles over accountability because the judiciary does not fill that space, while in South Africa court cases such as *Grootboom v Republic of South Africa* have had a more central role. In the United States, where there is a strong tradition of litigation, environmental justice groups have employed 'judicial activism', invoking civil rights and environmental legislation to hold polluters to account. By contrast, in India, despite the fact there is a strong tradition of using public interest litigation, there has also been resort to mock legal processes such as citizen hearings. And in Mexico, where there is little possibility of resolving accountability struggles through legal structures perceived to be convoluted and corrupt, social mobilisation around political objectives is key to increasing accountability. While law often allows for equity of treatment, it can also reinforce social inequities. In Bangladesh, the laws covering workers' rights date from the colonial period and heavily favour educated men. Women, who work almost entirely in the informal sector, do not fall under the auspices of these laws in practice. In Kenya and India the colonial Land Acquisition Act has been invoked to remove people from their land, often without compensation or redress.

An apolitical view of promoting accountability through law reform, capacity building, training judges and the like is unlikely to yield improved access for the poor unless structural barriers and social hierarchies that inhibit meaningful use of the law by the poor are also addressed. The high degree of attention given to law reform by key actors such as the World Bank needs to respond to other reports from the same institution emphasising that legal initiatives alone are not enough to tackle corruption and improve access to redress (Soopramien *et al.* 1999). If building accountability stops at the level of reforms to institutional procedures, it is unlikely to generate the sort of change that only comes through building coalitions to oversee and contest the translation of legal obligations into lived realities. We see from the chapters in this book the importance of this process of translation, of giving meaning to legal commitments.

More broadly, the chapters in this book also emphasise the different cultures of accountability that characterise specific contexts. In Bangladesh, a culture of accountability is slowly beginning to emerge that goes beyond the current culture of compliance, which is more concerned with meeting the short-term demands of contractors for observable enforcement of workplace conditions than in changing the relations of power that create abuses of workers rights in the first place. Paré and Robles also explore the meanings of accountability within rural indigenous communities in Southern Mexico, where, although the word 'accountability' does not exist in local languages, the meaning of accountability is encoded in certain traditions and practices. In this case, demands for accountability have become combined with prior notions of fairness and community obligation to produce a new definition of accountability based on co-responsibility. In Brazil, dissonant cultures of participation and a history of clientelism within the health care system make it difficult for clear lines of accountability to be drawn. In sum, there are different cultures of accountability grounded in different histories of conflict, trust and corruption.

Which strategies, when?

This book surveys a bewildering array of strategies for demanding accountability and realising rights, some of which are summarised in Table 1.1 below. Amid this diversity, however, some important trends emerge. In each case the factors that have inhibited or encouraged increased accountability are explored. The strategies are not static, however; there is often an evolution in strategy as accountability struggles change over time. This can involve a transition from resistance to dialogue and solution finding, as the case of the management of the watershed in Mexico shows, indicating ongoing processes of reflection within movements about which accountability strategies work, when, why and for whom.

Advances in accountability and rights claims are not linear, nor are they irreversible. In several of the studies in this book, setbacks in struggles for accountability have been as important as gains. A common feature across several of the cases, including Nigeria, Mexico and India, are the cycles of negotiation and conflict that have emerged as part of struggles for accountability. In Nigeria, as Abah and Okwori demonstrate, short-term demands for concessions by communities to oil companies have resulted in tangible results. But, at the same time, oil companies have reinforced and exacerbated internal divisions and conflicts within communities by granting concessions and financial

TABLE 1.1 SOCIAL ACTORS, STRATEGIES, RIGHTS AND RESOURCES

Who?	Types of strategies used		Rights involved	Resources involved
	Formal	Informal		
Indigenous groups in Chiapas and Veracruz, Mexico	Environmental round tables with government	Armed conflict Protests Re-settlement in reserve areas	Land rights knowledge rights	Environmental resources in general
Rural poor in South Africa	Court cases		Right to water	Water
Tenants' association in Mombasa, Kenya	Using international legal frameworks	Blocking illegal construction Gaining media attention Mobilising residents	Right to housing Right to information	Adequate housing
Community-based organisations in Cabo, Brazil	Participation in government-mandated health councils		Right to health	Adequate health care
Indigenous groups in Veracruz, Mexico	Negotiations with reserve management, municipal government Construction of alternative plans	Blockading dam to cut off water supply Citizen Water Management Council Participatory environmental audit	Right to water	Water

Who?	Types of strategies used		Rights involved	Resources involved
	Formal	Informal		
Landless groups in India	Court cases Complaints to government officials	Public hearings People's Development Plans Gaining media attention Citizen health and environmental monitoring	Land rights Right to work Right to a clean environment	Minerals Energy Water
Environmental justice movement, US	Civil rights legislation Court cases Legal clinics Public hearings	Protest Citizen health monitoring	Right to a clean environment	Water Air
Poor communities in the Niger Delta		Theatre Youth groups Womens' groups Protest Sabotage	Right to work Right to compensation Right to a clean environment	Oil
Municipal workers, US	Court cases State labour laws	Boycotts Gaining media attention	Right to a living wage	Labour
Garment workers, Bangladesh	Supplier-led standards State labour laws	Strikes/walkouts Forming workers' associations	Right to fair working conditions	Labour

windfalls to particular groups. Hence these concessions are only ameliora-tive and tend to fuel conflict rather than addressing the fundamental rights violations occurring in the Niger Delta. A similar though less violent situation has emerged in Mexico, where municipal governments appease rural indigenous communities by conceding certain rights and benefits without addressing the underlying causes of the lack of account-ability.

Many of the chapters focus on the interface between formal and informal strategies for accountability, and the potential for important advances towards outcomes positive to the poor when these strategies combine, as in the tenants' struggle in Mombasa and the living wage movement in the United States. Though much of the current debate about accountability focuses on formal mechanisms of accountability aimed at transparency and redress, for example, the chapters in this book show that informal approaches and strategies are often equally impor-tant. Struggles around accountability do not just take place through institutions, but between actors in civil society and the market and among communities. These groups also employ both 'inside' and 'outside' strategies, strategies that work within existing institutional channels as well as those that seek to contest and broaden formal spaces of engagement (see Chapter 12).

Several of the chapters also show how non-engagement in formal processes can also be an accountability strategy by contesting the boundaries of engagement and by opposing particular practices. In Chiapas, as discussed by Cortéz and Paré, the position of resistance of the Zapatista movement is predicated on non-engagement with the state. This position has forced the government to address the Zapatistas' demands in different ways to those it adopts when it deals with claims from other indigenous groups in Mexico. Given the limitations of tech-nocratic approaches to accountability, social movements are investing their efforts in new spaces for accountability such as creating new institutions; constructing economic and livelihood alternatives to exit exploitative relationships; and disengaging from interactions with the state when they are perceived to compromise the strength of the social movement.

In all cases where demanding rights is a strategy for achieving accountability, the key questions are: when, how, and for whom do rights make a difference? In many of the cases formal legal rights are an impor-tant first step (as in South Africa), but the implementation of rights becomes the central site of struggle. International legal rights can have a similar role. In the absence of national legislation granting the right to shelter, the tenants' association in Mombasa has drawn on international conventions on human rights, to which Kenya is a signatory, that protect this right. But appealing to national or international law and formal rights encoded in those laws can only take the attempts to establish accountability so far. Formal rights (whether derived from national or international legal frameworks) are insufficient on their own to guarantee substantive changes for poorer people. We also need to consider the fact that law and rights are as likely to work for powerful interests as for those without the power to advance rights claims, as we see in the cases of India and Kenya regarding legal provisions concerning land and property.

Implications

What are the implications of the key themes that we have identified above as emerging from the case studies in this book? In particular, what are the implications of what we have learned for predominant contemporary framings of accountability agendas in development debates?

We noted in the introduction a number of assumptions in contemporary debates about accountability in development: (1) that models of accountability can be transferred from one setting to another, and that what works in one place can be expected to work elsewhere; (2) that accountability is about accountancy; (3) that accountability is provided *by* states *to* citizens; (4) that the law is the primary vehicle for clarifying the respective duties and obligations of states and citizens; (5) that accountability can be created through institutional reforms; and (6) that promoting accountability is an apolitical project. Here we show how the contributions of this work challenge these assumptions and suggest the bases of a broader and more explicitly political understanding of accountability.

Cultures of accountability

There are many issues that arise from the framing of accountability as a problem of institutional engineering, legal reform and better accounting. One is denial of the political and historical context of accountabilities by which people make sense of rights, duties and obligations. Because they emerge from rooted experiences, defined by different cultural expectations of accountability, rights and duties are shaped by material conditions, which generate or subdue expectations of what is possible and affordable. Generic models of accountability reform necessarily encounter local realities, which will more often than not be at odds with how institutions are 'meant' to operate. Proscriptions of how to tackle accountability problems based on the experience of a limited number of countries tend to overlook the context-specific ways in which problems are understood and need to be confronted. This is true of World Bank 'model contracts' aimed at helping policy makers and bank executives 'discipline troubled banks' (Roulier 1995) as well as efforts by the same institution to 'transplant' institutions to Africa (Dia 1996).

The extent to which rights can be meaningfully exercised and enforced rests on institutional configurations and cultures of accountability that take distinct forms in different parts of the world. These cultures of accountability impose different rights, duties and obligations on 'accountability seekers' and 'accountability providers' (Goetz and Jenkins 2004). They assume reciprocal ties and social contracts between key elements within the state, civil society and the market. They derive from distinct historically constructed experiences of exclusion and expectations regarding the performance of institutions. Globally led efforts to promote accountability are often frustrated by such local realities.

This helps us to understand the process we observe in many of the chapters in the book, when accountability cultures imposed from the outside often conflict with more indigenous or traditional understandings of accountability. It is expressed, for example, in the difference between 'cultures of compliance' and 'cultures of accountability' discussed here in relation to Bangladesh. Universally proscribed protection only goes so far and there remains a key role for mobilisation around implementation. This book explores the difference between US labour movement strategies aimed at securing a living wage through an international standard and other struggles for that right in diverse settings. By looking at these forms of accountability politics in practice, we hope the insights contained in this book will contribute to an enhanced understanding of the embeddedness of strategies and institutions in particular social, cultural and political frameworks, which are important for making sense of those institutions.

Beyond accountancy

Technocratic framings of accountability generate a kind of naivety that reform processes can generate pro-poor change without challenging power inequities. This illusion arises through a focus on interventions that are easy to implement, monitor and evaluate (DfiD 2005). By constructing the problem as one of corruption and better service provision, for example (World Bank 2000; 2004), the systemic and institutional biases that permit conscious anti-poor decision making are left unchallenged.

Likewise, with debates about corporate accountability, emphasis is placed on improved systems of auditing, reporting and monitoring, often without questioning the indicators by which performance is measured or, more broadly, whether the activities of a firm are contributing to the achievement of wider societal and developmental goals. Again, the point is not to question the importance of greater transparency in political and financial affairs. Indeed a key theme throughout the book is the importance of rights to information as a precondition for effective mobilisation. Rather, the plea is not to reduce the concept of accountability to the pursuit of improved accountancy. The shift towards defining indicators and measuring accountability is problematic in this sense, with UNDP describing indicators for human rights advocacy as a 'cutting-edge area of advocacy' (UNDP 2000) and Narayan, writing for the World Bank, arguing that 'if empowerment cannot be measured, it will not be taken seriously in development policy making and programming' (Narayan 2005). For Shah, too, 'the power of accountability is significantly reduced if citizens are unable to measure their governments' performance in a meaningful way.... The abstract concept of government performance can only be an effective tool in public debate when there are concrete statistics measuring performance and benchmarks against which asset indicators can be compared' (Shah 2005). Accountability can and should be much more this, especially when viewed from the perspective of tackling those accountability deficits that serve to entrench poverty and frustrate attempts to combat it.

Multiple and embedded accountabilities

We lose a sense of the importance of prior processes of mobilisation and coalition building that generate demands for reform and sustain reform efforts when we assume that institutional change can occur in a social and political vacuum. In other words, without engaging broader processes of social change, institutional innovations, however far-reaching, are unlikely to deliver the sort of reform that is desired. Whether it is anti-corruption strategies that can be reduced to 'six steps' or emphasis on accountability through performance-related rewards for bureaucrats aimed at promoting civil service reform (Dia 1993), the assumption that intra-state institutional change should be the sole focus of policy attention seems increasingly at odds with the momentum for change generated above, beyond and below the state. This implies a wider focus on the diverse accountability strategies adopted by the poor to bring about change on their own terms. Hence the contribution of this book is to encourage the shift from an exclusive focus upon intra-state mechanisms of horizontal accountability to exploring more seriously the potential of society-centred models of vertical accountability discussed in Chapter 2. The state-centredness of prevailing approaches to accountability (DfiD 2001), noted above, is problematic, then, in the sense that it runs the risk of reinforcing the reliance of the poor on the very state institutions that have shown themselves to be singularly ineffective in responding to the needs of the poor.

In defence of the primacy of public accountability, Paul, writing about India, argues that 'government and its agencies are the key players in the poverty reduction arena, judged by their own public policy pronouncements and commitments' (2002: 1). By claiming that international institutions and NGOs are of 'marginal significance' in India, and that the commitment of business to poverty reduction is 'indirect and limited at best', Paul focuses on actors who identify themselves as key accountability brokers through their pronouncements and official mandates. In contrast, our approach is to examine critically the roles and performance of the broader range of actors who wield power over the lives of the poor in practice and in increasingly direct ways, rather than to read accountability politics from the formally proscribed accountability roles of actors.

This is clearly not a case for abandoning the state on the basis of its unreformability or structural inability to respond to the needs of the poor. Rather, it is a plea to recognise the many levels at which reform takes place; how informal strategies outside the immediate sphere of the state can serve to generate state reforms; but how also, on occasion, pro-poor accountability strategies emerge in ways and through arenas where the state is not, perhaps should not, be present. Cases in this book from India and Nigeria, for example, illustrate that it is often distrust of the state or an appreciation of the state's complicity in accountability abuses, experienced through resource conflicts, that drives people to construct alternative accountability mechanisms that do not rely on state endorsement or enforcement. The civil accountability that results (see Newell, Chapter 2) raises other significant issues for democratic politics, but failing to recognise its importance as an alternative site of accountability in the face of state negligence would be a mistake.

The importance of deepening accountability within civil society, particularly when representative functions are performed on behalf of the poor, is a theme that runs through the book. Power shifts resulting in part, but certainly not exclusively, from myriad processes of globalisation have altered profoundly the balance of rights and responsibilities and hence accountabilities between state, market and civil society actors (Newell et al. 2002). The ways in which this has occurred and its consequences are discussed at greater length in Chapter 2. Here the point is that we need to challenge the bias towards the state as the most appropriate and significant site of accountability reform. By looking in depth at struggles around corporate and civil society accountability, we hope this book takes forward thinking about the ways in which accountability can be deepened in new ways amongst a broader range of actors operating in multiple arenas. Increasing emphasis on 'citizen democracy' (UNDP 2004), 'citizen-centred governance' and 'global accountability' (Kovach et al. 2003) can be seen as evidence of the increasing acceptance, in some quarters at least, of a less state-centred approach to accountability. As Shah and Matthews note, 'technocratic approaches to public sector reform are unlikely to succeed.... Instead citizen empowerment through a rights-based approach to demand accountability from their governments and a rights-based culture of governance holds significant potential for success' (2005).

The politics of accountability

There is a tendency to assume that those actors supporting, funding and overseeing institutional reform for accountability do not have a stake in the reform process themselves. They do. And far from being neutral advocates of pro-poor accountability reforms, the way in which they intervene has an impact on rights that are respected or denied and accountabilities that are created or overlooked. The World Bank is an increasingly important actor in this area, but can hardly be said to be a neutral player in conflicts between competing rights claims, especially when revenues from natural resources are at stake. This book shows how the World Bank's association with the Plan Puebla Panama and the Global Environment Facility's role in local conservation projects in Mexcio have generated suspicion about the intentions of these actors regarding the control of environmental resources. The 2003 World Development Report on *Sustainable Development in a Dynamic Economy* advances the idea that the spectacular failure to tackle poverty and environmental degradation over the last decade is due to a failure of governance, 'poor implementation and not poor vision' (Foster 2002). As the report notes, 'Those [poverty and environmental] problems that can be coordinated through markets have typically done well; those that have not fared well include many for which the market could be made to work as a coordinator.' The challenge for governments is therefore to be more welcoming of private actors through, among other things, 'a smooth evolution of property rights from communal to private' (World Bank 2003). By pushing strongly for the protection of property rights as a solution to many conflicts over resources (Primo Braga *et al.* 2000), the rights of capital are automatically privileged over many communities with whom those rights may be in conflict.

Similarly, the neoliberal biases of many development institutions lead them to assume that clients and consumers are more effective accountability seekers and demanders than 'passive recipients' (or non-recipients) of state services. The World Development Report of 2004, for example, emphasises the importance of 'enabling the poor to monitor and discipline service providers' (World Bank 2004). Fiszbein, also writing for the World Bank, argues that the key issue in this regard is 'whether those responsible for designing and delivering services are accountable to the citizens who are demanding the services and also paying the taxes and fees that finance services' (2005). Power exercised through consumer choice in the market is said to improve basic services as firms compete to attract new customers. Corrupt, unresponsive firms will quickly lose customers in this model. The problem with such *marketised* notions of accountability is that they tend to overlook prior issues of exclusion and lack of access to key services. The very poorest, those most in need of services responsive to their needs, are of least interest to private utilities seeking to make a profit. For example, we shall see how in South Africa private contractors have cut off access to water when people are unable to pay, despite their constitutional right to water. Hence reducing accountability relationships to purchasing power invites an anti-poor bias (Whitfield 2001; Goetz and Gaventa 2001).

Placing power centrally, it becomes easier to discern why some forms of accountability politics are privileged over others, why some actors face more scrutiny than others, why some accountability deficits are addressed and others neglected. As we see in Chapter 2, this has to be understood in relation to the power wielded by key actors in development and their ability to project preferred discourses of accountability. For now, it is sufficient to note that, despite claims to the contrary, the politics of accountability are not value-neutral and key actors advancing the contemporary agenda in development are neither neutral bystanders nor indifferent to the outcomes.

Accountability and social justice

By framing the issue of accountability in narrow institutional terms we run the risk of failing to ask, let alone answer, the question of accountability *for what* and *for whom*? Who benefits, for example, from efforts to reform the state in ways prescribed by global economic institutions? If improved access for the poor is the aim, it is questionable that shifting service provision to private hands in the name of efficiency and combating corruption will achieve that, for some of the reasons stated above. On the other hand, promoting the accountability of corporations to the communities in which they invest through more effective use of public hearings or efforts to screen investment proposals – measures aimed at enhancing the exercise of social control over economic actors – may bring about a shift in the power imbalances that currently protect the powerful from scrutiny. A key theme emerging from the work presented in this book is that accountability struggles are invariably struggles for a broader social or economic good. They provide the means to an end which has to be specified in order to understand the utility and likely effectiveness of the strategy adopted.

Central to instances where these strategies lead to improved accountability are a set of methods that rely on the participation of poor and marginalised people. This book touches on a range of these methods, including citizen health monitoring and participatory development reports in India, community-based environmental audits in Mexico, local-level health councils in Brazil, and environmental justice clinics in the United States. Many of the chapters in this book are based on 'action research' engagements, where participatory methods for demanding accountability are part of the research process. Some important questions arise from these examples: how do these methods affect wider political structures and power relations; and what is their potential for contributing to the democratic processes that could contribute to wider social change? The potential of such strategies to contribute towards civil accountability is explored in Chapter 2, as well as more fully in the context of the case studies that describe the settings from which they are derived.

In sum, the project of accountability is not a politically neutral philanthropic exercise aimed at removing the obstacles that prevent the poor from realising rights and accessing justice. It can also seek to fulfil those aims, but it does not necessarily do so. Depending on the actor and the goal in mind, it may even be considered unlikely to do so. Misguided reforms can serve to further consolidate power if extra checks and balances are not introduced simultaneously – and not just within the formal institutions of governance but across society, creating new opportunities for democratic engagement about who performs which roles in society, on behalf of whom, and for what.

Neither is accountability a new concept. Rather it has been a narrative, albeit sometimes silent or subdued, running through the course of history, that describes the relations of power between those with more and less power. In this sense, the studies contained in this book suggest the need to reclaim the concept of accountability from the bureaucrats, the institutionalists and the development industry in general. It is a potentially powerful and emancipatory concept given that, at its core, it seeks to describe the appropriate relationship between state, market and civil society. Within the good governance agenda, this has been predominantly understood as a legal relationship, devoid of the social contracts that underpin it. This is a mistake, because it negates the politics and practice of accountability as it is experienced and lived by the world's poor on a daily basis. A conversation about accountability should be a conversation about democracy and rights, and how these can be constructed to reinforce one another. Acknowledging this allows us to engage in a more fundamental debate about what type of democracy we want. Struggles over resources provide one site for this conversation to begin, because access to resources is fundamental to substantive rights and the exercise of citizenship.

Conclusion: the citizenship dimension

Because rights frame the possibilities for making claims, and accountability frames the relationships between actors and institutions that are necessary for these rights to be realised, important implications for citizenship emerge.

Understanding the politics of the relationships between rights, resources and the politics of accountability draws attention to both the risks of greater exclusion and fragmentation, as powerful interests marshal control over important resources, and the potential for an increase in awareness and implementation of rights that can construct substantive citizenship. What is at issue here is the right to have rights, particularly where resources are at stake. Accountability struggles and strategies, through seeking to challenge the power relations that shield state and other actors from answerability, are an important element in making citizenship real.

Though we have argued that accountability, in the first instance, should be about the relationship between the powerful and those with less power, we have noted that state accountability is privileged over all other forms of accountability, not least within the good governance agenda. The assumption is that democracy will be achieved once the institutional mechanisms that allow citizens to hold states accountable are in place. Yet the strategies for demanding accountability explored in this book demonstrate a variety of actor-orientated forms of citizenship, where the boundaries between state and society are blurred, and citizen participation in accountability struggles is an essential element of how citizenship is constituted (see Leach, Scoones and Wynne 2005).

By shedding new light on diverse strategies and approaches to accountability, a more nuanced picture of citizenship emerges. Kabeer argues in *Inclusive Citizenship*, an earlier book in this series, that substantive citizenship from the perspectives of marginalised and excluded groups is based on justice, recognition, self-determination and solidarity. She goes on to make a case for recasting 'vertical' citizenship, based on the narrow relationship between people and states, into 'horizontal' citizenship, which recognises the multiple and overlapping connections and relationships that actually emerge from daily experiences. As many of the chapters in that volume show, collective action has been crucial in addressing 'situations where the state has proved consistently unresponsive to the needs of its citizens' (Kabeer 2005: 23).

Citizenship, then, is also understood in relation to processes of demanding accountability from powerful actors and institutions. Possibilities for accountability are, therefore, strongly shaped by how citizenship is exercised, enforced and denied. If making accountability demands (on the state, or even the private sector and civil society actors) is a way of expressing citizenship, then there are important linkages between accountability struggles and the character of citizenship. In order to be able to make accountability claims, there must be an implicit assumption about the roles and responsibilities of the state, as well as the rights and entitlements of citizens.

Several chapters in this book also point to how involvement in struggles for accountability can change people's perceptions of their rights, responsibilities and, indeed, their role as citizens. Because demands for rights are linked to accountability, these struggles can change the way people understand citizenship. In Bangladesh, the right of women to work in the garment industry has had important implications for citizenship. Despite the accountability problems in the garment sector, the right to work has challenged certain elements of patriarchy by giving a new sense of entitlement and citizenship to many women. Through increased financial independence, women have gained an awareness about rights and citizenship that might not have been possible otherwise.

In so far as citizenship confers material and political (process) rights, it also implies access to resources and channels of representation in decision-making processes that govern their use. Even with an increased awareness of rights, marginalised and excluded groups are unlikely to consider themselves true citizens if they are unable to access resources and entitlements such as adequate housing, health care, clean water and unpolluted living areas (see Wheeler 2003). When we use a resource lens to understand struggles for rights and accountability, the importance of daily struggles against material deprivations comes to the fore. This highlights the role that the lack of access to resources can play in denying substantive citizenship and unravelling shared imaginings of political community. Watts (2003: 5097) notes the importance of oil to the nation-building process and the creation of an 'oil nation'. He argues that it 'is a national resource on which citizenship claims can be constructed. As much as the state uses oil to build a nation and to develop, so communities use oil wealth to activate community claims.' The lack of access to resources and the politics of gaining that access are bound up not only in individual perceptions of citizenship, but also in the overall sense of belonging and recognition that underlies national citizenship.

Though we have sought to locate this book in relation to existing literatures and debates, and to summarise some of their insights for a broader audience, we hope that one of the greatest contributions of these studies will be to illuminate experiences of struggles for rights and accountability from around the world as *lived* experiences. As Eckstein and Wickham-Crowley note: 'A full understanding of rights begs for empirically grounded analyses, not philosophical "what ifs"' (2003: 1). 'Ordinary people ... respond to their lived experiences and their understanding of those experiences, not to the intellectual frames the scholarly community imposes to make sense of those experiences' (2003: 51). The studies that form the basis of this book attempt to engage people's own terms of reference for making sense of accountability and rights struggles. This helps to capture the diverse value systems people have and the cultural repertoires they employ to understand the politics of accountability. We hope that this book offers some insights into the prospects for substantive improvements in accountability, where poor and marginalised groups have a central role in achieving change.

Structure of the book

Chapter 2 provides a critical overview of debates about accountability in development, exploring competing notions of political, social, financial and civil accountability in relation to the key themes of the book.

The remainder of the book is divided into two sections. The first focuses on cases where the entry point for accountability struggles is formal and informal rights that are directly related to particular resources. The second brings together cases where accountability claims are broader than a specific right to a resource, framed around concerns with land, working conditions or access to resource revenues. This section includes examples where accountability struggles engage more specifically with corporate actors.

The first section of the book includes chapters where rights to a particular resource are at the heart of attempts to claim accountability. In Chapter 3 Lyla Mehta explores the case of South Africa, where there is a constitutional right to water, in order to understand issues of accountability where the state nevertheless fails to implement the right to water. It looks at how the right to water is implemented in practice – and at the contradictions between a rights-based approach to water and a market-driven approach. This chapter shows both the difficulties of operationalising formal rights, and how the right to water has had mixed effects on the lives of the poor in South Africa.

In Chapter 4 Luisa Paré and Carlos Robles focus on struggles for accountability by rural indigenous groups engaged in the sustainable management of a rapidly declining watershed in Veracruz, Mexico. There are many different actors and overlapping institutions involved, with often competing interests, including traditional/communal structures such as *ejidos*[2] and urban and rural municipal governments. Paré and Robles, on the basis of their long engagement as action researchers in the region, discuss how, together with the indigenous communities, they have been able to implement mechanisms to increase accountability, where the meanings of accountability are deeply rooted in local experiences and culture.

In Chapter 5 Carlos Cortéz and Luisa Paré, presenting another case from Mexico, compare the accountability issues emerging from two protected natural areas (PNAs) or reserves designed to conserve rainforest. As these PNAs are established, conflicts over the meaning of land rights and knowledge rights (especially traditional medicinal knowledge) emerge. These conflicts are in part a result of the overlapping web of actors and institutions involved in the PNAs. Within a context of conflict, where there are fundamental and underlying disagreements about what the environment and 'nature' mean, the prospects for accountability lie in political mobilisation.

In Chapter 6 Celestine Nyamu-Musembi documents the story of a tenants' association in Mombasa, Kenya, which is seeking to claim the right to housing and demand accountability from the local government. In the process, the association calls upon international legal frameworks that guarantee the right to adequate shelter. But when the local government proves unresponsive, residents use direct action to challenge the lack of accountability. This chapter help expose dilemmas facing community-based groups who use rights as an accountability strategy.

Finally, Chapter 7 by Andrea Cornwall, Silvia Cordeiro and Nelson Delgado focuses on the right to health in North-eastern Brazil. The main mechanism for accountability in this case is a local health council, mandated by the Brazilian constitution, that acts to oversee health care provision in a particular municipality. This chapter explores how the complex political dynamics involved in the council undermine the prospects for accountability.

The second part of the book explores questions of corporate accountability. Chapter 8 – by Peter Newell with Vaijanyanta Anand, Hasrat Arjjumend, Harsh Jaitli, Sampath Kumar, and A.B.S.V. Ranga Rao – uses three case studies from India to expose the frontline of corporate accountability where communities confront corporations in situations of huge power disparity. The case studies include the controversy surrounding the National Thermal Power Corporation power plant in Andhra Pradesh; the struggles around the development of the Lote Industrial area in Maharastra; and conflicts around tribal rights and mining in Jharkhand. Newell et al. catalogue some of the community-based strategies that have been used to challenge corporate power at a local level, reflecting on their effectiveness and the implications for corporate accountability.

In a similar vein, Chapter 9 by Rohit Lehki and Peter Newell also analyses community-based strategies for corporate accountability. It does so by bringing experiences from the global North into the book, focusing on the environmental justice movement in the United States. The chapter documents some of the strategies used by activists from communities of colour to demand greater accountability from state and corporate actors for the location of sites of hazardous and toxic waste in their neighbourhoods. Reflecting on the role of law in particular, this chapter shows both the importance of judicial activism and the ways in which the law can work against the poor.

Amidst the extensive literature on oil and the resource curse in Nigeria, Chapter 10 by Oga Steve Abah and Jenks Okwori explores community-level perspectives on accountability through drama and participatory research. The focus of this chapter is on the meanings and dynamics of accountability at the community level in a context of resource abundance where corporations exert significant influence. Perceived collusion between government and the oil companies operating in the Niger Delta has led to the creation of youth groups and womens' organisations, working with and at times claiming to represent communities in ways that themselves create new accountability challenges. Their activities are understood as a response to the failures of the state to guarantee accountability.

Chapter 11, by Naila Kabeer and Simeen Mahmud, considers the challenge of creating a culture of accountability around labour rights in the context of the garment industry in Bangladesh. They contrast a culture of compliance, deriving from buyer pressure for the adoption of international standards, with a culture of accountability that challenges more fundamental relations of power in the workplace. The competitive and globalised nature of the garment industry, and the poor track record of the state and labour unions in protecting labour rights, mean that garment workers are confronted with difficult choices in demanding accountability from their employers and articulating the rights that matter to them most.

Finally, also on the theme of worker rights, Stephanie Luce documents the experiences of the living wage movement in the United States. She shows how the movement has had to use strategies both within existing power structures (in direct negotiations with municipal government) and outside them (through public protest) in order to achieve greater accountability and the implementation of the living wage. Facing the difficulty of setting an acceptable and applicable living wage standard, workers' organisations have fought instead for the right to a living wage that can be tailored to the context in which it is to be realised.

NOTES

1 See, for example, Edwards and Gaventa 2001; Keck and Sikkink 1998; Cohen and Rai 2000.

2 *Ejidos* are traditionally communally-held plots of land, where the right of use is passed through inheritance.

REFERENCES

ADB (2005) 'ADB's accountability mechanism', Asian Development Bank, www.abd.org/ Accountability-mechanism/default.asp, 13 April, accessed 6 July 2005.

Anderson, M. (1996) 'Human Rights Approaches to Environmental Protection: an Overview', in A. Boyle and M. Anderson (eds), *Human Rights Approaches to Environmental Protection*, Oxford: Clarendon Press, pp. 1–25.

Bannon, I. and Collier, P. (2003) *Natural Resources and Violent Conflict: Options and Actions*, Washington, DC: World Bank, August.

Baviskar, Amita (2003) 'For a cultural politics of natural resources' in *Economic and Political Weekly* Vol. XXXVIII No.48, pp. 5051-5056.

Boyle, A. (1996) 'The Role of International Human Rights Law in the Protection of the Environment', in A. Boyle and M. Anderson (eds), *Human Rights Approaches to Environmental Protection*, Oxford: Clarendon Press, pp. 43–71.

Boyle, A. and Anderson, M. (eds) (1996) *Human Rights Approaches to Environmental Protection*, Oxford: Clarendon Press.

Cohen, R. and Rai, S. (2000) *Global Social Movements*, London: Athlone.

Cornwall, A. and Nyamu-Musembi, C. (2005) 'Why Rights, Why Now? Reflections on the Rise of Rights in International Development Discourse,' in Pettit, J. and Wheeler, J. (eds), *Developing Rights?* IDS Bulletin 36: 1, Brighton: Institute of Development Studies.

DfiD (2001) *Making Government Work for Poor People*, Governance Target Strategy, London: Department for International Development.

—— (2005) 'Public Financial Management and Accountability', Department for International Development, www.dfid.gov.uk/aboutdfid/organisation/pfma/pfma-pets.pdf, accessed 6 July 2005.

—— (2005a) *Promoting Institutional and Organisational Development*, London: Department for International Development.

Dia, M. (1993) *A Governance Approach to Civil Service Reform in Sub-Saharan Africa*, Washington: World Bank.

—— (1996) *Africa's Management in the 1990s and Beyond: Reconciling Indigenous and Transplanted Institutions*, Washington, DC: World Bank.

Dworkin, R. (1978) *Taking Rights Seriously*, London: Duckworth.

Eckstein, S. E. and Wickham-Crowley, T. (2003) *Struggles for Social Rights in Latin America* London: Routledge

Edwards, M. and Gaventa, J. (eds), (2001) *Global Citizen Action*, Boulder: Lynne Rienner Press.

Edwards, S. (1996) *Dismantling the Populist State: the Unfinished Revolution in Latin America and the Caribbean*, Washington, DC: World Bank, July.

Escobar, A. and Alvarez, S. (eds) (1992) *The Making of Social Movements in Latin America: Identity, Strategy and Democracy*, Boulder, Colorado and Oxford: Westview Press.

Evans, G., Goodman, J. and Lansbury, N. (eds) (2002) *Moving Mountains: Communities Confront Mining and Globalisation*, London: Zed Books.

Fabra, A. (1996) 'Indigenous Peoples, Environmental Degradation and Human Rights: a Case Study' in A. Boyle and M. Anderson (eds), *Human Rights Approaches to Environmental Protection*, Oxford: Clarendon Press, pp. 245–65.

Fiszbein, A. (2005) *Citizens, Politicians and Providers: the Latin American Experience with Service Delivery Reform*, Washington, DC: World Bank.

Foster, P. (2002) 'The WDR 2003: Greenwashing Globalization' in *Managing Sustainability World Bank Style: an Evaluation of the World Development Report*, Washington, DC and

London: Heinrich Boll Foundation and Bretton Woods Project, pp. 48–53.

Frynas, G. (1998) 'Political Instability and Business: Focus on Shell in Nigeria', *Third World Quarterly*, Vol. 19, No. 3, pp. 457–79.

Garcia-Guadilla and Blauert, J. (eds) (1994) *Retos para la desarallo y la democracia: Movimentos ambientales en America Latina y Europa* Mexico: Fundacion Fredrich Ebert de Mexico y Venezuela: Nueva Sociedad.

Goetz, A. M. and Gaventa, J. *et al.* (2001) 'Bringing Citizen Voice and Client Focus into Service Delivery', IDS Working Paper 138, Brighton: Institute of Development Studies.

Goetz, A. M. and Jenkins, R. (2004) *Reinventing Accountability: Making Democracy Work for Human Development*, Basingstoke: Palgrave.

Goldman, M. (1998) *Privatizing Nature: Political Struggles for the Global Commons*, London: Pluto Press.

Jones, P. (1994) *Rights*, Issues in Political Theory series, Basingstoke: MacMillan.

Keck, M. E. and Sikkink, K. (1998) *Activists Beyond Borders: Advocacy Networks in International Politics* Itacha and London: Cornell University Press.

Kovach, H., Negan, C. and Burrall, S. (2003) *Power without Accountability? The Global Accountability Report*, London: One World Trust.

Leach, M., Scoones, I. and Wynne, B. (eds) (2005) *Citizens and Science: Globalisation and the Challenge of Engagement*, London: Zed Books.

MacKay, F. (2002) 'The Rights of Indigenous People in International Law', in L. Zarsky (ed.), *Human Rights and the Environment: Conflicts and Norms in a Globalizing World*, London: Earthscan, pp. 9–31.

Mehta, L. (2003) 'Contexts and constructions of water scarcity' in *Economic and Political Weekly* Vol. 38, No. 48 pp. 5066–72.

Merills, J. G. (1996) 'Environmental Protection and Human Rights: Conceptual Aspects', in A. Boyle and M. Anderson (eds), *Human Rights Approaches to Environmental Protection*, Oxford: Clarendon Press, pp. 25–43.

Mintz, S. W. (1986) *Sweetness and Power: the Place of Sugar in Modern History*, New York: Penguin.

Narayan, D. (ed.) (2005) *Measuring Empowerment: Cross-disciplinary Perspectives*, Washington, DC: World Bank, April.

Newell, P., Rai, S. and Scott, A. (eds) (2000) *Development and the Challenge of Globalization*, London: Intermediate Technology Development Group (ITDG) Press.

Paul, S. (2002) 'New Mechanisms of Public Accountability: the Indian Experience', United Nations Development Programme (UNDP), www.undp.org/governance/discount/ new-mechanisms-accountability.pdf, accessed 6 July 2005.

Peet, R. and Watts, M. (1996) (eds) *Liberation Ecologies: Environment, development, social movements* London: Routledge

Pettit, J. and Wheeler, J. (eds) (2005) *Developing Rights?* IDS Bulletin 36:1 Brighton: Institute of Development Studies.

Piron, L-H. (2005) 'Rights-based Approaches and Bilateral Aid Agencies: More Than a Metaphor?' in Pettit, J. and Wheeler, J. (eds), *Developing Rights?* IDS Bulletin 36: 1, Brighton: Institute of Development Studies.

Primo Braga, C., Fink, C. and Paz Sepulveda, C. (2000) *Intellectual Property Rights and Economic Development*, Washington, DC: World Bank.

Puymbroeck, R. van (2001) (ed.) *Comprehensive Legal and Judicial Development: Towards an Agenda for a Just and Equitable Society in the Twenty-first Century*, Washington: World Bank.

Roulier, R. P. (1995) 'Bank Governance Contracts: Establishing Goals and Accountability in Bank Restructuring', World Bank Discussion Paper No. 308, Washington, DC: World Bank, November.

Sanchez Rubio, D., Solorzano Alfaro, N. J. and Lucena Cid, I. V. (eds) (2004) *Nuevos Colonialismos del Capital: Propriedad Intelectual, Biodiversidad y Derechos de los Pueblos*, Barcelona: Icaria y FIADH (Fundacion Iberoamericano de Derechos Humanos).

Shah, A. (2005) *Public Services Delivery*, Washington, DC: World Bank, June.

Shah, A. and Andrews, M. (2005) *Citizen-Centred Governance*, Washington, DC: World Bank.

Soopramien, R., Ofosu-Amaah, W. P. and Uprety, K. (1999) *Combating Corruption: a Comparative Review of Selected Aspects of State Practice and International Initiatives*, Washington, DC: World Bank, July.

Stephens, C., Bullock, S. and Scott, A. (2001) 'Environmental Justice: Rights and Means for a Healthy Environment for All', Special Briefing No. 7 (November), Swindon: Economic and Social Research Council.

Watts, M. (2003) 'Economies of violence: More oil, more blood' *Economic and Political Weekly* Vol. 38, No. 48, pp. 5089–99.

Wheeler, J. S., (2003) 'New Forms of Citizenship: democracy, family, and community in Rio de Janeiro, Brazil'. *Gender and Development*, Vol 11: No 3.

Whitfield, D. (2001) *Public Services or Corporate Welfare: Rethinking the Nation State in the Global Economy*, London: Pluto Press.

Wild, A. (2005) *Black Gold: a Dark History of Coffee*, London: Harper Collins.

UNDP (2000) 'Using Indicators for Human Rights Accountability', Chapter 5, *Human Development Report*, New York: Oxford University Press and United Nations Development Programme.

—— (2004) *Democracy in Latin America: Towards a Citizen's Democracy*, New York: United Nations Development Programme.

—— (2005) United Nations Development Programme website, (www.undp.org.fi/gold/accountability.ftm)

World Bank (1992) *Governance and Development*, Washington, DC: World Bank, May.

—— (1994) *Governance: the World Bank's Experience*, Washington, DC: World Bank.

—— (1998) *Beyond the Washington Consensus: Institutions Matter*, Washington, DC: World Bank.

—— (2000) *Anti-Corruption in Transition: a Contribution to the Policy Debate*, Washington, DC: World Bank.

—— (2003) *Sustainable Development in a Dynamic World: Transforming Institutions, Growth and Quality of Life*, World Development Report, New York: Oxford University Press.

—— (2004) *Making Services Work for Poor People*, World Development Report, New York: Oxford University Press and World Bank.

Zarsky, L. (2002) 'Global Reach: Human Rights and Environment in the Framework of Corporate Accountability', in L. Zarsky (ed.), *Human Rights and the Environment: Conflicts and Norms in a Globalizing World*, London: Earthscan, pp. 31–57.

CHAPTER 2

Taking accountability into account:
the debate so far

PETER NEWELL

> Accountability is a perpetual struggle when power is delegated by the
> many to the few in the interests of governability.... To these perennial
> problems, globalisation and political liberalisation have added new ones.
> Powerful non-state actors capable of influencing the lives of ordinary
> people have multiplied, often act with impunity across borders and can
> evade the reach of conventional state-based accountability systems.
> (Goetz and Jenkins 2004: 1)

The idea that accountability is central to ensuring that political and
market institutions respond to the needs of the poor has acquired the
status of a 'given' in mainstream development orthodoxy. However, the
popularity of the term in contemporary development debates, devoid of
an analysis of the power relations that it assumes, will do little to help us
understand the ways in which institutional and market failure and abuses
of power impact upon the lives of the poor. Though it has some potential
to identify and challenge the circuits of power that maintain and validate
social exclusion and inequity, the way accountability is currently understood and promoted in development debates is as likely to reinforce
hierarchy and marginalisation and miss important opportunities to
generate change. Politicising the term, on the other hand, provides for a
more fundamental set of conversations about power in development, for
whom it is exercised, how and with what consequences. Such a shift brings
to our attention how the webs of accountability that flow between dispersed and disaggregated decision makers and decision takers graft on to
the changing relations between state, market and society. It allows us to
ask:

- *what* is accountability for? (what broader political ends does it serve);
- *who* is it for? (who benefits, who articulates those claims, who bears
  rights to accountability);

- *how* is it practised? (through what means and processes);
- *where* is it practised? (in which sites and across what levels of political decision making).

Each of these questions is intimately connected to the others and implies a different set of strategies and claim making, as the discussion below reveals. At the same time, each allows us to explore different and volatile dimensions of the accountability debate. Goetz and Jenkins (2004: 4) argue, for example, that it is the dimension of the debate around '*for what*' the powerful are being held to account that is being most dramatically reinvented, as expectations proliferate about the functions of *governance* and the standards by which performance of these obligations should be judged. As we see in the section of the book on corporate accountability, this is as true of corporate actors (amid claims about their broader responsibilities to society) as it is of the state. Impact upon a community's human development, rather than compliance with narrowly defined financial and technical rules, is increasingly relevant as a standard of accountability for judging the private sector. Posing these critical questions provides a starting point for reclaiming the transformative potential of ideas about accountability to change structures and relations of power, and not merely to consolidate the power of the already powerful through better systems of reporting and auditing that validate their actions and omissions.

The argument developed in this chapter is, first, that the ability to demand and exercise accountability implies power. The right to demand and the capacity and willingness to respond to calls for accountability assume relations of power. This seemingly obvious observation is at odds with much of the contemporary debate, which seeks to render accountability claims manageable by reducing them to improved systems of management and auditing. Second, these power relations are in a state of flux, reflecting the contested basis of relations between the state, civil society and market actors. These relations both create and restrict the possibilities of new forms of accountability by generating novel dynamics of power through material change and changes in the organisation of political authority.

Beyond these material and political shifts, at a discursive level we find that exercises of power are justified and advanced by prevailing constructions of accountability and the entitlements they presume. These narratives, which are the product of a particular set of historical and material circumstances, validate some forms of power and delegitimise others. The interaction between political action, material change and discursive practices is what helps us to understand the distinct expressions of accountability politics explored in this book – in diverse settings and issue arenas, and as they are applied to different actors. These interactions also provide the basis for understanding the place of accountability in broader constructions of citizenship and discourses around rights, who gets to define these, and the implications of this for the poor. Challenging prevailing conceptions of accountability means engaging with change at the material, organisational and discursive levels that define the possibilities of alternative accountabilities.

Conceptualising accountability

In so far as an enquiry into the practice of accountability in development is an enquiry into how to control the exercise of power, we can view contemporary debates as a continuation of concerns that have driven political philosophy for several hundred years. Beginning with the ancient philosophers, political thinkers have been concerned to prevent abuses by restraining power within established rules. In contemporary usage, the notion of accountability continues to express this concern, attempting to apply checks, oversight and institutional constraints on the exercise of power. It implies both a measure of *answerability* (providing an account of actions undertaken) and *enforceability* (punishment or sanctions for poor or illegal performance) (Schedler *et al.* 1999). In its broadest sense, then, accountability is about the construction of a grammar of conduct and performance and the standards used to assess them (Day and Klein 1987).

During the last decade, the language of accountability has gained increasing prominence in development debates (Newell and Bellour 2002). Appropriated by a myriad of international donor and academic discourses, accountability has become a malleable and often nebulous concept, with connotations that change with the context and agenda. The widespread use of the term means that 'its field of application is as broad as its potential for consensus' (Schedler 1999: 13). It represents, nevertheless, 'an under-explored concept whose meaning remains evasive, whose boundaries are fuzzy and whose internal structure is confusing' (*ibid.*). For Brinkerhoff, the worrying implication of the lack of conceptual and analytical clarity is that 'Accountability risks becoming another buzzword in a long line of ineffectual quick fixes' (2004: 372). Its prevalent use in recent years can be explained by shifts in the strategic thinking of key development agencies with regard to the state, in particular, and the importance of creating mechanisms of accountability to citizens of the state (Goetz and Gaventa 2001). Though the term accountability generally refers to holding actors responsible for their actions, questions such as accountability for what, by whom, and to whom immediately arise (Cornwall, Lucas and Pasteur 2000). This, indeed, has been the entry point of the contributors to this book, who pose questions about accountability in exactly these terms.

Rather than attempting to formulate another definition of accountability or to refine one of the many existing formulations, in this book we have sought to interpret the conflicts of power through multiple lenses of accountability which derive from the contexts in which they are situated. There is no global grammar of accountability that makes sense across settings. The diversity of struggles explored in this book demonstrates the different expectations, histories and values that people bring to bear upon understandings of the respective rights, duties and responsibilities of social actors. Even agreeing a common working understanding of the term among the contributors to this book was a difficult task: for example, the very term accountability does not exist in Spanish. It is clearly a malleable and evolving concept that has to be understood in relation to the conflicts and struggles it is being used to describe. The following section explores some of the macro manifestations of shifting understandings of accountability politics.

Shifting accountabilities

In so far as accountability implies practices of power, it is unsurprising that its ideas and ideologies are promoted, sustained and contested by competing political actors. These discourses generate expectations, duties and conduct that change the practice of accountability politics. The historical and material context in which they are produced ensures that they relate strongly to the structures and actors that generate them. In this sense the construction of accountabilities, the definition of the rights and duties that flow from relations of accountability, is fundamentally a political process driven by broader economic and political agendas. For example, the predominant focus on state accountability can be understood in the light of prevailing notions about the appropriate relationship between states and markets, and assumptions within neoliberal ideology about the inefficiency and lack of responsiveness of states to the needs of citizens, defined as consumers.

From states...
From being the traditional subjects for the application of political and fiscal accountability measures, states are also becoming the principal

targets for improving the responsiveness of services to the poor. In the case of health sector reform, Brinkerhoff notes that concern with accountability derives from 'dissatisfaction with health system performance ... costs, quality assurance, service availability ... financial mismanagement and corruption and lack of responsiveness' (2004: 371). This market rationale for accountability is apparent in the way state functions are often equated with 'service delivery', a move which makes it easier for market advocates to argue that private actors may be able to provide the same services more cost-effectively and efficiently. As state service delivery systems have become more complex and as providers' roles have changed, it has become more difficult to assign responsibility, however. With service provision being increasingly shared with other actors, the boundaries of state accountability are blurring, as we see in Chapter 3 on water provision in South Africa.

Since initial conceptualisations of accountability have been derived from ways to improve state mechanisms, policies and processes, it is unsurprising that current debates should reflect and focus upon state-based notions of accountability. Indeed states remain the predominant reference point in debates about accountability and development despite the fact that accountability demands are increasingly made of non-state actors. The rhetoric of public accountability has grown with the increasing popularity of new public management approaches and renewed attention to state bureaucracy and administration associated with the 'good governance' agenda pursued by donors (Considine 2002). According to the United Nations Development Programme (UNDP), the concepts of responsiveness, accountability and transparency are among the core characteristics of good governance (UNDP 1997: 4). The turn back towards viewing the state as a key actor in development was in many ways led by the World Bank in its 1997 *World Development Report*, on 'The State in a Changing World' (World Bank 1997). Since then there has been repeated emphasis on enhancing accountability through increased state responsiveness.

Contemporary discourses of democracy have also highlighted the importance of state accountability to wider processes of democratisation (Luckham and White 1996). By promoting free and fair elections and mechanisms to hold governments accountable to their publics, international donors have emphasised themes of democratic governance (UNDP 1997: 3). While concepts of public accountability have long been associated with democratic theory and practice, the contemporary wave of transitions from authoritarian rule to democratic governance has highlighted the importance of answerability and enforcement mechanisms in new democracies (Oxhorn and Ducatenzeiler 1998). These trends have shown that without systems providing 'credible restraints' on power, many democratic regimes remain 'low-quality'. If deficiencies in accountability structures are often more visible in new democracies, demands for public accountability in old and new democratic states share a core assumption that elections are, by themselves, no guarantee of good governance. The experience of many new democracies provides evidence of this, as many continue to be haunted by human rights violations, corruption, clientelism and abuses of power, despite universal suffrage and multi-party elections (Schedler *et al.* 1999: 2).

There has also been increasing attention to the potential of decentralisation to deepen democracy through democratic local governance (Blair 2000; Posner 2003). The rationale is that decision making is more likely to be responsive to local needs the more it involves those directly affected by decisions, and that embedding decision making within strong webs of accountability that flow in all directions increases the probability of governance that benefits the poor, making such a regime both 'more responsive to citizen desires and more effective in service delivery' (Blair 2000: 21). Manor reports, however, that despite the assumption that decentralising decision making serves to enhance state responsiveness to the needs of the poor and popular control over decision making, he has 'yet to discover evidence of any case where local élites were more benevolent than those at higher levels' (Manor 1999: 91). Where enforcement mechanisms complement processes for creating answerability, the situation may be different. In Bolivia, for example, vigilance committees are entitled to monitor local budgets and can wield a legal instrument called a *denuncia* against local councils. This means that there is a process by which central funds to the local council that has been denounced can be suspended. As with other strategies aimed at enhancing the accountability of public and private actors, the combinations of tactics that will make an impact depend, amongst other things, on the responsiveness of the state, the sensitivity of the issue in question and the prevailing political culture.

... To markets ...

Recent global trends, however, are bringing into question the appropriateness of this focus on holding governments to account for decisions and actions that increasingly result from bargains with, and the actions of, non-state and private actors. The rapid growth in cross-border economic transactions in trade, production and finance has brought about changes in political authority at national and international levels and, as a result, transformed many traditional arenas of accountability. In the wake of globalisation and associated patterns of deregulation and liberalisation, global corporate power has gained increasing sway, leading to greater corporate influence over activities that traditionally have been the prerogative of states. With revenues that often dwarf the gross domestic products (GDPs) of many developing countries, transnational corporations (TNCs) are often more powerful than governments, and the mobility that allows them to locate their business in the most favourable regulatory environment gives them sufficient leverage to play one government off against another. We see from the chapters in this book on the pursuit of labour rights in the United States and Bangladesh that capital mobility also strongly and negatively impacts upon the ability of trade unions to hold corporations to account over the recognition of labour rights. As a result, it often seems that TNCs wield power without responsibility: they are as powerful as states, yet less accountable. As Vidal notes, 'Corporations have never been more powerful, yet less regulated; never more pampered by government, yet never less questioned; never more needed to take social responsibility yet never more secretive.... To whom will these fabulously self-motivated, self-interested supranational bodies be accountable?' (Vidal 1996: 263).

The imbalance between the rights and responsibilities of firms is also increasingly manifested at the global level where there is an imbalance between *regulation for* business rather than *regulation of* business (Newell 2001a). The entitlements and rights of corporations are enshrined in international agreements aimed at freeing up restrictions on investment. The attempt to negotiate a Multilateral Agreement on Investment, the conclusion by the World Trade Organisation (WTO) of the Trade-Related Intellectual Property Rights (TRIPs) accord and the General Agreement on Trade in Services (GATS) all provide evidence of this. Gill (1995) refers to this as the 'new constitutionalism', in which the rights of capital are affirmed, legally protected and upheld above those of states. Each of these agreements affords new rights to companies while circumscribing the powers of national and local authority over investors.

Not only has this brought about a renegotiation of relations between state and market, but there is also some evidence of a transformation of relations between actors such as TNCs, non-governmental organisations (NGOs), and international organisations. This has resulted in a more complex and dense set of obligations and responsibilities between different actors in development, creating both opportunities for the construction of new accountabilities and new *accountability gaps*. Accountability gaps can emerge where shifts of political authority take place, between state and market for example, without the creation of new accountability mechanisms. The way in which both the private sector and NGOs have become involved in the delivery of services that were traditionally the preserve of the state, such as health and education, has raised concerns about whether these new service providers have the same incentives, or channels of access, to respond to public demands and complaints in the way expected of states. When private actors perform public functions in this way, the issue of responsiveness to the poor is heightened, because they are working to a different mandate: profit maximisation and not service delivery for all (Whitfield 2001).

... to civil society

Just as the private sector plays an increasingly privileged role in service delivery, so civil society organisations are increasingly used by development agencies as aid deliverers because they are thought to provide more accountable, effective and equitable services, in many areas, than public or private agencies. As a result, large amounts of aid are channelled through NGOs. The very popularity of NGOs among donors and publics, which helps to explain their exponential rise, creates its own accountability gaps, however. Where NGOs have formed global alliances in order to enhance their effectiveness, questions arise about the identity of the constituency – if any – to which they are answerable. There are concerns, too, over the potential of NGO activity to become disembedded once groups become less dependent on a traditional support base and work instead to global donor or campaign agendas, set and negotiated with other partners.

Hence there has been a reappraisal of the role of NGOs, once the darlings of the development world, as service delivers and agents of democratisation (Najam 1996; Edwards and Hulme 1995). While NGOs do not necessarily perform less effectively than other public or private organisations, they often perform less well than the popular image suggests (Edwards and Hulme 1995: 6). NGOs can be as susceptible as other institutions to the problems of corruption, cooptation, opportunism and political manoeuvring. The issue here is not only accountability gaps, but also the potential for inconsistent standards and expectations regarding the conduct and degree of answerability of public and private actors. On these grounds, the World Bank has been criticised for demanding far higher standards of accountability from governments than from the NGO and private actors that increasingly also provide 'state' services.

The challenge of ensuring accountability is multiplied when political authority is shared, as it increasingly is, across a number of levels from the local to the national, the regional and the global. The term *multi-level governance* describes the layers of overlapping authority that characterise decision making in the current global system. The spectacular growth of supranational authorities and regionalism, with international regimes governing an increasingly broad spectrum of areas of social and economic life, add to this institutional complexity and potentially create further democratic deficits. The challenge, from a development point of view, is how to ensure that decisions that affect the lives of the poor, but are taken in arenas remote from those lives, remain responsive to local needs.

It is clear from this discussion that traditional definitions of accountability are being expanded to adjust to new realities. Indeed, many of the political and economic changes described in Chapter 1 have rendered increasingly permeable the categorisations of accountability described below. Blurred lines of authority, competing jurisdictions and shifting social expectations have produced messier and denser webs of accountability between states, market actors and civil society. The following sections explore *accountability types*: whether political, financial, social or civil, all are principally associated with a particular type of actor but also describe distinct approaches to, and practices of, accountability. For example, we see how financial accountability is increasingly demanded of private and civil society as well as state actors; how political accountability is no longer provided within the state but increasingly also by civil society actors acting as watchdogs of state action; and how civil accountability, traditionally pursued by pressure groups, is increasingly being sought by community-based groups in defence of their livelihood rights. Notions of accountability *to whom* and *for what* are continually evolving – a product of the coincidence of proliferating accountability gaps and an increasing sense in which, even if accountability is not a right, people have a right to claim it.

Political accountability

Traditional notions of political accountability are derived from the responsibilities of delegated individuals in public office to carry out specific tasks on behalf of citizens. It is this sense of accountability, in which rulers explain and justify actions to the ruled, that traditionally distinguished a democratic society from a tyrannical one. In the Athenian state, this meant holding officials accountable for their actions; more modern notions of political accountability have focused on ministerial accountability and the ability of parliament to call the executive powers to account. Thus democratic accountability is characterised not only by elections to determine who runs the affairs of society, but also by the continuing obligation of these officials to explain and justify their conduct in public. Though accountability is traditionally seen as a retrospective account of past actions (*ex post*), more radical constructions involve actors making public their intended actions before they are taken, promoting public engagement through consultation and deliberation (*ex ante*) (Day and Klein 1987).

In the modern state, with the growth of bureaucracies, the lines of political accountability have become more blurred, making traditional concepts more difficult to apply. Contemporary discussions of accountability have broadened to include both *horizontal* and *vertical* mechanisms of political accountability. Horizontal mechanisms amount to self-imposed accountability within the state machinery. Vertical accountability, on the other hand, is that which is demanded from below by citizens and civil society groups (Schacter 2000: 1). In this sense, horizontal accountability refers to the capacity of state institutions to counter abuses by other public agencies and branches of government through checks and balances on the powers of the judiciary, executive and legislature. In reality it may also be exercised by anti-corruption bodies, auditors general, electoral and human rights commissions and other ombudsmen. To be effective, horizontal accountability needs to be buttressed by strong vertical accountability, in which citizens, mass media and civil associations are in a position to scrutinise public officials and government practice in the ways suggested by approaches to social accountability discussed below.

We noted above the centrality of mechanisms of enforceability to practicable notions of accountability. Different forms of accountability rely on different enforcement mechanisms, but accountability is only as effective as the mechanisms it employs, and 'inconsequential accountability is not accountability at all' (Schedler *et al.* 1999: 17). To deliver answerability effectively, sanctions are key. Sanctions can be both 'soft' and 'hard'. Soft sanctions refer to tools aimed at bringing about change without the use of coercion. Moral appeals, expectations, exposure and embarrassment, and appeals to pride and responsibility are among these tools. Civil society scrutiny can play a key role here in exposing wrongdoing and non-compliance with commitments made by governments or industries. Without the ties to diplomatic routine and without having to face the costs of political fallout that prohibit public institutions from speaking out, NGOs can create and police accountability mechanisms that go far beyond what is conceivable in the realm of formal politics. As with all aspects of accountability, therefore, protest and exposure are key tools in enforcing compliance.

A great deal of importance is also attached to the law as a mechanism for enforcing political accountability. The law can be seen as a political mechanism for defining rights, allocating responsibilities and thereby helping to construct prevailing notions of citizenship. This form of accountability seeks answerability and enforceability through the courts, a process that we examine in relation to South Africa (Chapter 3), India (Chapter 8) and the United States (Chapter 12), where rights have been violated and/or compensation sought. Where the law governs access to key resources, determines economic entitlements and shapes the rules of participation in public life, it can be applied positively to create an enabling environment in which poorer groups can secure their rights.

Yet the law is not a neutral vessel and legal processes are not insulated from political pressures. Law creation is always for someone, for some purpose, responsive to state needs or the concerns of well-organised and well-resourced political groups. Attempts to use the law to hold corporations to account for their social and environmental responsibilities have often failed because of state support for the corporations that are the subject of the suit or discrimination against the communities trying to bring the case, as we see in Chapter 9. As an accountability tool of the poor, the law has limitations and opportunities depending on the system in question. Countries such as India have a strong tradition of public interest litigation, for example. It should be noted, however, that basic resource constraints, lack of legal literacy and distrust of legal processes often conspire to dissuade poorer groups from using the legal system to seek redress (Newell 2001b). The perceived limits of these and other strategies by which the state is meant to hold itself to account have resulted in increasing interest in broader forms of social and civil accountability.

Social accountability

Related in many ways to political accountability is the notion of social accountability (Smulovitz and Peruzzotti 2000; Peruzzotti and Smulovitz 2002). Lent legitimacy by emerging rights-oriented discourses, social accountability explores the way in which citizen action, aimed at overseeing political authorities, is redefining the traditional concept of the relationship between citizens and their elected representatives. Social mobilisations, press reports and legal cases are the repertoires of protest that produce such forms of accountability. The targets are often election processes, government restrictions imposed on access to information and instances of police violence (Stanley 2005). The aims are variously to tackle issues of citizen security, judicial autonomy and access to justice, electoral fraud and government corruption (Peruzzotti and Smulovitz 2002; Dodson and Jackson 2004). The strategies provide, in effect, extra sets of checks and balances on the proper conduct of government in the public interest, exposing instances of corruption, negligence and oversight that vertical forms of accountability are unlikely or unable to address. Social forms of political control intend to go beyond the limitations of relying upon traditional mechanisms of accountability: elections; the separation of powers; and the checks and balances that exist, in theory, between state agencies.

More radical notions of accountability might question the state-centred nature of such approaches, which (re)produce a reliance on the state as an agent of change. The emphasis is explicitly to explore the ways in which civil society 'adds to the classic repertoire of electoral and constitutional institutions for controlling government' (Smulovitz and Peruzzotti 2000: 149). To work, however, such strategies require a responsive state that demonstrates a level of concern for what citizens or voters think and is willing to implement reforms aimed at pacifying those concerns. Social accountability mechanisms often explicitly aim at activating or reinforcing the operations of other agencies of horizontal accountability, again assuming their existence, effectiveness and willingness to pursue public interest agendas. Their aim, for example, is to 'trigger procedures in courts or oversight agencies that eventually lead to legal sanctions' (Smulovitz and Peruzzotti 2000: 151), to catalyse state-based mechanisms of enforceability. Rather than being effective in their own right, therefore, societal mechanisms need to pull other levers of change through the law or media.

A problematic assumption in this regard relates not just to the limits of the law or of the critical capacity of the media to work in these ways, but to issues of the capacity of actors promoting social accountability to perform these watchdog functions on an ongoing and sustained basis. Besides issues of resourcing, there is an implied assumption that societal mechanisms provide a viable system for tracking and addressing instances of misconduct or acts of negligence. But what if the problems are systemic, deep-rooted, ingrained in the everyday administration of the state? The problem is then not one of temporary institutional failure, nor one of institutional failure at all, but of institutions working very well for those that benefit from prevailing concentrations of power, distributions of resources and institutional indifference or blindness towards the needs of poorer groups.

If the problem is more fundamental in nature, we can expect less to be achieved by single-issue campaigns targeted at particular abuses of power, well-intentioned as those may be, and in spite of their potential to draw attention to broader patterns of neglect. We see this in Chapter 9 of this volume, where environmental justice advocates claim that acts of environmental racism are not evidence of a breakdown in a decision-making process. Rather, they manifest a deliberate, state-endorsed strategy, one that works well for those who profit from the social and environmental externalities passed on to poorer groups. As Goetz and Jenkins claim more generally:

> Many of the initiatives that profess to promote accountability target only very 'soft' aspects of accountability ... treating the structural difficulties of democratic systems as temporary glitches requiring the application of technical expertise. Such initiatives side-step institutionalised anti-poor biases that prevent accountability institutions from recognising and responding to injustices that disproportionately, or even exclusively, affect marginalised groups. (Goetz and Jenkins 2004: 7)

A further limitation of approaches to social accountability is their applicability to contexts in which the state tolerates and accommodates such forms of protest and criticism; where a free media exists, willing and prepared to engage in critical exposé journalism; and an accessible and functioning legal system operates, able to back citizen claims against the state with financial support and expertise. Such conditions could be said to apply to an increasing number of developed and developing countries, but in many settings they remain a distant prospect. Even in contexts where these basic conditions are met in theory, in practice barriers to accessing the media and the justice system continue to frustrate change. Hence, although Peruzzotti and Smulovitz claim that 'The politics of social accountability has taken place under authoritarian contexts', they do acknowledge that

> Under authoritarianism, the struggle for access to information becomes a precondition for any initiative oriented at controlling government behaviour. Authoritarianism also weakens the politics of social account-ability in so far as it reduces the repertoire of institutional tools available to the citizenry for the exercise of control. (Peruzzotti and Smulovitz 2002: 226)

Exploring the limitations of strategies of social accountability is not to undermine their importance in generating significant and much-needed checks and balances on the often arbitrary exercise of state power. Work on law and development, in particular, explores the conditions in which poorer and marginalised groups have been able to secure change through legal systems (Crook and Houtzager 2001; McClymont and Golub 2000) and this book cites a number of cases in which legal challenges have yielded important pro-poor outcomes. Similarly, the fact that social accountability is stronger on answerability than enforceability does not render it insignificant. As Peruzzotti and Smulovitz argue, 'the fact that most societal mechanisms do not have mandatory effects does not mean that they cannot have important "material consequences"' (2002: 227).

Rather, raising such concerns about the possibilities of social accountability forms part of a generic concern articulated throughout this book to look at accountability in terms not defined exclusively by state power. Many of the chapters in this book explore the crucial roles of community-based and civil society groups that plug accountability deficits in public institutions or address their lack of responsiveness to the needs of the poor by taking action directly, albeit sometimes in ways which invoke rights or entitlements in theory conferred by the state. The state is rarely absent in accountability struggles, therefore. The question is whether it always makes strategic sense for it to be the primary focus of campaign energies. Again, the answer has to depend on the goal of an accountability struggle and the extent to which change is contingent on reform in state practice.

Financial accountability

Managerial and financial approaches to accountability describe specific practices of accountability, traditionally applied to states but increasingly also to the private sector and civil society. Managerial accountability generally refers to the answerability of those with delegated authority for carrying out tasks according to agreed performance criteria. This less explicitly political form of accountability is concerned with inputs, outputs and outcomes; monitoring expenditure as agreed and according to the rules; and making sure that the processes and courses of action are carried out efficiently to achieve intended results (Day and Klein 1987: 27). If political accountability focuses on questions of institutional engineering, financial accountability focuses on accountancy. Broader accountability challenges in such conceptualisations run the risk of being reduced to performative functions: institutional planning and the assembling of incentives to motivate rational actors. Hence, for health, standards, benchmarks, practice guidelines and compliance mechanisms are key to improving 'service utilisation and client satisfaction' (Brinkerhoff 2004: 372). In a simple logical sequence between incentives and outcomes, 'accountability is achieved through the application of the laws, standards and procedures these frameworks put in place, which shape the incentives for various actors to comply' (*ibid.*: 372).

In its origins, financial accountability can be distinguished from political accountability by virtue of its proclaimed status as a neutral, technical exercise essentially concerned with keeping accurate accounts, with using the tools of auditing, budgeting and accounting to track and report on the allocation, disbursement and utilisation of financial resources. Current notions of financial accountability have expanded beyond the balancing of public books to the management of resources, shifting from economy to efficiency. Fiscal accountability mechanisms and auditing practices are continuing to evolve and expand, moving away from being strictly accounts-based to incorporating new indicators of financial integrity and performance. The recent emergence of social and environmental auditing practices, discussed below, represents this shift.

Managerial accountability has also expanded to include notions of *administrative accountability*. In the arena of public service delivery, new management approaches aimed at enhancing financial accountability can generate competing accountability demands and conflicting trade-offs. Efficient performance of services, demonstrated through ever more elaborate and transparent systems of accounting, may be at odds with the need to widen the access and availability of services to poorer groups. Such conflicts are most visible in those public services of greatest importance to the poor, such as health, education or the supply of water (Paul 1992). In this sense, while the purposes of accountability can overlap, they can also yield tensions. Brinkerhoff notes that 'accountability for control, with its focus on uncovering malfeasance and allocating "blame", can conflict with accountability for improvement, which emphasises managerial discretion and embracing error as a source of learning' (2003: xii).

It is in the corporate sector, perhaps, that we see the clearest evidence of an audit culture taking root, combining elements of managerial and financial accountability. The range of indicators of corporate performance has been broadened, in some cases to include social and environmental factors. Clear performance indicators are difficult to quantify, however, stretching conventional auditing techniques that rest on the assumption that 'what can't be counted doesn't count', but their increased emphasis does indicate how auditing processes are responsive to evolving demands for the accountability of actors.

Increasing numbers of social and environmental reports and externally verified statements provide evidence of the attempt by corporate managers to demonstrate a commitment to the public at large (Beloe 1999), though it remains the case that in global terms very few companies make such data publicly available. Similarly, though the indicators of social and environmental reporting are becoming more numerous and sophisticated, there are as yet few standard formats for the type of information companies report, or how that information is collected, analysed and presented. Because of this, a variety of organisations and initiatives are attempting to standardise social and environmental reporting procedures to enable stakeholders to compare companies more easily across sectors and regions. Standards such as SA8000 (established in 1997 by Social Accountability International), and AA1000 (developed by the Institute of Social and Ethical Accountability in 1999) incorporate frameworks to improve performance and the quality of assessments.

Heightened public interest in questions of corporate accountability and responsibility has forced (some) companies to go beyond declarations of good intent and the self-enforcement of codes of conduct and to involve third-party consultants and accreditation agencies in the verification of their commitments. There has been a role for consultancy firms such as Ernst and Young and KMPG, verifying company claims once site inspections and interviews with employees have taken place. But cross-checking of these assessments rarely takes place and questions have been asked about their thoroughness and effectiveness. When there is pressure for a speedy audit, companies are given notice of inspections and interviews with workers take place in the work environment, where they may be less free to speak out (O'Rourke 1997).

The involvement of private auditors in verifying compliance also raises the question of who audits the auditors. Questions have been asked about the independence and commitment of consultancy firms, such as KPMG, since they perform these roles for profit and are paid by the companies whose activities they are meant to be monitoring (Simms 2002). The recent corporate governance scandals in the US involving corporations such as Enron and WorldCom have served to focus attention on the unhealthy degree of collusion between companies and those they employ to oversee their accounts. In this context, second-order accountability is an important issue: 'how can we hold institutions of accountability accountable themselves?' (Schedler et al. 1999: 25).

Unsurprisingly, this emphasis on accountancy has extended to civil society groups in development, given their heightened role in aid delivery. With regard to development projects, often the simplest mechanism by which an NGO can be held to account is accounting for expenditure. To demonstrate this, measures and indicators are needed, yet few agreed performance standards are available. Indicators of quality of organisational performance are rare, with most assessments favouring short-term visible results and evaluations that emphasise control and fiscal responsibility. The types of appraisal procedures insisted on by donors favour 'accountancy rather than accountability', audit rather than learning (Edwards and Hulme 1995: 13). Given tendencies towards loose oversight by a board, periodic elections of officers, minimalist reports of activities and summary financial records, Scholte suggests such 'pro forma accountability mainly addresses the bureaucratic requirements of govern-ments and donors.... Thus in civil society, just as much as in governance and market circles, formal accountability may well fall short of effective accountability' (2005: 107).

Towards civil accountability?

The conceptualisations above fail to capture an increasingly important type of accountability; civil accountability. Strategies of civil account-ability are non-state, often informal and distinct in form from political, social and financial accountability (see Table 1.1, page 18). They most closely resemble strategies of social accountability, but are less focused on achieving change in the state as an end itself and towards this end adopt different activist repertoires. Sometimes citizen action takes the form of problem solving as a self-help strategy, often in the absence of, or because of, a prior state intervention. Efforts to engage citizens in the manage-ment of water resources, explored in Chapter 4, are an example of this. At other times, the aim is raising awareness or improving consciousness about the ways in which accountability deficits frustrate the development prospects of the poor – as in the case of consciousmess raising through theatre in Nigeria, discussed in Chapter 10. Innovative participatory methodologies bring new citizen knowledge to the fore to challenge existing approaches to regulation. Participatory health assessments or pollution monitoring by citizens in India, discussed in Chapter 8, provide examples of these types of strategy in practice.

Building on the argument of the previous chapter that accountability is often a means to an end, by specifying the aim of a struggle it becomes easier to comprehend the strategies groups adopt to secure those ends. The strategic use of accountability tools shifts with time, so that it is unsurprising to find groups employing simultaneously a diverse range of tactics. In Mexico we find evidence of groups moving from registering dissent through cutting off water supplies to more proactive engagement in water management alternatives (Chapter 4). In practice then, multiple and hybrid forms of accountability are sought and practised by social actors working within available spaces and beyond them to construct new arenas of engagement, fusing strategies in combinations that make sense in the pursuit of diverse and shifting goals. This partly reflects a reading of existing political opportunity structures. As Eckstein and Wickham-Crowley note (2003: 4): 'State institutional arrangements ... can influence whether people turn to collective or individual, and formal or informal strategies to secure or protect social rights and to redress violations thereof.'

When such formal channels fail to operate or perform poorly, aggrieved citizens often resort to alternative mechanisms of redress. Arenas for the contestation of rights and duties can be created by movements and citizen groups where new spaces for accountability can be constituted. Indeed, as Goetz and Jenkins note, in many cases it is

> shortcomings in conventional accountability systems – secrecy in auditing, ineffective policy reviews in legislatures, the electorate's difficulty in sending strong signals to decision makers between elections, excessive delays in courts and inadequate sanctions for failure to apply administrative rules or respect standards [that] have created pressure for better channels for vertical information flows and stronger accountability mechanisms between state agents and citizens. (Goetz and Jenkins 2001: 2–3)

Sometimes activists imitate official accountability procedures in order to raise issues and highlight the limitations of existing mechanisms. The public hearings described in Chapter 8 of the book are an example in this regard, where formal hearings are called for, but often not undertaken, and communities and activists have sought to construct their own hearings for dealing with accountability claims. While to some extent mocking state procedures by staging them in informal ways, such experiments can yield institutional change. Often accountability mechanisms are fashioned in ways that seek to engage state actors without mimicking state-based accountability tools. Strategies of citizen water management in Mexico described in Chapter 4 aim to secure water supply in a context of acute conflict without resort to state mechanisms of redress.

Such experiments in accountability politics are often aimed at challenging prevailing political cultures of secrecy, official arrogance and institutional unresponsiveness. In so doing, they often contest the very purposes for which accountability tools are invoked. The 'new accountability agenda' includes the use of such experiments, whereby disenfranchised groups are provided with 'opportunities to operationalise rights and to shift the terrain of governance from technical solutions to a more immediate concern with social justice' (Goetz and Jenkins 2004: 3). The challenge is to move from *accountability as spectacle*, as it is practised in these events, useful as they are, to *accountability as norm*, a routine and mundane feature of everyday decision making.

There is clearly a difference between accountability that can be created *passively* and that which is produced *actively*. Passive accountability implies that the authority to act on behalf of others is conferred on leaders of communities, heads of NGOs, and, of course, governments. A mandate is given such that continual approval is not required for each and every decision that is made on behalf of a broader political community. This is the minimalist notion of democracy described by the term 'delegative democracy' (O'Donnell 1994). It is best represented in notions of political and managerial accountability, described above, which emphasise the self-regulating ability of state, private and civil society actors. Active accountability, on the other hand, is that which is continually (re) negotiated, where demands have to be vocalised and where closure is not reached on how accountability should be exercised and on whose behalf. This assumes both a right and a capacity to articulate accountability demands. It resonates more strongly with the notions of social and civil accountability where the focus is respectively on monitoring the state's ability to self-regulate or attempting to reproduce, compensate for or mimic state action in its absence. There is an important balance to strike, therefore, between building citizens' capacities to articulate rights *and* the capabilities of political-economic institutions to respond and be held to account (Gaventa and Jones 2002).

Conclusion

This chapter has shown that while accountability is an increasingly crucial reference point in development debates, its use in diverse discourses remains loose and under-specific as a result of the essentially contested nature of the term and the broad range of political claims it can be used to advance. This, indeed, is the whole point of our enquiry into the relationship between rights, resources and accountability. In understanding these processes, we have placed power centrally: power to define accountability, and power to create and enforce the mechanisms of accountability. We have seen throughout the discussion how power operates at different levels, reinforcing itself through discourse, process and the actions of actors. We noted a complex interplay between the way narratives of accountability construct rights and obligations (and notions of citizenship in so doing) and the way strategies of accountability generate new expectations about the appropriate conduct of others, contesting or reinforcing prevailing notions of accountability. In understanding predominant applications of accountability, we emphasised the importance of historical and material circumstances to the construction of rights and entitlements to accountability. It is to be expected, therefore, that future struggles for accountability will both reflect and help to redefine prevailing historical processes and material changes.

Inevitably, such a broad overview has raised as many questions as it has provided adequate answers to the key accountability questions we set out at the start of the chapter. Hard questions remain about whether accountability makes a difference, how much difference it makes, and for whom. As Chapter 10 on struggles over labour rights makes clear, there are social costs associated with accountability struggles. Despite claims to the contrary, they are neither win-win for all concerned, nor cost-free. In many of the contexts explored in this book, indeed, we have seen how people risk their lives in the face of violence and intimidation to protest abuses of power and advance accountability claims. More accountability may ultimately contribute both to the effectiveness and legitimacy of political institutions, but that hope must be demonstrated, not assumed. The question for many of the actors engaged in the accountability struggles described in this book is not what accountability does for those institutions that already wield power, but what it can do for the victims of institutional inaction, political oversight, economic marginalisation and overt repression.

REFERENCES

Beloe, S. (1999) 'The Greening of Business?' *IDS Bulletin*, Vol. 3 No. 3.

Blair, H. (2000) 'Participation and Accountability at the Periphery: Democratic Local Governance in Six Countries', *World Development*, Vol. 28, No. 1 (January).

Brinkerhoff, D. (2003) 'Accountability and Health Systems: Overview, Framework and Strategies', Technical Report No. 018 (January), Bethesda, Maryland: Partners for Health Reform*plus* project, Abt Associates Inc.

—— (2004) 'Accountability and Health Systems: Towards Conceptual Clarity and Policy Relevance', *Health Policy and Planning*, Vol. 19, No. 6, pp. 371–9.

Cornwall, A., Lucas, H. and Pasteur, K. (2000) 'Introduction: Accountability Through Participation: Developing Workable Partnership Models in the Health Sector', *IDS Bulletin*, Vol. 31, No. 1.

Considine, M. (2002) 'The End of the Line? Accountable Governance in the Age of Networks, Partnerships and Joined-up Services', *Governance*, Vol. 15 No. 1 (January).

Crook, R. C. and Houtzager, P. P. (2001) *Making Law Matter: Rules, Rights and Security in the Lives of the Poor*, IDS Bulletin, Vol. 32, No. 1, Brighton: IDS.

Day, P. and Klein, R. (1987) *Accountabilities: Five Public Services*, London and New York: Tavistock.

Dodson, M. and Jackson, D. (2004) 'Strengthening Horizontal Accountability in Transitional Democracies: the Human Rights Ombudsman in Central America', *Latin American Politics and Society*, Vol. 46, No. 4 (Winter).

Eckstein, S. E. and Wickham-Crowley, T. (2003) *Struggles for Social Rights in Latin America*, London: Routledge.

Edwards, M. and Hulme, D. (eds) (1995) *Beyond the Magic Bullet: NGO Performance and Accountability in the Post-Cold War World*, London: Save the Children Fund.

Gaventa, J. and Jones, E. (2002) 'Concepts of Citizenship: a Review', IDS Development Bibliography No. 19, Brighton: Institute of Development Studies.

Gill, S. (1995) 'Theorising the Interregnum: the Double Movement and Global Politics in the 1990s', in Hettne, B. (ed.), *International Political Economy: Understanding Global Disorder*, London: Zed Books.

Goetz, A. M. and Gaventa, J. *et al.* (2001) 'Bringing Citizen Voice and Client Focus into Service Delivery', IDS Working Paper 138, Brighton: Institute of Development Studies.

Goetz, A. M. and Jenkins, R. (2001) 'Hybrid Forms of Accountability: Citizen Engagement in Institutions of Public Sector Oversight in India', *Public Management Review*, Vol. 3, No. 3 (September).

—— (2004) *Reinventing Accountability: Making Democracy Work for Human Development*, Basingstoke: Palgrave.

Luckham, R. and White, G. (eds) (1996) *Democratization in the South: The Jagged Wave*, Manchester: Manchester University Press.

Manor, J. (1999) *The Political Economy of Democratic Decentralisation*, Washington, DC: World Bank.

McClymont, M. and Golub, S. (2000) *Many Roads to Justice: the Law-related Work of Ford Foundation Grantees around the World*, New York: Ford Foundation.

Najam, A. (1996) 'NGO Accountability: a Conceptual Framework', *Development Policy Review*, Vol. 14.

Newell, P. (2001a) 'Managing Multinationals: the Governance of Investment for the Environment' *Journal of International Development*, Vol. 13.

—— (2001b) 'Access to Environmental Justice? Litigation against TNCs in the South', *IDS Bulletin*, Vol. 32, No. 1.

Newell, P. and Bellour, S. (2002) 'Mapping Accountability: Origins, Contexts and Implications for Development', IDS Working Paper 168 (October), Brighton: Institute of Development Studies.

O'Donnell, G. (1994) 'Delegative Democracy', *Journal of Democracy*, Vol. 5 (January).

O'Rourke, D. (1997) 'Smoke from a Hired Gun: a Critique of Nike's Labour and Environmental Auditing in Vietnam as Performed by Ernst and Young', unpublished MS, available at http://www.corpwatch.org/trac/nike/ernst/.

Oxhorn, P. and Ducantenzeiler, G. (1998) *What Kind of Democracy? What Kind of Market? Latin America in an Age of Neoliberalism*, Pennsylvania: Pennsylvania State University Press.

Paul, S. (1992) 'Accountability in Public Services: Exit, Voice and Control', *World Development*, Vol. 20, No. 7, pp. 1047–60.

Peruzzotti, E. and Smulovitz, C. (2002) 'Held to Account: Experiences of Social Accountability in Latin America', *Journal of Human Development*, Vol. 3, No. 2, pp. 209–30.

Picciotto, S. and Mayne, R. (eds) (1999) *Regulating International Business: Beyond*

Liberalisation, London: Macmillan Press.

Posner, P. W. (2003) 'Local Democracy and Popular Participation: Chile and Brazil in Comparative Perspective', *Democratization*, Vol. 10, No. 3 (Autumn), pp. 39–68.

Schacter, M. (2000) 'When Accountability Fails: a Framework for Diagnosis and Action', Institute on Governance, Policy Brief No. 9.

Schedler, A., Diamond, L. and Plattner, M. (1999) *The Self-restraining State: Power and Accountability in New Democracies*, Boulder and London: Lynne Rienner Publishers.

Scholte, J. A. (2005) 'Civil Society and Democratically Accountable Global Governance', in Held, D. and Koenig-Archibugi, M. (eds), *Global Governance and Public Accountability*, Oxford: Blackwell, pp. 87–110.

Simms, A. (2002) *Five Brothers: the Rise and Nemesis of the Big Bean Counters*, London: New Economics Foundation.

Smulovitz, C. and Peruzzotti, E. (2000) 'Societal Accountability in Latin America', *Journal of Democracy*, Vol. 11, No. 4 (October), pp.147–58.

Stanley, R. (2005) 'Controlling the Police in Buenos Aires: a Case Study of Horizontal and Social Accountability', *Bulletin of Latin American Research*, Vol. 24, No. 1 (January), pp. 71–92.

UNDP (1997) 'Corruption and Good Governance', MDG (Millennium Development Goal) Discussion Paper 3.

Vidal, J. (1996) *McLibel: Burger Culture on Trial*, Basingstoke: MacMillan.

Whitfield, D. (2001) *Public Services or Corporate Welfare: Rethinking the Nation State in the Global Economy*, London: Pluto Press.

World Bank (1997) *The State in a Changing World*, World Bank Development Report, Washington, DC: World Bank.

Overview The political economy of resources and the cultural politics of rights: challenges for accountability

PETER NEWELL AND JOANNA WHEELER

The current focus on good governance in development debates implies some assumptions about accountability, in particular that increased accountability will lead to greater social, economic and political equity. By the same token, an inherent assumption in much of the current enthusiasm for rights-based approaches in development is that implementing rights will help create predictability for poor and marginalised groups by establishing clear relationships of responsibility between powerful actors and these groups. This section of the book will challenge both of these assumptions by examining, in rich empirical detail, the relationship between rights and resources in terms of accountability.

These chapters consider how marginalised groups contest access to a range of resources, including adequate housing, health care and water. These 'resources' are not defined in the narrow sense of extractable natural materials like oil and minerals, which are the focus of the literature on the 'resource curse', referred to in Chapter 10. Instead, these chapters take a wider view, exploring the interaction between the material features of resources and the social and political struggles over the control of their use. The starting point for understanding rights and accountability in relation to these resources is the deprivation of, or lack of access to, the resources in question. And while there is, in most cases, an important and pressing material deprivation (lack of adequate housing, lack of clean water, lack of appropriate health care), these chapters will focus on the political contestations to gain access to these resources. This section explores both the political economy of gaining rights to resources and the cultural politics of how resources are constituted and contested.

Within these processes of political contestation over resources, some key themes have emerged that shed some light on the relationship between rights and resources, and speak to the assumptions about accountability outlined above. In particular, these chapters focus on a variety of formal and informal strategies adopted by different groups to contest access to specific resources (see Table 1.1 in the Introduction). The rights claims in these cases can be categorised into two types. Some are claims of entitlement to a particular resource, as in the case of water in South Africa, housing in Kenya, and the health care system in Brazil. Others are claims of access to a resource, as in the case of the watersheds and natural reserves in Mexico. What is important is how these different rights claims are interrelated, and the intertwining of different types of rights (political, social and economic) in practice. While the claims to entitlement may spring from the immediate and pressing material deprivations people experience, the struggles over gaining access and control over these resources bring a whole range of other rights and accountability relationships into play. For example, the struggle of the Mombasa tenants' association to secure access to adequate housing has had to address the significant political corruption and lack of transparency in the council authorities, bringing political rights, such as the right to information, to the fore. For these tenants, securing access to housing is important for reasons beyond their physical needs – it is also about their sense of belonging and citizenship, which is tied to having a legitimate claim to their homes.

As we noted in the introduction, the cases in this book show not only how different types of rights are indivisible, but also how there can be conflicts between and among different rights. We see in the next section on corporate accountability how the rights of corporate actors can conflict with those of poorer communities, but there can also be conflicts between rights that emerge through the mobilisation strategies of communities. For example, in Mexico, the direct action of rural indigenous groups in cutting off a dam deprived downstream urban groups of their right to water. Yet this direct action was part of the informal strategies the rural indigenous groups used to demand accountability from municipal governments. These conflicts between rights have important implications for the extent to which they can be used as a strategy for demanding accountability.

The chapters in this section offer some important lessons about the circumstances in which these mobilisations to demand accountability can be successful. There is a clear division between short-term and long-term strategies for gaining access to resources. The short-term strategies of indigenous municipalities in the watershed in Veracruz, Mexico have led to a tokenistic response by the government in order to forestall direct social action. When the indigenous people shut down the dam and the water supply to the cities below, the municipal government reacted with offers of paved roads, funds towards clinics and schools for the indigenous communities. But these concessions, while couched in the language of fulfilling the rights of the indigenous communities, actually served as a palliative for defusing the social mobilisation without addressing the real issue of the responsibility for managing the watershed that is the essential basis of the right to water for both rural and urban communities. On the other hand, there is also the possibility that even short-term strategies, which result in rapid victories over marginal issues, can eventually have more transformative effects.

Another challenge for informal strategies and mobilisations around rights over resources is scale. In many cases – including Mexico, Brazil, South Africa and Kenya – mobilisations have led to key victories. But the challenge, given the complexity of actors and institutional relationships, is how to scale up (or down) these advances in a way that leads to substantive changes to government institutions. In South Africa, the right to water exists in the constitution, but in practice the right is not evenly upheld. In Kenya, gains at the local level by the tenants' association are difficult to sustain and scale up to council authority level because of political and financial pressure on the groups demanding accountability.

In Chapter 1, we discussed the limits of the law and the role of the state in the politics of how rights are defined. In addition, these chapters show how national and international legal frameworks have a central role in determining how rights over resources are realised and accountability relationships are established. But far from being a neutral enforcer of these obligations, the state plays a political role in terms of how resources are defined and allocated, so that the limits of the law and of legal frameworks become apparent. In the case of protected natural areas (PNAs) in Mexico, conflict continues over how natural resources are defined – indigenous groups are claiming knowledge rights in these areas, while international NGOs and others are constructing the rainforest as the object of conservation, and the government is attempting to enforce bans on using the rainforest for conservationist and geopolitical reasons. The chapters in this section reinforce the focus in the existing literature on ecological democracy (Watts 2003) and feminist political ecology (Rochelau et al. 1995) on 'how local communities resisted the incursions of the state, and how the state in turn attempted to "criminalise" local customary rights' over access to and control over resources (Watts 2003). These cases demonstrate how the state can act as a guarantor of accountability and also perpetuate a lack of accountability.

This section will explore the complex relationships between rights and resources in terms of accountability both by broadening the definition of resources and by focusing on the multiple strategies, informal as well as formal, for making rights claims in relationship to those resources. In so doing, these chapters raise some important challenges to dominant assumptions about the transformative effects of technocratic approaches to accountability and top-down versions of rights. By taking deprivation and the lack of access to resources as a starting point, these chapters investigate the political economy of gaining access to these resources, and the cultural politics of making rights claims. Within this complex landscape of actors, interests and discourses, it becomes clear that accountabilities must be claimed and negotiated by poor and less privileged people themselves if the fundamental issue of access to society's wealth and resources is to be addressed.

REFERENCES

Rocheleau, D., Thomas-Slayter, B. and Wangari, E. (eds) (1995) *Feminist Political Ecology*, London: Routledge.

Watts, M. (2003) 'Economies of Violence: More Oil, More Blood' *Economic and Political Weekly*, Vol. 38, No. 48, pp. 5089–99.

CHAPTER 3

Do human rights make a difference to poor and vulnerable people? Accountability for the right to water in South Africa[1]

LYLA MEHTA

To what extent is accountability key to realising rights? In struggles over access to water, conflicts between market- and rights-based frameworks imply distinct strategies of accountability. The former implies consumers holding service providers to account. In this understanding, citizens are consumers and accountability is exercised through the implied contract, mediated by the market, between customer and water utility, even if the state remains responsible for regulating private service providers to ensure they meet the needs of the poor. Rights-based frameworks, on the other hand, assume that accountability claims will be pursued through and mediated by the state. This confers upon the state the power to both respect and deny rights, the consequences of which are explored below.

In the past decade, the rights discourse has gained currency in international development. A human rights approach to development is seen as moving away from looking at charity or handouts to empowerment and securing firm rights to 'the requirements, freedoms and choices necessary for life and development in dignity' (Hausermann 1998). Despite the fact that support for the human rights movement has been growing considerably and a human rights approach to development is now fairly mainstream, there is a growing acknowledgement that many of the world's poor and marginalised have yet to enjoy the benefits of these rights. There are many possible reasons for this.

First, *sins of omission* may deny citizens access to social and economic rights. It is well known that poor states may not prioritise the provision of education, water and housing for all. Also, many developing countries lack the resources to make good the rights that allow all citizens to live a life of dignity, or the institutional capacity to establish these rights. Conversely, citizens may not be aware of their rights and may not have the capacity to mobilise around them. Second, *sins of commission* may deprive people of rights. The rights of vulnerable people may knowingly be put at risk or even violated for a variety of reasons. For example, freedom of speech and the right to protest are severely restricted under dictatorships. Moreover, as this chapter demonstrates, states and global players may introduce macroeconomic policies that violate basic rights in the name of development or growth. It is, however, the lack of mechanisms of accountability and poor regulation on the part of states that allow both sins of omission and commission to flourish, preventing economic and social rights from becoming real.

Accountability is usually seen as the means through which the less powerful can hold more powerful actors to account (Goetz and Jenkins 2004). Traditionally, it is governments that are mainly responsible for protecting people's rights, but there is an increasing need to hold private sector and global actors to account for policies and programmes that have a far-reaching impact on the rights and well-being of poor and vulnerable people. Diffuse and unclear rules of accountability for global players and non-state players are problematic when most human rights declarations focus on states as the primary deliverers and protectors of rights.

Rights claiming is a way to demand accountability from powerful players. But, as this chapter demonstrates, accountability is an issue that is still missing from many human rights debates. For the Millennium Development Goals and other processes to be successful, attention must be paid to several contradictions and questions. Do paradoxical outcomes arise from a dual commitment to markets and rights, compromising people's basic rights while making it difficult to enforce accountability mechanisms? Can poor institutional capacity and low resource allocation impede the realisation of economic and social rights? Do the necessary accountability mechanisms exist to hold the powerful to account? Is there an ambiguity about responsibilities and duty bearers when economic and social rights are violated?

This chapter focuses on these issues and questions by examining the right to water in South Africa.[2] In 2002, the UN Economic, Social and Cultural Council gave a lot of prominence to the right to water through its General Comment No. 15, which applies an authoritative interpretation of the International Covenant on Economic, Social and Cultural Rights (ICESCR, 1966), ratified by 148 states. The Comment, not a legally binding document, stated explicitly that the right to water is a human right and that responsibility for the provision of sufficient, safe, affordable water to everyone, without discrimination, rests with the state. States are thus clearly responsible for progressively realising the right to water.

Here I examine both the ideological currents underpinning the water debate in South Africa and its institutional, administrative and policy environment in order to understand the importance of accountability in realising the right to water. The chapter draws on empirical research conducted in 2002 and 2003. Interviews were conducted with NGO representatives, villagers, academics, policy makers and private sector representatives in Cape Town, Pretoria, Johannesburg and in the Eastern Cape province of South Africa.

Dancing to the two tunes of rights and markets?

South Africa is the only country that recognises the human right to water at both the constitutional and policy level. Moreover, its Free Basic Water (FBW) policy goes against the grain of conventional wisdom in the water sector, which stresses cost recovery mechanisms and shies away from endorsing the human right to water (Mehta 2003). Since early 2000, the Department for Water Affairs and Forestry has been investigating providing a basic level of water free to all citizens. In February 2001 the government announced that it was going to provide a basic supply of 6,000 litres of safe water per month to all households free of charge (based on an average household size of eight people). The Water Services Act 108 of 1997 states that a basic level of water should be provided to those who cannot pay, and the FBW policy emanates from the legal provisions of the Act. The main source of funding for this initiative is the Municipal Infrastructure Grant, a conditional capital grant for the provision of infrastructure, and the Equitable Share Grant, an unconditional grant from the central government to local authorities intended for operational expenditure. The latter amounts to about R7.5 billion a year (R1 = US$0.158) and is from national taxes for the provision of basic services.[3]

While the government of South Africa stands alone internationally in endorsing the constitutional right to water, its policies have been informed by several dominant water management frameworks, which include an emphasis on cost recovery as well as a shift in the role of the state from direct provider of water-related goods and services to a more regulatory function, with privatisation seen as the means to overcome the past failure of public systems to provide water to the poor. Government policies draw on a quasi-consensus amongst multilateral and bilateral agencies on issues such as cost recovery, user fees, and demand management, manifested in both poor countries and middle-income settings like South Africa. For example, several authors have demonstrated the extent to which the World Bank and the International Finance Corporation (IFC) have shifted South African government thinking away from its Reconstruction and Development Programme (RDP) commitments in infrastructure and service provision, based on entitlement and welfare, towards a cost-recovery approach that can deprive poor communities of their basic right to an adequate provision of water (Pauw 2003; Bond 2001; 2002). In 1996 total cost recovery became an official policy of the government when it adopted its fiscally conservative Growth, Employment and Redistribution macroeconomic policy (GEAR). The central features of the policy are a reduced role for the state, fiscal restraint and the promotion of privatisation.

Thus, alongside the remarkable commitments to providing free water, several policy changes were introduced under World Bank influence (Pauw 2003; Bond 2001). These include the 'credible threat of cutting service' to non-paying consumers, a move which has been linked by some to cholera and other gastrointestinal outbreaks (Pauw 2003; McDonald 2002). From 1997 municipalities began to witness widespread cut-offs of basic services to non-payers (*ibid.*). As the cost-recovery principle was applied, households that used more than the basic amount, and found themselves unable to pay, faced disconnections. In the case of Manquele *v* Durban Transitional Metropolitan Council 2001 JOL 8956 (D), the High Court found that the City Council had a right to disconnect the water supply of the applicant, Mrs Manquele, because she chose not to limit herself to the water supply provided to her free of charge. However, commentators argue that by completely disconnecting her water supply the municipality deprived Mrs Manquele even of the free basic amount; this was problematic, since the right to a basic level of water supply exists notwithstanding the ability to pay (Community Law Centre 2002). While cut-offs took place even during apartheid times (when non-payment for services was a form of political resistance),[4] the level of public indignation is undoubtedly higher today, not least because of the strong importance attached to economic and social rights in South Africa's constitution.

There are controversies over the number of people who have experienced cut-offs. According to the Municipal Services Project, using representative national survey data from the Human Sciences Research Council (HSRC), ten million people have experienced cut-offs in recent years (McDonald 2002). This figure is contested, however, and has been refuted by the Department for Water Affairs and Forestry (DWAF) (Kasrils 2003) and further revised by the HSRC to approximately 2 per cent of all connected households, or over 250,000 people. Despite

DWAF's admission that such numbers are a matter of serious concern, McDonald stands by the figure of ten million and has challenged DWAF and other agencies to research a more accurate figure (*Sunday Independent* 2003). DWAF maintains, nevertheless, that under certain conditions cut-offs are permissible on the legal basis of the Strategic Framework for Water Services.[5]

As part of GEAR, the South African government also reduced grants and subsidies to local municipalities and city councils. This forced cash-strapped local authorities to turn towards privatisation as well as to enter into partnerships in order to generate the revenue no longer provided by the national state (McKinley 2003). Since local government structures were incapable of dealing with past backlogs on their own, they began to privatise public water utilities by entering into service and management partnerships with external agencies. These ranged from multinational water corporations to South African firms. The role of consortia was also key. For example, Suez, which collaborated with the apartheid government in providing water largely to the white minority, formed Water and Sanitation Services Africa (WSSA). It subsequently won 'delegated management' contracts in Queenstown, Fort Beaufort and Stutterheim (all in the Eastern Cape) (Bond *et al.* 2001). Ruiters (in Pauw 2003), who researched water privatisation in these three towns, argues that water tariffs increased up to 300 per cent between 1994 and 1999. Pauw (2003) argues that by 1996 a typical township household was paying up to 30 per cent of its income for water, sewerage and electricity. Average income in the area at the time was less than US$60 per month, with more than 50 per cent unemployed. Those who could not pay their bills (the majority) were cut off and in Queenstown special debt collectors were appointed and a reinstatement fee was introduced that was almost twice the average township income.

Implementing FBW: experiences from the Eastern Cape

The Eastern Cape is the poorest of South Africa's nine provinces, with a predominantly rural population, high unemployment, and poor access to social services. Located on the south-eastern coast, the Eastern Cape province accounts for approximately 16 per cent of South Africa's population. Of all Equitable Share Grants to the nine provinces, the Eastern Cape receives 17–18 per cent (National Treasury 1999; 2004). Research was conducted in two district municipalities in the former Transkei.[6] The Alfred Nzo District Municipality (ANDM) is one of the poorest district municipalities in the Eastern Cape. It has 50 per cent unemployment and no manufacturing industry to curb the problem.[7] Across ANDM's large, poor rural population, 214 villages have a reliable water supply, whilst more than 400 villages do not have any water scheme whatsoever. ANDM is one of the poorest district municipalities in the Eastern Cape. The O. R. Tambo District Municipality is slightly larger, with a population of over 1.6 million and an unemployment rate of 51.8 per cent. Currently available statistics indicate that only 13.2 per cent have acceptable access to safe water (SSA 2002).

The FBW policy was conceived by DWAF at the national level, but its implementation rests with local authorities, including district and local municipalities, who are designated water services authorities (local municipalities, however, have to apply to be water services authorities). Although they are free to interpret it according to the resources and capacity available, operationalising the policy has been difficult. After all, the mere endorsement of the principle of social justice does not determine how resources are to be distributed. Instead, the distribution of resources and the implementation of rights-based approaches are usually at the discretion of professionals and bureaucrats in the public sector, who lack a clear directive on how to 'implement justice' (Plant 1992: 20). This certainly echoes the experiences of officials in South Africa's Eastern Cape. Many worked in bureaucracies of the former homelands and inherited a massive backlog in 1994. They also struggle to grapple with the many political and institutional changes arising through South Africa's decentralisation process.[8]

Many of the poorer district municipalities lack financial and institutional resources to implement the policy, despite Equitable Share Grants. Monitoring and rationing the quota of free water is also very difficult. Often, it can cost more to install a water meter than to provide the water free.[9] In some cases, the FBW policy has also made charging for water difficult. Many communities understood that they would now stop paying for water (Jackson 2002), making it increasingly difficult for cash-strapped district municipalities to raise the money required.

How do poor municipalities such as ANDM raise the money to ensure water delivery? The ANDM authorities believe that it is too costly to charge for water in rural areas. They have been down that road in the past and find it an administrative burden to try to collect tariffs. Moreover, many of the schemes were underutilised – Build–Operate–Train–Transfer (BOTT) schemes, for example, which relied on expensive technology and outside experts rather than local knowledge and expertise. Existing pre-paid schemes were highly underutilised and most people continued to use natural sources of water such as untreated streams. Those using the pre-paid scheme were only collecting an average of three litres of water per person per day, which meant that a million-rand investment could not yield the benefits intended and remained underutilised. Moreover, the scheme was not addressing the problems of health and the need to free women from long-distance water collection. It is for this reason that ANDM moved away from the policy of cost recovery and is now implementing the FBW policy. ANDM has not announced the policy to the entire district municipality, however, lest serious financial problems arise in implementing it. Thus many people in the Eastern Cape, especially in the remote rural areas, are not even aware of the policy of FBW.

Free water or basic water?
It has been argued that FBW is difficult to realise in rural areas dogged by a massive backlog with respect to water supply and sanitation. In ANDM in 2003, 132 villages (with a population of about 170,000 people) were being serviced with basic schemes. By 2010 the district municipality plans to serve 420 villages (a population of about 540,000 people), still only 63 per cent of the villages in the entire district.

Clearly a long road lies ahead in ensuring water for all. ANDM has to consider both the free basic water policy as well as basic water for all. In principle, basic water for all takes precedence in the work of ANDM, together with sanitation priorities. However, there is a trade-off in implementing free water for some and basic water for all. ANDM has contracted consultants to develop business plans for priority villages within the municipality. A village with a high population size, a clinic and/or a school is generally high on the list of priorities. However, if a priority village is next to a village with low priority, the consultants have to develop a business plan that encompasses both villages as one project, because people in the next village would fail to understand why they are being bypassed whilst the other village is earmarked to get a water scheme. Indeed, failure to recognise adjacent villages could result in pipes being destroyed and water theft.

In order to ensure that basic water is provided, ANDM has introduced play pumps as interim measures in villages unlikely to receive water in the near future.[10] The play pumps are also supposed to curb the problem of cholera, which in the beginning of 2003 was a problem in other district municipalities. Play pumps cost anything between R20,000 and R100,000 with a reservoir. Thus, despite good intentions, district municipalities such as ANDM and O. R. Tambo are finding it difficult to realise FBW for all. In part this delay is due to the legacy inherited in 1994, combined with both financial and institutional constraints. At the time of writing, 55.2 per cent of the country's poor population was being served by FBW (DWAF 2005). In 2003, two years after the policy had been announced, only 50 per cent of the communities had implemented FBW (COSATU 2003).

Livelihood and poverty reduction impacts
The FBW policy was not intended to address redistribution issues, and there are other provisions in the National Water Act (for example, compulsory licensing) that deal with these. Still, we need to ask how it contributes to poverty reduction and wider social justice concerns. For example, it is intended that the 25 litres of water will be used primarily for drinking and cooking purposes. However, the poor also need to be assured of water during scarcity periods for their farming activities based on subsistence. The 25 litres a day policy largely applies to domestic water supply, and not to wider concerns of livelihood security and how to restructure existing water-user practices.

While the Committee on Economic and Social Rights does not lay down particular standards on how much water should be provided, it states that water supply must be sufficient for personal and domestic use, correspondent to WHO standards stipulating a minimum of 50–100 litres per day with an absolute minimum of 20 litres per day (COHRE 2004: 8). Thus South Africa is providing close to the absolute minimum.[11] This is why trade union leaders and other advocates argue that the South African state should grant everybody at least 50 litres of water per day *per capita*. This, they argue, is the only way in which poor farmers can successfully maintain their livelihoods and thus escape the trap of poverty and dependence on pensions.

Do enforceable social and economic rights make a difference to people's lives and livelihoods? As demonstrated above, rights-based approaches may not necessarily radically redistribute resources in a society. But do they make a difference to poor people, and what are local-level village experiences of FBW? I draw on Zolile Ntshona's interviews in two villages in the Eastern Cape (see Mehta and Ntshona 2004) to show how the daily lives of three rural women, of which two are pensioners and one is unemployed, have been affected by FBW. Mabombo is 61 years old and is entitled to an old age pension. Before the implementation of the FBW policy, she used to collect water from the spring far from her house, and used a ten-litre container to make two or three trips to the spring before sunrise. Collection from the spring was difficult for her because she had to wait for the sediments to settle before pure water emerged. She now feels that life has improved. She does not have to wake up in the morning before the livestock make the spring water murky and can concentrate her energy on other work. She uses the FBW for washing, drinking and cooking, though she still visits the spring to wash blankets. Mathungu, 70 years old, also supports a large family with her old age pension grant. She could not afford the R10 to pay for water services in her village before the implementation of the FBW policy. She has also been relieved of the need to make arduous trips to the spring on a daily basis. Masakala is an unemployed member of the water committee. Her main complaints under the FBW regime are the rules for water use. She feels that when she paid R10 a month for water she used as much as she wanted, but since the FBW policy there are restrictions, and she occasionally needs to pay for additional water.

Clearly, FBW has made a significant difference to the everyday lives of people like Mathungu, Masakala and Mabombo. For one thing, it frees women from the time taken to collect water and the health benefits are clear, since they do not need to resort to unprotected streams. However, the issue of poverty alleviation raises questions because of the restrictions imposed by the FBW policy. For example, water cannot be used or is not enough for agricultural production, which could alleviate poverty in the area. The ANDM has stated categorically that it needs to prioritise basic water provision largely for drinking and washing for all the villages first, before upgrading schemes for agricultural production.

In Mdudwa village, a gravity-fed scheme was implemented in 2001. The scheme has seven standpipes, of which six were working when the scheme started operating. In 2003, only three taps were still in operation. There is a compulsory fee of R5 at Mdudwa, which every household is expected to contribute towards operation and maintenance. Most people in the village have refused to pay the fee because the standpipes closest to their households are not working, while others are not paying because they cannot afford to pay. Still others do not want to pay because they are unhappy with the conditions of the scheme. For instance, the communities require large amounts of water for cultural purposes, such as the practice of washing blankets for funerals and other ceremonies. The scheme does not provide enough water for these activities. Therefore, since the scheme has not improved people's livelihoods and has also imposed restrictions on water use for activities which are important to them, people generally perceive it as useless. Finally, there are also many people in Mdudwa who are not aware of the FBW policy.

Lessons from South Africa's Free Basic Water policy

The South African government stands alone in recognising the constitutional right to water. This is a great achievement. Yet, despite the existence of a constitutional right to water and related policies, millions in South Africa are either not aware of or not given access to this right. Thus, a right conceived at the national level is still to be realised on the ground in many parts of the country. The South African case highlights several lessons about rights as an accountability strategy in this regard.

Realising rights in practice

The FBW policy has not been implemented in a standardised way. Water service providers (who could be private companies, water boards, district municipalities or community-based organisations) interpret the policy in different ways. In some areas, the right to water has also been hindered by market processes such as cost recovery, leading to controversial cut-offs. This chapter has demonstrated that economic and social rights fail to be realised owing to sins of omission (the lack of funds and institutional capacity) and sins of commission (where rights are knowingly put at risk). The most persistent stumbling block to realising the right to water are sins of omission, as outlined in the section on the Eastern Cape. These include capacity problems on the part of local authorities and financial constraints. But one may also argue that cut-offs and high payments are sins of commission that put poor and vulnerable people's right to water at risk. The result is that some South African citizens still do not enjoy FBW and many are not even aware of their constitutional right to 25 free litres of water per day. Thus there is very uneven access to the right to water in South Africa.

The South African case highlights the difficulty in apportioning blame for rights violations and identifying who bears obligations and responsibilities to realise rights. This is a generic feature of the contemporary world, in which processes of economic globalisation have led to the proliferation of service provision by actors other than the state. As we saw in Chapter 2 of this book, this confuses lines of accountability, as channels of representation and redress central to accountability fail to keep pace with dispersed responsibilities.

Linking rights and poverty reduction

The FBW has certainly made a difference to the lives of poor people by addressing health issues and freeing women from time taken in collecting water. Still, the issue of poverty reduction seems to be lagging behind, especially with regards to water required for agricultural production purposes. The contentious issues concerning water for subsistence agriculture and cultural activities need to be resolved. The General Comment provides that states are required to ensure each person has access to sufficient, safe, acceptable, accessible and affordable water for personal and domestic use, and this is what the 25 litres per day per person achieves. But the Committee also states that while priority must be given to water for personal and domestic use, it is also important to recognise the need for water to meet the most essential aspects of each of the other relevant human rights (rights to livelihood, food, etcetera), for which the 25 litres do not suffice.

One reason why rights often do not make a great difference to poor people is because there is a marked lack of political will on the part of powerful stakeholders to enforce them in practice. The South African case highlights problems that arise when adequate financial resources are not provided to realise rights to water and when contradictions arise from market-based approaches. However, promoting the human right to water can only be the result of a conscious socio-political choice on the part of decision makers and local people. Continued attempts to mobilise around this right by communities and activists may provide governments with the mandate to stand by that right – for which they can subsequently be held to account, and which they can be pressured to enforce in an equitable manner.

Market dynamics versus rights
The discussion has highlighted the difficulty of implementing the principles of free basic water and cost recovery in tandem. The Committee clearly states that water should be affordable and not reduce a person's capacity to access other essential goods such as food and housing. This normally means that water must be subsidised for poor communities and provided free where necessary. This is the spirit of the FBW policy. But, the chapter has also demonstrated how cost recovery and privatisation dominate South Africa's water domain. Thus water is often unaffordable and cut-offs have contradicted and violated people's basic right to water. In rural areas such as the Eastern Cape, both willingness and ability to pay for water services were not very high, cost recovery was limited and there were many defaulters on payment for water use. There is thus a massive policy trade-off between thinking about free basic water for some and basic water for all. It is thus both dangerous and unrealistic to assume that cost recovery can be achieved amongst poor communities. When cost was an issue, a number of people

continued to use unprotected sources of water. Apart from health implications, the returns on investment for schemes where cost recovery applies could not be realised, since people did not always use them. It is compounded by the inherent tensions between rights-based and market-based frameworks, which assume and require different types of accountability politics. At times, though, markets may compromise social and economic rights since they 'can systematically deprive some individuals in order to achieve the collective benefits of efficiency' (Donnelly 1999: 628). Thus cost recovery and macroeconomic policies can have a direct negative impact on the right to water.

The politics of claiming rights and demanding accountabilities

Finally, how people demand accountability when their economic and social rights are violated is linked to the larger question of how rights are interpreted and deployed by local people. In urban areas, famous cases such as Grootboom (named after Irene Grootboom) have highlighted how poor people can be agents of change as they appeal to the Constitutional Court to advance their constitutional rights to basic services. In 2000, residents of Wallacedene, a large shantytown in the Cape Town area, made legal history when the Constitutional Court ruled in favour of their housing rights. Today, four years on, the people behind the historic Wallacedene settlement are still waiting for proper housing facilities. In fact, as one commentator argues, the only concrete building that the residents have is a stinking ablution block with broken pipes and inadequate sanitation (Schoonakev 2004). Since the Constitutional Court failed to specify which manifestation of the state – national, provincial or local – should honour the rights of the residents, there is a lack of clarity on where the locus of responsibility lies with regard to the implementation of the Grootboom judgement. The Constitutional Court also did not play any role in supervising or overseeing the implementation of the various orders, and the South Africa Human Rights Commission is only playing a monitoring role. Residents are angry because they now do not know where to turn. This highlights the difficulty of specifying duty bearers and their responsibilities in implementing economic and social rights.

In remote rural areas such as the Eastern Cape, the capacity of citizens to claim their constitutional rights to basic services is far lower than in the cities. Many people are not aware of their constitutional right to water. Therefore, they are less likely to hold the government to account if their rights are violated. In part this is because of their ignorance of these rights, and in part it is because the mediators of justice (courts, lawyers, activists) are more likely to operate in metropolitan areas than in remote rural ones.

These problems should not detract from the fact that constitutional endorsements of social and economic rights are very important. In acknowledging the right to water, the South African government has gone against the grain of conventional wisdoms, both on questions of the rights and entitlements of citizens and as reflected in donor debates on water provision. In this respect, the FBW is a remarkable achievement. Defending the constitutional right to water, poor people have successfully moved the courts to grant interim relief from disconnections. However, in order for rights to be more effective, attention needs to be paid to the caveats presented here: the lack of attention to poverty and livelihood questions; the problematic implementation of the policy; the lack of awareness; and the variable levels of accountability mechanisms to provide redress.

Implications for accountability

With the inclusion of new private actors, states are not merely enforcers of rights, but increasingly act as regulators and facilitators of rights (INTRAC 2003). Unfortunately, the General Comment and other such instruments do not explicitly identify private actors as accountable and responsible. Ironically, too, rights are denied at the 'behest of powers beyond the state itself' (INTRAC 2003: 3). For example, International Monetary Fund (IMF) and World Bank policies oblige states to curtail basic services and impose charges that exclude large numbers of vulnerable people. In this sense, global pressures have led to the state assuming a schizophrenic role as both the enforcer and violator of rights. Only the state can properly regulate the behaviour of markets and ensure that economic actors operate in a fair and transparent manner; only the state can provide adequate social protection to those who suffer insecurity and a loss of rights (ICHRP 2004: 60). But governments also become violators of rights by enforcing policies and programmes such as privatisation and structural adjustment that can erode people's rights. Protective provisions do exist. For example, under the Water Service Act no disconnections can take place on the grounds of inability to pay. But the onus of proving ability lies with the water user and will depend on the user's ability to access legal advice and representation – a minimal resource in many communities (COHRE 2004: 54). Thus links between ordinary citizens and their representatives in South Africa have become obscured through policy shifts towards GEAR and orthodox forms of neoliberal economic globalisation. This makes tracking processes of accountability difficult across these multiple scales.

This should not detract from the fact that rights do and should matter. The right to water is internationally recognised by both developing and industrialised countries as defined in General Comment 15. It includes clearly defined and realisable obligations, and thus forms the basis of concrete negotiations between the state, the communities concerned and civil society advocates. Moreover, the right to water in principle provides justiciable components to local claims and struggles around water and can also be used as a countervailing force against the commodification of water, which can impinge on poor people's rights. That few people in South Africa or around the world are demanding compliance and answerability on the right to water is another matter. But local struggles to realise the right to water are on the rise and the demand for accountability from water providers and those responsible for protecting this right will also therefore increase. If human rights are really to make a difference, we can only hope that more attention will be paid to the accountability mechanisms through which compliance and answerability become an indispensable aspect of the human rights regime.

NOTES

1 The empirical material in this chapter was generated through research conducted for the DfID-funded Sustainable Livelihoods in Southern African research programme and some sections of the chapter draw on Mehta and Ntshona (2004). I am very grateful to all my interview partners in South Africa for sharing their knowledge with me and to Zolile Ntshona for his insights and meticulous research. I thank Nurit Bodemann-Ostow and Paul Wright for their research assistance and competent internet searches. Comments by Carlos Cortez, the editors, Ian Scoones and Lisa Thompson helped strengthen the chapter. However, all responsibility for the errors that remain rests with me.

2 The Centre on Housing Rights and Evictions (COHRE) in Geneva, which has done extensive research on the right to water, clearly lays down the legal basis for the right to water (COHRE 2004). At the 1977 United National Water Conference, the Mar del Plata Declaration recognised that all peoples 'have the right to have access to drinking water in quantities and of a quality equal to their basic needs'. It has subsequently been recognised explicitly in several legally binding treaties, such as the Convention on the Elimination of all Forms of Discrimination Against Women (CEDAW, 1979), the Convention on the Rights of the Child (1989) and, more recently, in the General Comment 15.

3 DWAF official, personal communication by email, 16 May 2005.

4 Barry Jackson, personal communication, 23 December 2003.

5 DWAF official, personal communication by email, 16 May 2005.

6 See Mehta and Ntshona (2004) for more details.

7 Interview with the Deputy Director, Water and Sanitation, Alfred Nzo District Municipality, 10 December 2002.

8 Budget cuts have gone hand in hand with decentralisation in South Africa (Manor 2001). The function of water services provision is now performed by the municipality itself or by other public or private bodies. While this process devolves power to local authorities and gives more voice to ordinary citizens, it can also lead to shedding of functions and the dumping of 'unfunded mandates' on lower levels of government, which poor rural municipalities are not able to implement (Olver 1998).

9 Interview with DWAF official, Mount Ayliff, 23 April 2002.

10 Play pumps are designed in such a way that anyone can operate them. Children, who can get on and off the wheel as they play, can turn the horizontal wheel.

11 Of course what counts as 'sufficient water' is controversial. It is known that people can also survive on 10 litres of water a day (Mehta 2005).

REFERENCES

Bond, P. (2001) 'Privatisation, Participation and Protest in the Restructuring of Municipal Services: Grounds for Opposing World Bank Promotion of "Public–Private Partnerships"', The Water Page, www.thewaterpage.com/ppp_debate1.htm (accessed 16 November 2003).

—— (2002) 'Local Economic Development Debates in South Africa', Occasional Papers Series, No. 6, Municipal Services Project.

Bond, P., McDonald, D., Ruiters, G. and Greeff, L. (2001) Water Privatisation in Southern Africa: the State of the Debate, Cape Town: Environmental Monitoring Group.

COHRE (2004) 'Legal Resources for the Right to Water: International and National Standards', Geneva: Centre on Housing Rights and Evictions.

Community Law Centre, Socioeconomic Rights Project (2002) 'South African Cases: High Court Cases: Residents of Bon Vista Mansions v Southern Metropolitan Local Council 2002 (6) BCLR 625 (W)', http://www.communitylawcentre.org.za/ser/casereviews/2002_6_BCLR_625.php (accessed 18 March 2005).

COSATU (2003) 'Joint Submission by COSATU and SAMWU on the Draft White Paper on Water Services Presented to the DWAF', Congress of South African Trade Unions and South African Municipal Workers' Union, http://www.queensu.ca/msp/pages/Project_Publications/Reports/CosatuSamwu.pdf (accessed 18 March 2005).

Donnelly, J. (1999) 'Human rights, democracy and development', Human Rights Quarterly, No. 21, pp. 608–32.

DWAF (2005) 'Free Basic Water Project, Implementation Status', Department of Water, Agriculture and Forestry, http://www.dwaf.gov.za/FreeBasicWater/Defaulthome.asp (accessed 18 March 2005).

Goetz, A. and Jenkins, R. (2004) Reinventing Accountability: Making Democracy Work for Human Development, Basingstoke: Palgrave Macmillan.

Hausermann, J. (1998) A Human Rights Approach to Development, London: Department for International Development.

ICHRP (2004) Enhancing Access to Human Rights, Versoix, Switzerland: International Council on Human Rights Policy.

INTRAC (2003) 'Viewpoint: Rights or Values?', Newsletter of the International NGO Training and Research Centre, Oxford.

Jackson, B. (2002) 'Free Water – What Are the Chances of Serving the Poor', mimeo, Johannesburg: Municipal Infrastructure Investment Unit.

Kasrils, R. (2003) 'Minister Kasrils Responds to False Claim of 10 Million Cut-offs', www.dwaf.gov.za/Communications/Articles/Minister/2003/Cutoffs%20article%20WE BSITE.doc (accessed 4 May 2004).

McDonald, D. (2002) 'The Bell Tolls for Thee: Cost Recovery, Cut-offs and the Affordability of Municipal Services in South Africa', Municipal Services Project, http://qsilver.queensu.ca/~mspadmin/pages/Project_Publications/Reports/bell.htm (accessed 12 December 2003).

McKinley, D. (2003) 'Water is Life: the Anti-Privatisation Forum and the Struggle against Water Privatisation', Public Citizen, http://www.citizen.org/cmep/Water/cmep_Water/ reports/southafrica/articles.cfm?ID=10554 (accessed 12 December 2003).

Mehta, L. (2003) 'Problems of Publicness and Access Rights: Perspectives from the Water Domain', in I. Kaul, P. Conceiçao, K. Le Goulven and R. Mendoza (eds), *Providing Global Public Goods: Managing Globalisation*, Oxford: Oxford University Press.

—— (2004) 'From State Control to Market Regulation: behind the Border Policy Convergence in Water Management', IDS Working Paper No. 233, Brighton: Institute of Development Studies.

—— (2005) *The Politics and Poetics of Water. Naturalising Scarcity in Western India*, New Delhi: Orient Longman.

Mehta, L and Nshtona, Z. (2004) 'Dancing to Two Tunes: Rights and Market-based Approaches in South Africa's Water Domain', Sustainable Livelihoods in Southern Africa Research Report 17, Brighton: Institute of Development Studies.

National Treasury (1999) 'Provincial and Local Government Finances', *National Budget Review 1999*, Republic of South Africa, Chapter 4, http://www.treasury.gov.za/documents/budget/1999/review/chapter_4.pdf (accessed 7 May 2004).

—— (2004) 'Provincial and Local Government Allocations', *National Budget Review 2004*, Republic of South Africa, Chapter 7, http://www.finance.gov.za/documents/budget/2004/review/Chapter%207.pdf (accessed 7 May 2004).

Olver, C. (1998) 'Blueprint for the Business of Running Efficient Cities', *Sunday Times* (South Africa), 14 June 1998, http://www.suntimes.co.za/1998/06/14/insight/in04.htm (accessed 28 May 2004).

Pauw, J. (2003) 'Metered to Death: How a Water Experiment Caused Riots and a Cholera Epidemic', The Centre for Public Integrity, http://www.icij.org/water/report.aspx?sID=ch&rID=49&aID=49 (accessed 11 November 2003).

Plant, R. (1992) 'Citizenship, Rights and Welfare', in A. Coote (ed.), *The Welfare of Citizens: Developing New Social Rights*, London: Institute for Public Policy Research.

Schoonaker, B. (2004) 'Treated with Contempt', *Sunday Times*, 21 March.

SSA (2002) 'Measuring Rural Development: Baseline Statistics for the Integrated Sustainable Rural Development Strategy', Pretoria: Statistics South Africa.

Sunday Independent (2003) 'Attack the Problem not the Data: Report on the Number of People Affected by Water Cut-offs Was Based on Sound Methodology', 15 June 2003.

CHAPTER 4

Managing watersheds and the right to water: Indigenous communities in search of accountability and inclusion in Southern Veracruz

LUISA PARÉ AND CARLOS ROBLES[1]

The nature of the problem

Ecological degradation and economic injustice are often the result of the extraction or transfer of natural resources from poorer to richer, more influential regions. Dams, highway constructions and other major public works projects frequently generate conflict over natural resources that can be linked to a lack of accountability and adequate compensation mechanisms to address the impacts of natural resource extraction and exploitation. The story told in this chapter is one of imbalances of power between local communities and local, regional and national institutions; and of the conflicts and accountability problems related to these imbalances. The tensions that arise between these actors centre on the right to water; who exercises it and how; and the barriers to realising that right. A key issue that emerges in this case is the difficulty in realising the right to water and establishing accountability over how watersheds are managed, given the complex sets of actors and overlapping institutions and histories involved.[2]

Research for this chapter was carried out in the watershed of the Huazuntlán river (a tributary of the Coatzacoalcos) in southern Veracruz on the coast of the Gulf of Mexico, an area that provides 75 per cent of the water for industrial and human use in two petro-industrial urban areas with over half a million inhabitants, Coatzacoalcos and Minatitlán. To supply water needed to fuel the oil industry along the coast of south-eastern Mexico, water from the watershed is captured at the Yuribia dam (above the town of Tatahuicapan) in the rural mountainous rain forest region and transported for 60 kilometres by aqueduct to the cities below.[3] The compensation that these cities pay (or do not pay) to the indigenous communities living in the watershed is at the heart of a long history of conflict that has developed between these communities and the urban public water authorities.

This extraction accounts for water scarcity, both for urban dwellers and for rural people, because it has not been accompanied by the sustainable management of the watershed territory. After heavy rains, urban households often lack water for three days because of the excess of sediment that clogs the dam and water treatment facilities. This problem is related, on one hand, to a model of development that promoted forms of land use unsuitable to tropical soils, such as the extension of large-scale cattle ranching (Tudela 1989; Ewell and Poleman, 1980; Lazos and Paré 2000). On the other hand, it is related to inadequate planning and fragmented (sectorialised) public policies, and a centralised system of decision making. Decentralisation reforms in Mexico are intended to create spaces for public participation and accountability mechanisms, but these are often only consultative and not representative, and lack a permanent institutional life (Ribot 2002; Blauert 2004).[4]

Against this background, this chapter will examine the different strategies used by indigenous communities to realise the right to water and, in seeking compensation for water transfer, to build accountability in the way that the watershed is used and managed. It considers the governance issues, changes in perceptions of water and rights, mechanisms for participation and accountability (or their absence), and the conditions that prevent or lead to successful mobilisation for accountability. What this chapter reveals is that building accountability and co-responsibility between numerous actors with diverse and contradictory interests requires an ongoing process of negotiation and engagement through both formal and informal channels. For the rural indigenous groups living in the watershed, establishing accountability and protecting their right to water involves new challenges in establishing horizontal relationships of co-responsibility. These have to emerge within the communities themselves around the responsibility for maintaining the watershed, as well as between the indigenous communities, the urban municipalities and the reserve management. Our argument about accountability, therefore, is that the governance of (scarce) water requires a variety of mechanisms that can help to reconcile competing notions of accountability and correlate the associated rights and duties (see Mehta, Chapter 3). This chapter will show how traditional indigenous values can provide the basis for constructing a new, more solidly grounded culture of accountability.

The chapter includes a methodological and conceptual framework; a mapping of the social actors involved in water governance, and of their interests and perceptions; a description of the institutional and legal framework for water management and the gaps in mechanisms of accountability; and a discussion of the claims made by community organisations, and the resulting contestations, in the struggle to establish accountability. The chapter ends with some reflections on our role as researchers working to promote participatory and accountable natural resource management practices, and some conclusions about when particular strategies for demanding accountability around the right to water are successful. As an example of this, we present the strategy we designed in partnership with community groups for compensation of the environmental services they are providing.

Multiple strategies for natural resources management: a conceptual framework

In Mexico, the neoliberal development model's privileging of market forces has accelerated environmental destruction and the erosion of traditional local institutions. Major development projects have often deepened regional inequalities and the urban–rural gap as well as increasing social and political exclusion and poverty. The absence of an framework to address these inequalities is due to a lack of developed accountability mechanisms and rules, the poor enforcement of those that do exist, and the persistence of a political culture based on client–patron relationships (Paré 1975).

When communities lose control over their land, environmental degradation and poverty increases. In this case study, the transformation of land use, from slash-and-burn indigenous maize production into cattle ranching, has brought about not only the disruption of the rainforest landscape but also major social, cultural and political transformations.[5] Some authors define 'resilience' as the capacity of ecosystems to absorb disturbances or recuperate from natural events such as floods (Berkes 2004). But the capacity of ecosystems to regenerate is also influenced by the relationship between environmental and social change, and by social actors and institutions. In this case study, the relationship between environmental degradation and community institutions has an important influence on accountability issues.

Traditional notions of accountability are mostly limited to the obligation of governments to explain and justify their actions to citizens (Day and Klein 1987; Schacter 2000) and to electoral issues of ensuring 'free and fair elections'. A narrow notion of accountability, as discussed in the introduction to this volume, is often reduced within a good governance agenda to 'transparency',[6] focusing on the right to information. But a broader concept of societal accountability, as we saw in Chapter 2, 'involves social mechanisms outside the electoral sphere in which social movements supervise the legality of procedures carried out by politicians and public officials' (Smulovitz and Peruzzotti 2000: 32–3).[7] Also helpful to our discussion is the concept of co-governance for accountability, which 'confuses the boundary between state and society: in addition to co-producing specific services and pressuring government from the outside, social actors can also participate directly in the core functions of government itself' (Ackerman 2004: 451).

In terms of our case study, accountability is not reduced to a vertical claim by people against the state, but involves a two-way relationship in which different actors mutually claim their rights, and also define their obligations. Achieving accountability is not a question of merely creating institutional arrangements from above, but a process that requires new forms of negotiation and institutional arrangements for natural resource management that can benefit both those living within the protected areas and those outside them (Gaventa 2004).

Currently, and in relation to water specifically, there is a paradigm shift in the way that natural resources are seen. Water has moved from a common good to a tradable commodity (see Mehta, this volume), a shift that often distracts from community responsibilities for natural resource management. For example, in Mexico, payment for environmental services is seen, by the social movements organised around the opposition to mega projects and hydroelectric dams, as another attempt to privatise natural resources. In the final section of this chapter we describe our own experiences in relation to payment for environmental services, and examine the conditions under which it can provide better institutional arrangements that improve environmental conditions and livelihoods.

Starting with the premise that people are not necessarily a threat to ecosystems but can be a force for conservation (Buck et al. 2001), it has been our intention to carry out a joint enquiry with communities into arrangements over water use and how indigenous people have confronted the situation they face. Our concern is not only to increase academic understanding but to generate reflections that contribute to effective collective action, and to identify alternative solutions, consistent with strategies of civil accountability described in Chapter 2.

As action researchers and active promoters of proposals for how accountability could be improved, we saw our role as part of a creative process of collective learning (Leeuwis 2000) (see Box 4.1, p. 95).[8] Towards this end, we organised a range of activities including fora, workshops, focus groups with local actors, training programmes and community resource mapping. Sharing history, culture, environmental policies and landscape assessment with the local population opened the doors to an intercultural dialogue, which helped to create a common vision of the problems. Working on 'both sides of the equation' (that is, through dialogue with both government institutions and communities) aims to increase 'the receptivity of voice or responsiveness by the state' (Gaventa 2004: 17), although there was often resistance on the part of government institutions. In the conclusion to this chapter, we refer to the lessons learnt: the successes, difficulties and failures of this approach in building a new culture of accountability that connects rural and urban relationships to water management.

Mapping the different actors involved: conflicting uses, interests and perceptions

Figure 4.1 gives a picture of how the fluidity of water connects a variety of social actors. On its way down from the mountains in the reserve, the Texizapa river provides water for more than 13,000 people at local level. The Tecomaxochapan sacred spring has been transformed into a reservoir for the village of Tatahuicapan. Since 1985 the Yuribia dam has been diverting 800 litres per second from the Texizapa river to the industrial cities on the coast.

The current conditions of the watershed are not favourable to its conservation on a long-term basis. Pesticides, slash-and-burn agriculture on hills inclined at more than 35 per cent and cattle ranching produce erosion, pollution and sedimentation. The shrinking water volume seems to be of major concern to all the actors involved, including the people who live in the cities (especially the poor communities, who pay a disproportionately high cost for water), residents of the downstream villages, cattle ranchers using land on the reserve, and the urban municipalities authorities that control water distribution.

In Tatahuicapan, water is free and is seen as a common good. However the ecological conditions for resource management are now subject to individual or family-based decisions because the supportive societal norms either do not exist anymore or are not respected. The resilience of the system under these conditions is at risk. The fluidity of water streaming down the watershed is mirrored in the different interests and perceptions of different users regarding the nature of water and how it

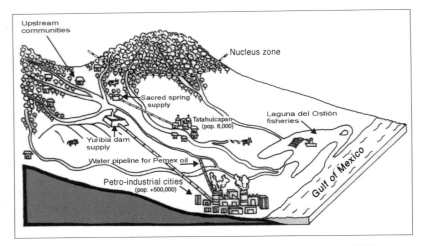

FIGURE 4.1 TEXIZAPA WATERSHED CATCHMENT: DIFFERENT WATER SUPPLY USES

should be used. Indigenous groups now claim the right to reciprocity for water extraction, and thereby to development, whereas the urban poor see water as a basic right. Indigenous communities base their claims to water on cultural and mythical tradition, as well as on specific livelihood needs. In the cities, people have no idea of the ecological problems upstream, the causes of water scarcity, or the threats regarding future supply. They perceive water service as expensive and inefficient; in moments of shortage, their interests and rights appear to be in conflict with those of the rural providers.

Table 4.1 helps to show the multiple actors and competing interests involved, including ourselves, as researchers.

Conflicting interests and perceptions over water

In order to understand the range of conflicting interests between so many different actors around the management of the watershed, how claims have developed and what strategies were used in different moments to build accountability, we sketch out a brief history of the institutional changes at local level, their effects on land use, the transformation of the rainforest, and perceptions of water. Across the region there is a strong sense of identity tied to the land. This is partly because at the end of the nineteenth century, before the Mexican Revolution, indigenous people

TABLE 4.1 MULTIPLE ACTORS AND COMPETING CLAIMS

Key accountability conflicts	Actors involved	Competing claims to water/watershed
Access to water	Ejidos/Ranchers	Agriculture
	Urban municipalities	Extraction for drinking water
	Rural municipalities	Drinking water/sacred resource
	Petrochemical industries	Extraction for industrial use
Distribution of water	Rural municipalities	Dam on municipal territory, watershed includes ejidos
	Urban municipalities	Water shortages affect urban residents
	Reserve management	Conserving rainforest
Watershed maintenance and conservation	Rural municipalities	Sustainable livelihoods
	Urban municipalities	Periodic compensation to rural municipalities for watershed maintenance
	Reserve management	Rainforest conservation and livelihood protection
	Universities/NGOs (including ourselves)	Environmental conservation, poverty reduction
	Federal and state government	Environmental conservation, economic development

lost part of their land to large landowners. Through agrarian reform, land was partially recuperated, but is now under the legal status defined by the state (*ejido* land tenure).

Prior to 1960, *ejido* land was owned in a communal way and traditional authorities – elder council, village chief (*jefe de pueblo*) – coexisted with *ejido* authorities recognised by the Agrarian Affairs Department (Velázquez 1997). The main crops were maize and beans. Water was perceived by the indigenous peasants of Tatahuicapan as a common good and local rules for its protection were strictly enforced through sanctions such as publicly exhibiting the offender or charging fines.[9] For example, logging was banned on common land, and river banks remained forested. Sporadically, Tatahuicapan cattle ranchers ran for the municipal presidency, and began to gain more influence.

Over the next twenty years, significant colonisation occurred as land was taken over, fenced in and virtually privatised into individual plots as government programmes gave priority to cattle ranching.[10] But small indigenous cattle ranchers fought to redistribute the land that had been monopolised, won a significant court case, and began to gain political force. Water was still perceived as a common good, with shared rules for access, independent of the individualisation of land holding. In losing power at local level, big ranchers also lost their positions in the municipal governments, and this contributed to their loss of control over land they had gained in the previous decades.

When the Yuribia dam was built in 1985, a large popular movement put pressure on the state government to respond to claims for education, health and public construction works for this marginalised area.[11] After the dam was seized by villagers from the whole watershed area in 1985, the city government of Coatzacoalcos signed an agreement where, in return for water, it would provide the necessary investment to improve urban infrastructure and services in Tatahuicapan. When the city later reneged on the agreement, further mobilisation by the residents of Tatahuicapan led to negotiations for additional concessions. Shutting down the valves of the dam was the best way that they could find to make their voices heard, and the success of this strategy has meant that water has become a weighty factor in the mechanics of social and political pressure.

Water has also gained an economic and a socio-political value for Tatahuicapan. Because the dam is on land owned by Tatahuicapan, the town itself has gained political clout and economic importance. Now in Tatahuicapan water transfer from the watershed to the cities is seen not only negatively but as an important instrument of negotiation. But despite concessions on services such as clinics and roads, no agreement was reached between the urban and rural municipal governments about watershed management. This brief description illustrates how perceptions of water have evolved following changes in landholding systems and patterns of water use.

Water management: gaps in mechanisms of participation and accountability

The fluid nature of water disperses its management between as many different institutions as the territories it crosses, resulting in atomisation of public interventions (land, water, forestry, agriculture, fisheries) and problematising greater inclusion and horizontal linkages between rural communities. The question of who is accountable to whom and on which issues becomes very complex as it involves multiple layers and chains of actors and institutions. In the next section, a short description of actors' interests and dynamics will help to contextualise our work as action researchers and the proposal to local government discussed later.

The dynamics of local institutions[12]
Specific conditions in the villages present a challenge to the adequate management of resources. It is through community institutions that the federal and state government applies its social, environmental and productive policies and programmes. For some indigenous people, water is sacred because they believe that revered spirits inhabit rivers and streams: this religious perspective is in paradoxical conflict with the poor management reflected by common practices such as pollution, deforestation and unsustainable fishery practices.[11]

At the local level, the most important spaces for public participation are the assemblies (by *ejido*, village and barrio) and the working commissions. Changes in these institutions wrought by external programmes and actors have reduced communal capacity to avoid negative impacts on their environment by creating or validating norms. Loss of community control is closely linked to changes in landholding systems, which have moved from communal to private tenure in 40 years. For instance, the government plan to regulate land tenure, the Programme for Secession of Ejido Rights, has contributed to the loosening of the assembly's powers to regulate land use, including sales and purchases. This practice has now expanded to include outsiders, who are not interested in local institutions such as the village assembly. Since the municipality was created, land-based governance institutions (*ejido* assembly, *comisariado ejidal* and vigilance council) have become isolated and have fewer connections with other local and regional institutions. Different political parties fight to control either the municipal government or agrarian authorities such as the Ministry of Agrarian Affairs. The current municipal government, in office for a three-year term, has become a protagonist in the politics around watershed management. But while the current municipal government is open to cooperation, the continuity of plans and possibilities for collaboration with non-governmental actors are subject to power shifts within and between political parties.

Although traditional indigenous community structures are being eroded, they still maintain principles of reciprocity and cooperation (Mauss 1967, Durstom 2002), as well as the necessary trust for the tasks required (Durstom 2000). These practices should not be romanticised, but they are important in understanding how accountability can function at the local level. For example, the *tequio* is a traditional institution used for public works based on *mano vuelta* (exchange of non-paid labour among peasants). While increasingly less common, these traditions do persist. Although the term 'accountability' does not exist in local indigenous culture, the values of reciprocity and cooperation, and the constant consultation between local authorities and the assembly on overarching issues, constitute a form of accountability in practice. Municipal government must respect decisions taken at the general public assembly. It is also on the basis of these values that villagers demand information from local authorities regarding their actions. However, there have been cases when accountability at the local level has broken down. For example, when the local water committee did not provide information on how fees villagers paid for the network maintenance were being used, people stopped paying and refused to participate in the committee's assemblies.[13] Local institutions are in constant interaction with external actors, including both the federal and state government, concerning social policies, financing and other issues. These interactions are regulated by a legal framework. The way that the legal framework is enforced, however, often does not contribute to the consolidation of long-term institutional arrangements based on consensus between the different actors involved. The next section examines this problem.

Governmental institutions

In Mexico, the legal framework for water is governed by the Law of National Waters and supported by other statutes such as the Environmental Equilibrium and Protection Law and norms related to water quality. According to the national constitution, water resources belong to the Mexican state. The National Water Commission is a semiautonomous federal authority, which is part of the Ministry of Environment. The official position of the federal government is that community participation should play a key role in the sustainable management of water. The National Hydraulic Programme for 2001–6 includes institutionalised social participation in water management through river basin councils, commissions and committees amongst its objectives. Among diverse strategies to achieve the sustainable management of water in Mexico is that of 'inducing societal recognition of water's economic value, and to consolidate organized society's participation in water management' (NHP 2001).

At the national level, 26 river basin commissions have been created to represent diverse users. However, providers from the catchment sites are not represented on these commissions. The authorities of the mountain villages such as Tatahuicapan are often unaware of the existence of their right to participate in this commission. They have not been included, although it is precisely the space where the integration between environmental, forestry and water policies could be addressed. There are some questions as to the scope for participation in the river basin commissions: this participation is relative and limited as the law confers on the National Water Commission the authority to decide whom to invite. This feature allows the Commission's officers to manipulate the balance of power and to direct decisions towards objectives already established at other levels (Castelán 2002: 183–4).

Sub-watershed and micro-watershed committees could be an important planning instrument but, throughout the country, very few have been created or function when they do exist. At the time of writing, we were still awaiting a response from a state government agency we invited to help with the formation of such a watershed committee in Texizapa. Each ministry defines its strategy without real coordination with other actors (even if legal instruments and formal agreements require holistic approaches). The result is that policies are not only uncoordinated but often contradictory. Water management institutions such as the Municipal Water and Sanitation Commission and even the National Water Commission seem to believe that their job starts from the tap down, as opposed to starting with watersheds where water is produced. Until very recently, these institutions did not coordinate their policies with the agencies in charge of the environment in the watershed such as the Management of the Reserve, the Federal Secretary for Environmental Protection and the Ministry of the Environment and Natural Resources. This fragmented vision erodes the capacity of government agencies (for both water provision and water use) to protect the ecosystems. According to the Coatzacoalcos Municipal Commission for Water and Sanitation, water supply is not guaranteed for more than eight years, yet there is no coordinated water policy for the whole mountain area. Neither have the municipalities and *ejidos* within the watershed issued norms or regulations for the protection of water resources.

The accountability issue in all of this relates to the difficulty of enforcing existing laws and procedures for a better-planned system, including coordinated institutional interventions that would benefit both the cities and rural municipalities through the creation of arrangements to mitigate future conflicts between rural and urban communities. Building accountability is difficult because local institutions lack information about their entitlements within this legal framework, and higher authorities lack political will to listen to the voice of indigenous people, even when they have sound proposals. Within this context, there is no simple recipe for creating accountability, nor will accountability be achieved merely by designing improved institutional structures. Instead, power inequities need to be confronted and new cultures of accountability nurtured.

Power struggles between these institutions are in evidence. The remit of the National Water Commission involves significant powerful interests and money. Conservation institutions such as the Ministry of the Environment and Natural Resources have smaller budgets than the ministries of Energy, Finance or Economy.[14] In a context of weak accountability and a lack of participation, it is not easy to create policy on local agreements for water conservation, or develop oversight and monitoring mechanisms that could lead to greater accountability. Given this landscape of institutional actors, the next section will explore the strategies used at the local level to build more accountable management of the watershed.

Conflicts, claims and strategies

Since the dam was built in 1985, Tatahuicapan has struggled to obtain the enforcement of state commitments concerning education, communication and health services. When the state did not deliver on these commitments, groups from Tatahuicapan cut the water supply to the cities by closing off the dam valves, which has led to further conflict. The main demand behind these cuts was and still is constructed around reciprocity as the basis of a fair exchange (water for services). However, what has developed is a cycle where conflict breaks out between the residents of Tatahuicapan and the cities' water authorities. Village residents cut the water supply or take other similar measures, and the cities respond by appeasing the residents with short-term benefits that do not address the underlying problem of sustainable watershed management. Through this pattern of conflict–negotiation–conflict, marginalised indigenous groups have obtained some short-term benefits, alleviating some social pressure for broader or more substantive changes.

However it does not always work out well for the political mediators. In 1985, when the community stopped the dam construction, community mobilisations overwhelmed the leaders. When people found out what type of negotiations their local authorities had agreed to regarding the construction of a health centre, they kidnapped the leaders and interrupted the construction until state authorities came to negotiate again. Traditional community practices of accountability required the leaders of the movement to exert pressure for compliance with the agreements.

The lack of accountability of the existing municipal authorities of Mecayapan (to which Tatahuicapan belonged at that time) in negotiations with the cities over their commitments to provide services to the villages resulted in the inhabitants of the watershed developing a strategy for direct action. In October 1993 some four thousand indigenous people, armed with bows, arrows and machetes, closed the valves of the dam and left the cities without water for three days. Four years later the new municipality of Tatahuicapan was recognised by the state Congress, which meant that the government had a responsibility to provide services to the municipality. Each case of direct action by indigenous groups against the dam is answered by the urban municipal governments with immediate material concessions, such as paving a road or contributing money towards a school. These responses do not address the underlying causes of conflict. The delay in the delivery of these concessions fuels the cycle of social mobilisation, which sometimes leads to violence. Water has become a tool to exert pressure on the government, and some groups in Tatahuicapan have clearly come to believe that cutting off the water supply is the only way to draw government attention to their needs.

It is difficult to discern if the city government's delay in introducing institutionalised accountability, such as formal procedures for compensations, is deliberate. The fact that urban authorities have managed to deal with such uncertain institutional arrangements for over 20 years shows that city governments were not under much pressure from their citizens to provide information about what really goes on in the water catchment areas and how the city water authority invests the funds from the fees paid for water. In the absence of predictable rules and durable institutions, the residents of Tatahuicapan (the weaker party) occasionally have been able to hold the city hostage in order to speed up the process of legal recognition of their territory as a separate municipality. The cost of this unpredictability for urban consumers is that they have had to put up with water shortages because city authorities do not honour agreements made with the rural mountain communities, and because the sustainable management of the catchment area seems not to be in the political interests of any of the institutional actors involved. The dynamics of conflict over water, and the strategies used by indigenous groups in Tatahuicapan to force government actors to deliver on their commitments, illustrate how accountability is a two-way relationship. Thus having adequate institutions in place does not necessarily lead to accountability in the absence of citizen action.

Building accountability through shared responsibility: a plan built through action research

Over the past three years of participatory research, we engaged in dialogue with the local government in Tatahuicapan to generate new concepts and practices for more accountable institutional arrangements over the long term. In our experience, Leeuwis's argument that solutions to the dilemma of contradictory interests are possible when the actors involved can create spaces for negotiating strategies, and find tools to strengthen trust, faces some significant challenges (Leeuwis 2000). Changes in some of the institutional relations analysed above, which are embedded in a context of conflict, clientelism, exclusion, lack of coordination, and the absence of spaces for participation, require new forms of negotiation and institutional arrangements. For instance, in practice, the government only pays compensation in some years and not in others. And as no conservation plans exist, the compensation funds are not invested in reforestation or sustainable land management projects, but in urban services in Tatahuicapan. The army manages government reforestation programmes without significant participation by local people. Only the district head municipality is allowed to participate in negotiations over the reforestation programme. The remainder of the villages in the watershed are excluded from this process.

The adoption of new political practices that can contribute to greater accountability is possible only if there is political will on both sides. Participatory governance is an alternative that can lead to increased accountability to marginalised groups, but it cannot be 'simply achieved from above with new policy statements, but ... requires multiple strategies of institutional change, capacity building, and behavioural change' (Gaventa 2004: 5). This section will explore the advances that have been made in building accountability and realising the right to water, in part through our own efforts as action researchers.

Over the past three years, we have developed an agenda around building mechanisms that would lead to greater accountability and sustainable management of the watershed, involving both rural and urban poor. We have started planning meetings in the villages to organise a regional committee to facilitate a redistribution of decision-making power to local and regional levels. This committee will also help to build trust between users and providers, and between rural and urban poor and government institutions. With the institutionalisation and long-term perspective of local and regional agreements where local actors have representation, the risk of conflict is diminished. A fund will be administered by the watershed committee, on the basis of land management plans, administering and monitoring the funds for the watershed restoration.[15] This proposal creates the possibility of financing rural development by taking into account the externalities in the cost of water. Several mechanisms, including payment for environmental services, taken either from the users' fees or from subsidies, would support development infrastructure and sustainable production.

Our approach to increasing accountability is summarised in a manifesto now signed by both local government institutions and community groups: A Strategy for Common Survival: Water and the Relationship between Tatahuicapan, Coatzacoalcos, Minatitlán and Cosoleacaque. It synthesises many discussions with all of the key actors involved, and represents a shift from the traditional form of negotiation because it is contingent upon the willingness of representative stakeholders from both the cities and the villages to discuss new arrangements of rules.

This shift towards increased dialogue between urban and rural political institutions does not exclude the possibility of social mobilisations. As Gaventa has argued, the possibility for social mobilisation is an important element in building accountability:

> Given that inequalities in power often exist, the struggle to attain authentic and meaningful voice by community leaders may involve conflict, as well as collaboration. While some approaches to partnership overemphasise consensus building to the exclusion of conflict, others point out that conflict and collaboration often must go hand in hand. (Gaventa 2004: 16)

But the contents of the new proposal address both spaces for citizen participation, and compensation mechanisms for watershed management.

Traditionally, in exchange for water, rural indigenous communities demanded development in kind: schools, roads, health centres and basic services. Now cash is required to finance watershed restoration. The president of the Tatahuicapan municipality, in his only appearance at the commission before his term ended, announced at a river basin commission meeting that part of the resources obtained from the fees paid for water would be deposited in a municipal fund as a form of 'social investment for sustainability' to finance projects for the watershed restoration.[16] This proposal has some advantages over the mainstream approach of payment for environmental services, as we explain below.

The federal government has initiated a 'Payment for Hydrological Environmental Services Programme'. However, in the Tuxtlas watershed, the failure of the government to deliver the payment promised during the first year in that part of the reserve provoked rejection by the local communities. The main problem with the programme (which entails a five-year period of obligatory conservation of forest cover) is that, rather than involving people in community participation for sustainable management, the programme offers individual contractual relationships between the government institution and the local authority that do not always deliver the correct amount of funds to the registered owner of the land. Significant internal conflicts have resulted from this ill-conceived approach.

Our alternative proposal involves community agreements and mechanisms to establish permanent norms and responsibilities. The participation of all the main actors – including watershed villagers, local rural authorities, urban municipalities, state and regional water bodies, the reserve director and local NGOs – in the fund's decisions would guarantee accountability. Despite the conciliatory nature of the president of Tatahuicapan's speech at the Coatzacoalcos river basin commission meeting, the main official response was to deny the commission the ability to deal with these demands, which would become a responsibility of the urban municipalities.

Accountability mechanisms

The tools to share decision making and enforce accountability that have been developed by the municipal president of Tatahuicapan and our team include an effective legal framework, mechanisms of technical/ environmental monitoring, and a social audit. While these are very specific institutional steps, they are being taken in conjunction with wider measures to build trust and dialogue between the different actors

BOX 4.1

LESSONS LEARNT ABOUT RESEARCHING ACCOUNTABILITY

Throughout the case described in this chapter, we played different roles, sometimes simultaneously. Sometimes we were interviewers, or advisers in resource management and farming techniques, and at other times our role was to provide information and lobby government officials. But we always worked towards the objective of trying to reconstruct trust between the rural indigenous communities with water institutions in the cities. Based on this wide range of activities and our long history of engagement in processes at the local level in Veracruz, we highlight here some of the key lessons we learned about researching accountability.

- *The importance of understanding historical and cultural context.* When we walked together with men and women from Tatahuicapan to their sacred spring for the first time, we were able to learn about the different perceptions of men and women, young and old, about the causes of deforestation and the different approaches to solving it. This experience showed how our vision for accountable management of the watershed is just one among many.

- *Creating new parameters for negotiation.* This requires ongoing discussion between different cultural perspectives and different values, and that all the actors involved should respect these differences. The values of reciprocity and cooperation, and a vision of the common good were important assets that communities brought to their struggles for greater accountability and the right to water.

- *Respecting the pace of political and social change.* When involved in interviews with bureaucrats within the water management authorities in the cities, sometimes we felt we were getting ahead of the local government rhythm of change and it was necessary to slow down. There is a risk that research can undermine existing processes of representation, and take on roles that are not legitimate.

involved. The legal framework must reflect local and regional agreements; a technical monitoring will verify the responsible use of resources according to the management plan; and a social audit will ensure social equity among the rural stakeholders.

Although this will be a long-term process, some results are already discernible. Improvements in village sanitation have been made, such as fencing in pigs that pollute local water supplies and spread disease. A geographical information system and management plan for the watershed communities now serves to raise funds and as a reference for monitoring results. Alliances with urban actors have raised awareness of the cause of problems and willingness to cooperate with this plan.

The three-year term for local government is short and processes to create a new culture of accountability can easily be interrupted. In our view, our most important achievement to date has been the formation of experimental groups of men and women that have opened discussion at a community level about how to develop an environmental agenda. These groups are now engaged in finding representatives to take forward their proposals, and to influence public policies. They have formed an environmental citizen committee to discuss water management with the cities and different institutions.

Conclusion

This chapter has shown how informal strategies for demanding accountability have a central role in securing the right to water. We can now offer some key conclusions about improving accountability within this context.

Contradictions between local perceptions of rights
Conflicting legal frameworks within the existing web of economic and political power make it very difficult to institutionalise accountability mechanisms. The principles that underpin indigenous institutions, such as reciprocity and cooperation, can be reframed in terms of the management of the common good. They can also perpetuate conflict and lead to a crisis of governance. In the past, some situations have led to successful mobilisations while others have presented difficulties. Even when the city governments respond to accountability claims by the indigenous communities, their impact has been fleeting and has not helped to forge new mechanisms for long-term accountability. The responses of cities and the reserve management did not address underlying inequalities in ways that would help to avoid future problems in water supply.

Long-term strategies for accountability
The negotiation process must be seen as a middle-term and long-term strategy dependent on many internal and external factors. The three-year terms of the municipal government are not long enough to consolidate new institutional arrangements, which emerge in large part through a slow process of consensus building, both internally and with external institutions.

Changing both sides of the equation
In order to increase the possibilities of a partnership or dialogue between actors with different degrees of power, changes are required on the government's side to create deliberative spaces open to all actors and respectful of the different perceptions, views, needs and proposals of others. For the community, there are also great challenges. On one side the water issue has to be perceived in a generalised way as a problem that concerns not only the cities but also the villagers' welfare and responsibilities. Much more has to be done to enable the villages to improve the management of their own water resources.

Building alliances for accountability
What is needed is increased awareness, both in the urban municipal governments and in the communities within the watershed, about what is necessary to improve the management of water resources. The strengthening of alliances between different levels and forms of government – even within Tatahuicapan, between the municipal government and the *ejido* – is an important first step for consensus to be built around a sustainable development plan. These processes offer hope that the cycles of conflict and environmental degradation that impede the realisation of the right to water in both rural and urban contexts can be ended. The formation of the watershed committee and the recent establishment of a plan for watershed management and restoration with the municipality of Coatzacoalcos may signal a new phase in conflict resolution and environmentally sustainable management, where the rights to water in both rural and urban areas will be protected.

NOTES

1 Luisa Paré and Carlos Robles are attached to Instituto de Investigaciones Sociales, Universidad Nacional Antónoma de Mexico (UNAM) and Desarrollo Comunitario de los Tuxtlas Asociación Civil (DECOTUX AC), respectively.

2 For example, within the area of the biosphere reserve (see Note 3) and the wider watershed, there are a variety of landholding patterns. Land tenure is both *ejido* and

communal. Over 1,500 *campesinos* (peasants) in eight villages, mainly Nahuas and Popolucas, inhabit the area. Some are the descendants of the indigenous population that has occupied the area since prehispanic times. *Ejido* is a form of social ownership in which land, previously held by powerful landowners or the nation, is given to peasants who, until the 1992 constitutional reforms, could not sell it (only inherit it). An *ejidatario* is a person entitled to this type of property.

3 The region is part of a biosphere reserve created in 1998, the Reserva de la Biostera de las Tuxlas.

4 Most of the actual decentralisation reforms are characterised by an insufficient transfer of powers towards local institutions, under strict control of central government. Often local institutions do not represent the communities, nor are they accountable towards them.

5 In Tatahuicapan, over a period of 30 years, the extent of grassland converted from rainforest increased by 300 per cent (Lazos 1996).

6 Transparency, now a popular idea with many social movements, is limited in the Mexican legislation to the obligation for governmental agencies to publish basic financial information on their web pages and the right of citizens to demand and obtain this information.

7 'By focusing on the workings of traditional mechanisms of accountability, such as elections or the division of powers and the existence of an effective system of checks and balance among them, these diagnoses tend to ignore the growth of alternative forms of political control that rely on citizens' actions and organizations' (Day and Klein 1987: 1).

8 In action research or participatory research, community groups are not research objects but subjects who participate in the definition of the objectives of the whole process.

9 Interviews with elder Nahua peasants.

10 In 1960, five cattle ranchers controlled 57 per cent of the existing stock (Lazos 1996).

11 A pre-Hispanic myth was revived during the excavations for the dam, when the machinery hit a huge serpent, a Nahuat symbol for water. In keeping with the legend, the machine's operator died of fright. The serpent was taken to the capital zoo. As told to us by an older member of the community: 'It was the male; the female serpent remained to protect the spring.' The operator's symbolic death re-established a kind of reciprocity that allowed the water to be removed (after demands were met). See Blanco *et al.* 1992.

12 Here we adopt Leach *et al.*'s (1997) concept of institutions, 'as regularised patterns of behaviour that emerge from underlying structures or sets of rules in use'.

13 Interview with the head of the Tatahuicapan water supply.

14 In 2005, the Ministry of the Environment and Natural Resources had a US$1,542 million dollars budget; Finance US$2,162; Rural Development US$3,376; and Energy US$2,396. http://www.shcp.sse.gob.mx/contenidos/presupuesto_egresos/temas/ppef/2005/ index.html

15 This plan includes agroecological alternatives such as agroforestry, intensive cattle ranching, soil conservation and the establishment of community norms concerning access to natural resources.

16 'Social investment for sustainability' involves raising funds for conservation and restoration of the resources that underlie the compensation for environmental services.

REFERENCES

Ayuntamiento de Tatahuicapan and Carlos Robles (2003) *Una Estrategia para la Sobrevivencia Común: el Agua y la Relación entre el Municipio Indígena de Tatahuicapan y la Región Industrial de Coatzacoalcos–Minatitlán, en el Sur de Veracruz, México.* Santiago de Chile: Fondo Chorlaví.

Ackerman, J. (2004) 'Co-Governance for Accountability: Beyond "Exit" and "Voice"', *World Development*, Vol. 32, No. 3, pp. 447–63.

Berkes, F. (2004) 'Knowledge, Learning and the Resilience of Social-Ecological Systems', paper prepared for the Panel 'Knowledge for the Development of Adaptive Co-Management'. IACSP '04 Conference, Oaxaca, Mexico, August.

Blanco, J. L., Paré, L. and Velásquez, E. (1992) 'El Tributo del Campo a la Ciudad: Historias de Chaneques y Serpientes', *Revista Mexicana de Sociología*, Vol. 54, No. 3, pp.131–7.

Blauert, J. (2004) 'Espacios de Consulta o de Decisión? Los Consejos de la Política Ambiental Regional en México, X', paper at IASCP '04 Conference, Oaxaca, August.

Buck, L. E., Geisler, C. C., Schelhas, J. and Wollenberg, E. (eds) (2001)*Biological Diversity: Balancing Interests through Adaptive Collaborative Management*, Boca Raton, FL: CRC Press.

Castelán, E. (2002) *Las Presiones Sobre los Recursos Hídricos en México*, Mexico DF: Centro del Tercer Mundo para el Manejo del Agua.

Cortéz, C. (2004) 'Social Strategies and Public Policies in an Indigenous Zone in Chiapas, México', *IDS Bulletin*, Vol. 35, No. 2 (April), pp. 76–84.

Day, P. and Klein R. (1987) *Accountabilities: Five Public Services*, London: Tavistock.

Durstom, J. (2000) 'Qué es el Capital Social Comunitario?', Serie Políticas Sociales, No. 38, Comisión Económica para América Latina (CEPAL), Santiago de Chile.

—— (2002) *El Capital Social Campesino en la Gestión del Desarrollo Rural: Díadas, Equipos, Puentes y Escaleras*, Santiago de Chile: Comisión Económica para América Latina (CEPAL).

Ewell, P. T. and Poleman, T. T. (1980) *Uxpanapa Reacomodo y Desarrollo Agrícola en el Trópico Mexicano*, Xalapa, Veracruz: INIREB.

Folke, C., Carpenter, S., Elmqvist, T. *et al.* (2002) *Resilience for Sustainable Development: Building Adaptive Capacity in a World of Transformations*, Rainbow Series No. 3, Paris: International Council for Scientific Unions (ICSU), http://www.sou.gov.se/mvb/pdf/resiliens.pdf

Gaventa, J. (2004) 'Representation, Community Leadership and Participation: Citizen Involvement in Neighbourhood Renewal and Local Governance', study prepared for the Neighbourhood Renewal Unit, Office of Deputy Primer Minister, Institute of Development Studies, draft, February.

Lazos, E. (1996) 'La Ganaderización de dos Comunidades Veracruzanas: Condiciones de Difusión de un Modelo Agrario', in L. Paré and M. J. Sanchez, *El Ropaje de la Tierra: Naturaleza y Cultura en 5 Zonas Rurales*, Mexico City: Plaza y Valdéz Editores/ Universidad Nacional Autónoma de México.

Lazos, E. and Paré, L. (2000) *Miradas Indígenas Sobre una Naturaleza Entristecida. Percepciones Ambientales entre Nahuas del Sur de Veracruz*, Mexico City: Plaza y Valdéz Editores/Universidad Nacional Autónoma de México.

Leach, M., Mearns, R. and Scoones, I. (1997) 'Environmental Entitlements: a Framework for Understanding the Institutional Dynamics of Environmental Change', Discussion Paper 359, Institute of Development Studies, Brighton.

Leewis, C. (2000) 'Reconceptualising Participation for Sustainable Rural Development:

Towards a Negotiation Approach', in *Development and Change*, Vol. 31, No. 5, pp. 931–61.

Mauss, M. (1967) *The Gift: Forms and Functions of Exchange in Archaic Societies*, New York: Norton.

Mearns, R. (ed.) (1996) *The Lie of the Land: Challenging Received Wisdom on the African Environment*, Oxford: James Currey Publishers Ltd.

Mehta, L. (2000) 'Problems of Publicness and Access Rights: Perspective from the Water Domain', working paper, Institute of Development Studies, Brighton.

National Hydraulic Programme 2001–6 (2001) Mexico DF: CNA, Ministry of the Environment and Natural Resources.

Newell, P. and Bellour, S. (2004) *El Mapeo de la Transparencia o Responsabilidad Social: Orígenes, Contextos e Implicaciones para el Desarrollo*, Cuaderno de Investigación No. 2, Xalapa: IIS-UNAM-UAM-IDS.

Paré, L. (1975) 'Caciquismo y Estructura de Poder en la Sierra Norte de Puebla', in B. Roger (ed.), *Caciquismo y Poder Político en el México Rural*, Mexico DF: Siglo XXI Editores.

Paré, L., Robles, C. and Cortéz, C. (2002) 'Participation of Indigenous and Rural People in the Construction of Developmental and Environmental Public Policies in Mexico', in Gaventa, J., Shankland, A. and Howard, J. (eds), *Making Rights Real: Exploring Citizenship, Participation and Accountability*, IDS Bulletin, Vol. 33, No. 2, pp. 83–90.

Ribot, J. C. (2002) *La Descentralización Democrática de los Recursos Naturales: la Institucionalización de la Participación Popular*, Washington: World Resources Institute.

Sachs, I. (1994) 'Urban Futures: Six topics for MOST', Management of Social Transformation programmes (MOST), United Nations Educational, Scientific and Cultural Organisation, www.unesco.org/most

Schacter, M. (2000) 'When Accountability Fails: a Framework for Diagnosis and Action', Policy Brief 9, Institute on Governance, Ottawa.

Sen, A. (1995) *Nuevo Examen de la Desigualdad*, Madrid: Alianza Editorial.

Smulovitz, C. and Peruzzotti, E. (2000) 'Societal Accountability in Latin America', *Journal of Democracy*, Volume 11, No. 4 (October), pp. 147–58.

Tudela, F. (ed.) (1989) *La Modernización Forzada del Trópico: el Caso de Tabasco*, México DF: Proyecto Integrado del Golfo, El Colegio de México.

Velásquez, E. (1997) 'Configuración y Reconfiguración de la Comunidad Indígena: el Caso del Parcelamiento de "Ejidos Comunales" en la Sierra de Santa Marta, Veracruz', paper presented at Social Sciences Doctorate Programme Seminar, El Colegio de Michoacán A.C.

Wainwright, H. (2003) *Reclaim the State: Experiments in Popular Democracy*, London: Verso.

CHAPTER 5

Conflicting rights, environmental agendas and the challenges of accountability: social mobilisation and protected natural areas in Mexico

CARLOS CORTÉZ AND LUISA PARÉ [1]

This chapter explores the contradictions between the agendas and accountability strategies of different social actors in two protected natural areas (PNAs) of rainforest in Southern Mexico. Different interests and perceptions over the actors' rights are at the root of these contradictions, which undermine the construction of accountable practices around conservation and sustainable development strategies in PNAs. The two case studies are both situated in south-east Mexico: the Tuxtlas Biosphere Reserve in Veracruz, and the Montes Azules Integral Biosphere Reserve in Chiapas. These cases highlight questions about how to establish formal accountability mechanisms for defining development policies for environmental resources.

Divergences over land rights and knowledge rights have resulted from historical power imbalances, institutional complexity, and the different political and economic interests of the actors involved. Conflicts over land rights centre on disputes about how land rights are guaranteed and how land is used. Conflicts over knowledge rights, on the other hand, have emerged from different views about 'traditional' or 'indigenous' knowledge, who has the right to knowledge about plants, medicine and other resources in the rainforest, and how these resources should be used. Given these conflicts over land and knowledge rights, and the institutional and historical complexity that underlies them, this chapter explores the difficulties in building meaningful accountability. What this chapter shows is that divergent and contradictory views of rights over resources can lead to and sustain conflict that makes building accountability extremely difficult.

The challenge of establishing accountability mechanisms in natural reserves in Mexico is sharpened by an underlying and fundamental tension: the different actors involved in the PNAs have radically divergent views and discourses about the nature of the resource (the environment) that should be protected and thus of the rights that follow from their competing conceptions. The most important actors involved in PNAs are federal, regional and local governments, multilateral and local NGOs, transnational corporations, universities, indigenous communities, and community-based organisations. For some of these actors, such as conservationist NGOs, natural resources should be conserved and protected because of their intrinsic value, while for others, such as transnational corporations, natural resources are considered as economic goods. Priorities for the indigenous population are access to land and territorial rights, which in some cases they were entitled to before the creation of the reserves.

Cooperation between these different actors is necessary to reach environmental, economic and social objectives, but it is not very common and has been unstable when it occurs. This can be explained in part by the lack of trust between different actors, which is an underlying factor that contributes to the difficulties in building accountability. The obstacles to accountability are compounded by the absence of spaces for participation in the way these resources are controlled and managed, where the different views of nature and the environment could also be expressed and at least partially reconciled. This chapter will explore how diverse interests generate conflict, contributing to a lack of accountability in the way that the environment is controlled and managed. It will also explore examples of when different actors have succeeded or failed in constructing accountability, where accountability is understood as a two-way relationship in which different actors mutually claim their rights and define their obligations (Gaventa et al. 2002).

The main issues at stake are, on one hand, that indigenous people have traditional as well as constitutional rights to their land, and, on the other, that they have physical access and knowledge rights to the natural resources contained there. However, these rights seem to be in conflict with the conservationist agenda, advanced by both the federal government and environmentalist international NGOs (INGOs), which asserts the need to conserve remaining natural resources. The approach to creating PNAs to achieve this goal has been pursued without establishing adequate procedures for the participation of the local population, or consideration for how to protect livelihoods – yet both these requirements are essential to making rights real as part of a broader agenda of human development.[2] This omission is important in the light of the different understandings of the environment that lie at the heart of some of the conflicts over rights and the lack of accountability in southern Mexico. Arturo Escobar's (1999) categories of different discursive formations on resource management are useful in terms of classifying these different understandings of nature as a resource because the range of views he presents are those expressed by the key actors in these cases:

1 The *globally centred* perspective is shared by most NGOs from the North, and is based on representations of threats to biodiversity. The extinction of species is a main focus. Nature is seen as a global resource that must be protected. This perception is related to three concepts: conservation, sustainable development and benefit sharing (either through intellectual property rights or other mechanisms).[3]

2 The *sovereignty* perspective, advocated by some governments, focuses on the ability of Southern countries to negotiate the terms of treaties and biodiversity conservation strategies. Nature is seen as a resource that individual countries should control, a principle that has been affirmed by successive environmental treaties.

3 The *biodemocracy* perspective focuses on democratic control of biological resources. The social movement against biodiversity prospecting, discussed in this chapter, would be an example of a social movement based on a biodemocracy perspective. Nature is seen as a resource belonging to communities who have traditionally held the land where the rainforests exist.

4 The *cultural autonomy* perspective is part of a critique of neoliberalism, and emphasises different cultural approaches to nature and the need for an intercultural dialogue. Many indigenous movements in Mexico and Latin America have adopted this perspective, including the Zapatistas in Chiapas. Other groups, less politically motivated, also try to conserve their modes of livelihood on the basis of a specific type of relationship with their environment. For example, one movement opposes the PNAs as top-down approaches to conservation, and advocates community-run reserves as an alternative. From this standpoint, autonomy from the government is a necessary precondition for demanding collective rights in a diverse and heterogeneous society. Nature is seen as a politically contested resource, with joint responsibilities for its conservation.

Each of these discourses about nature also connects to the co-construction of separate discourses and practices of accountability – with different approaches to who should control 'nature', the way the environment should be used and managed, and which rights claims should be upheld.

This case shows how different views about environment and nature, as well as conflicts over specific rights to concrete resources, contribute to a context in which institutional change alone cannot bring about accountability. Instead, competing and overlapping interests must be reconciled through a politics that brings these different perspectives to the fore. This chapter will focus on how social movements and political mobilisations around specific rights claims have a key role in constructing accountability through these means.

The first section of this chapter includes some general information about the institutional and legal frameworks and public policies in PNAs, and some key characteristics of both reserves. The second section explores the conflicting interests of different actors around land rights, and the implications of these differences for accountability. The third section focuses on conflicts between the actors' perspectives of knowledge rights, and identifies some accountability gaps in the relationships between the different actors involved. Finally, this chapter will explore some of the consequences for accountability of these conflicts over rights, and some of the changes that could lead to increased accountability and improved governance.

The institutional and legal framework of public policies in PNAs

In Mexico in the 1960s, when agrarian reforms led to demand for more land, the agricultural frontier moved out towards the tropical rainforests, the last refuge for landless peasants who were seen as a threat to large landowners' interests in different regions. From the 1960s to the 1970s different laws and programmes were implemented in order to colonise the rainforests, which were then transformed into grasslands: this process increased the diversity of ethnic groups living in these regions.

But from the 1980s, pressure from conservationist INGOs was mounting on the Mexican government to take steps to protect rapidly dwindling areas of rainforest. As a result, a series of PNAs were created across Mexico during the 1980s and 1990s. Many of the PNAs have been established in regions with a dense population. When reserves are created, the first policy tools used are the establishment of conservation and management zones (nucleus and buffer zones) and the definition of governance plans for the reserves.[4] The nucleus zone must be free of productive activities, while in the buffer zone local communities can engage in ecotourism or other environmentally sustainable activities. When reserves are created, land rights can be suspended on the basis of public interest. Reserve decrees have been criticised for being imposed without the participation of the communities affected by their creation, for not respecting promises of indemnities, and for the constraints the reserves place on local people's livelihoods, which is a factor that inhibits effective accountability relationships between the different actors involved. At a workshop on PNAs in Chiapas in February 2005, one participant explained:

> Our right to be consulted and to be part of the decision-making process in regions declared biosphere reserves is denied to us. We reject pressures made in different ways for relocation and disguised as peaceful – as they do not guarantee a future with dignity for us.

The essence of the actual conflicts between different actors' interests and agendas around PNAs cannot be understood without reference to the Plan Puebla Panama (PPP). The PPP, a mega-project for the economic integration of south-eastern Mexico and six Central American countries, is intended to promote investment, infrastructure and socio-economic and human development. As reactions to the PPP show, the creation of PNAs is seen by some as part of a politically contested process of gaining control of natural resources. The Mesoamerican isthmus, situated in the south-eastern part of Mexico, including Chiapas and Veracruz, is of immense strategic value as natural resources (oil, biodiversity and water) are plentiful. With generally high levels of poverty in the area, cheap labour is also abundant.

Over the past five years, in regional and international meetings held in Mexico and Central America, several social movements have wholly rejected the PPP. For example, the political leadership of the Zapatistas considers the PPP to be part of a geopolitical strategy designed to control natural resources and exploit the local labour force, to the detriment of the culture, territorial control and rights of the indigenous people (Resistencia Ciudadana al Plan Puebla Panamá 2002). This chapter will explore in greater detail two cases of PNAs where control of natural resources is being disputed: the Montes Azules Reserve in Chiapas and the Tuxtlas Biosphere Reserve in Veracruz.

Biosphere reserves in tropical rainforests: from agricultural frontier to biodiversity's last boundary

The Montes Azules Integral Biosphere Reserve, Chiapas
Three decades ago, the Mexican government, motivated by international environmental concern for conservation, created the Montes Azules

Integral Biosphere Reserve (Montes Azules Reserve) covering 331,200 hectares in the Lacandona rainforest in Chiapas. The reserve is located in the Usumacinta basin, which contains 30 per cent of the country's water resources and has the greatest levels of biodiversity in North America. But since the creation of the Montes Azules Reserve, the situation in Chiapas has changed dramatically with the emergence of a well-organised and militarised social movement, which is challenging the government's policies on the PNA.

Eleven years ago, in January 1994, on the same date that the NAFTA (North American Free Tree Agreement) came into force, the Ejercito Zapatista para Liberacion Nacional (Zapatistas) emerged as an armed movement in Chiapas, denouncing the situation of indigenous populations in Mexico and demanding changes at national level. Social mobilisation has been instrumental in pushing for changes in state-level legislation, and has also led to the creation of autonomous municipalities and *juntas de buen gobierno* (Good Governance Councils) as part of this process.

Since 1994, the government's response to the Zapatista movement has varied from a strictly military response to political negotiations, although these were suspended several years ago. The government has vacillated, sometimes accepting that the demands are just but at other times accusing the Zapatistas of manipulation by external interests. It has both dismissed the Zapatistas as a purely localised movement, and allowed Zapatista political leaders to present their position at the National Congress Tribune in 2001. Changes at national and state government level in 2001 have now slightly modified this perspective (Cortéz 2004). Despite the highly variable relationship between the Zapatistas and the Mexican government, the Zapatistas have come to play a central role in the politics of accountability around the Montes Azules reserve.

Tuxtlas Biosphere Reserve
Situated on the Gulf of Mexico coast in Veracruz, the Tuxtlas Biosphere Reserve was created in 1998 and covers 155,220 hectares (see Chapter 5). Within the boundaries of the reserve are over 121 poor rural communities, with a total population of 350,000 (including three medium-sized towns). Indigenous groups, including Nahuas and Popolucas, have lived in this area since pre-hispanic times. As in Chiapas, public policies promoting resettlement and cattle ranching have accounted for the destruction in about 50 years of more than 85 per cent of the original forest (Lazos and Paré 2000). Many previous initiatives to create a PNA in the region (1937, 1979, 1980) had no impact at all as they were only

formal declarations without any specific policies for implementation. The reserve created in 1998 is intended to promote the sustainable management and conservation of the Tuxtlas region. With water shortages affecting lowland urban areas with their petro-chemical industries, and flash flooding taking lives in the mountainous watershed, a general consensus had been reached that something needed to be done.

There are serious environmental concerns behind the creation of both of these reserves. But the process of establishing the reserves has generated conflict between competing sets of rights – and thrown into relief the radically different views of the main actors involved regarding nature as a resource. The lack of opportunities for participation by these different groups in the management of the reserves also contributes to the lack of accountability and the high levels of mistrust. These factors together have contributed to an extremely complex situation, one in which it is very difficult to establish lines of accountability. The next section will explore more closely the creation of the reserves as a source of conflict over land rights, and the strategies of poorer groups to claim their rights in response.

Competing claims and land rights

Montes Azules

The complex land tenure pattern in the Lacandona rainforest is the result of two processes. On one hand, for many decades the government's agrarian ministry has granted different groups endowments to the same lands, creating conflicts between them. On the other, many indigenous families have settled within the reserve area without governmental approval and claimed land for themselves according to traditional land tenure practices. These processes have contributed to competing claims to land rights. In some cases, formal land rights granted by the government are in direct contradiction with each other, and in other cases formal land rights clash with informal claims by indigenous people who are actually living on the land.

Without taking into account the reasons for emigration of indigenous people into the reserve, many government officials (including the director of the National Ecology Institute) and NGOs such as the World Wildlife Fund (WWF) and Conservation International have accused the recently settled population in the Biosphere Reserve of being responsible for environmental destruction caused by slash-and-burn agriculture and the shift to cattle ranching. In April 2000, WWF and a group of ecologists, concerned about conserving the rainforest in the reserve, called upon the Mexican government to stop the destruction of rainforest by indigenous people. The government and some conservation NGOs demanded their eviction, by force if necessary. In response, the federal government began to implement a plan to relocate the population to new settlements in locations outside the reserve, in order to relieve environmental pressure on the rainforest. While the conservationist NGOs and certain elements of the government advocate the forced resettlement of indigenous people living in the reserve area, indigenous groups are claiming the right to the land within the reserve.

An official from the Agrarian Ministry pointed out in an interview that the range of actors interested in Montes Azules makes it the most complicated reserve in Chiapas – with the most pressing environmental problems. Transnational companies (Grupo Pulsar), the World Bank (GEF in the Tuxtlas), international NGOs (Conservation International in Chiapas), the United States Agency for International Development (USAID), national or regional NGOs and academic institutions are all important actors.[5] The federal and local governments and indigenous groups settled around and in the reserves are also central actors.

A land rights and environmental sustainability round table was created in 1988 as part of an inter-institutional agreement between the federal and the state governments to reach workable solutions to the competing land rights and environmental problems.[6] But the interests, positionality, and negotiation capacity of the different actors involved are not equal. Some indigenous groups have been able to negotiate the conditions for their resettlement and protect their land rights. Others, particularly those who have only recently settled in the reserve, have very little capacity to negotiate.

The fundamental dispute between environmental conservationists and indigenous groups claiming land rights within the reserve has not been resolved. The underlying causes for this tension have been oversimplified by the polarised debate. According to the special officer from the Agrarian Reform Ministry in Chiapas:

> the causes of emigration to the rainforest must be considered in order to be able to define the most adequate responses…. [This perspective] created some internal dissent because the environmental sector was interested only in the irregular settlements, while we proposed to look at what is happening in the buffer zone in order to find out if we are creating conditions to allow people to have alternative livelihoods…. Many of the existing settlements in the Montes Azules reserve were generated by the land reform and the governmental policies…. This means that the deforestation process in Montes Azules was related not only to the illegal occupations of the reserve but to other issues.[7]

DEMANDS AND RESPONSES

The different groups established in the reserve have responded in different ways to this pressure from government and conservationist NGOs to relocate. Some have been willing to negotiate with the government and accept resettlement, while others have negotiated the recognition of their right to remain in the nucleus zone of the reserve. Other communities (especially those linked to the Zapatistas) have refused to negotiate with the government or give up their rights to the land within the reserve.

In contrast with the government's 'globally centred' perspective on the environment and nature, the principal demand of the Zapatista movement is the implementation of the San Andres Agreements signed by the Mexican government in 1994, accepting not only the recognition of indigenous people's rights and culture but also their territorial autonomy. One of the main factors in the breakdown of dialogue between the federal government and the Zapatistas is their different concepts of cultural and land rights. While the Congress Commission created to negotiate with the Zapatistas agreed on the central issues of cultural rights, the law approved in 2003 by the Congress dismissed this consensus and did not recognise the right to autonomy. This difference drove the Zapatistas to suspend negotiations and to resist all government-led neoliberal reforms. In the light of this general opposition, the Zapatistas consequently reject government-led environmental and development policies, including the attempts by the government to resettle people within the reserve area.

Although some of the Zapatista demands are related to land rights in the reserve, these land rights are linked to wider issues such as their cultural, social and political rights, self-determination, protection of their natural resources, and autonomy for the indigenous people within the national political agenda. For the Zapatistas, the Reserve is further evidence of the interests of global capital controlling natural resources, biodiversity and traditional knowledge. By having their land rights denied, the reserve settlers are also deprived of their rights to education, health and other services, which are tied to having land rights.

Tuxtlas

> The same federal government that gave us rights to the land was taking it away from us ten years later. (Peasant from a village in the Tuxtlas reserve)

In Tuxtlas, the creation of nucleus zones within protected natural areas has led to a range of effects on indigenous people's land rights: the expropriation of *ejido* land in its entirety,[8] the expropriation of a portion of village land, and the restriction of rights to communally held forests. In all, some 800 families have had their land rights affected by the creation of protected natural areas.

Although this land expropriation by the state has a legal basis (conservation in the public's interest), it directly clashes with the land rights granted by the state less than thirty years previously (see Paré and Robles, this volume). In the 1970s and 1980s, indigenous people in Tuxtlas received formal titles to their land after twenty years of struggle and attempts at land reform. In some cases, they received the formal rights to their land *after* the reserve decree, which then expropriated the same land for conservation.

In the process of land expropriation to create the PNA, the main grievance raised by the indigenous communities was the low price the government offered as compensation (US$200 per hectare, or less than a quarter of the land's commercial value). Losing land rights also meant giving up the rights to subsidies, which amount to half of the income of rural families in the region (Velázquez and Ramírez 2005; Leonard 2005). Communities rejected government reallocation offers as they meant emigrating from the region to locations without basic services such as roads, education and health facilities. Three of the villages filed injunctions against the government as a result of the land expropriations. But attempts to hold the state accountable for their actions in creating the reserve and perpetuating a situation of contradictory land rights have been impeded by the government's refusal to engage with communities:

> The government assumed that if they consulted people about the creation of the reserve, nobody would accept it. But there was no explanation, not even one attempt to create awareness or to negotiate. The same federal government that had given us the land was taking it away from us ten years later. For the majority of *ejidatarios* it was a betrayal. (Peasant from an expropriated community in Tuxtlas)

Conflicts between indigenous communities' rights to land and environmental conservation have been exacerbated by the top-down creation of protected natural areas. The lack of spaces for citizen participation in the creation and management of the reserve has contributed to increasing mistrust between the main actors involved and the politicisation of rights claims to land. Because of the reserve decree, there is an increased sense at the community level that the federal government has the responsibility to manage the reserve and resolve conflicts over land rights, but at the same time the communities themselves have increasingly fewer opportunities to contribute to the solutions to these problems. The strained relationships between key actors, and the apparently intractable conflict between rights, has important implications for accountability.

DEMANDS AND RESPONSES

For nearly five years the state government, responsible for the *ejido* land indemnities, was reluctant to enter into dialogue with the communities and resolve the conflicts over land rights. Two state elections (2000 and 2005) and the arrival of a host of new government officials has meant the suspension of previous agreements that had been reached between federal and state authorities concerning the reserve. The situation created by land expropriation and the fear of relocation rapidly became politicised as affected people turned to opposition political parties for solutions. In a vicious circle, state government repeatedly suspended negotiations because of this politicisation. Finally, after losing the injunction case in the courts, five years later, the communities accepted the low compensation price. In an attempt to defuse the situation, the state government construed the indemnities paid as a reward for communities' efforts at conservation rather than as compensation for expropriated land. But the conflict caused by the repeated delays in negotiations and the dispute over indemnities also undermined the ability of the federal authorities in charge of the reserve to promote sustainable development projects.

Other peasants and ranchers, on the contrary, would prefer the purchase by the state of the part of their land within the nucleus zone, as they cannot use this land productively. Although tree logging was illegal before the creation of the reserve, people saw the reserve as a threat to their land rights because they would lose formal rights to land they traditionally held. Some communities reacted to government attempts to ignore their previous land rights by threatening to burn the forests. Five years later a Payment for Environmental Services programme was launched, so that some communities would receive a small benefit (US$30 per hectare) for not cutting down the forest. The communities consider this an unsatisfactory offer and political rumours are spreading that the programme is a veiled attempt to privatise communal land. In contradiction with agrarian laws, and as one more example of lack of coordination between institutions even after the reserve decree, the Agrarian Reform Ministry gave individual titles to plots in the areas of the forest that had been communally owned. This contradictory policy strengthened a sense of individual rights to the forests within the nucleus zone which have now been cancelled as part of the reserve structure. This mistake deepened frustrations within indigenous communities and contributed to a sense of grievance over individual land rights. However, once again, the contradictions between the policies of different government agencies fuelled conflicts over the management of the reserve.

The increasing politicisation of government bureaucracies also serves to exacerbate disputes over land rights in Tuxtlas as mistrust between government officials at the state level is exacerbated by the differing political affiliations at various levels of government. In both cases, government slowness in resolving land problems linked to the creation of reserves has affected the lives of indigenous people living in communities within the reserves. In some expropriated communities, these issues have led to internal divisions within communities. While some rally around mobilisations or declarations against the reserve and in favour of its cancellation (Tuxtlas), others have invested indemnity payments to buy plots and turn to the reserve for investment funds. As we discuss below, a range of community-based strategies have emerged to address the lack of accountability and resolve the conflicts over land rights.

Knowledge rights and biotechnology research: hidden agendas?

The previous section has examined how conflicts over land rights have emerged around PNAs. Another important set of conflicts over rights has also developed as part of the trend towards conserving environmental resources: knowledge rights. Conflicts over knowledge rights in PNAs reflect radically different views of the environment: while government officials and conservationist NGOs see the environment as a resource to be conserved, some indigenous groups see the environment as part of their cultural heritage. Different (conflicting) rights are expressed here: the right of transnational pharmaceutical companies to invest in medicines backed by national laws protecting the rights of capital, the right of academic institutions to conduct research on the environment and use that knowledge, and the right of the local population to control how environmental resources are used, especially when the 'protection' of these resources does not result in any benefit for the communities themselves.

Natural resources are of strategic importance as a growing interest in genetics has changed the meaning of biodiversity for international corporations, especially the pharmaceutical and biotechnological industries.

The value of biodiversity is socially determined and elusive, as it depends on local as well as on scientific knowledge and does not require capital-intensive extractions of materials, as is the case with other natural resources (see Abah and Okwori, Chapter 10). As Baviskar points out, 'the process of decision making around resource-related issues often accords great weight to expertise, privileging technocratic knowledge' (Baviskar 2003: 5053). As in many other 'biodiversity hotspots', scientific research in the PNAs is now an issue of growing importance.

Within the context of the PPP, another reason to reject some projects that claim to be sustainable is that behind a discourse of protection lie real economical interests, which may be neither visible:

> We denounce the eviction and relocation policy and the imposition of PNAs, because it is in the interests of big transnational corporations such as Monsanto, Bayer, Aventis, Coca Cola, Nestlé, among others, interested in the appropriation of biological resources, of forests and water, all of which are of strategic value for our Nation.[9]

For some actors, actions linked with environmental protection that are promoted, organised or controlled by international organisations like the GEF, or leading INGOs like Conservation International or WWF, have important connections with transnational companies. These alliances are scientifically and technologically supported by academic groups, leading to conflation of the interests of transnational corporations with academic or scientific research initiatives. For some organisations working in PNAs, the principal interest of transnational corporations (chemical, pharmaceutical and biotechnological) and conservation NGOs is to identify biological material and patent it, so that it can be commodified. In the view of some of the indigenous social organisations, INGOs only offer incentives for rainforest conservation as a cover for bioprospecting ('biopiracy'), because the INGOs have prior agreements with companies to provide them with information gleaned through 'conservation'.

A general criticism by community groups is that actors engaged in bioprospecting do not consider indigenous people's rights, nor do they establish explicit lines of accountability and transparency with respect to these activities. The legal pressures and negative campaigning against people settled in the reserve on environmental grounds served the interests of other actors that can enter the reserve without similar restrictions. For example, the National Commission for Protected Areas does not regulate the intervention of researchers in PNAs very strictly. Official authorisation from the Ministry of the Environment and Natural Resources is required to collect samples in protected areas (Article 88), but the results of research are not available to the public without the researcher's agreement (SEMARNAT 2001: Articles 85 and 88).

In Chiapas bioprospecting has been the subject of important and ongoing discussion. As a result of public action by local and national civil society organisations, bioprospecting initiatives have been seriously questioned. In 1999, the ICBG-Maya project headed by the International Cooperative Biodiversity Group was revoked. This initiative, coordinated by the US National Institutes of Health, with participation from the University of Georgia and the Mexican academic institute Ecosur, was designed to do research on local knowledge of the medicinal properties of plants. Protest by the Indigenous Medical Organisations of the Chiapas State resulted in the suspension of the project. The position of some community-based organisations was set out in the San Gregorio, Biosfera de Montes Azules Declaration (2000):

> Indigenous people are not enemies of biodiversity, our culture is not destructive, as some ecologists have declared. Their critiques are welcome, but we also invite them to look for solutions to the problems of ecological destruction, marginality and poverty. Moreover, we call for the stewardship and the sustainable use and conservation of natural resources. And we denounce the genetic management of our environmental heritage by transnational and national enterprises through intellectual property rights. We call for trials, through the court system, on the patenting issue.

As recently as March 2005 this organisation, along with others, denounced a public consultation announced to discuss a biodiversity law proposed by the Chiapas state government. They argued that it was intended to legitimise bioprospecting by transnational corporations and to facilitate their control over biodiversity in Chiapas. In this perspective, the resettlement policy has been presented as part of a governmental counter-insurgency plan against the Zapatistas. Like conflicts over land rights, PNAs have become sites for disputes over knowledge rights. The interests of transnational corporations, conservationist NGOs, and academic researchers have become intertwined, and communities living in the reserve area are challenging this agenda. For those who see hidden agendas in the actions of scientific institutions and conservation NGOs, any proposal from these institutions is labelled as interventionist, and a violation of indigenous rights. Conflicts over knowledge rights contribute to lack of trust and antagonistic relationships between poor, rural indigenous groups and the government. The next section will explore how these various conflicts over rights impede attempts by community-based and civil society organisations to build mechanisms for accountability.

Challenges for building accountability: the politics of rights and resources

The foregoing sections have explored how the creation of PNAs has fuelled conflicts over rights within the context of disputes over the meaning and appropriate use of the environment as a resource. The institutional politics driving the different actors involved undermines the possibility of establishing accountability mechanisms. This section will review some of the interests that various civil society and community-based organisations have in terms of building accountability, and the obstacles that have emerged.

In both reserves, there is an array of organisations that have been active for years around land rights reform and other political demands, and have developed important expertise in agro-ecology, health and education. Before government programmes began to address these issues, community-based organisations had taken the lead in promoting environmentally sustainable practices, although the impact of these efforts was reduced by contradictory public policies and institutional infighting, as described earlier. These groups have been pursuing a range of strategies in order to resolve the conflicts over rights in the reserves, and increase accountability in the way that the environment is managed.

But these organisations do not represent a single position. Community-based organisations' perspectives are expressed in diverse agendas and practices, through different alliances, and from the local to the global level. These agendas include the recognition of cultural and political rights, as well as the implementation of specific development programmes. Some of these organisations are now receiving funds from government or from international NGOs (for initiatives such as CO_2 capture, and in Payment for Environmental Services initiatives) to strengthen sustainable production either for local use or for the global market. These organisations have had an important role in attempts to contribute to increased accountability around the management of the environment as a natural resource.

Both in the Montes Azules and the Tuxtlas reserves, some civil society organisations from academic, NGO or political backgrounds are more concerned with environmental issues and local development than with joining the national and international movements against neoliberal policies. With funds available from different government agencies and international non-governmental organisations, they carry out projects and initiatives to involve local people in the process of defining their own agendas and development plans. Others, more concerned with global issues and networks, provide information on wider environmental issues such as biopiracy, attempts to promote genetically modified organisms and megaprojects such as the PPP; these groups are involved in mobilisation to build community representation in wider forums. Yet another group of community-based organisations prefer to avoid collaboration with government programmes as they see them as incompatible with their own political positions, and do not want to risk government co-option of their constituency. In turn, some sectors of government see autonomous organisational processes as a threat.

There is considerable diversity in the types of community-based and civil society organisation involved in addressing the conflicts over rights and lack of accountability that have been highlighted by the creation of the PNAs. But they have had only mixed success in achieving these goals. Some community-based organisations are directly engaged in resolving these conflicts over rights. In Tuxtlas, in order to pressure the government to deliver the payment of indemnities, some of the indigenous groups in the affected communities changed strategies. They abandoned attempts at local mobilisation, filed a second injunction for the cancellation of the reserve, and joined a wider national movement against PNAs, mostly defined in opposition to the PPP megaproject. While the disputes over land rights remain unresolved, indigenous people occupy their land 'illegally'.

In Chiapas there have been lengthy negotiations over the complex landholding problems. The high levels of distrust in the whole process have been used by other social actors, such as environmental NGOs, to scale up the resistance to the PPP megaproject agenda. Possible government evictions of people from their land are denounced as a government strategy to privilege transnational corporations' bioprospecting interests. Because of constant protests against the possible eviction of people from the Montes Azules Reserve, some federal officials demanded that the Agrarian Reform and Environmental ministries change their policies in order to protect the indigenous peoples' rights established in the ILO 169 Agreement. (The International Labour Organisation's Convention Concerning Indigenous and Tribal Peoples in Independent Countries entered into force on 5 September 1991.) So far the state government has refused to comply. The lack of agreement between different parts of the government contributes to the gap in accountability around the management of the environment, and while there is no agreement over land rights, conservation projects have been put on hold.[10]

Meanwhile, the Zapatistas have declared an impasse. In October 2004, the Zapatista political leadership defined its position in a public statement:

Due to the offensive of paramilitary groups ... dozens of indigenous families had to move from their land and from small villages in the Montes Azules Biosphere. During this time they have been in a terrible situation, far from their original land, but displaced Zapatistas have been careful to obey our laws that require the protection of forests. However, the federal government, hand in hand with multinationals, intends to take control of the richness of Lacandonan rainforest. They have threatened once again to remove with violence all the settlements in the area, including the Zapatistas. *Los compañeros* and *compañeras* of different threatened communities have decided to resist, for as long as the government does not sign and respect the 'San Andres Agreement'. (Report from the Clandestine Indigenous Revolutionary Committee – Commander General of the Ejército Zapatista de Liberación Nacional (EZLN), Sub-comandante insurgente Marcos)

The cases of the Montes Azules and Tuxtlas reserves show how extremely complex institutional relationships and the overlapping interests of different actors can lead to increasing conflicts over rights. The question is what kind of accountability relationships can be established to avoid this type of clientelist approach to sustainable management of the environment. In the current situation of conflict, it is not possible to develop viable environmental and economical alternatives and build trust between community organisations and the government.

Conclusions

This chapter has shown how uneven relationships between the different actors and interests in the PNAs can undermine the construction of common agendas for conservation and development, and mechanisms for accountability. At the heart of this situation are different perspectives on rights and the nature of environment as a resource. The lack of spaces for participation in the institutions that manage the environment, especially within the PNAs, is also an important factor that restricts the potential for increased accountability.

PNAs are not always and everywhere a source of conflict and uncertainty. In many circumstances they represent an opportunity for local development and a better livelihood for poor communities. The integration of the local population into the sustainable management of the environment cannot be widely guaranteed at present, in large part because of the lack of recognition of their land and knowledge rights, and the lack of spaces for participation in the decision making that affects these rights. A participatory scheme should integrate local people's concerns and experiences with natural resource management and protection, while respecting their land rights through fair compensation and consensual relocation when unavoidable.

When decisions concerning PNAs are left in the hands of experts, progress towards a sustainable development model is minimal and the building of consensus around conservation very slow. On the other hand, when, as a result of social action, spaces for negotiation are opened and an intercultural dialogue is facilitated, the resolution of conflicts becomes possible, and problems can be solved (as in the case of the round table on land rights and environmental sustainability in Montes Azules). From the cultural autonomy standpoint, a condition for intercultural dialogue, and therefore for accountability, is that actors recognise each other as equals, and acknowledge each other's cultural, social and political rights.

The conflicts generated by the creation of both reserves have to do with lack of consultation and participation in reserve management. To reach the PNA objectives, it would be necessary to guarantee the participation of the different interest groups from the beginning, to involve them in a permanent way in activities and budget planning. Many factors, such as political interests at the local and regional level and internal contradictions or tensions between community-based organisations, make it difficult to construct participatory spaces in a short time. In both cases, the legally mandated regional reserve management councils either have not been formed, or, when formed, have been under the operational control of government agencies.

The cases in this chapter show that when institutional mechanisms and policies are insufficient to resolve disputes over rights and establish accountability, it is difficult to reach consensus between different actors to build common agendas around conservation and sustainable development. The lack of strong institutional coordination is also a source of social unrest and contributes to the loss of confidence in and lack of support for government conservation programmes. However, building greater accountability is not just an administrative issue that can be solved by changing rules or establishing certain guidelines. It is fundamentally a question related to power, and the struggle between different political interests.

Relationships characterised by the absence of co-responsibility, the lack of adequate institutions with the capacity to fulfil their functions, and the active presence of distrust, mean that accountability is limited on multiple levels. However, it would be naive to reduce the problem of accountability to questions of designing and establishing the correct procedures and participatory spaces. What we are facing is the existence of different visions regarding the nature of the environment in general and indigenous rights in particular. This explains why policies aimed at environmental sustainability, such as PNAs or Payment for Environmental Services programmes, are seen by some as part of the Plan Puebla Panama, and rejected for this reason.

The key implication for accountability from the cases examined in this chapter is that the competing and conflicting rights around resources, derived from radically different understandings of nature and subsequent discourses of accountability, are essentially irreconcilable through institutional change. It is in the politics and political mobilisation around rights claims that these differences about nature can be engaged. The steps taken to promote more accountable relationships demonstrate a certain capacity of the state to respond to people's demands. This shift has been possible because of the high degree of mobilisation by different community-based and civil society actors. But even acknowledging these advances, a culture of accountability is not deeply embedded, as shown by the refusal of the government to give information about megaprojects such as the PPP, which has provoked confrontation with community-based organisations.

The recent social movements focused on changing intercultural relations in Mexico, especially the Zapatistas and the indigenous movements, represent a political and cultural challenge to building accountability – and demonstrate the conflictual nature of cultural politics. An alternative autonomous position requires a new kind of dialogue between different cultural perspectives, one that obliges the different actors involved to state explicitly their social, economical, cultural and political interests, and assume co-responsibility for natural resources protection and social development. Accountability could then become not only a one-way relationship between indigenous groups and the government, but a two-way relationship involving respect for rights and responsibilities for all the actors involved.

NOTES

1 Carlos Cortéz and Luisa Paré are researchers with the Universidad Autónoma Metropolitana-Xochimilco (UAM-X) and Instituto de Investigaciones Sociales, Universidad Nacional Autónoma de Mexico (UNAM), respectively.

2 The human development approach is the process through which people's options and their functions and capacities are increased (a long and healthy life, access and

knowledge of their resources for a healthy life (UNDP 2000).

3 For instance, many environmental policy instruments such as carbon sequestration and the Clean Development Mechanism (CDM) are focused on reforestation in the South towards fulfilling the commitments of the Kyoto Protocol. Many of the projects derived from the CDM, however, do not take into account the structural causes of deforestation and loss of biodiversity in the South.

4 Environmental policies in Mexico are the responsibility of the Ministry of Environment and Natural Resources and among its policies is the System for Protected Natural Areas, managed by the National Commission for PNAs, which is responsible for the environmental protection of 7 per cent of the national territory. Regional Development Programmes, Global Environment Facility and European Commission funds, among others, are the main financing sources for PNAs.

5 UNAM in both reserves, Ecosur in Chiapas and a state university in Veracruz, in addition to foreign universities.

6 Interview with Martha Cecilia Díaz Gordillo, February 2005.

7 *Ibid.*

8 *Ejido* is a form of social property in which land, previously held by big landowners or the nation, is given in usufruct to peasants who, until the 1992 Reforms to the Constitution and Agrarian Law, could not sell it (only hand it on as an inheritance). An *ejidatario* is the person entitled to this type of property.

9 Second Encounter on PNAs, Chiapas, February 2005.

10 Neither in Chiapas nor in Veracruz were there processes of consultation for the declaration of the reserve, although according to the government's legal framework such a process is obligatory.

11 Disseminated on 13 October 2004 by the Mexican newspaper *La Jornada*.

REFERENCES

Baviskar, A. (2003) 'For a Cultural Politics of Natural Resources', in *Economic and Political Weekly*, Vol. 38, No. 48, pp 5051–6.

Coordinación General del Plan Puebla Panamá (2002) Proceso de Organización, Planeación y Resultados, Plan Puebla Panamá, June, Mexico DF: Presidency of Mexico.

Cortez, C. (2004) 'Social Strategies and Public Policies in an Indigenous Zone in Chiapas, Mexico', *IDS Bulletin*, Vol. 35, No. 2, pp. 76–84.

Escobar, A. (1999) *El Final del Salvaje. Naturaleza, Cultura y Política en la Antropología Contemporánea*, Bogotá: Instituto Colombiano Agropecuario and CEREC.

Foro de Información, Análisis y Propuestas (2001) 'El Libre Comercio y Asuntos Transfronterizos: el Pueblo es Primero Frente a la Globalización', *mimeo*, México DF.

Gaventa, J., Shankland, A. and Howard, J. (eds) (2002) 'Introduction – Making Rights Real: Exploring Citizenship, Participation and Accountability', *IDS Bulletin*, Vol. 33, No. 2.

Lazos E., and Paré, L. (2000) *Miradas Indígenas sobre una Naturaleza Entristecida. Percepciones sobre el Deterioro Ambiental entre los Nahuas del Sur de Veracuz*, Mexico City: Plaza y Valdéz Editores/Universidad Nacional Autónoma de México.

Leonard, E. (2005) 'Titularización Agraria y Apropiación de Nuevos Espacios Económicos por los Actors Rurales; el Procede en Los Tuxtlas, Estado de Veracruz", in E. Leonard, A. Quesnel and E. Velásquez (eds), *Políticas y Regulaciones Agrarias: Dinámicas de Poder y Juegos de Actores en Torno a la Tenencia de la Tierra*, Mexico City: Institut de Recherche pour le Développement (IRD), Centro de Investigaciones y Estudios Superiores en

Antropologia Social (CIESAS), and M. A. Porrúa Grupo Editorial, pp. 297–325.

Massieu, Y. and Chapela, F. (2002) 'Acceso a Recursos Biológicos y Biopiratería en México', *El Cotidiano*, Vol. 19, No. 114 (July–August), pp. 72–87.

Moguel, J. (2001) 'Claroscuros del Plan Puebla Panamá: de Cómo se Escamotean los Derechos Indios y se Traslada el Debate a los Presuntos Temas del Desarrollo', in A. Bartra (ed.), *Mesoamérica, los Iios Profundos. Alternativas Plebeyas al Plan Puebla Panamá*, Mexico City: El Atajo Ediciones.

Newell, P. and Bellfour, S. (2004) 'El Mapeo de la Transparencia o Responsabilidad Social: Orígenes, Contextos e Implicaciones para el Desarrollo', Cuaderno de Investigación No. 2, Instituto de Investigaciones Sociales, Universidad Nacional Autónoma de Mexico (UNAM), Universidad Autónoma Metropolitana (UAM), Development Research Centre (DRC)–Institute of Development Studies (IDS).

Resistencia Ciudadana al Plan Puebla Panamá (2002) *Serie Acción Ciudadana en las Americas*, No. 2 (September).

SEMARNAT (2001) *Reglamento de la Ley General del Equilibrio Ecológico y la Protección del Medio Ambiente en Materia de Areas Naturals Protegidas*, Secretaría de Medio Ambiente y Recursos Naturales (Ministry of the Environment and Natural Resources).

UNDP (2000) *Human Development Report*, New York: United Nations.

Velázquez E., and Ramírez, F. (2005) 'Las Impugnaciones Locales a las Políticas Estatales de Conservación de los Recursos Naturales: el Caso de la Reserva de la Biosfera Los Tuxtlas, Veracruz', paper presented at AMER, Vth Congress. Balance y perspectives del Campo Mexicano a Una Década del TLCA y del Movimiento Zapatista, Oaxaca, 25–28 May.

CHAPTER 6

From protest to proactive action: building institutional accountability through struggles for the right to housing

CELESTINE NYAMU-MUSEMBI

When are struggles for basic rights by weak social groups able to have an impact on public institutions and make them more responsive and accountable?[1] This chapter responds to this question by drawing from the experience of an ongoing struggle by council tenants in Mombasa, Kenya for decent housing conditions, secure tenure, functioning urban services, and an end to the grabbing of public land in the municipality.[2] Lessons from social movement literature suggest that in assessing the impact or effectiveness of such struggles it is necessary to pay attention not only to internal factors such as how the movement is organised, what resources it is able to mobilise, and the terms in which it articulates its claims, but also to external factors such as the nature of the state, the configuration of public institutions and the broader political context (Tarrow 1998; McAdam, Tarrow and Tilly 2001). In a paper exploring how citizens' exercise of voice may more directly influence policy and service delivery, and how public institutions can be more 'client-focused', Goetz and Gaventa employ a framework that breaks down this combined analysis of internal and external factors into three key questions (Goetz and Gaventa 2001: 10):

1 What is the social, cultural and economic power of the group? (This interrogates the extent to which there is a united and well-organised constituency that is able to articulate its entitlements clearly, able to attract allies in strategic places, and enjoys broad social support for its claims.)
2 What is the nature of the political system? (This interrogates the depth of procedural and substantive democracy: the manner in which executive, legislative and judicial power is organised, and the genuineness of political party competition based on ideas and programmes.)

3 , What is the nature of the state and its bureaucracies? (This interrogates the extent to which there is a professional and relatively autonomous civil service, a level of commitment to reform in the bureaucratic culture and practice, and pro-poor responsiveness.)

These questions provide a useful framework for taking stock of and accounting for gains and losses of the council tenants' ten-year struggle in terms of ability to have an impact on public institutions and make them more accountable. But first, what is the context of the struggle: who is involved and what are the main issues?

Background

The city of Mombasa is Kenya's sea port and its second largest city, with a population of about 700,000.[3] The city has an officially acknowledged housing crisis (Central Bureau of Statistics 1999: 15). The worst manifestation of the crisis is in the slums that have mushroomed in the city over the last ten years. But equally visible is the severe deterioration in the quality of existing low- and middle-income housing, which is also in short supply. Most people in this income group have only two options to choose from: on the one hand, the 'Swahili' type houses[4] (built out of mud and mangrove poles) occupied by several families, each household having a single room.[5] Cooking and toilet facilities are communal, with no proper sanitation services as they are located in unplanned, semi-permanent settlements. On the other hand, council-owned estates constructed in the colonial era that have not seen much maintenance since the mid-1980s. Among these estates are Tudor, Changamwe and Mzizima, where the tenants' associations' mobilisation work began.[6]

The tenants' associations from these three estates joined together in November 2002 to form the Shelter Committee of ILISHE[7] Trust, an umbrella organisation bringing together community-based groups in the Coast province. The Shelter Committee helps to mobilise other council tenants facing similar problems with the aim of ultimately getting all 18 council estates involved and active in the struggle. The tenants' struggle can be summed up as being about four issues: decent housing conditions, functioning urban services, secure tenure and fighting the grabbing of public land.

Decent housing conditions
Under the terms of the lease agreement, the council has an obligation to maintain the houses. The council has not undertaken routine maintenance

tasks such as painting of the exterior, or repairs and replacements of the fixtures, since the early 1980s. Tenants are forbidden to make any 'alterations or additions whatsoever' to the flat or 'any fixtures and fittings therein' without the council's consent. The council's established practice of withholding consent notwithstanding, those tenants who can afford it have been forced by circumstances to resort to self-help measures such as replacing sinks, toilets, doors and windows, and even improvised wooden staircases. However, for tenants living in blocks with shared ablution facilities, the deterioration has not seen such mitigation; these tend to be poorer tenants and also it would take the agreement and financial contribution of several households to tackle these problems.

Functioning urban services

The city has been in economic decline for the last ten years (Gatabaki-Kamau *et al.* 2000: 1). This economic decline was made worse by politically motivated clashes just prior to the 1997 elections. Key sectors of the economy, such as tourism, suffered huge setbacks, as did the urban infrastructure.[8] Water and sanitation services are poor in the city as a whole, but low-income areas are hardest hit. Estates such as Tudor have not had running water since 1995, a situation made worse by an ongoing dispute between the council and the state-operated National Water Conservation and Pipeline Corporation. Yet the tenants have continued to pay for water and sewerage services they do not receive, since these charges are included in their rent charges. Here, too, the tenants have resorted to self-help measures. A women's group in Tudor estate sank a borehole that sells water to the residents. People also buy water from vendors who cart water around the estates.

Secure tenure

As tenants with written lease agreements, the council tenants are more tenure-secure than most low-income residents of Mombasa. But tenure security is much more than having an official document: council tenants do not *feel* secure. Corrupt practices in the council's department of housing, irregular practices such as rigging waiting lists, and back-dated eviction notices used to evict people without the benefit of the notice period required by the tenancy agreement all contribute to the feeling of insecurity. The tenants speak of an increasing trend of people having to *teremka* (go down the slope) literally and figuratively into the *muoroto* (slum) on the periphery of the estate because they have either been unable to pay the rent, or unable to fight off an irregular reallocation of their lease to another tenant favoured by some council official or councillor. Thus the search for tenure security is expressed first and foremost in demands for an end to corruption. The search for tenure security also takes the form of demands for transfer of ownership to the tenants.

Fighting the grabbing of public land
In Kenya it is impossible to talk about the crisis in public housing without talking about land grabbing and therefore about corruption among bureaucrats and politicians. 'Land grabbing' has defined Kenyan politics, particularly in the 1990s, according to the Ndung'u Commission, which was set up in July 2003 to investigate illegal/irregular allocations of public land (Government of Kenya 2004). Land grabbing refers to irregular allocation of land set aside for public purposes, or any government-owned land, to private individuals or corporations. Many allocations did not follow the procedure laid down in the Government Lands Act. Allocations followed the exception rather than the rule: regular allocation procedure should go through an Allocation Committee. An exception permits the president (a power delegated to the Commissioner for Lands) in exceptional circumstances to bypass the allocations committee and give a direct grant through a letter of allocation. This became the standard procedure, doing away with scrutiny in all allocations.

Mombasa council tenants' mobilisation efforts sprang from resistance to land grabbing, since Mzizima and Tudor estates were threatened with this fate in the mid-1990s. The council's plans to sell off the estates were foiled by a combination of high-profile campaigns by the tenants and a hitch in the financing arrangements.

The next three sections analyse the tenants' struggle through the lens of an adaptation of the framework suggested by Goetz and Gaventa to respond to the central question: when are struggles for basic rights by weak social groups able to impact on public institutions and make them more responsive and accountable? The next section will address how to assess a group's social, cultural and economic power, which is necessary to hold public institutions to account.

What is the social, political, cultural and economic power of the group?

Social and political power
This can be assessed on two counts: first, does the struggle have broad membership so as to command social legitimacy? Second, does it offer incentives for people to join and stay engaged in collective action?

It is important to understand the membership of social movements. Who is in the tenants' struggle? Is its membership broadly representative of council tenants in Mombasa? As has already been stated, the struggle originated in three estates. The Shelter Committee formally started outreach activities in the other council estates in 2003. By December 2004 eight other estates had been added to the number. However, this represents a swelling in numbers rather than organic growth into a movement. It was precipitated by response to an immediate threat: in July 2004 the tenants received letters from the National Housing Corporation telling them that they would henceforth be required to pay their rent to the corporation, and also that the rent would be increased. This is on account of a dispute between the council and the corporation over outstanding amounts that the council owes to the corporation. The tenants mobilised and through ILISHE instructed a lawyer, who has since managed to secure a temporary injunction to prevent the National Housing Corporation from collecting any rent, pending hearing of a case filed by the tenants to determine whether the council or the corporation is the landlord.[9]

The links between the Shelter Committee and these eight estates are through key individuals rather than a critical mass, and therefore broad ownership of the struggle is something that needs to be cultivated. Discussion on how to expand the structure of decision making in the Shelter Committee so as to accommodate them is still at an exploratory stage. In terms of geographical spread, therefore, it is fair to say that the membership has not been broad enough to include a majority of the people affected by the issues central to the struggle.

Even within the three estates in which the struggle is most active, more could be done to achieve broader inclusiveness. With the discontinuation of the savings scheme there is no register of members as such, and so it is difficult to say with certainty how many are 'paid-up' members of the tenants' association in each estate. There is an identifiable core group that stays active, but mobilisation in the bulk of the estates has peaked and plateaued, depending on whether there was some imminent threat that called for unified resistance.

Does membership cut across divides? In terms of socio-economic class the group is relatively homogeneous. Therefore the divides that have mattered most are ethnicity and political party affiliation. The joint Shelter Committee has managed to function relatively smoothly, notwithstanding diversity in ethnic origin and political party affiliation. Coast province is characterised by a very particular politics of ethnicity that polarises 'indigenous' coastal peoples (*watu wa pwani*) and people from up-country (*watu wa bara*). The politically instigated clashes that preceded the 1997 general elections were fuelled by this polarisation. Political party affiliation broadly follows this pattern. The area has been a key stronghold of the former ruling party, KANU (the Kenya African National Union, in power for the last 40 years until the 2002 elections), and therefore coastal peoples are presumed to be KANU loyalists. Up-country people are presumed to support the former opposition, now in the governing coalition.

Tensions along these lines occasionally manifest themselves in relationships among the tenants and with external actors. There has been talk about the disruptive effect of the election campaigning seasons, when some tenants' association officials double up as party activists. If they undertake door-to-door recruitment exercises for their party, will people not identify them with that party the next time they come on a mobilisation exercise for the estate's tenants' association? There was one acknowledged incident of a tenants' association becoming deadlocked for months over unresolved differences between two officials belonging to rival political parties that had clashed during the campaign. This has subsequently been resolved following open discussion at the joint Shelter Committee level and binding arbitration.[10]

In order for the group to acquire and maintain membership it needs to show that it has something to offer. They need to demonstrate this to persons who remain aloof in the estates in which the tenants' associations have been active, as well as to the estates that have not experienced tenant organisation. Those active in the struggle cite solidarity and the amplification of voice (*kupaza sauti kwa pamoja*) as the most significant benefits of belonging to the tenants' struggle. One other benefit cited is membership in ILISHE Trust, which promises support in the form of connections to professional organisations (legal aid providers, for example), access to the media, and a means to secure funding (even though the latter is not guaranteed). What is lacking is a clear articulation and popularisation of the ultimate vision or desired outcome of the struggle, whether that be winning the right to own their houses or clarity in and implementation of the council's obligations to maintain the houses and deliver services. Clear articulation of the long-term goal is important in view of the weight of immediate disincentives to joining this type of struggle. Housing in Mombasa is difficult to come by. Therefore council housing – with all its problems – is still desirable. Many would not want to jeopardise a tenancy status that is already precarious and expose themselves to reprisals in the form of evictions or, even worse, job losses for those tenants who are also council employees. People need to be persuaded that there are long-term benefits that make the risks in the short term worthwhile.

Cultural power

'Cultural power' is a useful label for exploring a group's ability to influence public discourse on the issues that define the struggle. To paraphrase Goetz and Gaventa (2001: 41), it refers to the effective use of the media and other public forums to gain support for their cause and to shame and praise officials; the group's ability to successfully challenge presumptions (especially official presumptions) about the group and their struggle; and the ability to build credibility by combining protest with constructive engagement.

USE OF MEDIA TO GAIN SUPPORT AND TO SHAME AND PRAISE

The tenants' struggle has used the media and public forums quite effectively, particularly when a specific threat was imminent. It was a high-profile media campaign that thwarted the council's secret plans in 1997 to relocate Mzizima tenants (who are low-cadre employees of the council) so as to make room for a private housing development that would price out low-income earners from that neighbourhood.[11] In 2000 Mzizima tenants made their case before a presidential commission that had been set up to propose changes to the land law system.[12] Media publicity had earlier exposed planned evictions intended to make way for similar redevelopment in Tudor estate.[13] Tudor tenants credit their campaign for the decision by the National Social Security Fund to withdraw from negotiations for the financing of the redevelopment, which essentially halted the council's plans. In 1995 a concerted media campaign made the council shelve plans for a steep hike in rent, averting the full hearing of a court case that the tenants had initiated to challenge the rent increase.

The tenants now need to strategise for a more proactive media strategy that goes beyond mainstream media, particularly for the purpose of reaching into council estates in Mombasa. In order to win broad public support for reform of public housing policy nationally, the struggle also needs to be presented in terms of a vision for broader social transformation, articulating the struggle as being about offering an alternative vision rather than simply securing gains for the immediate constituency (Hunt 1990).[14] For instance, the campaign to resist private real estate developers is being pursued not only on the basis that tenants who cannot afford high rents will be displaced, but more broadly to ensure city policies that put people's basic shelter rights ahead of profits.

Shaming and praising of officials could be sharpened and made more evidence-based. In tackling land grabbing, for instance, Changamwe residents carried out impressive investigative work and compiled a list of the reference numbers of all the illegally allocated plots, along with the names of the people to whom they had been allocated. Missing from the list, however, were the names of the officials involved in the allocations. The obstacles to obtaining this information are enormous (as the Ndung'u Commission found out), but determined groups have been able to obtain it through a combination of formal and informal networks.

CHALLENGING PRESUMPTIONS

The importance of challenging presumptions (especially official presumptions) about the group and its struggle cannot be overemphasised. In official discourse the tenants are perceived as no more than ungrateful beneficiaries of heavily subsidised housing. The tenants' own account is that it is they who subsidise the council: with the council's failure to carry out routine maintenance since the mid-1980s, tenants have been forced to carry out major repairs at their own expense to make the houses habitable, knowing full well that the council will never reimburse these 'unauthorised repairs', nor will they be able to remove fixtures they have installed at the end of their tenancy, as this will be treated as vandalism.

This is common knowledge among the tenants, but in public discourse on council housing it is not. Making it more explicit could change the way in which 'subsidy' is understood, thus legitimising the tenants' alternative account. Literature on social movements and rights suggests that, in order for weaker social groups to be able to institutionalise and consolidate their gains, they must work towards legitimising their alternative vision so that it becomes the 'hegemonic' position (the taken-for-granted way of thinking or doing things) (Hunt 1990).

BUILDING CREDIBILITY BY COMBINING PROTEST WITH CONSTRUCTIVE ENGAGEMENT

Has the tenants' struggle worked to build credibility by combining protest with constructive engagement? It has been easier for the council tenants to agree on what they are against than to agree on a shared vision for proactive action. Whereas many who are active in the Shelter Committee see the ultimate aim of the struggle in terms of being able to purchase the houses from the council, there are some who will be content if the council carries out repairs, involves the tenants by allowing them to contribute through their labour and ideas, and takes this contribution into account in calculating the new rents so that the resulting rent increment is not too large.[15] There is also lack of agreement on the eligibility criteria for purchase, with some holding the view that only residents of at least ten years' standing should be allowed to participate (ILISHE 2002: 22). It will be necessary to carry out a detailed assessment of views among the residents so as to determine what vision is broadly representative. Engaging the council and other relevant public institutions on a constructive agenda will require the identifying and crafting of the key message, so that it can be targeted at the institutions most likely to intervene effectively. It will also require clear ideas for action, in the form of concrete, carefully budgeted proposals to the council.

Economic power
In the mid-1990s and into the late 1990s the tenants' associations in the three estates operated savings schemes, both to finance the struggle and to build up a funding base that would enable them to leverage financing for the purchase of the houses. These schemes have since lapsed. Except for *ad hoc* collections to deal with emergencies, there is no effort to fundraise among the membership. Now, since the joint Shelter Committee is one of the constituent committees of ILISHE Trust, ILISHE fundraises among donors and then makes allocations among the various areas of work. The tenants' work has made a significant contribution to ILISHE's funds by winning the 2002 Body Shop Award for Human Rights, which brought US$75,000 to the organisation. It is fair to say that the initial determination to build financial self-sufficiency through savings in preparation for the eventuality of purchasing the houses has been replaced by a reliance on fundraising from donors through ILISHE on a 'project' basis. The award served to weaken further the previous emphasis on linking grassroots mobilisation with building up savings. On the whole, the economic power of the tenants' associations is very weak, made worse by fluctuations in the number of people actively involved in the struggle.

What is the nature of the political system?

The following features of the political system have had significant implications for the tenants' struggle: political party competition; the relationship between central and local government; public institutions' accountability to Parliament; and the degree of protection of citizens' rights from the excesses of politicians and bureaucrats.

Political party competition
In an ideal situation, parties compete on the basis of programmes and ideologies, and therefore social movements are able to form strategic alliances with any party whose agenda is congruent with the movement's goals so as to advance their struggle. The situation in Kenya is far from this ideal. Party politics since independence has lacked genuine competition among alternative policies. Following ten years of legally imposed single-party rule, Kenya has had three multi-party elections: in 1992, 1997 and 2002, the last of these unseating KANU (from central government as well as from Mombasa) for the first time in 40 years. Even though the major parties publish manifestos, their political rallies and public discourse in general is dominated by ethnic posturing rather than by issues (Gatabaki-Kamau *et al.* 2000: 75; Southall and Wood 1996; Mutunga 1999). The politics of ethnicity has acquired a peculiar sharpness in Mombasa and in Coast province generally since the clashes of the 1997 elections, intended to flush out *watu wa bara* (up-country people who are not regarded as indigenous to the coastal region).

This context cannot be ignored in analysing citizen engagement with public institutions. The areas in which the council estates are located are densely populated and therefore any organised group constitutes an attractive vote bank for local politicians and aspirants. The tenants' struggle has not escaped the politics of ethnicity. Among the tenants there are suspicions that the reason why the council has paid no attention to the state of the estates is because the majority of tenants are *watu wa bara* – up-country people.

The political climate plays a big role in determining the types of strategies citizens' collective action will adopt. In a party-based political system that is not defined by issues and programmes, patronage sets in. There have been moments of setback in mobilisation efforts, when the respective tenants' associations that make up the joint Shelter Committee were in disagreement about whether to align their interests (and therefore political support) with a particular politician.

Relationship between central and local government
The relationship between central and local government in Kenya has been marked by determination by the former to control local affairs. The Local Government Act, which defines the functions of local authorities, gives a lot of oversight powers to the Minister for Local Government. For instance, local authorities need the Minister's approval for their budgets, employment decisions and the setting of local rates (such as property rates), as well as the Attorney-General's approval for any by-laws

enacted. The 1998 Local Authorities Transfer Fund (LATF) Act requires central government to designate 5 per cent of income tax revenue to local governments, which is then allocated among the various councils on the basis of population and subject to the councils' submission of a detailed budget and service delivery plan (Smoke 2004). This allocation, in addition to local rates and licence fees, makes up most of the local councils' revenue.

With few sources of revenue and an unpredictable flow of central government allocations,[16] municipal councils are still expected to provide a wide range of services. The pressure on local governments to raise revenue locally in meeting their service delivery mandate means that Mombasa municipality will be very reluctant to relinquish ownership of council estates that bring in a predictable and regular (though meagre) share of their revenue. It does not help that the economy of the city as a whole has been in decline since 1990 and therefore revenue from business licences and service charges has been falling (Gatabaki-Kamau *et al.* 2000: 1). Income from council housing accounts for 10 per cent of the council's revenue.[17] The biggest expenditure item is salaries for the council's bloated workforce and the councillors' generous allowances.[18] The irony was not lost on the tenants when a newspaper story on a council decision to increase rents by 30 per cent was published alongside a story on the councillors' vote to increase their own allowances by about 50 per cent.[19]

The relationship between central and local government is complicated further because the local government structure exists side by side with a provincial administration system under the Office of the President. This system is governed by a hierarchy that operates in a top-down fashion from Provincial Commissioner to District Commissioner, to a divisional administration at the sub-district level, then to a chief at the location level, assistant chief at the sub-location level and headman at the village level. The lines of authority and responsibility are not clearly defined and conflicts between councillors or council bureaucrats and district officials have often been bitter.[20]

The council tenants encountered this tension in their fight against the grabbing of public land. After obtaining the details of 'grabbed plots' they tabled these lists before the Municipal Physical Planning Liaison Committee, which set up a task force chaired by the District Commissioner, comprising the Municipal Engineer, Provincial Commissioner and Physical Planning Officer – a mix between council bureaucrats and provincial administration officials. The task force confirmed that these plots had indeed been irregularly allocated and that the buildings erected on them did not comply with the building code, primarily because many of them blocked off access to public amenities. The task force recommended revocation of the building approval. This revocation needed to be issued by the Town Clerk. The plot owners are wealthy and politically well connected, both on the local and national political scene. The Town Clerk was reluctant to take any action that the councillors would not approve of. Two months later no action had been taken. In April 2001 the tenants' association in Changamwe estate wrote to the committee requesting permission to demolish an illegally erected wall on one of the grabbed plots that was blocking a road, since the committee was afraid to take action against the grabbers. After a month of waiting in vain for a response from the committee, the residents mobilised and demolished the offending wall. In May 2001 the Provincial Commission wrote an urgent letter to the Town Clerk directing him not to approve any building plans for that plot, or 'any transaction that would provoke residents'.

In terms of protocol, the Provincial Commissioner has no authority to direct the Town Clerk. However, the Provincial Commissioner has a mandate to 'maintain law and order' within his jurisdiction, and the riotous demolition of the wall had turned this into a 'law and order' issue. The District Commissioner serving in Mombasa at the time (DC Rotich) was particularly responsive to citizens' complaints about land grabbing, and the tenants and other groups took full advantage of this and drew in the provincial administration whenever they could.[21] It is quite ironic that citizens would turn to the infamous provincial administration (reputed to be a top-down authoritarian and unresponsive structure) to reign in the excesses of their elected representatives (councillors). This should caution against too much faith in representative democracy as a means to secure accountability and responsiveness.

Public institutions' accountability to Parliament

If political accountability were functioning well, the tenants would be able to get their local MP to raise the issue in Parliament through questions to the Ministry of Local Government and/or Ministry of Lands and Housing and expect that action would be taken, for instance to compel the council to come up with a plan for proper maintenance of the estates or a plan for instituting a tenant purchase scheme. The tenants do not consider this to be a serious option because local MPs have been implicated in land grabs in the previous regime. Tough talk against corruption in the current regime notwithstanding, no action has been taken against them. Some MPs previously served as councillors and did nothing about poor housing conditions in the estates, and therefore the tenants seriously doubt that they can be relied upon to champion their cause in their new capacity as MPs. There is also a perception that approaching Parliament in Nairobi is a circuitous route, far removed from their reality, and there is no guarantee that the Ministry of Local Government will take action, let alone that the council will act on any directive the Ministry might issue. However, this route is worth a try, if for nothing else at least for the sake of building up a record and strengthening the case for more direct forms of accountability on the basis that the conventional representation-based system for political accountability has failed to serve citizens. The tenants' own proposal for Citizens' Committees in every ward as a forum for ongoing engagement with MPs and councillors expresses a desire for more direct forms of political accountability, but a case needs to be built up for them.

Protection of citizens' rights
Political power must be configured so as to ensure that the boundaries of the state–citizen relationship are observed and that citizens' rights are protected against the excesses of politicians and bureaucrats. In the case of council housing, protection is very weak and council tenants are rendered vulnerable. Kenya's constitution does not provide for a right to adequate housing[22] or a right to an adequate standard of living. However, these are internationally recognised in the International Covenant on Economic, Social and Cultural Rights, to which Kenya is a signatory.[23] A draft constitution produced in March 2004 after a broadly consultative process of constitutional review does make proposals for recognition of a broad range of economic and social rights, including housing, but it is not possible to predict whether or when this new constitution will be enacted.[24]

There is no statute dealing with housing. The Housing Act (Chapter 117 of the Laws of Kenya) relates narrowly to the activities of the National Housing Corporation. A proposal is underway to enact a Housing Act that deals with housing broadly (Draft Sessional Paper 2002). Kenya has not had a national housing policy since 1967 (Sessional Paper No. 5 1966/7). The most recent population and housing census indicates an urgent need for such a policy in view of a major housing crisis in urban areas (Central Bureau of Statistics 1999). An updated policy is only in the process of being drafted by the Department of Housing, and is yet to be presented in Parliament for endorsement (Draft Sessional Paper 2002).

The legal and institutional framework governing council tenancy specifically is also inadequate. There is no national legislative framework regulating the manner in which councils manage housing. This is left to each council's own by-laws, and many councils have not even enacted specific by-laws to deal with housing. Although the Minister for Local Government in 1995 issued a legal notice in 1995 stipulating standards of habitability for buildings, these relate to new construction and there is no provision for their retroactive application to existing housing, nor any clear indication that local councils are also bound by the order as owners of buildings, in addition to being the enforcers of the order.[25]

The laws that are intended to regulate landlord–tenant relations are not applicable where the government is the landlord. Councils as landlords are exempt from these general laws that spell out the obligations of landlords to their tenants. In addition, the law makes it less likely that council tenants will seek redress to hold councils to account. Government bodies (including local authorities) are exempt from the application of the Rent Restriction Act. The Rent Restriction Act sets up a Rent Restrictions Tribunal, which offers a cheap procedure for resolving disputes in a forum that is easier for low-income tenants to access. A low-income tenant is defined as any tenant paying less than Shs. 2,500 a month – just under US$40. Under this law, a low-income tenant cannot be evicted or have their rent increased without an order from the Rent Restrictions Tribunal (Bodewes and Kwinga 2003: 227). The exemption of government-owned housing from the jurisdiction of the tribunal means that low-income tenants of council housing are easier to evict. If they wish to challenge their eviction they must pay for the more expensive court process, which they are rarely able to do, not only on account of cost, but for fear of reprisals and loss of the lease altogether.

The argument for a change in this aspect of law is strengthened in the face of the breakdown of accountability mechanisms at the level of council and central government responsibility. Council tenants are effectively denied access to justice. In order to protect the rights of council tenants as citizens a mechanism for redress is necessary, even if it is not judicial redress. This could take the form of an ombudsperson for public housing, or a special dispute resolution tribunal that deals with such disputes involving government housing and government land.

In order to play a significant facilitative role in the institutionalisation of gains made by struggling groups, rights must be understood and employed as part of a broader strategy of political contestation (Hunt 1990: 318, 319). A clear legal framework setting out rights and responsibilities in concrete areas goes a long way. However, a struggle that focused narrowly on securing legal recognition of a right to adequate housing, for instance, would be missing the opportunity for broader political engagement. Such engagement would entail articulating a link between inadequate (or lack of) housing and disenfranchisement: how it begets other forms of deprivation such as generalised insecurity, inability to access quality health and education services, gross under-investment of city government revenues in those areas, and citizens' lack of voice over the way in which the city's or state's revenue is spent (Appadurai 2001: 28).

What is the nature of the bureaucracy?

How responsive is the bureaucracy to the citizens who rely on its services? Is the bureaucracy professional and relatively autonomous? Does it have systems of fiscal and administrative accountability that function reasonably well?

Degree of responsiveness and autonomy

Conventional understanding expects the relationships of responsiveness and accountability to function as follows: bureaucracies involved in service delivery will be responsive to citizen needs, and accountable to elected officials (Goetz and Gaventa: 2001). This expectation presumes that the bureaucrats have a measure of autonomy and that there exists a clear separation of powers between the civil service bureaucracy and the system of elected representatives. But bureaucrats in councils do not enjoy autonomy from councillors, and the functioning of the bureaucracy that runs council housing illustrates this. The council housing docket falls within the Directorate of Housing. But proposals by the director have to be endorsed by a resolution passed by the councillors. The tenants' associations learnt the hard way about the effect of the tangled relationship between bureaucrats and politicians in the council. One local councillor was very supportive of the tenants' efforts to get the estates converted into Tenant Purchase Schemes. The councillor managed to get the director of the housing development department on his side, and also cultivated support among a few more councillors. They planned to table a draft resolution at a full council meeting. Some tenants who are also council employees claim that the reason the proposals were never presented to the council is because as soon as the mayor got wind of it he summoned the director of housing and told him in no uncertain terms that if he tabled those proposals before the council he would be dismissed. Technically the mayor has no power to dismiss the director, since the director, like all civil servants, is recruited through the Public Service Commission, which is a central government body. He is therefore answerable to the Ministry of Local Government and not the council.

However, it is not uncommon for mayors and councillors to use their influence to get civil servants dismissed or transferred to less attractive postings. In this type of setting bureaucrats cannot afford to be responsive to citizens if to do so jeopardises their careers. Even leaving aside meddling mayors, the set-up gives no incentives to council bureaucrats to pay attention to complaints, views or suggestions of service users, because their terms of service are not linked to performance. The line of accountability only goes upwards to the Ministry, and no reference is made to citizens' assessment. Little wonder, then, that building alliances with bureaucrats has not been a feature of the council tenants' struggle. It would not make strategic sense for a movement to invest in cultivating long-term relationships with bureaucrats whose own tenure is so precarious.

Fiscal and administrative accountability
How efficient are the bureaucracy's systems of fiscal and administrative accountability? Fiscal accountability through formal systems of auditing and financial accounting for the use of public resources is extremely weak. Ideally, fiscal accountability would mean relying first on the council's own internal auditing procedures to detect abuses, and, second, on the general review function performed by the office of the Comptroller and Auditor-General, who reports to Parliament on the use of public resources in all government agencies, including local authorities. The tenants are able to estimate the revenue that the council gets from the rent they pay, but their demands that the council make public its expenditure statements have met with no response from the council. This information is essential in enabling the tenants to build a case showing that it is possible for the council to carry out essential and urgent repairs (to leaking roofs, for example), and that tenants' offers to make labour contributions would make such repairs feasible. The tenants' suspicion is that the council routinely deploys revenue from the rents to pay salaries and has no plan setting aside a portion of the revenue for routine maintenance of the estates, a perception that is not helped by frequent worker strikes or strike threats over delayed or missed salaries.[26] Complete lack of transparency in the management of council finances only fuels such suspicions.

There is some hope as awareness spreads about the Local Authority Transfer Fund (LATF) and about the requirement that, as a condition of accessing the fund, councils develop a Local Authority Service Delivery Action Plan (LASDAP) in a participatory process that involves citizens in identifying priority projects. However, central to enabling meaningful direct citizen participation is the ability to access information on how the council operates. There is no provision for monitoring the implementation process.

Administrative accountability operates through procedures that require bureaucracies to operate within their defined mandate and to report to ministers and legislatures. So in this case the directorate of the housing development department would be required to report to the Ministry responsible for housing, which would in turn be accountable to the relevant parliamentary committee, for instance the Public Investments Committee since the estates are public property. No such reporting appears to be required of the directorate. As a first step, such a report would provide an inventory of all housing owned by the council, which is important in the face of allegations that some have been 'privatised' informally; individual bureaucrats and councillors have sold them off or are collecting personal rents from them. That the Ndung'u Commission was unable to get such an inventory does suggest that councils have something to hide. The Commission complains that, of all the public institutions it had to interact with, local authorities were the most uncooperative. The Commission requisitioned from each local authority comprehensive lists of all public utility lands in its jurisdiction, as well as a list of all allocations to individuals and companies. The information supplied was grossly inadequate and the Commission concedes that it was unable to establish the full extent of land grabbing in areas administered by local authorities (Government of Kenya 2004: 39). This suggests that serious implementation of a simple reporting requirement has the potential to shake up the opaque council bureaucracy and expose irregularities.

The issue of land grabbing exposes administrative accountability failures at higher levels implicating the Commissioner of Lands and the Office of the President. As noted in the beginning, checks and balances such as the use of an Allocations Committee have been dispensed with in favour of unfettered allocation powers personified in the President or Commissioner. With respect to public land within townships the Commissioner of Lands is authorised to make such land available for sale subject to four conditions.[27] The first condition – only if such land is not required for public purposes – has evidently been breached. In Mombasa's council estates incidents of the sale of functioning marketplaces, school playgrounds, road reserves and parking lots attest to this. Second, the Commissioner must satisfy himself/herself that the land has been subdivided into plots clearly designated as suitable for residential or business purposes. This too has been breached: in Tudor, for instance, a commercial building with shops and bars has been built right in between residential blocks. Third, any buildings constructed on the plots must conform to specified building conditions. This must be verified by the Town Planning Officer and Town Engineer. This has been breached, as evidenced by structures on road or railway reserve land and others blocking off access to public amenities. Fourth, the land must be sold through an auction, preceded by advertisement and balloting 'unless the President otherwise orders in any particular case'. Records show that no auction for sale of public land has been held anywhere in the country in the last 50 years, and there is no documentation of a presidential order exempting specific plots from auction (Government of Kenya 2004: 11). A reasonable interpretation would presume that such presidential order must be in writing, even though the statute does not say so. It is difficult and futile to distinguish between allocations that had presidential exemption (issued verbally) and allocations made by low-level functionaries on the pretext of such presidential permission.[28]

Ultimately, the overall expectation that public land allocations will be in the public interest has been gradually eroded as the scrutiny mechanisms have disappeared altogether.[29] The Ndung'u Commission confirmed and substantiated Kenyans' suspicions that public land allocations were being used to reward political loyalty and to buy votes. The Commission found that allocations would intensify in the build-up to a general election (Government of Kenya 2004).

The tenants' fight against land grabbing draws attention to issues of scale in struggles for accountability: weak groups organising at the local level will focus on local manifestations of a problem, their immediate experience of deprivation of rights, but the accountability failures are on a nation-wide scale. The local-level organising may at best change the behaviour of local powerful individuals or officials, but without changes in the policy environment that makes corrupt behaviour possible, even such slight gains at the local level become difficult to sustain.

Conclusion

The analysis of accountability and responsiveness in citizens' engagement with public service delivery institutions in the case of the Mombasa council tenants' struggle, through the lens of the framework proposed by Goetz and Gaventa, shows a gap between ideals and context-specific realities. It becomes clear why, after ten years of struggle, the only victories that the tenants can point to have been about staving off the worst harms. These are not small achievements by any measure: keeping well-connected business interests at bay is remarkable. However, their efforts have not imprinted a legacy on the public institutions they have engaged with – in the form of a positive change in policy at local or national government level, for instance, or institutionalised changes in the specific practices and procedures of the Housing Development Department or municipal council. This absence of a lasting legacy is explained by a combination of the factors explored above, namely: the group's fluctuating social and cultural power and narrow economic base; inability to sufficiently distance the group from a politics of patronage and ethnicity and cultivate a new way of engaging; and a bureaucracy in which accountability systems have broken down and public officials have no incentive to be responsive to service users. With respect to the problem of land grabbing, issues of scale make it difficult for the tenants' localised actions to have impact on accountability failures on a national scale.

Inevitably, the tenants' ongoing struggle will continue to face one key dilemma: they need sustained action for long-term institutionalisation of accountability mechanisms in the larger political context and in the relevant bureaucracies that play a major role in shaping the struggle. Yet struggles for basic rights often have a sense of urgency about improvement in one's condition, and therefore in order for people to join and stay committed there must be some indication that this will materialise sooner rather than later. This is not easy to resolve, but it seems there is no shortcut to gradually building a genuine movement: the shift from protest to proactive action is imperative.

NOTES

1 Throughout this paper, the term 'accountability' is understood as comprising two dimensions: answerability (that public officials/institutions are under obligation to justify their actions) and enforceability (that sanction follows failure to account and failure to perform and that citizens have redress for harm suffered) (see Newell, Chapter 2). Responsiveness is used in the sense articulated by Goetz and Gaventa: 'the extent to which a public service agency demonstrates receptivity to the views, complaints and suggestions of service users, by implementing changes to its own structure, culture and service delivery patterns in order to deliver a more appropriate product' (Goetz and Gaventa 2001: 6).

2 The author is part of a team of Institute of Development Studies (IDS) researchers that has had close interaction with the Mombasa council tenants for three years (since 2002). Part of the participatory action research involved facilitating their strategic planning. It is hoped that the reflections in this chapter will make further contributions to that process of shaping a strategic vision for the struggle.

3 The last population census was held in 1999. Mombasa's population then was 643,168, with 181,849 households (Central Bureau of Statistics 1999: 15).

4 This is the most common type of housing available. The particular history of land tenure

and administration in the coastal region has produced a high incidence of absentee landlordism, so it is common to find that the owner of the house is not the owner of the land, but collects rent from tenants who each rent a room and share bathroom facilities. Technically their tenure is insecure because they could be evicted and the structures demolished should the landowner claim the land back.

5 This single-room living arrangement is not unique to Mombasa. The 1999 census found that 59 per cent of urban households nationally live in a single room. In the capital city, Nairobi, the figure is 67 per cent (Central Bureau of Statistics: 1999: 18–19).

6 Unless otherwise stated, the information presented here about the estates was generated by the Tenants' Associations from historical profiles, collective mapping exercises and interviews with key informants such as elderly residents and one active member of Changamwe Village Development Association who is a retired councillor and therefore had access to the council's archives. Their findings were then presented and discussed at a workshop in April 2003 which the author helped to facilitate. See 'Sharing Experiences and Mapping out Strategies for Advancing the Struggle for Shelter Rights' (Joint workshop for Tudor, Mzizima and Changamwe Tenants' Associations – Mombasa, Kenya, 15 and 24 April 2003).

7 ILISHE stands for 'Ilimu Sheria', Kiswahili for 'legal awareness'.

8 Following the 1997 clashes, average hotel occupancy fell to 26 per cent. The tourism sector suffered further setbacks with the embassy bombing in 1998. As of 1999, average hotel occupancy had fallen to 11 per cent (Gatabaki-Kamau et al. 2000: 2). The bombing of an Israeli-owned resort at the coast in 2002 further devastated Mombasa's economy.

9 Personal communication with Justus Munyithia, counsel for ILISHE, 18 April 2005. The case reference is Wilson Ndolo and others v Municipal Council of Mombasa and National Housing Corporation, Chief Magistrate's Court Case No. 4542 of 2004.

10 There is a tricky balance to strike between staying politically engaged as individual citizens free to form party or other affiliations, and at the same time building up (or at least not undermining) the inclusiveness and social legitimacy of the struggle. Open discussion is a good start and needs to become a regular practice, not just in response to extreme cases. In addition, perhaps it is time the group agreed to some general principles on their members' political engagement: for instance, agreeing not to use the tenants' association's name to further partisan activities, and not wearing party insignia to tenants' association events.

11 See Miano Kihu, 'We'll Resist Eviction by Council, Vow 114 Families', Sunday Nation, 24 October 1999.

12 Memorandum of Mzizima Staff Housing Estate to the Commission of Inquiry into the Land Law System in Kenya (the Njonjo Commission), 6 July 2000.

13 See Daily Nation, 19 July 1994.

14 Employing a Gramscian framework of analysis, Hunt refers to this process as one of counter-hegemony: 'the process by which subordinate classes challenge the dominant hegemony and seek to supplant it by articulating an alternative hegemony' (Hunt 1990: 312).

15 This divergence of views emerged at a review meeting held at ILISHE, Mombasa, 14 December 2004.

16 LATF is expected to make central government remittances more predictable but this is not yet the case. Using population as the basis for allocation is rigid and does not respond to changing needs, and is also contested (Smoke 2004).

17 The other revenue sources are: rates (taxes on land) 44 per cent; service charges 19 per

cent; market fees and commercial rents 10 per cent; business licences 8 per cent; other revenues (from user fees for health services, for example, or nursery school fees) 9 per cent (Gatabaki-Kamau *et al.* 2000).

18 Salary arrears are a frequent cause of confrontation between the council and its employees. See, for example, 'Council Unable to Pay Arrears', *Daily Nation*, 4 January 1995.

19 See 'Council Increases Rents', *Sunday Nation*, 9 July 2000, p. 4. The same story also exposed institutionalised nepotism in employment, whereby each councillor had a quota of employees to bring in, and some councillors had exceeded their quota, resulting in overemployment and causing a bitter row at the council meeting.

20 One source of conflict is with respect to a policy that was introduced in 1983, the District Focus for Rural Development. Under this policy, a District Development Committee is given the power to approve all development projects funded by the central government, even when those projects are proposed by the local authority (Government of Kenya 1987; Smoke 2004). The District Development Committee is chaired by the District Commissioner and in several cases DCs who did not have good relations with elected councillors have frustrated local authority projects.

21 See 'Squatters Paid Shs. 2.4m' *Daily Nation*, 10 April 2001; ILISHE Trust 2002.

22 The UN Committee on Economic, Social and Cultural Rights defines 'adequate housing' to include secure tenure. The other defining features are: availability of services (such as water, heating, lighting, refuse disposal), affordability, habitability (protection from damp, cold, heat, rain, structural hazards), accessibility (especially to vulnerable groups such as physically disabled, elderly, children), location (proximity to employment, schools, health services), and cultural adequacy. See UNCESCR, *General Comment No.4, Right to Adequate Housing*, 1991, available at http://www.ohchr.org/english/bodies/cescr/comments.htm

23 Kenya's constitution recognises a right to private property under Section 75 of the constitution, but this has been interpreted narrowly to refer to a right to compensation for compulsory acquisition of property by the state.

24 See http://www.kenyaconstitution.org.

25 *Kenya Gazette Supplement No. 44*, Legal Notice No. 257, The Local Government (Adoptive By-laws) Building (Amendment) Order, 7 July 1995.

26 See 'Council Unable to Pay Arrears', *Daily Nation*, 4 January 1995.

27 Sections 12–15 of the Government Lands Act, Chapter 280 of the Laws of Kenya (revised edition 1984).

28 In the absence of transparent processes, fraud has characterised the public land allocation system. Examples include: direct allocations by the Commissioner of Lands without presidential delegation of powers; allocation of government land that was already alienated for other purposes; multiple allocations of the same piece of land; forged letters of allocation bearing the President's name (which the Commissioner of Lands then acts upon to confer title); and even fake documents of title (Government of Kenya 2004: 75).

29 Similar breaches of procedure became the norm in dealing with 'special lands' – lands protected by law on account of their ecological integrity, cultural significance and strategic importance such as forests, wetlands, historical sites and lands set aside for research and scientific installations (Government of Kenya 2004: 15). Breaches also plagued settlement lands purchased by the government for purposes of settling landless people.

REFERENCES

Appadurai, A. (2001), 'Deep Politics: Urban Governmentality and the Horizon of Politics', *Environment and Urbanization*, Vol. 13, No. 2, pp. 23–43.

Bodewes, C. and Kwinga, B. (2003) 'The Kenyan Perspective on Housing Rights', in S. Leckie (ed.), *National Perspectives on Housing Rights*, The Hague: Kluwer Law International, pp. 221–40.

Central Bureau of Statistics (1999) *Kenya 1999 Population and Housing Census: Analytical Report on Housing Conditions and Household Amenities*, Nairobi: Government Printer.

Gatabaki-Kamau, R., Rakodi, C. and Devas, N. (2000) 'Urban Governance, Partnership and Poverty: Mombasa', Working Paper No.11, Birmingham: International Development Department.

Goetz, A. M. and Jenkins, R. (2004), *Reinventing Accountability: Making Democracy Work for Human Development*, Basingstoke: Palgrave Macmillan.

Goetz, A. M. and Gaventa, J. (2001) 'Bringing Citizen Voice and Client Focus into Service Delivery', IDS Working Paper No. 138, Brighton: Institute of Development Studies.

Government of Kenya (1987) *District Focus for Rural Development*, Nairobi: Office of the President, Government of Kenya.

—— (2002), Draft Sessional Paper on Housing, Ministry of Land and Housing, unpublished.

—— (2004), *Report of the Commission of Inquiry into the Illegal/Irregular Allocation of Public Land*, Nairobi: Government Printer.

Hunt, A. (1990), 'Rights and Social Movements: Counter-Hegemonic Strategies', *Journal of Law and Society*, Vol. 17, p. 309.

ILISHE Trust (2002) 'Land and Shelter Rights Struggles of Communities', unpublished mimeograph, ILISHE Trust.

McAdam, D., Tarrow, S. and Tilly, C. (2001) *Dynamics of Contention*, Cambridge: Cambridge University Press.

Mutunga, W. (1999), *Constitution Making from the Middle: Civil Society and Transition Politics in Kenya*, Nairobi: Swedish Department for Research Cooperation (SAREC).

Smoke, P. (2004), 'Kenya: Erosion and Reform from the Centre', in D. Olowu and J. Wunsch (eds), *Local Governance in Africa: the Challenges of Democratic Decentralization*, London: Lynne Rienner Publishers.

Southall, R. and Wood, G. (1996) 'Local Government and the Return to Multipartyism in Kenya', *African Affairs*, Vol. 95, No. 381, pp. 501–27.

Tarrow, S. (1998) *Power in Movement: Social Movements and Contentious Politics*, Cambridge: Cambridge University Press.

CHAPTER 7

Rights to health and struggles for accountability in a Brazilian municipal health council

ANDREA CORNWALL, SILVIA CORDEIRO AND
NELSON GIORDANO DELGADO

The right to health is enshrined in Brazil's 1988 constitution, dubbed 'the Citizens' Constitution' for giving legal form to the demands mobilised in the struggle for democratisation. The realisation of this right is intimately linked with the pursuit of accountability. The architecture of the Brazilian health system has at its foundation an acknowledgement of the contribution that citizens can make to equitable and efficient service delivery through their role in mechanisms of accountability. The right to health is instantiated in the monthly meetings of *conselhos de saúde*, health councils, at municipal, state and national level, in which representatives of civil society come together with health workers and representatives from the municipal government to audit health spending and approve health plans. Endowed with the power to make binding decisions, the *conselhos* are mandated by law to approve budgets, plans and accounts before monies can be released from the federal coffers.

The health of the population is a fundamental resource for the nation; and maintaining national health systems that can deliver services to the mass of the population, especially those who can least afford health care, is of symbolic as well as political and economic importance. Yet the provision of public health services also requires resources. It involves significant investment and management of public monies, and difficult decisions over allocations of ever-diminishing budgets. Throw in the complications of a mixed health system, where there is statutory acknowledgement of the limits of state provision and the need to contract out particular services to the private sector, and add historic distrust on the part of citizens in the probity of its bureaucrats, and the interplay between the realisation of rights and demands for accountability become all the more complicated.

This chapter is about how citizens in the small north-eastern Brazilian municipality of Cabo de Santo Agostinho, in the state of Pernambuco, have sought to realise the right to health through efforts to exact accountability from their municipal government. It tells the story of the evolution of the town's municipal health council, and reflects on some of the challenges for the realisation of the right to health that persist. It begins by introducing the health councils, their structure and functions, and the political context out of which they arose. It then goes on to explore the origins and evolution of the municipal health council in Cabo. Focusing on some of its successes and shortcomings in the pursuit of accountability, the chapter reflects on some of the challenges faced by citizen actors in pursuing the right to health through these institutions.[1]

Brazil's health councils: new democratic spaces?

Popular participation in the governance of health services has been on the international health agenda since the 1970s (Loewenson 1999). In many of the co-management and consultative institutions established as part of health sector reforms, citizens are provided with opportunities for involvement in discussion, and sometimes in decision making, over making the delivery of health services more effective (Cornwall, Lucas and Pasteur 2000). Less commonly found are institutions that offer citizens a role in deliberation over health policy and the nature of health service provision, matters that are often retained as functions of the state. Rarer still are institutions that endow social actors – not merely individual citizens but the representatives of organised civic associations – with the legal right to approve budgets and health plans, and play a part in ensuring accountable governance. This is the function of Brazil's innovative participatory health councils (Coelho 2004; Coelho and Nobre 2004; Coelho, Pozzoni and Cifuentes 2005). Operating at each of the three levels of government – municipal, state and national – the health councils lend shape to a set of norms and institutional arrangements for the provision and governance of health care that provide new opportunities for citizens to engage directly in holding the state to account for their right to health. Each municipal and state government in the country is obliged to have a health council, with a structure that is predetermined by national decree.

The Brazilian health system – the Sistema Único de Saúde (SUS) seeks to embody the basic principles of universality, equity, decentralisation and *controle social*, a term which constitutes only part of what the word 'accountability' has come to mean in English. Health councils are organs of accountability in a number of senses.[2] They are sites for the pursuit of fiscal accountability, in which citizen representatives can literally audit the accounts of the local government, and pick up and pursue any anomalies. They are also sites for answerability, as public sphere institutions to which public officials are obliged to present accounts and explanations for health spending. And they are sites that provide citizen groups with a direct interface with health policy decision makers at every level, and which serve − in theory at least − to maintain the accountability of these public officials to diverse publics. They are open to members of the public and, whilst only elected councillors have the right to vote, all present have the right of voice.

Brazil's health councils represent a form of governance institution that has gained considerable popularity in recent years as a space for 'cogovernance' (Ackerman 2004). Writing on the challenges for accountability of these new governance institutions, Cornwall, Lucas and Pasteur (2000) suggest that one of their most pressing challenges is overcoming embedded hierarchies that are so much a feature of the health sector, especially in the constitution of expertise and 'ignorance'. In Brazil, an unusual confluence of influences has made these dynamics more complex. For the generation of medical professionals now in senior positions within the public health system and in non-statutory health organisations, the national health system and its participatory institutions was the fruit of a long and intense struggle by the radical public health movement (the *movimento sanitarista*) of the 1970s and 1980s, in which many of them took part as medical students. A deep commitment to public health and to the right to health arose out of this movement, and inspired a generation of visionary doctors, whose agency has been so crucial at every level to the success of democratising health reforms.

The system of participatory health councils was envisaged by the health reformers who mobilised for its institutionalisation both as a means of creating an interface for civil society with the government and as a further political means of democratising Brazilian society, by stimulating the engagement of associations, movements and other forms of popular organisation with the process of governance. The councils were seen as providing a complement to the representative democratic system, involving representation of a different kind − of civil society organisations rather than elected politicians. The councils are composed according to strict rules of parity. Civil society organisations constitute 50 per cent of the council's representatives. They are elected by civil society delegates at municipal conferences or in municipal assemblies.

Representatives of health workers make up 25 per cent of the council's members, and include primary health care auxiliary nurses and outreach workers, doctors and specialist health workers. The last 25 per cent is made up of representatives from the municipal health secretariat and contracted-out service providers, consisting of the Secretary of Health, and managers of municipal hospitals and clinics in the public and private sector.

The notion of *controle social*, literally 'social control', represents at once the idea of 'the people' controlling what is rightly theirs *and* the enlistment of publics in the auditing of health spending. The term is often taken to extend to citizen engagement in health policy and planning, and to represent the right to participate at every level and in every aspect of health sector decision making. Yet in practice, as we go on to suggest, there are limits to citizen participation in this context that confine the possibilities for engagement to a narrower auditing role.

Background

The municipality of Cabo de Santo Agostinho, with a principally urban population of just over 150,000 people, lies in the Greater Recife area in the state of Pernambuco. The town is an important economic centre because of its strategic location, its established industrial facilities and its expanding service sector, especially in the tourism, health and retail sectors. Despite those economic potentialities, Cabo de Santo Agostinho has low human development and infant development indices, substantial populations of people below the poverty line and a high rate of illiteracy. Its mixed epidemiological profile reflects the diseases of poverty and those associated with urban living, such as cardiovascular and degenerative disease. Health services are provided at neighbourhood health posts, and by referral to municipal and private hospitals in the town of Cabo de Santo Agostinho itself. The successful implementation of a national primary health care programme – which involves teams of community health agents, who are linked to health posts staffed by a doctor and nurses, doing regular house-to-house visits – has brought marked improvements over the last seven years in a range of health outcomes, from a drop in the infant mortality rate (from 41/1000 to 18/1000) to reduced hospital admissions figures.

Cabo has a rich history of social movement mobilisation, dating back to agrarian struggles, the engagement of the progressive Catholic church, informed by Liberation Theology, during the period of the dictatorship, and a strong feminist movement with regional and national connections.

Immediately after the return to democratic rule, a progressive democratic party held the municipal government until shortly after the first wave of implantation of the *conselhos*. A diversity of social movements, NGOs and corporate social actors exist in both urban and rural areas in the municipality. Some of these are long-standing organisations, supported by the progressive Catholic church's work with base communities. Others came into being as a result of the first wave of democratisation in the late 1980s with support from the municipal government, and continue to benefit from municipal government *subvenções* (literally subsidies, grants to support their activities). Others still are directly contracted through *convênios*, statutory agreements, with the municipal government for the delivery of social and health services. There are around 130 registered civil society organisations in the municipality, and many more small community-based organisations dealing with issues in their immediate locality. The character of the state and of civil society, the nature of mutual dependencies and of cross-cutting links that exist across their borders, mediated by the church and by political parties, is extremely significant in making sense of the struggles for accountability in the municipality.

Cabo's municipal health council: laws, structures and purpose

Cabo's municipal health council (*conselho municipal de saúde*, CMS hereafter) was officially inaugurated by Municipal Law 1.687 on 12 May 1994, according to Federal Laws 8080/90 and Law 1840 /90. It was established with the following goals:

1 To define municipal health priorities;
2 To establish guidelines to be followed when making the municipal health plan;
3 To act on making strategies and controlling the application of the health policy;
4 To propose criteria for financial and budget planning and application of the municipal health fund, auditing transfers and use of resources;
5 To follow, evaluate and audit health services provided to the population by public and private institutions with SUS service contracts in Cabo;
6 To define quality criteria for the functioning of public and private health services within the SUS;
7 To call the municipal health conference every two years, together

with the executive, according to the Lei Orgânica da Saúde (Basic Health Law).

Cabo's CMS is made up of 20 members and 20 substitutes, distributed as follows: 10 service users; 5 health professionals; 3 public managers; 2 representatives of private services with contracts with SUS. Its legal status is that of a collective body of public administration linked to the executive branch of government. The CMS meets once a month for 3–5 hours, meetings are open to the general public and take place in a central location in Cabo, in a building – the Casa de Conselhos ('House of the Councils') - provided by the municipal government.

The CMS was established in Cabo just as the progressive Partido do Movimento Democrático Brasileiro (PMDB) government lost office to the conservative Partido da Frente Liberal (PFL). In its initial years, there was little opportunity to develop its potential. As in many parts of Brazil, the council came to be an extension of the municipal government, filled with appointments made by government and serving as a mechanism for rubber-stamping the government's decisions. This period of crisis was extremely significant in shaping the current CMS. Popular movements, progressive Church interests, unions and the feminist movement joined forces in a popular front to pressurise the municipal government to democratise the health council. The return of progressive government in 1997 was accompanied by the recruitment of an energetic, radical reformer into the position of Secretary of Health, and the revitalisation of the CMS and reforms to the health system that ushered in what is today's SUS in the municipality.

While citizens can attend and have rights of voice in health council meetings, councillors are elected as representatives of civil society organisations. Terms are for two years, renewable for a further term. In 2000, the health council elected its first civil society chair – one of the first in Brazil, where it is usually the municipal health secretary who takes up this position. During 2000–2, intense discussions within the CMS gave rise to internal regulations that sought to further democratise the action of the council. Rules of representation were evolved to ensure a diversity of communities of place and of interest, with half of the civil society seats being allocated to representatives of neighbourhood associations and the remaining half to those representing particular interest groups, such as the women's movement, the black movement and disabled people. These efforts culminated in the largest municipal health conference held to date, in 2003, at which new councillors were elected by several hundred delegates who had been elected at pre-conferences in four regions of the municipality. Ranging in age from their early 20s to their late 60s, most of Cabo's councillors are lower-middle-class or working-class, on average having no more than secondary schooling and often only primary level education. During 2003–5, the council's civil society complement consisted of civil society organisations as diverse as an Afro-Brazilian cultural centre, a herbal medicine non-governmental organisation (NGO), an association representing 'progressive' elements of the Protestant church, a Catholic workers' movement and a feminist NGO, along with residents' associations from all over the municipality. To extend the health council's scope yet further, in recent years efforts have been made to inaugurate local health councils in neighbourhoods in the municipality.

The health council is notionally autonomous and thus independent of the municipal government. In practice, however, it is reliant on the secretariat of health to provide resources for it to function effectively, including paying for the costs associated with administrative support. This support is critical to the council's viability, as the administrator not only keeps records of meetings, prepares documents for councillors to read and convenes meetings, but also reminds the councillors of the meetings, keeps them up to date with any changes in policy at state or national level that are communicated to her by councillors involved at those levels, and helps to organise training, transport of councillors and logistics for participating in events such as conferences. Charged with functions that require both significant investments of time and money, this infrastructure and resourcing is critical – underfunding undermines both the possibility of the council being able to exercise social control effectively, and the trust that members have in the seriousness with which their work is taken by the government.

Council members are entitled to demand access to public health accounts and explanations about certain investment and spending decisions, as well as to pay visits to clinics, health units, and hospitals to carry out spot checks. An auditing committee, composed of two CMS councillors and a member of the public, is charged with carrying out a number of such checks, examining stock cupboards for expired or badly stored medicines and inspecting the facilities. The mandate of the councillors extends beyond that of a watchdog, however, in their function as representatives of broader community interests. One of their tasks is to consult broadly amongst their constituents about local health plans, and to become directly involved in organising biannual health conferences, where such plans are opened to discussion. Councillors' own perceptions of what being a member of the CMS entails varies significantly, as does the way in which they frame their role in relation to the task of holding government to account. In a participatory workshop, councillors gave the functions of the health council as follows:[3]

- To facilitate popular participation in health public policies; to define priorities, audit resources and evaluate results.
- To develop projects as well as to audit what is approved by the council.
- To promote social control, with popular and democratic participation.
- To contribute to the system's better functioning, with popular participation.
- To enforce peoples' rights, already guaranteed by SUS.
- To audit users' demands for good service.
- To exercise social control through organised civil society, playing a central role and directing public policies for the sector.
- To jointly discuss and establish the best options for public policy.
- To propose and to follow public policies.
- To be a deliberative body where members have the opportunity to audit and to contribute to health policies.
- To provide citizens with conditions conducive to participation in public health policies in the community.
- To contribute to the management, auditing and construction of health policy.

A lack of clarity over what the role of the council ought to be, and what its limits actually are, is one of the factors that hampers the work of the council. Newly appointed councillors are sent on training courses, of variable quality, which teach them the basics about what their role involves, and instruct them in the various technical procedures that are part of health budgeting and planning. This is, however, a rather rudimentary education: necessarily so, as the costs of providing such training are significant. Councillors talked about how useful and important the training they had received was for them, and how much they valued opportunities to go on further courses and attend events in the nearby metropolis, Recife, including state-level conferences on a range of health-related topics. For those who had been able to take up these opportunities, they were regarded as an invaluable opportunity for personal as well as professional growth, expanding their horizons and bringing them into contact with similar people from other municipalities. Not everyone, however, is interested in taking up these opportunities or able to do so, and there is a general feeling in the council that people do not have enough of an idea of what exactly they are there to do.

People enter the council with expectations that are shaped by their previous experiences, whether in political parties, social movements or their own communities. Their own interpretations of what *controle social* ought to be all about play a part in defining what for them are the appropriate concerns of the council, as well as the boundaries of their own interventions in this space. How do these different perceptions of the function of the health council play out in practice? The next section explores some of the everyday dynamics of the health council, and the meanings of accountability and rights that citizen representatives, health workers and managers bring to their engagement with the health council.

Accountability in practice

The everyday business of the CMS ranges from listening to presentations by organisations who deliver services, to being informed about the plans of the municipal health secretariat, to discussing specific incidents that have been reported by members of the public concerning the provision of health services. There is little deliberation on matters of health policy; health plans are prepared by the government, without any attempt to engage the participation of health councillors in their formulation, and presented to the council for their approval, along with periodic presentations of the accounts. There is equally little expectation on the part of health councillors that they will be involved in the health policy and planning process, even though some see their responsibility in these terms.

Examination of the minutes of the CMS for the last three years reveals a series of patterns of interaction between health bureaucrats, citizens and health workers. One is a pattern of information provision followed by question and answer, which generally involves one of the managers, and most often the Secretary of Health. There is often little or no deliberation over the issues brought for consultation, nor does there appear to be any expectation of a more broad-ranging discussion: they are presented as matters of fact, questions are asked, and the matter is closed. This is the way that the municipal health plans tend to be treated. Another pattern is one of clarifying or contesting the way in which things are being done by debating whether something should be on the agenda, whether the council needs to have a position or a policy, and so on. At times, this appears to be about the council exploring the boundaries of what they are expected to do, at times about finding ways of working more effectively. Yet another interaction is more adversarial, generally involving denunciations of the quality of care or lack of services available in public health facilities, but also extending to critique of particular medical staff or failures to provide certain services. Rarely does this turn into constructive debate as to what to do about it, taking a more predictable pattern of making a complaint, and the complaint being recorded.

The minutes of the health council meetings support the impressions that we gained from our conversations with representatives. Users talked of the need for persistence, of wearing down a reluctant bureaucracy until they gave in to demands; managers spoke of the frustration of dealing with users who clearly did not understand either technical issues or the bigger picture; and workers spoke of the difficulties they faced in meetings, being unable to speak out against managers, but equally feeling on the receiving end of the criticisms levelled by users in their denunciation of health service provision. These tensions are played out in the space of the meeting. Styles of interaction echo the different purposes that the council serves, from the adversarial, distrustful stance of user representatives in contests with the state through to the posture of consultation, with users and workers listening to and asking questions of the managers, to a more collaborative relationship, with users and workers making suggestions together, and management agreeing with them. These different purposes are held in a permanent tension and create significant paradoxes for what participation in the council comes to mean to different members.

Deliberation in the council often appears to be less about content than procedure; quite what councillors actually understand deliberation to mean says more about their perceived role in auditing and authorising decisions than in deliberating the nature of health policy and the content of health plans, as the following quote from a user representative illustrates:

> We are not a consultative body; we are a body that deliberates. The manager has his/her own planning team ... he or she makes an action plan, what is going to be spent on health ... he or she comes here and presents to us what is going to be spent within the plan for each account. It comes to us, we take a good look at it and then we say if we approve the plan or not. If it is approved the government can go ahead with it, it can spend the money approved ... it is up to me, as a councillor, each three months, to say where it has advanced, because accounts are rendered every three months.... The council audits them really closely, members have the right to go to take a look for themselves; if it is wrong, we can stop it. That is the role of the council.

Framed in this way, realising the right to health involves making sure the municipal health secretariat and the medical staff they employ do their job: discussions rarely stray outside the frame of what that job is defined as by the government. There are strict rules that are set by central government about the proportion of money that should be spent on primary care, and guidelines and models for the delivery of care at that level that municipal governments can opt out of, but doing so may present political risks, which are better avoided. Municipal health secretariats can, however, contract out a greater proportion of secondary and tertiary care to the private sector, if they wish, and pursue health plans that give less priority to the health rights of the poor. As one union activist – a former CMS representative and a regular and vocal figure in CMS meetings – pointed out, it was the job of the CMS to hold the government to account for the resolutions made in the health conference, not to make policy. Yet even he conceded that the long shopping list of promises that constituted these resolutions necessitated prioritisation, and that the lack of citizen engagement in that prioritisation process potentially undermined the prospects citizens had for holding the government to account for its role in realising their right to health.

The worlds of the bureaucrat and the citizen tend to intersect most on questions of probity, and very rarely around issues that might be regarded as 'technical'. There have been notable exceptions. The current chair combed through the epidemiological report for the previous year and found a large number of untreated cases of one prevalent condition, which he brought to the health council as a concern. It was, however, not a concern that was debated: he simply informed them that he had composed a letter to the authorities noting the incidence of this condition, and calling for more attention to be paid to providing effective medical treatment. It was evident that his own technical knowledge did not extend to knowing exactly what that treatment might be – unlike treatment activists in other contexts, including parts of Brazil, who would be able to demand specific medication. What mattered, for him, was putting on the record that not enough was being done: a form of interaction with the authorities that was as familiar to him, from his activist background, as it was to a number of his fellow councillors. It needs to be remembered that he, like many user representatives, has rudimentary education and does not come from a medical background. To take up an issue like this is in itself evidence of the kinds of changes that the CMS has made possible. It is, however, an exception: many of the most effective challenges to the municipal health secretariat tend to come from people with medical training, who are able to directly pursue lines of argumentation that are simply not available to ordinary citizens.

Making a difference

Despite difficulties and contradictions, CMS actors have been relatively capable of taking initiatives, speaking out, expressing criticism, proposing and resisting in their role as civil society representatives. Acting autonomously, they have sought allies in social movements and within the state on certain issues of mutual concern, such as outsourcing of services. Common political sympathies – such as anti-privatisation sentiments – create bridges across the health council, and have worked to strengthen the power of the CMS in seeking to withstand the tide of marketisation that threatens the public health system. Where the municipal government's policies are in the interests of poorer members of the community – and this could be said, by and large, for the Partido Popular Socialista (PPS) government that was in office when we carried out this research – then this auditing role within the broader ambit of a SUS that delivers on its promises of equity and equality makes management and political sense. Yet much comes to depend on the character of individual bureaucrats, as on the broader agenda of the municipal government. The scope for conflict and co-option is as present in these spaces as that for collaboration, and civil society representatives may adopt a range of strategies for engagement, which put them into conflict with each other.

Shifting alliances and commonalities between health bureaucrats, health workers and user representatives complicate attempts to categorise actors as part of bounded interest groups. These alliances take shape in other spaces – the space of the party office, the church, the neighbourhoods in which councillors live. Party affiliation may make more of a difference when it comes to some issues; belonging to a common faith may matter more when it comes to others. Debates in the space of the council call on these allegiances, and on cultural styles familiar from other spaces: they are often characterised less by the kind of detached rational argumentation that is evoked in the writings of deliberative democrats than by other processes of persuasion that are laden with power, whether bound up with personal loyalty, religious belief or belief in superior knowledge or expertise, and political strategies and tactics that make the CMS an intensely political arena.

When councillors were asked what difference the council had actually made to the well-being of people in the municipality, the answers were often couched in terms of the kinds of successes claimed by the municipal health secretariat. Health bureaucrats emphasised the importance of the CMS in creating a bridge with civil society, as much as some acknowledged the limitations that civil society representatives had in understanding the complexities of health provisioning. For a number of the user representatives, the successes of the CMS were closely identified with making the health system function better: they pointed to the successes of the CMS in dealing with demands to guarantee service provision and improve the quality of care, thus contributing to the accomplishment of municipal health plans and improving basic health care units, access to tests, specialised outpatient centres, social mobilisation for municipal conferences, and the establishment of local health councils.

There seems to be a broad acknowledgement by the actors involved that the existence of the council has made some contribution to reducing the practice of clientelism and exchange of favours as the predominant form of access to health services in Cabo. Similarly, there has been an increase in public recognition and identification of privileges existing in the sector as well as the possibility of fighting to end them. Yet a number of current as well as former user representatives were much more circumspect about the successes of the CMS. Yes, they said, there had been gains: the council is an institution worth having. But they highlighted a wide range of concerns, from the 'party-isation' of the space of the council, to the compacts between government and user representatives benefiting from service contracts that complicate prospects for accountability, to the lack of voice of more marginal members, silenced as much through fear of the repercussions of speaking up as through their own lack of confidence in what they might have to say. For some, these factors neutralised the potential of the council as a mechanism of *controle social*; for others, they were an inevitable part of it, something which required constant vigilance as well as active strategies for its further democratisation.

A further dimension of reflections on the council concerns the gap between the ideals of the SUS and the realities of scarce resources, and the difficulties of ever overcoming the barriers to access experienced by those with complex and expensive conditions that simply could not be treated effectively at this level because of shortcomings in the ways services are articulated. These raise larger concerns about the very way in which the SUS is organised, and about the tensions between democratising priority setting and the medical exigencies with which planners of public health have to deal in order to be able to contribute to guaranteeing the right to health.

Realising the CMS as an accountability space

Even when the practice of participatory governance institutions does not meet the expectations that were created as part of the political struggle that led to their institutionalisation, most case studies conducted in Brazil stress their 'positive impact on the process of construction of a more democratic culture in Brazilian society' (Dagnino 2002: 162). The significance of this impact cannot be underestimated in a country with such an entrenched authoritarian tradition as Brazil, which combines state centralisation with local clientelism, and where economic modernisation and the location of Brazil within international capitalism has been conducted under an authoritarian regime, worsening its elitist and exclusionary character. Institutionalised participatory spaces such as the CMS contribute, by and large, to the collective political effort to democratise the implementation of public policies in Brazil, since (1) they confront elitist conceptions of democracy, (2) they challenge authoritarian conceptions about the primacy of 'technicians' and 'the technical' in state decision-making processes, (3) they challenge state monopoly over the definition of what is public and what the public agenda should be, and (4) they contribute to reducing clientelism and to more transparency in government actions (Dagnino 2002).

From what we gathered in Cabo, the signs are there that the process of creating spaces for accountability is having some effect on the culture of politics, with the hope expressed by some councillors that the expansion of local councils will serve to further open, and broaden, spaces for participation. It is evident, however, that simply creating spaces for citizen participation is no guarantee that old political practices will not simply be reproduced within them (Cornwall 2002). The council is an intermediary space. It is one that lies in between a series of other spaces: those of associations, of the bureaucracy, of health providers, of political parties and a range of other social and governmental actors. It is one threaded through with relationships, with party political alliances, clientage relationships and tensions. Social actors representing civil society are far from autonomous vis-à-vis a municipal government which gives many of them small grants to support their activities, and has contracts with others to deliver services. Neither civil society nor the state can be thought of as constituting a homogeneous bloc; and amidst the universe of civil society organisations in Cabo there exists tremendous diversity in terms of capabilities to engage in these spaces, as much as in their own internal democracy and accountability and claims to legitimacy, which further complicate their interactions within the space of the council.

To be effective in holding the state to account, health councils require a range of resources – the provision of which goes beyond the means and the responsibility of civil society members. Funds are needed to support the everyday functioning of the council, to provide a space to meet and someone to organise meetings, keep records and notify councillors of any pertinent changes in policies or upcoming events that require their attention. Financial resources are also required to support the training of representatives, not just from the users' segment – who require information on the structure and functioning of the health system, and on interpreting accounts and budgets to be effective – but also from the health workers and managers' segments, to equip them with the capabilities to participate in this kind of forum. Beyond these material resources, there are further technical and symbolic resources that are critically important if councils are to have 'teeth'. Active participation by user and health worker representatives is often not matched by commitment from managers, whose inaction and perceived lack of respect for councillors undermines the potential of the CMS as a space for accountability.

Although managers often voice professions of intent and eulogies regarding the importance of citizen participation in *controle social*, their conduct is perceived by many user representatives to reveal a very different attitude. The municipal government was charged by some user representatives with failing to provide adequate and timely information; seeking to drive through plans and budgets at short notice; giving councillors very little chance to find out and debate what they entailed; and exerting 'pressure' at key decision-making moments. There is a significant consensus among user representatives – shared by some health worker councillors – that the lack of value given to the CMS by the bureaucracy acts as a critical brake on its effectiveness. There remains amongst bureaucrats a very real tension between the legitimacy the CMS can offer them, and a perception that 'the council wants to be the manager', displacing what they see as properly their prerogative in making decisions about public health.

Contests over the meaning of *controle social* lie at the heart of the ambivalent relationship between managers, workers and users in the CMS. Conflicts and tensions between users and managers can be interpreted in terms of contestation over two distinct although not entirely incompatible conceptions about accountability through participation. One conception (commonly held by managers) sees participation as a model for the management of public policies and another one (generally that of users) understands participation as a process of democratisation of those policies. Of course, that does not mean that managers are not interested in democratising the process, or that users do not see management as relevant. But it does shed light on why the demarcation of issues as 'technical' becomes so important in the conflicts that arise in spaces of *controle social* over public policies, and it is linked precisely to the struggle for effective power sharing between state and civil society actors in those spaces. On one hand, acknowledging the legitimacy of politicising the technical is a way for civil society actors to demand power sharing. On the other hand, the constant reaffirmation of the essentially technical character of decisions is an argument enabling state bureaucracy to retain maximal power. Which direction the balance tilts in will depend on actors' political forces in distinct scenarios, and the result is always provisional.[4]

Conclusion

For all the shortcomings people identified – and there were many – everyone we spoke to, without exception, viewed the CMS as critical to the very possibility of accountability, and as an institution worth preserving no matter what difficulties were experienced in making it effective. People across the board – from the director of a maternity clinic to a temporary auxiliary health worker, to a worker at a programme for black youth, to the founder of a centre for herbal medicine – all felt that being part of this institution had provided them with opportunities for hearing new perspectives, learning new things and contributing to improving public health in Cabo. The very newness of this institution, and its counter-cultural nature in a political context marked by pervasive authoritarianism and clientelism, means that the potential for change may only be realised over a much longer term. The challenges are many, from changing the very dispositions of political society to transforming relationships in a sector marked by the hegemony of hierarchies of expertise. But there is every indication that, slowly, the CMS is beginning to make a difference, turning users into citizens who are aware that access to decent health services is not a favour, nor a privilege, but a right, and transforming a culture of clientelism into a culture of accountability.

Realising that right and enabling the cultural shifts that are required for accountability calls for continued efforts to change relations of power that enable managers to frame consultation and control the agenda, that deny lower-level health workers a voice, and that work to undermine the possibility of democratising health policy and planning. Overcoming these obstacles is a challenge that calls for new and imaginative ways of breaking and remodelling the old cultural patterns that limit the exercise of citizenship. As one councillor put it:

> When you begin to get the rights you have, and the way to seek those rights without the need for an intermediary, without favours or party-political

bargains, then you change the character of the life of a society into one in which citizens have awareness, in which you know what you are entitled to.

To fulfil their democratising potential, participatory governance institutions like health councils require more than citizen awareness and active citizen engagement – although this, and the further democratisation of the public sphere that would lend greater legitimacy and representativity to civil organisations, is a vital precondition for their role in making the work of *controle social* effective. What is also needed is an active, engaged and enabling state, a state whose bureaucrats recognise the role of accountability in democratic governance and who respect their obligations in creating the conditions and providing the resources that can facilitate citizen engagement – both material and symbolic. On one hand, efforts to enhance accountability need to reckon not only with an often idealised model of 'civil society participation' but with particular and shifting configurations of state–society relations, and the extent to which such configurations condition the possibility of accountability and require a range of potential strategies on the part of social actors – whether inside 'invited spaces' such as the health council or in 'popular spaces' outside them. On the other hand, they need to take account not only of the possibilities presented by enabling legislative and institutional frameworks, but also of pervasive political culture. There are, in short, no easy recipes, and for all the enabling conditions that would seem to exist in this case – supportive legislation, a municipal government that has at least provided some material support and had a public commitment to participation, a strong and organised civil society – the struggle for accountability in Cabo continues.

NOTES

1 This chapter is based on participatory research carried out in collaboration between the three authors – the ex-chair of Cabo's Municipal Health Council and director of the Centro das Mulheres do Cabo, a local feminist NGO; a political economist from the Rural University of Rio de Janeiro; and an anthropologist from the IDS, Sussex – and members of Cabo's health council and of the municipal administration. Parts of this paper are drawn from a longer paper (Cordeiro, Cornwall and Delgado 2004) prepared as part of the DfID-ActionAid Brazil *Olhar Crítico* ('A Critical Gaze at Practices of Citizenship and Participation in Brazil') project. Thanks to Alex Shankland for comments.

2 See Newell (Chapter 2) and Goetz and Jenkins (2004) on different dimensions of and interpretations of 'accountability', and Cornwall, Lucas and Pasteur (2000) on these issues with reference to the health sector.

3 Derived from cards produced at a participatory workshop held in Cabo on 12 April 2004 which included users' and health workers' representatives. Health managers chose not to attend.

4 In countries with authoritarian political cultures such as Brazil, it is probably more realistic to assume that the balance has a fatal attraction to state actors.

REFERENCES

Ackerman, J. (2004) 'Co-governance for accountability: beyond "exit" and "voice"', *World Development*, Vol. 32, No. 3, pp. 447–63.

Coelho, V. S. and Nobre, M. (2004) *Participação e Deliberação: Teoria Democrática e Experiências Institucionais no Brasil Contemporâneo* [Participation and Deliberation: Democratic Theory and Institutional Experiences in Contemporary Brazil], São Paulo: 34 Letras.

Coelho, V. S. (2004) 'Conselhos de Saúde Enquanto Instituições Políticas: o Que Está Faltando?', in V. S. Coelho and M. Nobre, *Participação e Deliberação: Teoria Democrática e Experiências Institucionais no Brasil Contemporâneo* [Participation and Deliberation: Democratic Theory and Institutional Experiences in Contemporary Brazil], São Paulo: 34 Letras.

Coelho, V., Pozzoni, B. and Cifuentes, M. (2005) 'Participation and Public Policies in Brazil', in J. Gastil and P. Levine, *The Deliberative Democracy Handbook*, San Francisco: Jossey Bass.

Cordeiro, S., Cornwall, A. and Giordano Delgado, N. (2004) 'A Luta Pela Participação E Pelo Controle Social: O Caso Do Conselho Municipal De Saúde Do Cabo De Santo Agostinho, Pernambuco', Rio de Janeiro: ActionAid/DfID.

Cornwall, A. (2002) 'Making Spaces, Changing Places: Situating Participation in Development', IDS Working Paper 170, Brighton: Institute of Development Studies.

—— (2004) 'New Democratic Spaces? The Politics and Dynamics of Institutionalised Participation', *IDS Bulletin*, Vol. 35, No. 2.

Cornwall, A., Lucas, H. and Pasteur, K. (2000) 'Accountability through Participation: Developing Workable Partnership Models in the Health Sector', *IDS Bulletin*, Vol. 31, No.1.

Dagnino, E. (2002) 'Democracia, Teoria e Prática: a Participação da Sociedade Civil', in R. Perissinotto and M. Fuks (eds), *Democracia. Teoria e Prática*, Rio de Janeiro/Curitiba: Relume Dumará/Fundação Araucária.

Goetz, A. M. and Jenkins, R. (2004) *Reinventing Accountability: Making Democracy Work for Human Development*, Basingstoke: Palgrave Macmillan.

Loewenson, R. (1999) 'Public Participation in Health: Making People Matter', IDS Working Paper 84, Brighton: Institute of Development Studies.

Young, I. M. (1996) 'Communication and the Other: Beyond Deliberative Democracy', in S. Benhabib (ed.), *Democracy and Difference: Contesting the Boundaries of the Political*, Princeton: Princeton University Press.

Overview: Rights, resources and corporate accountability

PETER NEWELL AND JOANNA WHEELER

> The rapid expansion of global investment, production and consumption, in short, has collided in many places and in many ways with local communities. The collisions take place in both developed and developing countries.... Lacking the protection of either national or global norms and institutions, poor and marginal communities in developing countries are either left to suffer or fight or both. (Zarsky 2002: 2)

This section of the book explores the ways in which poorer groups mobilise to hold powerful corporate actors to account for their social, environmental and developmental responsibilities. We noted in Chapter 1 the way in which the state has assumed a central place in discussions about accountability in development amid the attention given to the good governance agenda. Embodying the technocratic approach to accountability that we are questioning in this book, the good governance agenda has privileged sound accounting, reporting and transparency as the central pillars of accountability. It is thus unsurprising that many such notions of accountability have been picked up and put into practice by the private sector. Indeed, there is an intimate relationship between the state and corporate accountability that lies at the heart of initiatives such as 'publish what you pay', recognising the key role of the private sector in attempts to combat government corruption.

Nevertheless, there is a broader and more fundamental accountability agenda that is neglected when we pose the issue in terms of sound financial management and clear reporting requirements. In a context of globalisation, businesses have assumed new forms of power which derive from the legal protection they now operate under as well as unprecedented access to new areas of the world. Investor agreements and global trade accords have enshrined these new powers, described by some as the 'new constitutionalism' (Gill 1995). While the rights of capital are more protected than ever before, the same cannot be said of the labour companies employ or the communities that host them. Questions about who regulates companies which increasingly operate beyond the control of any one state and who, therefore, is responsible when they fail to act responsibly, acquire central importance in development.

This raises issues about the ability of conventional tools of accountability to operate effectively in this new context and, in particular, to serve the needs of poorer and more marginalised groups. International regulation, and in particular international law, is seen to be weak and underdeveloped, and the capacity and willingness of states to regulate business have been thrown into doubt. Businesses themselves have proposed voluntary forms of self-regulation, but issues regarding their enforceability and scope have generated scepticism about whom they serve and how effectively. In this governance gap, NGOs, social movements and community groups have been constructing new mechanisms of accountability through a diversity of means. Though the breadth of strategies adopted towards this end demonstrates a remarkable diversity, and the range of both sectors and regions that we explore in this section of the book reflects a vast geographical canvas, the interesting, notable and politically significant point is the similarities and connections between the ways in which poorer groups in the global North and South are organising to put power into accountability.

Engaging allies across levels of decision making and beyond national borders, groups have mobilised through imaginative and incredibly broad repertories of protest to register dissent, amplify voice and construct alternatives. Some strategies are aimed at enforcing rules and regulations set by others. Mobilisations around labour laws in the United States bear this out in the form of the living wage campaign and efforts to contest the racialised (non)-enforcement of environmental protection measures. Others are aimed at questioning deeper assumptions about who bears the costs and secures the gains from development. In the Niger delta, the contest is centred around the distribution of oil revenues, raising in turn complex and fraught questions of land ownership and entitlement, and magnifying ethnic divisions and sensitivities. In India, marginalised groups question why they are being asked to bear the social costs of adjustment by hosting large industrial projects that primarily benefit wealthier urban élites. Often, then, the issue at stake is the right to say no and the right to claim accountability. Positive rights that do exist are often systematically violated, or lack of awareness about their existence makes it easy for governments to overlook them.

Though played out through localised contests, these conflicts very rapidly assume much wider political dimensions. While garment workers in Bangladesh find their working conditions under scrutiny as a result of civil society campaigns about 'sweatshop' working conditions, activists in the North attempt to exert pressure on oil companies in order to change their operations in Nigeria. To some extent, companies force the spotlight on themselves, engaging in global claim making regarding their responsibilities and invoking the language of citizenship while continuing to be involved in controversial projects on the ground. The case of the National Thermal Power Corporation in India bears this out clearly.

The politics of promoting and ensuring corporate accountability is played out across many arenas simultaneously, therefore, implying a range of actors and raising awkward questions about where the lines of responsibility are drawn between state, market and civil society. The nature of the accountability contest inevitably changes according to the context, reflecting unique histories of conflict and distinct cultures of accountability. The materiality of the resources over which these contests and claims are fought brings into sharp relief questions of power over production and distribution, and, in so doing, raises questions of equity and justice. In Nigeria these controversies are often played out along ethnic lines. In the United States racial dimensions assume a higher profile in debates about environmental racism. Despite these differences, what we find are surprising similarities between the way groups mobilise to contest their fate as the social and environmental sinks that absorb costs associated with other people's development. From using 'weapons of the weak' (Scott 1985) and strategies of resistance, to various forms of engagement with formal institutions, what we see amid the empirical diversity is convergence around many of the themes we highlighted in Chapter 1 about the importance of cultures of accountability, the limits of strategies that rely upon change produced through the law, and the importance of viewing accountability struggles not as an end in themselves, but rather as a surrogate for the pursuit of a variety of forms of social and environmental justice.

REFERENCES

Gill, S. (1995) Globalisation, market civilisation and disciplinary neoliberalism *Millennium: Journal of International Relations* Vol.24, No.3, pp. 399–423.

Scott, J. C. (1985) *Weapons of the Weak: Everyday Forms of Peasant Resistance*, New Haven: Yale University Press.

Zarsky, L. (2002) 'Introduction', in L. Zarsky (ed.), *Human Rights and the Environment: Conflicts and Norms in a Globalizing World*, London: Earthscan.

CHAPTER 8

Corporate accountability and citizen action: cases from India[1]

PETER NEWELL WITH VAIJANYANTA ANAND,
HASRAT ARJJUMEND, HARSH JAITLI, SAMPATH
KUMAR AND A. B. S. V. RANGA RAO

> We have a social responsibility to the community ... a moral responsibility ... we have to give something back ... we take this very seriously.[2]

> We are being sacrificed for the national interest. We are the victims of this cause. What do we get in return?[3]

Given the imprecision of the term accountability as a guide to identifying who is responsible to whom and for what, it is unsurprising to find that in India, as in the other case studies featured in this book, competing notions of accountability feature prominently in conflicts over resources. Cultures of blame and shame collide amid a fog of claims and counterclaims regarding the respective responsibilities to one another of states, business, civil society and the communities at the centre of the conflict. Unlike the Nigerian case discussed in Chapter 10, the conflicts described below have been less violent in their conduct, less global in their scope, but no less political or intractable as a result.

Many companies, particularly multinational enterprises, are increasingly employing the language of citizenship to describe their relationship to society in the context of debates about corporate social responsibility. The limitations and dangers associated with corporate co-option of the language of citizenship, where entitlements are often claimed without assuming corresponding obligations, have been explored elsewhere (Newell 2002; 2005). In liberal notions of citizenship, rights claims are validated and mediated by the state. In the context of debates about corporate accountability, this becomes problematic in so far as the dual roles of the state as promoter and regulator of investment may create conflicting responsibilities. In circumstances in which the state fails to enforce the responsibilities of corporations under its jurisdiction, we may expect to find evidence of groups exposed to the harmful side of weakly regulated investment adopting their own self-help strategies to seek responsiveness from the corporations they host. The citizenship that is expressed by such actions is an active, living citizenship, a version of the concept that is often lost in more legal-constitutional and state-based notions of the term. Exploring the ways in which the poor seek to define and practise their own notions of citizenship should not, however, allow for a negation of the core responsibilities of the state towards its citizens, including the proper regulation of the social and environmental consequences of industrial development.

These competing notions of citizenship manifest themselves in contests over the nature of rights and responsibilities that apply to states, corporations and communities in the context that provides the case studies for this paper: India. While companies such as the National Thermal Power Corporation (NTPC) invoke a globally constituted notion of good corporate citizenship derived from the UN Global Compact (Global Compact 2005), the communities with which they are in conflict, employing a different and more localised notion of citizenship, invoke rights to work, to a secure livelihood and to a pollution-free environment. The claims they make refer to rights that the state is duty-bound to provide for its citizens, but in this case fails to enforce. The citizenship companies project through philanthropic acts and references to responsible conduct is a voluntary concept of 'good citizenship', in theory backed by rights and obligations articulated in legal statutes, in practice often not enforced.

This then is the link to accountability, a concept with two elements at its core: answerability and enforceability (see Chapter 2). The active forms of citizenship that groups express in the cases explored in this chapter aim to produce new forms of answerability: obligations to account for actions and to acknowledge the claims of communities. The particular focus here is relations between corporations and communities in three sites in India, though implicated in this relationship are many other actors from government as well as local NGOs, their national counterparts and the media. This focus provides interesting insights from the frontline of corporate accountability where communities confront corporations in situations of huge power disparity. The three case studies discussed here are, first, the controversy surrounding the NTPC power plant in Paravada, Visakhapatnam (Vizag), Andhra Pradesh; second, the struggles around the development of the Lote Industrial Area in Chiplun, Maharastra; and, third, conflicts around tribal rights and mining in Dumka, Jharkhand.

The first case concerns the siting and operation of the NTPC near the port city of Visakhapatnam in Andhra Pradesh (AP). The Simhadri Thermal Power Project (STPP) under the aegis of the NTPC was commissioned in Paravada, 40 kilometres from Vizag. The AP State Electricity Board signed a power purchase agreement with NTPC in 1997, and construction work started in 1998 after land was acquired from 13 villages spread over three mandals in Vizag district. The plant only started operating fully in May 2002. The company at the centre of this controversy, NTPC, is in many ways a national flagship company, a symbol of national pride, enjoying a significant degree of government backing. NTPC is not just a powerful player within Indian politics, but the sixth largest thermal power corporation in the world and a member of the UN's Global Compact.

The second case concerns the Lote-Parshuram Industrial Area, located in Ratnagiri district of Kokan region in Maharashtra. Following an announcement in 1988 by the Government of India of the development of 'growth centres', the Maharashtra Industrial Development Corporation (MIDC) was given the primary responsibility for selecting 140 sites for mini-industrial areas, acquiring land, and the planning and development of the basic infrastructure (Anand 2002). Many petrochemical companies have established themselves there, including Rallis, Gharda chemicals, Van Organics and National Organic Chemical Industries Limited (NOCIL), producing pesticides, fertilisers, paints and a variety of organic and inorganic chemicals. Like Vizag, the area has attracted the interest of these industries because of an abundance of cheap labour, bountiful natural resources and access to coastlines for the convenient disposal of effluent. Indeed, MIDC has explicitly invoked the availability of creeks for the disposal of treated effluent in campaigns to lure prospective investors (Anand 2002).

The third case centres on the mining industry and its relationship to tribal communities in and around Dumka, Jharkhand. It focuses on small-scale mining activity in Santal Pargana, particularly the 57 stone mines and associated stone factories in three villages of Dumka district. Though the Government of India has recognised the inalienability of tribal rights to land,[4] there is much evidence, including in this case, of their transfer to non-tribals. The incentives for land grabs, corruption and violence are high, since both the government and the private sector have a keen interest in gaining access to and control over the land the tribals occupy and its associated mineral wealth. The conflict is fuelled, as in the previous cases, by both the indiscriminate use of the Land Acquistions Act and pressures for regional commercial development, this time in the form of the World Bank/IMF-assisted Bihar Plateau Development Project, which have resulted in large-scale industrial, mining, irrigation and power projects being undertaken on tribal lands (Arjjumend 2004).

Differences between the three sites in terms of the nature of the companies involved and the responses of the affected communities generate interesting and important lessons about the possibilities and limitations of different accountability strategies. What is striking, however, is the very many similarities in terms of the ways in which decisions were made regarding the investments and the ways in which communities were both affected and sought to mobilise to defend their interests. The cases are used as a basis for identifying the key factors determining the conditions in which it is possible for communities to protect their interests through the construction of new mechanisms of accountability with the corporations they host. These are discussed in turn below. The issues raised by these case studies have a wider resonance than the regions or sectors to which they refer, as we see in Chapter 9 on environmental justice struggles in the United States. The challenges they imply are confronted by many communities around the world faced with similar dilemmas and engaged in struggles that might be advanced by an understanding of what has happened in these three locales in India.[5]

Limits of the law

Accessing the law and realising the rights it is meant to protect presents an enormous challenge for marginalised groups. At the centre of battles over land, livelihoods and compensation in the cases explored here is the Land Acquisitions Act of 1894, a remnant of colonial legislation which allows authorities to remove people from land according to some loose and poorly defined notion of the 'public interest'.

While some people receive compensation, many do not, and these cases suggest important limitations of viewing financial compensation as the ultimate goal of an accountability struggle or as an adequate substitute for political reform. In Vizag, while some families received compensation for their land at a rate above the commercial value of the land (at Rs225,000 or Rs2.25 Lakhs per hectare),[6] many receiving compensation were not entitled to any employment within the plant once constructed, jeopardising the employment opportunities of younger members of those families. Many of those most affected by the industrial development, such as landless labourers, do not have an entitlement to the land on which they work, and are therefore not able to receive any compensation. In Chiplun, for example, herders who grazed their cattle on land owned by the Maratha or Brahmin community got nothing, because the landowners sold it to MIDC (Anand 2002: 17). Community groups have demanded that the government secure compensation for these affected groups on the basis that the company has a 'social obligation' if not a legal obligation to pay for the damage it has caused. But most negotiations have resulted in a bad deal for the local communities and have taken place in private and with no formal records kept. Even where formal agreements have been reached, such as those between mineowners and landholders in Dumka, Jharkhand, none of the landholders who gave over land on mining lease have been given copies of the lease documents, despite having signed or thumbed those documents. None of the mineowners countersigned the settlements, leaving them unaccountable for their obligations (Arjjumend 2004).

An additional problem is that much land is not registered, as it was considered ancestral property and there are no village records, so no entitlement to compensation exists. Land acquisition officers in Hyderabad reported that the land around the NTPC site was 'wasteland', land that is not fertile or productive, so that all cultivation that has taken place on the land is illegal. It is perhaps unsurprising, therefore, that some community leaders accuse the government of 'behaving like monarchs' in driving people off what they perceive to be their land. This suggests the importance (in positive and negative terms) of property rights to the exercise of rights-based claims, either in clarifying the customary rights of communities or, more insidiously, in concentrating access rights in the hands of the powerful. The problem in realising rights, however, is brought out in the Jharkhand case, where 'when they saw the opportunity to gain economically and to get regular employment in return for foregoing their land rights, the tribal families engaged with the mining industry' (Arjjumend 2004: 77).

While maintaining scepticism about legally based accountability strategies, there are some cases of positive change. For example, in Chiplun, a petition was filed by a number of affected individuals against the State of Maharashtra, MIDC, the Collector and the Pollution Control Board (Anand 2002: 22). The High Court advised the appointment of a committee to examine the extent of land, water and air pollution, and the committee produced an extensive report. Though not all of the measures were implemented, it confirmed the extent of pollution and the Court ordered the provision of green belts, setting up effluent treatment plants, water and air monitoring centres and 'corrective measures for industries to prevent the pollution of the Dabhol Creek' (Anand 2002: 22). In the case of Jharkhand, too, organised NGOs have filed public interest litigation suits to contest the acquisition of land for mining and the degradation that has ensued from existing mines, but delays and the costs of the legal process, as well as 'threats' from powerful local figures, prevent many tribals from going to court (Arjjumend 2004).

Capital over community

It is has been common in India for large companies to buy up large swathes of land with the help of state governments and then sell it on at a higher price for a profit, without having delivered the promised industrial development in a region. This 'grab and run' strategy has been encouraged in the past by the use of subsidies and tax breaks by competing states in order to lure investors. For example, Jharkhand's State Industrial Policy of 2001 delivers commercial incentives and fast-track clearances in order to create 'a friendly business environment'. Towards this end, land has been made available at concessional rates, advances have been provided at favourable rates of interest and businesses have been offered nominal tax rates or in some cases relieved of a tax burden altogether. Additional promises to investors include reviews of forestry, mining and tenancy laws, priority supply of power and no 'unnecessary inspections' (Arjjumend 2004: 18). The use of such measures has been justified by the anticipated employment and broader developmental gains to be made by accepting a proposed industrial plant. Such justifications have also been invoked to secure community support for the developments.

One of the consequences of the 'grab and run' strategy has been that state governments have constructed programmes of infrastructure to accommodate industry's needs, which are either discontinued or not maintained when the investor moves on, so that the local communities do not even receive this 'knock-on' benefit. While some are happy to receive any infrastructure at all from governments that normally neglect them altogether, others express anger that their demands for these developments were only met when they coincided with a similar demand from a powerful industry. More controversially still, in Lote, the people are being asked to pay for a pump and pipeline to bring the water in from elsewhere since existing water supplies have been contaminated by industrial activity. In Vizag, promises to the communities included access to a supply of free power that has not been forthcoming, despite their proximity to the plant.

Contested science, contested impact

One of the key sources of grievance for communities is the negative effect on their health of living in close proximity to the industries in question. In Vizag, for example, communities report a number of complaints that they attribute to the plant, including illnesses associated with water contamination and respiratory problems such as coughing and throat infections.[7] Ranga Rao and Sampath Kumar note that 'The presence of upper respiratory infections as reported by the villagers has also been corroborated by the PHC [primary health care] doctors, who said that there has been a substantial increase after the establishment of STPP' (2003: 7). Establishing such connections in a way that would satisfy a law court is another matter, however, underlining again the limits of strictly legal strategies. For example, to make the case that it is the Lote industrial estates that are directly responsible for the damage to their health or their livelihoods means sending samples to laboratories in Mumbai for testing, yet many cannot afford the costs of sending such samples. The NGO PRIA has been able to provide communities with water testing kits to check themselves for levels of pollution.[8] The equipment required is often not very sophisticated: litmus tests to check for levels of acidity, for example. The pollution testing kits provide a useful means by which to challenge the Pollution Control Board's own pollution monitoring figures, nevertheless, which, according to their critics, routinely downplay and underestimate levels of pollution.

In Jharkhand, many of the key health impacts derive from the combined effect of water pumped from the mines being discharged into neighbouring croplands, streams and other water bodies. In Chitragarhia village an epidemic of water-borne diseases including diahorrea, dysentery, cholera and jaundice broke out in July–August 2002, claiming several lives. Dust generated by mining activity and exacerbated by the movement of trucks in and out of the quarries, has affected crops grown in nearby areas and human health. Environmentally, the forests that are traditionally home to many tribals have been devastated by the quarries and stone crushers (Arjjumend 2004: 62). In terms of regulation, it is claimed that the mineowners have not even registered their operations with the regional office of the Central Pollution Control Board, hence studies of the effects of stone quarrying in the area simply do not exist. Besides health and environmental impacts felt 'outside' these operations, occupational health hazards for those working within them are numerous given the nature of work employees are expected to undertake: boulder splitting, exploding, drilling and other heavy-duty extractive tasks.

Workplace conditions are hardly enhanced by the absence of running water and toilets. Minimum wages, insurance and health services, Arjjumend concludes, are 'distant dreams' (Arjjumend 2004: 60).

There have nevertheless been attempts to develop alternative methodologies to capture the disparate and multidimensional effects of the industrial plants in these areas, which are often overlooked in conventional environmental impact assessments. Anand, in her work in Chiplun (2002), encouraged people to identify 'key events' that depicted the impact of the industrial belt upon their lives. The Bhoi community, in particular, spoke of the how dead fish floated to the surface of the creek: 'due to a sudden release of toxic chemicals in the creek … the whole crop of fish died in one single blow' (2002: 18). Besides alternative ways of recording and gauging impacts, activists have also challenged the ways in which current assessments of social and environmental impact are made. For example, claims that rates of malaria have increased in the communities surrounding the NTPC plant were dismissed as ridiculous until people were able to show the relationship between the pollution of the water wells, the resulting stagnation, and the increasing numbers of malaria-carrying mosquitos attracted to the area.

It is indicative of the desperate situation that confronts several communities that many people we spoke to said they would tolerate these adverse human health impacts if they were to be offered some work as compensation. It is the sense that they are suffering the negative side of this industrial development without reaping any benefits that fuels their sense of injustice. One person declared angrily: 'We are being sacrificed for the national interest. We are the victims of this cause. What do we get in return?'[9] Often the absolute dependence created by the presence of an industry in a remote area serves to suffocate community demands for accountability. This is true of the struggle in Jharkhand. Tribal residents in Chitragarhia attempted to block the passage of trucks along the road through their village in protest at the health and environmental problems being exacerbated by the traffic to the mines. Yet 'when people saw their employment at stake, the last livelihood resort … they calmly withdrew the struggle for accountability' (Arjjumend 2004: 68).

Citizen action: barriers and opportunities

Having described some of the obstacles that stand in the way of justice for these communities, this section of the chapter analyses some of the strategies adopted within the community and civil society to contest these injustices and accountability deficits.

Local NGOs, supported by wider networks, have tried to advance the cause of these communities in a number of ways. In Vizag, Sadhana,[10] a Paravada-based NGO, has been the frontline organisation in the campaign around the NTPC plant. The group has conducted surveys of the villages most affected by the plant to compile data and evidence of the impact on their lives; it has also recorded their demands and how they would like to see them met. The findings from these surveys will be presented at a local *gram sabha* (local assembly) as well as at panchayat (village government) meetings, and will feed into the People's Development Plan to be presented at a public hearing.

Public hearings and People's Development Plans

In Vizag, there has been one public hearing so far. It is hoped that the second will provide both an important opportunity to reflect on the process surrounding the construction and development of the NTPC, and to identify necessary changes in time for the consultation process regarding the proposed 'Pharma Park' in the same area. Whereas a public hearing was not required for the NTPC plant, a decision was made subsequently that future developments required such a hearing. The challenge for concerned NGOs is to ensure that people get to know about the public hearing and are aware of the implications of the proposed development for their livelihoods. As things stand, a company is required to provide one month's advance notice of a public hearing. The notice must appear in one local English-language and one Telegu-language newspaper. Details are also meant to be kept at local Panchayat offices that people can visit to read the documents. Of course, many people in the area cannot read the documents and would not be aware of where they are being held because they cannot read the notices in the newspapers.

Activists also complain that, in the past, industries have deliberately placed announcements in the least widely read newspapers in the area (a discretion in their power) and often only run the announcement for one edition on one day, so that news of the public hearing is unlikely to spread very far. Given this, there have been calls to extend the time between the announcement of the hearing and the actual event, to allow people to discuss the implications and prepare submissions, and for NGOs and others to spread news of the meeting to a broad range of potentially affected constituencies, and to assist, for example, with their transportation to such an event.

Potentially, however, the public hearings provide an important opportunity to raise concerns, and to hold the company and government publicly accountable for their past track records regarding promises concerning employment, compensation and the like. Using the hearings effectively in such a way, however, requires significant advance preparation of materials and networking with other groups who have experience of previously affected communities in order to compile evidence and testimonies that can be used in the hearing. One of the key lessons from the NTPC experience has been that if bargaining takes place once the proposed industrialisation has the go-ahead or construction work has already taken place, the chances of getting the company to respond to demands and grievances are significantly reduced. This is why significant efforts are now being put into ensuring that the process surrounding the proposed 'Pharma Park' is more transparent and inclusive, and that concerns are raised early enough in the process to secure action.

Ensuring that companies such as NTPC will attend the proposed public meeting is a difficult task in itself, given previous refusals to attend.[11] Direct appeals for meetings from NGOs, on behalf of the communities, have been consistently refused or not acknowledged.[12] While the company claims not to have received correspondence, NGOs claim to have sent numerous letters requesting meetings and raising specific issues of concern. It is hoped that the company will view future hearings as an opportunity to clarify expectations regarding the scope of its obligations to the community. Often, of course, claims of abuse of due process are aimed at state bodies responsible for overseeing these investments. In the case of Jharkhand, land acquisitions are taking place without prior consultation with local people and the *gram sabhas* of concerned villages in direct contravention of administrative provisions for panchayats and other legislation (Arjjumend 2004: 21). Those public hearings about the mines that have been organised were conducted in a 'biased and discreet manner where the local administration, the statutory bodies for clearing the projects and the mining companies are in close collusion to ensure that there are no effective objections raised by the public' (Arjjumend 2004: 85).

Local NGOs in both Vizag and Chiplun, with the support of the Society for Participatory Research in Asia (PRIA), are also in the process of constructing People's Development Plans. These are constructed on the basis of the surveys conducted by NGOs and following extensive consultations with groups in the area over a number of months. The findings are compiled as a plan of desired development for the region: the types of industrial and other activities that people are willing to accept and would like to see, and those they want to avoid. There has even been some support from companies such as NTPC for the idea of a plan. The appeal for the company is the opportunity to receive a consolidated set of demands and ideas as opposed to a steady stream of disparate and bilateral demands from communities around the plant.

Working through the local NGO Parivartan, PRIA has also assisted in the development of a People's Development Plan and in establishing public hearings in Chiplun. The first public hearing was held in 1999. Many chemical companies operating in the area, such as Rallis, only undertook a full public hearing concerning their activities after they had been operating for seven years and after much of the environmental degradation had already been caused. In setting up the hearings the groups have relied, for example, on the assistance of local medics and union activists working in the area to provide inputs for the People's Development Plan, and have tried to facilitate communication between villages along the coastal industrial belt.[13] The public hearing organised by Parivartan was the first time that industries, MIDC and people came together face to face to air their views. One successful outcome was that industry accepted the major responsibility for setting up an effluent treatment plant (Anand 2002: 22).

The People's Development Plans that feed into the hearings provide an important opportunity for inter-community learning through know-ledge sharing around their experiences with particular forms of industrial development. Such exchanges of experience allow communities faced with the prospect of a development in their area to inform themselves of the risks and benefits associated with the new investment by involving communities that have already been exposed to the same industries' activities. Having heard testimonies about the pollution of a creek which led to the death of cattle, water pollution has been a key focus of villagers' concern in Lote, for example.

Despite the many benefits of such informal tools, many communities continue to channel their concerns and grievances through state authorities. In the absence of corporate responsiveness, this makes some sense and mirrors the companies' own preference for operating through the state rather than talking to people directly.

NGO accountability

In addition, a key danger for NGOs adopting these strategies is that they become cast as the legitimate representatives of the community interest in dialogues directly with industry, either in the run-up to specific events or in ongoing bilateral discussions. Many affected communities are clear about their desire for leadership from groups with the perceived expertise, resources and networks to carry forward their concerns in seeking action from government and the company. The onus is then on the NGOs themselves to manage these expectations as best they can. NGOs such as Sadhana in Vizag are keen to see that the communities themselves take a lead on these issues with themselves in a supporting role, but it is clear from conversations with these communities that they do expect the group to play a leadership role.[14]

It may also be preferable from the company's point of view to engage with an articulate NGO that enjoys some credibility with the local community, rather than have to face the strength of feeling of the affected communities directly. But such arrangements inevitably raise issues of how adequately the interests of the community are being represented and whether NGOs' own agendas are always consistent with the community's needs. In the Jharkhand struggle, only two of the four NGOs are from within the tribal community. Indeed, there are suspicions that the 'outsiders' were at least partly involved in order to seek material gain and personal benefits by negotiating with the mineowners (Arjjumend 2004: 67). There may also be a difference between communities being happy for NGOs to register their concerns with companies and governments and to use their expertise to 'validate' their claims, on one hand, and, on the other, their consenting to a process whereby an NGO brokers deals and negotiates terms with a company on their behalf. The consequences and the scale of the accountability challenge are certainly more significant in the latter case, where issues of trust and transparency are more critical.

Strategic alliances with the state

There have also been attempts by community activists to form strategic alliances with lower levels of the state such as mandals and panchayat rajs. Legally, panchayats can demand information from, sanction or even stop industrial operations in their jurisdiction. Nevertheless, while aware of the problems reported to them through NGOs, or directly by the villagers themselves, state officials at this level feel relatively powerless compared to the district government, which has greater powers; officials emphasise that they have no legal control over NTPC, for example, despite its being a government undertaking. P. Jagannadha Rao (MPP), local elected head of the mandal in Paravada, feels that decisions are being made above their heads. He said: 'We have no choice but to accept these investments: they are driven by the state governments; this is government policy.'[15]

It is difficult in such settings to differentiate between genuine incapacity on the part of the state to effect change and inaction justified by claims of limited power. In raising critical concerns about the direction of industrial development in the area, these government bodies would be pitting themselves against the strong state-level support for the NTPC plant as well as the proposed 'Pharma Park'. These projects form part of former AP Chief Minister Chandrababu Naidu's vision of constructing a 'new economic zone' in the Vizag area. It would be costly for local leaders to appear to be against these developments, especially when they are from the same political party – in this case Telegu Desam, the majority party in many mandals and panchayats in the Vizag area. That said, there are fractures within the local state that open up opportunities for new alliances. Some officers in the local mandal office, for example, express sympathy towards villagers' claims about the human health and environmental impacts of the NTPC plant.[16] The Medical Officer appeared in a video about the conflict supporting community claims that the plant's activities were damaging health.

Importance of the media

Given this failure of information flow, the media potentially play a key role in promoting accountability. Many journalists have taken a personal interest in the NTPC issue, for example, and are keen to work with activists to build coalitions around it. Following our meetings with the communities surrounding the NTPC plant, several journalists attended a press conference we hosted to discuss the issues raised by the visit and many published stories in influential newspapers as a result (*Deccan Herald* 2003; *The Hindu* 2003). Though downplaying their role in drawing the company into a public dialogue about its operations, activists are clear that it is negative publicity that has made the company more receptive to their demands for meetings and dialogue. *The Hindu* and *Deccan Chronicle*, two of the region's most widely read daily English-language newspapers, have started to publicise the issue, sparking debate within élite policy circles. When *The Hindu* carried a story about an information-sharing meeting organised by PRIA on the impact of the plant, the following day tests for water pollution were undertaken when the Pollution Control Board and district officials arrived. In addition, following media reports of security guards at the plant beating villagers climbing the walls of the plant to escape a fire sweeping across their villages, the company distributed 10 kilograms of rice to villagers in the immediate area to pacify anger about the incident.[17]

While publicity to the cause is welcome, there is concern that too much media attention could encourage the company to retreat from public debate. Once a level of trust between intermediary NGOs, such as

PRIA, has been achieved it may be counter-productive to continue to air grievances through the media, as the company may see this as a breach of trust. In the case of NTPC, proceedings have not got that far, and there is little discernible evidence that the company is as yet willing to involve the NGOs in its decision making or to partner them in exploring possible solutions of mutual benefit. In addition, the threat of negative coverage should the company fail to act and renege on its promises has to remain a plausible one to encourage compliance. The danger remains that media coverage serves to identify opponents of industry as a nuisance, inviting unwanted and potentially hostile action on the part of industry or the state.

Democratic space

At a basic level, citizen action for accountability is also affected by a culture of tolerance towards protest. While in theory this culture is an accepted feature of political life in India, in all these cases there have been complaints about the repression of protest activities. For example, there are allegations that threats of beatings were issued by the police when a community refused removal from their land in Vizag.[18] They refused to move on the basis that they had records of money paid to the government for the hire of the land for work, contradicting government claims that the land was not theirs. The law can also be used to break up protests that do take place. Protests of more than five people can be broken up and the people imprisoned under the colonial Criminal Procedures Act, on the basis that the protests constitute a public nuisance. The Act has been used in this way to disband protests over both proposed future petro-chemical investments in the Chiplun area and the controversial Daebol-ENRON project in the region (Mehta 1999).

Corporate responsiveness

Corporate responsiveness to citizen action, particularly in the absence of effective state action, is clearly also critical to the prospects of change. If answerability is one of the two pillars of accountability, it depends both on actors feeling obliged to justify their actions and to recognise that the accountability claims made of them are valid. NTPC, for its part, has denied allegations of human health impacts and environmental degradation resulting from its activities. It has, nevertheless, sought to defend its track record. The company's web site pronounces:

> As a responsible corporate citizen, NTPC is making constant efforts to improve the socio-economic status of the people affected by its projects. Through its

Rehabilitation and Resettlement programmes, the company endeavours to improve the overall socio-economic status of Project Affected Persons. (NTPC 2003)

Elsewhere, the company claims that its 18 power stations have received ISO14001 certification and proudly proclaims its membership of the UN's Global Compact initiative. The company also draws attention to its community development efforts, where Rs4 Crores (Rs40 million) have been spent over four years, according to the Resettlement and Rehabilitation Officer.[19] Displayed on the company office walls are photographs of family planning programmes, eye-testing clinics and water sanitation projects sponsored by the company.

In spite of company claims that its community development efforts are 'needs-driven',[20] it mainly funds projects tackling problems that do not implicate the company in any way. For example, clinics to test hearing, which many community members claim has been impaired by the noise the plant generates, would be useful – but would allow people to document damage to their hearing, for which the company might then be liable. The major environmental contribution that the company has made, and which adorns all its public relations material, is the plantation of 100,000 trees grown next to the plant to absorb the pollution generated by its activities and to 'offset' its emissions. This 'forest' is the source of many jokes in the communities, expressing cynicism about the green credentials of NTPC.

Again, we find competing notions of accountability at work. From the company's point of view, discretionary philanthropy is an adequate response to demands for accountability by the community. For the company, accountability is first and foremost to the state. In a typical response, one NTPC official said that the company's involvement in a public hearing would be conditional on the participation of the district collector. The challenge for PRIA and other groups working both in Chiplun and Vizag is to not only to get the state (re-)involved in such processes, but to expand the boundaries of what is up for discussion; to improve corporate responsiveness on livelihood issues such as land and employment; and to displace the more convenient and seemingly political neutral emphasis on 'soft responsibility', or philanthropic health and education projects which firms are happier to discuss.

While increasingly willing to engage in tentative discussions with groups such as PRIA, NTPC is unrepentant about the process to date: 'The past is past … there is no point having grievances,' one representative said to us.[21] Inevitably, with such a mega-project there are some 'adjustment' costs to be borne and a level of 'dislocation' that has to take place. The firm claims that all its actions are legal and were conducted with the acquiescence and support of the government. Its deal with the government was over land and no legally binding commitments were made regarding jobs and infrastructure. Indeed, it seems the government is equally to blame over the growth of misperceptions about the number of jobs that would be made available to the local community. Many villagers claim that it was the former Chief Minister Chandrababu Naidu who promised that 99 per cent of the jobs associated with the plant would be provided to local people. Equally, the company has no legal obligation regarding rehabilitation, despite having made efforts in this direction.

In Jharkhand, we find a more extreme case of reluctance on the part of the companies to engage in dialogue with communities affected by their activities. Negotiation through intermediaries has taken the place of direct dialogue, and companies employ influential staff members as 'diluting agents' or 'informers' to quell resistance and contain demands for change (Arjjumend 2004: 72). This is in addition to their use, noted above, of middlemen to broker deals needed to secure access to tribal land – despite legal protections, which are routinely overridden in the rush to claim property rights. Arjjumend cites the case of a village headman and supervisor in Madan Rathi's quarry. With little knowledge of local land or the leases held on it, and allegedly ignorant of customary norms, he supported mining interests by offering consent to the illegal and arbitrary transfer of lands for mining operations (Arjjumend 2004: 72).

Conclusions

This analysis highlights a number of key issues about the conditions which affect the ability of communities to secure accountability from key actors in these regions.

First, the importance of multi-pronged strategies: we saw above how media exposure, direct dialogue with companies and government officials, public hearings, and the law have been used to seek a fair deal for the communities that host these industrial projects. Often these strategies are pursued simultaneously and in ways that reinforce their impact. Decisions about which strategy it makes most sense to adopt at which time, and by whom, depend upon the nature of the change sought. At different times, these strategies have served respectively to expose, to embarrass, to engage and to seek redress. We have emphasised throughout the use of citizen-based methodologies of accountability. Citizen health monitoring, video, public hearings and People's Development

Plans have been among the tools employed to document concerns that have been overlooked, to give a platform to voices that have been ignored, and to generate new expectations about the conduct of powerful actors.

Second, mobilising early in order to shape discussions about a proposed investment is vital. This is the overriding lesson of the struggle around the NTPC plant that is now being applied in relation to the proposed 'Pharma Park' in the same region. Once land has been acquired and licences issued, it becomes increasingly difficult to raise objections or negotiate better terms for the communities that will host the project. Building an effective case requires sharing information and experience of communities that have hosted the same industry or even the same company. This issue emerges strongly from the Chiplun case study, where inter-community learning was used to feed into the development of a People's Development Plan and the public hearing – to hear testimony of the companies' conduct elsewhere, and whether promises made to other communities had been fulfilled.

A third key factor is the importance of rights (to land, compensation, and information). Much of the social dislocation caused by the Lote Industrial Area and the NTPC plant resulted from the fact that the poorest workers had no land entitlement and therefore were not in a position to receive compensation. Having rights is not enough, however. Being aware that you have those rights and knowing how to use them is what makes a difference. For example, many villagers affected by pollution from the NTPC plant were unaware that the information they need to support their claims already resides in the offices of the Pollution Control Board and that they are entitled to access it. In the Jharkhand struggle, people were unaware of the constitutional provisions pertaining to their land rights and process, and their decision-making rights with regard to consultation and participation. The barriers to realising those rights should not be underestimated, however, where governments systematically override legal obligations they have set for themselves, as they did with regard to tribal rights in Jharkhand.

A fourth factor that comes through strongly in the case of the NTPC plant is the importance of party politics and relations with the state in general. There has been systematic discrimination in favour of those villages that were under the control of the ruling party to the neglect of other villages, often those most affected by the plant. We noted how local panchayat and mandal officials felt relatively powerless in the face of strong state-level government support for the NTPC project, particularly from officials of the same political party. When the backing of state and federal government is so strong, strategies of negotiation are less likely to be effective. In the Jharkhand case, we saw how contests over tribal rights quickly became embroiled in broader party political struggles in which tribal communities were associated with the left and the communist parties in particular, an association which invited further marginalisation and repression from state officials (Arjjumend 2004: 72). We also saw (occasional) examples, however, of the potential for alliances with sympathetic elements within government able to lend their support and authority to community claim making.

Ultimately, these cases underscore the problem of reducing accountability to acts of corporate responsibility that rely on various forms of philanthropy. Such approaches assume not only a willingness on the part of the companies to engage in an open and public dialogue about their responsibilities, admit wrongdoing when necessary and take remedial action when negligence has occurred, but also a proactive approach to accommodating the needs of the communities with which they are working. This is particularly problematic for communities affected by irresponsible investment practices: they are rarely identified as legitimate stakeholders by business and lack sufficient influence within government policy making to articulate and defend their concerns. In this context, their resort to informal and often confrontational strategies can hardly be considered surprising. In this sense, the accountability struggles we describe here are a far cry from notions of corporate responsibility, which tend to confer on business the power to set the terms of its own conduct. The notion of accountability is more helpful in this context, for it lays bare the power relations that the seemingly benign language of 'responsibility' and 'citizenship' seeks to deny or transgress.

NOTES

1 We would like to thank Aruna Katragadda, Shagun Mahotra, Randeep Singh Saini, Shaikh Ismail and Ashok Kadam for help in setting up meetings with government and company officials, and for organising the visits to the villages that made this research possible. Thanks also to Jutta Blauert and John Gaventa for very useful comments on an earlier draft of this chapter. Some of the material in this chapter draws from Newell (2005a) and I am grateful to Ranjita Moharty and Rajesh Tandon for permission to reproduce it.

2 Representative from NTPC. Interview with Peter Newell, Aruna Katragadda and Shagun Mahotra, February 2003.

3 Villager from the area surrounding the NTPC plant. Village meeting with Peter Newell, Aruna Katragadda and Shagun Mahotra, February 2003.

4 These have been recognised in amendments to the Indian constitution in 1990, Provisions of the Panchayats Act, 1996, the Supreme Court judgement (Samatha),

1997 and the Environmental Protection Act of 1986.

5 The discussion of the case studies is based on two visits to the sites in Vizag (2002) and Chiplun (2001) in which meetings and discussions were held with affected communities, government officials, local NGOs and company officials (in the case of NTPC). It also draws on case reports by Anand (2002), Ranga Rao and Kumar (2003) and Arjjumend (2004). Recording and analysing the claims made by the different parties involved in these disputes should not be taken to imply that the authors endorse all reported claims and allegations.

6 The market rate for the land was said to be Rs45,000 per acre (*The Hindu* 22 November 2002). STPP officials claim that the land was worth between Rs40,000 and Rs100,000 (or Rs1 lakh).

7 Meeting with Peter Newell, Aruna Katragadda and Shagun Mahotra, February 2003.

8 The Society for Participatory Research in Asia (PRIA), an advocacy and research NGO (PRIA 2005).

9 Meeting with Peter Newell, Aruna Katragadda and Shagun Mahotra, February 2003.

10 The full name of the organisation is 'Visishta Gramodaya Swayam "Sadhana" Parishad'.

11 For example, prior to the construction and operation of the NTPC plant, unrecorded bilateral discussions took place between communities and individuals from the firm. Because there is no record of these meetings, promises made there have no legal standing.

12 Meeting with Peter Newell, Aruna Katragadda and Shagun Mahotra, February 2003.

13 Interviews by Peter Newell and Randeep Singh Saini with a number of activists, Chiplun, 2002.

14 Meetings with Peter Newell, Aruna Katragadda and Shagun Mahotra, February 2003.

15 Interview with Peter Newell, Aruna Katragadda and Shagun Mahotra, February 2003.

16 *Ibid*.

17 *Ibid*.

18 Meetings with Peter Newell, Aruna Katragadda and Shagun Mahotra, February 2003.

19 Interview with Peter Newell, Aruna Katragadda and Shagun Mahotra, February 2003.

20 *Ibid*.

21 Interview with Peter Newell, Aruna Katragadda and Shagun Mahotra, February 2003.

REFERENCES

Anand, V. (2002) *Multi-party Accountability for Environmentally Sustainable Industrial Development: the Challenge of Active Citizenship. A Study of Stakeholders in the Lore Parshuram Chemical Industrial Belt, Chiplun, Maharastra*, College of Social Work, Mumbai University, paper produced for Society for Participatory Research in Asia (PRIA) New Delhi.

Arjjumend, H. (2004) *Tribal Rights and Industry Accountability: the Case of Mining in Dumka, Jharkland*, New Delhi: Society for Participatory Research in Asia (PRIA).

Deccan Chronicle (2003) 'Acquisition Policy Draws Flak', 21 February.

Global Compact (2005) www.unglobalcompact.org, accessed 3 August 2005.

Mehta, A. (1999) *Power Play: a Study of the ENRON Project*, Hyderabad: Orient Longman.

Newell, P. (2002) 'From Responsibility to Citizenship: Corporate Accountability for Development' *IDS Bulletin* Vol.33 No.2 'Making Rights Real: Exploring Citizenship, Participation and Accountability' Brighton: IDS.

—— (2005) 'Citizenship, Accountability and Community: the Limits of the CSR Agenda', *International Affairs*, Volume 81, No. 3 (May), pp. 541–57.

—— (2005a) 'Corporate Citizenship and the Politics of Accountability: Communities and Companies in India', in R. Moharty and R. Tandon (eds), *Identity, Exclusion and Inclusion: Issues in Participatory Citizenship*, New Delhi: Sage.

NTPC (2003) http://www.ntpc.co.in/aboutus/rrpol.pdf, National Thermal Power Company website, accessed 10 January 2003.

PRIA (2005) www.pria.org, Society for Participatory Research in Asia website, accessed 9 August 2005.

Ranga Rao, A. B. S. V. and Sampath Kumar, R. D. (2003) *Multi-party Accountability for Environmentally Sustainable Industrial Development: the Challenge of Active Citizenship. A Study of Stakeholders in the Simhadri Thermal Power Project, Paravada, Visakhapatnam District, Andhra Pradesh*, Department of Social Work, Andhra University, paper produced for Society for Participatory Research in Asia (PRIA) New Delhi.

The Hindu (2003) 'Adverse Impact of Pharma City Feared', 19 February.

The Hindu (2002) 'Villagers Brood over a "Hazy" Future', 22 November.

CHAPTER 9

Environmental injustice, law and accountability

ROHIT LEKHI AND PETER NEWELL

> Poor people bear the brunt of environmental dangers – from pesticides to air pollution to toxics to occupational hazards – and their negative effects on human health and safety. At the same time, poor people have the fewest resources to cope with these dangers, legally, medically or politically. (Cole 1992: 620)

Work on environmental racism in the United States (US) shows that communities of colour are often targeted by firms engaged in the production of hazardous materials such as chemicals and toxics, because they anticipate a more compliant workforce that can be paid lower wages and where they expect political resistance to be less forthcoming. If these are the 'drivers' of environmental racism, its consequences include much higher levels of exposure to toxics and subsequently increased rates of illnesses related to exposure to these hazards among minority communities. Taking just one statistic to illustrate the point, the famous 1987 study by the United Church of Christ (UCC) Commission for Racial Justice found that three out of every five African and Hispanic-Americans live in communities with uncontrolled toxic waste sites (Commission for Racial Justice 1987).

Given the limitations of voluntary patterns of business-based self-regulation and state interventions to protect the rights of poorer communities – either excluded from mechanisms of corporate responsibility, or more often than not the victims of acts of corporate irresponsibility – there is growing interest in the role of community-based strategies for corporate accountability (Garvey and Newell 2005). Though it is often assumed that it is communities in the South that are more heavily reliant on strategies of self-help, in a prevailing context of a 'weak' state and a private sector not yet subject to the pressures and disciplines of corporate social responsibility (CSR), we suggest in this chapter that important insights can be gained from the community-based struggles around environmental racism, principally in the US, which manifest many of the basic conditions confronting poorer communities the world over. Our aim is to review and consolidate insights emerging from these struggles in order to explore parallels with other campaigns for corporate accountability explored in this book (see chapters 8 and 10).

The purpose of this chapter is not to document the evidence of the poor being exposed to disproportionate levels of environmental degradation or to engage with debates that seek to establish whether the principal drivers of such patterns are race, class or some other hierarchy of social exclusion. Our enquiry is focused instead on the question of strategy: how poorer groups mobilise to defend their interests, to articulate rights claims and to secure a degree of accountability from the powerful economic actors that are located 'where we live, work and play', to borrow a phrase from the environmental justice movement.

Amid the many state-based, company-based and community-based factors that impinge upon the effectiveness of community-based strategies for corporate accountability, our enquiry centres on the potential and limitations of legally based strategies for corporate accountability. This reflects the fact that the strategic orientation the environmental justice (EJ) movement has been shaped, in large part, by the experiences of the civil rights movement. As a result, many of the strategies employed by EJ activists during the past three decades have sought to use and extend pre-existing frameworks oriented to addressing racial injustice. As a result, the EJ movement in the US has placed a great deal of strategic emphasis on the use of law as a primary mechanism for defending the interests and articulating the rights of poorer communities of colour.

This is not to suggest that the law is the only or even the best means of realising the rights of those communities, but rather that the orientation of the EJ movement has been shaped by the historic importance of the legal arena as the major location of challenges to racial discrimination in the US. Indeed, this emphasis on the law has generated numerous tensions within the EJ movement. As we note below, there are many within the EJ movement who argue that the limits of what can be realised through legal challenge necessarily requires an alternative strategic orientation towards grassroots mobilisation and the direct empowerment of local communities. Our aim in what follows is not to dispute that this may be the case. Instead, in seeking to analyse the use (and equally importantly, the limits) of law as a strategic tool, we hope to shed light on

those alternative strategies that may be more appropriately employed when those limits are reached.

In pursuing this aim, we hope to identify parallels, lessons and insights that may resonate with struggles defined in opposition to similar patterns of injustice elsewhere. Lessons generated from the experiences of the environmental justice movement in the US cannot be unproblematically imported into other settings. Even work from outside the US, from South Africa for example, suggests the importance of studying the interface between race and environment in particular settings (Ruiters 2002). Nevertheless, the patterns of exclusion and inequality which define struggles for environmental justice in the US resonate strongly with the experience of poorer groups the world over, even if the contours of injustice and the forms of accountability politics express different histories, cultures and politics.

The first part of the chapter explores the historical, political and conceptual contexts that have shaped the development of the environmental justice movement in the US in order to better understand the origin and evolution of particular rights-based claims and their relation to broader accountability struggles. In the second part, we construct a framework for understanding the factors that facilitate or inhibit the success of community-based organising for corporate accountability, based on the experience of the environmental justice movement. In the concluding part of the chapter, we discuss how accountability struggles in the US share similarities with, and offer insights for, poorer groups engaged in similar struggles in other parts of the world.

The origins and development of the US environmental justice movement

Defining environmental racism
For many, the origins of the environmental justice movement in the US can be traced back to the protests that took place in 1982 against the decision to build a toxic waste landfill for PCB-contaminated dirt in Warren County, North Carolina, which is a largely African American and extremely poor area of the state. In the course of these protests, involving the arrest of both local people and high-profile civil rights activists, the relationship between race and environmental impact was given national prominence for the first time. 'While the protests did not succeed in keeping the landfill out of Warren county, an interracial movement was forged, linked to the larger civil rights and poverty

movements, with the goal of empowering people to protect themselves and their communities from environmental harms' (Babcock 1995: 8). It was in the aftermath of the Warren County protests that the concept of 'environmental racism' was first advanced by the civil rights activist, Dr Benjamin Chavis. According to Chavis, environmental racism refers to:

> racial discrimination in environmental policy making and the unequal enforcement of the environmental laws and regulations. It is the deliberate targeting of people-of-colour communities for toxic waste facilities and the official sanctioning of a life-threatening presence of poisons and pollutants in people-of-colour communities. It is also manifested in the history of excluding people of colour from the leadership of the environmental movement. (Quoted in Sandweiss 1998: 36)

The idea of 'deliberate targeting' suggests, unequivocally, that the causes of environmental racism are intentional. However, as a basis from which to challenge inequitable distributions of environmental impact, the standard of proof required to demonstrate the existence of 'environmental racism' defined in this way has been notoriously difficult to establish – requiring as it does, *explicit* evidence of intent. Consequently, others have argued for a shift in the burden of proof required to establish the fact of environmental racism away from a notion of explicit intentionality to one premised on disparate outcomes or impacts of decisions. This can refer to policies, practices or directives (whether intended or unintended) that differentially affect or disadvantage individuals, groups or communities based on race or colour, or unequal protection against toxic and hazardous waste exposure and systematic exclusion of people of colour from decisions affecting their lives (Bryant 1995).

Whatever the precise nature of the mechanisms that generate specific inequalities in respect of environmental decision making, it is clear that an overt focus on causation has been unhelpful to the extent that it has deflected attention from the more important question of what to do about the inequalities (intentional or otherwise) that clearly do persist in respect of communities of colour and low-income communities – inequalities that include not just siting decisions but also standard setting, enforcement, clean-up, and opportunities (or the lack of them) to participate in regulatory processes.

From environmental racism to environmental (in)justice

The pursuit of remedial action in respect of such inequalities is represented in the shift in focus – both politically and conceptually – from environmental racism to environmental justice. If environmental racism is based upon problem identification, environmental justice is based on problem solving. For many social activists environmental degradation is just one of many ways in which their communities are under attack. Environmental racism, therefore, is often understood in relation to multiple forms of deprivation and exclusion experienced in daily life:

> Because of their experiences, grassroots activists often lose faith in government agencies and elected officials, leading those activists to view environmental problems in their communities as connected to larger structural failings – inner-city disinvestment, residential segregation, lack of decent health care, joblessness, and poor education. Similarly, many activists also seek remedies that are more fundamental than simply stopping a local polluter or toxic dumper. Instead, many view the need for broader, structural reforms as a way to alleviate many of the problems, including environmental degradation, that their communities endure. (Cole and Foster 2001: 33)

It is through this articulation of the problems to be addressed within the framework of EJ as, inseparably, those of racism *and* social justice that the environmental justice movement builds on the rhetorical legacy of the civil rights movement. Furthermore,

> The collective action frame of the civil rights movement – which emphasised such values as individual rights, equal opportunities, social justice, full citizenship, human dignity, and self-determination – provided a 'master frame' that legitimised the struggles of other disenfranchised groups. By framing the problem of disproportionate exposure as a violation of civil rights, the environmental justice movement was able to integrate environmental concerns into the civil rights frame. (Sandweiss 1998: 39)

This has allowed for a significant expansion of the civil rights movement into the environmental arena, bringing with it all the 'moral force, compelling emotion, dedication, activism, sympathetic response and relentless commitment to the pursuit of rights that have characterised civil rights activism during the past 30 years' (Jones 1993: 28).

In order to operationalise its demands, the environmental justice movement has advanced two sets of rights-based claims (Pulido 1994). First is the demand for procedural rights to participate equally in the process of environmental regulation. This is seen as a primary mechanism to ensure that communities of colour and poorer communities are able to gain 'voice' in those fora where decision making occurs. As codified in the 'Principles of Environmental Justice' adopted by the First National People of Colour Environmental Leadership Summit, this is 'the right to participate as equal partners at every level of decision making including needs assessment, planning, implementation, enforcement and evaluation' (Bullard 1994: 274–5). However, in and of itself, the demand for equity in decision making around the distribution of hazards signals a clear limit in respect of the strategic goals that the environmental justice movement can hope to realise. As Heiman argues:

Should the quest for environmental justice merely stop with an equitable distribution of negative externalities, business could proceed as usual. This time it would be with assurance from the Environmental Protection Agency (EPA) and other regulatory agencies that we will all have an equal opportunity to be polluted or – the flip side – protected from pollution, however ineffectively. Such assurance comes complete with procedural guarantees that we may participate in the equitable allocation of this pollution and protection, if we so choose. (Heiman 1996)

As a consequence, the environmental justice movement has also sought to advance a second set of rights claims. This is a demand for rights to live free from environmental hazard, not just to distribute that hazard more equitably. These substantive rights are oriented to the demand for preventative strategies to ensure that threats are eliminated before they create harm. As expressed in the aforementioned 'Principles' this is 'the fundamental right to clean air, land, water and food'.

Strategic orientation to realising rights: law vs activism

Within the environmental justice movement there are significant differences in respect of how these rights claims can best be pursued. Some argue that meaningful solutions can only be realised through the active intervention of federal government, and this requires a prioritisation of legislative/procedural strategies of reform (Ferris 1995). For others, grassroots mobilisation and the empowerment of local communities are the key strategic goals in any attempt to overcome environmental injustices (Schafer 1993; Bullard 1993a). For yet others, the meaningful realisation of procedural and substantive rights will only be secured through systemic changes in the very basis of economic production (Faber and O'Connor 1993).

As might be expected, given the framing of EJ issues in terms of civil rights, the use of constitutional and statute law features prominently in the tactical arsenal of the EJ movement. The first moves in this direction were to pursue EJ claims under the constitutional right to equal protection – the use of which had been pivotal in helping to secure African American civil rights during the 1950s and 1960s. The first EJ claim to be brought under these auspices was *Bean v. Southwestern Waste Management Corporation* in the late 1970s. This involved a challenge by local residents in Houston, Texas to the siting of a hazardous waste facility in a predominantly African American area. However, in this case – and in others brought subsequently under the auspices of equal protection – the US Supreme Court rejected the claim of unequal protection on the basis that it is necessary in such cases to show discriminatory *intent*.

Given the difficulties in establishing direct proof of intentionality in such cases, the EJ movement has sought to employ a civil rights approach that has been less onerous in the standards of proof demanded. Of greatest importance in this regard has been the use of Title VI of the 1964 Civil Rights Act, which prohibits racial discrimination in all activities and programmes in receipt of federal funding. Claims pursued under Title VI have sought to deny federal funds to those states that are involved in enacting discriminatory environmental decisions. In these cases, however, the standard of proof required is one of discriminatory outcome or impact rather than intent. Plaintiffs need only prove that the result of the policy or practice impacts disproportionately on (discriminates against) the community, not that it was the intent of policy or practice to do so.

However, the pursuit of legal remedies, while fostering some limited successes, is not the favoured strategic orientation of many EJ activists. As Cole and Foster (2001: 33) note,

> grassroots environmentalists are largely, though not entirely, poor or working-class people. Many are people of colour who come from communities that are disenfranchised from most major societal institutions. Because of their backgrounds, these activists often have a distrust for the law and are often experienced in the use of non-legal strategies, such as protest and other direct action.

Mobilisation

In pursuit of alternative strategies oriented to grassroots mobilisation as opposed to the law, the historical and strategic relationship of the civil rights movement to the EJ movement has again been crucial. According to Sandweiss (1998: 39), there are two aspects to this:

> First, environmental justice activists have been able to draw on the organizational resources and institutional networks established during the previous struggle for racial equality. Churches, neighbourhood improvement associations, and historically black colleges and universities have furnished the environmental justice movement with leadership, money, knowledge, communication networks and other resources essential to the growth of any social movement. Second, environmental justice activists have successfully borrowed many of the tactics associated with the civil rights movement to call attention to their demands – both direct action tactics, such as protests and boycotts, as well as more conventional activities, such as lobbying and litigation.

It was precisely these roots in civil rights and church-based advocacy that led to the UCC's landmark 1987 study, *Toxic Wastes and Race in the United States* and the 1991 First National People of Colour Environmental Leadership Summit (Commission for Racial Justice 1987). Both of these facilitated, for the first time, a national voice and national-level coordination of what until then had been largely localised struggles around specific instances of environmental injustice. The Summit itself, which brought together EJ activists from across the US and other parts of the world, also provided a platform for the first concerted attempt to articulate a coherent vision of environmental justice, embodied in its seventeen 'Principles'.

A further goal was to develop greater coordination of EJ activities at the regional level. In addition to the already-formed Southern Network for Economic and Environmental Justice (SNEEJ), further regional coordination was facilitated in the development of the Asian Pacific Environmental Network (APEN), the Indigenous Environmental Network (IEN), the North-east Environmental Justice Network; the Midwest/Great Lakes Environmental Justice Network and the Southern Organising Committee for Economic and Environmental Justice. These regional networks have played a crucial role in ensuring the coordination of activism and mobilisation, while at the same time recognising the diverse needs and concerns of specific ethnic and geographic communities (Pellow 2002: 77).

Accounting for mobilisation

Having provided an overview of the contexts in which the environmental justice movement emerged, this section organises insights regarding factors that impact upon the effectiveness of strategies employed by groups that are the victims of environmental racism. Given the many links, suggested above, including the forms of injustice and the ways in which these are contested, between the environmental justice movement and other forms of community-based activism for corporate accountability, we want to suggest there is a broad resonance in these insights that extends well beyond the contexts from which they are derived.

Planning, process and representation

Minority and poorer groups generally lack access to and representation within government, particularly at the national level (Babcock 1995). Beyond voice in areas traditionally considered to be environmental, lack of representation in planning and zoning commissions is particularly relevant here. Bullard (1993: 23) suggests that 'Many of the at-risk communities are victims of land-use decision making that mirrors the power arrangements of the dominant society. Historically, exclusionary zoning has been a subtle form of using government authority and power to foster and perpetuate discriminatory practices.' Even accepting that state laws are to some extent not generating inequalities, Cole and Foster note that 'State permitting laws remain neutral or blind toward these inequalities; they therefore perpetuate, and indeed exacerbate, distributional inequalities' (Cole and Foster 2001: 75).

Corporate penetration of such decision-making processes further reduces their responsiveness to community demands. Discussing attempts by communities in Illinois to hold the company Clark Oil to account for its social and environmental responsibilities, Pellow (2001: 63) shows how the city council's environmental and industrial committee, charged with evaluating Clark Oil's health and safety record, included a former Clark Oil employee. These patterns of influence hint at deeper cracks in the democratic process and the inherent tensions faced by liberal democracies in balancing economic growth with democratic decision making. In this regard, Krauss (1989: 230) argues that 'The state must in one and the same moment achieve two conflicting aims: it must maintain the conditions for profitable capital accumulation and economic growth while legitimating its own power by appealing to the principle of democracy.'

Even where channels of representation within the state are made available, it is often very difficult for groups to make use of them. During the permit application process for the Genesee power station in Michigan, public hearings were held. However, community members were made to sit for hours while the committee undertook other business, and when the group finally got a chance to testify, 'the decision makers talked among themselves, laughed and paid little attention. Moreover, the hearing took place at a location more than an hour from the proposed site, forcing residents to rent a bus' (Cole and Foster 2001: 124). Citizen input is often seen as a nuisance and limited to a short period of time, signalling to residents (1) that they must make a quick decision; (2) that their input was deemed irrelevant during the planning phase of the proposal; and (3) that their input has been reduced to 'we want it' or 'we don't want it' (Allen 2003: 156).

It is predictable, then, that local authorities decide upon sites where residents are least likely to oppose such developments, which a 1984 report for the California Waste Management Board suggested would be 'rural communities, poor communities, communities whose residents have low educational levels ... and whose residents were employed in resource-extractive jobs' (Cole and Foster 2001: 3). The Cerrell report, a strategy manual for industries needing to set up polluting facilities such as incinerators, aimed to 'assist in selecting a site that offers the least potential of generating public opposition' (cited in Cole and Foster 2001: 71). Its recommendations were: (1) avoid middle- and higher-income neighbourhoods; (2) target communities that are less well educated; (3) target conservative or traditional communities, preferably with fewer than 25,000 residents; (4) target rural or elderly communities; and (5) target areas whose residents are employed in resource-extractive jobs like mining, timber or agriculture (Cole and Foster 2001: 3).

At the level of enforcement, there are also oversights, acts of negligence or patterns of exclusionary decision making that activists have sought to contest. Activism, in this sense, can serve to plug gaps in state enforcement of environmental regulations, highlighting both the limits of law and the reluctance of states to enforce it in circumstances in which private investors may be deterred from making further investments. Pellow suggests that corporate–community compacts and good neighbourhood agreements (GNAs) have become more common as a result of the weakening of state policy-making authority, as corporations have become both policy makers and the new targets of challengers (Pellow 2001). He defines GNAs as 'instruments that provide a vehicle for a community organisation and a corporation to recognise and formalise their roles within a locality and to foster sustainable development' (Pellow 2001: 55). They became more popular as a non-litigious method of dispute resolution among companies, workers, environmentalists and local communities in the wake of an increase in industrial disasters. Combating exemptions that allow corporations to keep certain information out of the public sphere, GNAs encourage broad disclosure so that communities and NGOs can play a role in the enforcement of codes of conduct. Even their proponents are clear, however, that GNAs are not a substitute for governmental regulation: they are simply a response to the lack of, and need for, such regulation.

Community activists often seek to address weaknesses in state-based processes through their own informal sanctions. Process requirements and resources available to corporate actors can make official sanctions difficult to impose, so that community groups adopt what Cable and Benson call (1993: 471) 'informal sanctions' (such as press conferences denouncing the company, pickets outside company offices, and attempts to attract media attention through rallies and protests). Informal sanctions are also important in incentivising the take-up of the sort of informal and 'soft' community-based policy tools described above.

Beyond drawing attention to an injustice through protest or media coverage, community groups have also sought to train and educate themselves, to find ways of exchanging experience about successful accountability strategies, and to build a degree of learning and reflection into their struggles. Activists, as well as setting up literacy programmes and field trips, have run programmes on participatory citizenship skills. Environmental justice clinics also play an important role. The clinics function, according to Babcock, 'as laboratories for exploring different ways to overcome legal and institutional barriers ... and as catalysts for reforming the legal system' (Babcock 1995: 50). They provide high-quality legal services to communities at risk, including requests for disclosure of information and analysis and distillation of technical reports for local residents. As Babcock notes, 'Victories may be as seemingly insignificant as securing the release of information from a recalcitrant government official; however, even these exercises have led to changes in official attitudes toward public requests for information and reforms in their process of responding' (Babcock 1995: 56).

Law and its limits

These patterns of exclusion from decision making help to explain why legal battles to contest the outcomes of these processes have been commonplace. Allen argues that citizen groups end up with their complaints in the courts precisely because the legislative and executive branches have been co-opted by corporate lobbyists (Allen 2003: 90). She suggests that 'regulatory agencies such as DEQ are easily co-opted by industry because top-level officials often alternate between agency posts and positions in industry. The judicial branch is the last option for residents otherwise disenfranchised by the close liaisons between the chemical industry and their elected and regulatory officials.'

Nevertheless, legal strategies are seen as a key strategy by mainstream groups such as the Sierra Club, whose executive director of legal defence believes that 'Litigation is the most important thing the environmental movement has done over the past fifteen years' (quoted in Cole and Foster 2001: 30). However, there are many resource and procedural barriers to bringing, successfully pursuing and enforcing legal cases. Barriers for poorer groups are multiple and include: lack of legal literacy, lack of resources, distrust of the legal process, and inability to pay costs if the case is unsuccessful (Newell 2001). Babcock (1995: 22) notes that 'some members of a disempowered group may be initially hostile toward, or intimidated by, lawyers and the judicial process, or may have been trained in the confrontational tactics of the civil rights or poverty movements'. There are also process barriers to the successful pursuit of legal strategies, such as high demands for expertise required to engage the legal system effectively. Many environmental laws have 'created complex administrative processes that exclude most people who do not have training in the field and necessitate specific technical expertise' (Cole and Foster 2001: 30).

Besides these barriers and process issues, many environmental justice activists are wary of 'legalising' a problem. The concern, as noted earlier, is that legal strategies take the struggle out of the realm in which the community has control of it. Broader social justice claims get pressed into legally cognisable claims. In these instances, 'collective struggle is translated into an individual lawsuit with the result that the momentum of the community's struggle is lost' (Cole 1992: 652). Though successful in bringing attention to a case, the diverse and spontaneous forms of community organising that groups employ to contest their fate as victims of environmental justice are largely redundant within the legal process. Moral claims, the use of symbolic power and a variety of 'weapons of the weak' which poorer groups deploy to counter the structural and material forms of power that corporates benefit from become less visible and less relevant once a struggle is reframed in legal terms, shifting the balance of power towards those with resources, expertise and influence. Cole argues that 'Even if the law is "on their side", unless poor people have political or economic power as well, they are unlikely to prevail.... Tactically, taking environmental problems out of the streets and into the courts plays to the grassroots movement's weakest suit' (Cole 1992: 648, 650).

Beyond the limits of legally based strategies in general, there are also questions about the value of poorer communities seeking protection through environmental law. Because they are risk-oriented, environmental laws tend to support decisions as long as emissions comply with minimal state regulatory thresholds. As Cole notes (1992: 646), 'while we may decry the outcome, environmental laws are working as designed. Such a disproportionate burden is legal under US environmental laws.... Thus decisions to place unwanted facilities in low-income neighbourhoods are not made in spite of our system of laws, but because of our system of laws.'

The positive potential of the law
Our emphasis on the many limitations of legally based strategies should be tempered by an acknowledgement that cases can and have been won

when the rights of poorer communities have been violated. Landmark legal settlements can pave the way for change. Allen (2003: 40) describes a court ruling in which it was determined that citizens' environmental protection must be given fair weight alongside economic and social factors. The groups bringing the case 'effectively changed the face of environmental planning in the state' according to Allen (2003: 40). Though enforcement remains a problem, following the ruling, chemical companies that sought to locate in the area had to prove that they had fully considered alternative sites and projects as well as environmental mitigation measures. In cases in Dallas and Alabama, out-of-court settlements have been achieved by communities affected by environmental racism, including, in the case of Olin Chemicals, an agreement to clean up residual PCBs and DDT, allocate money for long-term health care costs and pay cash settlements to individual residents.

Community groups have used to positive effect provisions that require the government to respond to each public comment on an environmental impact report, for example. In the case, *Pueblo para el Aire y Agua Limpio v County of Kings*, a community successfully filed a complaint against the environmental impact report on grounds of its inadequacy under the California Environmental Quality Act, and the court blocked the project. The legal challenge was based upon the principle of discrimination against Spanish speakers in the decision-making process, given the lack of Spanish translation in public consultation meetings and documentation.

Before they can locate a toxic waste facility in a community, companies have to obtain permits. Public notices of plans are issued, a comment period is allowed and public hearings are held where there is a significant degree of public interest, including published notices in area newspapers. In theory, if the content of the notice or the procedures for publicising it do not meet the regulatory requirements, a court may order the notice process to be repeated (Perkins 1992). While agencies are reluctant to deny permits, if an agency does issue a permit over community objection, administrative and judicial appeals are available, as with the case in California described above.

There are also community right-to-know laws, despite numerous attempts to revoke them. Some statutory schemes for hazardous waste siting have progressive potential. The Massachusetts scheme, for example, requires the hazardous waste developer to negotiate an approved siting agreement with the host community to offset any adverse impacts. State assistance is also sometimes available to the host community to obtain any technical studies and other material it needs to negotiate effectively

(Colquette and Robertson 1991). Provision of state legal aid can be important. Because they are free, for many people in low-income communities legal-aid services are the only option available and logically become 'part of the first line of defence for [those] facing environmental dangers' (Cole 1992: 656).

Beyond building legal capacity, the state can also facilitate less confrontational approaches to conflict mediation by initiating dialogues between companies and communities. Pellow and Park (2002) describe 'Project XL' under the Common Sense Initiative, a multi-stakeholder project aimed at reconciling the respective demands and expectations of companies and communities. The problem, however, was that rather than going beyond existing regulations, regulatory flexibility was traded in exchange for increased community involvement and concessions on improved environmental performance, worker safety and environmental justice criteria. In addition, companies have insisted that meetings would not be open, decisions would not be made by consensus and local stakeholders would not be able to veto the agreement or an element of the agreement.

Concessions to business are seen by community activists as part of a broader pattern of bias evident in the planning process. Allen (2003: 3) quotes a resident from Louisiana's chemical corridor complaining that while the Department for Environmental Quality spent 'hours and weeks with the applicant polluter to help them get their permitting applications legally and technically correct and to help the polluters stay in business … the time for citizens just isn't there'. Cole (1992a: 1995) also takes issue with the presumption of state neutrality in such disputes:

> Increasingly, states have set up processes to site toxic waste facilities over local opposition – whether the opposition is by people of colour or not. Additionally, the US Environmental Protection Agency has threatened at least one state … with loss of superfund monies if it does not site a toxic waste incinerator.

Far from being a neutral arbiter in such conflicts, the state is often aligned in direct opposition to those advocating environmental justice.

The purpose of this section has been to highlight the ways in which particular legal mechanisms and strategies can help to advance corporate accountability claims and the circumstances in which this is possible. In previous sections we noted the very many procedural barriers that make the legal process a difficult one for community activists to navigate, raising issues such of access, cost and representation. We have also emphasised the ways in which, by its very nature, the law validates certain forms of claim making and delegitimises others. This has important consequences for accountability struggles, which often aim at broader political change and seek to tackle the causes of injustice and discrimination – at times embodied by the law. It raises key dilemmas of strategy and brings to the fore awkward trade-offs between the prospect of short-term gains and the imperative of longer-term change.

Conclusions: parallels and insights

The parallels between what we have found here and other work documented in this book are striking. First, there is a sense in which the most controversial industrial developments are often located in the poorest areas of a country, whether it is areas in the US predominantly inhabited by black and Latino communities or the poorest states of India, where tribal communities are most likely to be victims. The pattern of privatising profit and socialising costs also appears to be similar. Just as Louisiana's cancer corridor has been described as a 'massive human experiment' and a 'national sacrifice zone' (Perkins 1992: 390), so poorer communities in India ask 'We are being sacrificed for the national interest. We are the victims of this cause. What do we get in return?' (Chapter 8). Often the target is a particular category of the poor, based on broader patterns of racial and social discrimination. In India, it is tribals, in the US native Americans have found themselves disproportionately exposed to toxic waste, while in South Africa forced relocation of poorer communities of colour was employed by the apartheid regime to make way for mining operations (Madihlaba 2002: 158).

Second, the luring of high-polluting industries as a state strategy emerges as a theme with global resonance. Just as an 'industrial tax exemption' has been used to attract the chemical industry into poor areas of the US, so it is has been common in India for large companies to be offered financial concessions in exchange for promised industrial development that is often not delivered. The importance attached to attracting chemical and pharmaceutical companies to the state of Andhra Pradhesh in India is seen by activists there as a constraint on state action and community mobilisation around claims of negligence.

Such trends serve to compound intra-state practices of 'economic blackmail', where companies threaten to relocate in the face of new labour or environmental legislation or when confronted by organised opposition. This creates extra challenges for community organising where capital mobility can have the effect of setting impoverished communities, in need of investment, against one another in the search for the least-cost and most trouble-free investment location (Gaventa and Smith 1991). Within the United States cooperative action between social justice and environmental groups has been seen as one of the best ways of weakening the hold of 'job blackmail' – threats of job loss or plant closure – on working-class areas and communities of color (Bullard and Wright 1990: 302). The immense structural advantage afforded to capital by its mobility clearly applies to some sectors more than others. As we shall see in Chapter 10 on the oil industry in Nigeria, the nature and availability of a resource, its materiality, shapes the options available to an industry in terms of where it operates and the form of politics which surrounds its exploitation, management and distribution. The industries discussed in this chapter have many more options open to them about where to locate, a factor that greatly enhances their bargaining leverage.

A third, interrelated, feature common to many of the situations we describe here is the conscious location of hazardous production activities in areas populated by groups from whom low levels of political resistance are expected. Impoverished communities generally lack the financial and technical resources necessary to resist environmentally hazardous facilities, as well as having less access to traditional remedies to ameliorate those burdens under environmental and civil rights laws. This is compounded by the lack of mobility of the poor in terms of employment and residence.

Fourth, the poorest groups in these conflicts are often the least visible. Migrant labour from some of the poorest states in India provides a pool of cheap and informal labour for industry. Even in high-tech sectors, immigrant populations face disproportionate exposure to toxic hazards (Pellow and Park 2002). Not only is mobilisation harder for migrant, transient populations with fewer resources and networks to draw on, but the often illegal nature of their work renders them less able to secure the forms of protection bestowed upon more formal types of employment. Inhabiting unregulated, unprotected spaces, immigrant, seasonal, temporary and child labour are most vulnerable to exploitation.

A fifth theme we have sought to highlight with global resonance is the importance of the law in both a positive and negative sense. Legal contests characterise many of the conflicts between communities, corporations and governments, raising issues of access and legal literacy as well as the enforceability of decisions and the regulations they invoke. While potential resides in existing state provisions for those that know about them and have the resources, time and confidence to make use of them, this positive potential is often diminished by deliberate oversight, manipulation of procedures by powerful interests or non-enforcement of the terms and conditions of regulations. Just as they did in Vizag, Andhra Pradesh, companies choose media with restricted reach to advertise hearings and notices of proposed developments. Residents of 'Chemical valley' in the US complain that public notices of siting decisions do not work because they 'can be placed anywhere in the newspaper – in the legal section, the classified and even the social section' (cited in Allen 2003: 36). Even far-reaching legal protection afforded to poorer groups is often bypassed in practice when the economic stakes are raised. Whether it is civil rights laws in the US or provisions for the protection of tribals in India, non-accessibility and the mobilisation of bias against poorer groups diminishes the utility of the law as a tool of accountability.

This is how what start as campaigns about particular siting decisions become struggles over decision-making processes that allocate risks in unjust ways. In this sense, Cole argues that 'many in the grassroots environmental movement conceive of their struggle as not simply a battle against chemicals, but a kind of politics that demands popular control of corporate decision making on behalf of workers and communities' (1992: 633). Anti-toxics activists, through the process of local struggles against polluting facilities, came to understand discrete toxic assaults as part of an economic structure in which, 'as part of the "natural" functioning of the economy, certain communities would be polluted' (Cole and Foster 2001: 23). This, in turn, raises many strategic questions, such as whether merely calling for environmental equity reproduces a naive faith in procedural justice and the ability of distributional notions of fairness to tackle the structural and institutional sources of injustice (Ruiters 2002: 118).

Our purpose in drawing these parallels is not to suggest that the settings are identical, permitting successful strategies to be exported to other locales unproblematically. How the factors are weighted in terms of political significance, and how they play out in practice, will always be context-specific – a function of the alliances between community, civil society and the state in any particular setting. And whilst we have suggested parallels with the insights emerging from work on environmental justice movements in the US, it is always important to bear in mind the ways in which accountability struggles are strongly defined by the context in which they emerge and the end for which they are employed.

REFERENCES

Allen, B. L. (2003) *Uneasy Alchemy: Citizens and Experts in Louisiana's Chemical Corridor Disputes*, Cambridge MA: MIT Press.

Babcock, H. (1995) 'Environmental Justice Clinics: Visible Models of Justice', *Stanford Environmental Law Journal*, Vol. 14, No. 3, pp. 3–57.

Bryant, B. (1995) *Environmental Justice: Issues, Policies and Solutions*, Washington: Island Press.

Bryant, B. and Mohai, P. (1992) *Race and the Incidence of Environmental Hazards: a Time for Discourse*, Boulder, CO, San Francisco and Oxford: Westview Press.

Bullard, R. D. (1990) *Dumping in Dixie: Race, Class and Environmental Quality*, Boulder, CO, San Francisco and Oxford: Westview Press.

—— (1993) 'The Threat of Environmental Racism', *NR&E*, Winter, pp. 23–6 and 55–6.

—— (1993a), *Confronting Environmental Racism: Voices from the Grassroots* (Boston: South End Press).

—— (ed.) (1994) *Unequal Protection*, San Fransisco: Sierra Club Books.

—— (1994a) 'Decision Making', in L. Westra and P. Wenz (eds), *Faces of Environmental Racism*, London: Rowman and Littlefied.

Bullard, R. D. and Wright, B. H. (1990) 'The Quest for Environmental Equity: Mobilizing the African-American Community for Social Change', *Society and Natural Resources*, Vol. 3, pp. 301–11.

Cable, S. and Benson, M. (1993) 'Acting Locally: Environmental Injustice and the Emergence of Grassroots Environmental Organisations', *Social Problems*, Vol. 40, No. 4 (November), pp. 464–78.

Cole, L. (1992) 'Empowerment as the Key to Environmental Protection: the Need for Environmental Poverty Law', *Ecology Law Quarterly*, Vol. 19, pp. 619–83.

Cole, L. (1992a) 'Remedies for Environmental Racism: a View from the Field', *Michigan Law Review*, Vol. 90, pp. 1991–7.

Cole, L. and Foster, S. (2001) *From the Ground Up: Environmental Racism and the Rise of the Environmental Justice Movement*, New York: New York University Press.

Colquette, K. M. and Robertson, E. H. (1991) 'Environmental Racism: the Causes, Consequences and Commendations', *Talane Environmental Law Journal*, Vol. 5, pp. 153–207.

Commission for Racial Justice United Church of Christ (1987) *Toxic Wastes and Race in the United States: a National Report on the Racial and Socio-Economic Characteristics of Communities with Hazardous Waste Sites*, New York: Public Data Access.

Faber, D. and O'Connor, J. (1993) 'Capitalism and the Crisis of Environmentalism', in R. Hofrichter (ed.), *Toxic Struggles: the Theory and Practice of Environmental Justice*, Salt Lake City: University of Utah Press.

Ferris, D. (1995), 'A Broad Environmental Justice Agenda', *Maryland Journal of Contemporary Legal Issues*, Vol. 5, No. 1, pp. 115–27.

Garvey, N. and Newell, P. (2005) 'Corporate Accountability to the Poor? Assessing the Effectiveness of Community-based Strategies', *Development in Practice*, Vol. 15, Nos 3–4 (June), pp. 389–404.

Gaventa, J. and Smith, B. (1991) 'The De-industrialisation of the Textile South: a Case Study', in J. Leiter, M. Schulman and R. Zingraff (eds), *Hanging by a Thread: Social Change in Southern Textiles*, Ithaca, NY: Ithaca Press.

Heiman, M. (1996) 'Race, Waste and Class: New Perspectives on Environmental Justice', *Antipode*, Vol. 28. No. 2, pp. 111–12.

Jones, S. C. (1993) 'EPA Targets 'Environmental Racism', *The National Law Journal*, 9 August, pp. 28, 34, 36.

Keeva, S. (1994) 'A Breath of Justice', *ABA Journal*, February, pp. 88–92.

Krauss, C. (1989) 'Community Struggles and the Shaping of Democratic Consciousness', *Sociological Forum*, Vol. 4, pp. 227–39.

Madihlaba, T. (2002) 'The Fox in the Henhouse: the Environmental Impact of Mining on Communities', in McDonald, D. (ed.), Athens and Cape Town: Ohio University Press and University of Cape Town Press, pp. 156–68.

McDonald, D. A. (ed.) (2002) *Environmental Justice in South Africa*, Athens and Cape Town: Ohio University Press and University of Cape Town Press.

Newell, P. (2001) 'Access to Environmental Justice? Litigation against TNCs in the South', *IDS Bulletin*, Vol. 32, No. 1.

—— (2005) 'Citizenship, Accountability and Community: the Limits of the CSR Agenda', *International Affairs*, Vol. 81, No. 3 (May), pp. 541–57 .

—— (2005a) 'Race, Class and the Global Politics of Environmental Inequality', *Global Environmental Politics* Vol.5, No.3, August, pp. 70–94.

Pellow, D. N. (2001) 'Environmental Justice and the Political Process: Movements, Corporations and the State', *The Sociology Quarterly*, Vol. 42, No. 1, pp. 47–67.

—— (2002), *Garbage Wars: the Struggle for Enivronmental Justice in Chicago*, Cambridge, MA.: Massachusetts Institute of Technology (MIT) Press.

Pellow, D. and Park Sun-Hee, L. (2002) *The Silicon Valley of Dreams: Environmental Injustice, Immigrant Workers and the High-tech Global Economy*, New York and London: New York University Press.

Perkins, J. (1992) 'Recognising and Attacking Environmental Racism', *Clearinghouse Review*, August, pp. 389–97.

Pulido, L. (1994), 'Restructuring and the Contraction and Expansion of Environmental Rights in the United States', *Environment and Planning A*, No. 26.

Ruiters, G. (2002) 'Race, Place and Environmental Rights: a Radical Critique of Environmental Justice Discourse', in McDonald, D. (ed.), Athens and Cape Town: Ohio University Press and University of Cape Town Press, pp. 112–27.

Sandweiss, S. (1998) 'The Social Construction of Environmental Justice', in D. Camacho, (ed.), *Environmental Injustice, Political Struggles: Race, Class and the Environment*, Durham: Duke University Press.

Schafer, K., with Blust, S., Lipsett, B., Newman, P. and Wiles, R. (1993) *What Works: Local Solutions to Toxic Pollution*, Report No. 2, Washington, DC: The Environmental Exchange.

Szasz, A. and Meuser, M. (1997) 'Environmental Inequalities: Literature Review and Proposals for New Directions in Research and Theory', *Current Sociology*, Vol. 45, No. 3 (July), pp. 99–120.

White, H. L. (1998) 'Race, Class and Environmental Hazards', in D. Camacho (ed.), *Environmental Injustice, Political Struggles: Race, Class and the Environment*, Durham: Duke University Press.

CHAPTER 10

Oil and accountability issues in the Niger Delta

OGA STEVE ABAH AND JENKS ZAKARI OKWORI

The politics of oil in Nigeria has attracted considerable activist and academic attention in recent years (Rowell and Goodall 1994; Okonta and Douglas 2003; Frynas 2000; Naneen 2004). Amid allegations of human rights abuses, environmental devastation and state corruption, the Niger Delta has come under increasing global scrutiny. Accountability in the region is intimately tied to the politics of resource extraction and the governance of abundance. The lack of accountability over how oil is extracted and who benefits in the Niger Delta has led to demands by many different community-based groups for their rights to the resource to be respected and guaranteed. They demand accountability from different actors, including the state and transnational corporations. The emergence of these community-based groups, especially youth organisations and women's groups, has resulted in the creation of new informal structures of governance.

The focus of this chapter is on community-level processes and politics as the site for accountability struggles, though these are linked to a wider context in which the state (federal and local), and transnational corporations are important actors. In order to understand how community-based politics relates to overarching questions of accountability and oil, this chapter draws on participatory research conducted using popular theatre, in which communities tell their own stories about rights and exclusion, and in this way identify for themselves where change is needed. Given the context of conflict and tension in the Niger Delta, drama is an important tool because it provides insights into the community-level politics of accountability, a topic neglected in many of the other studies on oil and politics in the region. The meanings and representations of oil at the local level challenge the idea of a 'resource curse' and open up the relationship between community-level politics and processes and the wider context of political and commercial interests.

Many studies on the Niger Delta, especially following the death of activist Ken Saro-Wiwa in 1995, have focused on the federal government and its failure to deliver development to communities in the region (see Johansen 2002; Ekeh 1999); even Shell's shortcomings are explained through the failure of the federal government to enforce rules and regulations. In contrast, our focus is on the accountability of other actors, including the private sector. To explore these issues, we begin with an overview of how the abundance of oil contributes to a lack of accountability in the Niger Delta. We briefly summarise the literature focusing on oil as a 'resource curse' that undermines the prospects for improving accountability, as well as on other contributory factors. We discuss the complex relationships between actors – including the government, transnational corporations (TNCs) and communities – and the accountability demands they make. The main focus of this chapter, however, will be community-level politics, explored through performance, drama and their relationship to state and corporate accountability.

The Niger Delta and the politics of abundance

The abundance of oil in Nigeria has made the country dependent on oil for revenue generation. Revenue from oil is controlled and distributed by the government. Corruption has made politics in Nigeria very lucrative, with politicians spending huge amounts to get into office. Once in office they and their business collaborators become the active beneficiaries of the centralised system of bureaucracy, through which they are then able to manipulate the distribution of the state's resources to enrich themselves through corrupt means. Since oil alone accounts for 80 per cent of Nigeria's budgetary allocations, there is a lot of wealth at the disposal of those in political office, which has led to capital-intensive projects in which overhead costs far outstrip actual disbursements to people-centred programmes (Mutizwa-Mangiza 1990: 43; Olowu and Wunsch 2004: 65). The crude oil output from Bayelsa and Delta states accounts for 90 per cent of Nigeria's foreign exchange earnings and over 80 per cent of its GDP (Okon 2003: 4). With each election, politicians promise to return more oil revenue to the communities from which it was derived, yet once in power these promises are largely unfulfilled and frustration mounts, often leading to violence.

The term Niger Delta refers to both the immediate area where the River Niger shreds into tributaries and empties into the Atlantic Ocean and the contiguous zones and communities that are geographically defined by the creeks that have formed as a result of the interaction of the Niger and the ocean. It covers an area of about 70,000 square kilometres extending from Akwa-Ibom State through Cross River, Rivers, Bayelsa, Delta and Edo to Ondo State. In its extended form it also includes Abia and Ebonyi states. The region is made up of several ethnic groups including Annang, Efik, Egi, Ibibio, Ijaw, Isoko, Ikwerre, Itsekiri, Ndokwa, Ndoni, Ogba, Oron,Urhobo, Ibo and Yoruba (Okon 2003: 1).

The people of this region are traditionally fishers and farmers. A large part of the population was also involved in trading, production of crafts, oil palm milling, timber extraction, boat building and local gin brewing. With the discovery of oil, there has been a remarkable shift from these means of livelihood to other sources centred on oil and oil exploration. In this sense, the production of oil has redefined livelihoods, the economy and politics in the region (Eson et al. 2004: 197). In comparison to other parts of the country, the region has inadequate infrastructure and high unemployment rates. There is, therefore, a correspondingly high level of tension and community-based conflict. Another effect of oil extraction and processing is the diminishing sustainability of livelihoods from forest products and marine resources due to environmental pollution and degradation caused by oil exploration activities.

At the same time, the advent of oil extraction has raised awareness among different groups of people in the area. Women's and youth organisations, as well as development unions and associations such as Ijaw national youth organisations (mostly formed after the discovery of oil), have become highly mobilized. This growing involvement in the politics of oil is informed by feelings of oppression and marginalisation, and alienation from the 'dividends' of oil manifested in an absence of education and employment. In turn, this contributes to a crisis of citizenship in Nigeria, where national citizenship has little meaning in comparison with other geographical and ethnic identities (Abah and Okwori 2005: 73).

There is consensus that a crucial way to address poverty, and the lack of accountability poor people experience, is to gain more control over resources, especially oil; people in the Niger Delta have been trenchant in calling for this (Eson et al. 2004). They believe that only through self-determination and direct control of the oil found on their land will they be able to use the revenue from oil to better their lives. The reality is that oil wealth is seen in Nigeria as a 'national cake' and politicians, the military and civilians scramble to get a slice of it.

Production from joint ventures (JV) accounts for nearly all of Nigeria's crude oil production. The largest JV, operated by Shell, produces nearly 50 per cent of Nigeria's crude oil.[1] The federal government generates revenues that it disburses to all states and local governments in Nigeria for development purposes. In doing this, it takes into account certain allocation principles, especially those of population, the need for equality between states, internal revenue generation, land mass and terrain. The current constitutional provision, however, is that the principle of derivation shall be constantly reflected in any approved formula as being not less than 13 per cent of the revenue accruing to the federation account directly from any natural resources (Udeh 2002: 3). This is in recognition of the need to compensate the oil-producing states for their contribution to wealth generation. Yet, despite the high levels of oil production from the Delta region, it remains one of the poorest in the country.

Given the pervasive and often perverse effects of oil on politics and development in Nigeria, it is important to highlight the contextual factors that contribute to the situation, including colonialism. There is also a growing body of literature exploring the idea that oil and other natural resources can constitute a 'resource curse' destructive of developmental and democratic prospects. The next section will summarise some of the key arguments from this literature, in order to contextualise the community-level perspectives on oil that will be the focus of this chapter.

Conflict and control: resource curse and neocolonialism

Neocolonialism

Scholars over the years continue to link the conflict in the Niger Delta region to British colonial arrangements and control of the Niger area. Agbonifo (2004) argues that Nigeria, from its inception, was treated as a business enterprise by British colonisers. Therefore, from the slave trade to the palm oil trade and subsequently petroleum, the terms of trade have always been unfavourable to Nigeria. He asserts that the discriminatory strategy of granting licences and leases to British subjects provided the basis for the entrepreneurial underdevelopment of Nigeria, and the entrenchment of the hegemony of foreign capital.

As argued by Akpobibo (2001), Alamieyeseigha (2002) and Ajakorotu (2004), ethnic competition laid the foundation for political and economic competition in the Nigerian state. They maintain that the division of the country into three regions and the subsequent linking of representational power to population size meant that minorities had little opportunity to demand access to resources or developmental projects in regional assemblies. In response, ethnic minorities in the region began to mobilise for self-determination. Against this backdrop, Ajakorotu insists that at the core of the Niger Delta crisis in the post-independence era has been the concentration of power and resources in the hands of the federal government through constitutions and decrees, making governments insensitive to the grievances of local people. Into this context of inadequate representation, and a history of exploitative resource extraction, came the discovery of oil and drilling on a large scale in 1958, creating the conditions for what has been described as a 'resource curse'.

Resource curse
The idea of the resource curse brings together political, economic, social and cultural dimensions of natural resource conflict and control:

> It is both difficult and artificial to distil out the narrowly defined biological and geophysical properties of 'crude' or 'raw' petroleum from the social relations (institutional practices, ideological associations and meanings, forms of extraction, production and use) of petroleum, a commodity not only saturated in the myths of the rise of the West but also indisputably one of the most fundamental building blocks of twentieth-century industrial capitalism. (Watts 1998: 2)

Work on the resource curse seeks to explain how abundance of natural resources can often stunt economic development, and contribute to a lack of accountability (Karl 1997; Shafer 1994; Sachs and Warner 1995). There are both economic and political explanations for this (Ross 1999). Some centre on the short-sightedness among policy makers that resource abundance produces (a 'get rich quick mentality'/'petromania'/'petro-fetishism'), while other accounts emphasise the way in which resource exports tend to empower sectors, classes or interest groups that favour growth-impeding policies. Another set of explanations focuses on the institutional weakness that derives from resource booms. Karl, for example, argues that 'dependence on petroleum revenues produces a distinctive type of institutional setting, the 'petro-state' which encourages the political distribution of rents' (1997: 16). In so far as state élites are able to accumulate revenues from resource exploitation without the need to raise taxes from citizens (who would then be entitled to a say in how those taxes are spent), they are able to insulate themselves from popular pressure. Rentier states 'are freed from the need to levy domestic taxes and become less accountable to the societies they govern' (Ross 1999: 312). This leads to poor governance in so far as state officials can use resources to meet unpopular, controversial or illegal objectives with low taxes and high patronage dampening pressures for democracy (Ascher 1999). Rentier states are able to concentrate wealth earned from resource extraction in activities that deepen and sustain their political power through economic pay-offs and military means. In many ways, this reflects the current situation in Nigeria.

The net effect of oil on Nigeria's growth, despite the ostensible wealth, is often negative. Sachs and Warner in their study on resource abundance and growth (Sachs and Warner 1995) show that states with a high ratio of natural resource exports to GDP in 1971 had abnormally slow growth rates between 1971 and 1989. Resource exporters are then left with resource enclaves that produce few knock-on benefits to other parts of the economy (Ross 1999: 302). Oil has been described as a resource curse because, despite its value, the effects of its extraction include increased violence, environmental degradation and loss of livelihoods, decreased economic growth, and a lack of accountability by governments and corporations to the people affected. As Watts notes (2003: 5089): 'oil capitalism produces particular sorts of enclave economies and governable spaces characterised by violence and instability'. Violence resulting from resource conflicts represents perhaps the most extreme expression of an accountability breakdown (Watts 2003; Dalby 2003; Collier 2000; Peluso and Watts 2001).

The value of resource extraction to companies, which determines where they can operate, means that they are often willing to tolerate adversarial operating conditions, conflict and even civil war. Though it is generally assumed that multinational companies prefer conditions of political and economic stability, Frynas suggests that, in certain circumstances, firms benefit from a lack of clarity about rules and expectations (Frynas 1998). Cultures of corruption can actually benefit those with the financial resources and political clout to secure deals to their advantage (Frynas and Wood 2001). It is not only in deals with government that financial resources are important. Our research has shown that funds from oil companies can contribute to inter-community divisions, which can lead to violence.

Firms, including Shell in Nigeria, have come under attack for encouraging the privatisation of security services, whereby state police services are supplied with arms to protect their investment sites or paid to see off attacks and acts of sabotage from those disputing their proclaimed right to operate in the area. Ross suggests that even when property rights are poorly enforced, 'resource extraction can still proceed since firms earning resource rents can afford to pay criminal gangs, private militias or nascent rebel armies for the private enforcement of their property rights while still earning a normal profit' (1999: 320). Contrary to popular assumptions, therefore, that investors tend to demand and benefit from good governance in the form of minimal corruption, transparency in transactions and respect for the rule of law and human rights, there is some suggestion that for some firms, weak forms of governance provide them with a degree of freedom of manoeuvre and discretion that would not otherwise be possible (Frynas 1998). In such contexts, claims by corporations to be uninvolved in politics ring hollow. For example, in the primary elections for local councils for the People's Democratic Party (PDP), Nigeria's ruling party, in Nembe in July 2003, 'officials of Shell and Agip were on hand to lend support to the governor…. Helicopters provided by Shell airlifted the cards and other electoral material from Creek House, to Nembe … Agip also airlifted voting material directly to its own terminal in Brass instead of Twon, the local council headquarters designated by the party's national executive as the voting centre (Okonta 2004: 23–4).

Each of these dimensions serves to fuel the current conflict in the Niger Delta, sustained by people's feeling of dissatisfaction over the distribution of the resources accruing from the oil wealth of the Niger Delta (*This Day* newspaper, 29 October 2004: 2). In addition, each of the actors involved views the other as neglecting its role, or expecting too much of others. There is an overwhelming perception of corruption and mismanagement of oil resources involving the national, state and local governments. Our research in Bayelsa and Delta states also revealed that at the community level within the oil-producing communities, the chiefs, local élite and youth are thought to be caught up in corruption and mismanagement. Likewise, TNCs are perceived to be engaged in the intensive extraction of oil without adequate and commensurate attention to the protection of the environment and the communities it sustains.

Drama as a tool for researching rights and accountability

In circumstances of fear and lack of voice, drama becomes a vehicle to discuss the accountability failures, dilemmas and issues facing the community by creating linkages between different communities; to take

forward actions discussed during meetings. Within the drama, community members would explore narratives about their experiences of
accountability failures, recreating their stories through the lens of breakdowns in relationships with government and the oil companies.

Drama drew out a diversity of opinions and brought submerged
perspectives into open engagement in public. It is a tool for generating
information, engaging in analysis and eliciting community discussions.
But it also allows groups to broach taboo issues, and to talk about issues
without holding any one individual responsible for raising delicate
subjects, especially those involving actors from government, TNCs and
the militia. In addition to the drama, the Theatre for Development
Centre (TFDC), a research unit of the Nigerian Popular Theatre
Alliance based at Ahmadu Bello University, has also combined other
research approaches such as participatory learning and action (PLA) in
order to develop 'methodological conversations' (Abah 2003: 125) that
help to democratise the research process.

This research has generated some key questions for accountability:

• What do we learn about accountability from working directly with
  community-based groups?
• What is the significance of oil at the local level and how is this
  represented through drama? Do these representations challenge or
  support the idea of oil as a 'resource curse'?
• What is the relationship between community-level politics and processes and the wider context of political and commercial interests?

Community perspectives on the politics of accountability

All over the Niger Delta region, oil exploration and exploitation
activities have adversely affected the environment and human welfare.
The issues and problems range from environmental pollution, unemployment and the lack of potable drinking water to the absence of health
facilities and an overall lack of say in the control and use of the natural
resources from the region.

The drama in Otuegwe chronicles the story of two brothers pitted
against each other in a fight to the death because oil had been found on
land that belongs to one of them. Out of jealousy, the one without oil on
his farm fights the other and kills him. In the midst of the brothers'
mortal conflict the oil rig bobs up and down irreverently, ceaselessly. The
constant refrain of 'Na wetin de happen here?' (What is going on here?),

demonstrates the agony, the frustration and confusion of the community. The drama may also have been forward-looking in warning against the kind of greed and conflict that the presence of oil in a community could cause without effective management. The paramount chief in Otuegwe said: 'I know there is a problem with oil everywhere. Nevertheless, I believe that oil in itself is not the problem. It is the way it is managed.' These issues were interrogated in the drama performances, articulating a critique of TNCs and government for unmet responsibilities and offering suggestions for action beyond the drama.

The Sanubi drama titled 'Unfulfilled Promises' was a performance that rolled together several issues from denial of rights through to collusion, corruption and violence. In the drama, oil is found on the farm of one of the community members. The chief tries hard to deny him the compensation money on the grounds that his forefathers were slaves and therefore he could not claim to be indigenous to the place. The women and the youth are excluded from discussions with Shell and therefore denied some of the benefits that should accrue to them. When the Shell contractors destroy farms to lay pipes, hell breaks loose. The women and the youth join forces declaring "Shell o! Emo! Emo!" (Shell o! It is war! It is war!). What these dramas show is that oil is linked to accountability in complex ways within particular communities. Inter-community and even inter-family divisions are part of the experience of lack of accountability. Indigeneity and citizenship also appear to shape rights claims and the demand for accountability.

A resource curse? Meanings of oil at the local level

We heard from people in the communities that agricultural production has diminished significantly as vegetation cover and soil have deteriorated since drilling began. In Samagidi, Ethiope East Local Government, for instance, the thick vegetation cover has been replaced by a scanty vegetation of trees and certain species of weeds which the people now refer to as 'Shell'. Residents also complained of dwindling marine resources. Fish have either migrated or have been badly depleted by oil spills. Although the group we worked with acknowledged that there is, in general, an increase in capital inflow to the community, funds go mainly to the village élite.

Other concerns as expressed in Otuokpoti, Nyambiri and Tuburu included lack of proper transportation to and from the village. The boats are few and irregular; they are overcrowded; very often they sink and passengers drown. There is no potable drinking water in the village. The creek water is used for drinking, for washing and for waste disposal, including human waste. In the words of one of the community elders, 'We are not known by government here. The many young people here have nowhere to go.' The elders argued that this explains why they are very restless and get involved in violent acts.

The community also accused Shell and other TNCs of differential treatment and marginalisation. Leaders argued that while Shell pays monthly fees to elders and youth in Isoko, Itsekiri and Ijaw communities, they are refused such benefits. According to Samagidi elders, 'oil wealth is not in the hands of Samagidi sons and daughters because our children are not employed in the oil industry, except in menial jobs'. They cited the example of Shell Petroleum Development Company (SPDC), where no local people are employed.

In contrast to this catalogue of complaints, Shell paints a picture of its good environmental record, which contradicts the reality of the oil communities' lived experiences. According to Chris Finlayson, Chairman of Shell in Nigeria, the corporation has 'continued to work to mitigate the impact of our operations on the environment. Five years ago, the company began voluntary certification to international standards through the ISO 14001 process. All our major facilities are now independently certified' (SPDC, *People and Environment Report*, 2003). He goes on to say that Shell has a major commitment to end gas flaring by 2008, but then ends by saying that it was not feasible. He acknowledges that the volume of associated gas flared in 2003 was 700 million standard cubic feet per day over and above previous volumes. He acknowledges that, 'oil spills remain a persistent cause for concern, damaging the environment, posing health hazards, and disrupting production'. In 2003, there were 221 such incidents, in which a total of some 9,900 barrels of oil were spilled. He blames two-thirds of the spills on wilful damage to facilities, however, suggesting that Shell is 'particularly concerned about the high proportion of incidents that are caused by theft, or motivated by the prospect of compensation payments and/or employment opportunities in the resulting clean-up' (SPDC, People and Environment Report, 2003: 7–8).

However, the reality from the field, also documented by other research, tells a different story that does not tally with Finlayson's claims. According to the Executive Governor of Bayelsa State, Chief Diepreye Alamieyeseigha, (2004)

> the atrocities of oil companies have reached scandalous proportions. There has been systematic violation of environmental safety laws especially as relates to pollution. One good illustration of this is the volume of natural gas flared in the country. The average rate of gas flaring in the world is about 4 per

cent. In Nigeria, over 70 per cent of associated gas is flared. Nigeria has the notorious record of 25 per cent of all gas flared in the world.

In addition, community members deny the location of blame for most of the spills on theft and sabotage. They argue that pipeline vandalism requires expert knowledge of petroleum technology, which is beyond the capacity of ordinary people. They charge that vandalism and spills are done at the insistence of, or in connivance with, oil officials who stand to benefit from monies allocated for cleaning and repairs.

Changing livelihood and altered community ethos

Oil has contributed immensely to the rural–urban divide because of the destruction of rural and community livelihoods arising from exploration and mining, as well as the job prospects offered by oil operations. On one hand, the discovery of oil in the Niger Delta enhanced the status of several urban centres where the oil company's major operations are based or headquartered. On the other hand, it has altered livelihoods and community life in significant ways. Many young people drifted into cities, notably Warri, which employed thousands in the construction industry. When construction eased in the early 1970s, however, a deluge of unwanted labour remained. Today, many of them are in the 'militia industry'.

Additionally, oil workers introduced new modes of consumption and altered social life and behaviour within the communities. Where in-kind contribution was common, cash has replaced traditional systems of exchange in a context in which every facet of life has become monetised. This has reduced and diminished the value of communality and hard work, and set the stage for a culture of greed to flourish around the unbridled quest for money. A local prayer in Urhobo that captures the new culture is very telling: 'May your workload lessen while your money triples.' While some degree of commodification of work is inevitable as a result of these changes, a key accountability challenge is how to manage it in a productive and positive way.

A resource can sometimes be a curse when its abundance breeds complacency instead of the creativity that scarcity seems to elicit. In Nigeria, resource abundance has produced a culture of rent seeking. In order to protect the rent, the rent seeker must ignore some unaccountable practices and human rights abuses in the bid to keep the tenant engaged. The materiality of the resource in this sense, and the incentives to exploit it, constitute a serious constraint on efforts to hold corporations to account. The lack of ownership and control of the structure of oil production also mean that the Nigerian government cannot monitor the activities of TNCs effectively. The concentration of knowledge about production rests in the hands of non-Nigerian entities, in turn creating a dependency which undermines prospects for accountability. Such regulations as do exist are often not enforced because of the power the oil companies wield. In addition, the boundaries between the state and the private sector are often unclear when the latter, as in the example above, is involved in providing logistical support to government campaigning. There are, nevertheless, trends in the Niger Delta towards increased agency and action by excluded groups, even if it is currently of an *ad hoc* and temporary nature.

From community politics to accountability

In this section we argue that the discovery and extraction of oil in the Niger Delta have altered community life and ethos in ways that impact upon accountability relations.

The politics of abundance and who benefits, particularly those communities that live in the oil producing areas, are critical issues. The social costs of development were sharply brought to the attention of the youth groups at the time of the 'Million People march in March' for Abacha's self succession campaign in 1999. At this time the gap between the wealth accumulated in Abuja and their own experience of rural deprivation became clear raising questions about how revenue earned from oil was being allocated.

The close collaboration between governments and TNCs in profit-sharing and the TNCs' support of the government's political activities have compromised the government's ability to hold TNCs to account. The operations of the TNCs have also affected traditional systems of accountability at the local level through chiefs and elders, and led to new formulations of rights (such as the right to control natural resource extraction) and contestation for those rights. Power has shifted away from a culture of respect centred on the authority of chiefs to a culture of greed in which people increasingly seek direct access to resources through the state and corporations. As a result of the failures of government and traditional institutions, other 'governance' structures have emerged. Some of these are independent, while others are set up by government as a way of promoting participation and giving voice to the people in the development of their areas.

Community-based groups and accountability
There are different types of community-based groups. There are the umbrella organisations such as the Ijaw National Youth Organisation,

which has formed itself into an umbrella body under which various groups in the Ijaw diaspora operate, from Bayelsa through Delta and Rivers to Ogun states. There are also other ethnic groups, such as the Ogoni, Urhobo and Itsekiri. In addition to these groups, there are a plethora of community organisations and women's groups. The Ogulaha Development Council (ODC) and the Niger Delta Women's Association in Warri are examples.

These ethnic, youth and women's groups have emerged for a number of reasons. First, the breakdown in governance results from the government's failure to provide basic social development in terms of education, employment or infrastructure. In response, women's and youth groups have been created, seeking to be heard and respected in community affairs. Second, these groups have a sense that they are not benefiting from the proceeds of natural resource extraction. Third, there is a lack of trust in the elders and chiefs to do business on their behalf, because they are seen as complicit in corruption. Finally, there is a strong feeling that the government does not care about their loss of livelihood. The perception of these groups is that the different tiers of government, from federal through state to local, have become highly unaccountable and dysfunctional.

In cases of perceived breaches of agreement by TNCs or the government, the groups may press their cases through protest. Examples of such protests include the Niger Delta Women for Justice protest (January 1999), Kenyabene Women Action (10 June 2002), Ugborodo Women's Action (July 2002), and the Ekpan Women's blockade (30 July 2002). In all of these instances, groups demanded, among other things, the provision of basic social services and employment. In some cases, it is claimed women were shot at, beaten up and injured by state armed police officers and security personnel from TNCs (Okon 2003: 10). This is one of the many reasons different communities are hardly able to separate the government from the TNCs. They see them both as collaborators in undermining accountability. These new groups see their role as (informal) law enforcement to ensure transparency and accountability. On this basis, they now engage in negotiation with government and TNCs on behalf of their communities. They also monitor the award of contracts and the employment of workers in the oil sector, functioning as watchdog pressure groups. The informal practices produced by this action may not give rise to governance in a formal sense, but these groups have been able to produce a certain form of order. They have been able to undertake a critical analysis of their own predicament and given voice to many groups previously ignored by government. They have also been able to develop and take actions to address this situation. Whilst not all of these contributions may be deemed positive, they do nevertheless provide forms of governance or social regulation in the absence of government responsiveness.

However, in addition to these apparently altruistic motives, some of the groups have agendas of personal enrichment. The militias fall into this category, despite their rhetoric of fighting for the welfare of the Niger Delta people. Initially, the militias were instruments for claiming from the oil companies and the Nigerian government what the communities perceived to be their entitlements from oil, but which they had been denied. It was soon realised, however, that they could also be used to extract concessions for personal and group enrichment.

This interest has since taken on new dimensions in which different communities have armed factions that war against each other for traditional chieftaincy titles. The rivalry over chieftaincy is explained by the fact that to control oil-bearing land and access to the oil companies is to be wealthy and powerful. This generates intra-and inter-communal conflicts as local élites jostle for access to the resources. Such dynamics explain the apparent contradiction between promoting the interests of the community and seeking law enforcement and the conflicts generated by these intra- and inter-communal conflicts, which produce more short-term and self-interested strategies.

A large number of unemployed youths, already alienated by their own social condition and with very little hope for the future, have become the crack troops of ethnic-based conflicts in the Delta (Naanen 2004: 5). Some of the wars are exacerbated by the way the oil companies allocate wells and pipes to communities. During field research in Odovie and Samagidi, we heard from youth groups that oil companies sometimes deliberately label the wrong communities on well or pipe sites, provoking conflict where they are the beneficiaries because common platforms of complaint become harder to articulate. We also heard how the oil companies employ the services of the militias to protect their installations, encouraging inter-militia conflict. A study commissioned by Shell supports the idea that TNCs are heavily implicated in the security crisis of the Niger Delta: 'It is clear that SCiN (Shell Companies in Nigeria) is part of the Niger Delta dynamics and that its social licence to operate is fast eroding', that Shell uses 'a quick-fix, reactive and divisive approach to community engagement expressed through different areas of policy, practice and corporate culture' (SPDC, Peace and Security in the Niger Delta (PaSS), December 2003: 5).

In staking their rights to control the resource found on their land, the groups breed abuses of other kinds of rights. The different levels of conflict that exist between the various groups in the communities are caused by the fact that the élite members of the community, as well as chiefs or leaders who represent the communities before the TNCs and or government, negotiate for themselves instead of the communities. The self-seeking attitude of persons in positions of power was reflected in the Eku drama, *If You Give Even a Madman a Hoe and Tell Him to Farm, He Will First Till the Soil Towards Himself!* The struggles for accountability can also produce their own accountability problems: groups that set out to fight for rights and accountability have ended up being unaccountable in their operations and activities, pursuing shorter-term material gains over broader community concerns. Demanding accountability can itself reveal accountability deficits.

Conclusions

What the above discussions demonstrate is the strong link between the nature of oil as a resource and the lack of accountability in the Niger Delta. The problems of accountability produced by resource abundance are compounded by cultures of corruption and a lack of transparency. Many people do not know how much oil is extracted and how much money the state earns from this. The refusal of the government to make this clear is related to how much profit is being made. Transparency about this would reveal what was earned and the government could then be held to account for its (lack of) expenditure on development. Lack of clarity allows the Nigerian government maximum discretion over how to use the resources.

What we observe is an accountability culture defined by corruption and patronage. We noted above how the activities of the youth groups, for example, help to create new structures of governance, but do so in ways that we would not usually associate with practices of governance. Yet, the degree of organisation of the youth groups makes them attractive to politicians, who usurp them for their own ends. Nonetheless, the youth group discourses of emancipation, enfranchisement and control now shape the conduct of politics and the terms of debate in the Niger Delta. While rights and responsibilities are in theory defined, they are often not enforced in practice; it is difficult for meaningful accountability to be established when transparency is lacking and rights and responsibilities are contested. There is a gap between the rhetoric of corporate citizenship and the local reality of poverty, conflict and failed expectations in which companies are implicated. This seems to reflect more fundamental conflicts within communities and between communities, the state and TNCs over who should be accountable, to whom, and for what.

The federal government is torn between protecting and fending for its citizens in the Niger Delta and ensuring an enabling environment for business to earn revenue. So far, the balance is lacking and the government is, in general, viewed by citizens in the Niger Delta as choosing to protect business. The Niger Delta, therefore, continues to be an area where contestation over resources and conflict over rights and responsibilities will remain unresolved for some time yet.

When all of these events and facts unfold in the dramatic performance, they suggest a need for action. This action is situated in the afterlife of both the drama and the research. However, the links between the immediacy of the events in the performance and the action afterwards are many: the performance has identified gaps and established a basis for further dialogue; eventually leading to a congruence of concern between community members, a common agenda and the will to act.

The research process democratises in three ways. It creates a space in which people can speak and bring issues forward for discussion. It allows them to make suggestions about what is to be done. It challenges power relations within the community, creating a space to question roles and hierarchies within the community. Yet, while individual actions can be questioned, the positions of traditional rulers cannot be challenged, and therefore only certain relations of power are subject to scrutiny through drama. The limitation of drama as an accountability strategy is that inevitably it only reaches a limited number of people at any one particular time. It is harder to engage higher levels of decision making. The challenge, therefore, is to connect these local experiences of accountability failure, as explored through drama, with the politics of state decision making.

NOTE

1 The state-owned oil firm, Nigerian National Petroleum Corporation (NNPC), has a 55 per cent interest in the Shell JV. NNPC also has 60 per cent stakes in JVs with ExxonMobil (US), ChevronTexaco (US), ConocoPhilips (US), Eni SPA (Italy), and Total SA (France). (see 'Country Analysis Briefs' 2004).

REFERENCES

Abah, O. S (2003) 'Methodological Conversations in Researching Citizenship: Drama and Participatory Learning and Action in Encountering Citizens', in Oga S. Abah (ed.), *Geographies of Citizenship in Nigeria*, Zaria: Tamaza Publishing Company Ltd., pp.114–43.

Abah, O. S. and Okwori, J. Z. (2005) 'A Nation in Search of Citizens: Problems of Citizenship in the Nigerian Context', in Kabeer, N. (ed.), *Inclusive Citizenship: Meanings and Expressions*, London, Zed Books, pp. 71–84.

Agbonifo, J. (2004) 'The Colonial Origin and Perpetuation of Environmental Pollution in the Postcolonial Nigeria State', pp. 4–5, available at http://www.lilt.llstu.edu/critique/fall2002docs/jagbonifo.pdf, accessed 8 December 2004.

Ajakorotu, V. (2004) 'Oil Minorities and the Politics of Exclusion in the Niger Delta of Nigeria', p. 11, available at www.sidos.ch/method/RC28/abstract/Victor per cent200jakorotu.pdf-similar, accessed 8 December 2004.

Akpobibio, O. (2001) 'Sustainable Development as a Strategy for Conflict Prevention: the Case of the Niger Delta', pp. 6–8, available at http://www.waado.org/NigerDelta/Essay/resourceControl/Onduku.html, accessed 8 December 2004.

Alamieyeseigha, D. (2004) 'The Environmental Challenge of Developing the Niger Delta', p. 6, available at http://www.newsAfrica.net/article.php?section=9 , accessed 8 December 2004.

—— (2004a) 'The Niger Delta and Youth Restiveness: a Way Forward', paper presented to the Nigerian Union of Journalists, Abuja Chapel, 16 September 2004.

Ascher, W. (1999) *Why Governments Waste Resources: the Political Economy of Natural Resource Policy Failures in Developing Countries*, Baltimore: Johns Hopkins University Press.

Collier, P. (2000) 'Economic Causes of Conflict and their Implications for Policy', paper for World Bank, 'The Economics of Crime and Violence', online research project.

Country Analysis Briefs (2004), pp. 1–2, available at www.eia.doe.gov/emeu/cabs/nigeria.html, accessed 1 January 2005.

Dalby, S. (2003) 'Environmental insecurities: Geopolitics, Resources and Conflicts' *Economic and Political Weekly*, Vol. 38, No. 48, pp. 5073–9.

Ekeh, P. (1999) 'What the Federal Government of Nigeria is Doing in the Niger Delta is Wrong', available at www.waado.org/.../BayelsaInvasion/EkehWritesToPresidentObasanjo.html

Eson *et al.* (2004) 'Contesting Control of Resource Allocation: Power Relations, Actors and the policy process in Bayelsa State, Nigeria' in K. Brock (ed.), *Unpacking Policy: Knowledge, Actors and Spaces in Poverty Reduction in Uganda and Nigeria*, Kampala: Fountain Publishers, p. 197.

Frynas, G. (1998) 'Political Instability and Business: Focus on Shell in Nigeria', *Third World Quarterly*, Vol. 19, No. 3, pp. 457–79.

—— (2000) *Oil in Nigeria: Conflict and Litigation between Oil Companies and Village Communities*, Hamburg, New Brunswick NJ and London: LIT/Transaction.

Frynas, G. and Wood, G. (2001) 'Oil and War in Angola', *Review of African Political Economy*, Vol. 28, No. 90, pp. 587–606.

Johansen, B. E. (2002) 'Nigeria: the Ogoni: Oil, Blood and the Death of a Homeland. Indigenous Peoples and Environmental Issues: an Encyclopedia', available at www.ratical.org/ratville/IPEIE/Ogoni.html, accessed 25 June 2005.

Karl, T. L. (1997) *The Paradox of Plenty: Oil Booms and Petro-States*, Berkeley: University of California Press.

Mutizwa-Mangiza, N. D. (1990), 'Decentralization and District Development Planning in Zimbabwe', *Public Administration and Development*, Vol. 10, No. 4, pp. 355–72.

Naneen, B. (2004) 'The Political Economy of Oil and Violence in the Niger Delta',

Association of Concerned African Scholars (ACAS) Bulletin, No. 68 (Autumn), pp. 4–9.

Okon, E. J. (2003) 'Women's Issues and Women's Action in Claiming Citizenship Rights in the Niger Delta', Zaria: Theatre for Development Centre (TFDC), pp. 1, 10.

Okonta, I. (2004) 'Death-Agony of a Malformed Political Order', *Association of Concerned African Scholars (ACAS) Bulletin*, No. 68 (Autumn), pp. 23–9.

Okonta, I. and Douglas, O. (2003) *Where Vultures Feast: Shell, Human Rights and Oil in the Niger Delta*, London: Verso.

Olowu, D. and Wunsch, J. S. (2004) *Local Governance in Africa: the Challenges of Democratic Decentralization*, Boulder, Colorado: Lynne Rienner Publishers.

Peluso, N. and Watts, M. (2001) *Violent Environments*, New York: Cornell University Press.

Ross, M. (1999) 'The political economy of the resource curse', *World Politics*, Vol. 51, No. 2 (January), pp. 297–322.

Rowell, A. and Goodall, A. (1994) *Shell-shocked: the Environmental and Social Costs of Living with Shell in Nigeria*, Amsterdam: Greenpeace International.

Sachs, J. D. and Warner, A. (1995) 'Natural Resource Abundance and Economic Growth', Development Discussion Paper No. 517a, Cambridge: Harvard Institute for International Development.

Shafer, D. M. (1994) *Winners and Losers: How Sectors Shape the Developmental Prospects of States*, Itacha, NY: Cornell University Press.

SPDC (2003) *People and Environment Report*, Shell Petroleum Development Company, http://www.shell.com/static/nigeria/downloads/pdfs/2004rpt.pdf.

SPDC (2003a) *Peace and Security in the Niger Delta (PaSS)*, Shell Petroleum Development Company, December, http://www.shell.com.

This Day newspaper (2004) Vol. 10, No. 3476, 29 October, pp. 1–2.

Udeh, M. (2002) 'Petroleum Revenue Management: the Nigerian perspective', available at www.earthinstitute.columbia.edu/.../Nigeria/Nigeria%20petroleum%20Revenue%20 Management%20UdehPaper.pdf, accessed 4 January 2005.

Watts, M. (1998) 'Some Notes on Petro-violence', paper prepared for the workshop on 'Environment and Violence', University of California, Berkeley, 24–26 September.

—— (2003) 'Economics of Violence: More Oil, More Blood', *Economic and Political Weekly*, Vol. 38, No. 48, pp. 5089–99.

CHAPTER 11

Compliance versus accountability: struggles for dignity and daily bread in the Bangladesh garment industry

SIMEEN MAHMUD AND NAILA KABEER

The women workers in the Bangladesh garment industry have had more public attention to their rights than any group of workers in the entire history of the country. (Journalist, Development Research Centre (DRC) Inception Workshop on Inclusive Citizenship, Bangladesh, 2001)

I believe that the 'culture of compliance' is far ahead in the garment manufacturing sector and changes in the RMG [ready-made garments] sector are dramatic compared to other sectors. (Director, Labour Department, Bangladesh, 2004)

The process of globalisation has brought workers in the poorer countries of the global South into direct competition with workers in the wealthier countries of the global North, exposing the stark inequalities in the conditions under which they work to the full glare of international publicity. Trade unions, the media, human rights activists and others in prosperous Northern countries have made consumers aware as they never were before about the conditions under which some of their regularly purchased consumer items are made. The international garment industry is one that has consistently attracted the attention of these groups and given rise to various campaigns, including Students against Sweatshops, the Clean Clothes Campaign and OXFAM's Make Trade Fair (See Luce, Chapter 12).

The working conditions of Bangladeshi export garment workers, predominantly women, have featured regularly in these campaigns: the absence of written contracts, long working hours, delayed payment of wages and routine violations of health and safety standards. Since working conditions in the garment industry are no worse, and generally are considered to be better, than those prevailing in the rest of the economy, the intense concern with garment workers' rights, referred to in the first quote above, reflects both the publicity generated by international campaigns as well as the unusual visibility of its largely female workforce in a society in which women have historically been regarded as a vulnerable group, in need of protection and hence confined to the shelter of the home. Currently the export garment industry employs 1.8 million workers, of whom 1.5 million are women. The mass entry of women workers into a sector hitherto dominated by men dramatically changed the character of the urban manufacturing labour force in the span of a few years[1] and explains some of the attention they receive domestically.

The second quote comes from the Director of the Labour Department, the government department responsible for ensuring that workers' rights are upheld. It testifies to one of the consequences of the intense public scrutiny on the working conditions prevailing within the export garment industry. This is the proliferation of codes of conduct imposed by the various international buyers operating in the export garment sector and anxious to avoid adverse attention from their consumers at home. The Director pointed out that the attempt at self-regulation on the part of garment manufacturers reflected the fact that non-compliance with basic labour standards in this sector carried real penalties in the form of lost orders from their international buyers.

It is worth noting that these observations were couched in the language of 'compliance' and that the compliance in question was to a voluntary code of conduct drawn up by the affected section of the private sector. He was not referring to compliance with national labour laws drawn up by the state to set out the rights of all citizens of Bangladesh, including its garment workers. There is clearly a gap between compliance of the kind the Labour Director is referring to and the kind of accountability that this book is about.

As we saw in Chapter 2, there are two key elements to the concept of accountability: *answerability*, the right to make claims and demand responses; and *enforceability*, the mechanisms for ensuring that answers are backed by actions and for sanctioning non-responsiveness. Accountability thus gives 'teeth' to the concept of rights and hence is indispensable to the status and practice of citizenship. A 'culture of compliance', on the other hand, refers to the willingness to abide by a given set of regulations (whether laws or codes). It is not the same as a culture of accountability, but it need not be incompatible with it, and may even contain the seeds from which such a culture can emerge. Whether it has done so or not in Bangladesh is a matter for empirical investigation, one that will be addressed in this chapter. We will be basing our analysis on in-depth interviews with 20 garment workers, with relevant officials of the Department of Labour, employer representatives and factory managers, with trade union officials and NGO workers. The chapter also draws on previous research carried out by the authors as well as media reports and the secondary literature. In the next section, we sketch out the context in which our analysis is located.

The context: poverty and patriarchy in a labour-surplus economy

There are a number of features of the Bangladesh context which represent 'the initial conditions' from which cultures of compliance and accountability have had to grow. Bangladesh was, and remains, a poor, largely agrarian economy, with 45 per cent of its population below the poverty line; it is one of 49 'least developed countries' in the world, according to the United Nations (2002). Although industrialisation dates back over a hundred years, it has been very narrowly based, confined largely to the processing and manufacture of jute, until recently its main export. The spread of market relations and infrastructural development has led to increased rates of economic growth and a small but steady decline in poverty over the 1990s. However, growth in agriculture has not been sufficient to absorb this annual increment and there has been increasing diversification into off-farm activities in rural areas, partly assisted by the spread of microfinance activities, and migration into urban areas.

Bangladesh was, and remains, a society that continues to be largely governed by patron–client relations. The intersection of patron-clientelism and a modern state apparatus with monopolistic control over rules and resources created a particular type of patrimonial ruling élite in Bangladesh (Khan 2001), whose search for political power and personal profit is pursued through the granting of special privileges to politically influential actors – including industrialists and trade unions – in return for their support at national and local level.

Finally, Bangladesh was and remains an extremely patriarchal society, with strict cultural constraints on women's participation in the public sphere and their confinement to reproductive work and the domestic domain. Socialised into this role from an early age, denied independent access to economic resources and defined as life-long dependents of male breadwinners and guardians, women occupy a subordinate position within the family as well as the wider society. Women have consequently constituted a significant proportion of the country's pool of 'surplus' labour, particularly in more close-knit communities in rural areas, where gender-specific constraints on their ability to take up paid work are more severe.

The expansion of export-oriented garment manufacturing in Bangladesh coincided with a period of radical economic reform. Under the aegis of the World Bank/IMF, the Bangladesh government had undertaken a series of measures since the late 1970s to move away from a strategy of protection for import-substituting domestic industry towards a more liberalised, open and export-oriented economy. Various incentive schemes channelled domestic investment into the export sector so that around 95 per cent of garment factories in the country are owned by local private capital (Kabeer and Mahmud 2004a). However, foreign direct investment was also encouraged through the establishment of export processing zones (EPZs) outside Dhaka and Chittagong, where the country's few joint ventures are located.

The dramatic expansion of the export-oriented RMG sector has also seen a substantial expansion of its workforce from a few thousand workers in the early 1980s to around 1.8 million workers in recent years, of whom 80 per cent are women (Kabeer and Mahmud 2004a). There has been a gradual growth in the share of knitwear to woven garment manufacturing and here there is a somewhat higher percentage of men. Although the export garment sector is, strictly speaking, in the formal economy and hence subject to national labour legislation, it is characterised by informal economy characteristics: easy entry and exit, an absence of written contracts, irregularity of payments, violations of health and safety regulations, long hours of overtime, low levels of unionisation and high rates of turnover in the workforce. The main exceptions to this are to be found in the country's EPZs, where more formal conditions exist, but these account for a very small proportion of total garment employment.

These working conditions, which are not unique to Bangladesh but prevail to a lesser or greater degree in export garment factories across the world, have led to various campaigns by coalitions of trade unions, students, NGOs and consumers including the living wage campaign described in Chapter 12. Faced by the threat of boycotts of their goods, the major buyers in the global market for clothing have adopted codes of conduct to regulate the conditions under which those goods are produced.

The question we are addressing in this paper is the extent to which the proliferation of these codes in the Bangladesh garment industry have brought about a 'culture of accountability'. Their adoption is only the beginning of a process of translation, and a variety of different actors have a role to play in ensuring that the translation does indeed occur. Along with the buyers who draw up the codes and the employers who are responsible for their implementation, there is the state, which has overall responsibility for upholding the rights of workers; the trade unions, who are considered to be the organised voice of workers; and, of course, the workers themselves, who have most to gain from the growth of a culture of accountability. We will consider the views and roles of each group in turn.

Monopoly power and consumer clout in buyer-driven global value chains

Competition in the clothing market revolves around prices and brand names. The major clothing retailers are constantly driven by the need to respond to fashion-led fluctuations in the demand for clothing at increasingly competitive prices. The fact that it is a highly labour-intensive industry means that this price competition has revolved to a significant extent around the cost of labour. The production process lends itself to subdivision into an increasing number of routine tasks, each of which can be carried out by increasingly unskilled, and hence increasingly cheaper, labour.

The increasing divisibility of the production process allows different stages of garment manufacturing – from design to delivery – to be located across the globe on the basis of comparative advantage, giving rise to an internationally networked production system in which the same item of clothing may be designed in one location, cut in another, assembled in another and delivered for final sale in yet another. The producers of garments, particularly those involved in its labour-intensive assembly stages, are mainly based in the low-wage countries of the South, so that these countries enter the production chain as providers of cheap labour, competing with each other for orders from buyers of clothing in the international market for garments.

The restructuring and concentration of the clothing retailers over time mean that today buyers are operating in a buyer-driven commodity chain in which large numbers of producers compete for orders from a relatively small number of transnational volume retailers. They are consequently in a position to use their monopolistic power to threaten to withdraw orders from a factory or a country and to dictate conditions to producers. At the same time, their drive to reduce costs continuously has led them in search of ever-cheaper labour working in ever-more exploitative conditions.

However, this footloose strategy and its consequences have attracted the attention of trade unions, consumers and labour activists across the world. As a result of the threat of adverse publicity and consumer boycotts exercised by their campaigns, most of the major garment retailers now espouse the principle of 'corporate social responsibility'. They have drawn up their own codes of conduct regarding the conditions on which they are prepared to place orders, and have set up departments and full-time staff to promote the socially responsible face of their business.

The state and public policy in an era of deregulation

While the interest of the buyers is focused on profits and working conditions in the export sector of Bangladesh, the state is, in principle, responsible for promoting the economic growth of the country and the welfare of its citizens. The pursuit of growth and foreign exchange explains why the state played an extremely active and innovative role in the promotion of the export garment industry from its inception. The fact that many of those in government own garment factories may have also contributed to their active engagement.

The New Industrial Policy of 1982 introduced various incentives to encourage local entrepreneurs, including tax concessions and special duty-free import facilities. However, as far as the interests of its workers are concerned, the state has displayed an attitude of apathy bordering on indifference. The Bangladesh constitution, adopted in 1971 after independence from Pakistan, spelt out the fundamental rights of its citizens and asserted the state's responsibility for emancipating 'the toiling masses' from their exploitation. In reality, however, less than 3 per cent of the workforce is protected by the existing legislative framework (Mondol 2002: 121). Instead, labour legislation in Bangladesh both reflects and reproduces a dualistic economic structure in which a small formal sector coexists alongside a large and growing informal economy.

A great deal of existing labour legislation is inherited from the period of colonial rule in the subcontinent, when it was formulated for the benefit of workers in the urban industrial sector who had the potential to make trouble for their rulers. In the Bangladesh context, this was largely confined to a small number of textile and jute-related manufacturing units. At present there are 51 labour laws in existence: while only 13 of these were actually passed in the colonial period, most of the others draw on rules and regulations which originated in that period (Mahmud and Ahmed 2005). Today they mainly benefit the urban, male workforce employed by the public sector and a tiny formal private sector found in financial services and larger-scale manufacturing. The vast majority of the workforce – which is employed in agriculture, services and cottage industry, the informal or so called 'unorganized' sectors[2] – has little or no legal protection.

Labour legislation in Bangladesh not only excludes the majority of workers in Bangladesh, but also fails to protect those it formally includes. There is an elaborate and hierarchical infrastructure for ensuring compliance with national regulations within the labour ministry, also inherited from the British period, which exists only on paper.

Because the number of inspectors is far lower than is required, there is an implicit institutional bias in the inspections carried out in favour of more dramatic accidents and 'dangerous occurrences' at the expense of the routine violations of labour rights that the more vulnerable sections of the workforce are likely to face. And a blind eye is often turned to those violations that do come to the attention of inspectors if factory owners obtain necessary clearances through the payment of bribes to poorly paid and generally overworked inspectors. Finally, officials interviewed for the research suggested that penalties for non-compliance with the existing laws were not severe enough to act as a deterrent. The flaws in the procedures for enforcing labour legislation are evident from the fact that over 10,000 court cases are pending and collection of fines in the last 10 years has been miniscule (personal communication with Director of Labour Department, Bangladesh, 2004).

The government took a decision in the early 1990s to reform its labour laws in order to bring them up to date to deal with the challenges of the contemporary economy. A high-powered commission was set up in 1992 with a view to dropping or modernising old laws, introducing new ones and developing a unified labour legislation that would cover workers in both formal and informal sectors. A draft code was drawn up in 1994, but with changes in governments has yet to be finalised and adopted. There has been a long process of consultation around these changes and unprecedented participation by different sections of civil society, including the trade unions. The next challenge, of course, is to get the law finalised and, even more challengingly, implemented. The country's track record on implementation does not inspire optimism: in the words of a senior official from the Department of Labour, 'We will need a law to implement the new law.' However, one of the new trade union federation leaders was hopeful:

If the new Labour Code were passed, it will improve the situation a great deal. The New Labour Code has had much more airing than any other. There was a tripartite consultative committee, and workers had more input. If this code is passed, we can make more reasonable demands – demands that we can stand by.

Employers' strategies and the informalisation of the labour contract

The initial emergence of the export garment industry in Bangladesh was almost accidental, a product of the search by East Asian firms using 'quota-hopping' strategies to bypass the Multi-Fibre Arrangement (MFA) regulations in the late 1970s. The subsequent adoption of a more liberal trade regime brought into existence a number of domestic entrepreneurs, many with no previous experience of running industry but who were able to take advantage of the opportunities available in a largely informal economy with a large pool of cheap and already 'flexible' female labour. Despite its *ad hoc* beginnings, however, it became clear early on to the garment employers that they needed to organise themselves to deal with the challenges of operating in the global economy.

The Bangladesh Garment Manufacturing and Exporters Association (BGMEA) was established in 1987. While it began by lobbying with government for the interests of the industry, inevitably it has been drawn into international controversies about labour standards and played an increasingly proactive role in this issue, undertaking various social programmes in collaboration with the International Labour Organisation (ILO), the United Nations Children's Fund (UNICEF) and various national and international NGOs. In 1998, it set up procedures for arbitration between workers and management in collaboration with the leading trade union federations in the garment sector in order to avoid time-consuming processes of resolving these through the labour courts. As many as 10 federations of garment workers, representing several thousand union and even more 'non-union' members, are institutional partners in these procedures. Disputes frequently go in favour of workers, primarily because employers have been accustomed to violating workers' rights with impunity and, therefore, do not take precautions to disguise their actions. Evidence that they now search for pretexts to sack 'troublesome workers', or seek to make their lives so difficult that they leave of their own accord, suggests that the threat of immediate arbitration is having some effect.

With the proliferation of codes of conduct among the international buyers, the BGMEA has also taken on the task of developing a uniform code of conduct as the basis of future contracts in the industry. The BGMEA has thus become a key actor in developing institutional mechanisms for establishing responsibility for labour standards. This role did not emerge out of sudden conversion to the principles of corporate social responsibility, but out of the recognition that, in a ruthlessly competitive market, demonstration of compliance was becoming a source of competitive advantage. Employers have thus gone through a process of education about the nature of global competition in their sector. As the Managing Director of V Apparels commented: 'In the beginning it was beyond the imagination of factory owners to provide such facilities for the workers. But now owners believe that without compliance it is not possible to stay in this highly competitive business. So there is no alternative.'

However, while employers have formalised their relationships with each other and with the government, their relationships with their workers, and their attitudes towards them, remain rooted in the mindset of the informal economy. Interviews with 13 employers carried out in the late 1980s concluded that they could be positioned on a continuum extending between those who viewed their workers as commodities to be exploited as ruthlessly as possible and those who viewed them in clientelist terms, to be treated with benevolent paternalism (Kabeer 2000). None saw their workers as citizens with rights and obligations.

Little has changed today. There is a new breed of employers who have been shamed by the negative image that the industry has acquired in the international arena or influenced by the rising tide of women's activism in the country, and made considerable efforts on their own initiative to improve working conditions in their factories. However, they remain a minority. Of the rest, there is at best paternalism and, at worst, ruthless commodification. Some employers present themselves as responsible for the welfare of the young girls from the countryside who have left their parents and their homes to work in the city: 'they are like my daughters'. Others regard their workers as little more than bonded labour, hired to provide maximum labour at minimum cost. Some expect gratitude and loyalty in return for the privilege of a job, other use threats and coercion to impose discipline.

Such attitudes serve to reproduce and justify the informalised labour practices of employers. Some employers thought workers behaved like workers in the informal economy, coming and going as they pleased, and neither expected nor deserved to be treated like workers in the formal sector. This construction of garment workers as lacking 'professionalism' and hence undeserving of formal treatment is evident in the description provided by one managing director interviewed: 'Actually they don't like to work under any rules. They work for some days, if they need to go home they leave without any notice and come back to join another factory.'

From the perspective of most employers, the imposition of codes of conduct by buyers is seen as simply another set of conditions (along with meeting their deadlines and observing quality control) that have to be met in order to stay in business. Consequently, working conditions have improved over time in their factories, most visibly in the EPZs, but also in factories which deal directly with buyers rather than on the basis of subcontracted orders. Improvements relate mainly to paid leave, maternity leave, overtime pay and medical care. However, there were two telling indicators of the limits of what company codes achieve: less than 5 per cent of the garment workers reported a presence of a trade union in their workplace (none of the workers outside the export industry did so) and only around 20 per cent had heard of the country's labour laws (Kabeer and Mahmud 2004b). Codes thus appear to have more impact on workers' welfare than their rights.

It could be argued that since Bangladesh generally lacks a culture of rights, these employers are simply reproducing the attitudes of their society. However, these employers as a group have also benefited from state largesse a great deal more than their employees or, for that matter, employers in other sectors. An equally persuasive counter-argument might be that they owed a great deal more by way of social responsibility to their workers than the simple generation of jobs. Company codes of conduct could thus be seen as the attempt by international buyers to enforce this social responsibility, given the failure of employers to do so voluntarily and the state to compel them. On the face of it, therefore, codes of conduct may indeed be planting the seeds of a culture of accountability within the corporate sector in Bangladesh.

Unfortunately, there is a great deal of well-founded scepticism on the part of Bangladeshi employers towards these codes, which somewhat undermines this interpretation. Many see them as a public relations exercise on the part of international brand name companies, concerned about their public image, to maintain a facade of social responsibility with their consumers while covertly passing the cost of compliance to their producers. A number of employers complained with bitterness about the double standards of these companies, who combined their demands for increasingly onerous and expensive quality and labour standards with a steady reduction in the prices they offered to their producers. One employer who has been in the industry for many years commented:

We follow factory laws which say that after three months, you have to make your workers permanent, that if we sack a worker, we have to 'show cause', have an enquiry. But our factory laws are not enough for US buyers. They each have their own codes – how many square feet per workers, how much light, how high the fire extinguisher should be. [...] Still I am prepared to comply with all their codes if they increase the price they give me. Smaller factories are closing down because prices are falling.

Another employer pointed to the implications of flexible business practices:

There is no such thing as a permanent contract in this business. None of the buyers will give you a permanent contract and say okay, we have booked orders with your factory for at least the next two years.... They will work from contract to contract and demand shorter and shorter delivery times.

Thus, if garment producers profit from keeping their relationships with their workers as informal as possible, using the threat of dismissal to discipline their workers, international buyers in turn use their monopoly power in the global market for clothing to keep their relationship with their producers as informal as possible, using the constant threat of relocation to create a permanent condition of insecurity among their suppliers across the world.

Trade unions and the politics of collective action

Although not all buyers include the right to organise in their codes, international campaigns to promote improved working conditions in the export garment industry have placed particular emphasis on this. Trade unions are seen as the concrete expression of this right. Both law and constitution in Bangladesh recognise the right of workers to freedom of association, to join unions and, with government approval, to form unions.[3] Unions in Bangladesh are enterprise-based and registered with the Ministry of Labour if 30 per cent of workers in the enterprise become members. These unions form the basis of larger federations which tend to be organised by sector.

However, trade unions are virtually absent, not only from the garment industry, but from the economy at large. Our recent survey found that only 5 per cent of EPZ garment workers, 1 per cent of export garment workers outside the EPZs and none of the non-garment informal-economy women workers reported the presence of a trade union at their place of work (Kabeer and Mahmud 2004b). One important factor has been the hostility of employers. Unions were generally regarded as troublemakers. Some used paternalistic relationships to ensure worker loyalty, the rest resorted to a variety of coercive tactics, having workers beaten up or arrested, lodging criminal cases against them, and so on. There is therefore a high cost associated with exercising the right to organise in Bangladesh.

However, the problem also lies with the trade unions themselves. They tend to be associated in the public mind with confrontational struggles in pursuit of their own interests by a privileged and protected minority of workers. Trade unions have a history of aggressive politics towards employers, because prior to Bangladesh's independence in 1971 most employers were non-Bengalis, reinforcing the nationalist case that Bengalis faced discrimination in their own country (Mondol 2002). Nationalisation of major banks and industries, after Bangladesh's independence meant that most trade unions have been confined to public sector administration, banks and industries where units are larger and easier to organise, but which are also among the better-paid sections of the workforce. Trade union membership thus accounts for less than 3 per cent of the total workforce and only one-third of the formal workforce (Mondol 2002: 121).

In addition, all the major unions are affiliated to political parties. Consequently, they tend to represent the competing political agendas of their parties rather than the interests of their members. During periods of political unrest, quite frequent in Bangladesh, union federations organise on partisan lines, calling for nation-wide stoppages and strikes –which, of course, lead not only to the well-publicised losses of the country's industrialists, but also to the less well-publicised loss of income of the working poor, including their own members, across the country.

There are currently about 14 federations of garments workers unions working in the country, but some exist in name only and are not registered with the Directorate of Labour (Khan 2001). They do not have a great deal of incentive to be accountable to their membership because their bargaining power with employers comes from their party-political affiliation and is largely independent of their membership base. Some factory owners describe union leaders as 'brokers' who 'milk' both sides. They allege that, in times of industrial conflict, federations take money from owners in order to 'buy off' prospective troublemakers. At the same time, federation leaders take money from their largely female member-ship by promising protection from the police or the employers' muscle-men (Khan 2001).

The lack of accountability to their membership on the part of the federation leaders also reflects the social distance between the two. The leadership is almost overwhelmingly male and drawn from activists in political parties or former student leaders who have had very little previous involvement with the garment sector or its workers. They tend to blame the workers themselves for their lack of unionisation. Many have a university degree and view the passivity of female garment workers as the product of their rural backgrounds, their illiteracy and their general backwardness: 'Since the women are illiterate they do not understand what a labour union is and that we are trying to improve their working conditions. We visit them but they hardly listen to us because they cannot grasp the idea of solidarity and unity' (Dannecker 2002: 222).

Workers in turn do not appear to have much faith in unions. They spoke of past betrayals, of collusions between union leaders and management either because of shared political affiliation, in which case management is given an easy ride, or because they have been bought off. They complained that federation leaders were only visible when some factory conflict or agitation captured the newspaper headlines, but had little to do with the everyday demands and struggles of workers. As one male factory leader observed: "During our agitation, I saw lots of federations. I don't know why they all came here, however, they don't come here now. I can't say why they don't come [...]'

However, not all attempts to organise workers can be dismissed as politically motivated machinations on the part of union leaders. As the importance of the industry has become established, as the slow but steady rise in female labour force participation across the economy has become evident, and as human rights activism has grown across the country, some of the more progressive parties have begun to devote more attention to the challenge of organising women workers and addressing their grievances.

The Textile and Garment Workers' Federation, for instance, has been active in the industry since 1990 and has around 6,000 unionised members who pay dues and 40,000 'non-unionised members' in those workplaces where employers do not recognise unions. The latter pay a fee when they join but do not pay dues. Most of their members are in the larger factories, as they find it too difficult to organise the workforce in the small subcontracting factories. The federation is moving towards a more formalised mode of representational politics in place of the adversarial politics which has been the hallmark of employer–union relations so far. As one of its leading representatives put it:

> Unions are a right under the ILO, but they are also the law of the land. I recognise why employers won't want a union, but the government sides with the employers. I am much more angry with the government about this than

with employers…. We have agreed on procedures for negotiation. When we agree on a demand, we sign, but the employers gradually violate the agreement. The government should enforce this. … I favour social monitoring systems – civil society, unions, workers – to pressure the government to enforce laws.

The Bangladesh Independent Garment Workers Union Federation (BIGUF) was founded with United States Agency for International Development (USAID) funds and supported by the Solidarity Foundation in the US, an affiliate of the American Federation of Labour–Congress of Industrial Organisations (AFL–CIO). It has also been extremely active. It calls itself 'independent' because it is not affiliated to any political party, although of course in the view of some of the labour activists, it is seen as dependent on the goodwill of USAID and the AFL–CIO. However, its leadership is made up of active, rather than token, women members who were themselves once garment workers, in contrast to the middle-class origins of most other union leaders. It pursues a variety of strategies to organise garment workers, visiting them in their homes, organising cultural programmes to motivate them, encouraging them to engage in collective bargaining with management and providing legal education as well as legal support in disputes with management.

Kormojibi Nari (Working Women) is the other federation led by a woman. Founded in 1991, it is affiliated to the leftist Workers' Party, and partly financed by more progressive international NGOs like War on Want. It has also opted for neighbourhood-based organisation of women workers and the provision of legal education and support but, unlike the BIGUF, it focuses its efforts on all women workers, not just those involved in the export garment sector:

> First, we have to organize the women, then we promote the union. We work by forming cells…. In Dhaka, we work in 12 areas: *bidi*, shrimp, construction, home-based work, industrial, digging for construction, handicrafts, printing and dyeing. Half our membership is from the informal sector …. Trade unions are very important – *true* trade unions. Those that are working to implement laws, enforce workers' rights. Those that are truly in support of the workers. You can't solve any problem if workers have no union of their own. Even the health and safety laws – you can have the law, but only the workers can enforce it…. Ours is a culture of favours…. We say, don't go asking for favours: demand your rights!

There are, along with trade unions, a range of other civil society organisations which focus primarily or exclusively on issues related to rights. Prominent among these is Ain O Salish Kendra (ASK), which has been working on legal issues since 1994. Initially it worked with two trade unions to provide training to garment workers on labour law and trade union rights. However, it found that workers tended to turn to them for advice on family-related rather than work-related problems. Workers were not interested in forming trade unions or in taking legal action against their employers. They preferred to change jobs if they had a grievance against an employer. The initiative closed down but the organisation continued, in collaboration with a number of NGOs, to provide legal support and education to workers through its six legal clinics in Dhaka. Discussing the culture of accountability within the industry, one ASK representative felt the problem lay partly with the nature of the workforce, who 'haven't developed any kind of professionalism yet. Most of them do not think of this job as a career.' He believed that women workers took on these jobs temporarily, that many would not continue to work after marriage and that, in any case, the levels of exploitation in the workplace ruled out working for more than a few years. However, he also believed that training succeeded in bringing about some change in the attitudes of workers, giving them greater self-confidence and the willingness to challenge exploitative practices at work, something that had been almost unheard of in the early stages of the industry.

Women workers and the struggle for dignity and daily bread

As we have seen, women workers have been variously constructed by employers as unprofessional and lacking in workplace discipline; by trade union leaders as illiterate, backward and rural, and unable to grasp concepts of unions and solidarity; and by other civil society actors as 'temporary' workers, likely to leave once they get married. These negative stereotypes are not devoid of an element of truth. Certainly the vast majority of garment workers are young women, socialised into docility and subservience to authority, mostly illiterate or with very low levels of education. They have migrated from the countryside, where notions of workplace discipline, trade union organisation and worker solidarity have little purchase.

What is also relevant, however, is the fact that these women come from poor households, with few options in the labour market and only their family as a safety net to fall back on should they lose their jobs. Such factors would tend to constrain militancy on the part of any worker. But additionally, in an economy in which women historically have been confined to a limited number of economic activities and where there is an apparently unlimited supply of female labour in search of jobs in the garment sector, women with jobs are particularly likely to be cautious about making demands or taking stands that might jeopardise their employment. Thus, while their illiteracy, gender and origins may play an initial role in explaining women's reluctance to protest their conditions, it is the larger structural constraints on their capacity to act on their own behalf, and the costs they may incur if they were to try to do so, that prevent the majority of women workers from standing up for their rights.

However, like other actors in the economy, women workers have not remained untouched by the forces of change in the larger society. Intense media coverage of their working conditions, increased attempts to mobilise them and the involvement of a wider range of actors than traditional trade unions have all served to raise their knowledge and awareness of their rights. How has this affected their capacity to take action?

Statistics on trade union membership and knowledge of labour laws may underestimate the actual degree to which workers know about their rights and are willing to take action to claim them. Time, both personal and historical, emerges as a key factor in the evolution of workers' consciousness. Each young woman who arrives fresh from the country-side needs time to adapt to the very different rhythm of work in the urban factories compared to the rural economy, and she also needs time before she understands what her entitlements are. Recent cohorts of workers may be coming into the factory with a different level of consciousness than earlier cohorts, however. People in the countryside are now better connected with what is going on elsewhere in the country than they were in the early years of the industry because of improvements in transport, communications and media, while rising levels of female education mean that recent garment workers are at least more aware of what is going on around them. According to Shefali, a female garment leader,[4] NGOs have also played an important role in disseminating information about workers' rights:

> Earlier it used to be much more difficult to make the workers understand different issues. But now they understand the importance of organisations, when a worker loses their job but eventually gets it by filing a case through the labour court they stand to gain much.... Now they understand about the ILO convention and the law, and they ask for information.

Workers may also have become less willing to put up with instances of injustice in the workplace. Many take action as individuals. Resigning from the factory is still the most frequent individual response to injustice, a silent form of protest, and one that women resort to more frequently than men, but there were also instances of workers taking a more collective approach to dealing with problems, such as staging walk-outs or threatening the manager. From our interviews, it was clear that many women are learning the principles of collective bargaining. There were a number of cases when workers got together, sometimes spontaneously, sometimes in a planned and co-ordinated way, to undertake factory-wide protests which often spilled out onto the streets. Most of these protests revolved around issues of wages and overtime rather than workplace conditions, because, as workers themselves said, 'getting paid their wages on time is the biggest problem of garment workers'. These incidents are often reported in newspapers. In one case, workers agitating over three months' wage arrears were arrested on charges of assault: 72 of them, all women, were given bail but 13 were taken into custody (*Daily Star*, 12 November 2004). In another case (*Daily Star*, 5 September 2004), women workers took to the street in support of a male worker who had been struck by his manager for demanding workers' overtime dues. The management later fixed dates for settling the workers' dues in phases.

Accounts of such spontaneous street-level protests make two points clear. First of all, women workers are active participants in many of these protests. The second point is that, perhaps predictably, the protests are generally led by male workers. One female worker explained male leadership partly in terms of their greater physical strength – which meant they were better able to look after themselves in a confrontation – as well as their greater knowledge of their rights. Another pointed to the importance of women's earnings for their families and their fear that they would not easily find another job. Clearly greater activism among women suggests they have been able to overcome some of the fears and inhibitions associated with being women – but not all of them.

Finally, there were examples of more organised forms of collective action by garment workers that provide insights into some of the potentials and limitations of workers' struggles in the garment sector in Bangladesh. One example of organised collective action came from Alam, who had had long-standing connections with a union federation. He had participated in the campaign when a number of federations got together and put five basic demands to the BGMEA: recognition of the right to organise; maternity leave; an appointment letter; a weekly holiday; and a minimum wage. His view with regard to a strike he had led in 2001 against an employer who did not observe the five demands was that although they did not win their demands, the day-to-day abusive behaviour towards workers decreased:

Certainly our agitation had an impact in reducing the verbal abuse of workers. Due to the agitation, they saw that the workers had become united, if they continued their agitation, it might get spread throughout the country and in that case the buyers would also create a fuss.

There is thus no linear story of progress that emerges out of these accounts, of victories gained leading on to further victories. Some workers felt that conditions had improved after a protest, some felt they had worsened. Employers made promises in order to quell a disturbance, but used every pretext subsequently to victimise or get rid of the leaders. However, changes in consciousness were often permanent and the leadership that developed did not simply fade away when a struggle was lost but went on to other factories to start the job of organisation once again.

Compliance and accountability in Bangladesh

The question that we set out to answer in this chapter is the extent to which the emergence of what a government labour official described as a 'culture of compliance' within the export garment sector in Bangladesh has contributed to the growth of a culture of accountability. We have described some of the elements in the process by which this perceived 'culture of compliance' came into existence. We noted that efforts of trade unionists, students, consumers and human rights activists to exert pressure on buyers to take greater responsibility for working conditions have resulted in the proliferation of codes that garment manufacturers now have to accept before they can win an order from these buyers. Indeed, the BGMEA, at least (though not necessarily all its members), has realised that compliance with codes holds the key to future survival in the post-MFA competitive environment. As a result, there has been a marked improvement in health and safety standards in the major factories as well as a range of other benefits, such as payment on time, proper overtime rates, maternity leave, and so on.

The setting up of arbitration procedures by the BGMEA has reduced the employers' prerogative of sacking workers and also given rise to some degree of cooperation between the BGMEA and unions, in place of the relentless confrontations of earlier encounters. Representatives of both workers and management have come to recognise that submitting to a joint process of conflict resolution is likely to yield longer-term gains for both parties outweighing any short-term defeats. From the point of view of the federations, having a place at the negotiating table has opened up a novel way of recruiting members, by responding to their most pressing everyday concerns (being paid on time, getting proper overtime, increasing their wages) rather than relying on the promise of political patronage. For women workers in particular, the former is a far more appealing incentive to join unions than the latter.

While these various developments are certainly steps in the right direction, do they constitute evidence of a 'culture of compliance' within the garment sector? There is certainly evidence of greater compliance in the garment sector than in other industries, as asserted by the Director of the Labour department, but this is primarily because other sectors are not under the same external pressures to comply. It is thus the vulnerability of the export garment producers within a buyer-driven global value chain which has led to 'compliance' on their part.

The concept of a *culture* of compliance, by contrast, suggests the internalisation of the norms embedded in the codes of conduct, so that they become a routine and accepted part of the way that business is done. We did not find widespread evidence that this is the case in the garment industry. Despite the fact that higher labour standards did prevail within the industry, and that some garment employers have clearly embraced the principles of corporate social responsibility, we found persistent attempts by many, perhaps most, employers to evade their responsibilities. Many sought to comply only with the more visible aspects of the codes while they reneged on the less visible, some of which were of greater importance for their workers. Moreover, the codes are not applied to the smaller factories, which are not members of BGMEA and deal only indirectly with the buyers.

While many workers expressed the belief that buyers were their allies against the owners, since they had introduced the codes of conduct, it was clear from the employers' accounts that they had a less benevolent view of buyers for very good reasons. If most Bangladeshi employers have not internalised the concept of corporate social responsibility, neither have most of their buyers. Consequently, employers sought to comply with buyers' codes of conduct in response to the threat of withdrawal of orders, while buyers sought to impose the codes in response to the threat of negative publicity and the accompanying loss of sales. Although they made sure that their suppliers were monitored for code compliance, they generally used the threat of withholding orders rather than any positive incentives to promote compliance. In fact, their demands for compliance have been accompanied by the demands for shorter delivery times and lower unit prices. Not surprisingly, employers in Bangladesh do not generally view codes of conduct as a manifestation of social responsibility on the part of international buyers, but as a cynical marketing strategy which allows the latter to keep their brand image with their consumers 'clean' while passing on the costs of maintaining this image to the former.

From this perspective, it is difficult to describe changing practices on the part of employers in the garment industry as evidence of a culture of compliance, although there is certainly evidence of the enforcement of compliance. To what extent, then, has the enforcement of compliance led to a growth in the culture of accountability? A similarly qualified response is required. There is certainly a greater willingness on the part of many workers to make claims and demand responses from employers, while the adoption of the arbitration procedures by the BGMEA has also certainly contributed to the enforceability of some of these claims. However, changes in the visible segments of the garment industry should not be conflated with changes in the entire industry.

The reality is that many of the workers in the export garment sector are to be found in small units in the informal economy, beyond the reach of buyers (and their complicated codes of conduct), the BGMEA and the major trade union federations. Furthermore, the vast majority of workers in the country are not in the export sector at all. For them, the new accountability structures of the garment industry have very little relevance. Of greater relevance to them are the activities of the government and of organisations prepared to represent their interests. For this larger and generally poorer work force, there are a number of developments, directly or indirectly triggered by the rise of the export garment industry, that could have positive future implications. First of all, the new labour code is a step in the right direction – but getting the law right is, of course, only a first step in changing the reality.

Second, there are proposals to reform the trade unions themselves. The widespread politicisation of trade unions in Bangladesh is a product of the structure of political parties in the country rather than of the nature of trade unionism itself. Not only have the political parties failed to curb the rent-seeking activities of trade union leaders, but they have actively benefited from their partisan activities. It is, therefore, the responsibility of the political leadership in Bangladesh to transform their relations with the trade union movement in such a way that they can perform their function of representing the interests of their membership and ensuring that employers are held accountable. Such reform is difficult but essential if an environment is to be created that will allow a genuine workers' movement to flourish.

Finally, and most hopefully, in spite of the unpromising political situation in Bangladesh, we may be seeing the emergence of a 'new' form of trade unionism that is more responsive to the needs and interests of its membership, and to its women members in particular. These new forms of labour organisations are seeking to reach out to women workers who have been bypassed by both development NGOs and by trade unions. Like women workers all over the world, women workers in Bangladesh need organisations that address their needs and interests as women as well as workers. These new organisations provide hope that a genuine labour movement may yet emerge in Bangladesh, one that is more closely aligned to the interests of the workers that make up its membership. They appear to be far more cognisant of this than the older, male-dominated unions, indeed, some are led by articulate and experienced women activists. Furthermore, a number of these organisations have moved beyond the focus on codes and conditions in the export garment sector, which has been the sole preoccupation of global campaigns for labour standards, to organising all women workers, both within the export sector and outside it, both within the formal economy and outside it. It is in this willingness to take on the challenge of organising those who are most vulnerable within the economy, who have little strategic importance internationally because they do not earn the country's foreign exchange or compete with workers in the North, but who nevertheless make up the majority of the working poor in the country that we may find the seeds of a genuine culture of democratic accountability being sown.

NOTES

1 The percentage of working women in manufacturing rose from around 4 per cent in 1974 to 55 per cent in 1984–5, while urban female labour force participation rates rose from around 12 per cent in 1883–4 to 26 per cent in 1999–2000 (Kabeer and Mahmud 2004a).

2 In 2000 three-quarters of the workforce was employed in the informal sector (calculated from the 1999–2000 Labour Force Survey, 2002).

3 The exceptions are government civil servants and security-related employees who are forbidden to join unions. Until recently, unions were banned in the EPZs. Under pressure from the US government, limited trade unionism will be allowed in the EPZs from 2006.

4 We use the term 'garment leaders' to refer to those who are active within their own units but may or may not have connections with any of the larger federations.

REFERENCES

Dannecker, P. (2002) *Between Conformity and Resistance: Women Garment workers in Bangladesh*, Dhaka: University Press.
Daily Star, 5 September 2004.
Daily Star, 12 November 2004.

Kabeer, N. (2000) *The Power to Choose: Bangladeshi Women and Labour Market Decisions in London and Dhaka*, London: Verso.

Kabeer, N. and Mahmud, S. (2004a), 'Rags, Riches and Women Workers: Export-Oriented Garment Manufacturing in Bangladesh', in *Chains of Fortune: Linking Women Producers and Workers with Global Markets*, London: Commonwealth Secretariat.

Kabeer, N. and Mahmud, S. (2004b), 'Globalization, Gender and Poverty: Bangladeshi Women Workers in Export and Local Markets', *Journal of International Development*, Volume 16, Issue 1, pp. 93–109.

Khan, S. I. (2001) 'Gender Issues and the Ready-made Garment Dector of Bangladesh: the Trade Union Context', in R. Sobhan and N. Khundker (eds), *Globalisation and Gender. Changing Patterns of Women's Employment in Bangladesh*, Dhaka: University Press.

Bangladesh Bureau of Statistics (2002) *Report of Labour Force Survey Bangladesh 1999/2000*. Dhaka: Ministry of Planning, Government of the People's Republic of Bangladesh.

Mahmud, S. and Ahmed, N. (2005) 'Workers Rights' and Working Conditions in the Export Garment Sector in Bangladesh: A Review', Draft, Bangladesh Institute of Development Studies (BIDS), Dhaka, March.

Mondol, A. H. (2002) 'Globalisation, Industrial Relations and Labour Policies: the Need for Renewed Agenda', in M. Muqtada *et al.* (eds), *Bangladesh: Economic and Social Challenges of Globalisation*, Geneva and Dhaka: International Labour Organisation and University Press.

Personal Communication (2004) Director of Labour Department, Bangladesh.

UN (2002) *The Least Developed Countries Report 2002. Escaping the Poverty Trap*, New York: United Nations.

CHAPTER 12

Accountability begins at home:
the living wage movement in the United States

STEPHANIE LUCE

This chapter deals with mobilisations around the right to a living wage in the United States. This implies a form of accountability politics that is at once global and local, public and private. The outcomes of the living wage movement demonstrate that accountability cannot be assumed, but must be fought for by stakeholders, through a variety of means. This case study highlights the importance of accountability processes and the contested relationship between rights and standards, and provides an exploration of the relationship between the rights of capital and the rights of labour. It engages with the themes explored in the previous chapter on workers' rights in the garment sector in Bangladesh, showing how workplace and national labour struggles connect to global commercial and political arenas. If working conditions in Bangladesh have become the *site* of global scrutiny, this chapter shows how US campaigns on these issues have become a *source* of global scrutiny.

The US struggle for a living wage, which developed in the 1990s as a local struggle, emerged parallel to a global debate about international labour standards. In labour and policy circles, much attention was focused on apparel industry employers that violate domestic labour law or international labour codes. As manufacturing facilities proliferated in the global South, NGOs and Northern unions raised awareness around their working conditions, building up a moral outrage by consumers and students who viewed large retailers as exploiting children and young women to produce garments and other items for export. From this grew the so-called 'anti-sweatshop movement'. The idea of an anti-sweatshop movement itself is not new: similar campaigns have been waged in various countries at various times for more than a century. But the current campaign differs in that it has focused largely on an effort to hold transnational corporations (TNCs) accountable to their workers as they move around the globe.

There is a growing body of literature on the global anti-sweatshop movement, such as the work of Armbruster-Sandoval (2005), which examines cross-border organising campaigns in the US and Latin America, and the work of Esbenshade (2004), which examines efforts to monitor factories for compliance with labour standards.[1] Recent work by Elliot and Freeman (2003) and Fung, O'Rourke and Sabel (2001) engages in debate about whether international labour standards should be included in trade agreements and international institutions like the World Trade Organisation, or whether other mechanisms would be more effective at improving wages and working conditions.

These scholars, along with anti-sweatshop activists, saw that it was hard enough to hold corporations accountable within one country, let alone across borders. For this reason, activists have looked for various points of leverage that could be used in the absence of binding international law. One such point of leverage was universities. Students came together to pressurise their universities to adopt codes of conduct regarding the purchase of apparel and goods with the university logo. These campaigns were relatively successful in getting universities to adopt the codes and join international monitoring agencies (such as the Worker Rights Consortium). Soon, these students began to realise that sweatshop conditions prevailed in garment factories at home as well as abroad. In addition, they saw that workers in the university towns, and indeed, on the university campuses themselves, often suffered similar conditions as the garment workers in other countries: low wages, little job security, and resistance to unionisation efforts. Eventually, college sweatshop activists began to get involved in 'living wage' campaigns in their cities and on their campuses.

Living wage campaigns are part of another social movement that arose in the US around the same time as the anti-sweatshop movement. Rather than mobilising pressure in the North to affect working conditions of TNCs in the South, the living wage movement began by looking for leverage to affect corporate behaviour and local government spending in the US. While the approach of the living wage movement is different from the anti-sweatshop movement, and there are some important differences between the two struggles, the living wage movement can offer valuable lessons for those searching for ways to hold corporations accountable to their workforce and host communities. The processes of privatisation, deregulation and deunionisation that are central to the emergence of the living wage movement can be found in many parts of the world. The movement provides findings useful for understanding the relationships between processes of accountability, rights and resources. In particular, it has discovered that it is not enough to vote in legislation that specifies the right to a living wage. Because low-wage workers have few resources and little power, they must find ways to hold those with greater resources and power – employers and governments – accountable for enforcing those laws.

Living wage supporters have also found that processes can be as important as outcomes. Specifically, processes that create conditions for implementing laws – including mechanisms for workers to file complaints about non-compliance and to form unions – may matter more in the end than setting a particular wage standard. This chapter examines the US living wage movement to draw out these lessons for other movements for worker rights.

The material presented here is based on research conducted by the author over the past eight years. This includes reviews of city documents, surveys of employers and employees, and over 100 interviews with living wage advocates and opponents, city council members, city administrative staff, researchers and journalists.[2]

Context and background

The US labour movement fought hard to win certain gains for workers over the past century. These include the establishment of state-provided services and public sector employment to provide those services; a federal minimum wage law passed in 1938, which set a mandated hourly wage;[3] and the 1960s–1970s wave of unionisation of many public sector jobs that created good wages, benefits and job security.

However, by the late 1970s and 1980s, the rise of a neoliberal agenda began a backlash against these gains. Congress failed to pass regular raises to the minimum wage (which is not adjusted automatically with inflation), and by the mid-1990s the real value of the minimum wage was 30 per cent below its 1968 peak value and far below the hourly amount needed to raise a worker with a family to the federal poverty line. City managers pursued an agenda of privatisation of public services, which resulted in an attack on public sector unions and savings based on reduced wages, benefits and job security. They also pursued a 'business climate' model of economic development, using tax breaks and economic subsidies to lure firms to their region (and to retain existing firms).

One result of these trends was a sharp decline in the real wage for the average worker, as well as those at the very bottom. Although the US is the richest country in the world, there are a substantial number of people who can be considered the 'working poor': those who do not earn enough to meet the federal poverty lines despite having jobs. In 2003, approximately a quarter of all US workers did not earn an hourly wage high enough to meet the poverty threshold for a family of four (Mishel, Bernstein and Allegretto 2005).

At the same time, a fall in unionisation density rates and union power took away one avenue for raising wages. This was compounded by an unfavourable political climate at the national level. Even after Bill Clinton was elected in 1992, ending twelve years of Republican rule, there appeared to be little political commitment to raising the federal minimum wage.

By 1994, pastors in Baltimore, Maryland observed that a number of the people coming for free food from their churches were people who had jobs yet did not earn enough to feed themselves and their families. For the previous few decades, city leaders had persuaded citizens that if they supported the city's economic development plans ('revitalising' the downtown), jobs would follow. While some jobs did come, the bulk of these were low-wage and non-benefited, resulting in a growing population of the working poor. The pastors, members of a faith-based community organisation, joined forces with a local public sector union to demand that city leaders respond to this problem.

The end result was a 'living wage ordinance': legislation requiring that any private sector firm providing city services pay its workers an hourly wage high enough to meet the federal poverty line for a family of four. Although this would only raise wages for a small percentage of all workers in the city, the policy was an initial step toward making the city accountable to low-wage employers for its decisions to privatise city services.

The Baltimore ordinance inspired activists in other cities to pursue living wage campaigns. Soon, activists were looking to expand coverage of the ordinances. In addition to covering firms providing city services, some ordinances also included firms receiving economic development financial assistance (tax breaks and subsidies), firms operating on city property (such as retailers and restaurants in airports and sports arenas), and direct city or county employees. By 2004, three cities even passed city-wide minimum wage laws, establishing higher wages for most workers working within city borders.[4] Many of these ordinances include automatic indexing for inflation, correcting for the weakness in the federal minimum wage. In addition to higher wages, some ordinances began to require that employers provide health benefits, paid overtime and paid days off.

After five years, over 40 ordinances have been passed in cities and counties. The campaigns turned into a social movement, with coalitions developing at the grassroots around the country. After ten years, more than 120 ordinances had been passed in cities, counties, universities, school boards and other agencies.

The right to a living wage?

Living wage campaigns were so successful in part because the language used resonated strongly with the public. Since the federal minimum wage was established, the US population has favoured the idea that the rate be raised regularly.[5] The idea of a fair wage for work is supported perhaps in part because the idea of work has powerful moral and social connotations in the country: people are often judged by whether they have a job and what kind of work they do. In addition, despite its wealth, the US has always had a relatively weak welfare state. Those without access to jobs that pay a fair wage will likely live in poverty. Work is not only one of the few avenues for subsistence, but it is also a crucial means of achieving full citizenship. For example, many US cities have outlawed homelessness (vagrancy laws) and asking for money (anti-panhandling laws). There are few and dwindling government resources available to help the poor.

Despite this, no one has the 'right to work' in the US.[6] In fact, courts have interpreted the law in such a way that jobs are seen to be the private property of employers, not employees. As Michael Yates points out so clearly in *Naming the System: Inequality and Work in the Global Economy*, no capitalist economy ever has solved the problems of unemployment and underemployment (Yates 2003). This means that there are never enough jobs that pay a living wage, and that people must compete for those jobs that do exist. Competition over living wage jobs occurs within countries and, increasingly, between countries. Despite spot shortages in particular occupations and countries, there exists an excess supply of labour in the global labour market. In this context, even if a laws exists giving workers the right to a living wage, the conditions of globalisation make it almost impossible to realise this in practice.

But this raises a larger issue around the idea of labour standards and labour rights. Some scholars point out that there is an important distinction between rights and standards: for example, the right to organise, the right to collective bargaining, the right to be free from danger and discrimination, versus standards that may vary from country to country, such as the minimum wage level. Labour rights may be about processes, while standards are about outcomes. This means that labour rights, such as the right to organise unions, create a *process* by which labour market *outcomes*, such as wage levels, are determined. Some suggest that rights should not vary from country to country, whereas standards might.[7]

Elliot and Freeman (2003) add that there is a difference between standards that are relatively free or low-cost and those that cost money, or 'cash versus non-cash' standards. They suggest that the main concern of labour activists should be to win the right to collective action. Once workers have the right to unionise, they have a mechanism to bargain over other standards, such as wages. Robin Broad echoes this, writing that focusing on basic rights, such as the right to freedom of association, 'avoids a major pitfall: having to determine which standards are appropriate for which corporations or which levels of development – a potentially messy judgment call' (Broad 2001: 44).

While focusing on the right to organise seems a possible solution to improving conditions of work, there are critics of this approach. Some proponents of labour standards say that the right to organise is not enough. For example, Heintz (2004) argues that within the current global commodity chain structures, workers simply do not have enough power to bargain over wages. Indeed, even a large swath of unionised workers in the US find themselves relatively powerless to bargain wages upward – let alone keep their jobs. While stories of mass outsourcing are mostly exaggerated in terms of their impact on total jobs in the US, a recent study found that in the first quarter of 2004, 39 per cent of all jobs leaving the country were unionised jobs (compare this to a national private-sector union density of only 8 per cent) (Bronfenbrenner and Luce 2004). Clearly, simply having a union does not provide workers in global industries with much bargaining power.[8] In these cases, labour standards advocates argue that it is necessary to establish wage standards that serve as a floor, preventing a 'race to the bottom' in wages even when unions are present.

Esbenshade raises another important point concerning the difference between rights and standards. She argues that the anti-sweatshop movement's 'focus on working conditions rather than rights put the movement in a vulnerable position' as it allowed corporations to make minor changes in working conditions and declare the problems fixed (Esbenshade 2004: 202). The focus on working conditions also ignores the crucial fact of worker rights. Labour is a unique 'input' into production precisely because there is a 'non-cash' element involved in human labour.

The living wage movement has provided an interesting twist to this debate. Some of the ordinances have worked to include labour rights or processes in the ordinance: for example, some include protections for workers trying to form a union or organise around wage issues. Many include specific language giving workers the right to file charges of non-compliance against employers without risk of retaliation or job loss. Yet the living wage campaigns have also tried to make the living wage itself – a labour standard – into a right. In particular, the campaigns declare that a living wage is at a minimum a moral right, which should be made into a legal right. Clergy members have been active in campaigns, citing scripture to argue that all humans do, in fact, have the 'right' to a living wage in return for their work. For example, in 2000 the United Methodist Church passed the following resolution: 'The United Methodist Church recognises the responsibility of governments to develop and implement sound fiscal and monetary policies that provide for the economic life of individuals. Every person has the right to a job at a living wage.' (United Methodist Church 2000: 55.) Catholics point to several teachings in their tradition that call for a living wage, such as Catechism of the Catholic Church 2434: 'A just wage is the legitimate fruit of work. To refuse or withhold it can be a grave injustice. In determining fair pay both the needs and the contributions of each person must be taken into account' (United States Catholic Conference 1997).

The campaigns are also often posed as a counter to the expanding rights of capital to relocate, privatise, and control the terms of debate. Indeed, the Montgomery County, Maryland living wage campaign quotes President Franklin D. Roosevelt, who stated in 1933: 'No business that depends for its existence on paying less than living wages has any right to continue in this country … and by living wages I mean more than a bare subsistence level. I mean the wages of decent living' (Progressive Maryland 2005). In some cases, living wage supporters frame their campaign as being about the right of municipalities to attach standards or requirements to private companies that receive economic development subsidies or contracts for performing city services. In this way, citizens have mobilised to struggle for what they considered a right of workers and governments against the rights of capital.

The campaigns have involved a mix of 'inside' and 'outside', or formal and informal strategies, to get the laws passed. The outside strategies include building coalitions of sympathetic organisations, public education on the issues of wages and inequality, public rallies and protests designed to get media and public attention, and, at times, tactics such as marches and civil disobedience. The inside strategies involve developing alliances with city leaders and staff, and direct lobbying of and negotiating with city council members and mayors. Throughout the campaign activists emphasize a range of arguments in favour of the living wage, but particularly underline the idea of the living wage as a right.

Implementation struggles

Using the argument that working people have the right to a living wage, the movement saw considerable success throughout the 1990s. But, as new campaigns continued to emerge, the original activists turned to the question of implementation. The challenge was how to hold governments and employers accountable: to ensure that employers were paying the mandated living wage, and that the city governments were taking the necessary steps to monitor workplaces and enforce the law.

In almost no city has the city, left on its own, pursued strong enforcement of the living wage ordinance. While city councillors subject to re-election are sensitive to voters' wishes to pass ordinances, city administrators are not as eager to enforce laws that they see as running counter to the dominant neoliberal economic development paradigm that suggests cities need to focus on creating a positive business climate in order to grow. In other words, passing and enforcing regulations on businesses is seen as having a negative impact upon the business climate. In this case, there may be *ideological opposition* or resistance to reform.

Even where city staff may be personally committed to enforcement, either due to personal sympathies with the law or simply the desire to do their jobs well, cities are not likely to devote many resources or much staff time to monitoring and enforcement. Often, reluctant to hire new staff to implement laws effectively, the city merely adds the job of enforcement to the workload of existing personnel. This means living wage enforcers are overworked and stretched between multiple tasks, revealing a *lack of state capacity* to enforce the laws.

The accountability issues were not confined to a vertical demand of activists against the state and employers, however. Living wage advocates had to hold themselves accountable to make implementation a priority. The fact is that, in most places, the workers who were to be covered by the ordinances were not the main activists involved in passing the ordinances. Rather, the coalitions comprised representatives from labour unions, community organisations, faith-based groups, student groups, women's groups and others. To be sure the workers eventually got the living wage, living wage advocates had to themselves pursue avenues to monitor compliance. For example, after getting the ordinance passed in Baltimore, activists soon turned to efforts to organise the covered workers into a new organisation of low-wage workers called the Solidarity Sponsoring Committee (SSC). SSC organisers went to bus yards to talk to school bus drivers and monitors covered by the Baltimore living wage law. They soon found workers who did not know about the ordinance, and who were not receiving the higher wage. SSC helped the workers file complaints with the city. They then launched a public pressure campaign, holding rallies and getting large crowds to turn out for city hearings, in order to force the city to implement the law. Eventually, the city ruled in favour of the workers and ordered the bus companies to raise the wages and give back-pay to their employees.

In addition to the efforts in Baltimore, activists in other cities had similar concerns about implementation. However, in Los Angeles living wage coalition members realised that in order to ensure more systematic enforcement they would need to find ways to institutionalise their role in implementation. After the city council passed the ordinance, coalition members worked with their allies on the council to write the regulations and include the right of non-profit organisations to provide training to covered workers to educate them about the living wage policy. This provision allowed living wage advocates regular access to covered workers, greatly improving the chances of successful implementation. The coalition also pressured the city to hire an adequate number of staff to enforce the law, including Spanish-speaking staff that could answer workers' questions and complaints.

Activists in Boston, Massachusetts went one step further. They got the city to pass regulations establishing a Living Wage Advisory Board, comprised of government, business, union and community members, which would meet every month to review contracts covered by the ordinance, examine complaints of non-compliance, and oversee general implementation. This Advisory Board has since recommended revisions to the ordinance which were passed by the City Council and mayor, substantially expanding coverage and raising the wage. The Advisory Board has also played a key role in reviewing the applications for exemption submitted by employers. In almost every city, the living wage ordinance includes language that allows for 'hardship waivers': employers who claim that they will suffer undue economic harm from paying the higher wage are allowed to request exemption. In many cities these requests are granted with little investigation, but in Boston the Advisory Board has been strict about requiring employers to open their books and prove their case of hardship. The Advisory Board has turned down a number of these requests, even from non-profit child care agencies.

Another important tactic pursued by some living wage coalitions was to include language in the ordinances giving citizens the 'right to know'. This means that the ordinances specifically state that cities must make public information about their contracting and economic development, and/or that firms receiving service contracts or economic development assistance must make their payroll records available. In some cases, the disclosure provision is the one that employers fight most vigorously. For example, the Toledo Chamber of Commerce did not put up much resistance to a general living wage ordinance: rather, they put their energy into keeping the disclosure provision out.

The battle over disclosure can be found in other labour standards struggles as well. In the anti-sweatshop movement, students quickly found that it was not enough to pressure large retailers to improve their labour conditions, since they would just say that they had subcontracted all their manufacturing work to other firms all over the world. Therefore, the students had to develop ways to get the TNCs to disclose the location of their factories. This access to information was a crucial first step to determining whether the factory owners were complying with labour codes. Disclosure has also been an issue in the movement for corporate accountability in the US, around the issue of 'corporate welfare'. Activists have pressured their local and state governments to disclose details about the subsidies that they give out to corporations.[9] This is a key lesson for accountability struggles: stakeholders must have equal and reliable access to information in order to assess implementation progress and outcomes.

Civil society involvement: inside and outside strategies

The above examples highlight the various mechanisms that living wage advocates have used to improve implementation outcomes. Parallel to the strategies used initially to pass the ordinances, inside and outside strategies have been utilised in implementation struggles as well. In Baltimore, activists relied on outside strategies: applying public pressure to force the local government to enforce its law. In Los Angeles and Boston, activists used inside strategies: establishing mechanisms to institutionalise their role in the implementation process and work from within the state. Including disclosure provisions in ordinances also helps systematise the implementation process, as it allows an opening for citizens to get information to which they would not otherwise have access.

Relying solely on outside or inside strategies has limitations. In Baltimore, public pressure resulted in a victory for bus drivers and monitors. However, in 2003 the union which represents the food and beverage workers at the city sports stadium discovered that the employer, Aramark, had not been in compliance with the overtime provision of the ordinance. The union filed complaints with the city and, again using public pressure and media attention, was able to get the city to force the employer to comply and provide back-pay for the unpaid overtime. These examples led to successful outcomes, but they suggest that, without systematic scrutiny, there may be many other workers not receiving the mandated living wage who are in fact entitled to it. Organisations with the motivation to do so, investigated conditions for the workers they were trying to organise or already represented, but what about the other workers? The city expended few resources to implement the living wage, and did not conduct its own workplace investigations.

In Los Angeles and Boston living wage advocates were able to have greater systematic monitoring. Yet this did not solve all implementation problems. While advocates had won a place in the monitoring process, they did not have the power to enforce. In both cases, the city council and mayor had the final say over all implementation issues. This meant that, in a few cases, employers resisted compliance with the ordinance.

For example, the Los Angeles living wage ordinance was intended to cover the airport, but employers at the airport – restaurants as well as airlines – claimed that the law did not apply to them. In this case, the Los Angeles living wage coalition resorted to 'outside pressure' tactics in order to pressure the city council to amend the ordinance and close loopholes, making it explicit that the ordinance did in fact cover the airport employers.

In Boston, KTI, the firm holding the contract to provide recycling services to the city, announced that it would not comply with the ordinance. The Advisory Board told KTI that it needed to prove its case that compliance would cause a hardship, but the firm refused. The Advisory Board recommended that the city not grant a waiver, but the mayor did not accept that ruling. Instead, he has been granting temporary contract extensions to the firm for several years. Living wage advocates have resorted to outside strategies: leafleting the public to call the mayor, and working with advocates in nearby cities where living wage ordinances also covered KTI to develop strategies to get the company to comply. Although these efforts have not yet resulted in victory, they have raised awareness in the community about the living wage issue. A major city newspaper that had initially opposed the ordinance came out in favour of the city denying the KTI waiver.[10]

These examples provide several important lessons. Whether due to ideological opposition or lack of state capacity, cities are not enforcing the ordinances on their own and holding employers accountable to pay the living wage. Living wage advocates must work to hold the state accountable for implementing the laws. This can be done by outside tactics – 'protest politics' – which can improve the chances of enforcement. At the same time, these outside tactics often fail to result in systematic changes in the implementation process, such as increased numbers of city personnel to monitor worksites.

In Los Angeles and Boston, living wage supporters pursued inside strategies that institutionalised improvements and enhanced state capacity. At the same time, because this still did not give the advocates decision-making power, they needed to maintain their ability to utilise pressure politics when necessary. This outside pressure is important for keeping the public educated and engaged on the issues, and to demonstrate that city officials must remain accountable to the citizenry that demands living wages. Outside pressure is also important because it can give city staff the political cover they need to make demands of powerful employers. Finally, maintaining the avenue for outside pressure is important to ensure that individuals or organisations serving in formal Advisory Boards are not 'co-opted' by employers or city officials. These individuals may also benefit in the same way that city staff do: outside pressure gives them political cover to stick to their demands for strong enforcement.

Although civil society participation can lead to more accountability from governments, one cannot assume that it will solve all implementation problems or replace the state as the chief implementation agent. Community organisations are subject to some of the same constraints as states – for example, they too may have weak capacity or the social movements they are a part of may fade away over time. As mentioned above, individual activists are subject to 'capture', much like government officials.

In addition, many of the organisations involved in the campaigns lack a direct incentive to monitor the ordinances. It is not enough for cities to create the space for community involvement: those actors must be motivated to do an effective job. For example, in Cleveland, although there were two seats for union representatives on the living wage task force, one member never came to meetings, and the other attended but offered little input. Apparently, according to Policy Matters Ohio researcher Dave Focareta, the union representatives had little or no incentive to put time into living wage enforcement. This may be because they did not see the connections between the living wage and organising opportunities for their union, or because they saw living wage enforcement as a low priority compared to other tasks they had to do. In contrast, activists in Baltimore, Boston and Los Angeles saw specific connections between living wage enforcement and representing or organising workers. We cannot assume that all civil society organisations will possess similar incentives to monitor the ordinances. Because they face numerous constraints on their own ability to do the work, and they do not have the force of law behind them, they should only be seen as a complement to state enforcement, not a substitute. The issue of motivation to monitor, and to hold governments accountable is key, and one that deserves further attention.

Conclusion

The living wage movement highlights the fact that accountability should be understood as a process rather than an outcome. While activists had won certain struggles to prioritise workers' rights, particularly in the 1930s–1960s, employers and the state failed to maintain their commitment to these gains. Instead, power shifted in favour of capital and against workers, leading to a situation where many were denied access to jobs that paid a living wage.

In response, activists mobilised at the local level, where they felt they had greater resources vis-à-vis capital. Successful in these efforts, they got cities to pass local living wage ordinances. But as Kerry Miciotto, an organiser in the Baltimore campaign, notes, 'It takes one kind of power to get a law passed. Getting it enforced takes a whole other kind of power.' The lessons of the struggles to implement living wage ordinances highlight the fact that passing laws alone is often not enough to improve conditions for workers, or those without power. Top-down legislative strategies will not address power imbalances. Laws can give workers points of leverage, but it takes work to enforce them. Living wage activists have found a combination of inside and outside (or formal and informal) strategies are needed to provide the best chance of enforcement.

In addition to these lessons about accountability, the living wage movement also demonstrates that workers in the global North often experience the same kinds of challenges faced by those in the global South: poverty-level wages, lack of benefits, work insecurity, and attacks on any gains won, such as unionisation. The 'business-climate' model used to lure investors with tax relief and other financial incentives is similar to that employed by state governments in India, discussed in Chapter 8. The struggle for US-style living wage ordinances has emerged in other Northern countries (such as the UK and Canada), but, certainly, general living wage struggles can be found in the South as well as the North. South Africa was home to an active campaign for living wages in the 1980s. According to the Congress of South African Trade Unions (COSATU), that campaign was aimed at uniting workers across sectors under some common goals. Some of the demands were then adopted under the new regime, but the living wage campaign re-emerged in the late 1990s. COSATU General Secretary Zwelinzima Vavi noted that the executive committee met in 2002 and 'agreed that the struggle for a living wage must be at the core of creating a better life for all South Africans'.[11] As a result, COSATU has made a demand for a basic income grant that all citizens would receive.

As mentioned in the introduction, the United Students Against Sweatshops (USAS) have also linked their anti-sweatshop campaigns to local living wage campaigns. On some campuses, members of USAS began to realise that garment sweatshops were not only found in the global South, but in the US as well. Furthermore, the conditions faced by workers on their own campuses were often poor. Many universities were also privatising services, attacking unions, and paying low wages. In some cases, students launched campus-based living wage campaigns to fight for better conditions for the janitors, food service workers and housekeepers at the university. In other cases, students linked up with local living wage campaigns aimed at the municipal government. And in a few cases, students realised that they themselves were workers who deserved better wages and working conditions. In 2002 undergraduate students working in the dormitories at the University of Massachusetts-Amherst formed their own union to bargain for better working conditions. The focus on labour issues prompted graduate students working as teaching assistants at several public and private universities to undergo unionisation drives.[12] Today, USAS considers campus-based workers' rights movements and living wage campaigns to be a core part of its work. This story shows how students began with an effort to hold corporations accountable for their wages and working conditions in factories in other countries, but soon began to see connections between the working conditions of garment workers in the global South, gatekeepers on their campus, and even themselves as workers. This also involved a realisation that 'accountability begins at home'.

There are at least two important questions that remain unanswered. The first involves the relation between the local and the global. If a living wage is a right in the US – if activists succeed in passing ordinances in most cities that declare this – what does this mean for workers in other countries? Specifically, if the US living wage ordinances declare that employers have the responsibility to pay their workers enough to live on, shouldn't that responsibility apply to the employer no matter where they are located? Or if the right to a living wage is attached to the worker, should that worker not be entitled to that right no matter where he/she is located? Although the rhetoric of the living wage movement calls for a universal right to living wages, the ordinances provide only an opening to attach a right and responsibility to worker and employer in a particular relationship (employment in a given city, or under a given contract). In this sense, there is a disconnect between the rhetoric of the campaign and the outcomes. However, this raises interesting questions about the relationship between rights and accountability. The discussion of the difference between rights and standards brought this out clearly, where rights may deepen accountability means or processes, guaranteeing representation, association and freedom of speech, for example, while standards specify accountability outcomes or ends in a material sense. The relationship between the two and the ability of one to reinforce the other is not always clear-cut, however.

The second question is related to the first. To what extent can living wage ordinances really bring about change? Activists have found mechanisms to hold their local governments more accountable for enforcing living wage ordinances, and to hold certain employers accountable for complying with the law. But there is a widespread problem of accountability when it comes to enforcing labour law in the US, which stems from a gross imbalance of power and a system of labour law that privileges capital over workers. Living wage enforcement can be improved to achieve marginally better outcomes, but can it alter the balance of power between employees and employers? In order for living wage activists to win real rights, and the real ability to hold corporations and governments accountable, much more fundamental changes are needed. So far, the movement has enjoyed success in part because it does not always have to address deeper ideological debates. Some living wage advocates are business leaders who see higher wages as compatible with healthier markets. Some are trade unionists that like to hark back to a New Deal economy, or advocate a 'high road' solution. But as the living wage opponents themselves realize, living wages are ultimately not sustainable under an economic system that has built-in business cycles and a permanent pool of unemployed workers. This remains the next challenge for the living wage movement: shifting the terms of debate so that it confronts the real ideological battles at the core of the issue: should governments make decisions based on the right to profit-maximization, or based on human needs as the utmost concern?

NOTES

1 There are many more books on the topic, such as R. J. S. Ross, 2004; A. Ross, 2004; A. Ross 1997; Bonacich and Appelbaum 2000; and E. I. Rosen 2002.

2 Further description of the research methods and data can be found in Luce (2004).

3 The minimum wage was part of the Fair Labour Standards Act of 1938. Not all workers were covered, although over time Congress amended the law to expand coverage.

4 Whether a city government has the right to pass a city-wide minimum wage law differs by state: only those states with 'home rule' allow cities to pass laws of this kind. Currently, San Francisco, California, Santa Fe, New Mexico, Madison, Wisconsin, and Washington, DC are the cities with city-wide minimum wage laws. Voters passed a city-wide minimum wage in New Orleans, but the state legislature passed a law overriding home rule in the case of minimum wages.

5 Polls have tended to show widespread and consistent support for raising the minimum wage in the US. Data shows majority support for raising the minimum wage for most years since 1945 (Waltman, 2000 p. 50). As inequality continued to rise through much of the 1990s, even with a booming economy, public support for 'economic fairness' increased. See, for example, a 1998 Gallup Poll, 'Have and Have-Nots: Perceptions of Fairness and Opportunity'. A number of measures in this poll suggest that Americans generally support a 'reduction in the degree of economic inequality' in the US (Meyerson 1999).

6 In fact, the term 'right to work' in the US generally refers to state legislation that limits the ability of trade unions to require workers to join a union in a worksite covered by a collective bargaining agreement. In this sense, 'right to work' is used to mean 'right to hold a job and not have to join a union'. Unionists counter this by referring to these laws as 'right to work for less'.

7 Guy Standing of the ILO argues that 'In developing a strategy [for labour standards], you need to identify a core of standards that are a floor of human decency; then practices that accord with a country's capacities and a firm's size and structure; and then standards that are reasonable aspirations.' (Standing 2001: 72).

8 It is not only in mobile industries that unions suffer from weak bargaining power. Even in industries such as retail, janitorial services, daycare and hotels, workers do not always see significant increases in pay with the presence of a union. In fact, in a few places unions that have been unable to win significant wage increases through bargaining have supported local living wage ordinances as a way to raise union members' wages through legislation.

9 According to the research organisation Good Jobs First, the states of Minneapolis and Maine have the 'cadillacs' of disclosure laws. These states require state and local agencies to name the companies that receive subsidies, along with the dollar value of the subsidy, the number of jobs expected to be created/retained, the wage and benefit levels of those jobs, and this information must be available to the public in a centralised location and on a regular basis (LeRoy and Hinkley 2002).

10 Editorial, *Boston Globe*, 'Recycling Wages', 22 February 2003, p. A14. The editorial states, 'Though the company [KTI] has a right to charge what it wants for its services, Boston has an obligation to recognise where there is economic room for higher wages.'

11 Editorial, COSATU Weekly, 7 June 2002. http://www.cosatu.org.za/news/weekly/20020607.htm. Accessed 20 March 2005.

12 Graduate students had already unionised at a handful of campuses, starting with the University of Wisconsin-Madison, in 1966. However, the resurgence of interest in labour issues led to an upsurge in graduate student unionisation efforts in the 1990s.

REFERENCES

Armbruster-Sandoval, R. (2005) *Globalization and Cross-Border Labor Solidarity*, New York: Routledge.

Bonacich, E. and Appelbaum, R. (2000) *Behind the Label: Inequality in the Los Angeles Apparel Industry*, Berkeley: University of California Press.

Broad, R. (2001) 'A Better Mousetrap? A Response to "Realizing Labor Standards"', in A. Fung, D. O'Rourke and C. Sabel, *Can We Put an End to Sweatshops? A New Democracy Forum on Raising Global Labour Standards*, Boston: Beacon Press.

Bronfenbrenner, K. and Luce, S. (2004) 'The Changing Nature of Corporate Global Restructuring: the Impact of Production Shifts on Jobs in the US, China, and Around the Globe', Washington, DC: US–China Economic and Security Review Council.

Elliot, K. A. and Freeman, R. (2003) *Can Labour Standards Improve under Globalisation?* Washington, DC: Institute for International Economics.

Esbenshade, J. (2004) *Monitoring Sweatshops: Workers, Consumers and the Global Apparel Industry*, Philadelphia: Temple University Press.

Fung, A., O'Rourke, D. and Sabel, C. (2001) *Can We Put an End to Sweatshops? A New Democracy Forum on Raising Global Labour Standards*, Boston: Beacon Press.

Heintz, J. (2004) 'Globalization and Sweatshops, Comments', MacArthur Research Network on the Impacts of Inequality on Economic Performance, Sloan School of Management, Massachusetts Institute of Technology, 8–10 October.

LeRoy, G. and Hinkley, S. (2002) 'No More Secret Candy Store: a Grassroots Guide to Investigating Development Subsidies', Washington, DC: Institute on Taxation and Economic Policy.

Luce, S. (2004) *Fighting for a Living Wage*, Ithaca: Cornell University Press.

Meyerson, H. (1999) 'Gray Davis Takes Over', *LA Weekly*, 15 January, p. 15.

Mishel, L., J. Bernstein and S. Allegretto (2005) *The State of Working America 2004/2005*, Ithaca: Cornell University Press.

Progressive Maryland (2005) 'Introduction to Living Wages', Webpage. http://progressive-maryland.org/page.php?id=148, accessed 27 May 2005.

Rosen, E. I. (2002) *Making Sweatshops: the Globalisation of the US Apparel Industry*, Berkeley: University of California Press.

Ross, A. (2004) *Low Pay, High Profile: the Global Push for Fair Labor*, New York: New Press.

Ross, A. (ed.) (1997) *No Sweat: Fashion, Free Trade, and the Rights of Garment Workers*. London: Verso.

Ross, R. J. S. (2004) *Slaves to Fashion: Poverty and Abuse in the New Sweatshops*, Ann Arbor: University of Michigan Press.

Standing, G. (2001) 'Human Development: a Response to 'Realising Labour Standards,' in A. Fung, D. O'Rourke and C. Sabel, *Can We Put an End to Sweatshops?: A New Democracy Forum on Raising Global Labour Standards*, Boston: Beacon Press.

United Methodist Church (2000), *Book of Resolutions*. Washington, DC: The United Methodist Church.

United States Catholic Conference (1997), *Catechism of the Catholic Church*. Washington, DC: United States Catholic Conference. http://www.usccb.org/catechism/text/pt3sect2chpt2art7.htm, accessed 27 May 2005.

Waltman, J. (2000). *The Politics of the Minimum Wage*, Urbana: University of Illinois Press.

Yates, M. D. (2003) *Naming the System: Inequality and Work in the Global Economy*, New York: Monthly Review Press.

Index

Abacha, Sani 216
Abia State 207
Abuja 216
accountability, active and passive 55;
administrative 51, 54, 65, 118,
136-8; alternative forms of 54-5; as
answerability and enforceability 7,
13, 15, 17, 28, 39, 41-2, 46-7, 50,
76, 90, 140n, 146, 151, 164, 167,
189-90, 195, 198, 201, 224, 242,
247, 252-9; auditing the auditors
52; and citizenship 28, 144-60,
166-7, 179, 181, 213, 224, 231,
254; and civil society 44-50, 53-5,
115-19, 146, 149-51, 155-60, 165,
173, 229, 236, 254, 256; and commodification 14, 82, 215, 227, 231;
and community, 8, 10, 18, 32, 45,
72, 102, 112, 114-16, 119, 164,
205, 212, 216-17, 252, 256; and
'compliance' 223-4, 231, 240-3;
and conflicting rights 25, 60, 63,
90, 104-5, 110-19; conceptualising
28, 39-40; consumers and 26, 40,
63, 223-4, 226-8, 232, 240, 242,
245; corporate 42-4, 47, 51-3, 163-
5, 166-83 (India) 186-8, 193-4,
199, 206, 210, 214-16, 228, 231-2,
241; cultures of 21-2, 83, 90, 96,

119, 159, 165, 219, 224, 227, 232,
237, 240, 242-3; and democracy
28, 41-2, 45-6, 55, 146, 149-50,
157-60, 179, 194, 243; and development 21, 39, 52-3, 101-2;
dynamic relationships with rights
and resources 4-13; and the environment 12, 81; financial accountability 50-3, 137, 146-8, 150-1,
153-4, 163; four key questions
about 4, 37-8, 56; gaps in 43-4, 81,
116, 164, 173, 224; and globalisation 8, 11, 13, 22, 163-5, 230-1,
241, 243, 245, 249-50, 254, 257-8;
as a grammar of conduct and performance 39-40; and indigenous
people 213; institutional aspects of
1, 11-13, 20-4, 29, 46, 48-50, 87-
97, 104, 115, 117-19, 122-40, 145-
6, 157, 159; and investment
globally 9, 27, 43, 163, 166-9, 171,
175-7, 179, 182-3, 195, 200-1,
210-11, 226, 257, 226, 257; and
law 6, 13, 16, 26, 47, 50, 135, 148-
9, 164-5, 169, 181, 186-202, 247-
8, 252-9; and markets 42-4, 165,
231; measurement of 23; and
media 14, 18-19, 46, 48-9, 127-9,
167, 174, 178-9, 181, 195-6, 202,